THE ADVENTURE ZONE

Petals to the Metal

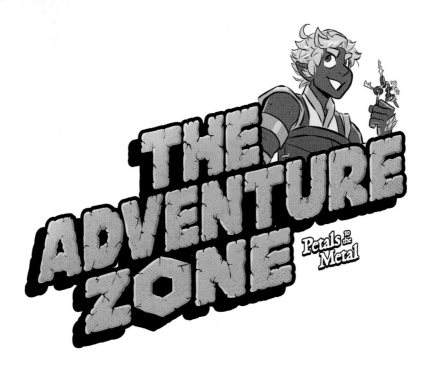

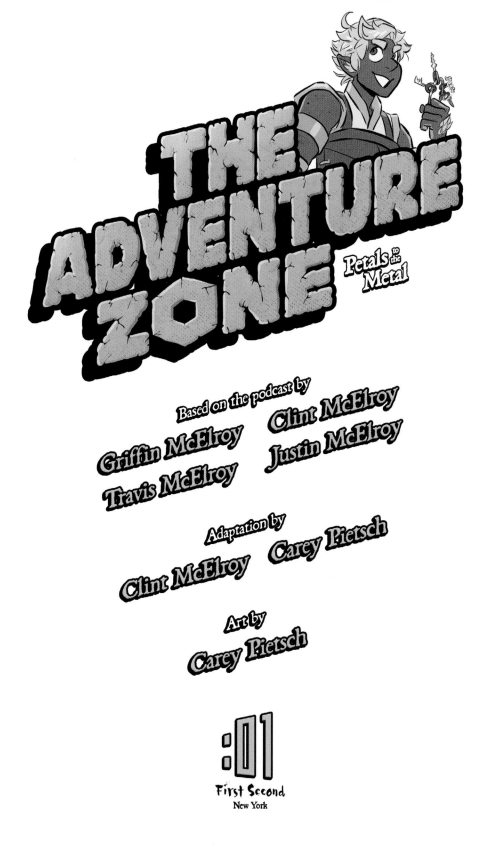

THE ADVENTURE ZONE

Petals to the Metal

Based on the podcast by

Griffin McElroy   Clint McElroy

Travis McElroy   Justin McElroy

Adaptation by

Clint McElroy   Carey Pietsch

Art by

Carey Pietsch

:01

First Second

New York

First Second

Letterer: Tess Stone
Flatters: Megan Brennan, Ensley Chau, Leigh Davis,
Suzanne Geary, Luke Healy, Hien Pham, and Cassandra Tassoni
Authenticity Readers: Mey Rude and Kori Michele Handwerker
Game board photo copyright © 2020 by Megan Brennan and Lisa Aurigemma
Fan art gallery copyright © 2020 by (respectively):
Andrew Soman
Angela Tong
April Leong
Emily K. Smith
Julia Maddalina
Gabriela Epstein
Kory Bing
Mhuyo
Myra Hild
Nathanael Whale
Nick Leerie
Pati Ćmak
Alexandra Maria Flis

Published by First Second
First Second is an imprint of Roaring Brook Press,
a division of Holtzbrinck Publishing Holdings Limited Partnership
120 Broadway, New York, NY 10271

Don't miss your next favorite book from First Second!
For the latest updates go to firstsecondnewsletter.com and sign up for our newsletter.

Library of Congress Control Number: 2019938061

ISBN: 978-1-250-23263-2 (Paperback)
ISBN: 978-1-250-23262-5 (Hardcover)
ISBN: 978-1-250-76215-3 (Special Edition)
ISBN: 978-1-250-76684-7 (Special Edition)
ISBN: 978-1-250-76216-0 (Special Edition)

Our books may be purchased in bulk for promotional, educational, or business use.
Please contact your local bookseller or the Macmillan Corporate and Premium Sales Department
at (800) 221-7945 ext. 5442 or by email at MacmillanSpecialMarkets@macmillan.com.

First edition, 2020
Edited by Calista Brill and Alison Wilgus
Cover design by Molly Johanson and Carey Pietsch
Series design by Andrew Arnold
Interior book design by Molly Johanson
Printed in the United States of America

Penciled with a 2B pencil-style tool in Procreate. Inked with a brush-style
digital nib in Clip Studio Paint and colored digitally in Photoshop.

Paperback: 10 9 8 7 6 5 4 3 2 1
Hardcover: 10 9 8 7 6 5 4 3 2 1

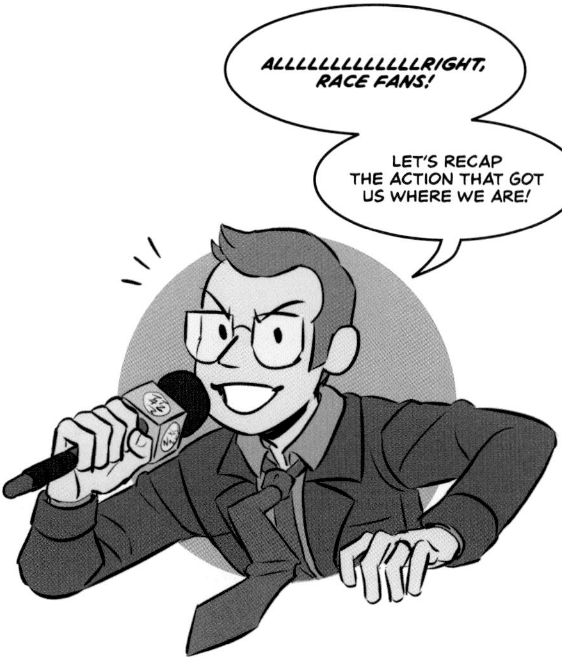
ALLLLLLLLLLLLLLLRIGHT, RACE FANS!
LET'S RECAP THE ACTION THAT GOT US WHERE WE ARE!

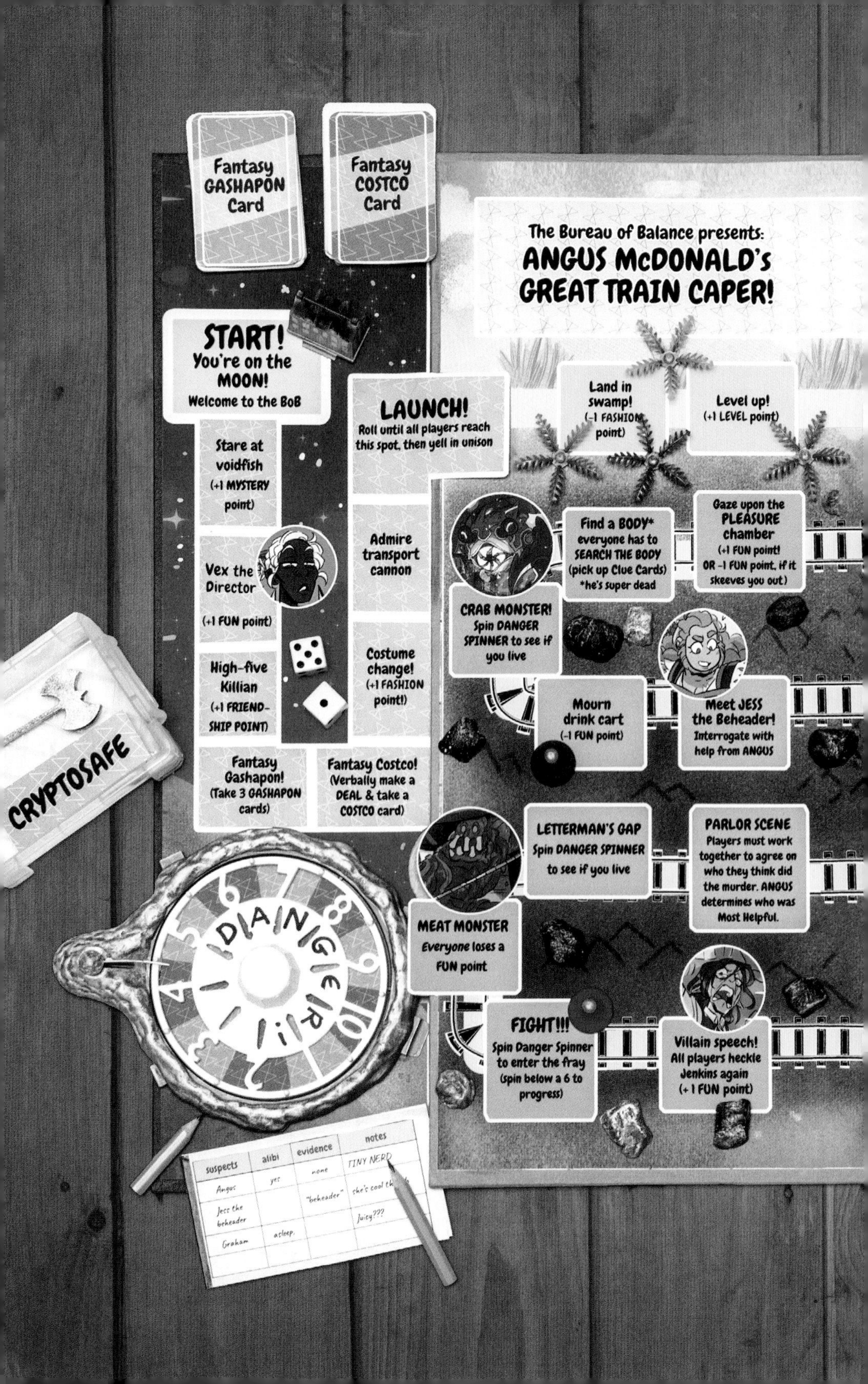
Fantasy GASHAPON Card
Fantasy COSTCO Card
The Bureau of Balance presents:
ANGUS McDONALD's GREAT TRAIN CAPER!
START! You're on the MOON! Welcome to the BoB
Stare at voidfish (+1 MYSTERY point)
Vex the Director (+1 FUN point)
High-five Killian (+1 FRIEND-SHIP POINT)
Fantasy Gashapon! (Take 3 GASHAPON cards)
Fantasy Costco! (Verbally make a DEAL & take a COSTCO card)
LAUNCH! Roll until all players reach this spot, then yell in unison
Admire transport cannon
Costume change! (+1 FASHION point!)
Land in swamp! (-1 FASHION point)
Level up! (+1 LEVEL point)
Find a BODY* everyone has to SEARCH THE BODY (pick up Clue Cards) *he's super dead
Gaze upon the PLEASURE chamber (+1 FUN point! OR -1 FUN point, if it skeeves you out)
CRAB MONSTER! Spin DANGER SPINNER to see if you live
Mourn drink cart (-1 FUN point)
Meet JESS the Beheader! Interrogate with help from ANGUS
LETTERMAN'S GAP Spin DANGER SPINNER to see if you live
PARLOR SCENE Players must work together to agree on who they think did the murder. ANGUS determines who was Most Helpful.
MEAT MONSTER Everyone loses a FUN point
FIGHT!!! Spin Danger Spinner to enter the fray (spin below a 6 to progress)
Villain speech! All players heckle Jenkins again (+1 FUN point)
CRYPTOSAFE
DANGER
suspects | alibi | evidence | notes
TINY NERD
Angus | yes | none
Jess the beheader | "beheader" | she's cool th
Juicy???
Graham | asleep.

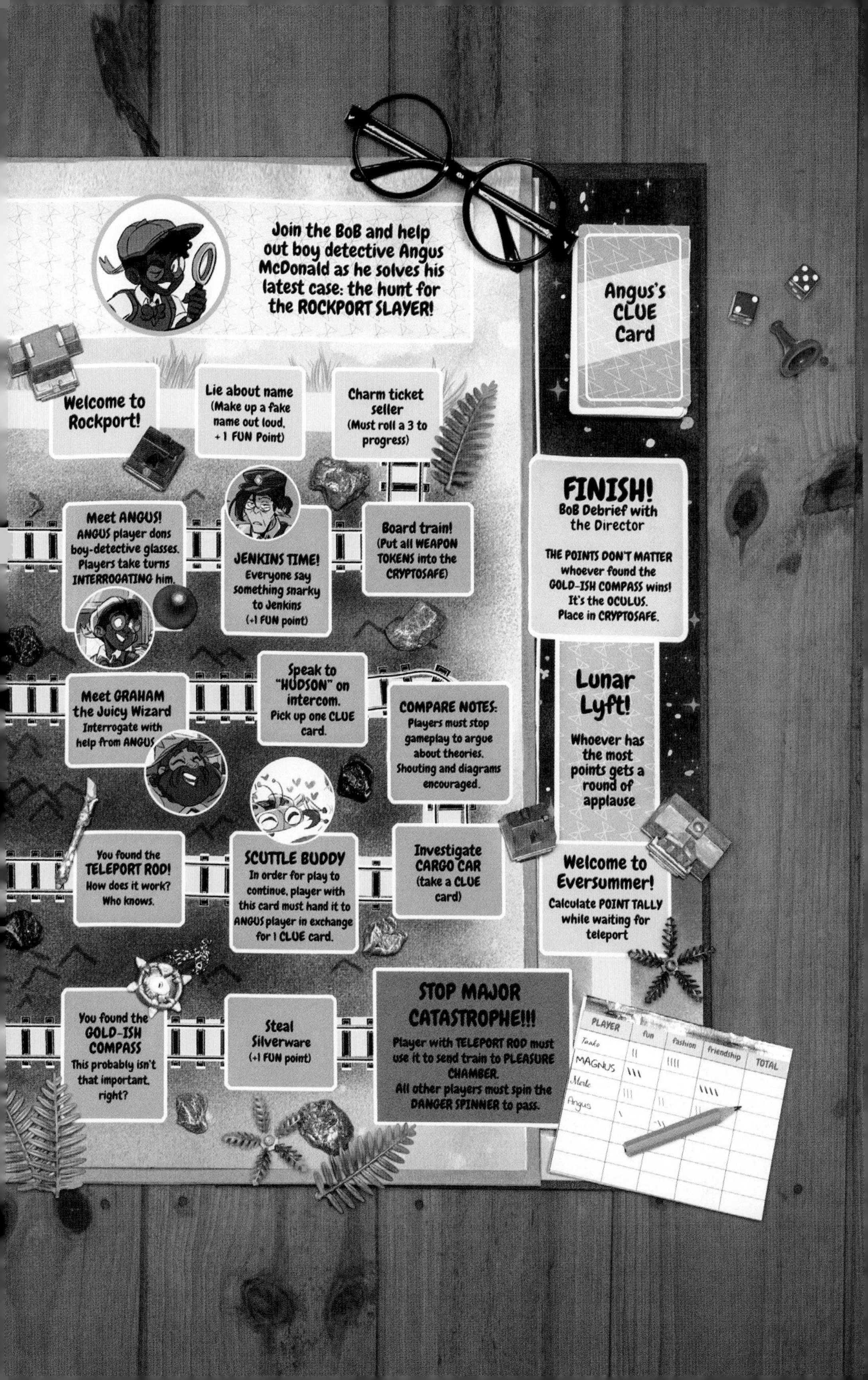
Join the BoB and help out boy detective Angus McDonald as he solves his latest case: the hunt for the ROCKPORT SLAYER!
Angus's CLUE Card
Welcome to Rockport!
Lie about name (Make up a fake name out loud, +1 FUN Point)
Charm ticket seller (Must roll a 3 to progress)
Meet ANGUS! ANGUS player dons boy-detective glasses. Players take turns INTERROGATING him.
JENKINS TIME! Everyone say something snarky to Jenkins (+1 FUN point)
Board train! (Put all WEAPON TOKENS into the CRYPTOSAFE)
FINISH! BoB Debrief with the Director
THE POINTS DON'T MATTER whoever found the GOLD-ISH COMPASS wins! It's the OCULUS. Place in CRYPTOSAFE.
Meet GRAHAM the Juicy Wizard Interrogate with help from ANGUS
Speak to "HUDSON" on intercom. Pick up one CLUE card.
COMPARE NOTES: Players must stop gameplay to argue about theories. Shouting and diagrams encouraged.
Lunar Lyft! Whoever has the most points gets a round of applause
You found the TELEPORT ROD! How does it work? Who knows.
SCUTTLE BUDDY In order for play to continue, player with this card must hand it to ANGUS player in exchange for 1 CLUE card.
Investigate CARGO CAR (take a CLUE card)
Welcome to Eversummer! Calculate POINT TALLY while waiting for teleport
You found the GOLD-ISH COMPASS This probably isn't that important, right?
Steal Silverware (+1 FUN point)
STOP MAJOR CATASTROPHE!!! Player with TELEPORT ROD must use it to send train to PLEASURE CHAMBER. All other players must spin the DANGER SPINNER to pass.
PLAYER
fun
fashion
friendship
TOTAL
Taako
MAGNUS
Merle
Angus

Chapter 1

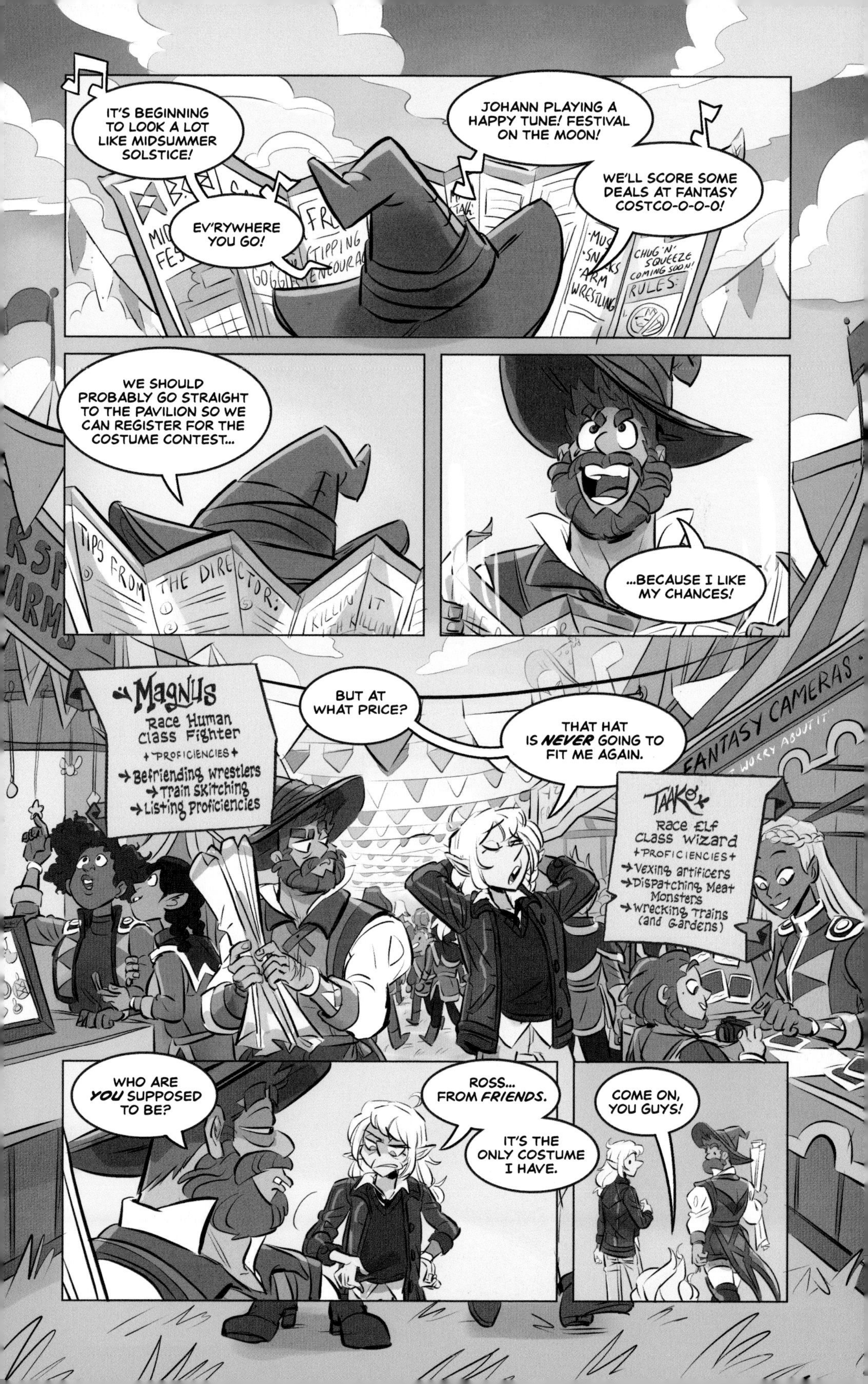
IT'S BEGINNING TO LOOK A LOT LIKE MIDSUMMER SOLSTICE!
EV'RYWHERE YOU GO!
JOHANN PLAYING A HAPPY TUNE! FESTIVAL ON THE MOON!
WE'LL SCORE SOME DEALS AT FANTASY COSTCO-O-O-O!
CHUG 'N' SQUEEZE COMING SOON!
RULES
WE SHOULD PROBABLY GO STRAIGHT TO THE PAVILION SO WE CAN REGISTER FOR THE COSTUME CONTEST...
TIPS FROM THE DIRECTOR:
...BECAUSE I LIKE MY CHANCES!
Magnus
Race Human
Class Fighter
PROFICIENCIES
Befriending wrestlers
Train Skitching
Listing Proficiencies
BUT AT WHAT PRICE?
THAT HAT IS NEVER GOING TO FIT ME AGAIN.
FANTASY CAMERAS
TAAKO
Race Elf
Class Wizard
PROFICIENCIES
Vexing artificers
Dispatching Meat Monsters
Wrecking Trains (and Gardens)
WHO ARE YOU SUPPOSED TO BE?
ROSS... FROM FRIENDS.
IT'S THE ONLY COSTUME I HAVE.
COME ON, YOU GUYS!

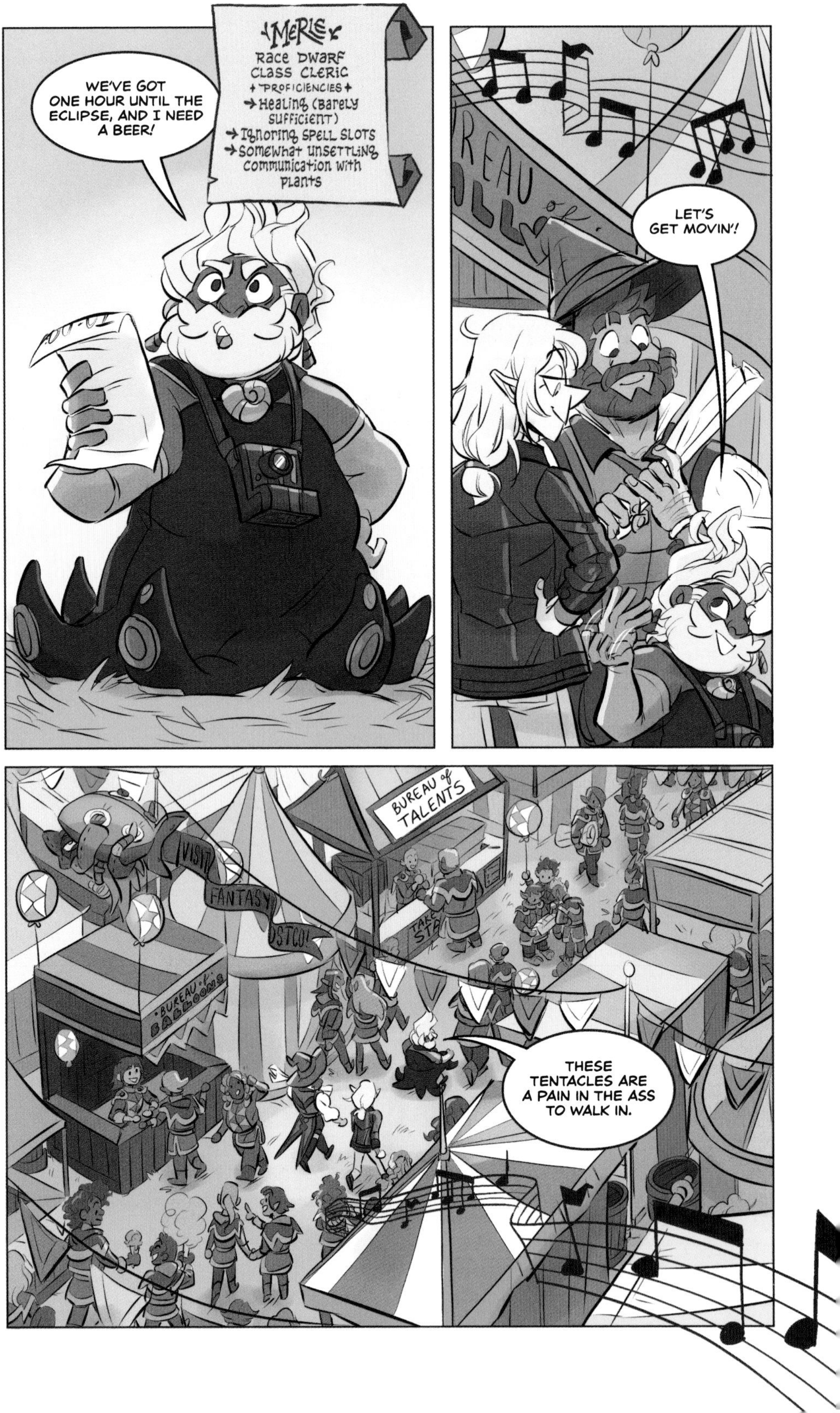
WE'VE GOT ONE HOUR UNTIL THE ECLIPSE, AND I NEED A BEER!
MERLE
Race Dwarf
Class Cleric
PROFICIENCIES
→ Healing (barely sufficient)
→ Ignoring spell slots
→ Somewhat unsettling communication with plants
LET'S GET MOVIN'!
BUREAU of TALENTS
VISIT FANTASY COSTCO!
BUREAU of BALLOONS
THESE TENTACLES ARE A PAIN IN THE ASS TO WALK IN.

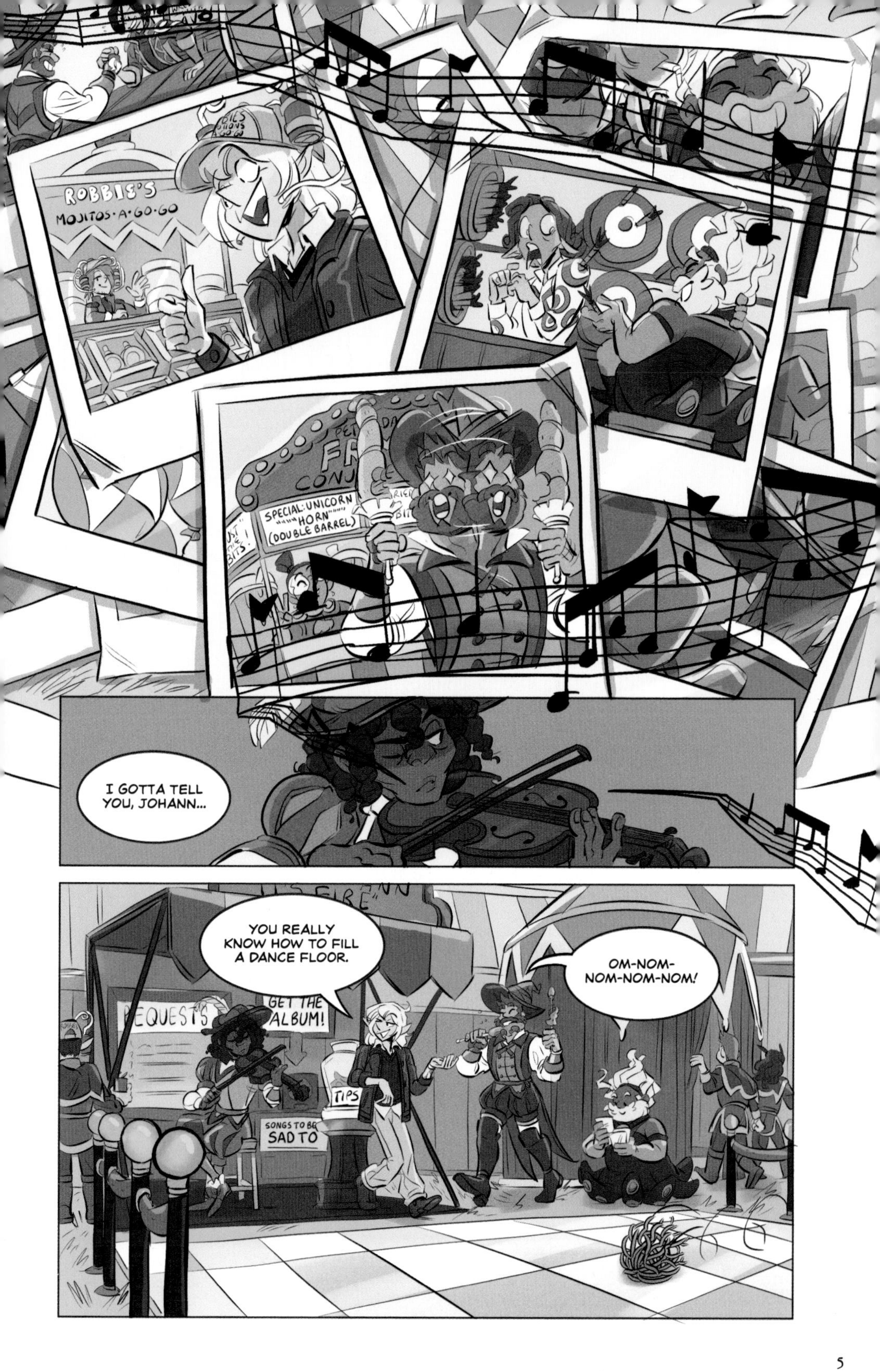
ROBBIE'S
MOJITOS-A-GO-GO
SPECIAL: UNICORN "HORN" (DOUBLE BARREL)
I GOTTA TELL YOU, JOHANN...
YOU REALLY KNOW HOW TO FILL A DANCE FLOOR.
OM-NOM-NOM-NOM-NOM!
REQUESTS
GET THE ALBUM!
TIPS
SONGS TO BE SAD TO

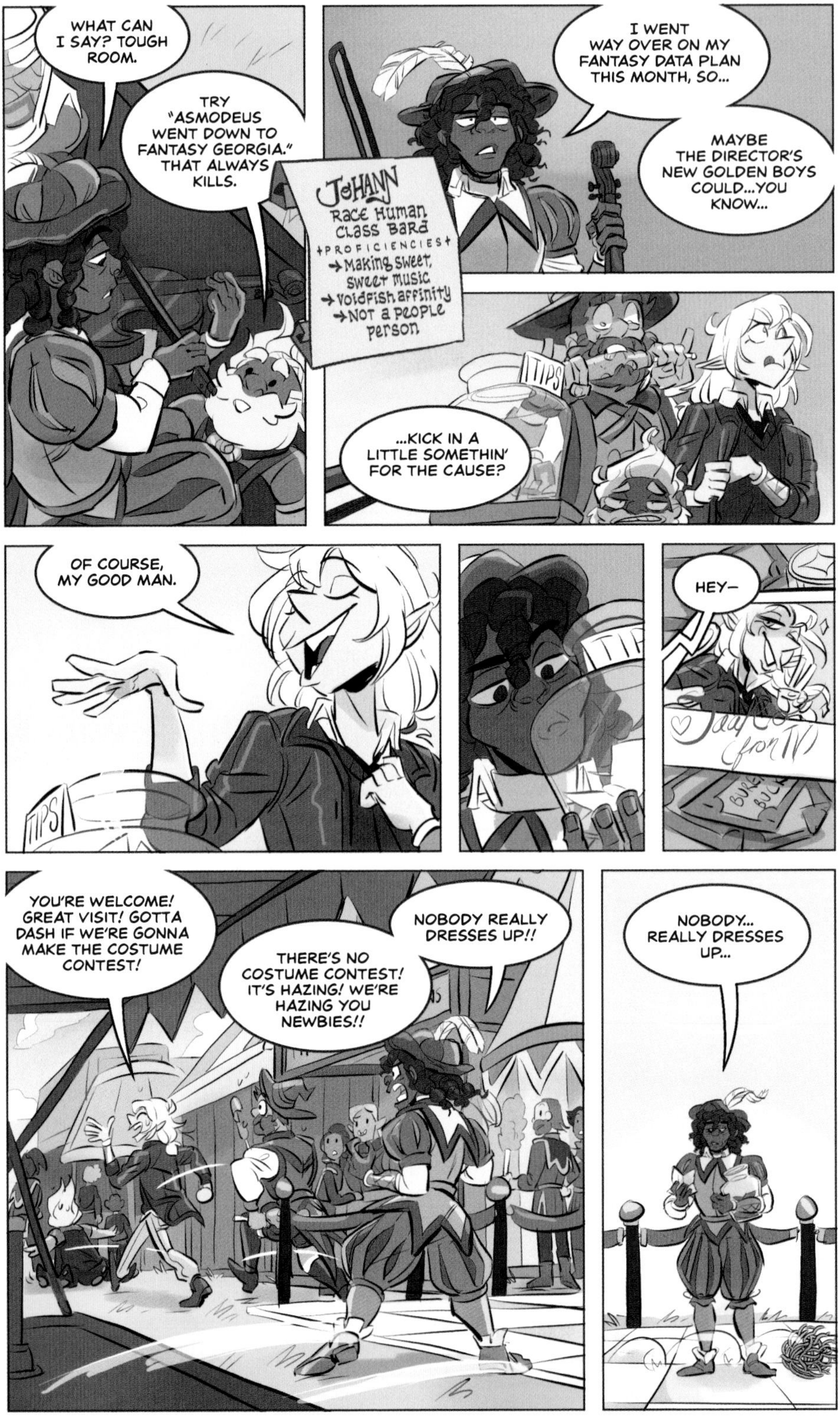
WHAT CAN I SAY? TOUGH ROOM.
TRY "ASMODEUS WENT DOWN TO FANTASY GEORGIA." THAT ALWAYS KILLS.
JOHANN
Race Human
Class Bard
PROFICIENCIES
→ Making sweet, sweet music
→ Voidfish affinity
→ Not a people person
I WENT WAY OVER ON MY FANTASY DATA PLAN THIS MONTH, SO...
MAYBE THE DIRECTOR'S NEW GOLDEN BOYS COULD...YOU KNOW...
TIPS
...KICK IN A LITTLE SOMETHIN' FOR THE CAUSE?
OF COURSE, MY GOOD MAN.
TIPS
TIPS
HEY—
YOU'RE WELCOME! GREAT VISIT! GOTTA DASH IF WE'RE GONNA MAKE THE COSTUME CONTEST!
NOBODY REALLY DRESSES UP!!
THERE'S NO COSTUME CONTEST! IT'S HAZING! WE'RE HAZING YOU NEWBIES!!
NOBODY... REALLY DRESSES UP...

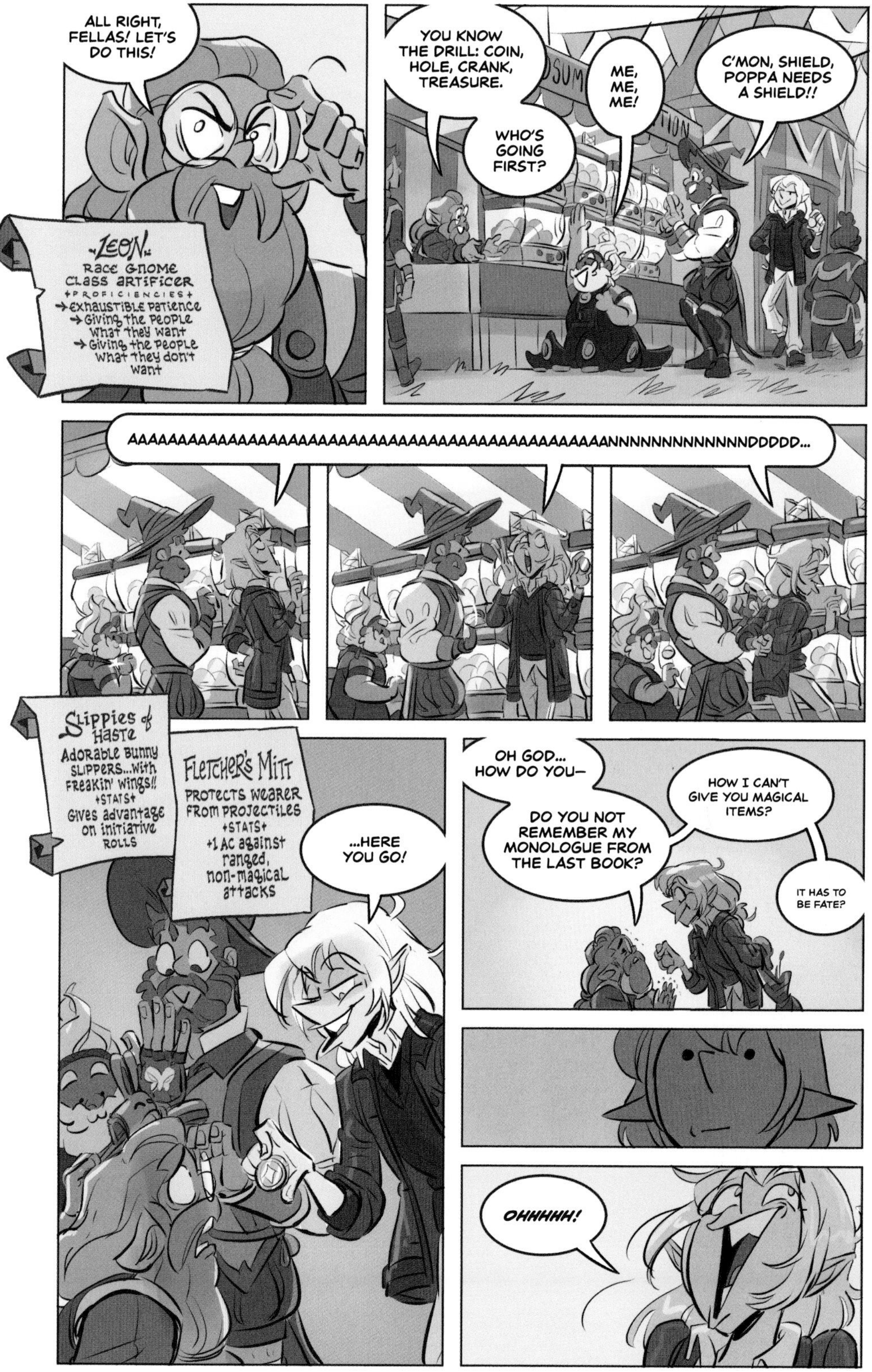

ALL RIGHT, FELLAS! LET'S DO THIS!
LEON
RACE GNOME
CLASS ARTIFICER
PROFICIENCIES
→EXHAUSTIBLE PATIENCE
→GIVING THE PEOPLE WHAT THEY WANT
→GIVING THE PEOPLE WHAT THEY DON'T WANT
YOU KNOW THE DRILL: COIN, HOLE, CRANK, TREASURE.
WHO'S GOING FIRST?
ME, ME, ME!
C'MON, SHIELD, POPPA NEEDS A SHIELD!!
AAAAAAAAAAAAAAAAAAAAAAAAAAAAAAAAAAAAAAAAAAAAAAAAANNNNNNNNNNNNNDDDDD...
SLIPPIES OF HASTE
ADORABLE BUNNY SLIPPERS...WITH FREAKIN' WINGS!!
STATS
GIVES ADVANTAGE ON INITIATIVE ROLLS
FLETCHER'S MITT
PROTECTS WEARER FROM PROJECTILES
STATS
+1 AC AGAINST RANGED, NON-MAGICAL ATTACKS
...HERE YOU GO!
OH GOD... HOW DO YOU—
DO YOU NOT REMEMBER MY MONOLOGUE FROM THE LAST BOOK?
HOW I CAN'T GIVE YOU MAGICAL ITEMS?
IT HAS TO BE FATE?
OHHHHH!

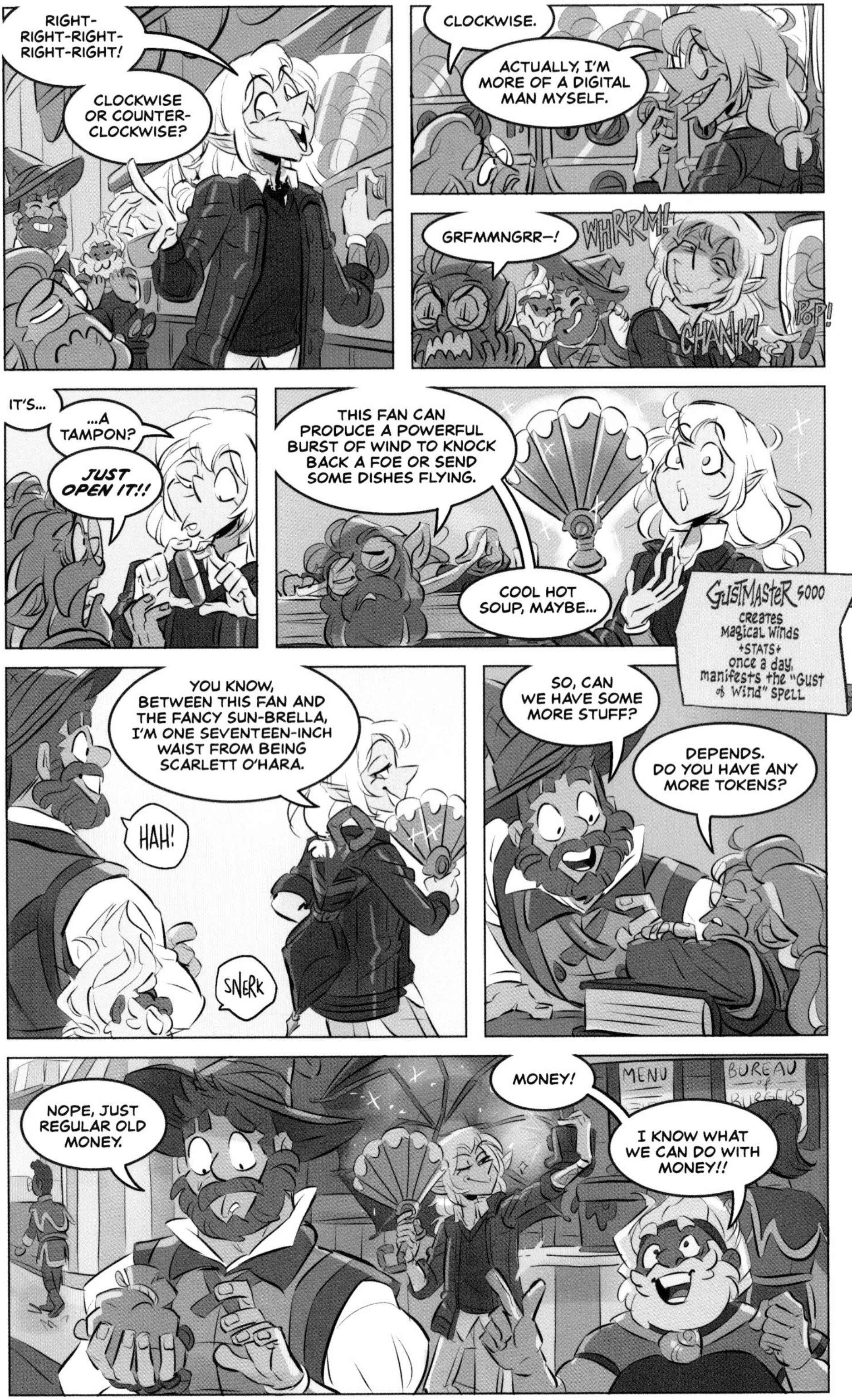
RIGHT-RIGHT-RIGHT-RIGHT-RIGHT!
CLOCKWISE OR COUNTER-CLOCKWISE?
CLOCKWISE.
ACTUALLY, I'M MORE OF A DIGITAL MAN MYSELF.
GRFMMNGRR—!
WHRRM!
CHANK!
POP!
IT'S...
...A TAMPON?
JUST OPEN IT!!
THIS FAN CAN PRODUCE A POWERFUL BURST OF WIND TO KNOCK BACK A FOE OR SEND SOME DISHES FLYING.
COOL HOT SOUP, MAYBE...
GUSTMASTER 5000
creates Magical Winds
+STATS+
once a day, manifests the "Gust of Wind" spell
YOU KNOW, BETWEEN THIS FAN AND THE FANCY SUN-BRELLA, I'M ONE SEVENTEEN-INCH WAIST FROM BEING SCARLETT O'HARA.
HAH!
SNERK
SO, CAN WE HAVE SOME MORE STUFF?
DEPENDS. DO YOU HAVE ANY MORE TOKENS?
NOPE, JUST REGULAR OLD MONEY.
MONEY!
MENU
BUREAU of BURGERS
I KNOW WHAT WE CAN DO WITH MONEY!!

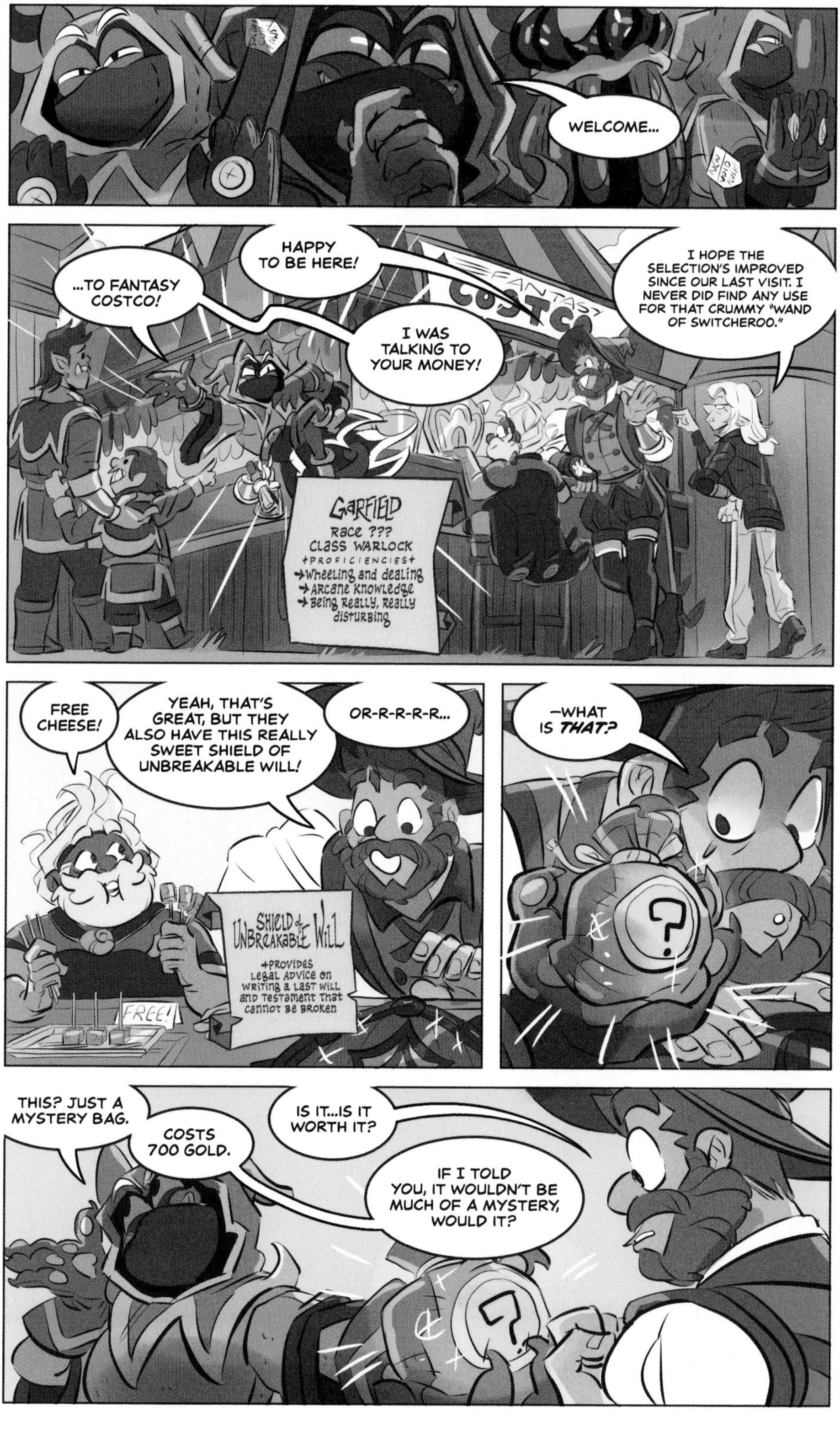
WELCOME...
...TO FANTASY COSTCO!
HAPPY TO BE HERE!
I WAS TALKING TO YOUR MONEY!
I HOPE THE SELECTION'S IMPROVED SINCE OUR LAST VISIT. I NEVER DID FIND ANY USE FOR THAT CRUMMY "WAND OF SWITCHEROO."
FANTASY COSTCO
GARFIELD
Race ???
Class Warlock
+PROFICIENCIES+
→Wheeling and dealing
→Arcane knowledge
→Being really, really disturbing
FREE CHEESE!
YEAH, THAT'S GREAT, BUT THEY ALSO HAVE THIS REALLY SWEET SHIELD OF UNBREAKABLE WILL!
OR-R-R-R-R...
SHIELD of the UNBREAKABLE WILL
+PROVIDES LEGAL ADVICE ON WRITING A LAST WILL AND TESTAMENT THAT CANNOT BE BROKEN
FREE!
—WHAT IS *THAT?*
THIS? JUST A MYSTERY BAG.
COSTS 700 GOLD.
IS IT...IS IT WORTH IT?
IF I TOLD YOU, IT WOULDN'T BE MUCH OF A MYSTERY, WOULD IT?

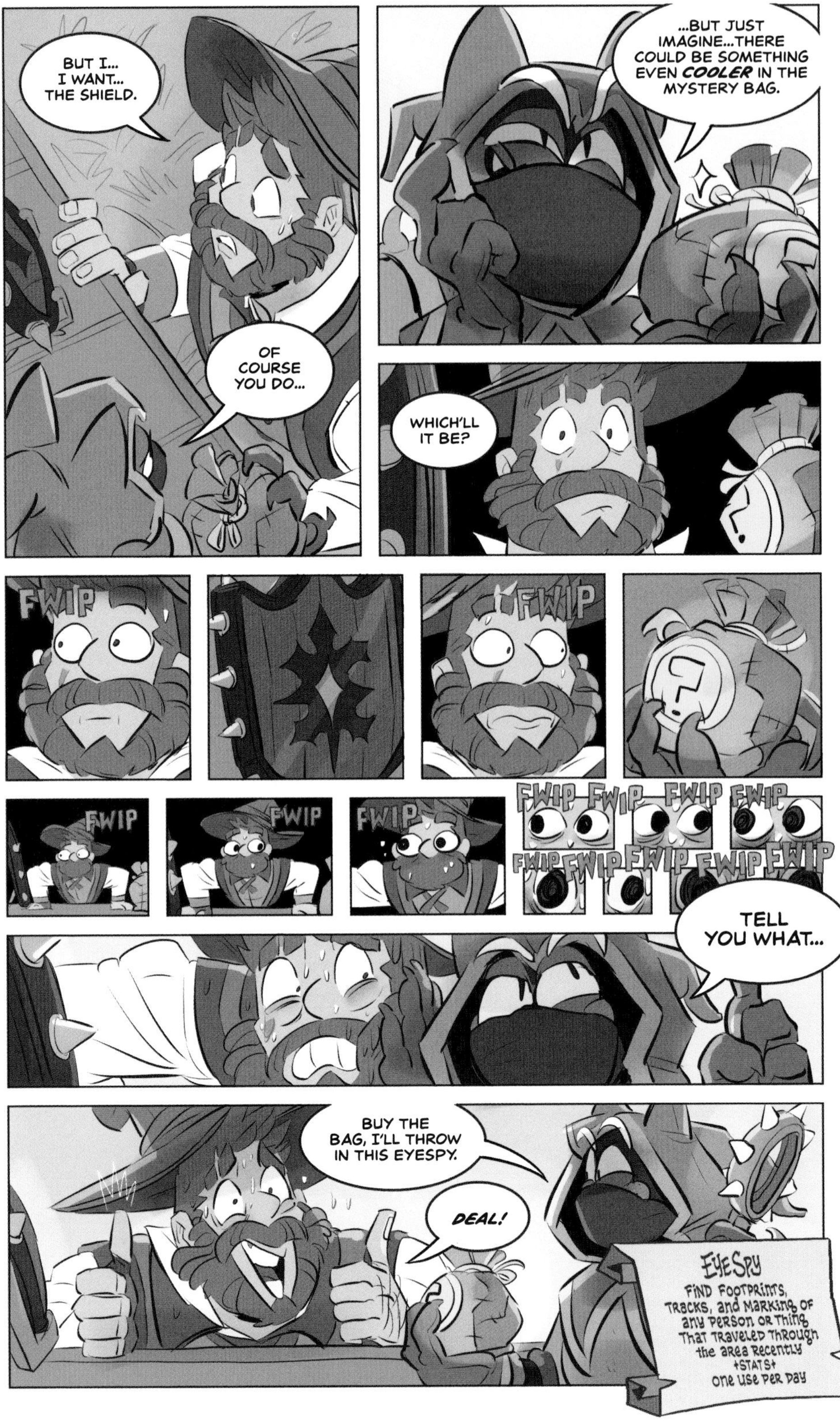
BUT I... I WANT... THE SHIELD.
...BUT JUST IMAGINE...THERE COULD BE SOMETHING EVEN COOLER IN THE MYSTERY BAG.
OF COURSE YOU DO...
WHICH'LL IT BE?
FWIP
FWIP
FWIP
FWIP
FWIP
FWIP FWIP FWIP FWIP
FWIP FWIP FWIP FWIP FWIP
TELL YOU WHAT...
BUY THE BAG, I'LL THROW IN THIS EYESPY.
DEAL!
EyeSpy
Find Footprints, Tracks, and Marking of any Person or Thing That Traveled Through the area Recently
+STATS+
One Use Per Day

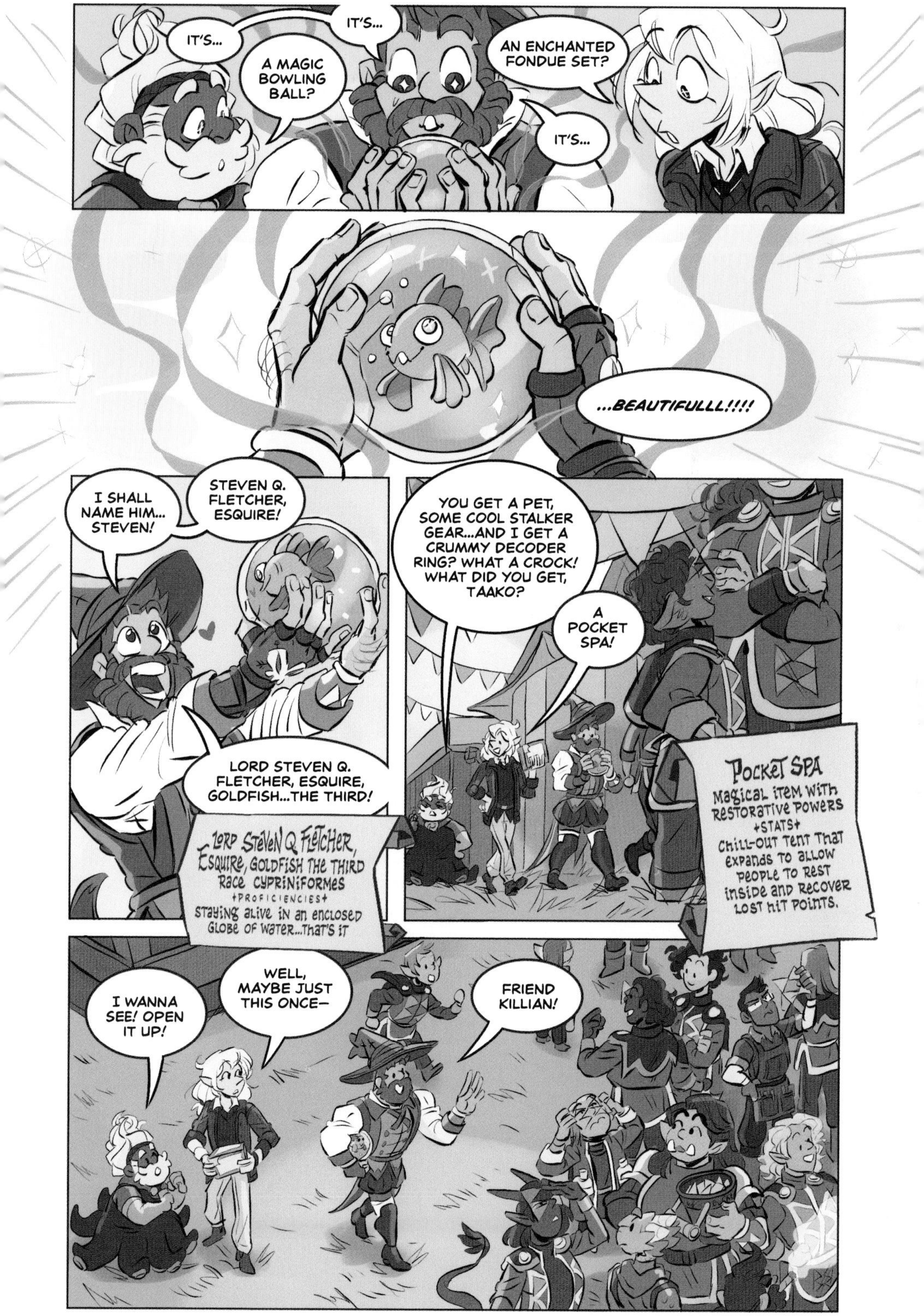
IT'S...
A MAGIC BOWLING BALL?
IT'S...
AN ENCHANTED FONDUE SET?
IT'S...
...BEAUTIFULLL!!!!
I SHALL NAME HIM... STEVEN!
STEVEN Q. FLETCHER, ESQUIRE!
LORD STEVEN Q. FLETCHER, ESQUIRE, GOLDFISH...THE THIRD!
LORD STEVEN Q FLETCHER, ESQUIRE, GOLDFISH THE THIRD
RACE CYPRINIFORMES
+PROFICIENCIES+
STAYING ALIVE IN AN ENCLOSED GLOBE OF WATER...THAT'S IT
YOU GET A PET, SOME COOL STALKER GEAR...AND I GET A CRUMMY DECODER RING? WHAT A CROCK! WHAT DID YOU GET, TAAKO?
A POCKET SPA!
POCKET SPA
MAGICAL ITEM WITH RESTORATIVE POWERS
+STATS+
CHILL-OUT TENT THAT EXPANDS TO ALLOW PEOPLE TO REST INSIDE AND RECOVER LOST HIT POINTS.
I WANNA SEE! OPEN IT UP!
WELL, MAYBE JUST THIS ONCE—
FRIEND KILLIAN!

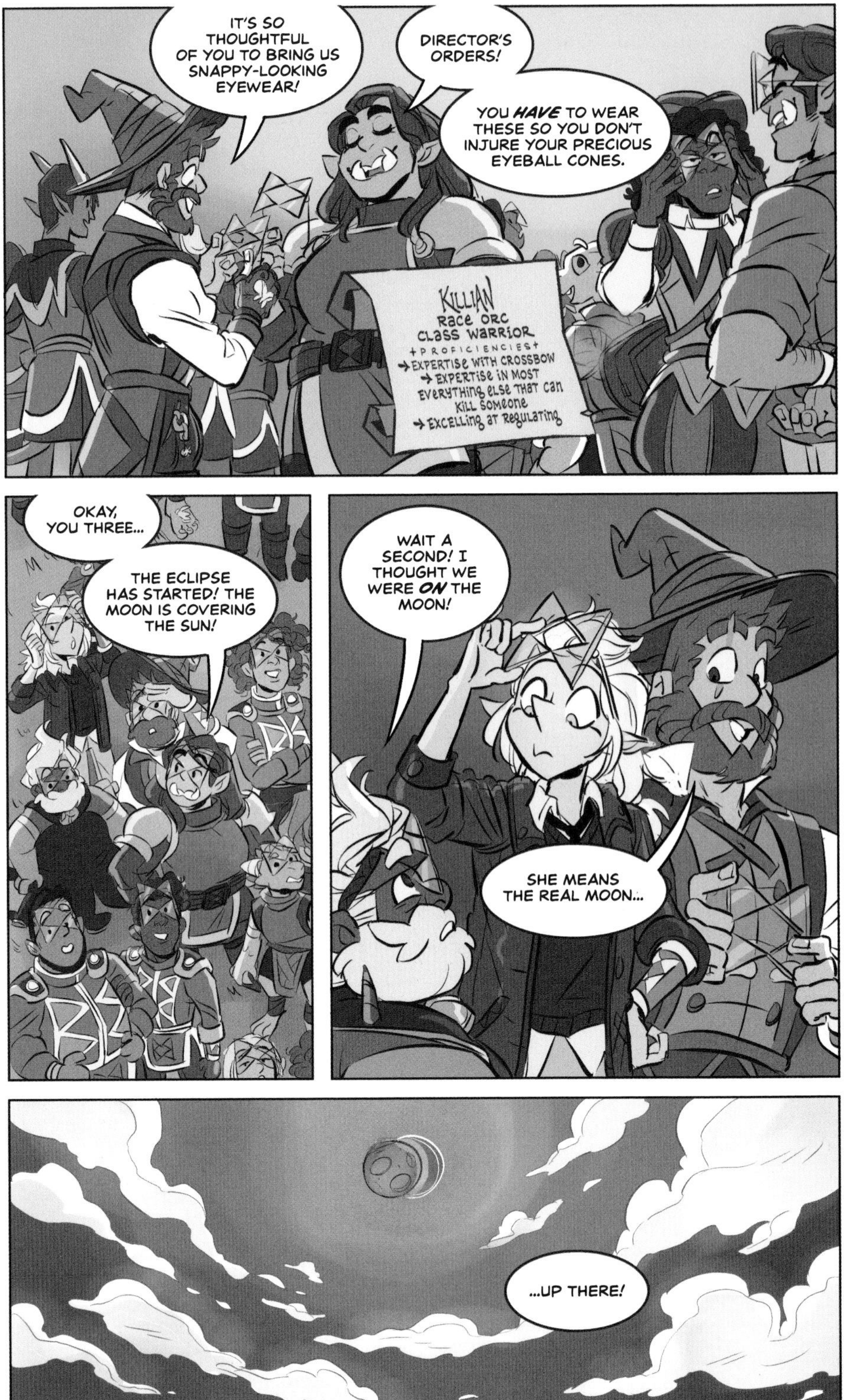
IT'S SO THOUGHTFUL OF YOU TO BRING US SNAPPY-LOOKING EYEWEAR!
DIRECTOR'S ORDERS!
YOU HAVE TO WEAR THESE SO YOU DON'T INJURE YOUR PRECIOUS EYEBALL CONES.
KILLIAN
Race Orc
Class Warrior
PROFICIENCIES
→ Expertise with crossbow
→ Expertise in most everything else that can kill someone
→ Excelling at Regulating
OKAY, YOU THREE...
THE ECLIPSE HAS STARTED! THE MOON IS COVERING THE SUN!
WAIT A SECOND! I THOUGHT WE WERE ON THE MOON!
SHE MEANS THE REAL MOON...
...UP THERE!

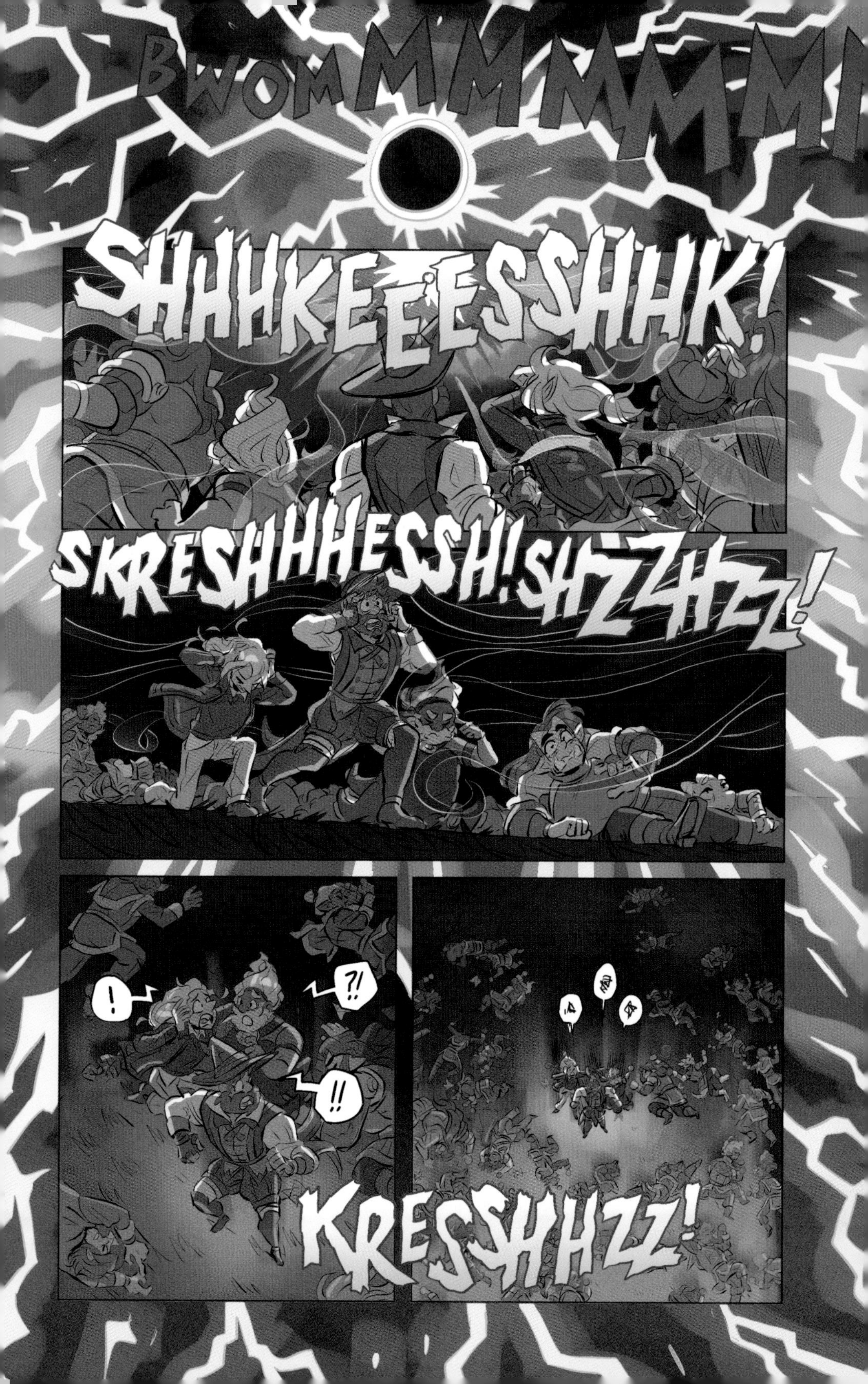
BWOMMMMMMM
SHHKEEESSHHK!
SKRESHHHESSH! SHZZHZZ!
!
?!
!!
KRESSHZZ!

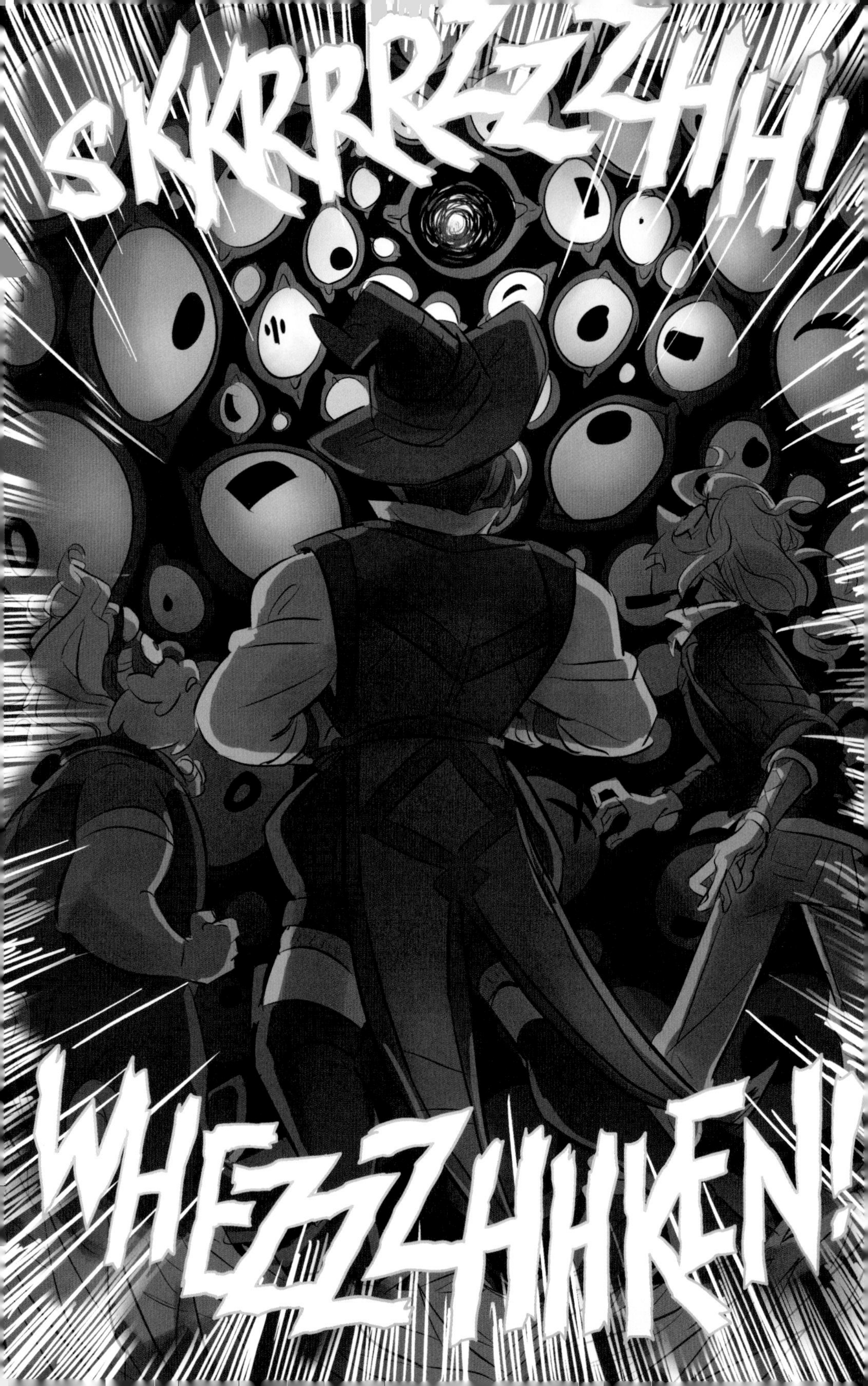
SKRRRZZHH!
WHEZZZHHKEN!

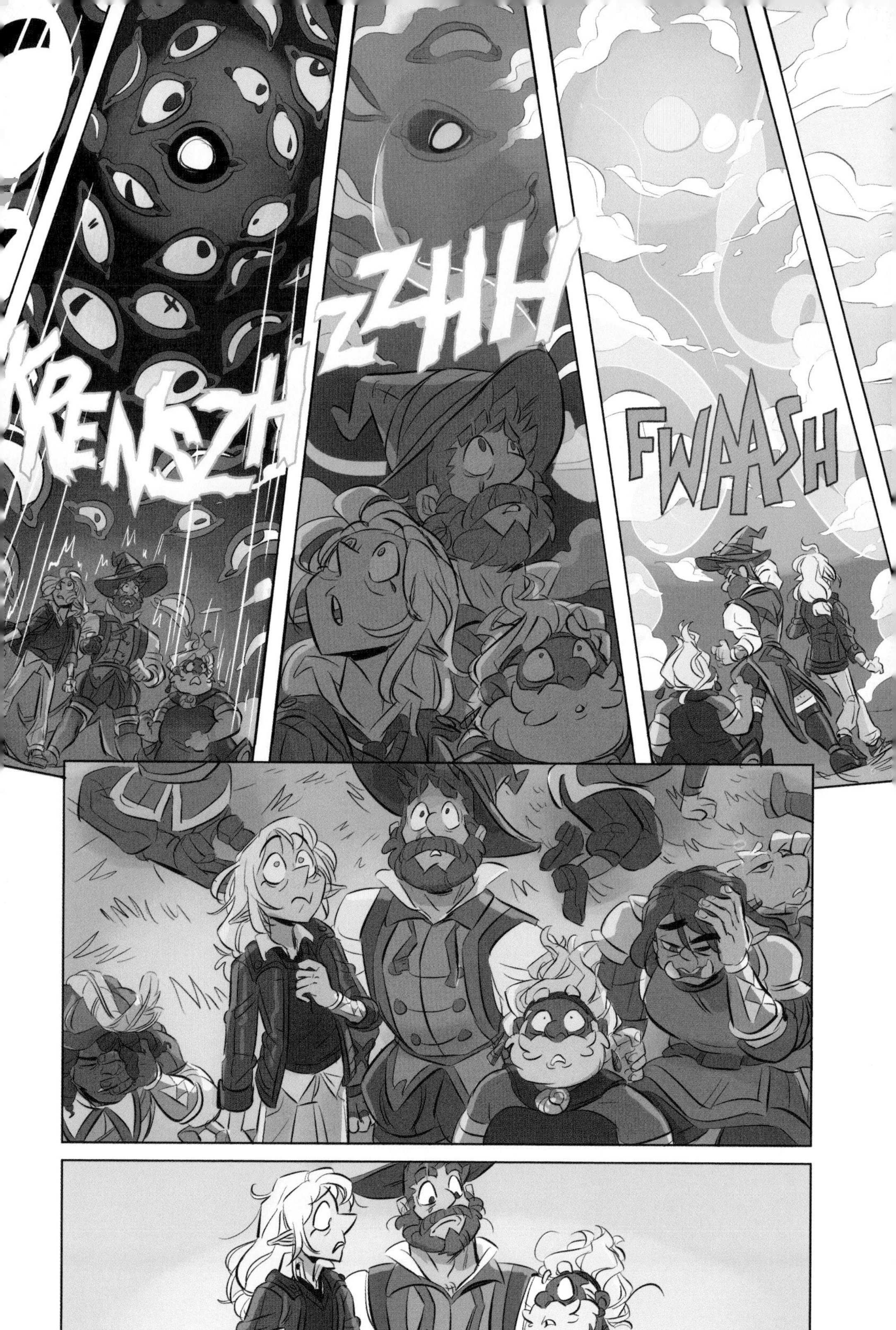
KRENSZHZZHH
FWAAASH

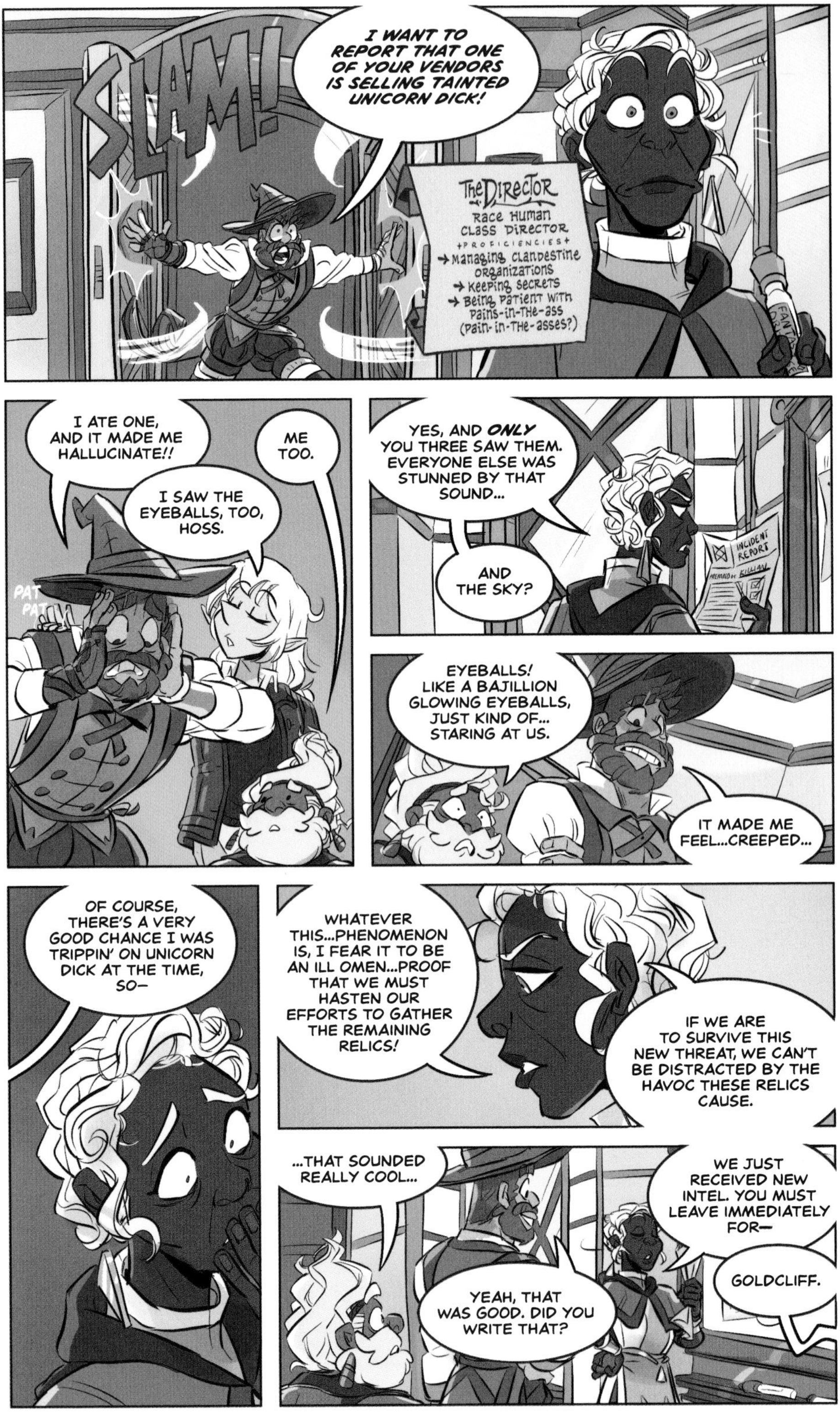
SLAM!
I WANT TO REPORT THAT ONE OF YOUR VENDORS IS SELLING TAINTED UNICORN DICK!
The Director
Race Human
Class Director
Proficiencies
→ Managing clandestine organizations
→ Keeping secrets
→ Being patient with pains-in-the-ass (pain-in-the-asses?)
I ATE ONE, AND IT MADE ME HALLUCINATE!!
ME TOO.
I SAW THE EYEBALLS, TOO, HOSS.
PAT PAT
YES, AND ONLY YOU THREE SAW THEM. EVERYONE ELSE WAS STUNNED BY THAT SOUND...
AND THE SKY?
EYEBALLS! LIKE A BAJILLION GLOWING EYEBALLS, JUST KIND OF... STARING AT US.
IT MADE ME FEEL...CREEPED...
OF COURSE, THERE'S A VERY GOOD CHANCE I WAS TRIPPIN' ON UNICORN DICK AT THE TIME, SO—
WHATEVER THIS...PHENOMENON IS, I FEAR IT TO BE AN ILL OMEN...PROOF THAT WE MUST HASTEN OUR EFFORTS TO GATHER THE REMAINING RELICS!
IF WE ARE TO SURVIVE THIS NEW THREAT, WE CAN'T BE DISTRACTED BY THE HAVOC THESE RELICS CAUSE.
...THAT SOUNDED REALLY COOL...
YEAH, THAT WAS GOOD. DID YOU WRITE THAT?
WE JUST RECEIVED NEW INTEL. YOU MUST LEAVE IMMEDIATELY FOR—
GOLDCLIFF.

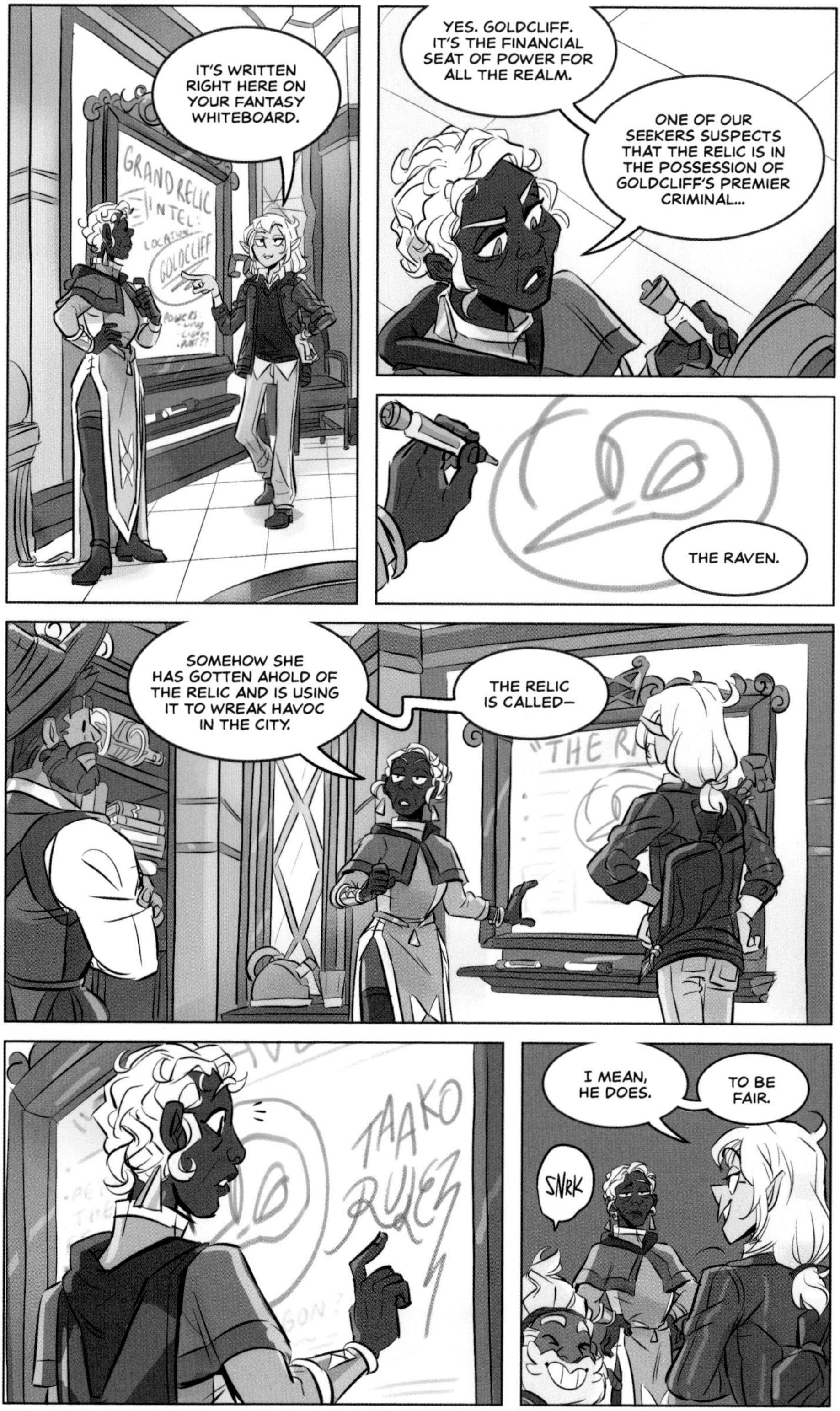
IT'S WRITTEN RIGHT HERE ON YOUR FANTASY WHITEBOARD.
GRAND RELIC INTEL:
GOLDCLIFF
YES. GOLDCLIFF. IT'S THE FINANCIAL SEAT OF POWER FOR ALL THE REALM.
ONE OF OUR SEEKERS SUSPECTS THAT THE RELIC IS IN THE POSSESSION OF GOLDCLIFF'S PREMIER CRIMINAL...
THE RAVEN.
SOMEHOW SHE HAS GOTTEN AHOLD OF THE RELIC AND IS USING IT TO WREAK HAVOC IN THE CITY.
THE RELIC IS CALLED—
TAAKO RULEZ
I MEAN, HE DOES.
TO BE FAIR.
SNRK

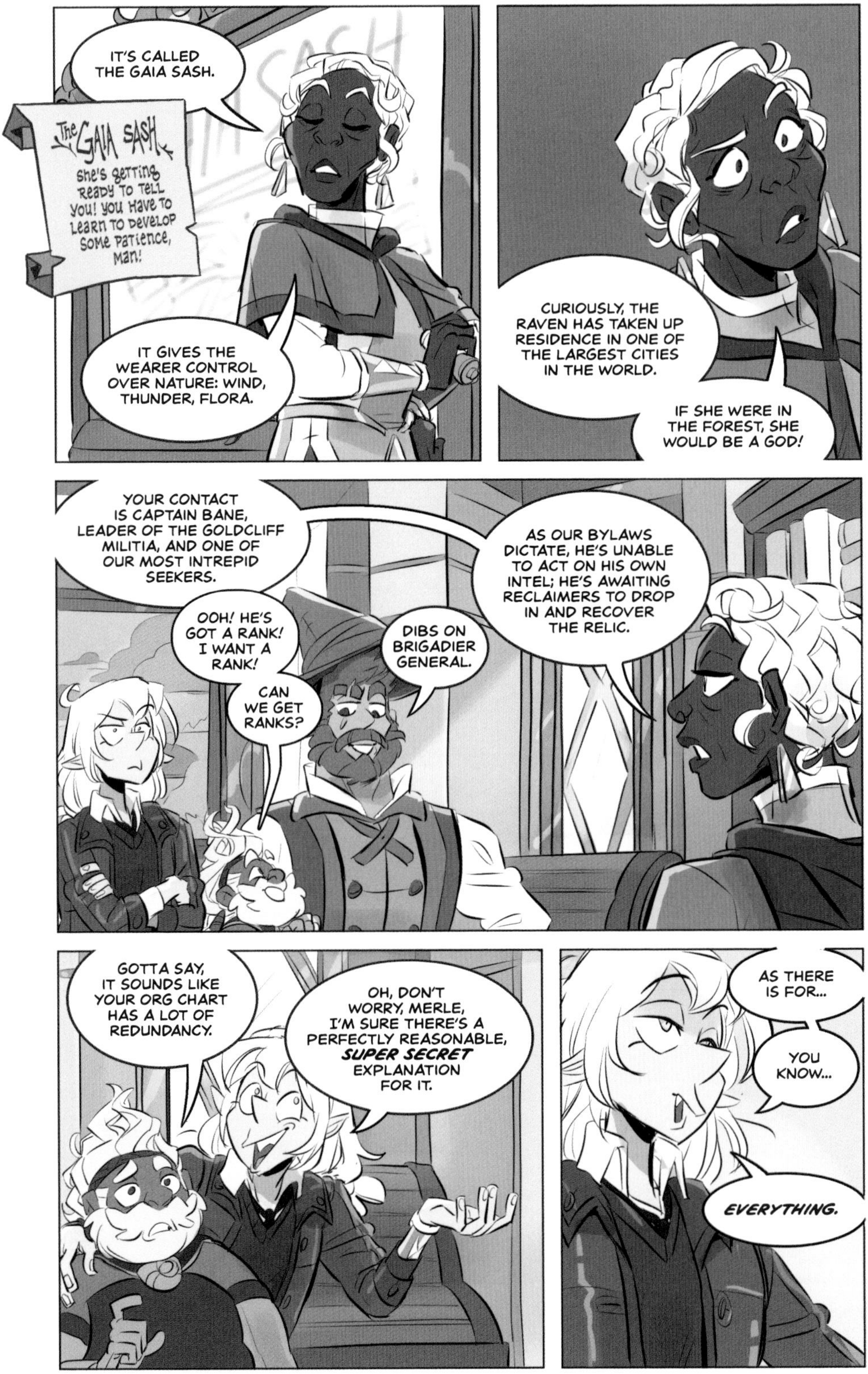
IT'S CALLED THE GAIA SASH.
The GAIA SASH
She's getting Ready To Tell You! You Have To Learn To Develop Some Patience, Man!
IT GIVES THE WEARER CONTROL OVER NATURE: WIND, THUNDER, FLORA.
CURIOUSLY, THE RAVEN HAS TAKEN UP RESIDENCE IN ONE OF THE LARGEST CITIES IN THE WORLD.
IF SHE WERE IN THE FOREST, SHE WOULD BE A GOD!
YOUR CONTACT IS CAPTAIN BANE, LEADER OF THE GOLDCLIFF MILITIA, AND ONE OF OUR MOST INTREPID SEEKERS.
AS OUR BYLAWS DICTATE, HE'S UNABLE TO ACT ON HIS OWN INTEL; HE'S AWAITING RECLAIMERS TO DROP IN AND RECOVER THE RELIC.
OOH! HE'S GOT A RANK! I WANT A RANK!
DIBS ON BRIGADIER GENERAL.
CAN WE GET RANKS?
GOTTA SAY, IT SOUNDS LIKE YOUR ORG CHART HAS A LOT OF REDUNDANCY.
OH, DON'T WORRY, MERLE, I'M SURE THERE'S A PERFECTLY REASONABLE, SUPER SECRET EXPLANATION FOR IT.
AS THERE IS FOR...
YOU KNOW...
EVERYTHING.

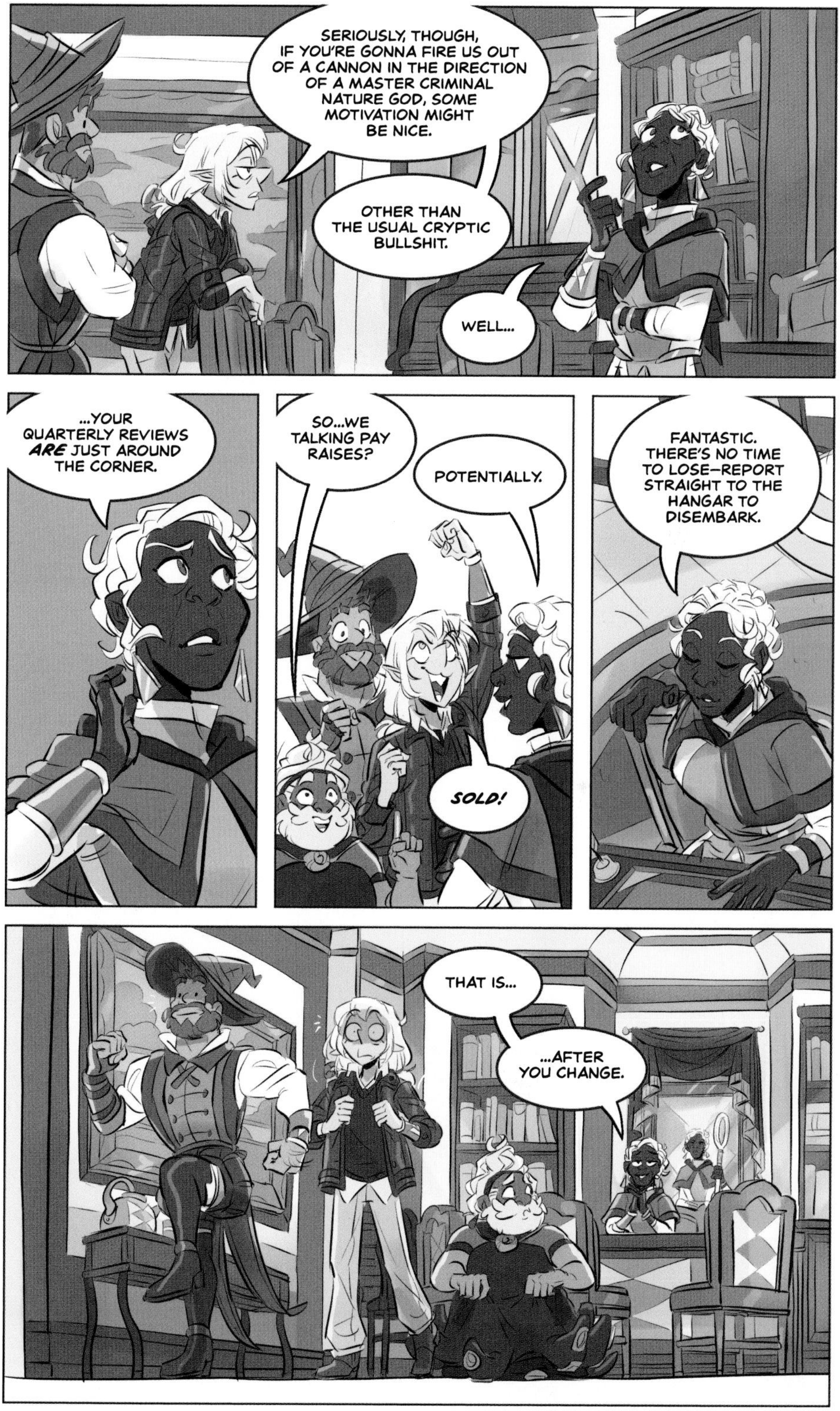
SERIOUSLY, THOUGH, IF YOU'RE GONNA FIRE US OUT OF A CANNON IN THE DIRECTION OF A MASTER CRIMINAL NATURE GOD, SOME MOTIVATION MIGHT BE NICE.
OTHER THAN THE USUAL CRYPTIC BULLSHIT.
WELL...
...YOUR QUARTERLY REVIEWS *ARE* JUST AROUND THE CORNER.
SO...WE TALKING PAY RAISES?
POTENTIALLY.
SOLD!
FANTASTIC. THERE'S NO TIME TO LOSE—REPORT STRAIGHT TO THE HANGAR TO DISEMBARK.
THAT IS...
...AFTER YOU CHANGE.

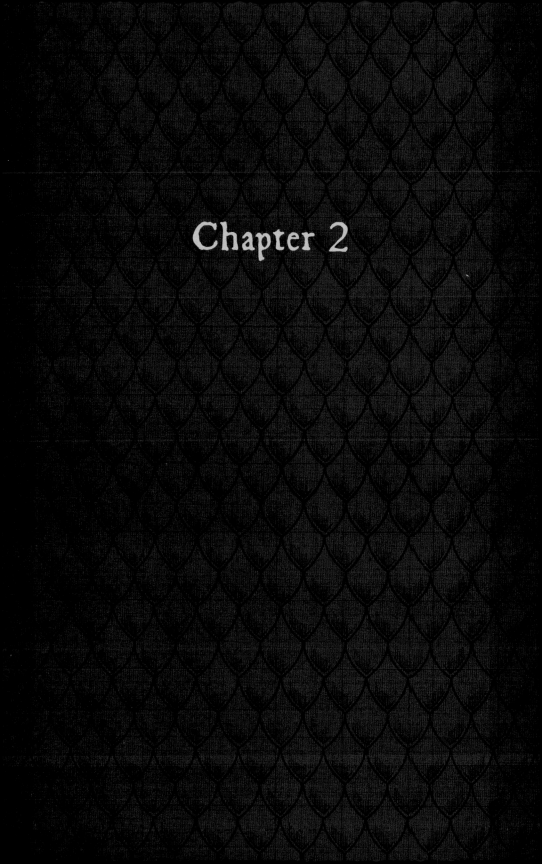

Chapter 2

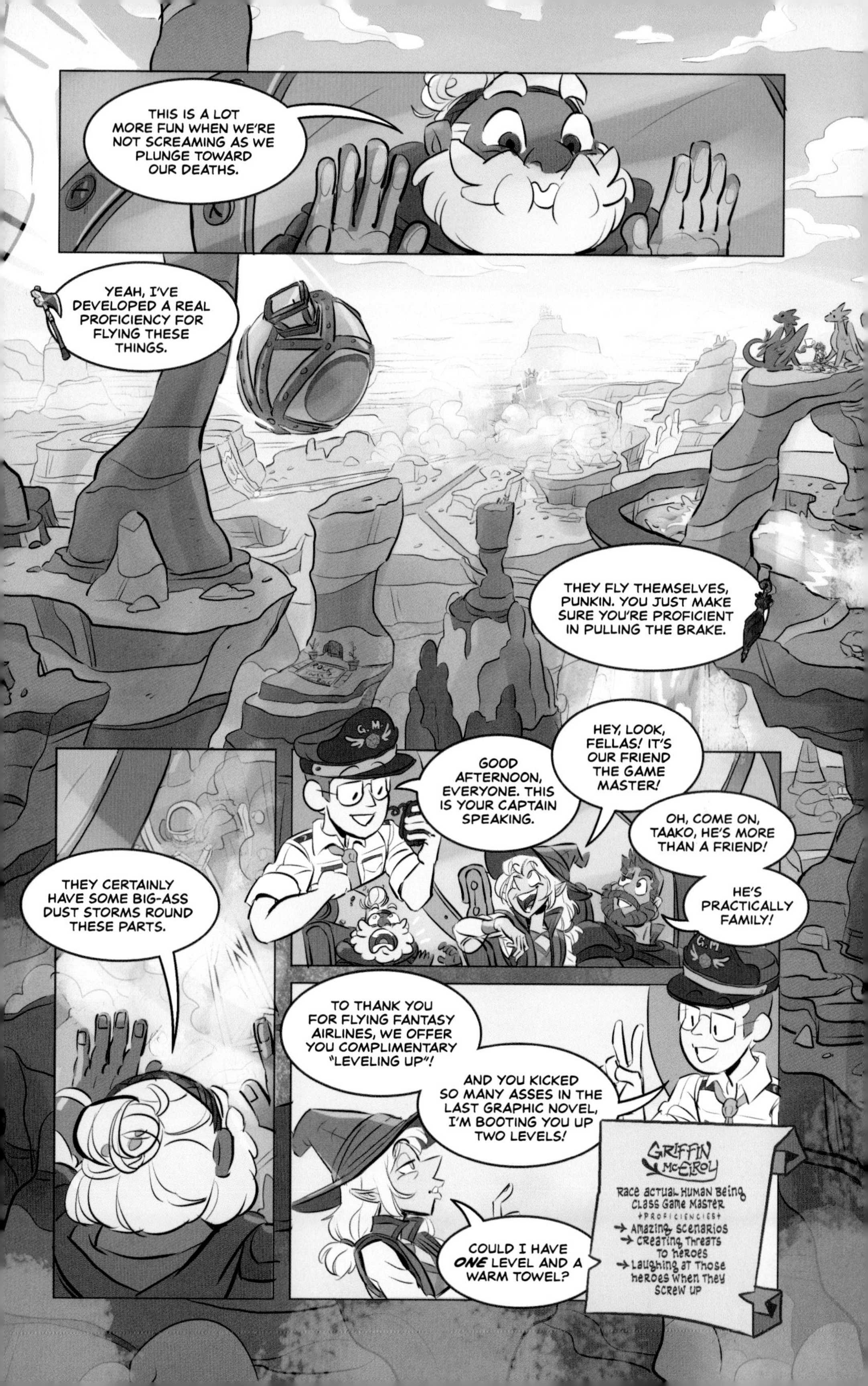
THIS IS A LOT MORE FUN WHEN WE'RE NOT SCREAMING AS WE PLUNGE TOWARD OUR DEATHS.
YEAH, I'VE DEVELOPED A REAL PROFICIENCY FOR FLYING THESE THINGS.
THEY FLY THEMSELVES, PUNKIN. YOU JUST MAKE SURE YOU'RE PROFICIENT IN PULLING THE BRAKE.
THEY CERTAINLY HAVE SOME BIG-ASS DUST STORMS ROUND THESE PARTS.
GOOD AFTERNOON, EVERYONE. THIS IS YOUR CAPTAIN SPEAKING.
HEY, LOOK, FELLAS! IT'S OUR FRIEND THE GAME MASTER!
OH, COME ON, TAAKO, HE'S MORE THAN A FRIEND!
HE'S PRACTICALLY FAMILY!
TO THANK YOU FOR FLYING FANTASY AIRLINES, WE OFFER YOU COMPLIMENTARY "LEVELING UP"!
AND YOU KICKED SO MANY ASSES IN THE LAST GRAPHIC NOVEL, I'M BOOTING YOU UP TWO LEVELS!
GRIFFIN McELROY
Race actual Human Being
Class Game Master
PROFICIENCIES
→ Amazing scenarios
→ Creating Threats to heroes
→ Laughing at those heroes when they screw up
COULD I HAVE ONE LEVEL AND A WARM TOWEL?

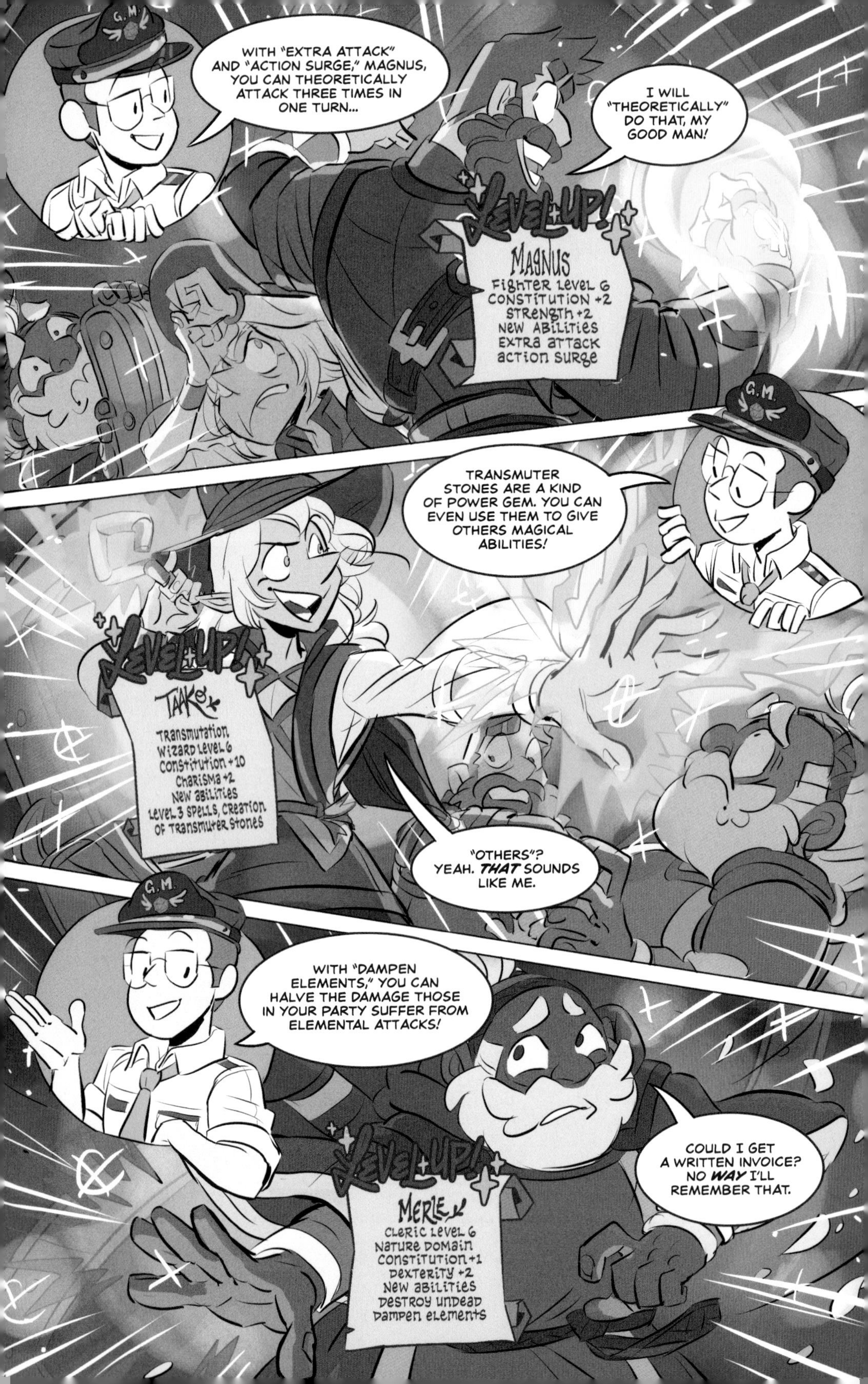
WITH "EXTRA ATTACK" AND "ACTION SURGE," MAGNUS, YOU CAN THEORETICALLY ATTACK THREE TIMES IN ONE TURN...
I WILL "THEORETICALLY" DO THAT, MY GOOD MAN!
LEVEL UP!
MAGNUS
Fighter Level 6
Constitution +2
Strength +2
New Abilities
Extra attack
action surge
TRANSMUTER STONES ARE A KIND OF POWER GEM. YOU CAN EVEN USE THEM TO GIVE OTHERS MAGICAL ABILITIES!
LEVEL UP!
TAAKO
Transmutation
Wizard Level 6
Constitution +10
Charisma +2
New abilities
Level 3 spells, Creation of Transmuter Stones
"OTHERS"? YEAH. *THAT* SOUNDS LIKE ME.
WITH "DAMPEN ELEMENTS," YOU CAN HALVE THE DAMAGE THOSE IN YOUR PARTY SUFFER FROM ELEMENTAL ATTACKS!
LEVEL UP!
MERLE
Cleric Level 6
Nature Domain
Constitution +1
Dexterity +2
New abilities
Destroy Undead
Dampen Elements
COULD I GET A WRITTEN INVOICE? NO *WAY* I'LL REMEMBER THAT.

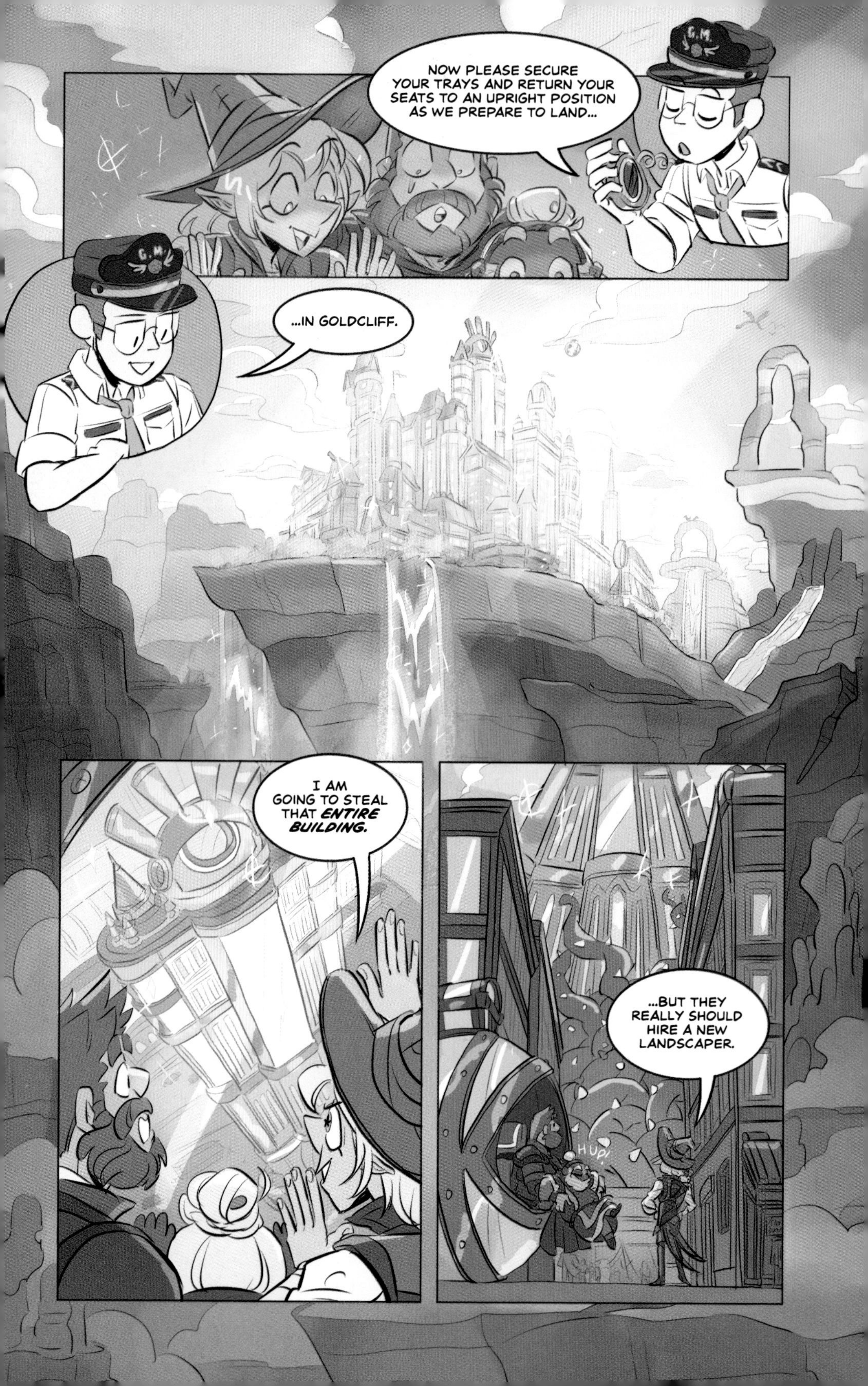
NOW PLEASE SECURE YOUR TRAYS AND RETURN YOUR SEATS TO AN UPRIGHT POSITION AS WE PREPARE TO LAND...
...IN GOLDCLIFF.
I AM GOING TO STEAL THAT *ENTIRE BUILDING.*
HUP!
...BUT THEY REALLY SHOULD HIRE A NEW LANDSCAPER.

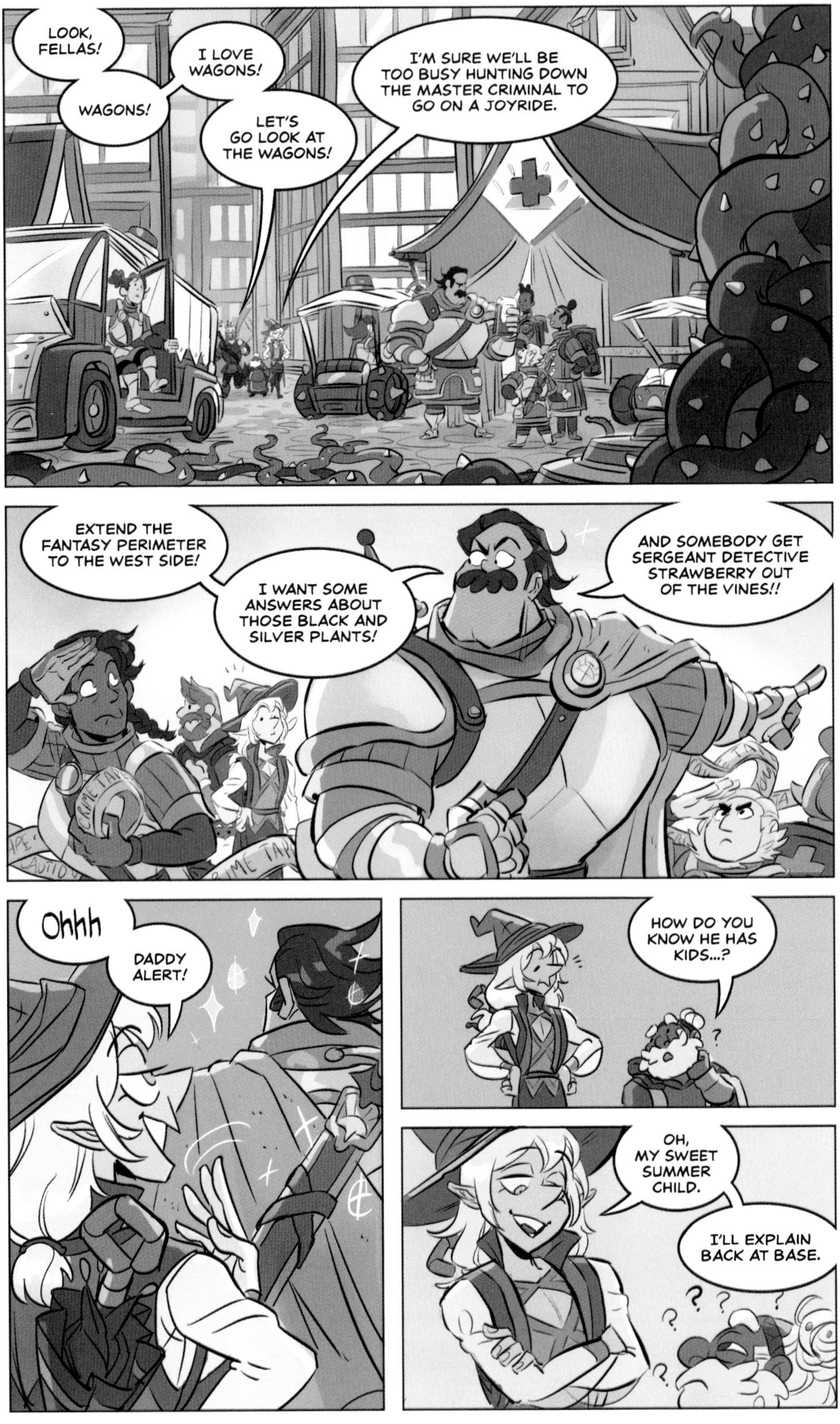
LOOK, FELLAS!
WAGONS!
I LOVE WAGONS!
LET'S GO LOOK AT THE WAGONS!
I'M SURE WE'LL BE TOO BUSY HUNTING DOWN THE MASTER CRIMINAL TO GO ON A JOYRIDE.
EXTEND THE FANTASY PERIMETER TO THE WEST SIDE!
I WANT SOME ANSWERS ABOUT THOSE BLACK AND SILVER PLANTS!
AND SOMEBODY GET SERGEANT DETECTIVE STRAWBERRY OUT OF THE VINES!!
Ohhh
DADDY ALERT!
HOW DO YOU KNOW HE HAS KIDS...?
?
OH, MY SWEET SUMMER CHILD.
I'LL EXPLAIN BACK AT BASE.
? ? ? ? ?

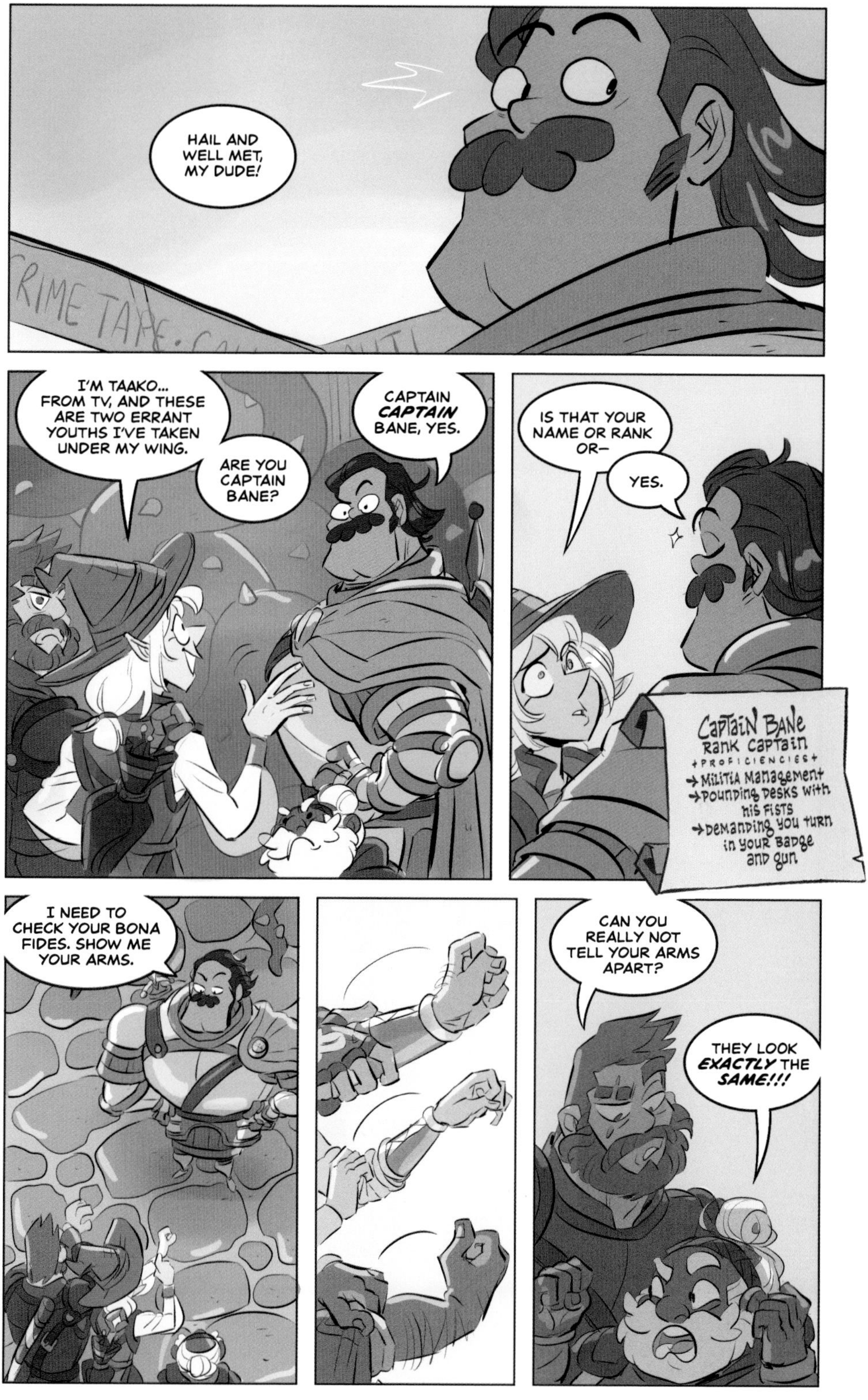

HAIL AND WELL MET, MY DUDE!
I'M TAAKO... FROM TV, AND THESE ARE TWO ERRANT YOUTHS I'VE TAKEN UNDER MY WING.
ARE YOU CAPTAIN BANE?
CAPTAIN *CAPTAIN* BANE, YES.
IS THAT YOUR NAME OR RANK OR—
YES.
Captain Bane
Rank Captain
+PROFICIENCIES+
→Militia Management
→Pounding desks with his fists
→Demanding you turn in your badge and gun
I NEED TO CHECK YOUR BONA FIDES. SHOW ME YOUR ARMS.
CAN YOU REALLY NOT TELL YOUR ARMS APART?
THEY LOOK *EXACTLY* THE *SAME!!!*

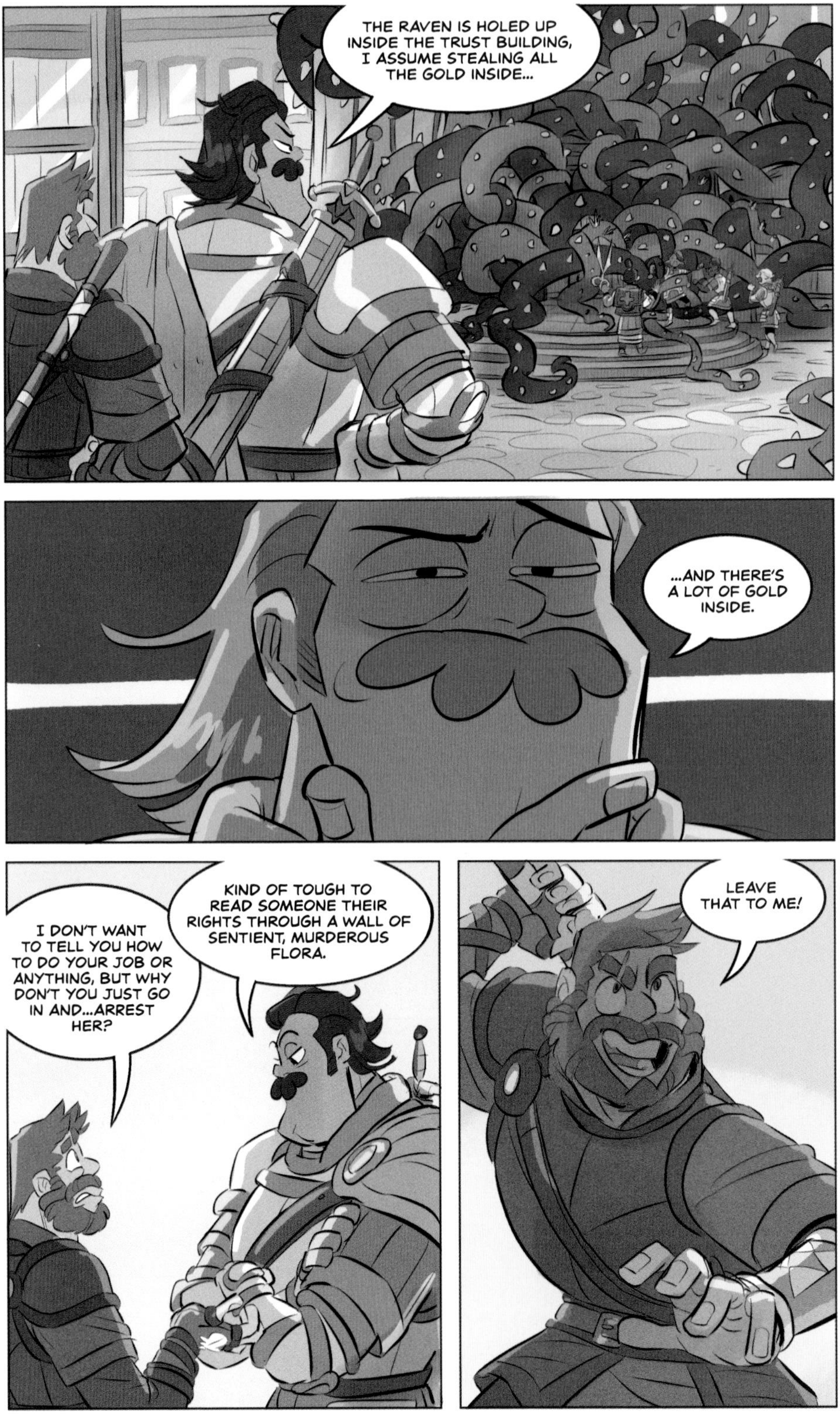
THE RAVEN IS HOLED UP INSIDE THE TRUST BUILDING, I ASSUME STEALING ALL THE GOLD INSIDE...
...AND THERE'S A LOT OF GOLD INSIDE.
I DON'T WANT TO TELL YOU HOW TO DO YOUR JOB OR ANYTHING, BUT WHY DON'T YOU JUST GO IN AND...ARREST HER?
KIND OF TOUGH TO READ SOMEONE THEIR RIGHTS THROUGH A WALL OF SENTIENT, MURDEROUS FLORA.
LEAVE THAT TO ME!

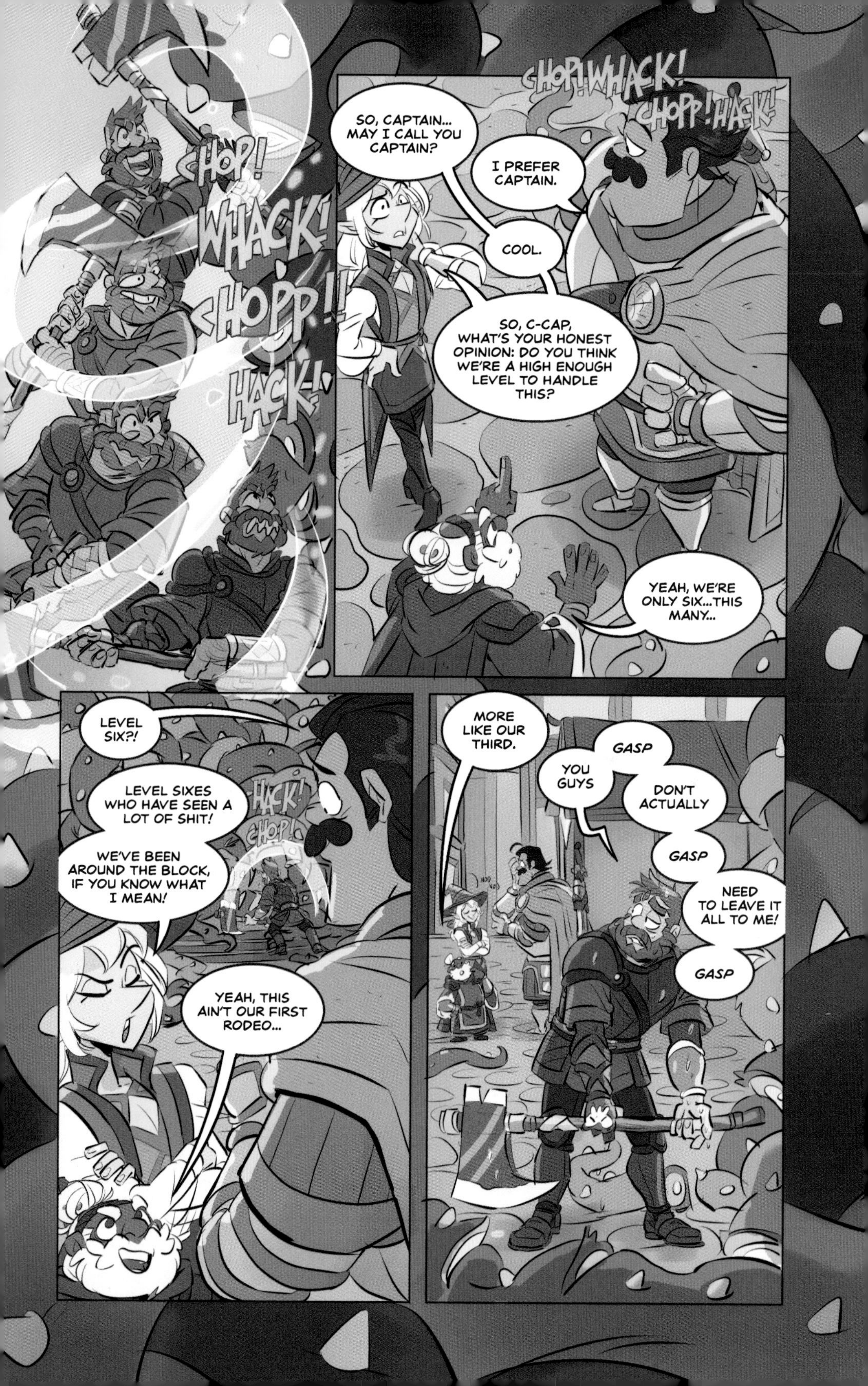
CHOP!
WHACK!
CHOPP!!
HACK!
CHOP! WHACK!
CHOPP! HACK!
SO, CAPTAIN... MAY I CALL YOU CAPTAIN?
I PREFER CAPTAIN.
COOL.
SO, C-CAP, WHAT'S YOUR HONEST OPINION: DO YOU THINK WE'RE A HIGH ENOUGH LEVEL TO HANDLE THIS?
YEAH, WE'RE ONLY SIX...THIS MANY...
LEVEL SIX?!
HACK!
CHOP!
LEVEL SIXES WHO HAVE SEEN A LOT OF SHIT!
WE'VE BEEN AROUND THE BLOCK, IF YOU KNOW WHAT I MEAN!
YEAH, THIS AIN'T OUR FIRST RODEO...
MORE LIKE OUR THIRD.
YOU GUYS
GASP
DON'T ACTUALLY
GASP
NEED TO LEAVE IT ALL TO ME!
GASP

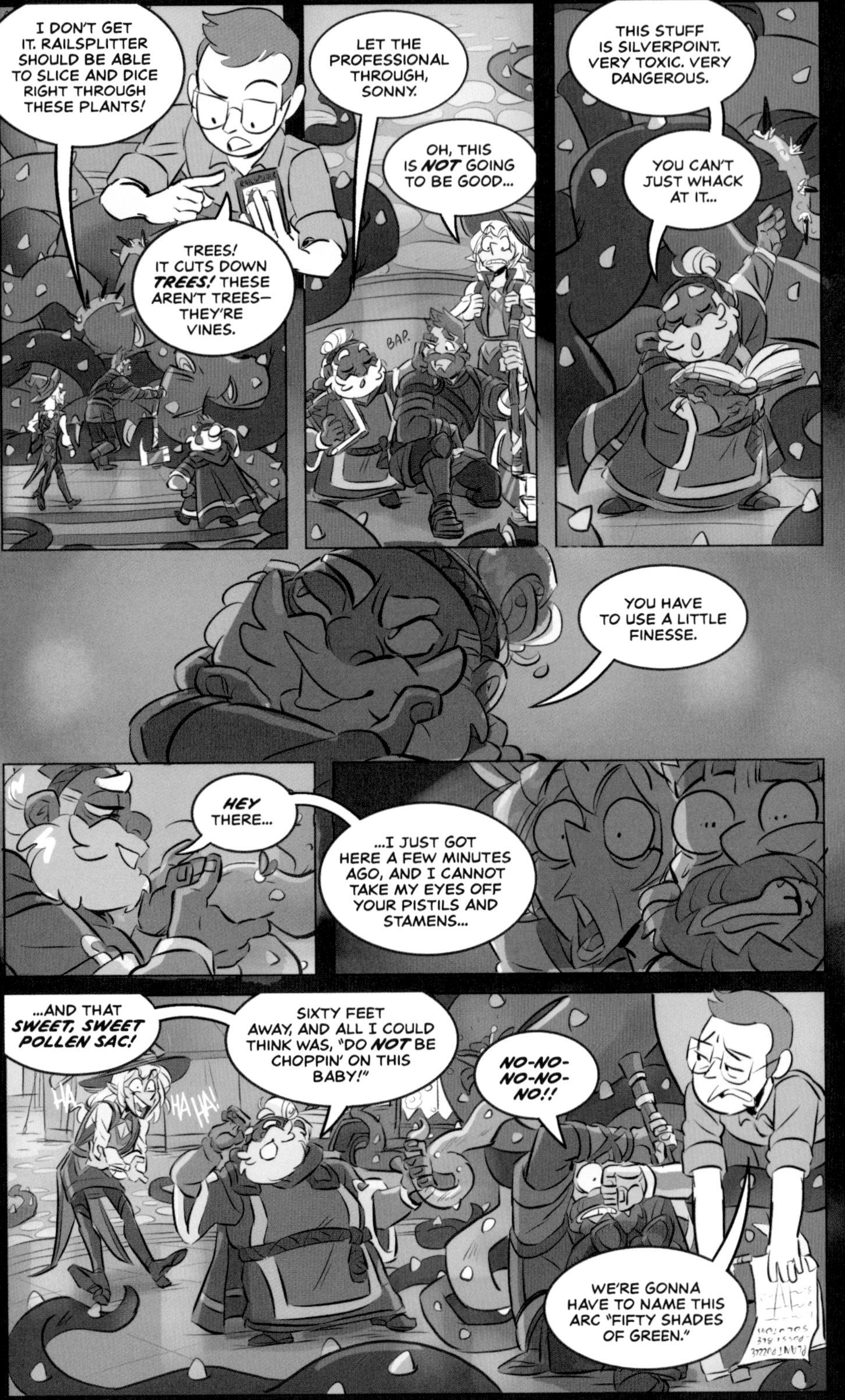
I DON'T GET IT. RAILSPLITTER SHOULD BE ABLE TO SLICE AND DICE RIGHT THROUGH THESE PLANTS!
TREES! IT CUTS DOWN TREES! THESE AREN'T TREES—THEY'RE VINES.
LET THE PROFESSIONAL THROUGH, SONNY.
OH, THIS IS NOT GOING TO BE GOOD...
BAP.
THIS STUFF IS SILVERPOINT. VERY TOXIC. VERY DANGEROUS.
YOU CAN'T JUST WHACK AT IT...
YOU HAVE TO USE A LITTLE FINESSE.
HEY THERE...
...I JUST GOT HERE A FEW MINUTES AGO, AND I CANNOT TAKE MY EYES OFF YOUR PISTILS AND STAMENS...
...AND THAT SWEET, SWEET POLLEN SAC!
SIXTY FEET AWAY, AND ALL I COULD THINK WAS, "DO NOT BE CHOPPIN' ON THIS BABY!"
HA
HA HA!
NO-NO-NO-NO-NO!!
WE'RE GONNA HAVE TO NAME THIS ARC "FIFTY SHADES OF GREEN."

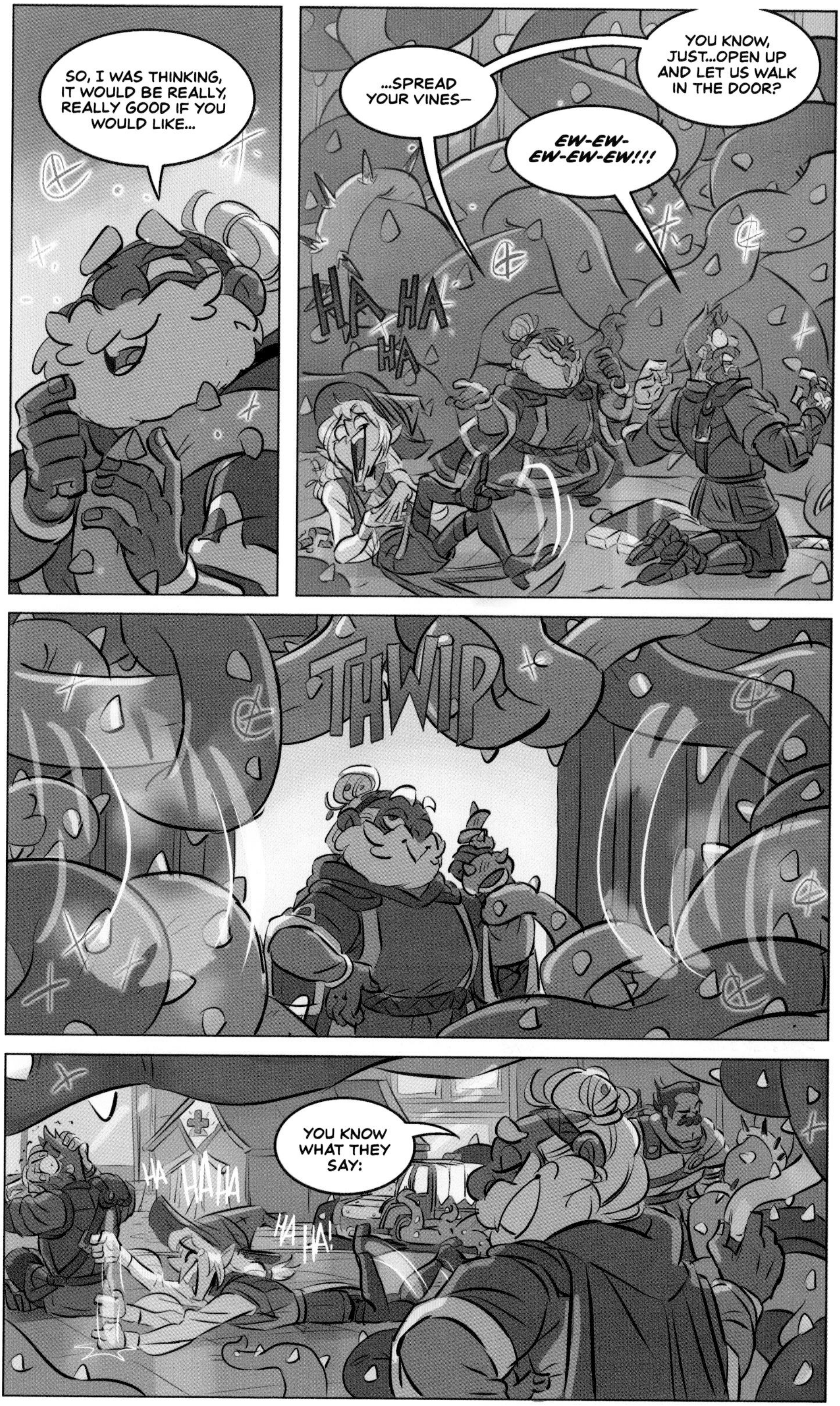
SO, I WAS THINKING, IT WOULD BE REALLY, REALLY GOOD IF YOU WOULD LIKE...
...SPREAD YOUR VINES—
YOU KNOW, JUST...OPEN UP AND LET US WALK IN THE DOOR?
EW-EW-EW-EW-EW!!!
HA HA HA
THWIP
YOU KNOW WHAT THEY SAY:
HA HAHA
HA HA!

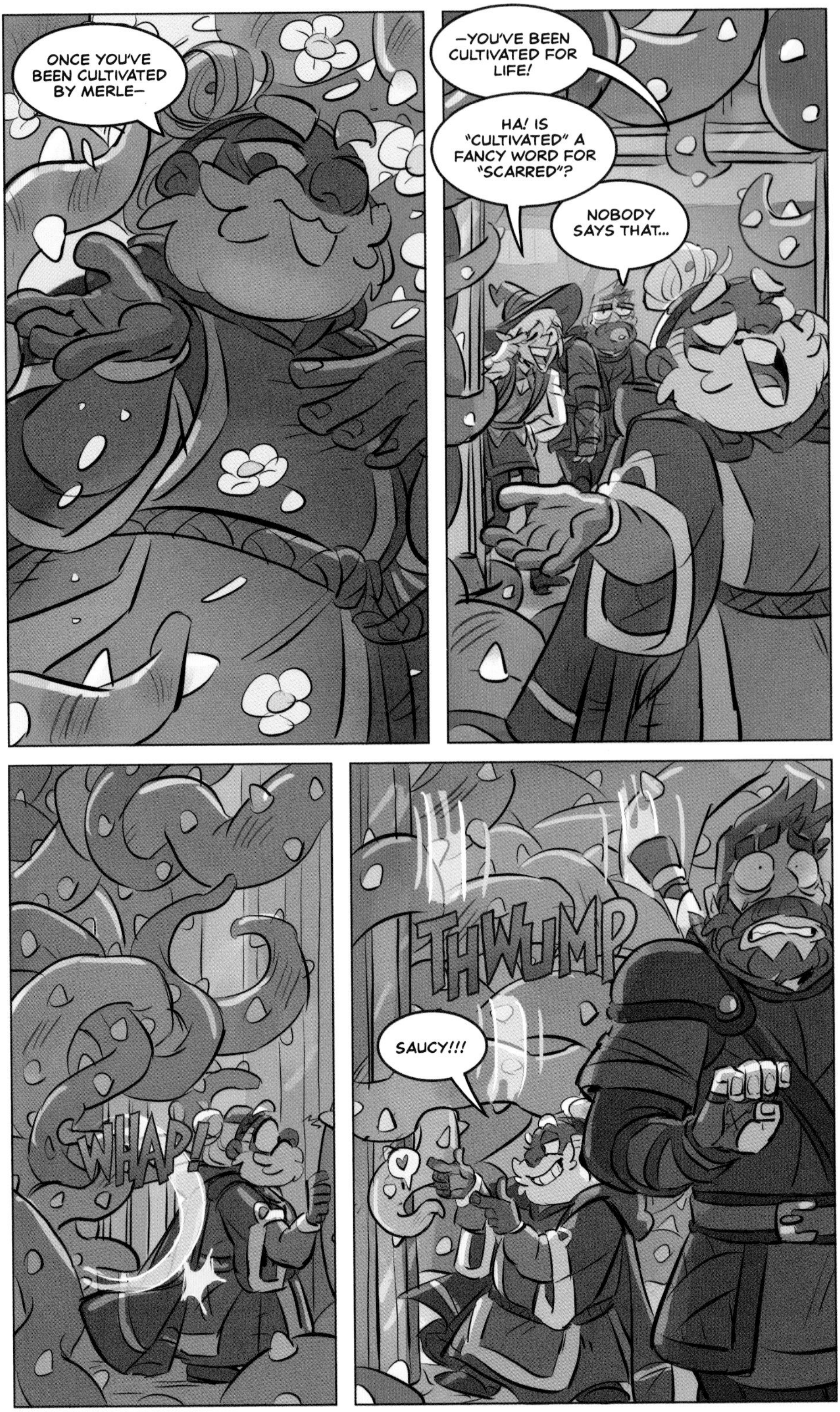
ONCE YOU'VE BEEN CULTIVATED BY MERLE—
—YOU'VE BEEN CULTIVATED FOR LIFE!
HA! IS "CULTIVATED" A FANCY WORD FOR "SCARRED"?
NOBODY SAYS THAT...
WHAP!
THWUMP
SAUCY!!!

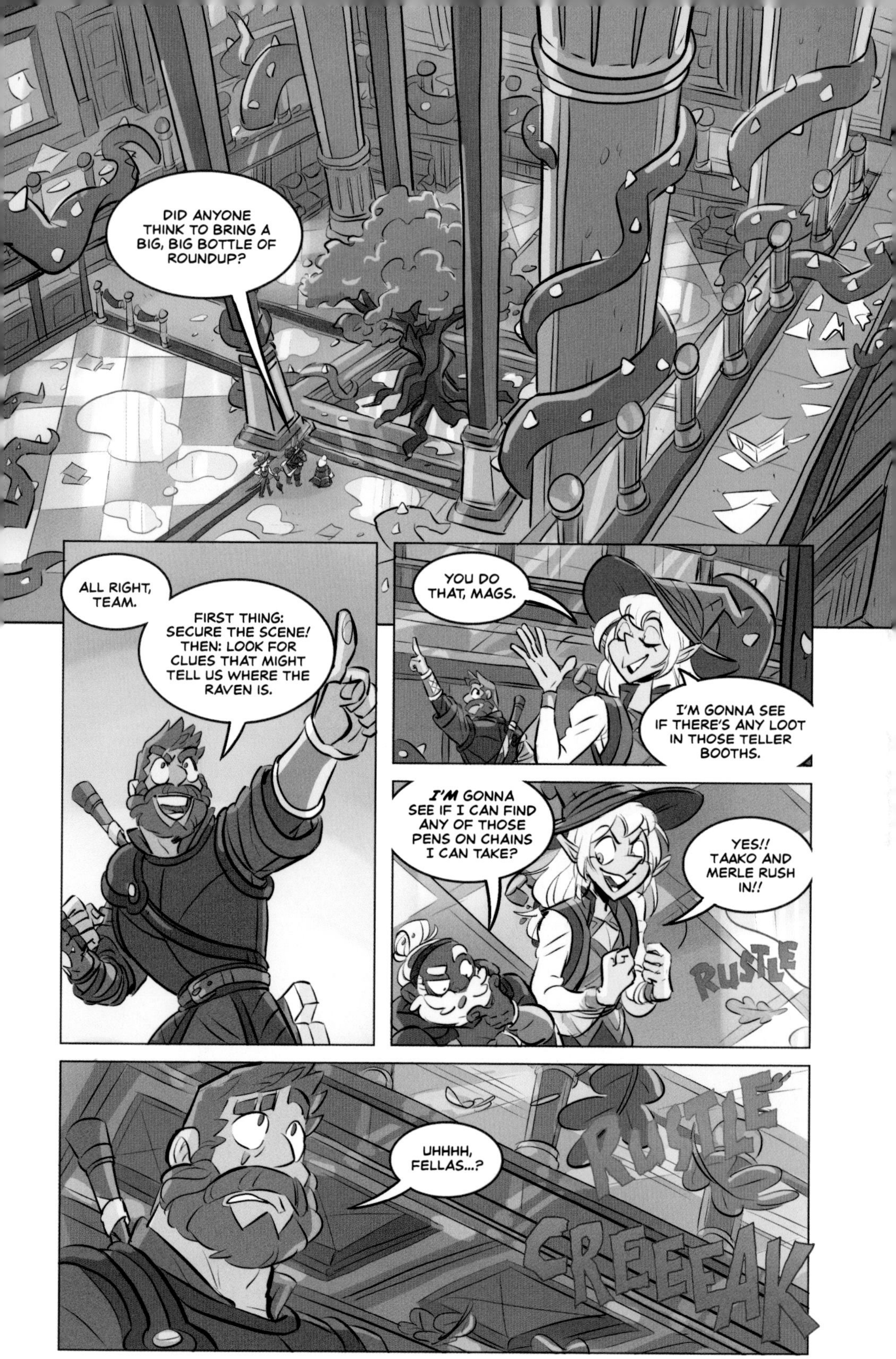
DID ANYONE THINK TO BRING A BIG, BIG BOTTLE OF ROUNDUP?
ALL RIGHT, TEAM.
FIRST THING: SECURE THE SCENE! THEN: LOOK FOR CLUES THAT MIGHT TELL US WHERE THE RAVEN IS.
YOU DO THAT, MAGS.
I'M GONNA SEE IF THERE'S ANY LOOT IN THOSE TELLER BOOTHS.
I'M GONNA SEE IF I CAN FIND ANY OF THOSE PENS ON CHAINS I CAN TAKE?
YES!! TAAKO AND MERLE RUSH IN!!
RUSTLE
UHHHH, FELLAS...?
RUSTLE
CREEEAK

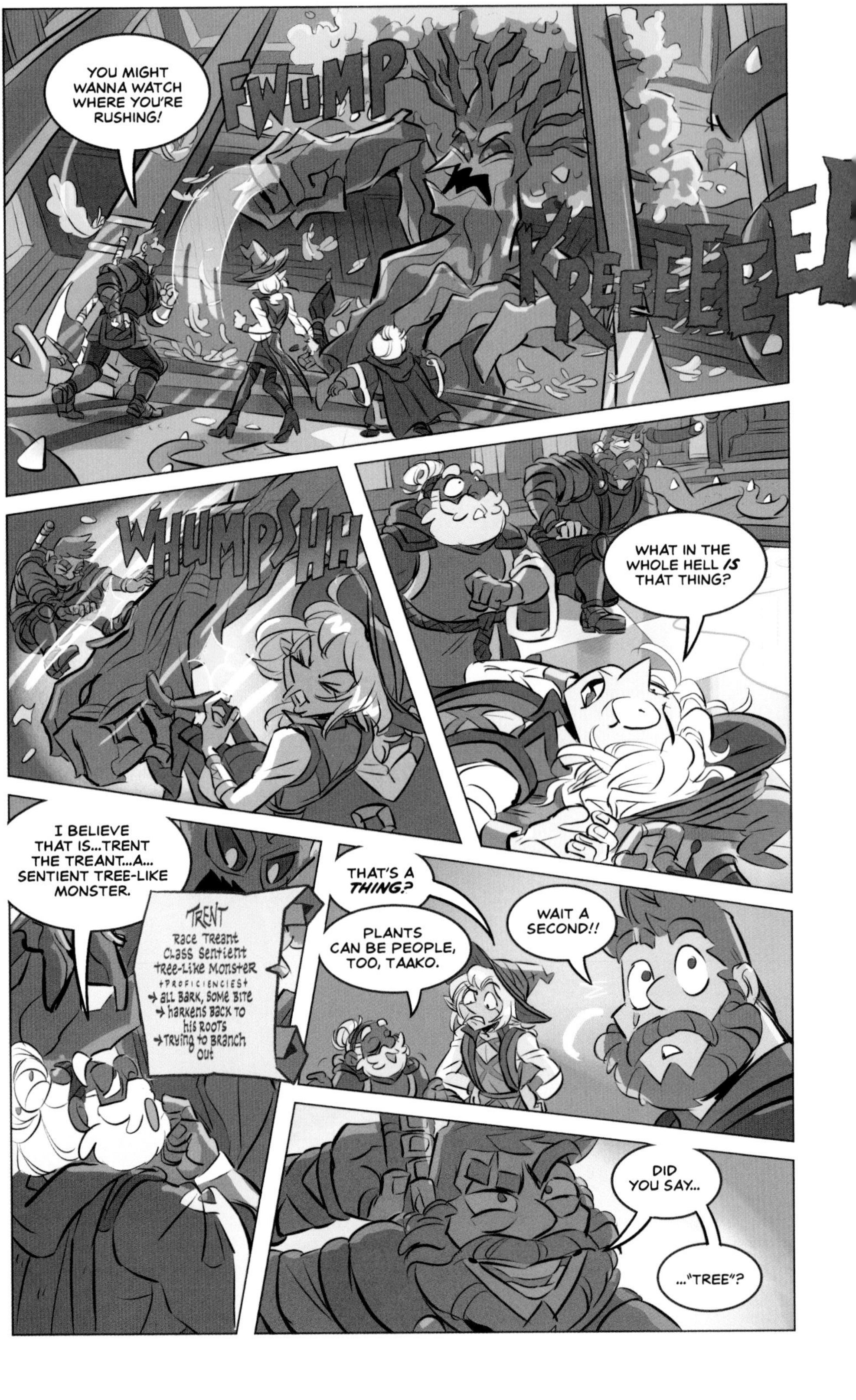
YOU MIGHT WANNA WATCH WHERE YOU'RE RUSHING!
FWUMP
KREEEEEE
WHUMPSHH
WHAT IN THE WHOLE HELL *IS* THAT THING?
I BELIEVE THAT IS...TRENT THE TREANT...A... SENTIENT TREE-LIKE MONSTER.
TRENT
Race Treant
Class Sentient Tree-Like Monster
PROFICIENCIES
→ all Bark, Some Bite
→ harkens Back to his Roots
→ Trying to Branch Out
THAT'S A *THING?*
PLANTS CAN BE PEOPLE, TOO, TAAKO.
WAIT A SECOND!!
DID YOU SAY...
..."TREE"?

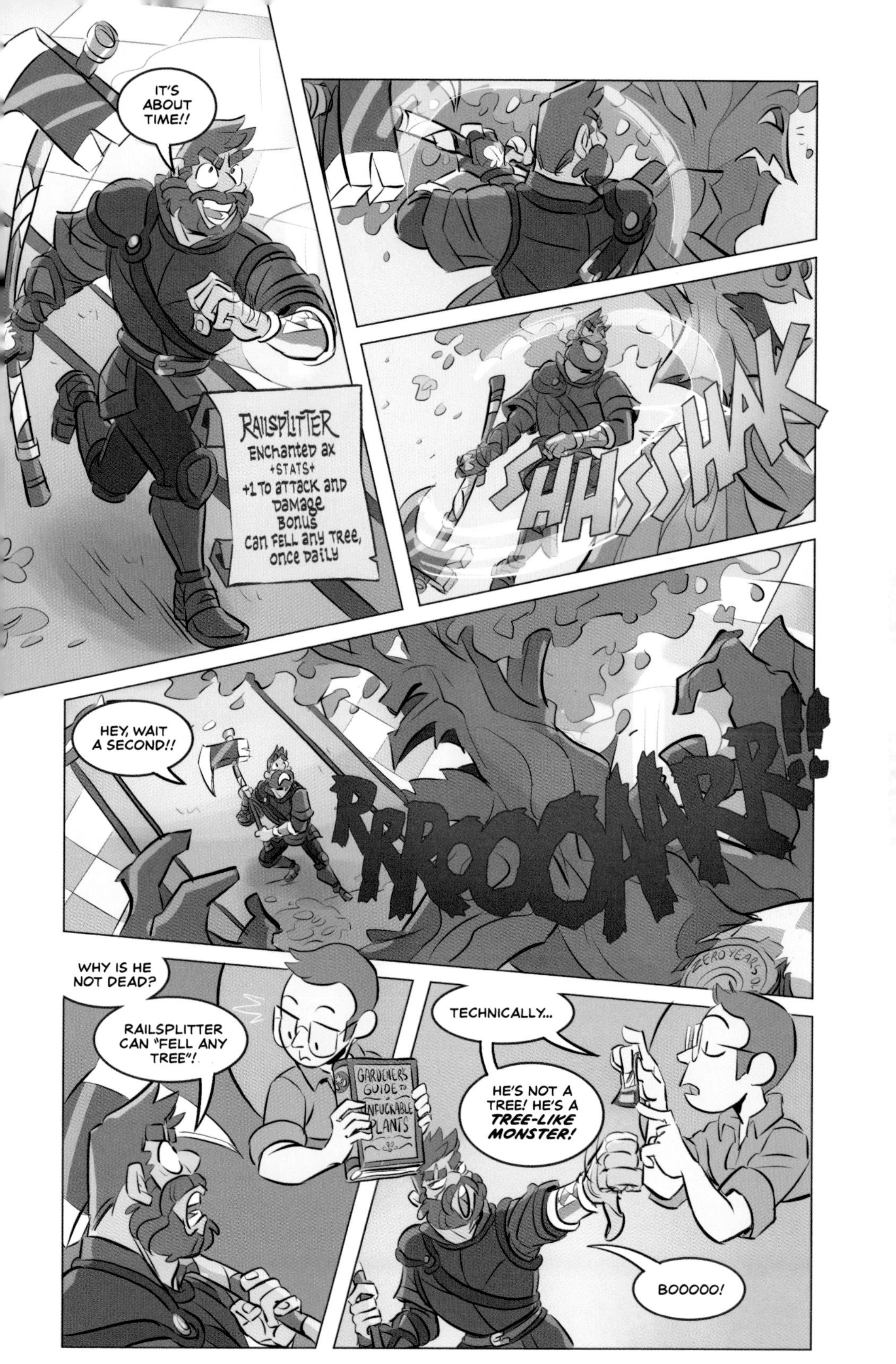
IT'S ABOUT TIME!!
RAILSPLITTER
Enchanted ax
+STATS+
+1 to attack and damage bonus
can fell any tree, once daily
SHSSSHAK
HEY, WAIT A SECOND!!
RRROOOARR!!!
ZERO YEARS O
WHY IS HE NOT DEAD?
RAILSPLITTER CAN "FELL ANY TREE"!
GARDENER'S GUIDE TO UNFUCKABLE PLANTS
TECHNICALLY...
HE'S NOT A TREE! HE'S A ***TREE-LIKE MONSTER!***
BOOOOO!

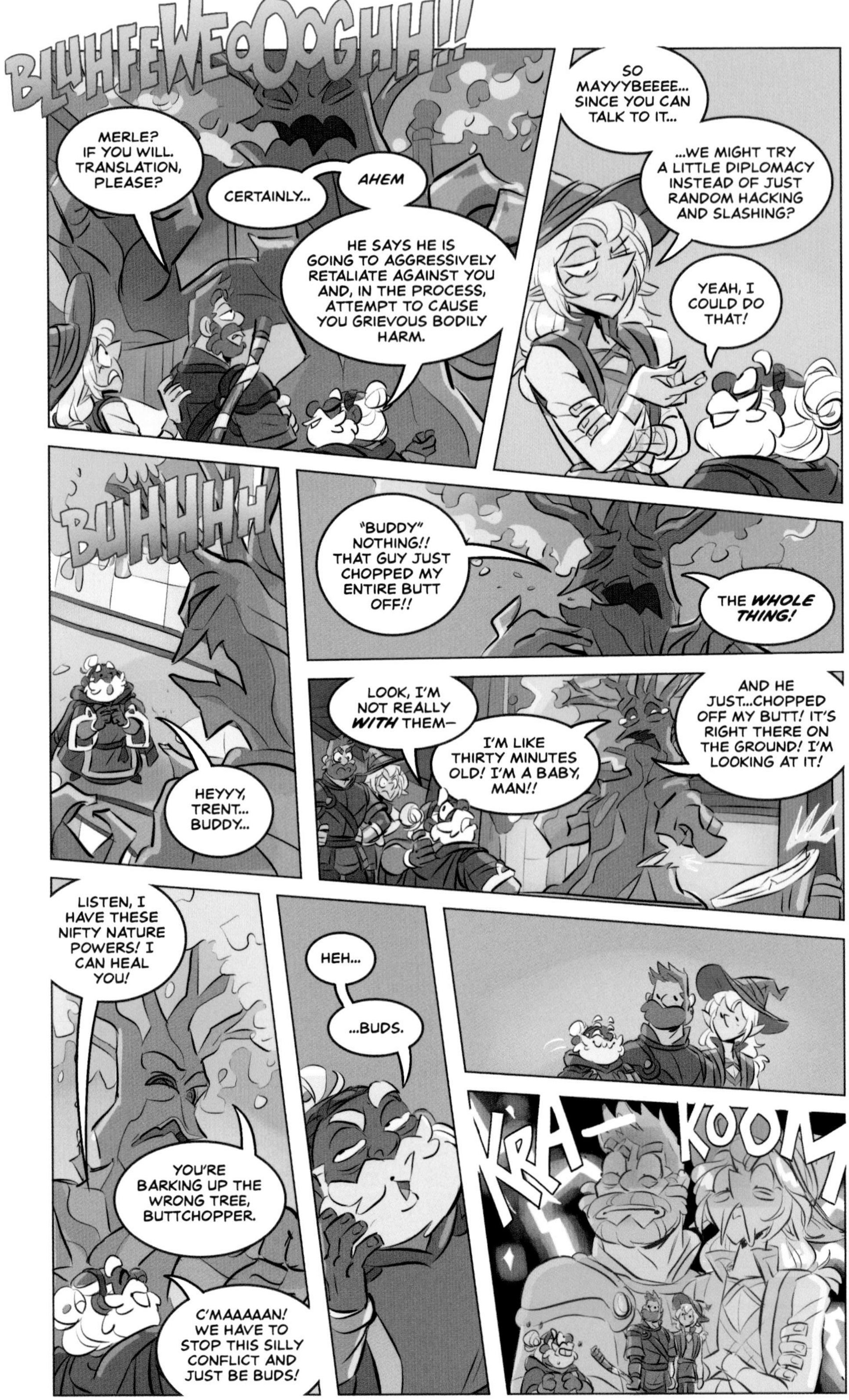
BLUHFEWEOOOGHH!!
MERLE? IF YOU WILL. TRANSLATION, PLEASE?
CERTAINLY...
AHEM
HE SAYS HE IS GOING TO AGGRESSIVELY RETALIATE AGAINST YOU AND, IN THE PROCESS, ATTEMPT TO CAUSE YOU GRIEVOUS BODILY HARM.
SO MAYYYBEEEE... SINCE YOU CAN TALK TO IT...
...WE MIGHT TRY A LITTLE DIPLOMACY INSTEAD OF JUST RANDOM HACKING AND SLASHING?
YEAH, I COULD DO THAT!
BUHHHH
HEYYY, TRENT... BUDDY...
"BUDDY" NOTHING!! THAT GUY JUST CHOPPED MY ENTIRE BUTT OFF!!
THE WHOLE THING!
LOOK, I'M NOT REALLY WITH THEM—
I'M LIKE THIRTY MINUTES OLD! I'M A BABY, MAN!!
AND HE JUST...CHOPPED OFF MY BUTT! IT'S RIGHT THERE ON THE GROUND! I'M LOOKING AT IT!
LISTEN, I HAVE THESE NIFTY NATURE POWERS! I CAN HEAL YOU!
YOU'RE BARKING UP THE WRONG TREE, BUTTCHOPPER.
C'MAAAAAN! WE HAVE TO STOP THIS SILLY CONFLICT AND JUST BE BUDS!
HEH...
...BUDS.
KRA—KOOM

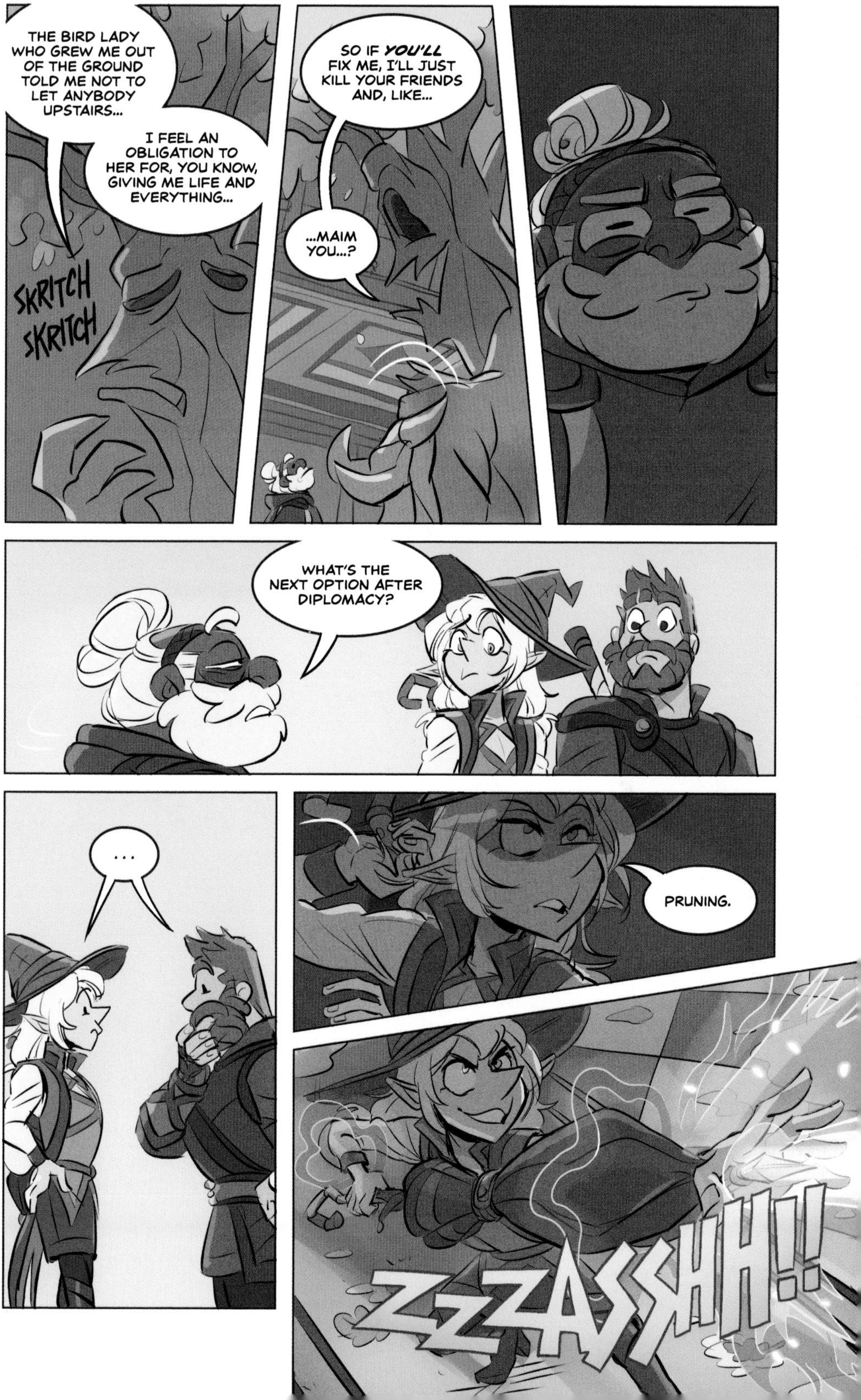
THE BIRD LADY WHO GREW ME OUT OF THE GROUND TOLD ME NOT TO LET ANYBODY UPSTAIRS...
I FEEL AN OBLIGATION TO HER FOR, YOU KNOW, GIVING ME LIFE AND EVERYTHING...
SKRITCH SKRITCH
SO IF YOU'LL FIX ME, I'LL JUST KILL YOUR FRIENDS AND, LIKE...
...MAIM YOU...?
WHAT'S THE NEXT OPTION AFTER DIPLOMACY?
...
PRUNING.
ZZZASSHH!!

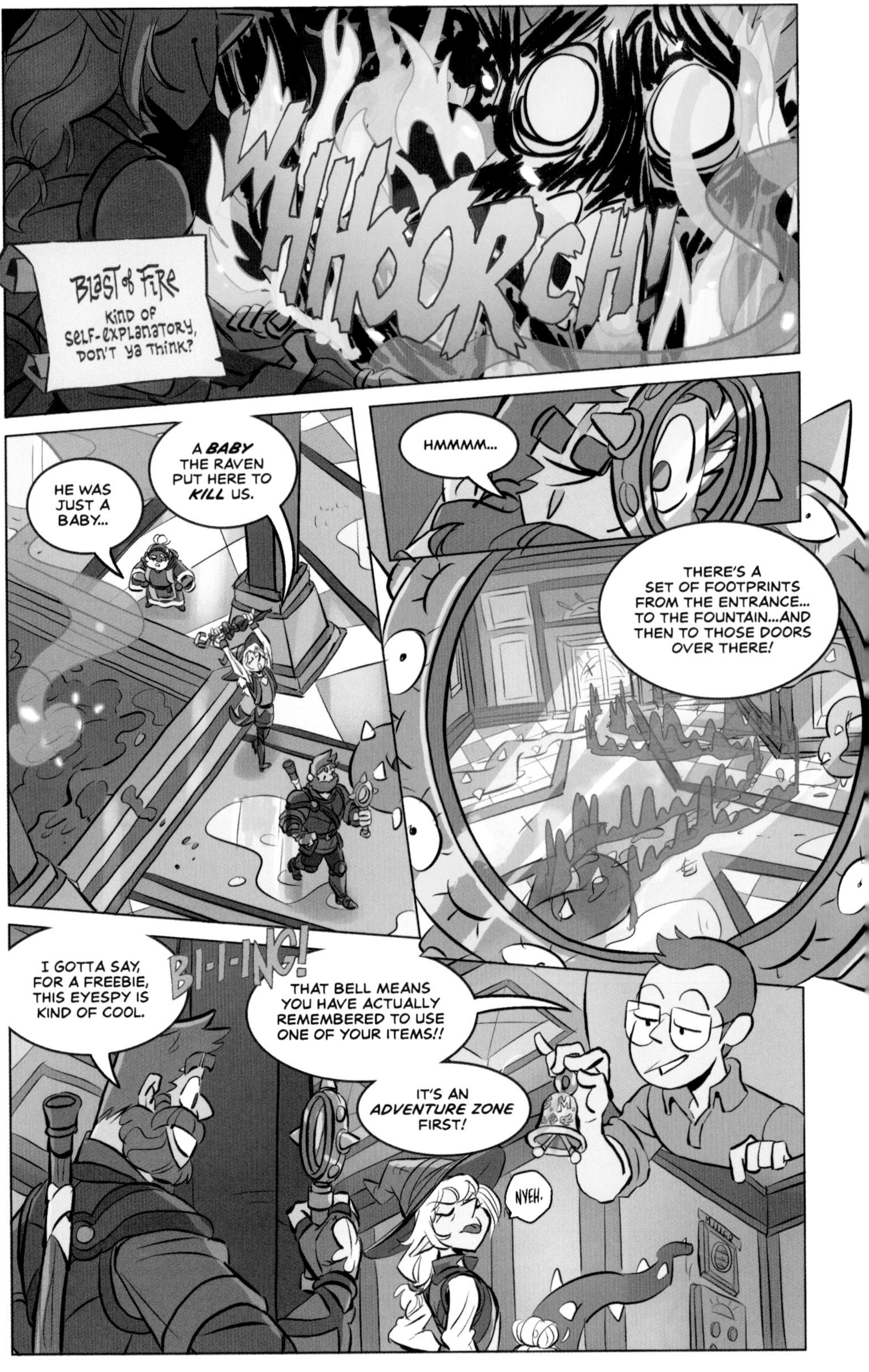
WHHOORCH!
BLAST OF FIRE
KIND OF SELF-EXPLANATORY, DON'T YA THINK?
HE WAS JUST A BABY...
A BABY THE RAVEN PUT HERE TO KILL US.
HMMMM...
THERE'S A SET OF FOOTPRINTS FROM THE ENTRANCE... TO THE FOUNTAIN...AND THEN TO THOSE DOORS OVER THERE!
I GOTTA SAY, FOR A FREEBIE, THIS EYESPY IS KIND OF COOL.
BI-I-ING!
THAT BELL MEANS YOU HAVE ACTUALLY REMEMBERED TO USE ONE OF YOUR ITEMS!!
IT'S AN ADVENTURE ZONE FIRST!
NYEH.

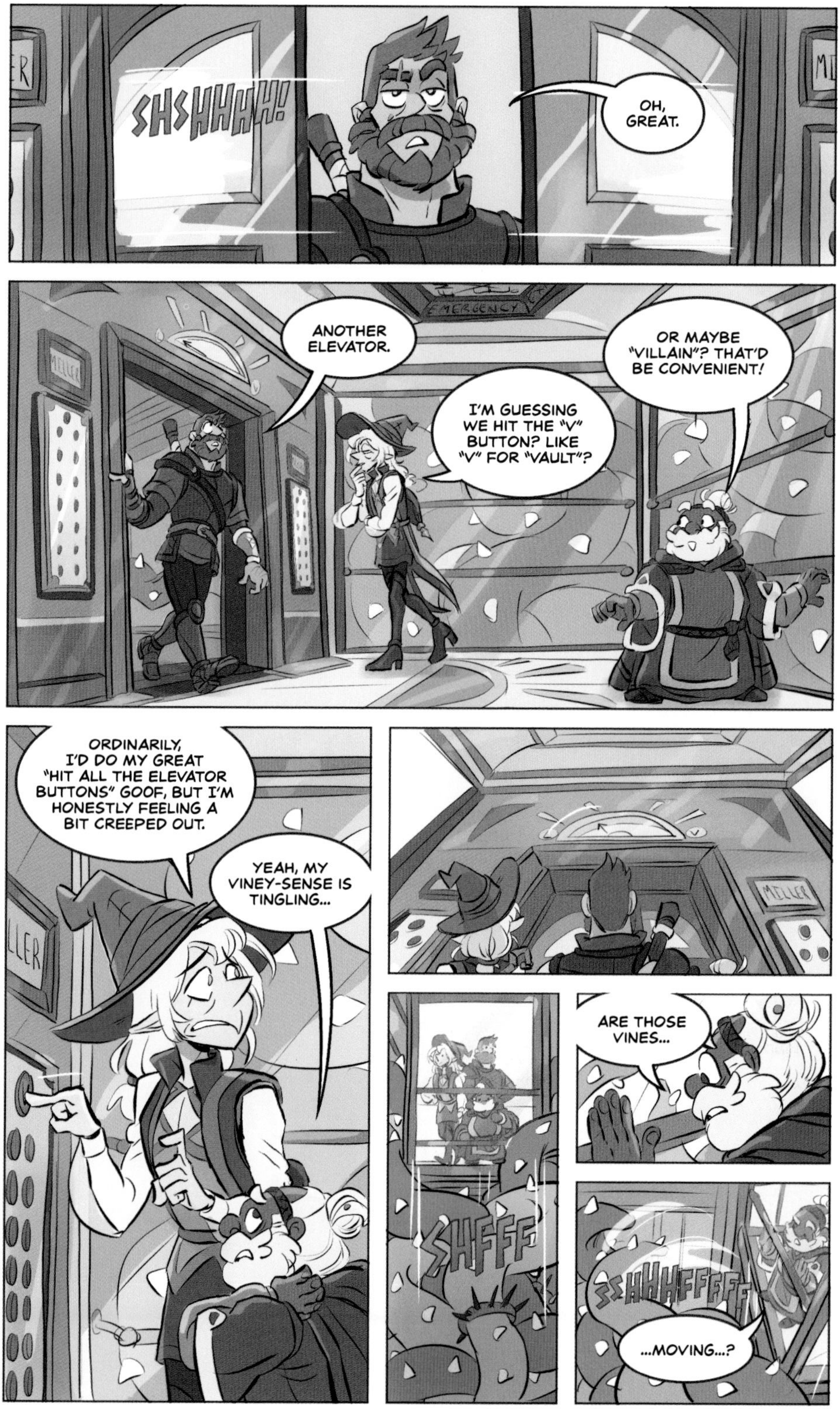
SHSHHHHH!
OH, GREAT.
EMERGENCY
ANOTHER ELEVATOR.
I'M GUESSING WE HIT THE "V" BUTTON? LIKE "V" FOR "VAULT"?
OR MAYBE "VILLAIN"? THAT'D BE CONVENIENT!
ORDINARILY, I'D DO MY GREAT "HIT ALL THE ELEVATOR BUTTONS" GOOF, BUT I'M HONESTLY FEELING A BIT CREEPED OUT.
YEAH, MY VINEY-SENSE IS TINGLING...
SHFFF
ARE THOSE VINES...
SSHHHFFFFF
...MOVING...?

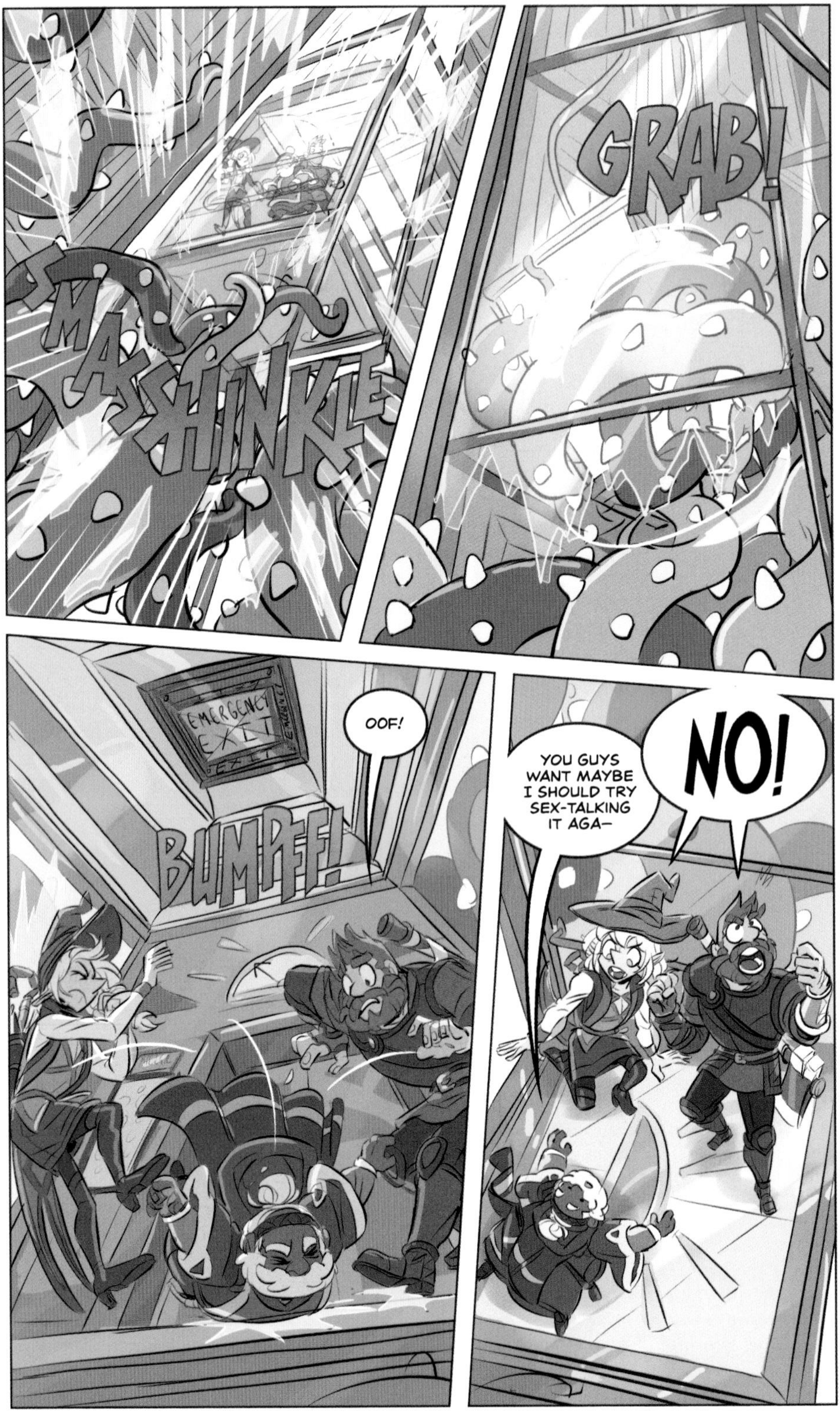
SMASSHINKLE
GRAB!
EMERGENCY EXIT
BUMPFF!
OOF!
YOU GUYS WANT MAYBE I SHOULD TRY SEX-TALKING IT AGA—
NO!

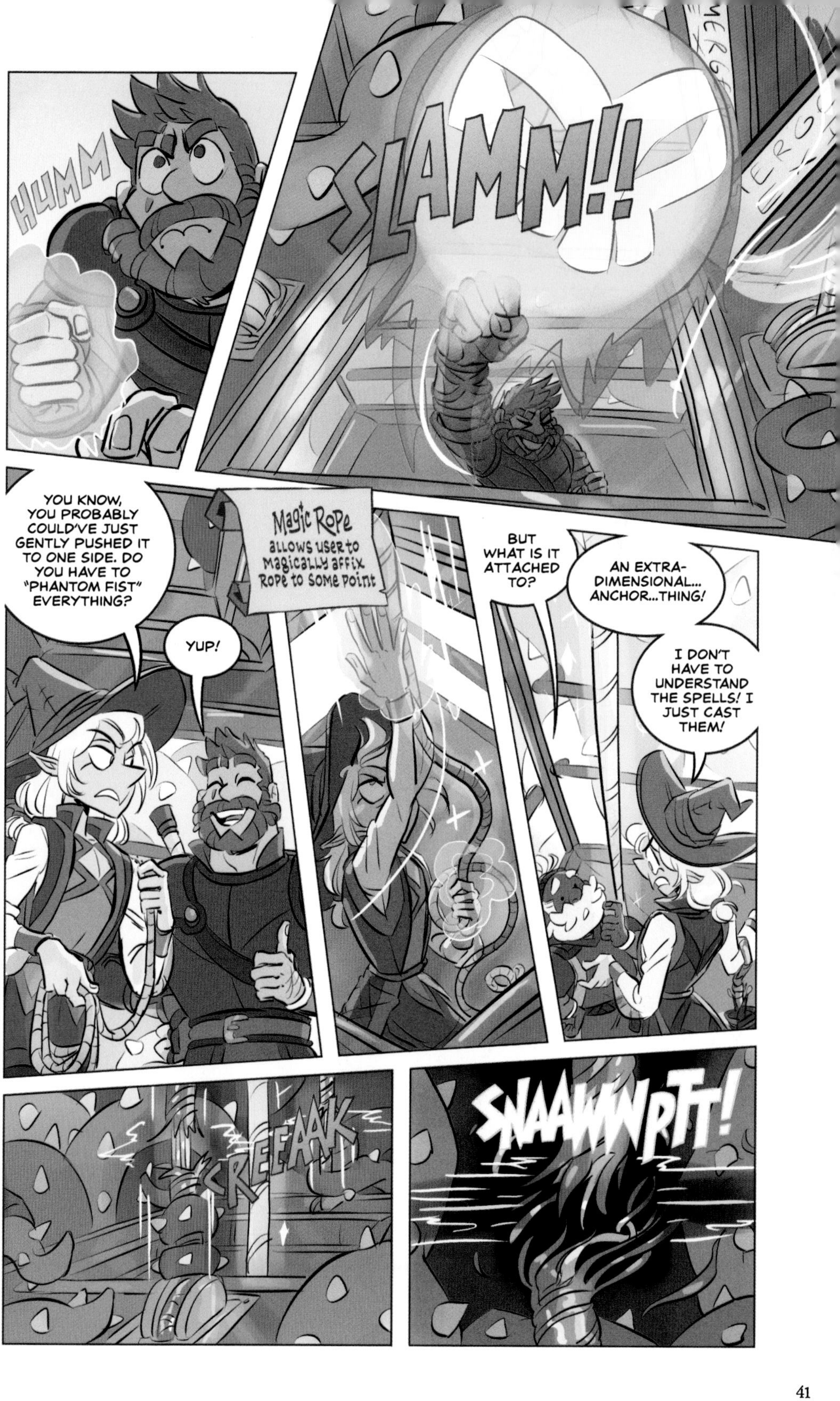
HUMM
SLAMM!!
YOU KNOW, YOU PROBABLY COULD'VE JUST GENTLY PUSHED IT TO ONE SIDE. DO YOU HAVE TO "PHANTOM FIST" EVERYTHING?
YUP!
Magic Rope allows user to magically affix Rope to some point
BUT WHAT IS IT ATTACHED TO?
AN EXTRA-DIMENSIONAL... ANCHOR...THING!
I DON'T HAVE TO UNDERSTAND THE SPELLS! I JUST CAST THEM!
CREEEAAK
SNAAWNRTT!

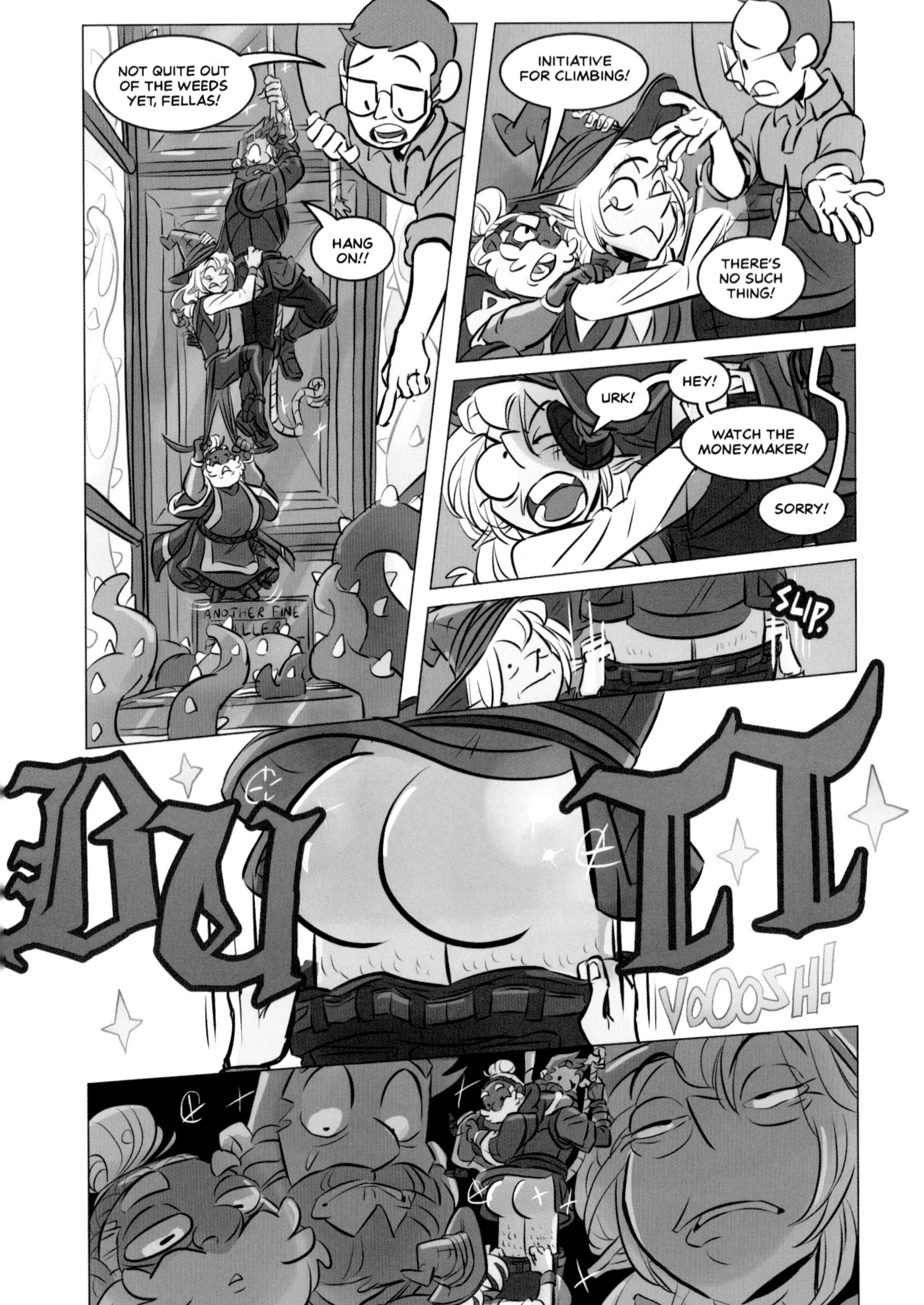
NOT QUITE OUT OF THE WEEDS YET, FELLAS!
HANG ON!!
INITIATIVE FOR CLIMBING!
THERE'S NO SUCH THING!
URK!
HEY!
WATCH THE MONEYMAKER!
SORRY!
SLIP.
BUTT
VOOOSH!

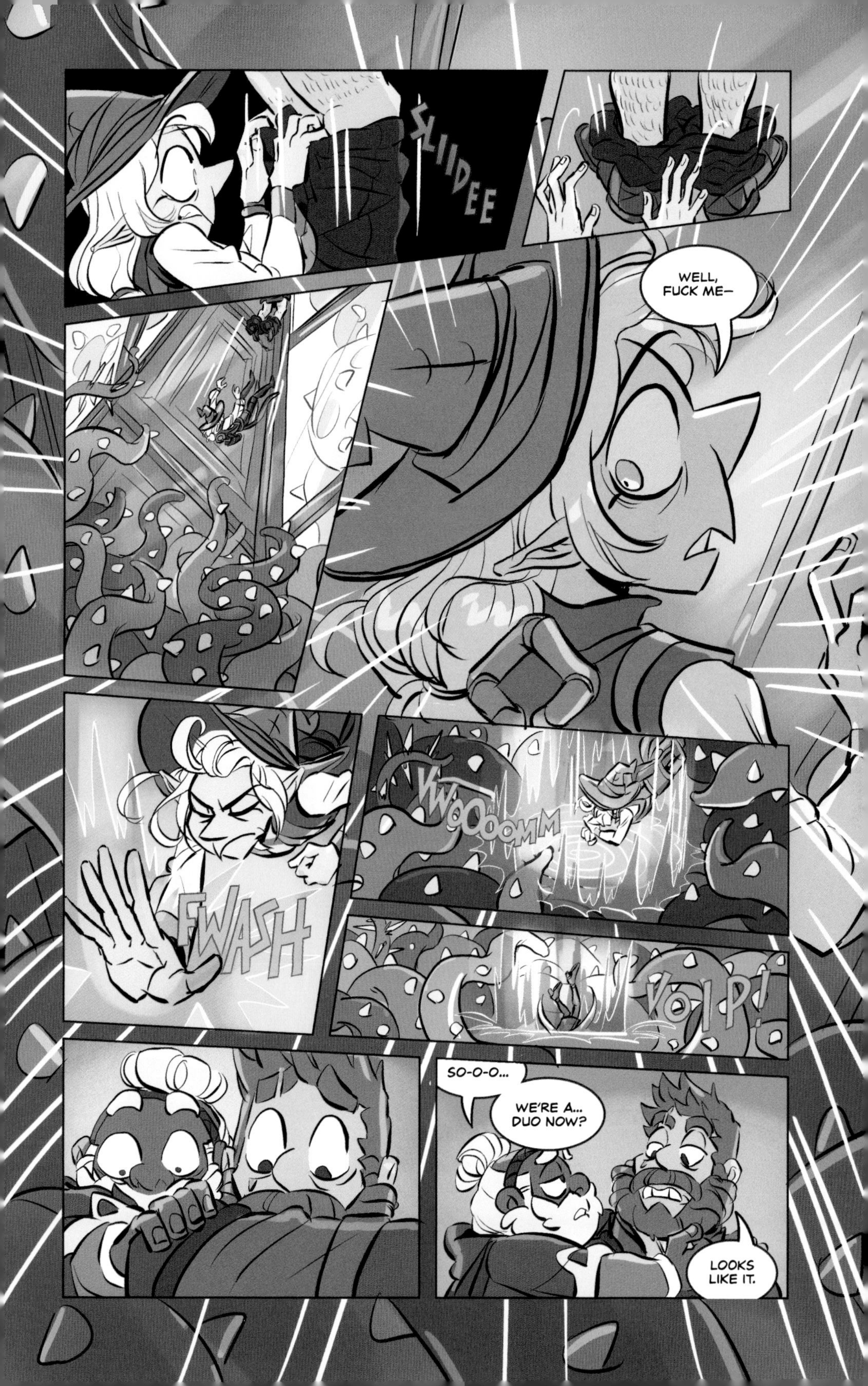
SLIIDEE
WELL, FUCK ME—
FWASH
VWOOOOOMM
VOIP!
SO-O-O...
WE'RE A... DUO NOW?
LOOKS LIKE IT.

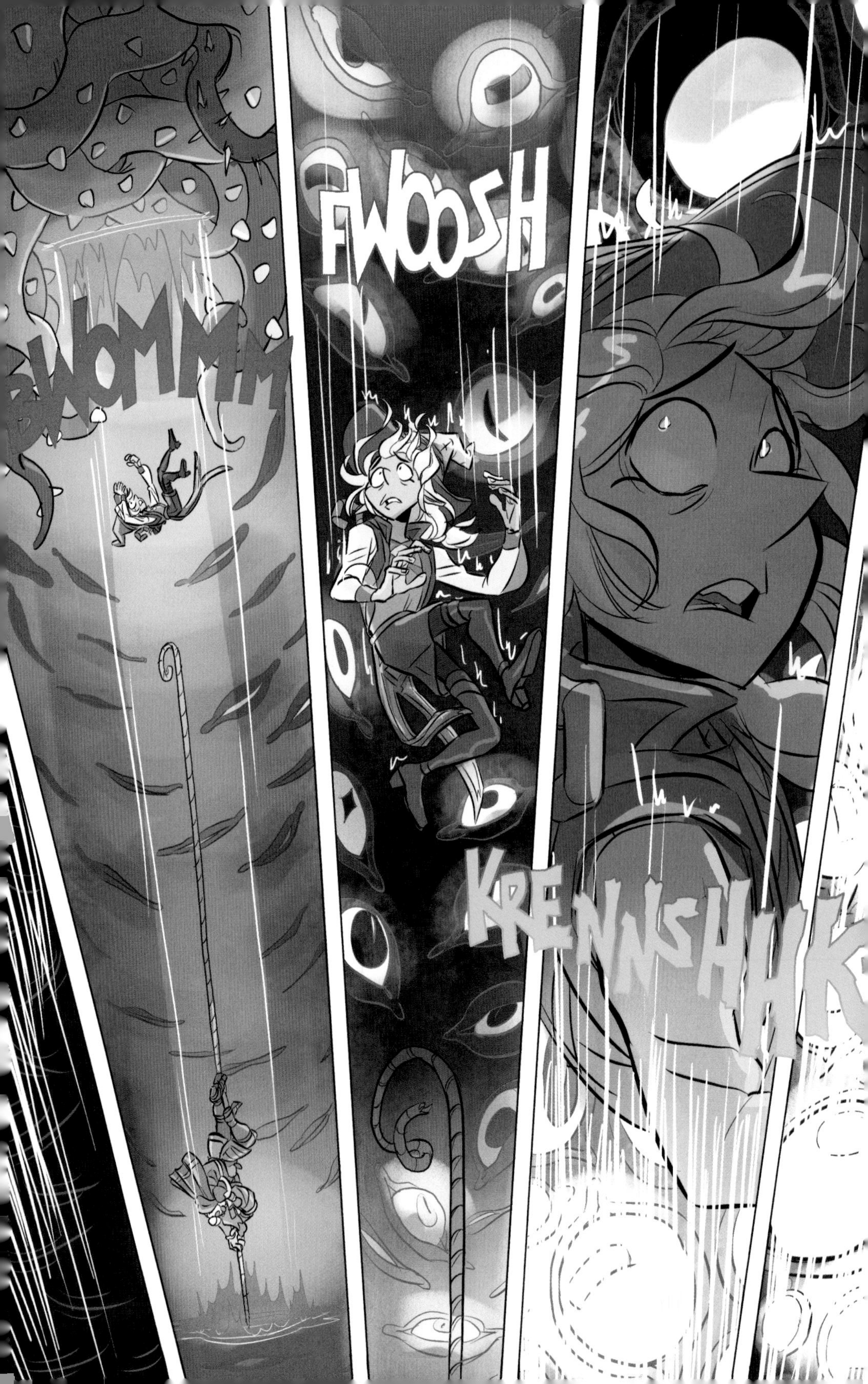
BWOMMM
FWOOSH
KRENNSHHK

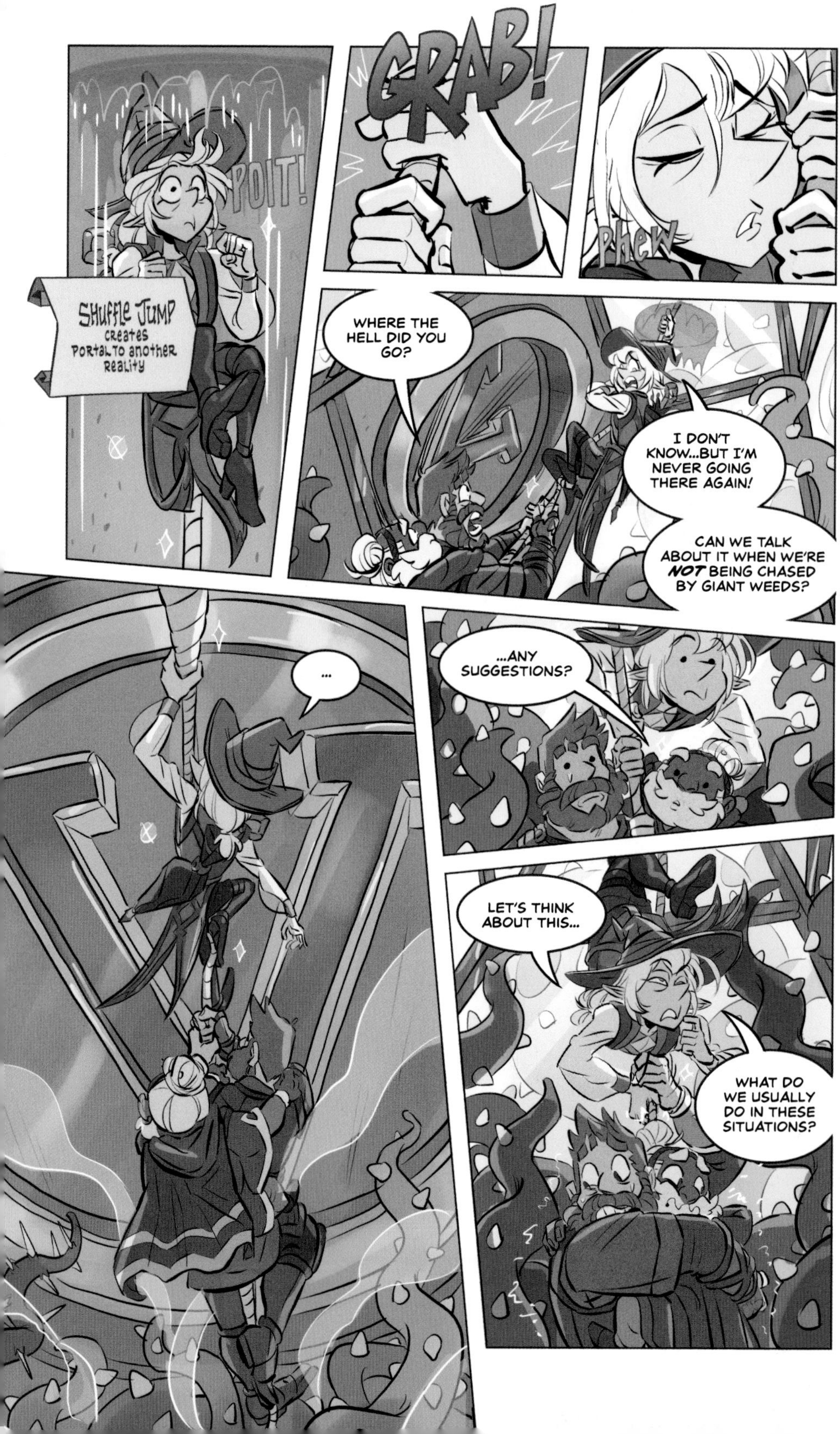
POIT!
SHUFFLE JUMP
CREATES
PORTAL TO ANOTHER
REALITY
GRAB!
PHEW
WHERE THE HELL DID YOU GO?
I DON'T KNOW...BUT I'M NEVER GOING THERE AGAIN!
CAN WE TALK ABOUT IT WHEN WE'RE NOT BEING CHASED BY GIANT WEEDS?
...
...ANY SUGGESTIONS?
LET'S THINK ABOUT THIS...
WHAT DO WE USUALLY DO IN THESE SITUATIONS?

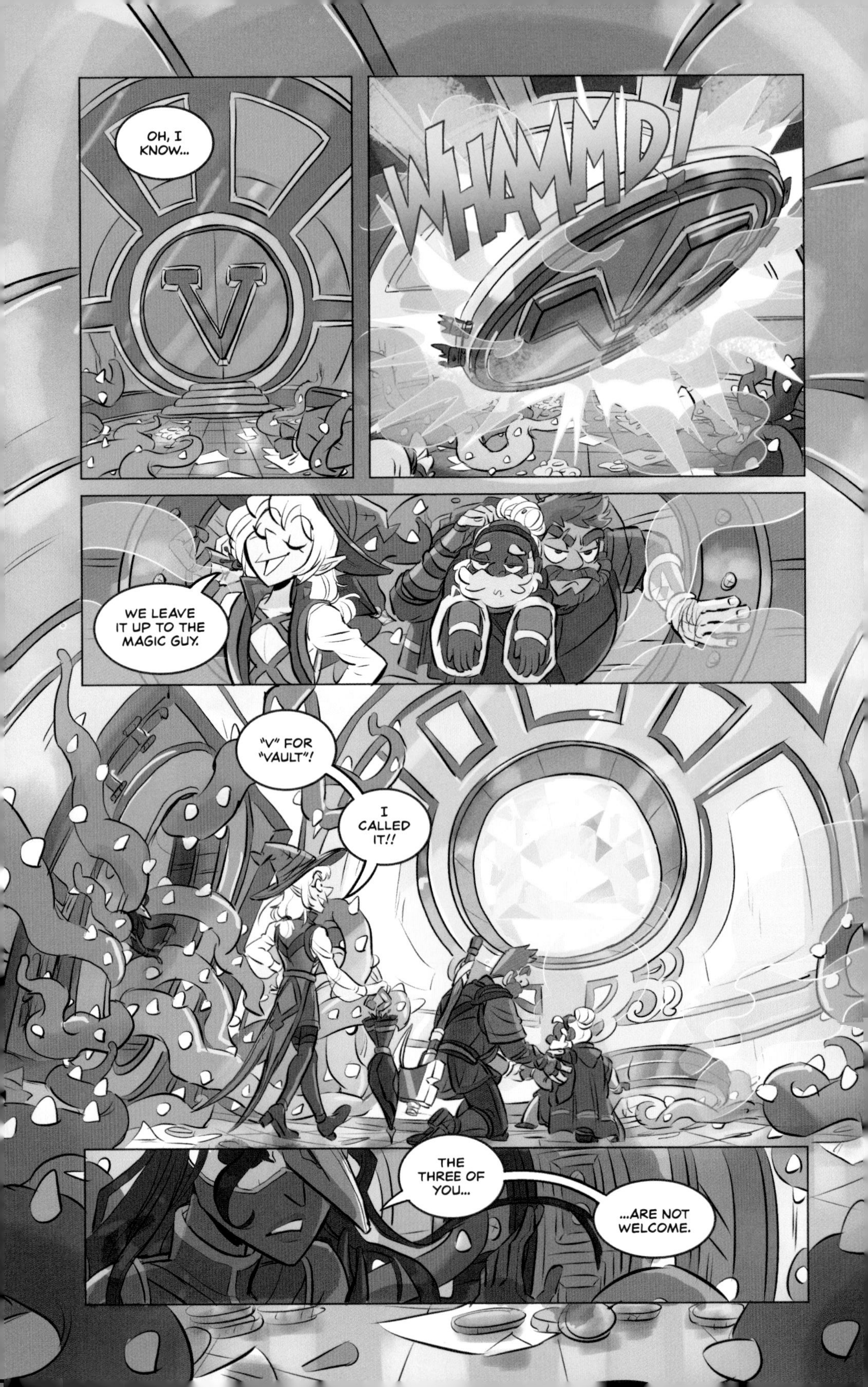
OH, I KNOW...
WHAMMD!
WE LEAVE IT UP TO THE MAGIC GUY.
"V" FOR "VAULT"!
I CALLED IT!!
THE THREE OF YOU...
...ARE NOT WELCOME.

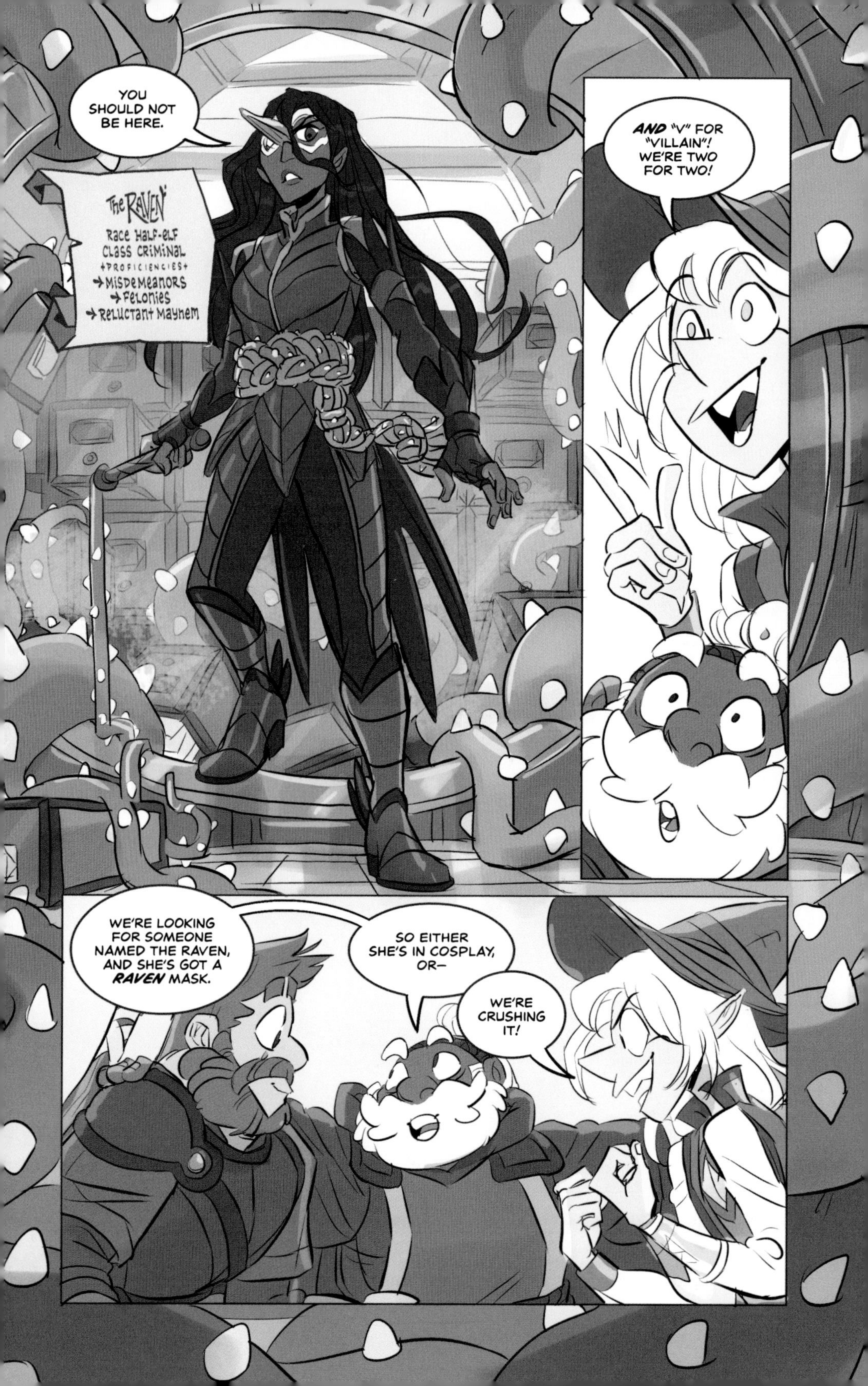

YOU SHOULD NOT BE HERE.
THE RAVEN
RACE HALF-ELF
CLASS CRIMINAL
PROFICIENCIES
→MISDEMEANORS
→FELONIES
→RELUCTANT MAYHEM
AND "V" FOR "VILLAIN"! WE'RE TWO FOR TWO!
WE'RE LOOKING FOR SOMEONE NAMED THE RAVEN, AND SHE'S GOT A RAVEN MASK.
SO EITHER SHE'S IN COSPLAY, OR–
WE'RE CRUSHING IT!

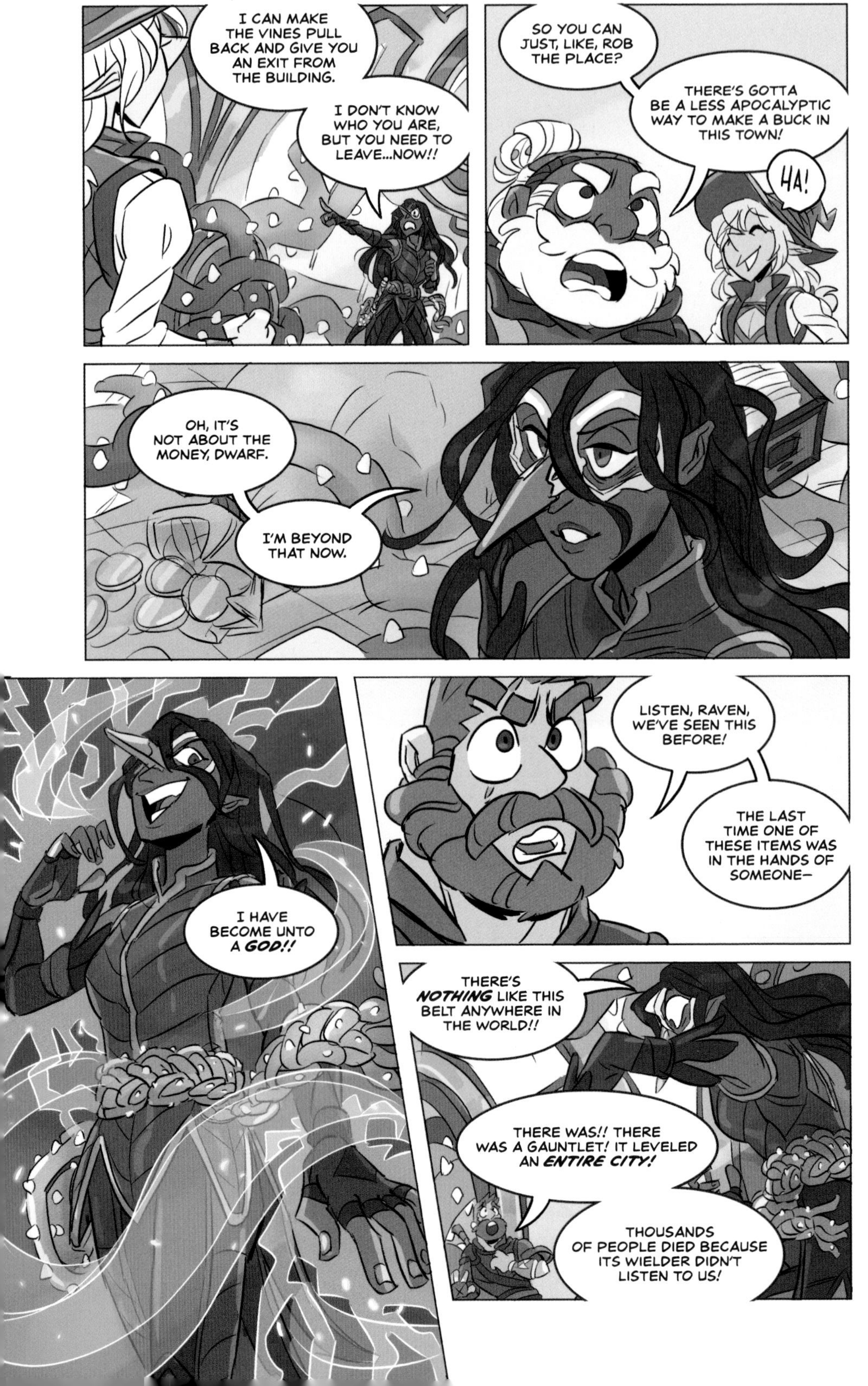
I CAN MAKE THE VINES PULL BACK AND GIVE YOU AN EXIT FROM THE BUILDING.
I DON'T KNOW WHO YOU ARE, BUT YOU NEED TO LEAVE...NOW!!
SO YOU CAN JUST, LIKE, ROB THE PLACE?
THERE'S GOTTA BE A LESS APOCALYPTIC WAY TO MAKE A BUCK IN THIS TOWN!
HA!
OH, IT'S NOT ABOUT THE MONEY, DWARF.
I'M BEYOND THAT NOW.
I HAVE BECOME UNTO A ***GOD!!***
LISTEN, RAVEN, WE'VE SEEN THIS BEFORE!
THE LAST TIME ONE OF THESE ITEMS WAS IN THE HANDS OF SOMEONE–
THERE'S ***NOTHING*** LIKE THIS BELT ANYWHERE IN THE WORLD!!
THERE WAS!! THERE WAS A GAUNTLET! IT LEVELED AN ***ENTIRE CITY!***
THOUSANDS OF PEOPLE DIED BECAUSE ITS WIELDER DIDN'T LISTEN TO US!

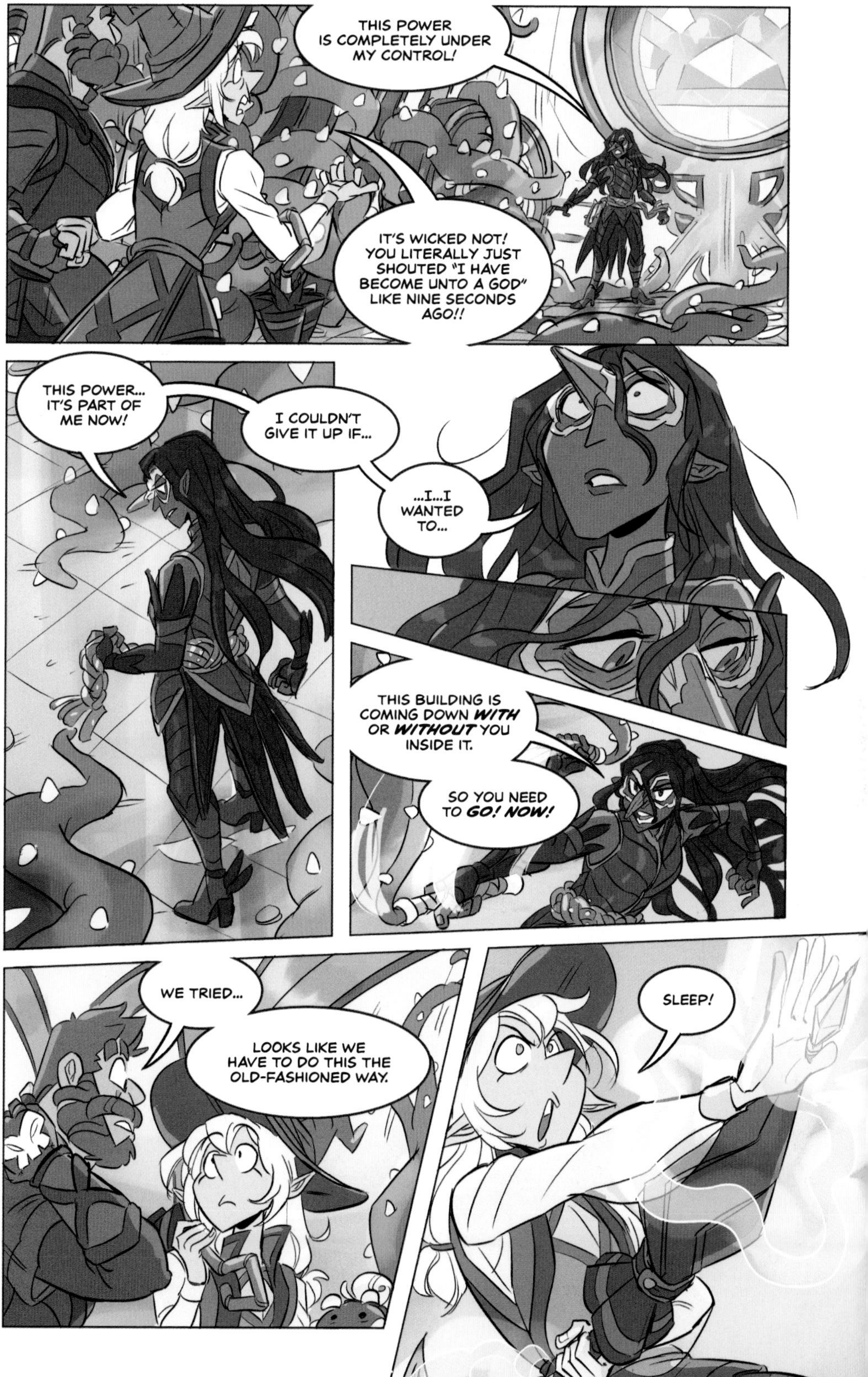
THIS POWER IS COMPLETELY UNDER MY CONTROL!
IT'S WICKED NOT! YOU LITERALLY JUST SHOUTED "I HAVE BECOME UNTO A GOD" LIKE NINE SECONDS AGO!!
THIS POWER... IT'S PART OF ME NOW!
I COULDN'T GIVE IT UP IF...
...I...I WANTED TO...
THIS BUILDING IS COMING DOWN *WITH* OR *WITHOUT* YOU INSIDE IT.
SO YOU NEED TO *GO! NOW!*
WE TRIED...
LOOKS LIKE WE HAVE TO DO THIS THE OLD-FASHIONED WAY.
SLEEP!

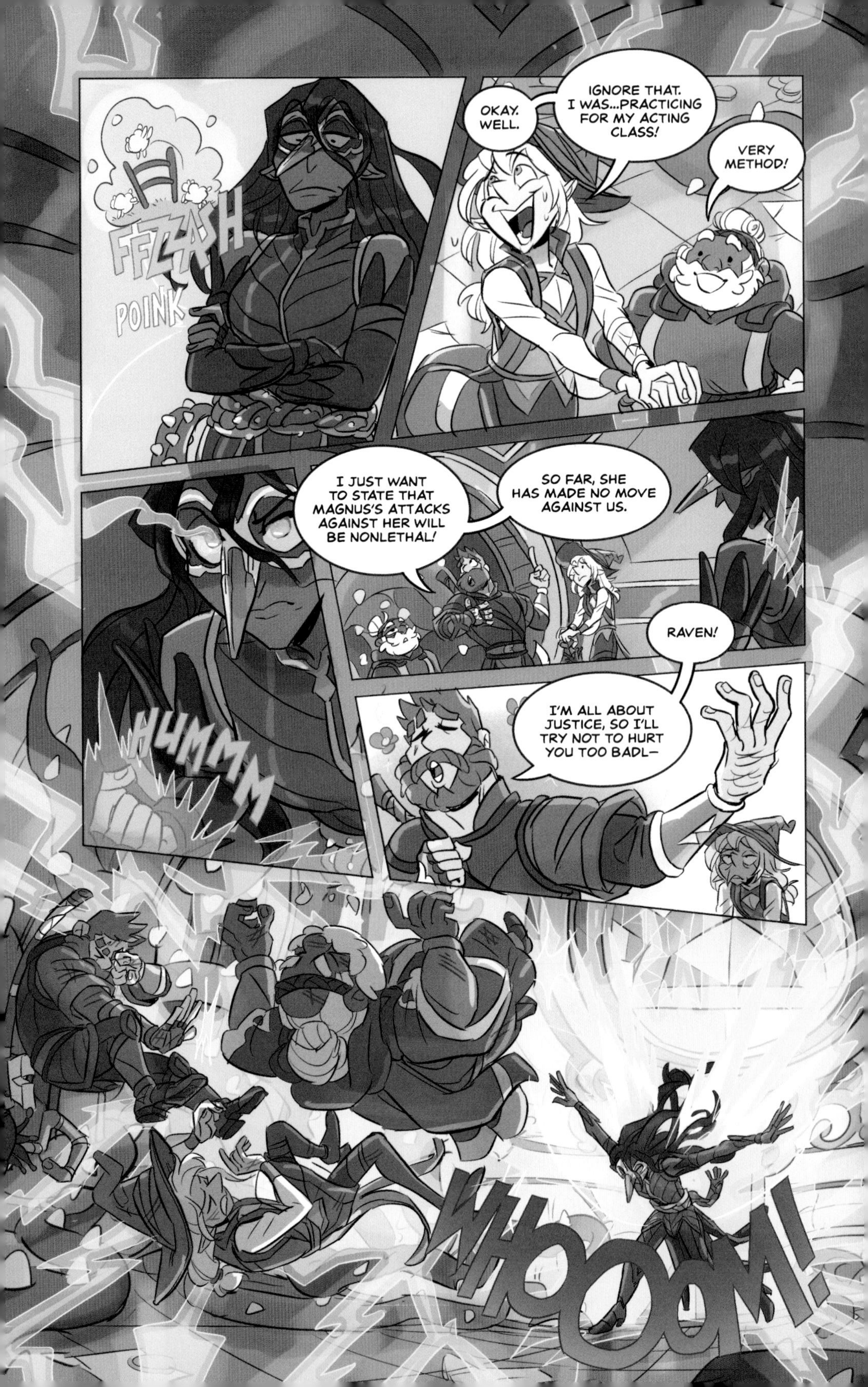
FFZZASH
POINK
OKAY. WELL.
IGNORE THAT. I WAS...PRACTICING FOR MY ACTING CLASS!
VERY METHOD!
I JUST WANT TO STATE THAT MAGNUS'S ATTACKS AGAINST HER WILL BE NONLETHAL!
SO FAR, SHE HAS MADE NO MOVE AGAINST US.
HUMMM
RAVEN!
I'M ALL ABOUT JUSTICE, SO I'LL TRY NOT TO HURT YOU TOO BADL—
WHOOOM!

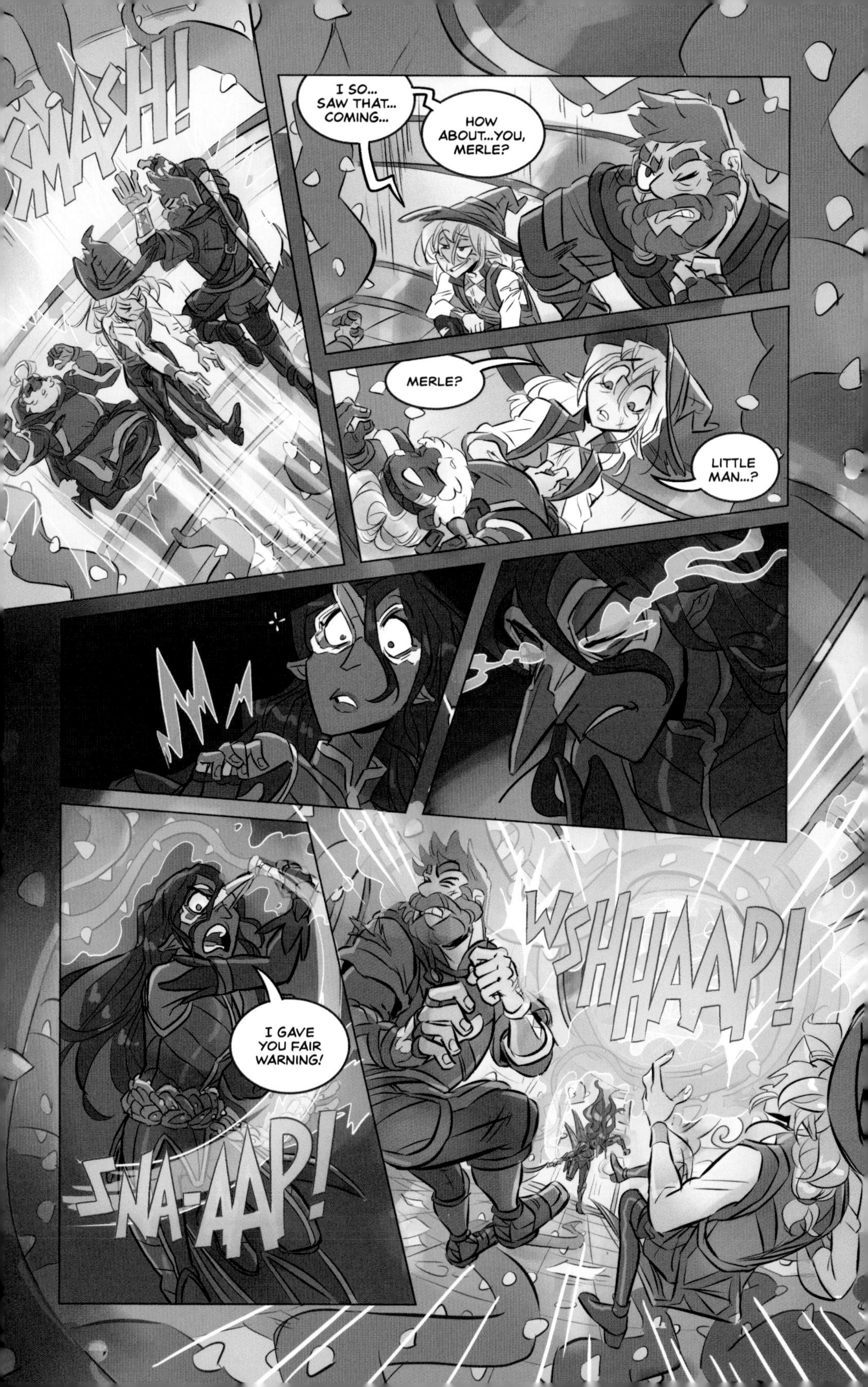

SMASH!
I SO... SAW THAT... COMING...
HOW ABOUT...YOU, MERLE?
MERLE?
LITTLE MAN...?
I GAVE YOU FAIR WARNING!
WSHHAAP!
SNA-AAP!

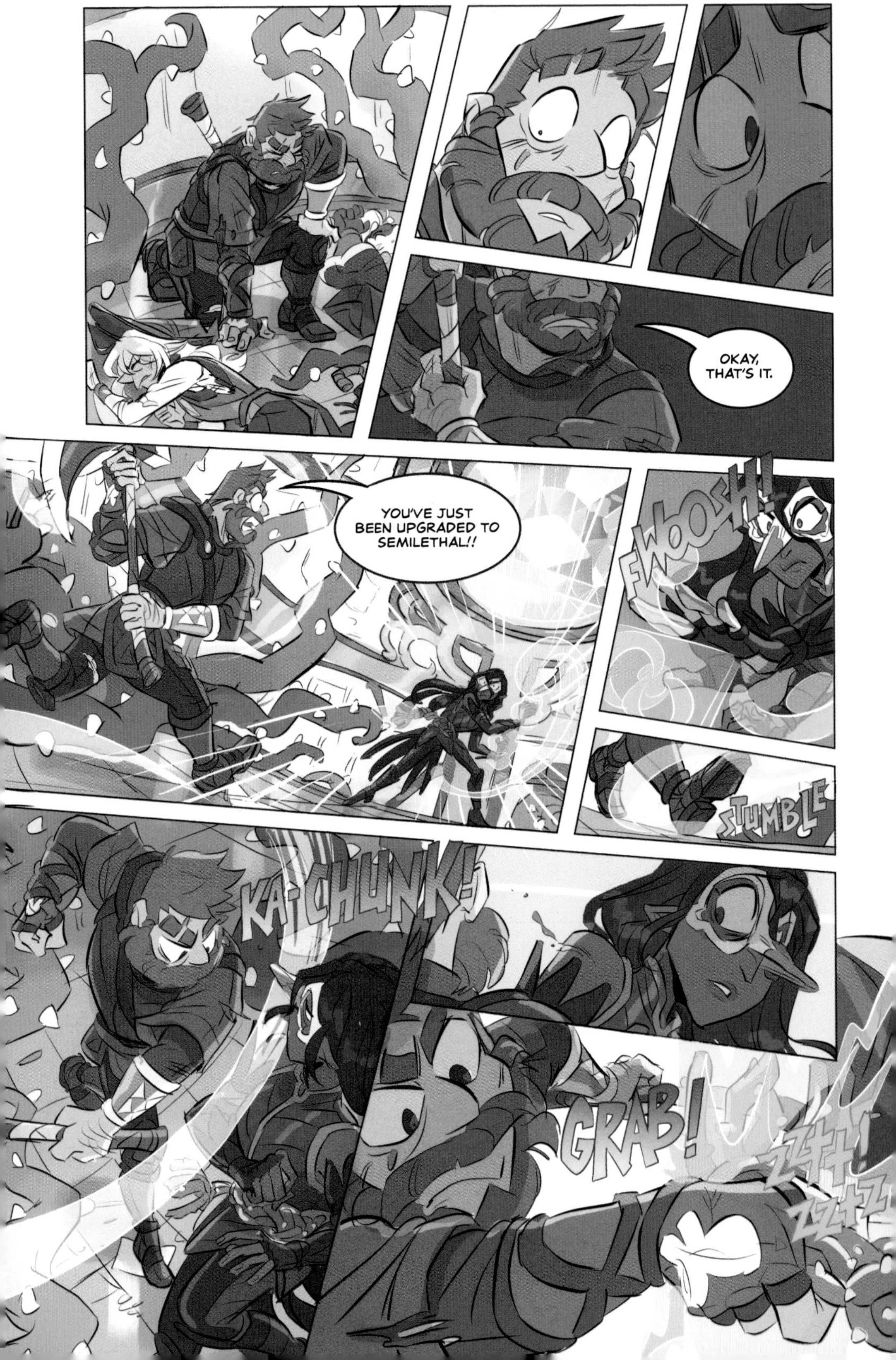

OKAY, THAT'S IT.
YOU'VE JUST BEEN UPGRADED TO SEMILETHAL!!
FWOOSH!
STUMBLE
KA-CHUNK!
GRAB!
ZZT
ZZT

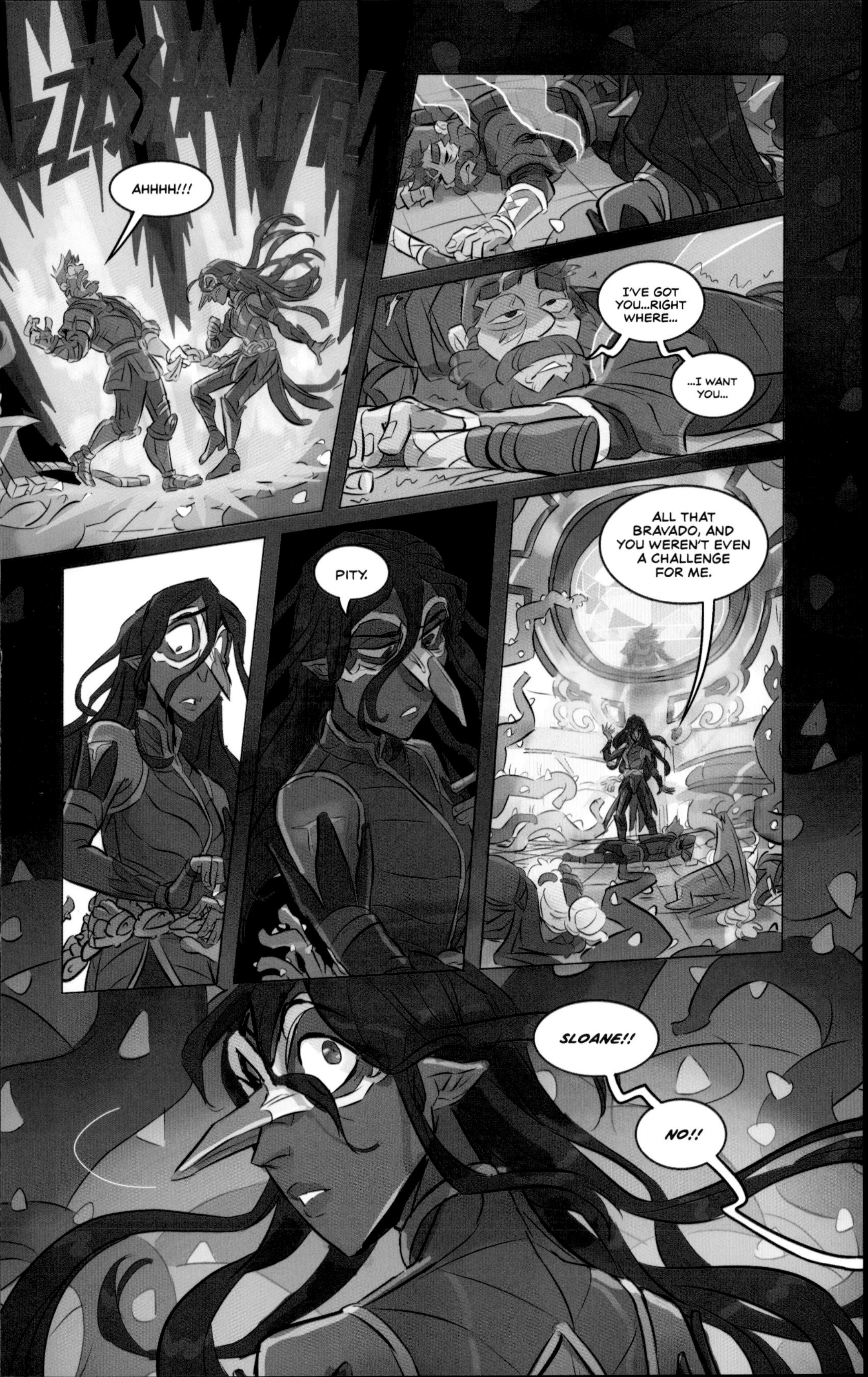

ZZZZAAAAKKKK!
AHHHH!!!
I'VE GOT YOU...RIGHT WHERE...
...I WANT YOU...
ALL THAT BRAVADO, AND YOU WEREN'T EVEN A CHALLENGE FOR ME.
PITY.
SLOANE!!
NO!!

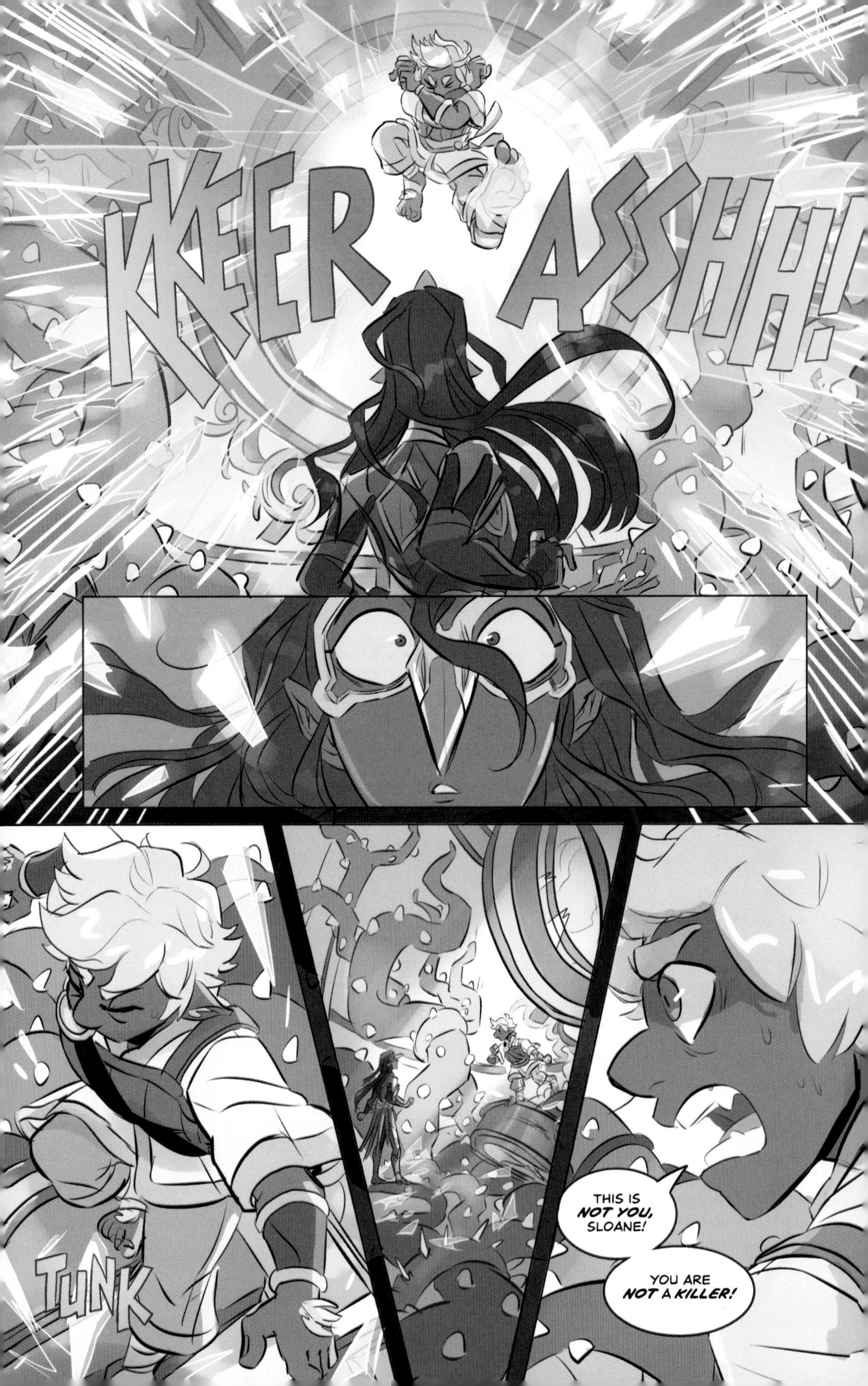
KKEER ASSHH!
THIS IS **NOT YOU,** SLOANE!
YOU ARE **NOT A KILLER!**
TUNK

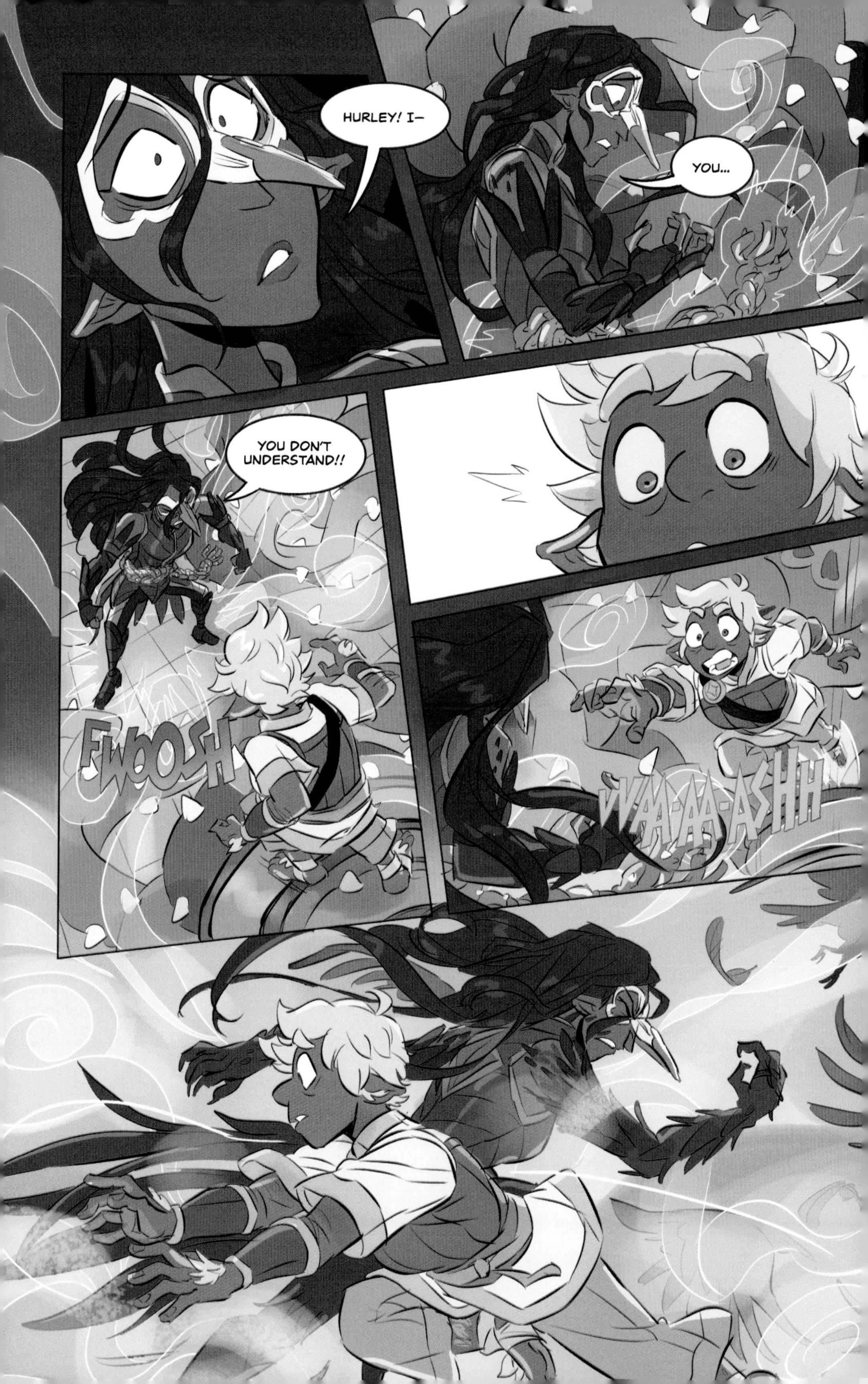
HURLEY! I—
YOU...
YOU DON'T UNDERSTAND!!
FWOOSH
VVAA-AA-ASHH

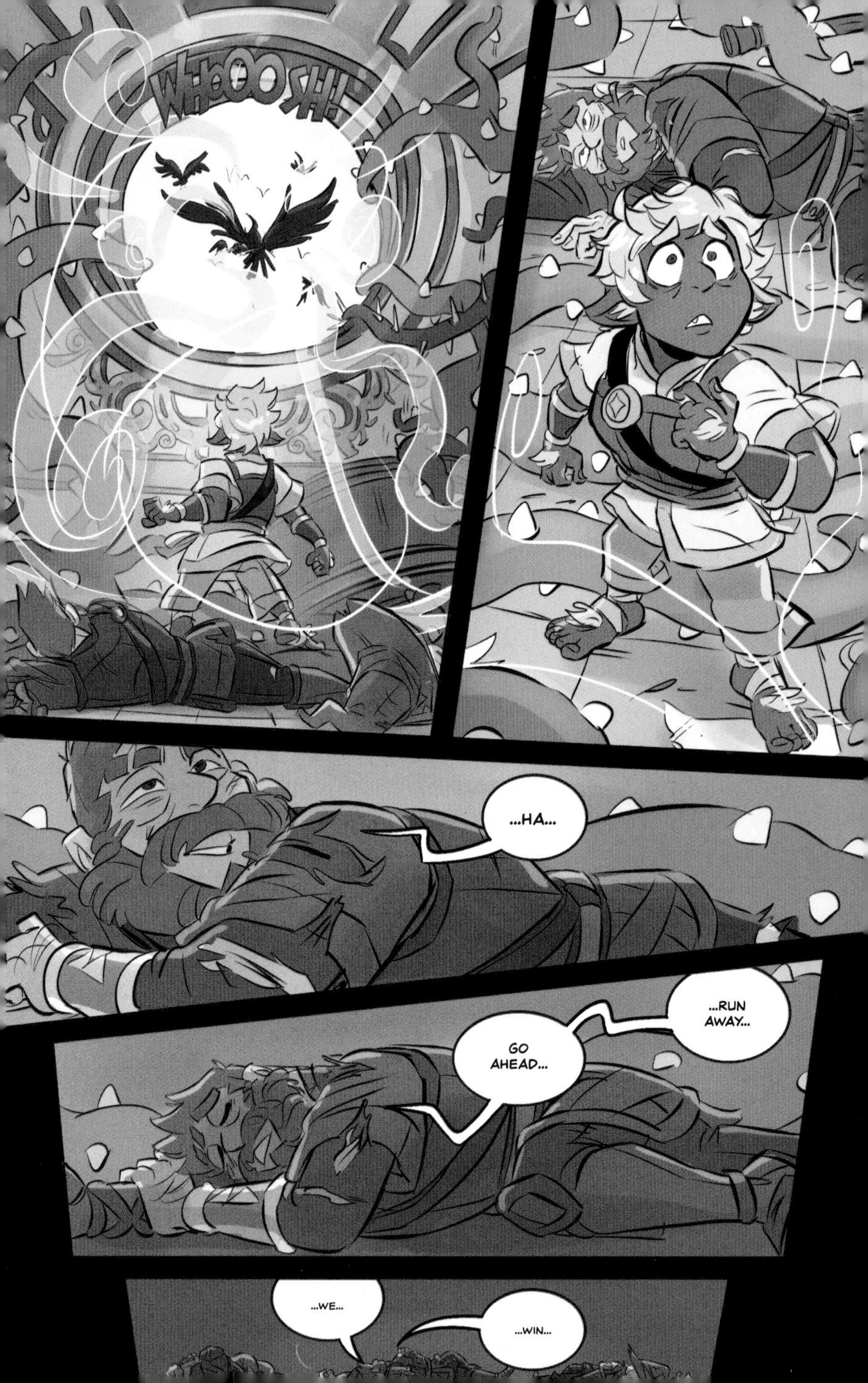
WHOOOSH!
...HA...
GO AHEAD...
...RUN AWAY...
...WE...
...WIN...

Chapter 3

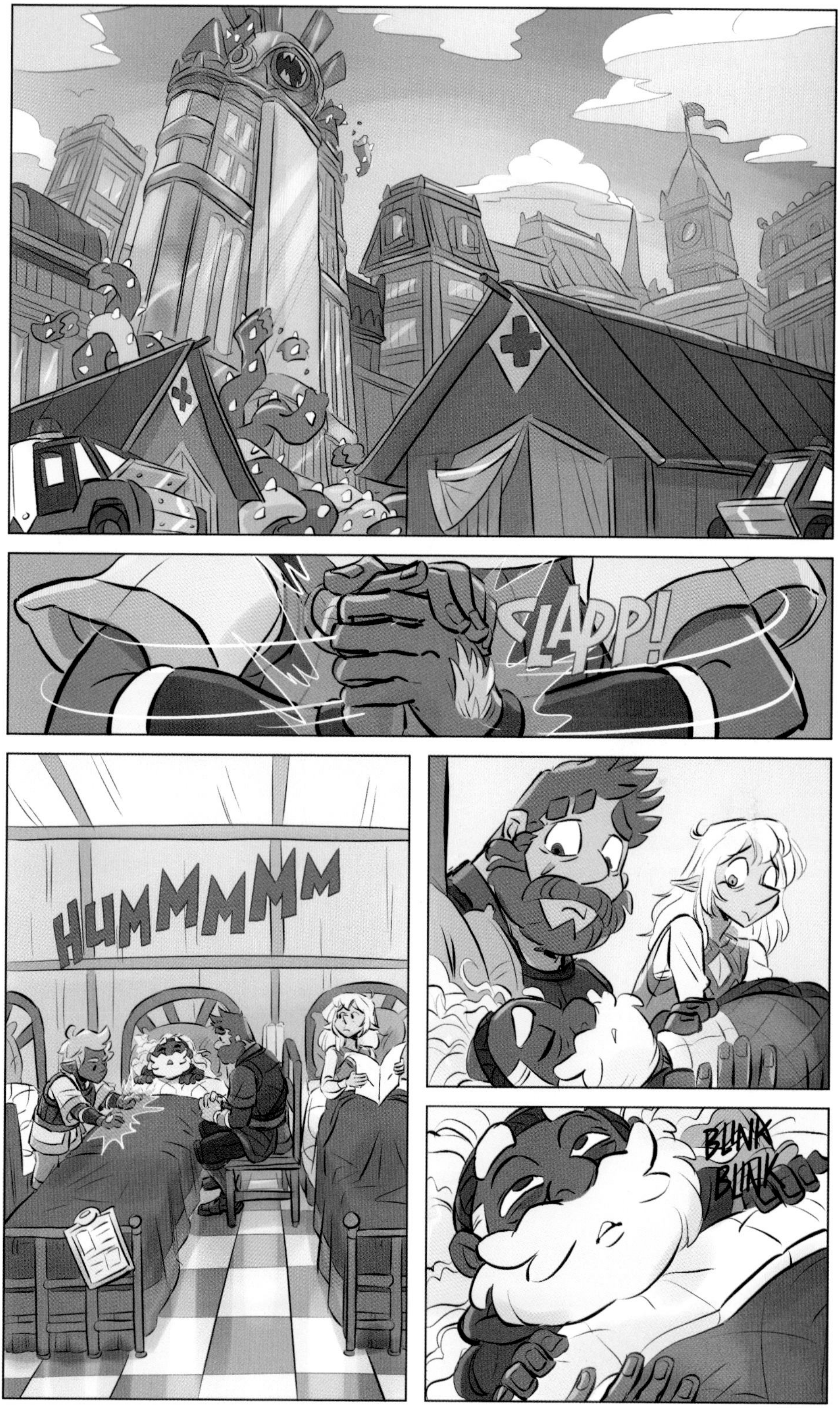
SLAPP!
HUMMMMMM
BLINK
BLINK

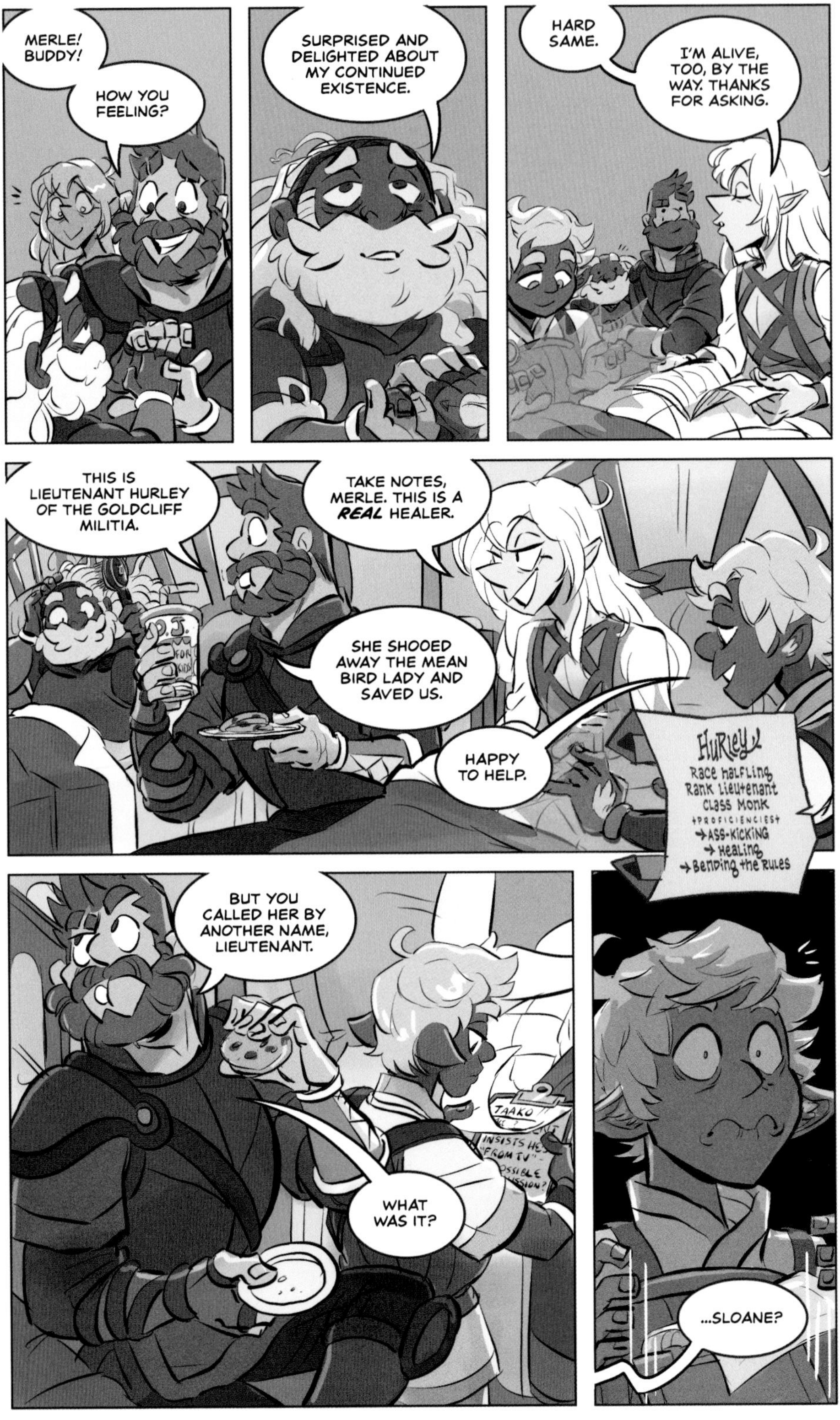
MERLE! BUDDY!
HOW YOU FEELING?
SURPRISED AND DELIGHTED ABOUT MY CONTINUED EXISTENCE.
HARD SAME.
I'M ALIVE, TOO, BY THE WAY. THANKS FOR ASKING.
THIS IS LIEUTENANT HURLEY OF THE GOLDCLIFF MILITIA.
TAKE NOTES, MERLE. THIS IS A *REAL* HEALER.
SHE SHOOED AWAY THE MEAN BIRD LADY AND SAVED US.
HAPPY TO HELP.
HURLEY
Race halfling
Rank Lieutenant
Class Monk
PROFICIENCIES
→ASS-KICKING
→Healing
→Bending the Rules
BUT YOU CALLED HER BY ANOTHER NAME, LIEUTENANT.
WHAT WAS IT?
TAAKO
...SLOANE?

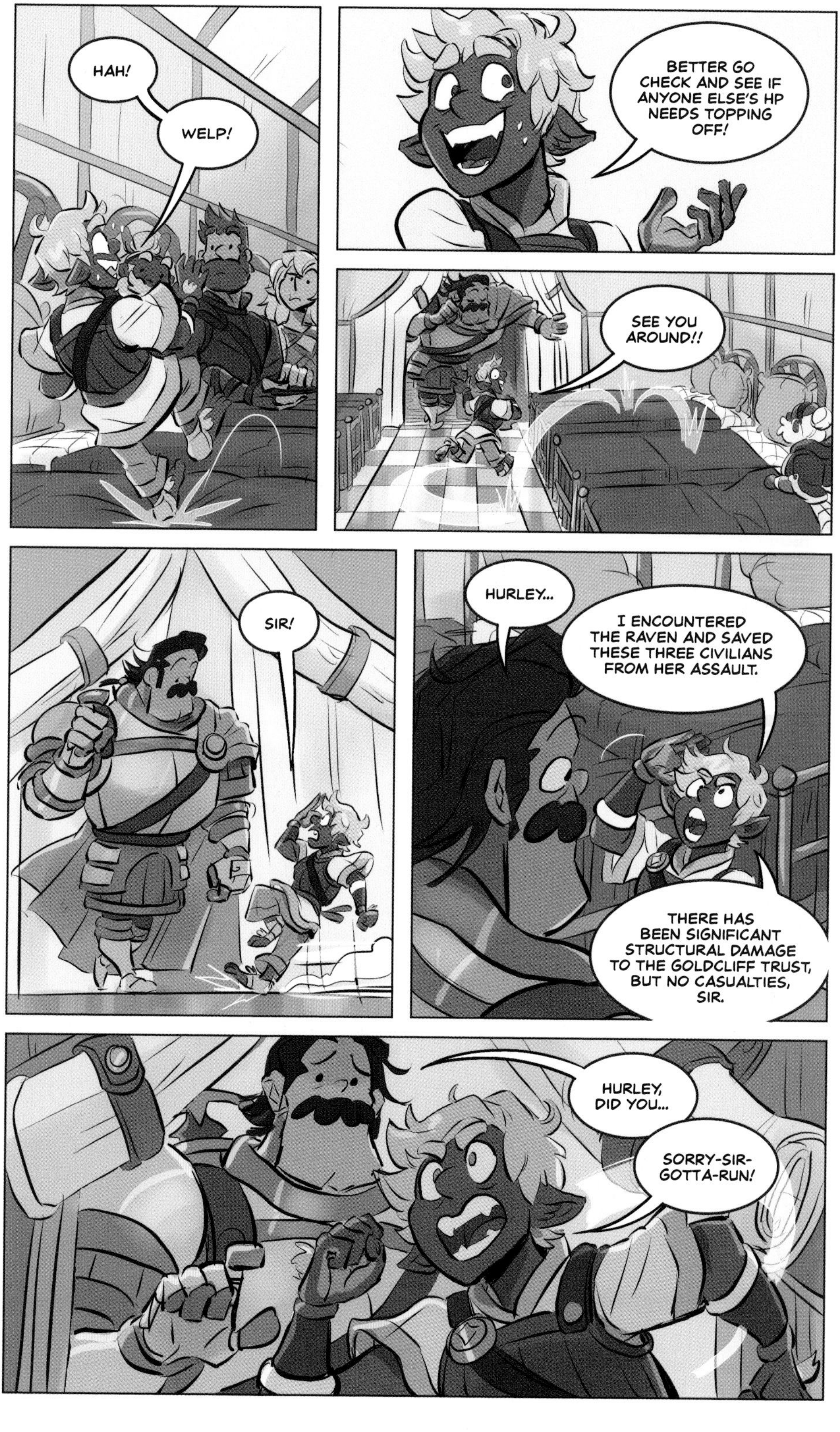
HAH!
WELP!
BETTER GO CHECK AND SEE IF ANYONE ELSE'S HP NEEDS TOPPING OFF!
SEE YOU AROUND!!
SIR!
HURLEY...
I ENCOUNTERED THE RAVEN AND SAVED THESE THREE CIVILIANS FROM HER ASSAULT.
THERE HAS BEEN SIGNIFICANT STRUCTURAL DAMAGE TO THE GOLDCLIFF TRUST, BUT NO CASUALTIES, SIR.
HURLEY, DID YOU...
SORRY-SIR-GOTTA-RUN!

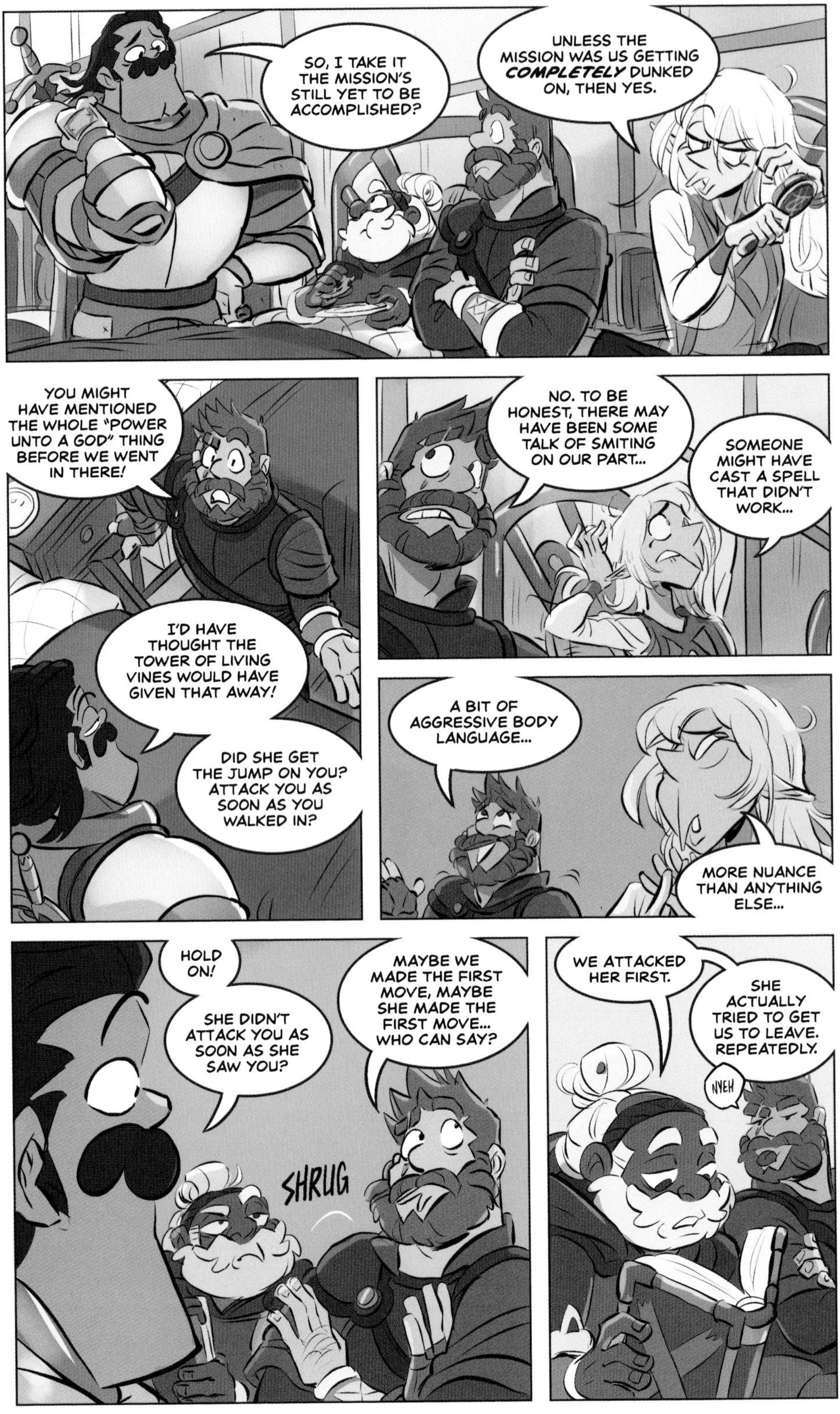
SO, I TAKE IT THE MISSION'S STILL YET TO BE ACCOMPLISHED?
UNLESS THE MISSION WAS US GETTING *COMPLETELY* DUNKED ON, THEN YES.
YOU MIGHT HAVE MENTIONED THE WHOLE "POWER UNTO A GOD" THING BEFORE WE WENT IN THERE!
I'D HAVE THOUGHT THE TOWER OF LIVING VINES WOULD HAVE GIVEN THAT AWAY!
DID SHE GET THE JUMP ON YOU? ATTACK YOU AS SOON AS YOU WALKED IN?
NO. TO BE HONEST, THERE MAY HAVE BEEN SOME TALK OF SMITING ON OUR PART...
SOMEONE MIGHT HAVE CAST A SPELL THAT DIDN'T WORK...
A BIT OF AGGRESSIVE BODY LANGUAGE...
MORE NUANCE THAN ANYTHING ELSE...
HOLD ON!
SHE DIDN'T ATTACK YOU AS SOON AS SHE SAW YOU?
MAYBE WE MADE THE FIRST MOVE, MAYBE SHE MADE THE FIRST MOVE... WHO CAN SAY?
SHRUG
WE ATTACKED HER FIRST.
SHE ACTUALLY TRIED TO GET US TO LEAVE. REPEATEDLY.
NYEH

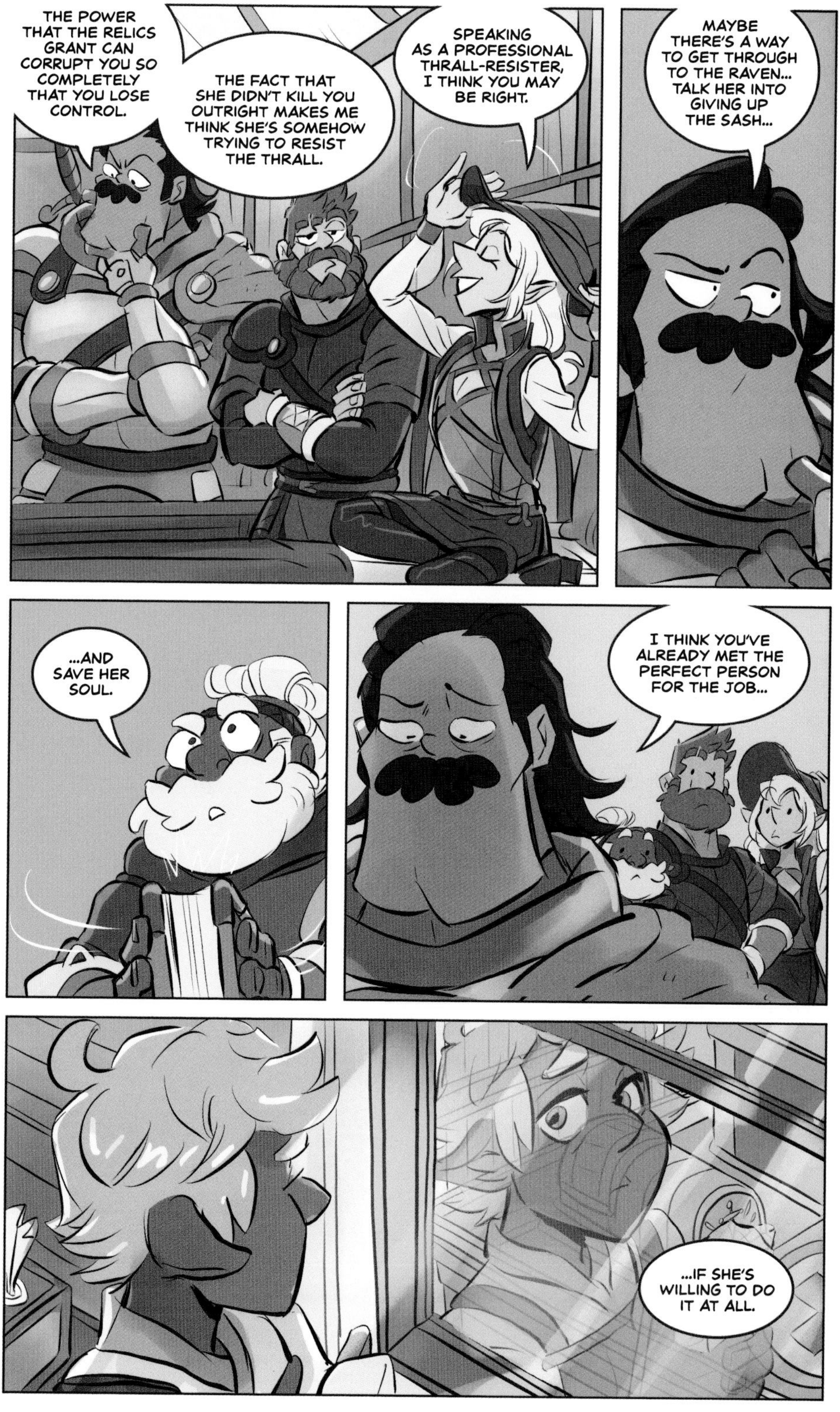
THE POWER THAT THE RELICS GRANT CAN CORRUPT YOU SO COMPLETELY THAT YOU LOSE CONTROL.
THE FACT THAT SHE DIDN'T KILL YOU OUTRIGHT MAKES ME THINK SHE'S SOMEHOW TRYING TO RESIST THE THRALL.
SPEAKING AS A PROFESSIONAL THRALL-RESISTER, I THINK YOU MAY BE RIGHT.
MAYBE THERE'S A WAY TO GET THROUGH TO THE RAVEN... TALK HER INTO GIVING UP THE SASH...
...AND SAVE HER SOUL.
I THINK YOU'VE ALREADY MET THE PERFECT PERSON FOR THE JOB...
...IF SHE'S WILLING TO DO IT AT ALL.

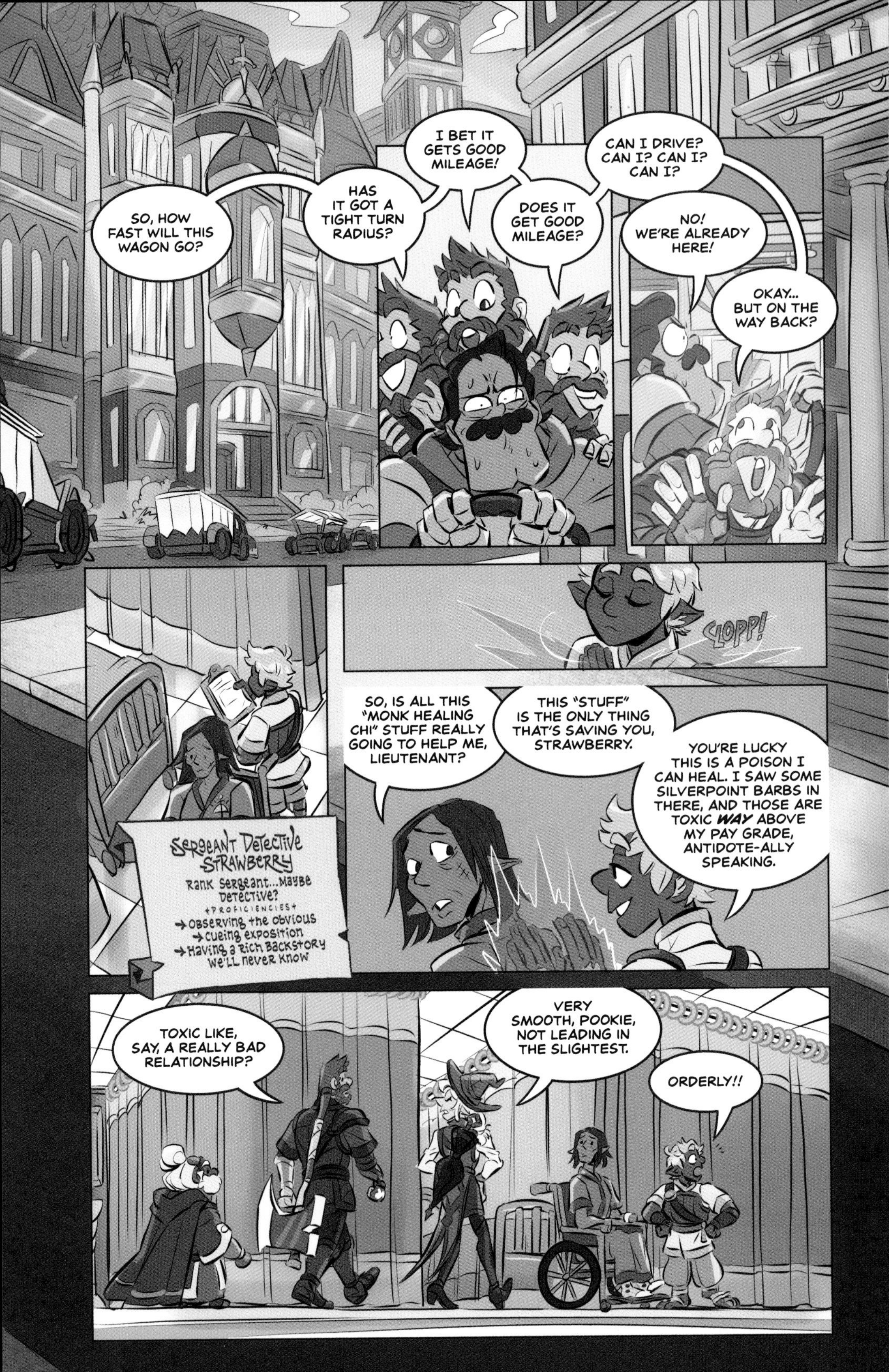
SO, HOW FAST WILL THIS WAGON GO?
HAS IT GOT A TIGHT TURN RADIUS?
I BET IT GETS GOOD MILEAGE!
DOES IT GET GOOD MILEAGE?
CAN I DRIVE? CAN I? CAN I? CAN I?
NO! WE'RE ALREADY HERE!
OKAY... BUT ON THE WAY BACK?
CLOPP!
Sergeant Detective Strawberry
Rank Sergeant...Maybe Detective?
PROFICIENCIES
Observing the obvious
Cueing exposition
Having a Rich Backstory We'll never Know
SO, IS ALL THIS "MONK HEALING CHI" STUFF REALLY GOING TO HELP ME, LIEUTENANT?
THIS "STUFF" IS THE ONLY THING THAT'S SAVING YOU, STRAWBERRY.
YOU'RE LUCKY THIS IS A POISON I CAN HEAL. I SAW SOME SILVERPOINT BARBS IN THERE, AND THOSE ARE TOXIC WAY ABOVE MY PAY GRADE, ANTIDOTE-ALLY SPEAKING.
TOXIC LIKE, SAY, A REALLY BAD RELATIONSHIP?
VERY SMOOTH, POOKIE, NOT LEADING IN THE SLIGHTEST.
ORDERLY!!

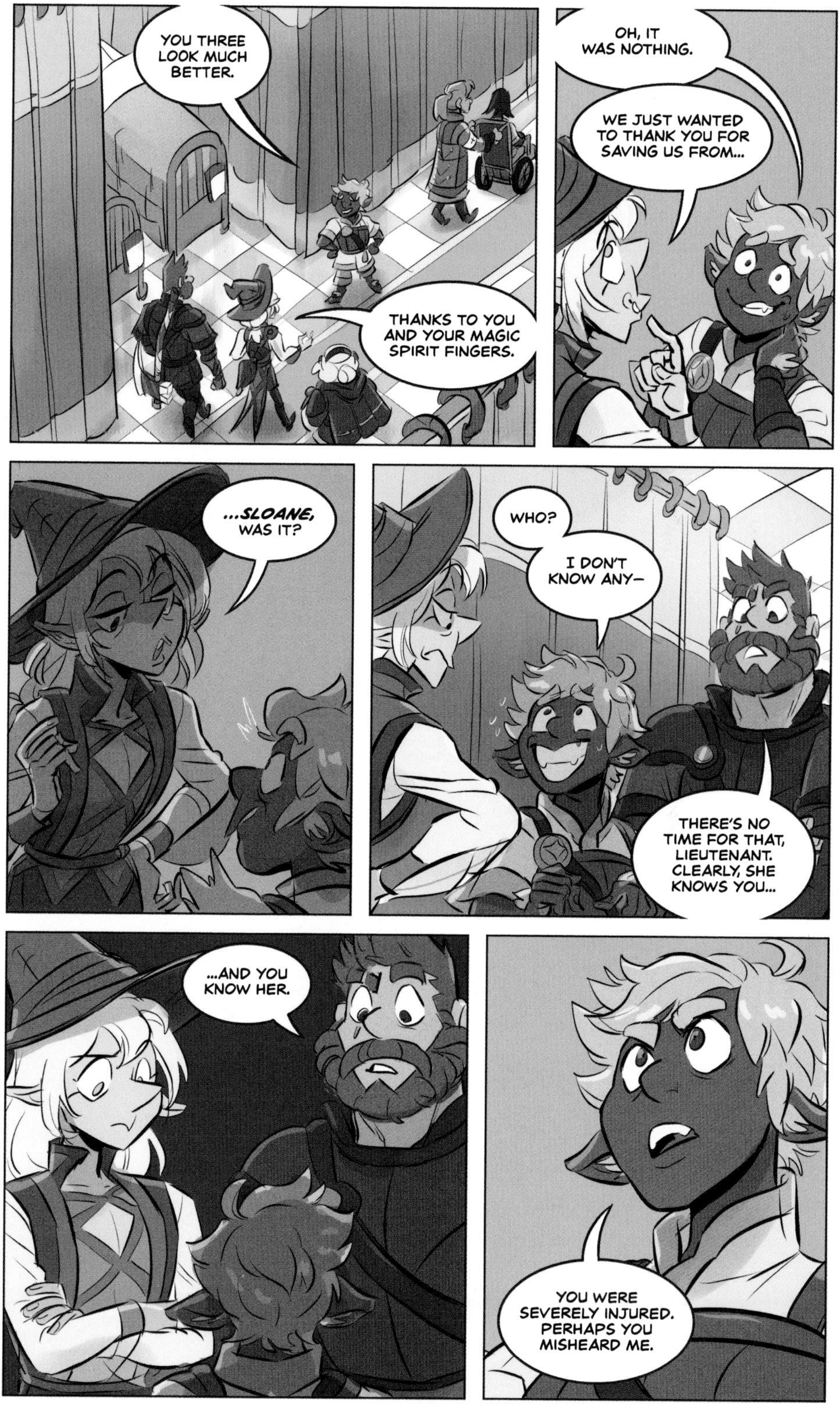
YOU THREE LOOK MUCH BETTER.
THANKS TO YOU AND YOUR MAGIC SPIRIT FINGERS.
OH, IT WAS NOTHING.
WE JUST WANTED TO THANK YOU FOR SAVING US FROM...
...SLOANE, WAS IT?
WHO?
I DON'T KNOW ANY—
THERE'S NO TIME FOR THAT, LIEUTENANT. CLEARLY, SHE KNOWS YOU...
...AND YOU KNOW HER.
YOU WERE SEVERELY INJURED. PERHAPS YOU MISHEARD ME.

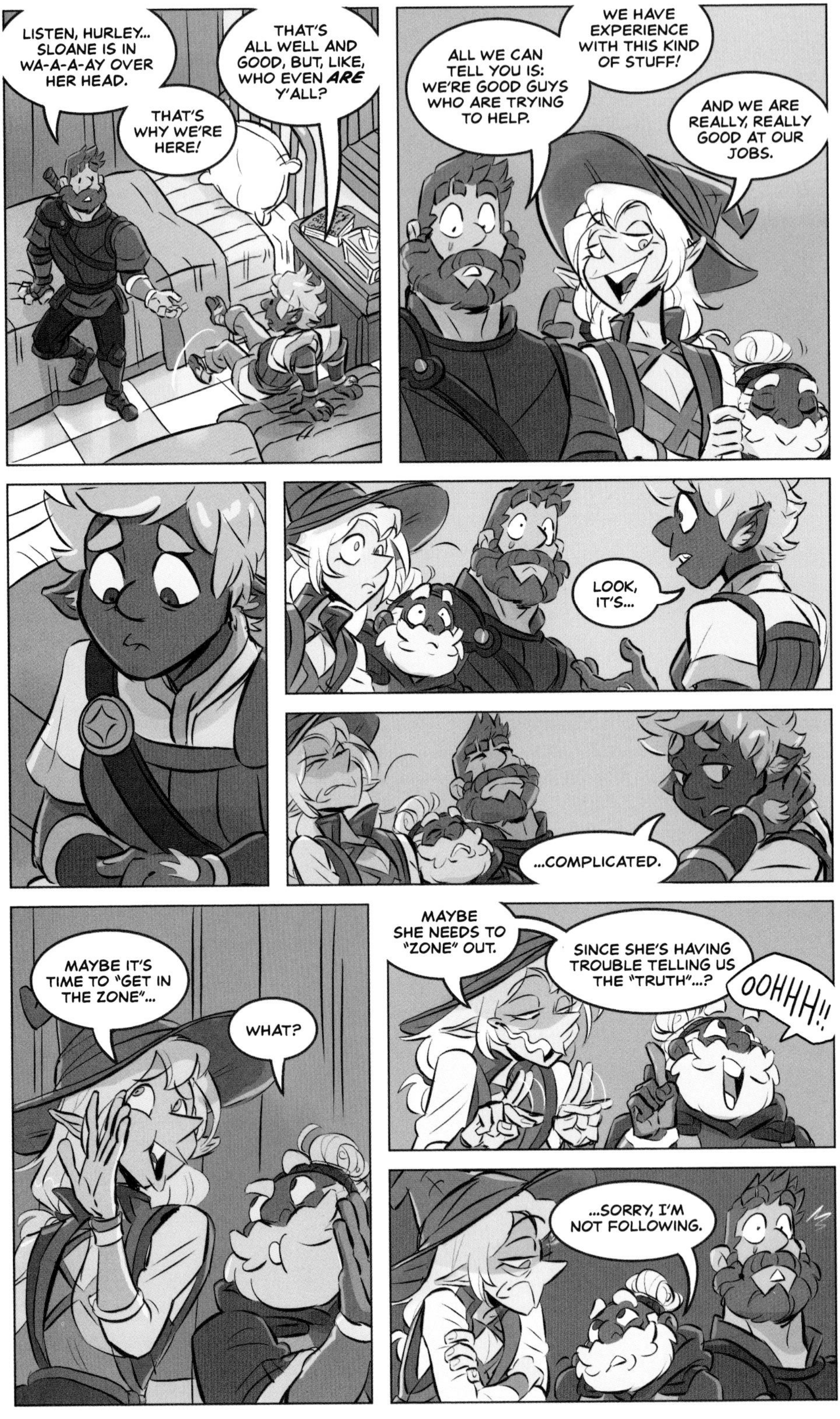
LISTEN, HURLEY... SLOANE IS IN WA-A-A-AY OVER HER HEAD.
THAT'S WHY WE'RE HERE!
THAT'S ALL WELL AND GOOD, BUT, LIKE, WHO EVEN ARE Y'ALL?
ALL WE CAN TELL YOU IS: WE'RE GOOD GUYS WHO ARE TRYING TO HELP.
WE HAVE EXPERIENCE WITH THIS KIND OF STUFF!
AND WE ARE REALLY, REALLY GOOD AT OUR JOBS.
LOOK, IT'S...
...COMPLICATED.
MAYBE IT'S TIME TO "GET IN THE ZONE"...
WHAT?
MAYBE SHE NEEDS TO "ZONE" OUT.
SINCE SHE'S HAVING TROUBLE TELLING US THE "TRUTH"...?
OOHHH!!
...SORRY, I'M NOT FOLLOWING.

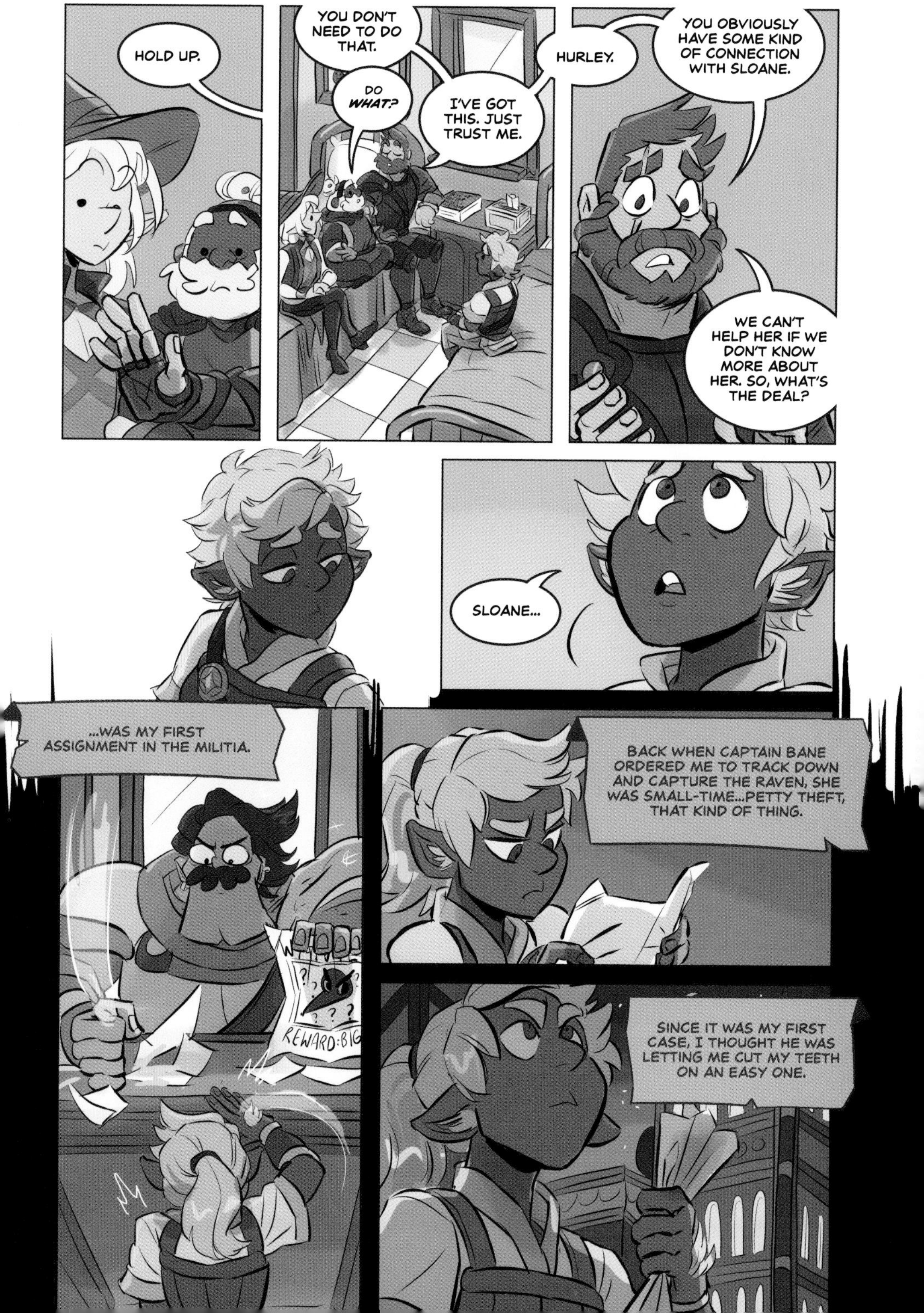
HOLD UP.
YOU DON'T NEED TO DO THAT.
DO *WHAT?*
I'VE GOT THIS. JUST TRUST ME.
HURLEY.
YOU OBVIOUSLY HAVE SOME KIND OF CONNECTION WITH SLOANE.
WE CAN'T HELP HER IF WE DON'T KNOW MORE ABOUT HER. SO, WHAT'S THE DEAL?
SLOANE...
...WAS MY FIRST ASSIGNMENT IN THE MILITIA.
BACK WHEN CAPTAIN BANE ORDERED ME TO TRACK DOWN AND CAPTURE THE RAVEN, SHE WAS SMALL-TIME...PETTY THEFT, THAT KIND OF THING.
REWARD: BIG
SINCE IT WAS MY FIRST CASE, I THOUGHT HE WAS LETTING ME CUT MY TEETH ON AN EASY ONE.

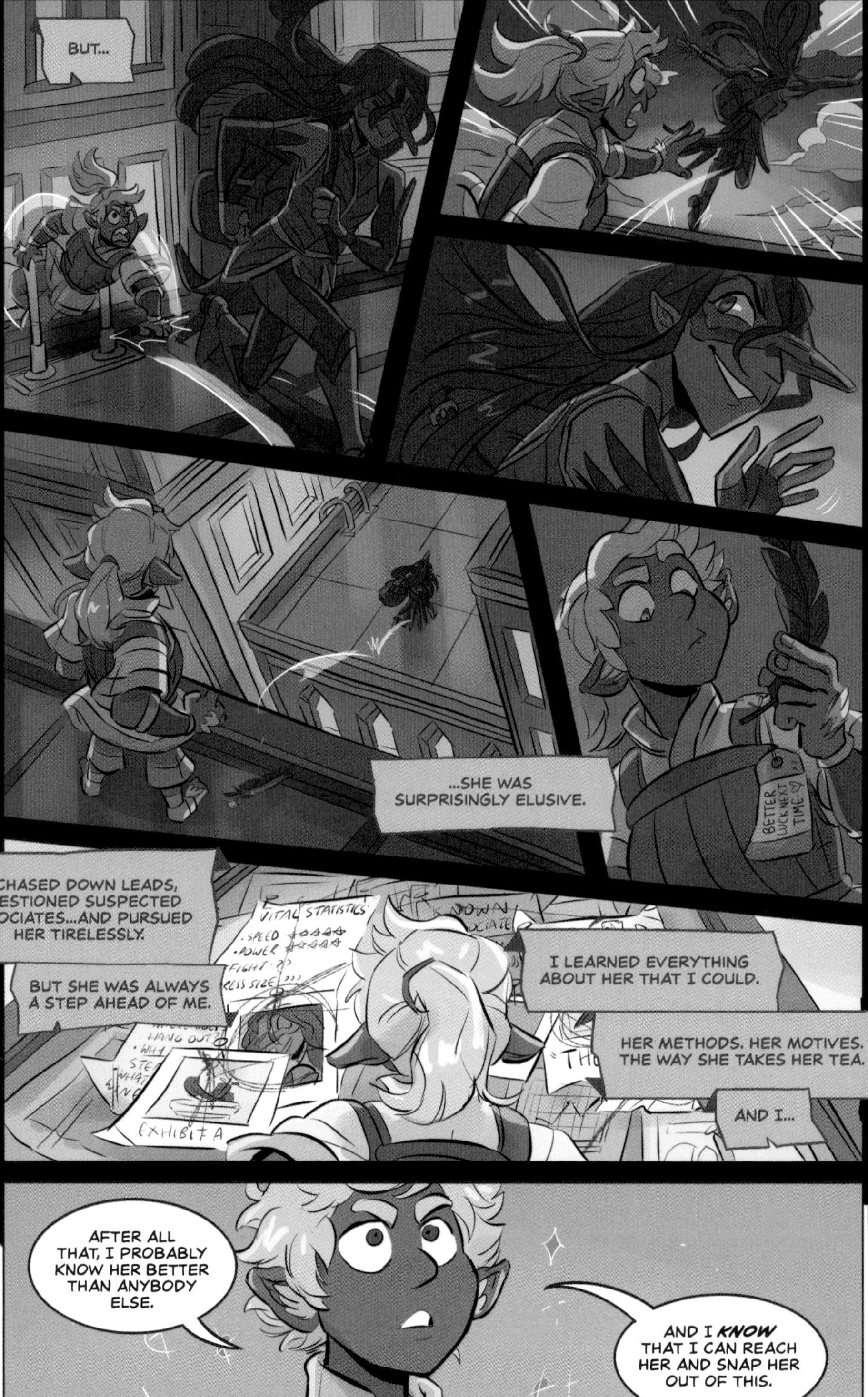
BUT...
...SHE WAS SURPRISINGLY ELUSIVE.
BETTER LUCK NEXT TIME
I CHASED DOWN LEADS, QUESTIONED SUSPECTED ASSOCIATES...AND PURSUED HER TIRELESSLY.
BUT SHE WAS ALWAYS A STEP AHEAD OF ME.
VITAL STATISTICS
EXHIBIT A
I LEARNED EVERYTHING ABOUT HER THAT I COULD.
HER METHODS. HER MOTIVES. THE WAY SHE TAKES HER TEA.
AND I...
AFTER ALL THAT, I PROBABLY KNOW HER BETTER THAN ANYBODY ELSE.
AND I *KNOW* THAT I CAN REACH HER AND SNAP HER OUT OF THIS.

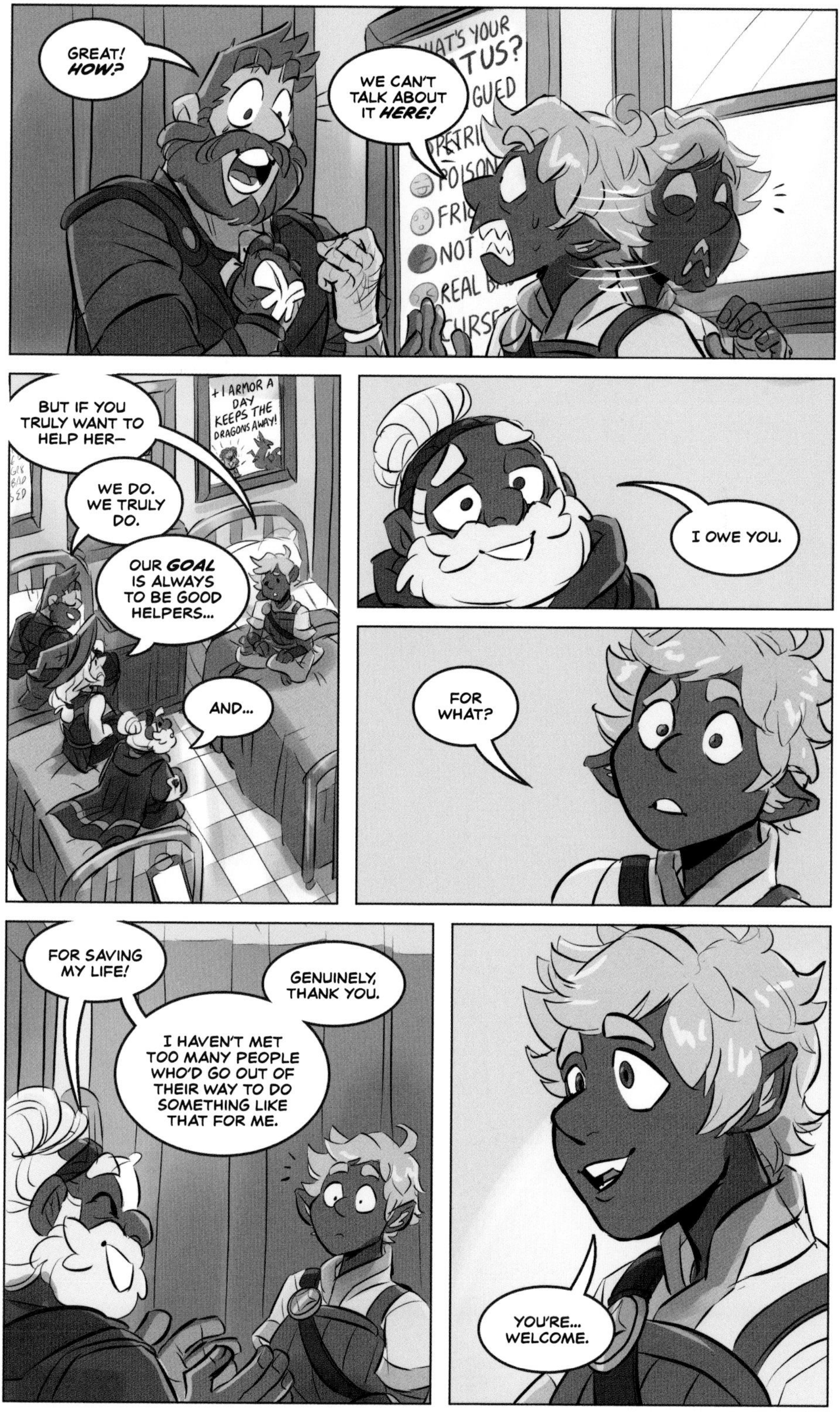
GREAT! HOW?
WE CAN'T TALK ABOUT IT HERE!
BUT IF YOU TRULY WANT TO HELP HER—
+1 ARMOR A DAY KEEPS THE DRAGONS AWAY!
WE DO. WE TRULY DO.
OUR GOAL IS ALWAYS TO BE GOOD HELPERS...
AND...
I OWE YOU.
FOR WHAT?
FOR SAVING MY LIFE!
GENUINELY, THANK YOU.
I HAVEN'T MET TOO MANY PEOPLE WHO'D GO OUT OF THEIR WAY TO DO SOMETHING LIKE THAT FOR ME.
YOU'RE... WELCOME.

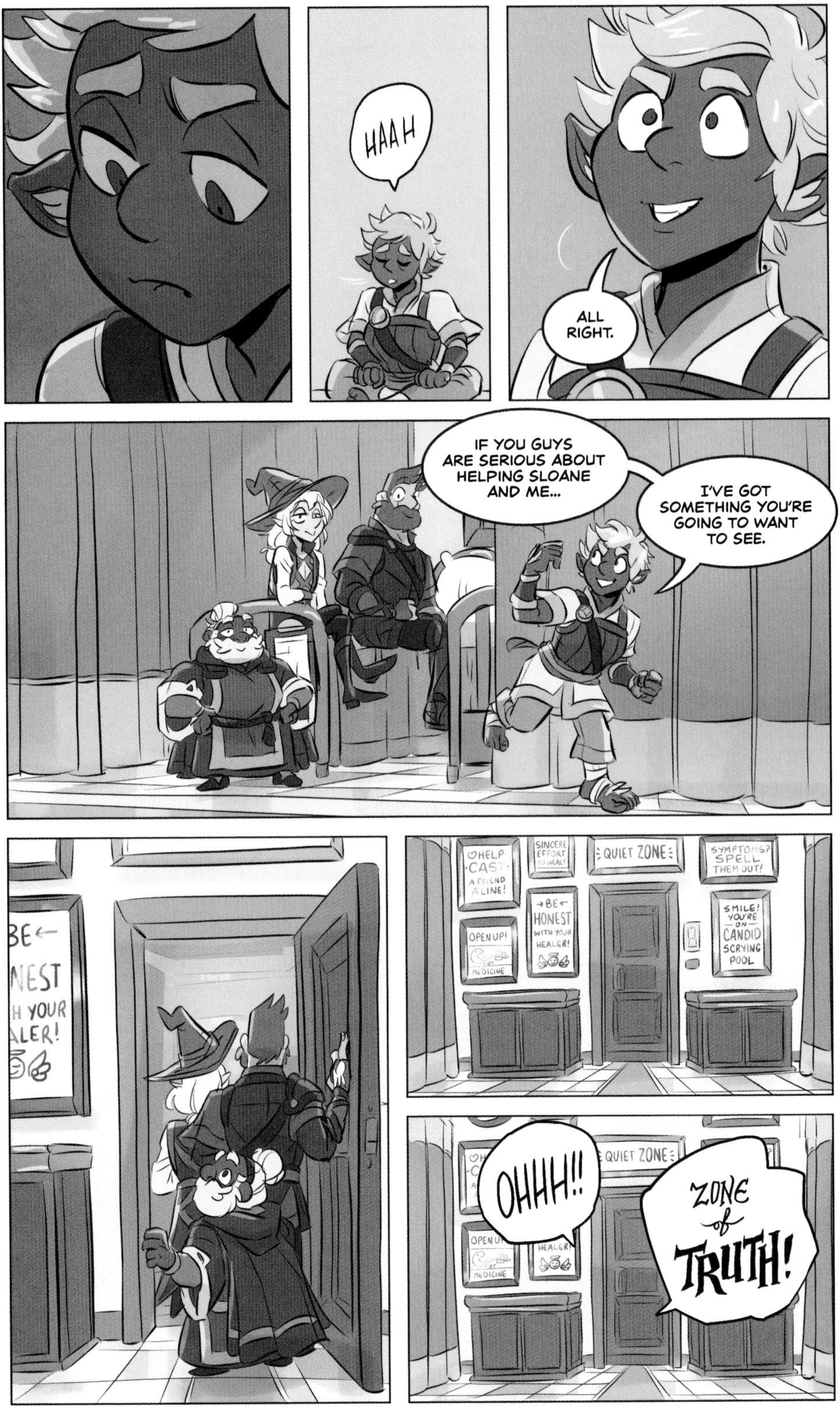
HAAH
ALL RIGHT.
IF YOU GUYS ARE SERIOUS ABOUT HELPING SLOANE AND ME...
I'VE GOT SOMETHING YOU'RE GOING TO WANT TO SEE.
BE← HONEST WITH YOUR HEALER!
♡HELP-CAST- A FRIEND A LINE!
SINCERE EFFORT TO HEAL!
QUIET ZONE
SYMPTOMS? SPELL THEM OUT!
OPEN UP! MEDICINE
→BE← HONEST WITH YOUR HEALER!
SMILE! YOU'RE ON CANDID SCRYING POOL
OHHH!!
ZONE of TRUTH!

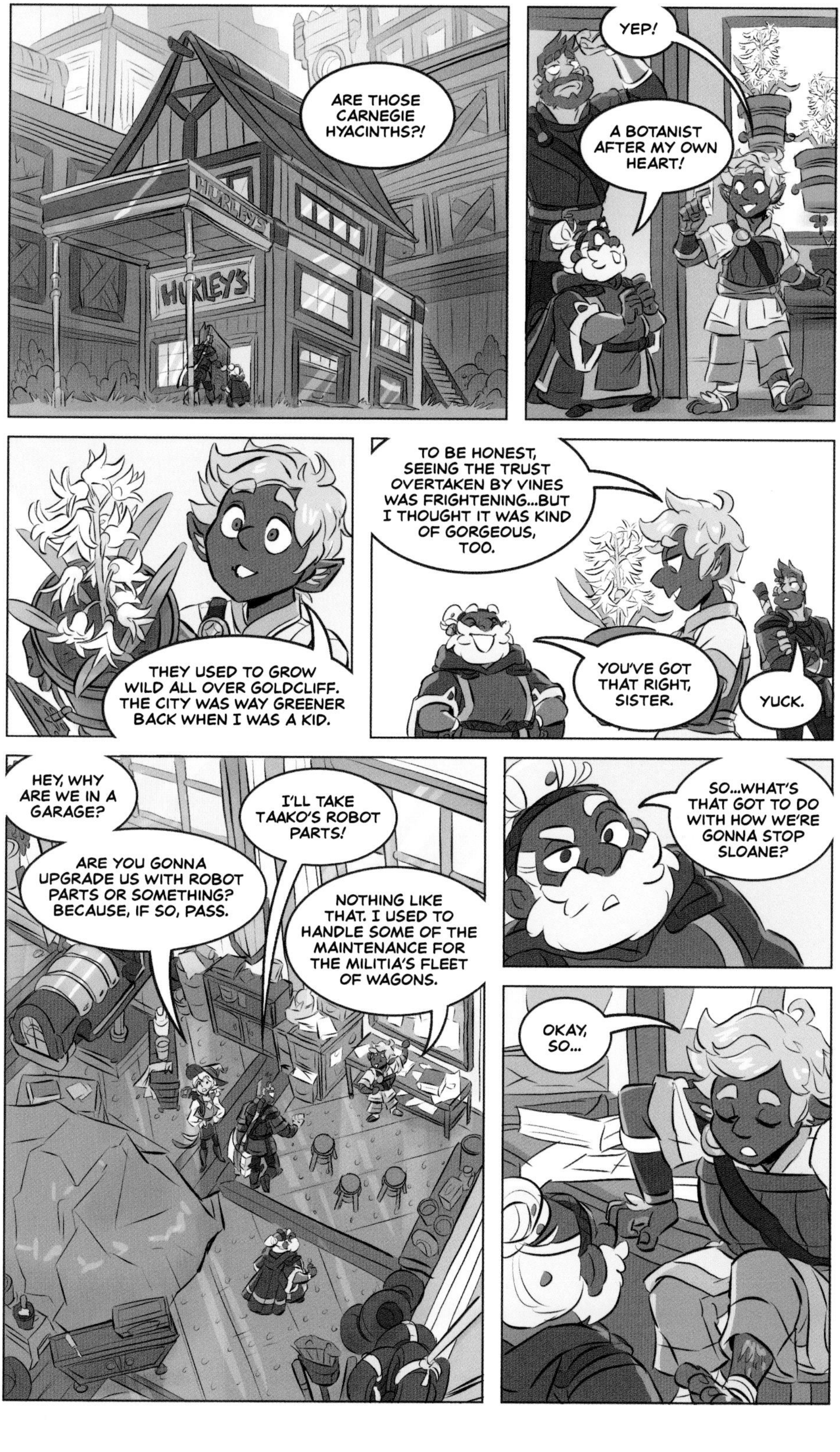

HURLEY'S
ARE THOSE CARNEGIE HYACINTHS?!
YEP!
A BOTANIST AFTER MY OWN HEART!
THEY USED TO GROW WILD ALL OVER GOLDCLIFF. THE CITY WAS WAY GREENER BACK WHEN I WAS A KID.
TO BE HONEST, SEEING THE TRUST OVERTAKEN BY VINES WAS FRIGHTENING...BUT I THOUGHT IT WAS KIND OF GORGEOUS, TOO.
YOU'VE GOT THAT RIGHT, SISTER.
YUCK.
HEY, WHY ARE WE IN A GARAGE?
ARE YOU GONNA UPGRADE US WITH ROBOT PARTS OR SOMETHING? BECAUSE, IF SO, PASS.
I'LL TAKE TAAKO'S ROBOT PARTS!
NOTHING LIKE THAT. I USED TO HANDLE SOME OF THE MAINTENANCE FOR THE MILITIA'S FLEET OF WAGONS.
SO...WHAT'S THAT GOT TO DO WITH HOW WE'RE GONNA STOP SLOANE?
OKAY, SO...

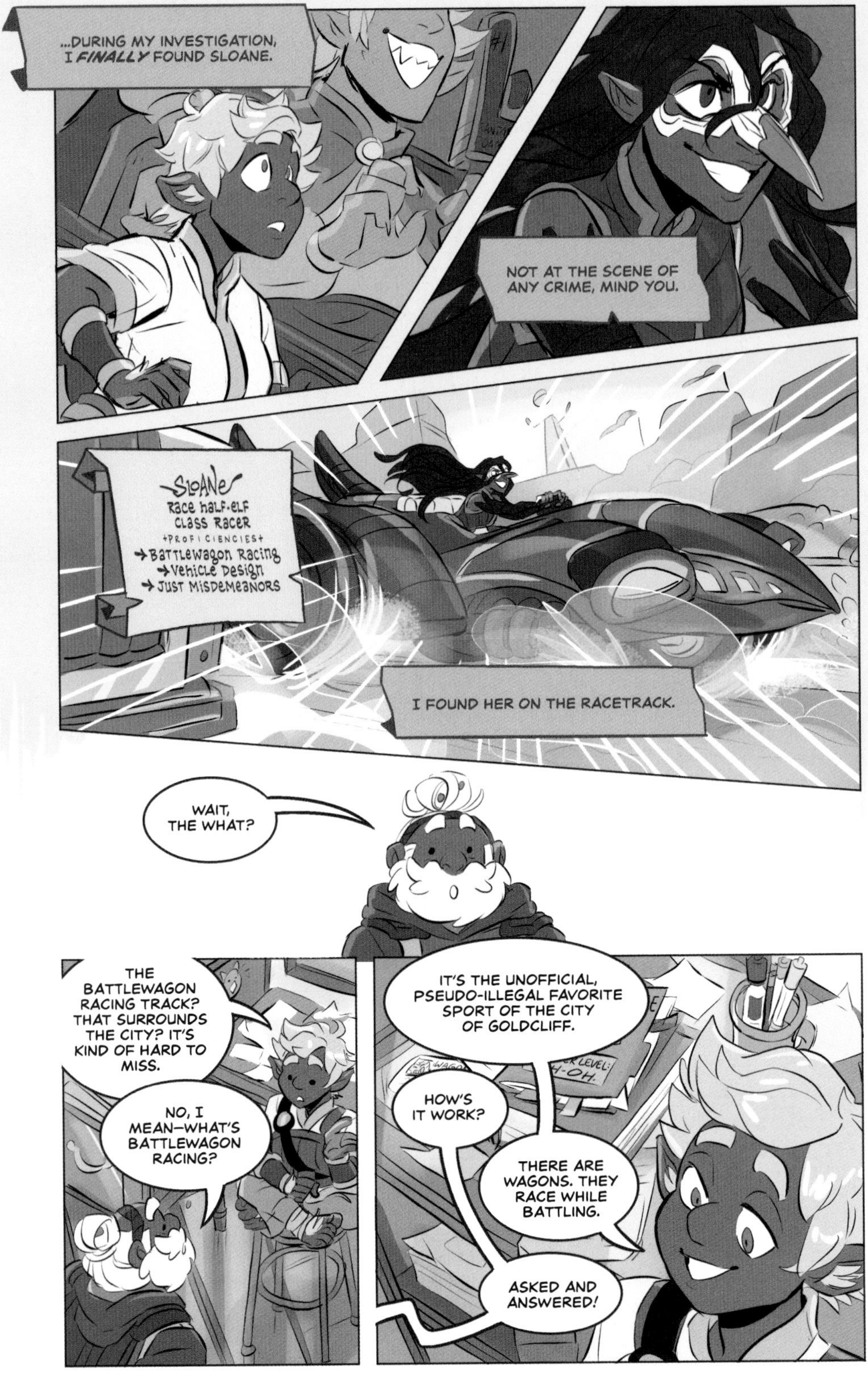
...DURING MY INVESTIGATION, I FINALLY FOUND SLOANE.
NOT AT THE SCENE OF ANY CRIME, MIND YOU.
SLOANE
Race half-elf
Class Racer
PROFICIENCIES
→Battlewagon Racing
→Vehicle Design
→Just Misdemeanors
I FOUND HER ON THE RACETRACK.
WAIT, THE WHAT?
THE BATTLEWAGON RACING TRACK? THAT SURROUNDS THE CITY? IT'S KIND OF HARD TO MISS.
NO, I MEAN—WHAT'S BATTLEWAGON RACING?
IT'S THE UNOFFICIAL, PSEUDO-ILLEGAL FAVORITE SPORT OF THE CITY OF GOLDCLIFF.
HOW'S IT WORK?
THERE ARE WAGONS. THEY RACE WHILE BATTLING.
ASKED AND ANSWERED!

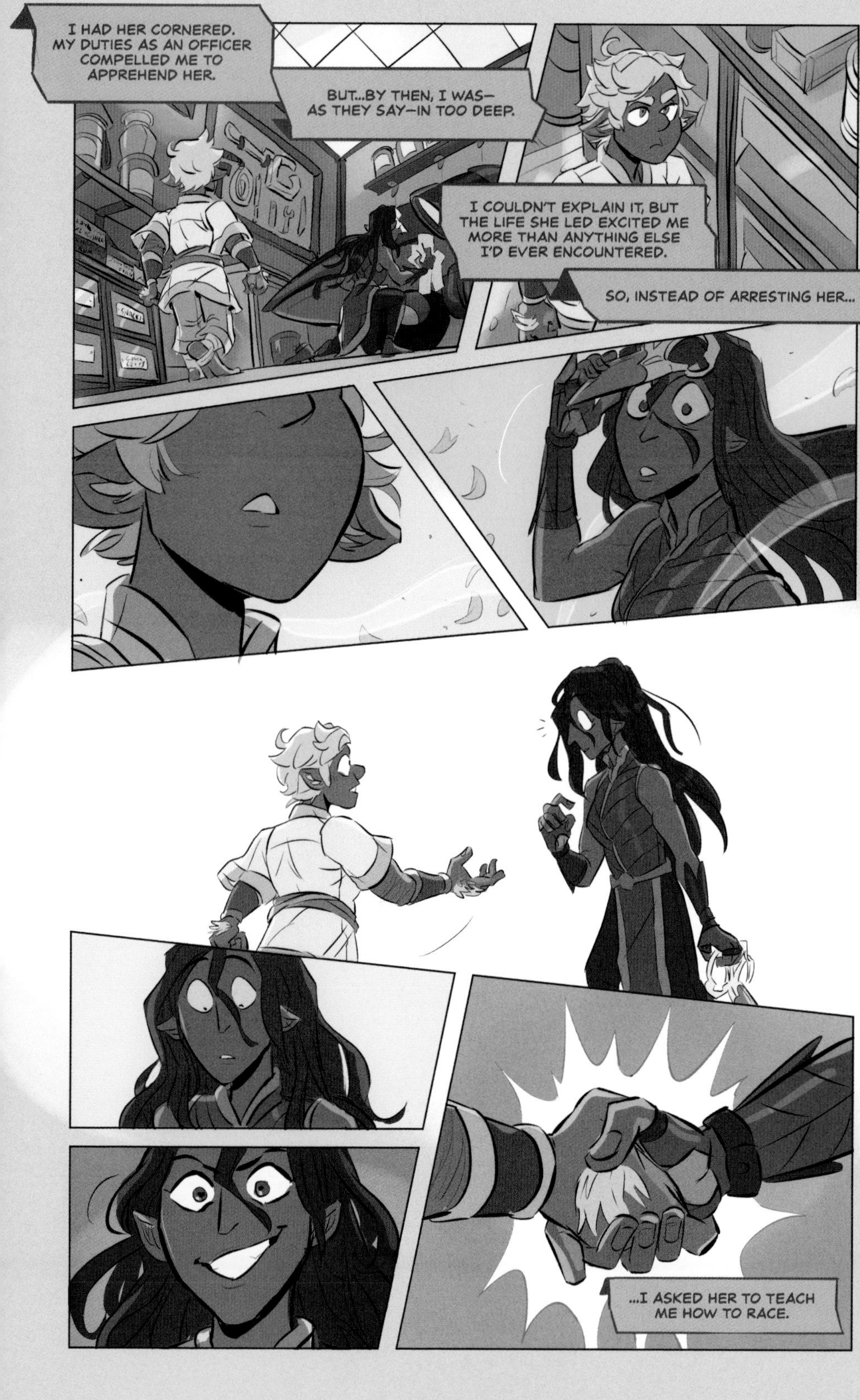
I HAD HER CORNERED. MY DUTIES AS AN OFFICER COMPELLED ME TO APPREHEND HER.
BUT...BY THEN, I WAS—AS THEY SAY—IN TOO DEEP.
I COULDN'T EXPLAIN IT, BUT THE LIFE SHE LED EXCITED ME MORE THAN ANYTHING ELSE I'D EVER ENCOUNTERED.
SO, INSTEAD OF ARRESTING HER...
...I ASKED HER TO TEACH ME HOW TO RACE.

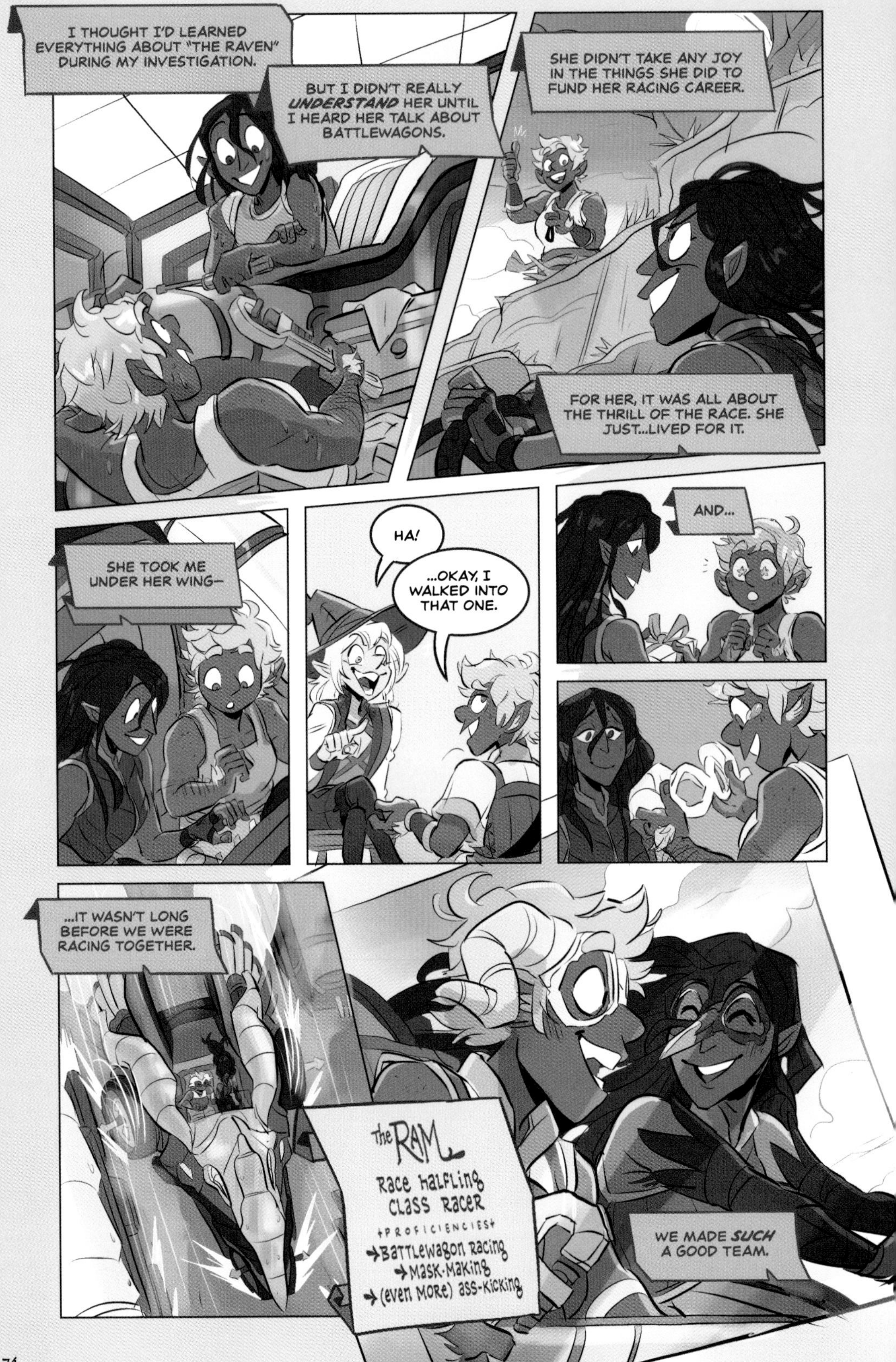

I THOUGHT I'D LEARNED EVERYTHING ABOUT "THE RAVEN" DURING MY INVESTIGATION.
BUT I DIDN'T REALLY UNDERSTAND HER UNTIL I HEARD HER TALK ABOUT BATTLEWAGONS.
SHE DIDN'T TAKE ANY JOY IN THE THINGS SHE DID TO FUND HER RACING CAREER.
FOR HER, IT WAS ALL ABOUT THE THRILL OF THE RACE. SHE JUST...LIVED FOR IT.
SHE TOOK ME UNDER HER WING—
HA!
...OKAY, I WALKED INTO THAT ONE.
AND...
...IT WASN'T LONG BEFORE WE WERE RACING TOGETHER.
The RAM
Race halfling
Class Racer
PROFICIENCIES
→Battlewagon Racing
→Mask-Making
→(even More) ass-Kicking
WE MADE SUCH A GOOD TEAM.

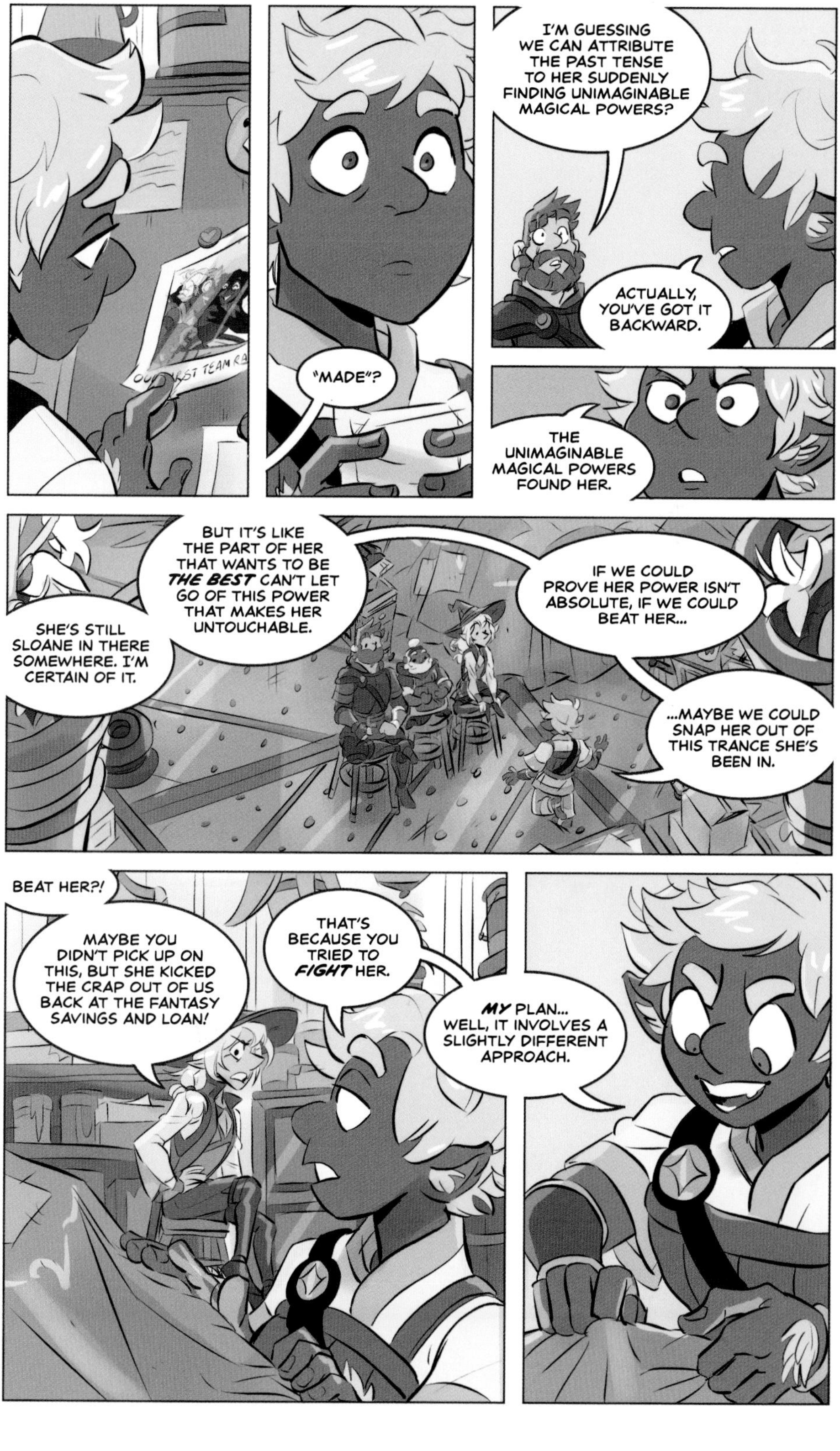
OUR FIRST TEAM RA
"MADE"?
I'M GUESSING WE CAN ATTRIBUTE THE PAST TENSE TO HER SUDDENLY FINDING UNIMAGINABLE MAGICAL POWERS?
ACTUALLY, YOU'VE GOT IT BACKWARD.
THE UNIMAGINABLE MAGICAL POWERS FOUND HER.
SHE'S STILL SLOANE IN THERE SOMEWHERE. I'M CERTAIN OF IT.
BUT IT'S LIKE THE PART OF HER THAT WANTS TO BE *THE BEST* CAN'T LET GO OF THIS POWER THAT MAKES HER UNTOUCHABLE.
IF WE COULD PROVE HER POWER ISN'T ABSOLUTE, IF WE COULD BEAT HER...
...MAYBE WE COULD SNAP HER OUT OF THIS TRANCE SHE'S BEEN IN.
BEAT HER?!
MAYBE YOU DIDN'T PICK UP ON THIS, BUT SHE KICKED THE CRAP OUT OF US BACK AT THE FANTASY SAVINGS AND LOAN!
THAT'S BECAUSE YOU TRIED TO *FIGHT* HER.
MY PLAN... WELL, IT INVOLVES A SLIGHTLY DIFFERENT APPROACH.

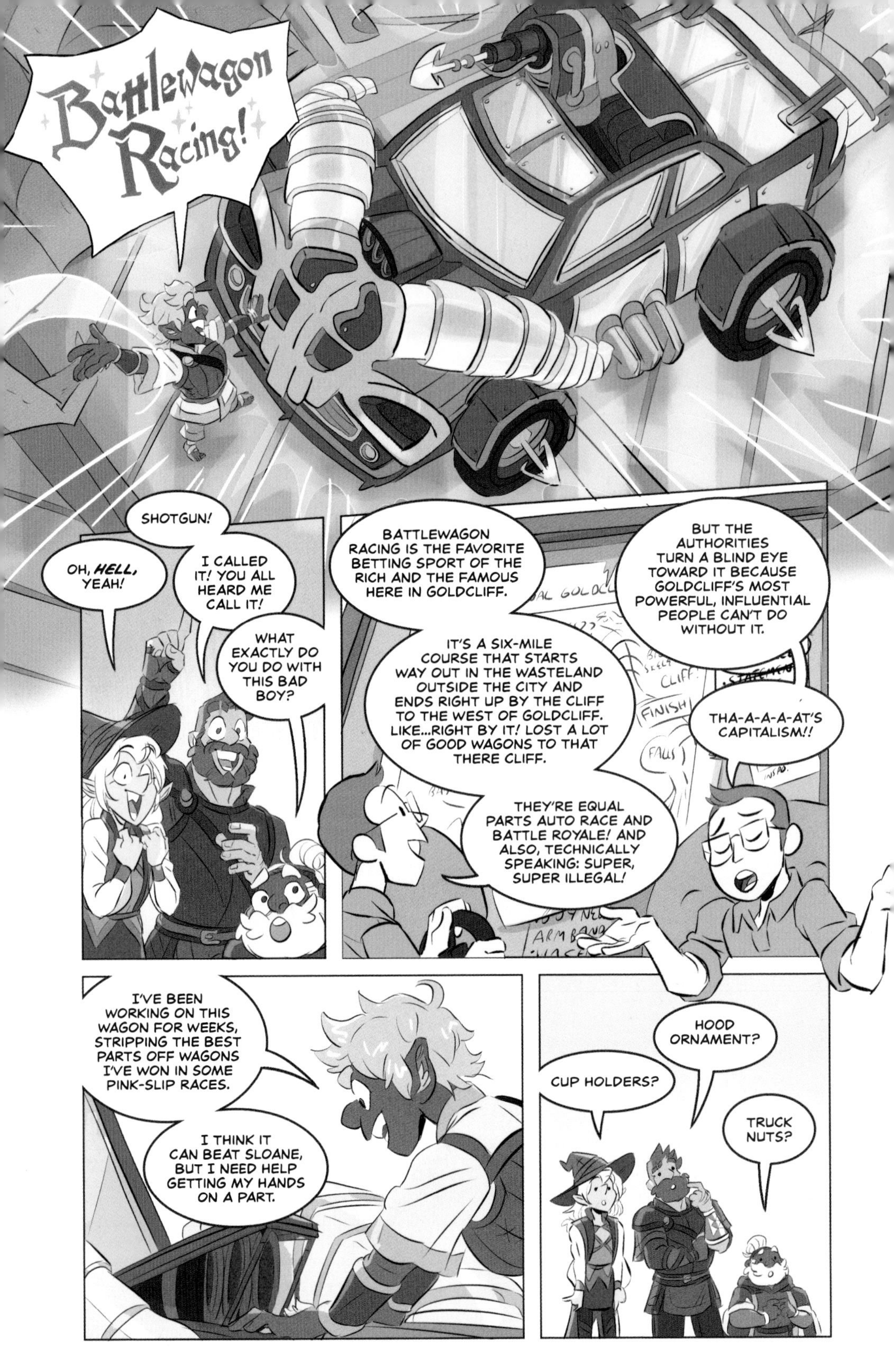

Battlewagon Racing!
SHOTGUN!
OH, **HELL,** YEAH!
I CALLED IT! YOU ALL HEARD ME CALL IT!
WHAT EXACTLY DO YOU DO WITH THIS BAD BOY?
BATTLEWAGON RACING IS THE FAVORITE BETTING SPORT OF THE RICH AND THE FAMOUS HERE IN GOLDCLIFF.
IT'S A SIX-MILE COURSE THAT STARTS WAY OUT IN THE WASTELAND OUTSIDE THE CITY AND ENDS RIGHT UP BY THE CLIFF TO THE WEST OF GOLDCLIFF. LIKE...RIGHT BY IT! LOST A LOT OF GOOD WAGONS TO THAT THERE CLIFF.
THEY'RE EQUAL PARTS AUTO RACE AND BATTLE ROYALE! AND ALSO, TECHNICALLY SPEAKING: SUPER, SUPER ILLEGAL!
BUT THE AUTHORITIES TURN A BLIND EYE TOWARD IT BECAUSE GOLDCLIFF'S MOST POWERFUL, INFLUENTIAL PEOPLE CAN'T DO WITHOUT IT.
THA-A-A-A-AT'S CAPITALISM!!
CLIFF!
FINISH
I'VE BEEN WORKING ON THIS WAGON FOR WEEKS, STRIPPING THE BEST PARTS OFF WAGONS I'VE WON IN SOME PINK-SLIP RACES.
I THINK IT CAN BEAT SLOANE, BUT I NEED HELP GETTING MY HANDS ON A PART.
CUP HOLDERS?
HOOD ORNAMENT?
TRUCK NUTS?

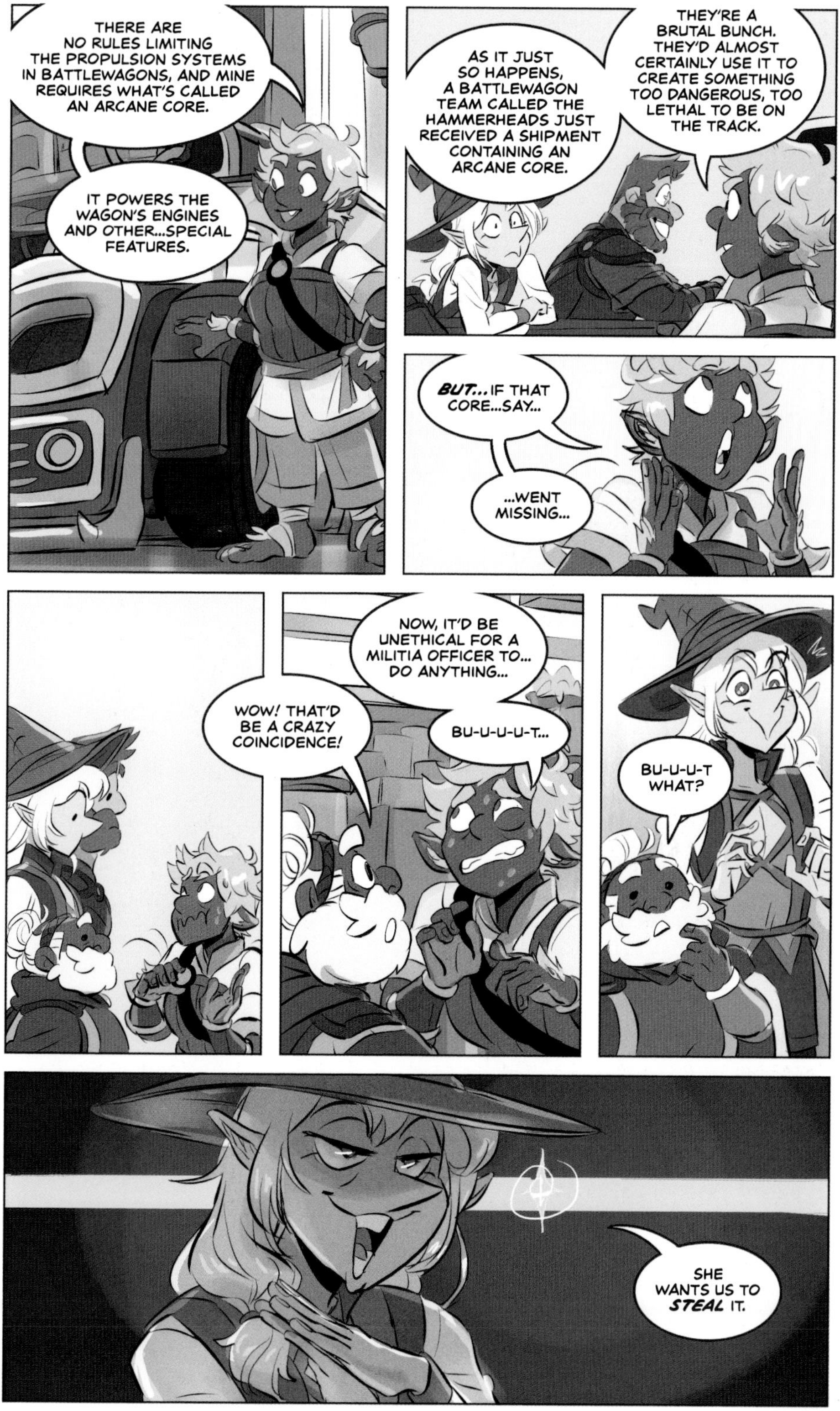
THERE ARE NO RULES LIMITING THE PROPULSION SYSTEMS IN BATTLEWAGONS, AND MINE REQUIRES WHAT'S CALLED AN ARCANE CORE.
IT POWERS THE WAGON'S ENGINES AND OTHER...SPECIAL FEATURES.
AS IT JUST SO HAPPENS, A BATTLEWAGON TEAM CALLED THE HAMMERHEADS JUST RECEIVED A SHIPMENT CONTAINING AN ARCANE CORE.
THEY'RE A BRUTAL BUNCH. THEY'D ALMOST CERTAINLY USE IT TO CREATE SOMETHING TOO DANGEROUS, TOO LETHAL TO BE ON THE TRACK.
BUT... IF THAT CORE...SAY...
...WENT MISSING...
WOW! THAT'D BE A CRAZY COINCIDENCE!
NOW, IT'D BE UNETHICAL FOR A MILITIA OFFICER TO... DO ANYTHING...
BU-U-U-U-T...
BU-U-U-T WHAT?
SHE WANTS US TO ***STEAL*** IT.

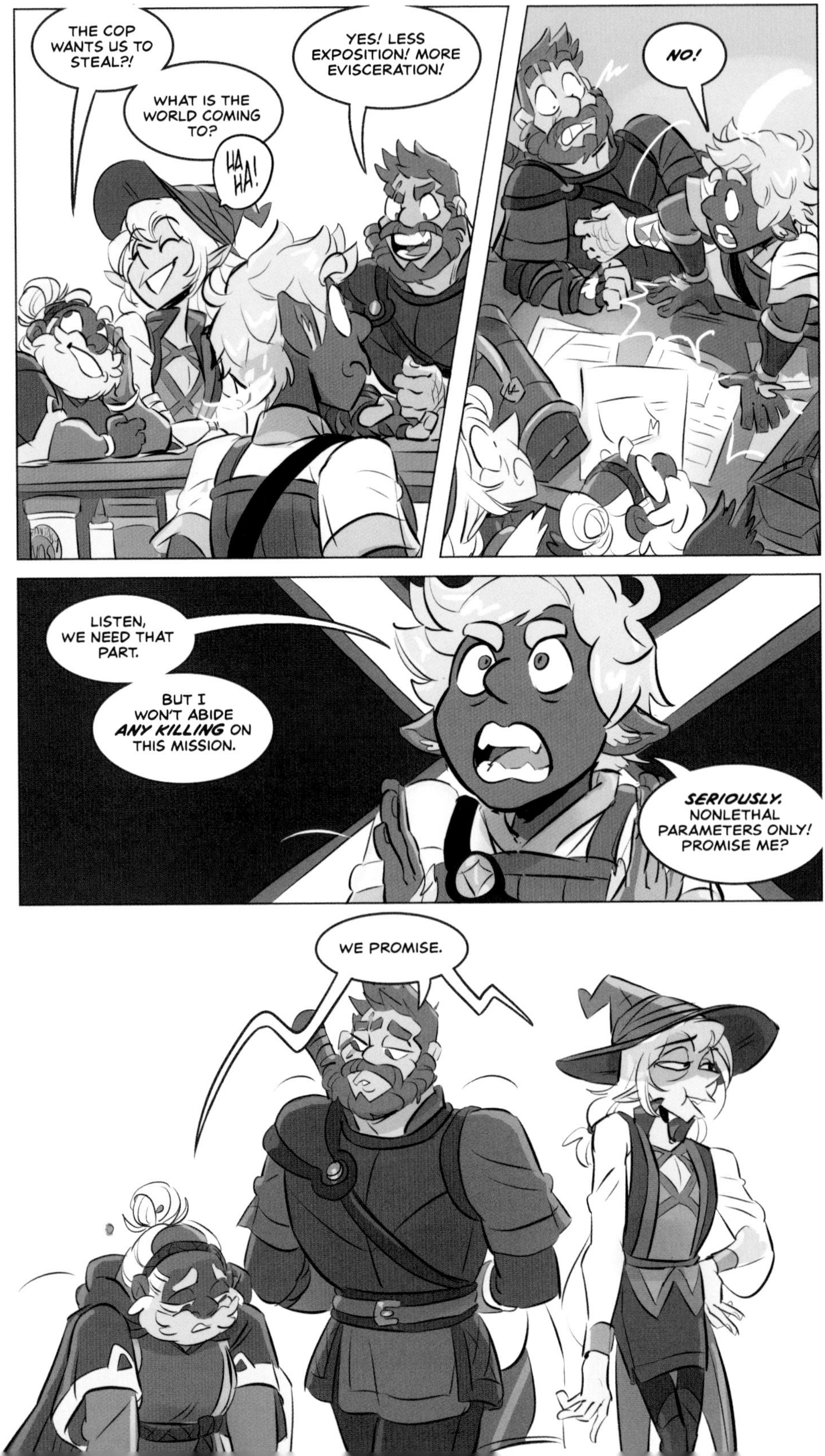
THE COP WANTS US TO STEAL?!
WHAT IS THE WORLD COMING TO?
HA HA!
YES! LESS EXPOSITION! MORE EVISCERATION!
NO!
LISTEN, WE NEED THAT PART.
BUT I WON'T ABIDE *ANY KILLING* ON THIS MISSION.
SERIOUSLY. NONLETHAL PARAMETERS ONLY! PROMISE ME?
WE PROMISE.

Chapter 4

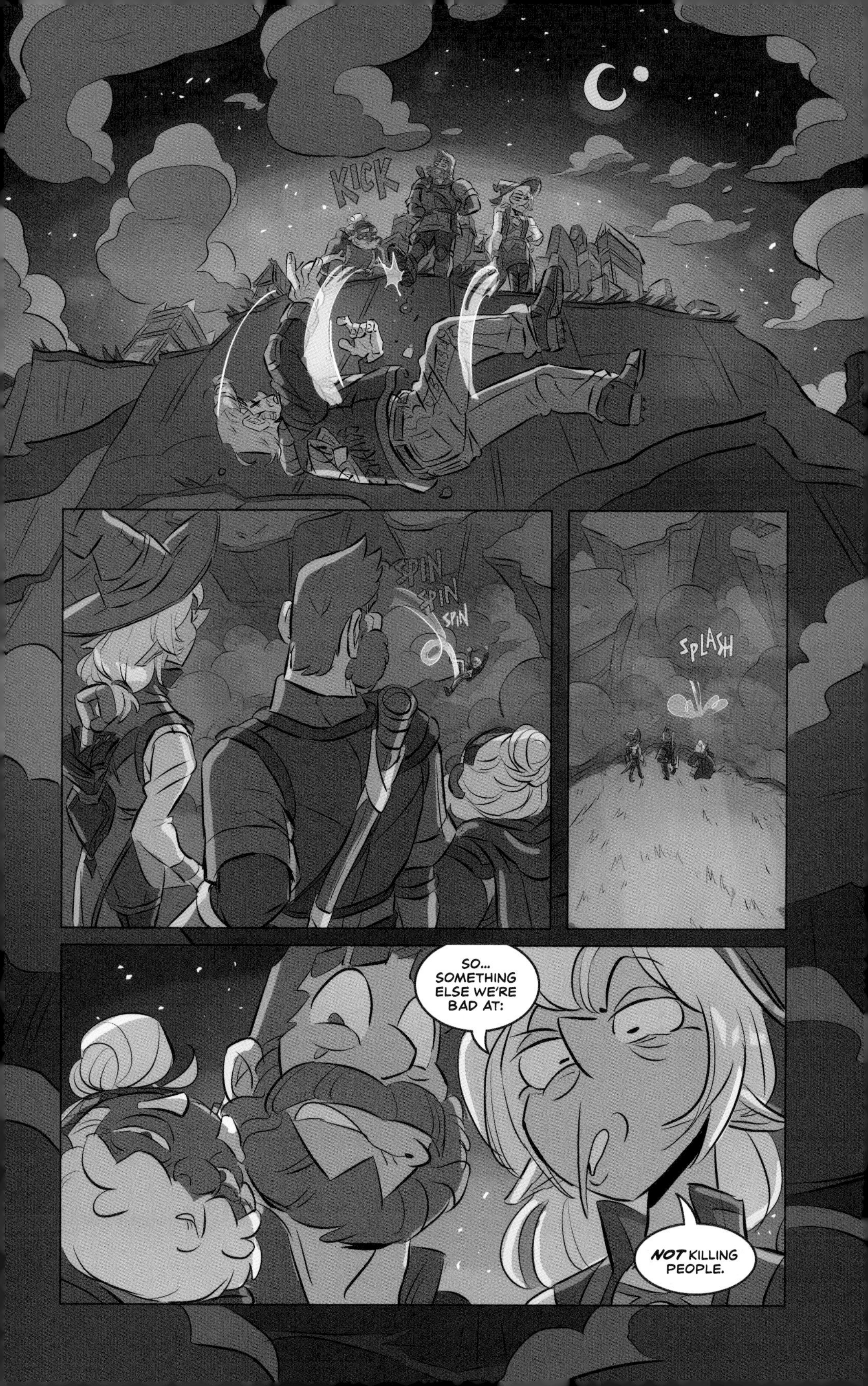
KICK
SPIN
SPIN
SPIN
SPLASH
SO... SOMETHING ELSE WE'RE BAD AT:
NOT KILLING PEOPLE.

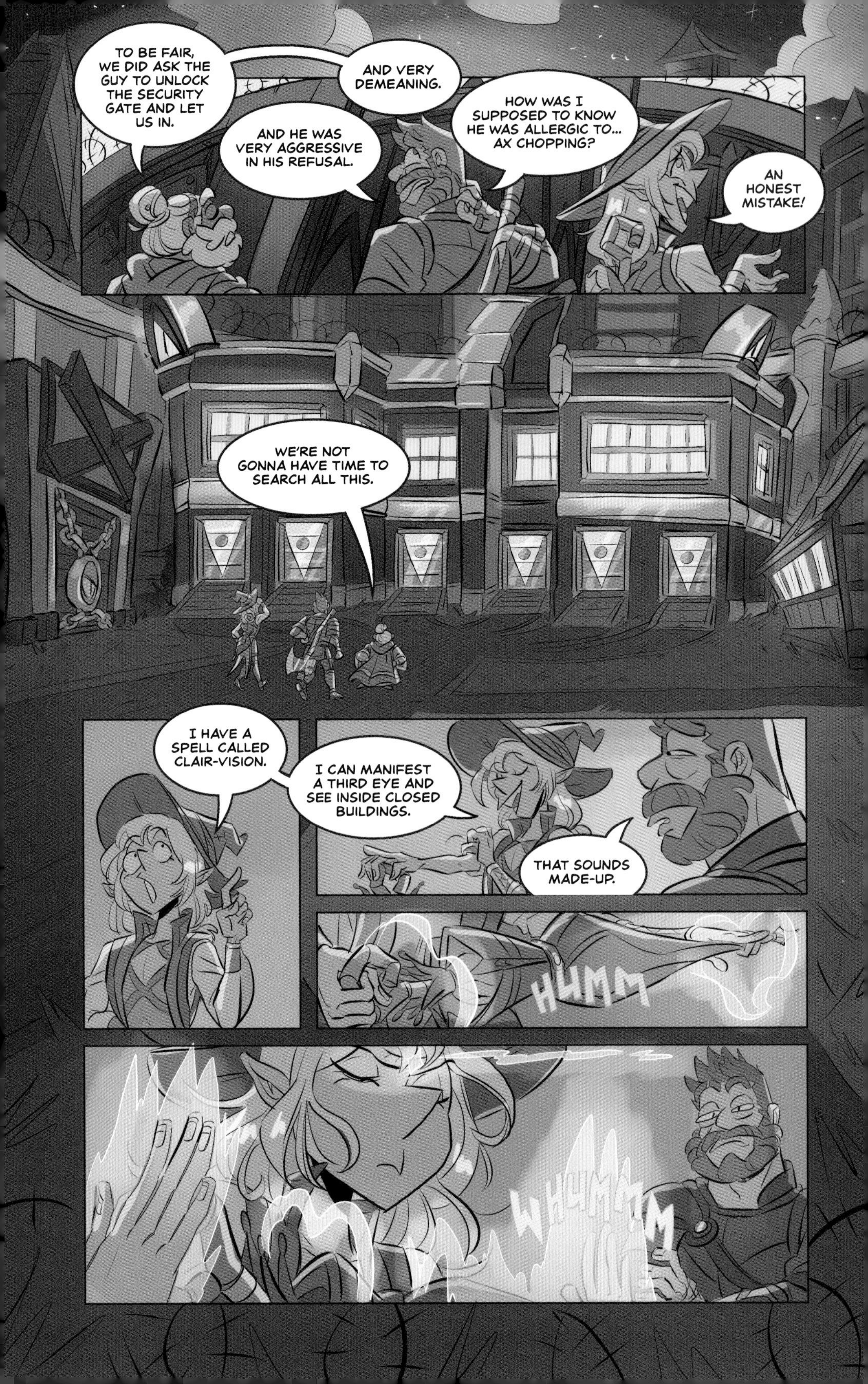
TO BE FAIR, WE DID ASK THE GUY TO UNLOCK THE SECURITY GATE AND LET US IN.
AND HE WAS VERY AGGRESSIVE IN HIS REFUSAL.
AND VERY DEMEANING.
HOW WAS I SUPPOSED TO KNOW HE WAS ALLERGIC TO... AX CHOPPING?
AN HONEST MISTAKE!
WE'RE NOT GONNA HAVE TIME TO SEARCH ALL THIS.
I HAVE A SPELL CALLED CLAIR-VISION.
I CAN MANIFEST A THIRD EYE AND SEE INSIDE CLOSED BUILDINGS.
THAT SOUNDS MADE-UP.
HUMM
WHUMMM

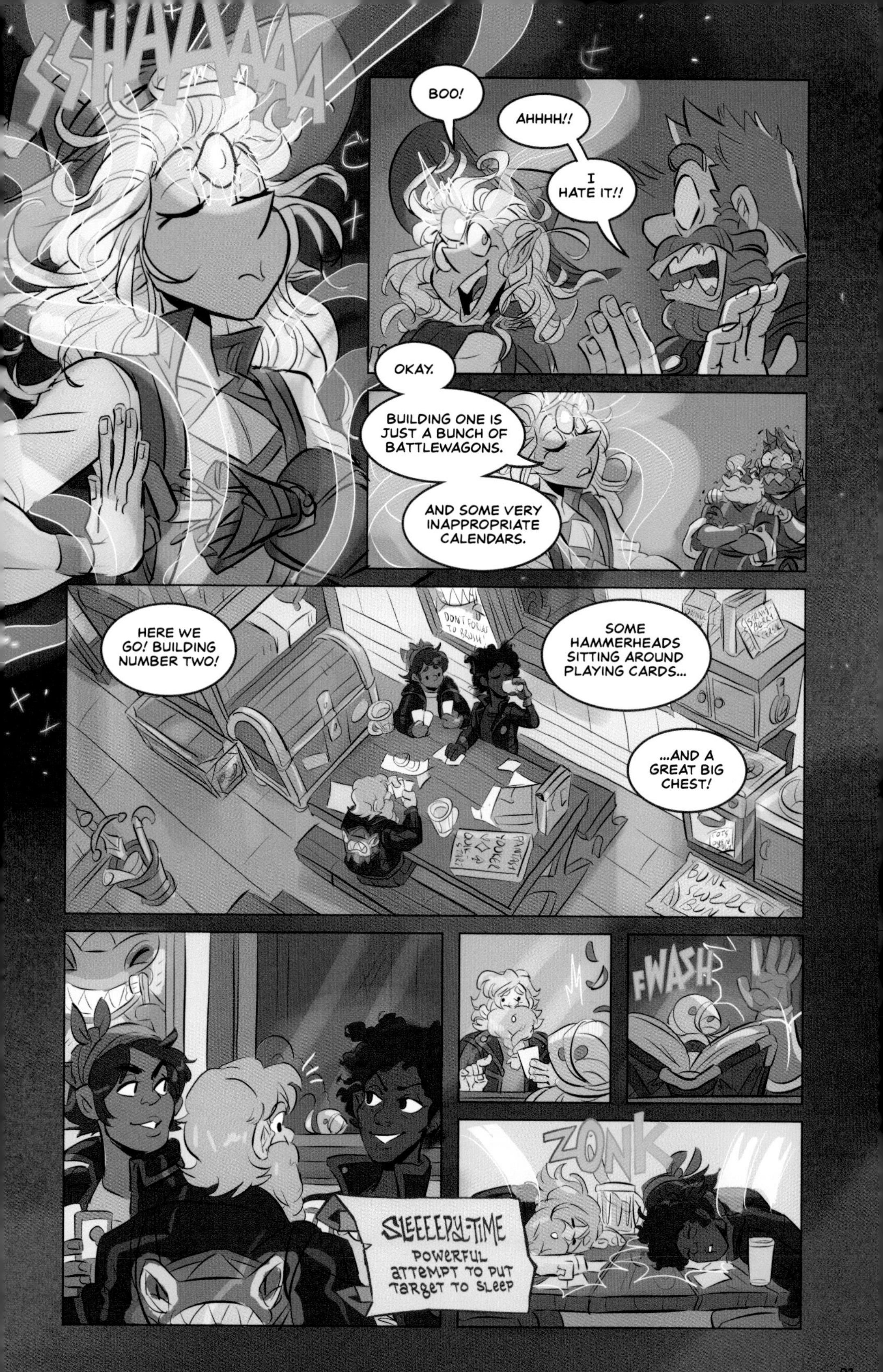
SSHAAAAA
BOO!
AHHHH!!
I HATE IT!!
OKAY.
BUILDING ONE IS JUST A BUNCH OF BATTLEWAGONS.
AND SOME VERY INAPPROPRIATE CALENDARS.
HERE WE GO! BUILDING NUMBER TWO!
SOME HAMMERHEADS SITTING AROUND PLAYING CARDS...
...AND A GREAT BIG CHEST!
DON'T FORGET TO BRUSH!
FWASH
ZONK
SLEEEEPY-TIME
POWERFUL ATTEMPT TO PUT TARGET TO SLEEP

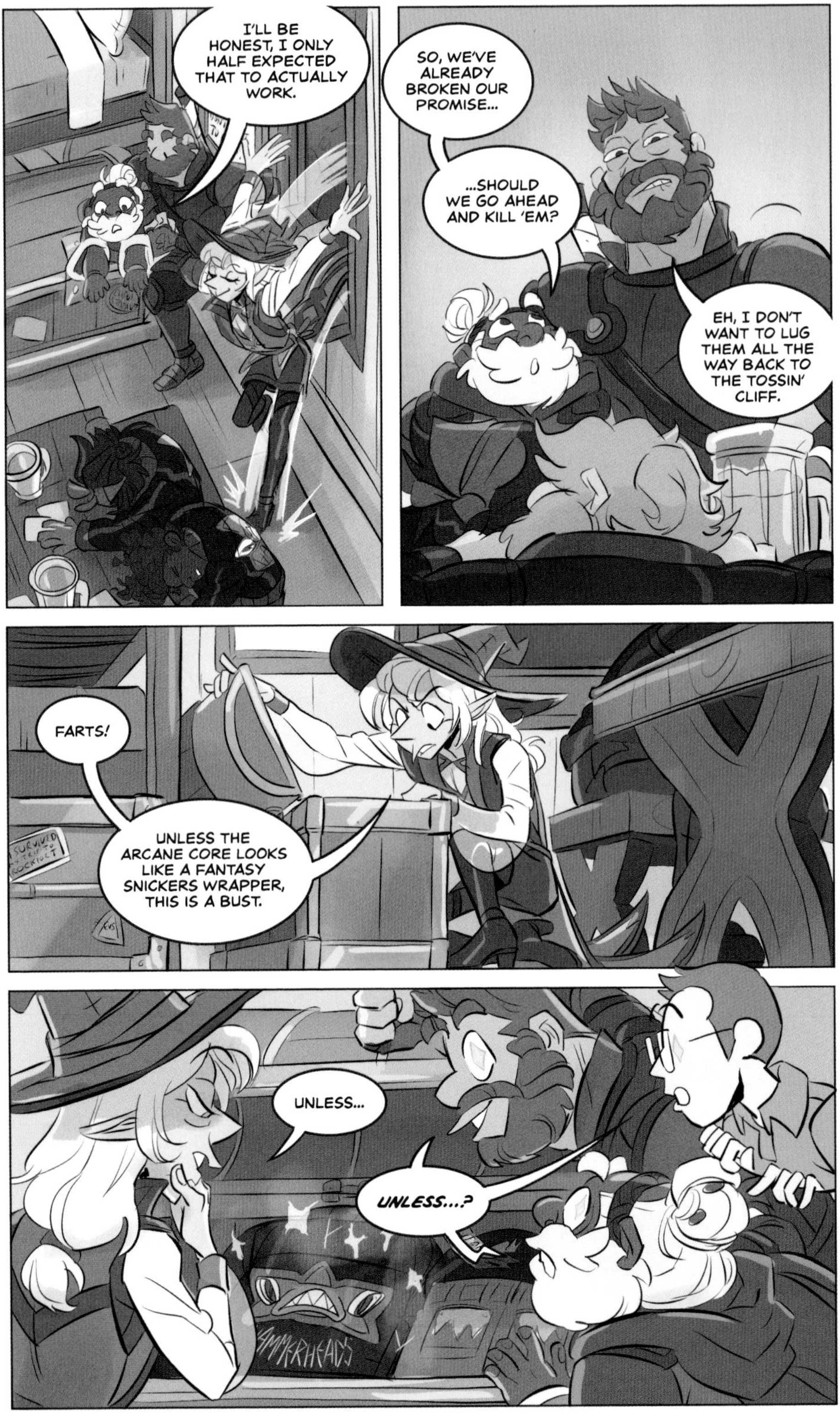
I'LL BE HONEST, I ONLY HALF EXPECTED THAT TO ACTUALLY WORK.
SO, WE'VE ALREADY BROKEN OUR PROMISE...
...SHOULD WE GO AHEAD AND KILL 'EM?
EH, I DON'T WANT TO LUG THEM ALL THE WAY BACK TO THE TOSSIN' CLIFF.
FARTS!
UNLESS THE ARCANE CORE LOOKS LIKE A FANTASY SNICKERS WRAPPER, THIS IS A BUST.
UNLESS...
UNLESS...?

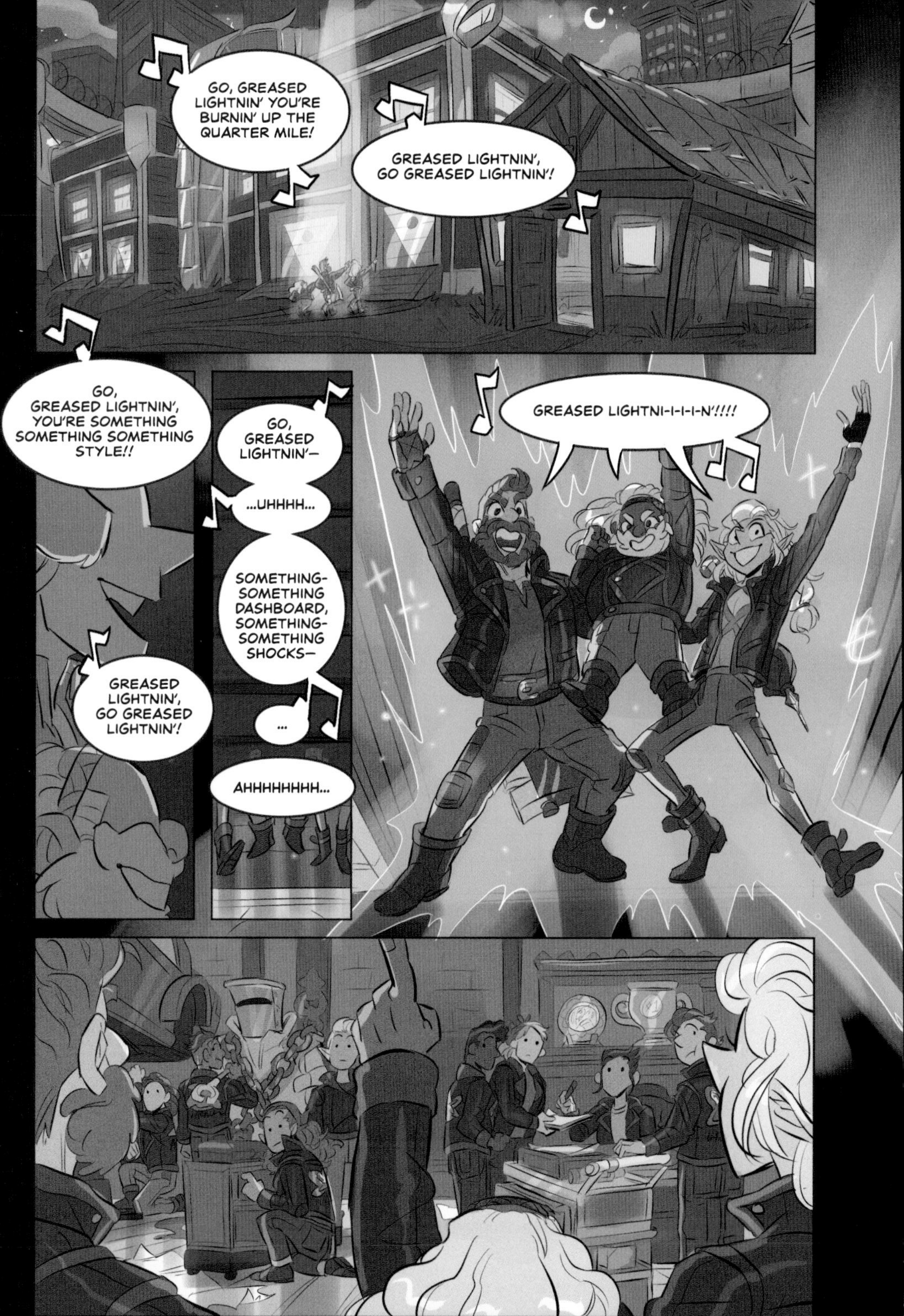

GO, GREASED LIGHTNIN' YOU'RE BURNIN' UP THE QUARTER MILE!
GREASED LIGHTNIN', GO GREASED LIGHTNIN'!
GO, GREASED LIGHTNIN', YOU'RE SOMETHING SOMETHING SOMETHING STYLE!!
GREASED LIGHTNIN', GO GREASED LIGHTNIN'!
GO, GREASED LIGHTNIN'—
...UHHHH...
SOMETHING-SOMETHING DASHBOARD, SOMETHING-SOMETHING SHOCKS—
...
AHHHHHHHH...
GREASED LIGHTNI-I-I-I-N'!!!!

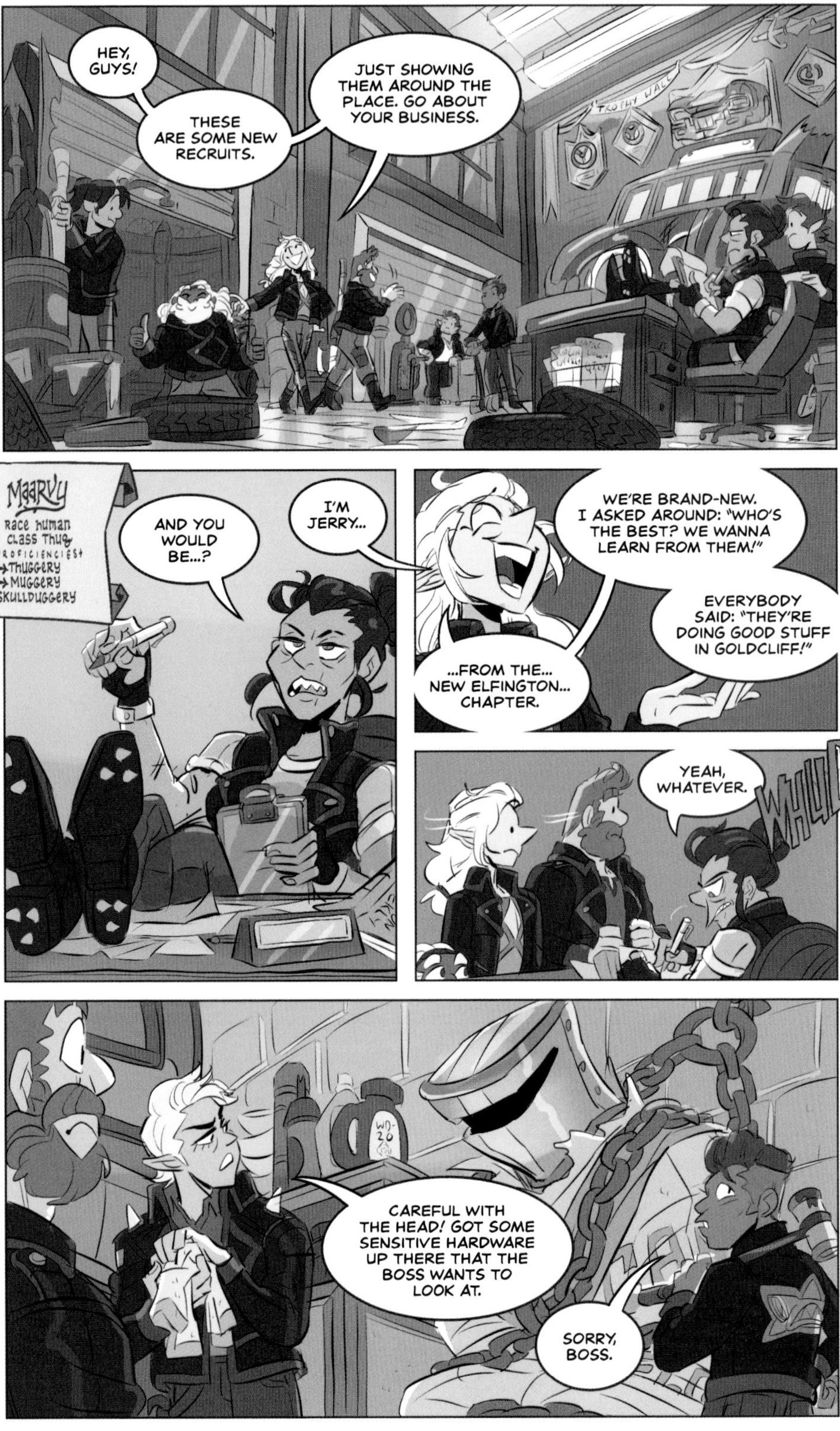
HEY, GUYS!
THESE ARE SOME NEW RECRUITS.
JUST SHOWING THEM AROUND THE PLACE. GO ABOUT YOUR BUSINESS.
TROPHY WALL
MAARVY
Race human
Class Thug
PROFICIENCIES
→THUGGERY
→MUGGERY
→SKULLDUGGERY
AND YOU WOULD BE...?
I'M JERRY...
...FROM THE... NEW ELFINGTON... CHAPTER.
WE'RE BRAND-NEW. I ASKED AROUND: "WHO'S THE BEST? WE WANNA LEARN FROM THEM!"
EVERYBODY SAID: "THEY'RE DOING GOOD STUFF IN GOLDCLIFF!"
YEAH, WHATEVER.
WHUD!
CAREFUL WITH THE HEAD! GOT SOME SENSITIVE HARDWARE UP THERE THAT THE BOSS WANTS TO LOOK AT.
SORRY, BOSS.

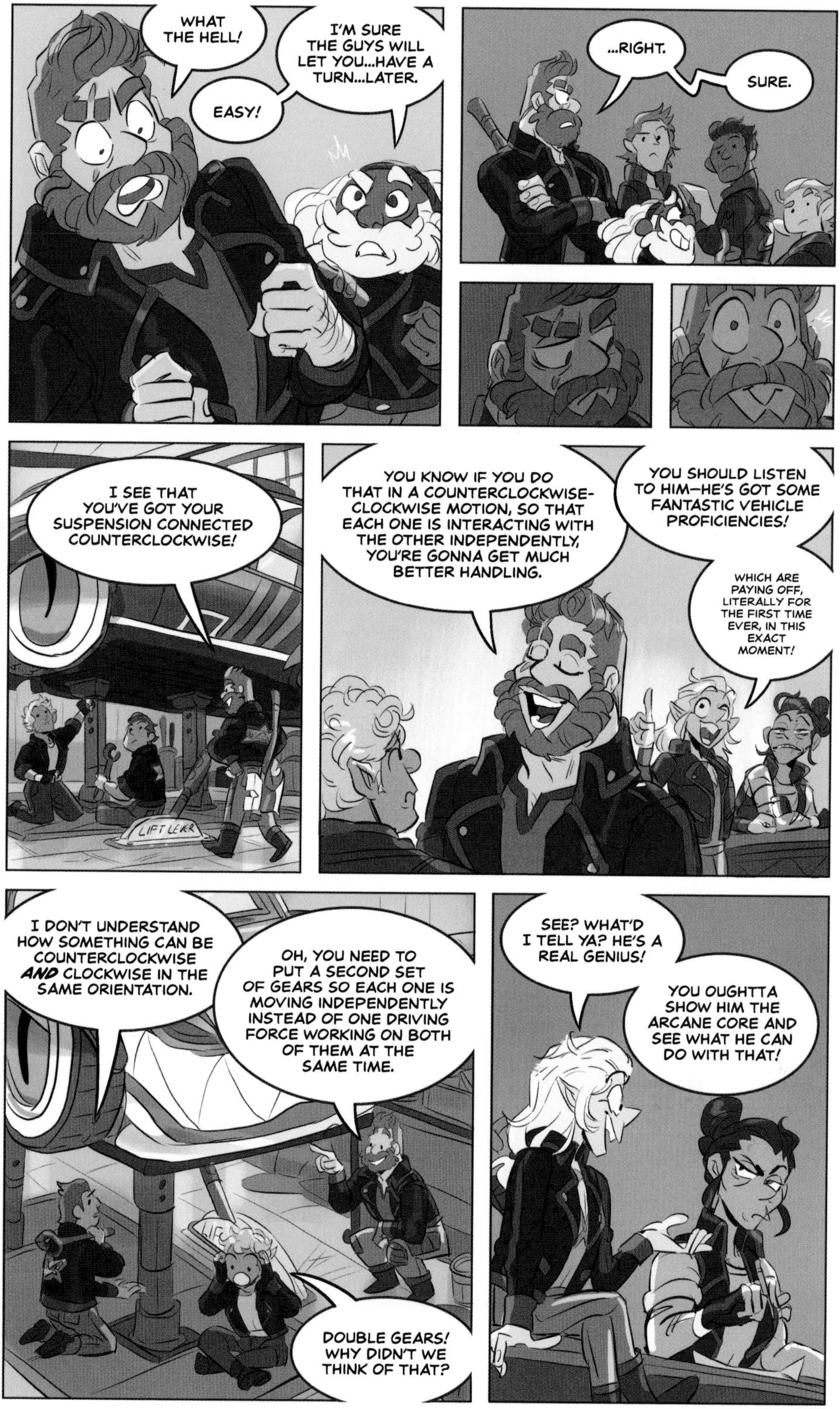
WHAT THE HELL!
EASY!
I'M SURE THE GUYS WILL LET YOU...HAVE A TURN...LATER.
...RIGHT.
SURE.
I SEE THAT YOU'VE GOT YOUR SUSPENSION CONNECTED COUNTERCLOCKWISE!
LIFT LEVER
YOU KNOW IF YOU DO THAT IN A COUNTERCLOCKWISE-CLOCKWISE MOTION, SO THAT EACH ONE IS INTERACTING WITH THE OTHER INDEPENDENTLY, YOU'RE GONNA GET MUCH BETTER HANDLING.
YOU SHOULD LISTEN TO HIM—HE'S GOT SOME FANTASTIC VEHICLE PROFICIENCIES!
WHICH ARE PAYING OFF, LITERALLY FOR THE FIRST TIME EVER, IN THIS EXACT MOMENT!
I DON'T UNDERSTAND HOW SOMETHING CAN BE COUNTERCLOCKWISE AND CLOCKWISE IN THE SAME ORIENTATION.
OH, YOU NEED TO PUT A SECOND SET OF GEARS SO EACH ONE IS MOVING INDEPENDENTLY INSTEAD OF ONE DRIVING FORCE WORKING ON BOTH OF THEM AT THE SAME TIME.
DOUBLE GEARS! WHY DIDN'T WE THINK OF THAT?
SEE? WHAT'D I TELL YA? HE'S A REAL GENIUS!
YOU OUGHTTA SHOW HIM THE ARCANE CORE AND SEE WHAT HE CAN DO WITH THAT!

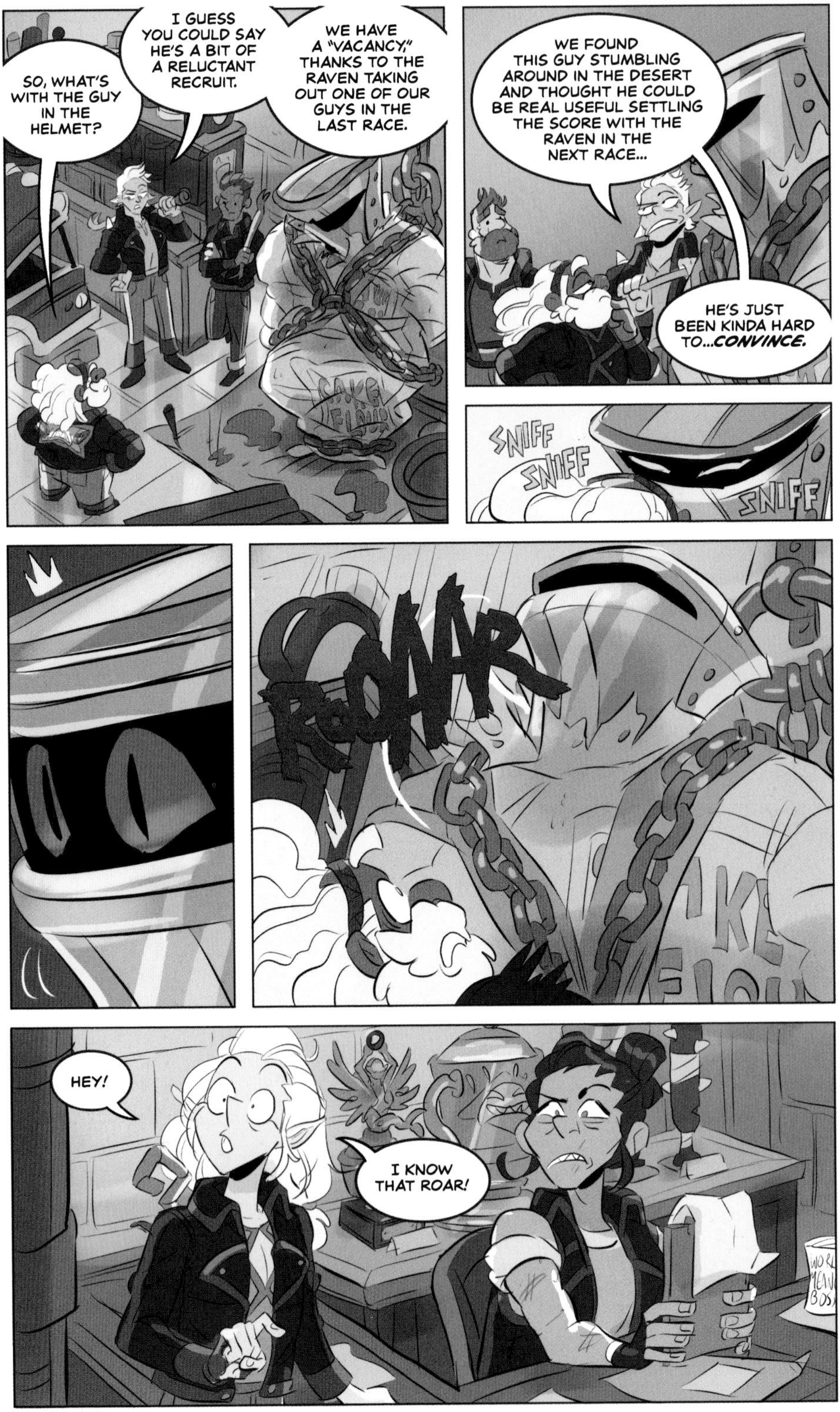
SO, WHAT'S WITH THE GUY IN THE HELMET?
I GUESS YOU COULD SAY HE'S A BIT OF A RELUCTANT RECRUIT.
WE HAVE A "VACANCY," THANKS TO THE RAVEN TAKING OUT ONE OF OUR GUYS IN THE LAST RACE.
WE FOUND THIS GUY STUMBLING AROUND IN THE DESERT AND THOUGHT HE COULD BE REAL USEFUL SETTLING THE SCORE WITH THE RAVEN IN THE NEXT RACE...
HE'S JUST BEEN KINDA HARD TO...CONVINCE.
SNIFF
SNIFF
SNIFF
ROAAR
HEY!
I KNOW THAT ROAR!

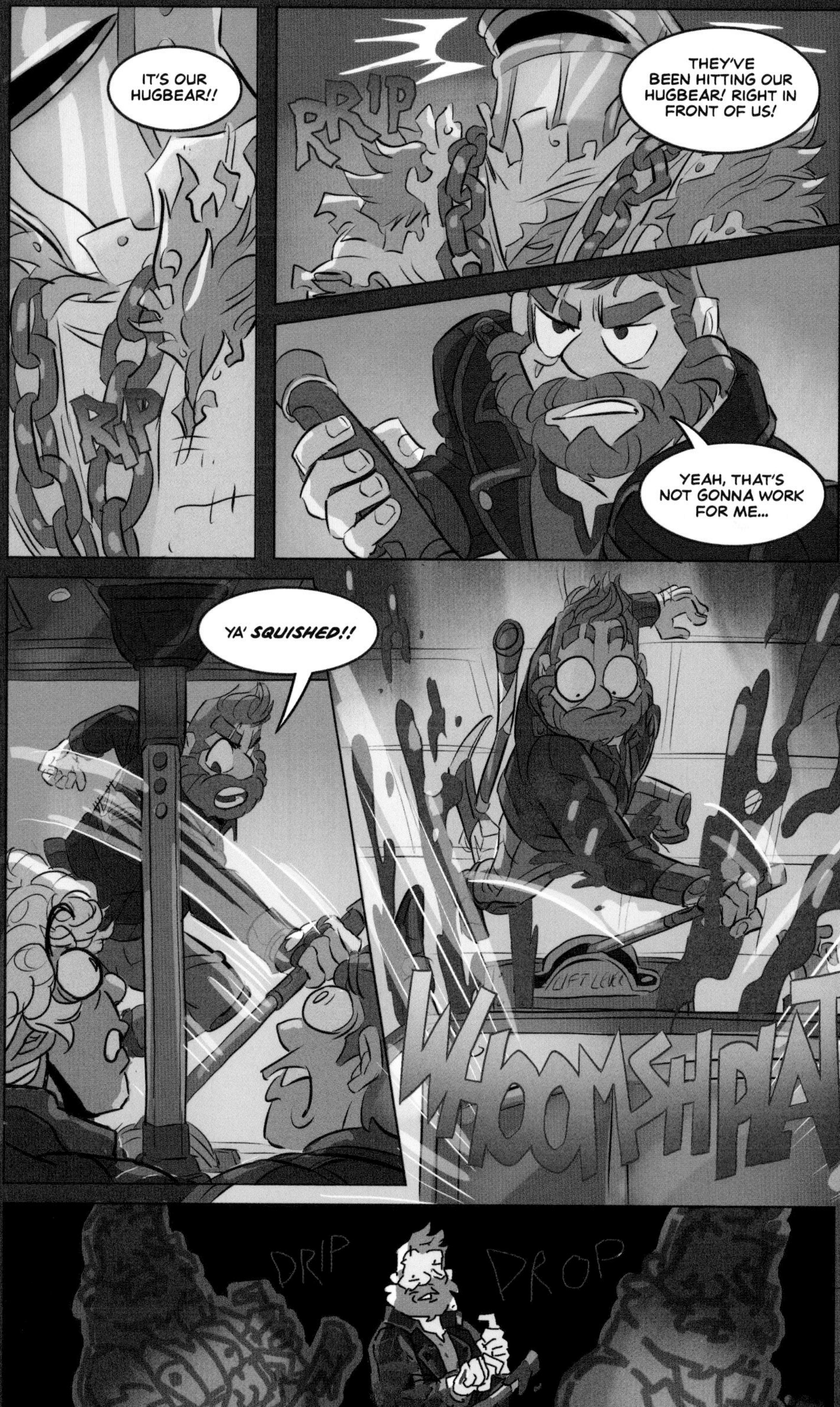
IT'S OUR HUGBEAR!!
RRIP
RIP
THEY'VE BEEN HITTING OUR HUGBEAR! RIGHT IN FRONT OF US!
YEAH, THAT'S NOT GONNA WORK FOR ME...
YA' *SQUISHED!!*
WHOOMSHPLAT!!
DRIP
DROP

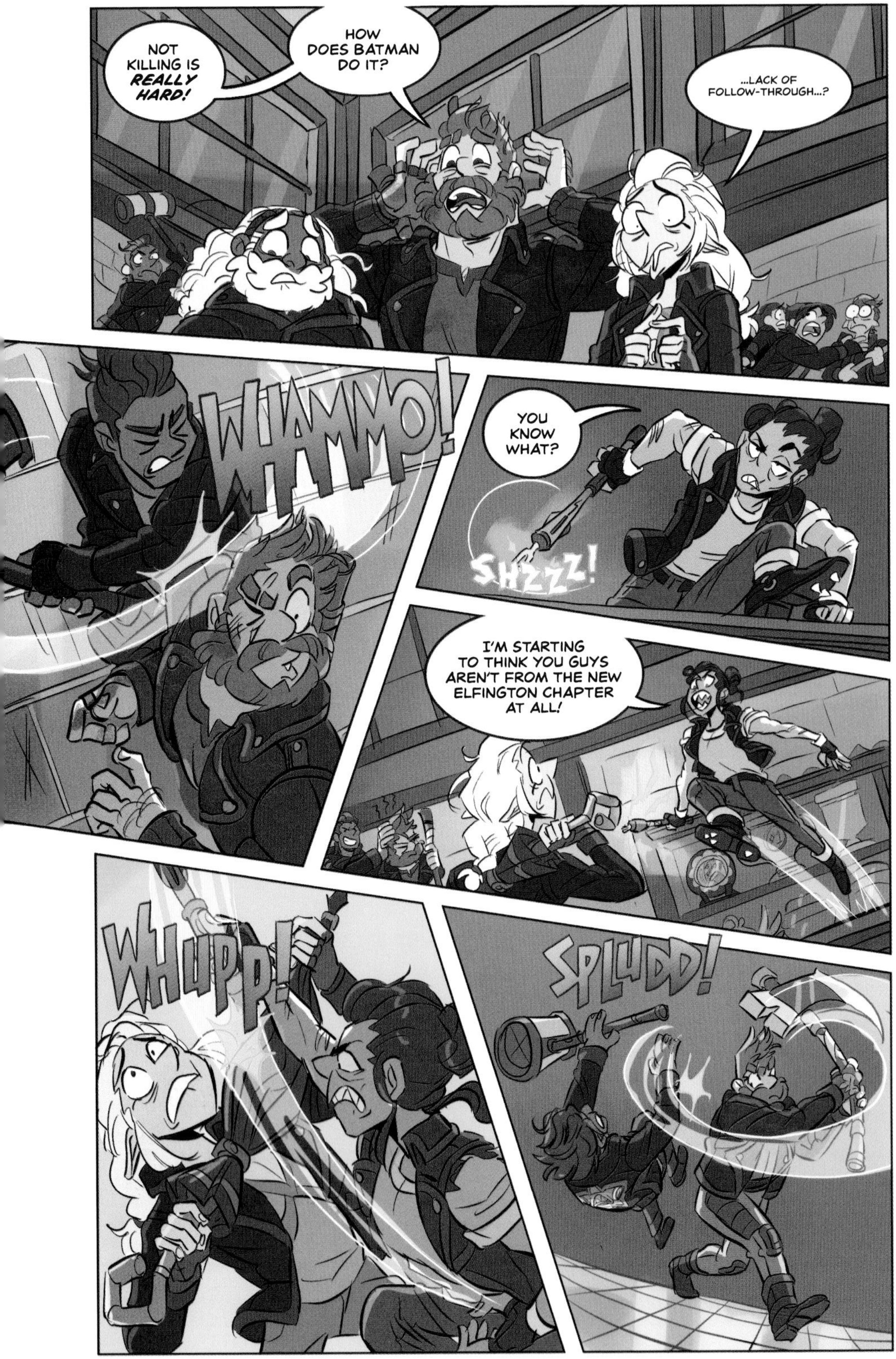
NOT KILLING IS *REALLY HARD!*
HOW DOES BATMAN DO IT?
...LACK OF FOLLOW-THROUGH...?
WHAMMO!
YOU KNOW WHAT?
SHZZZ!
I'M STARTING TO THINK YOU GUYS AREN'T FROM THE NEW ELFINGTON CHAPTER AT ALL!
WHUPP!
SPLUDD!

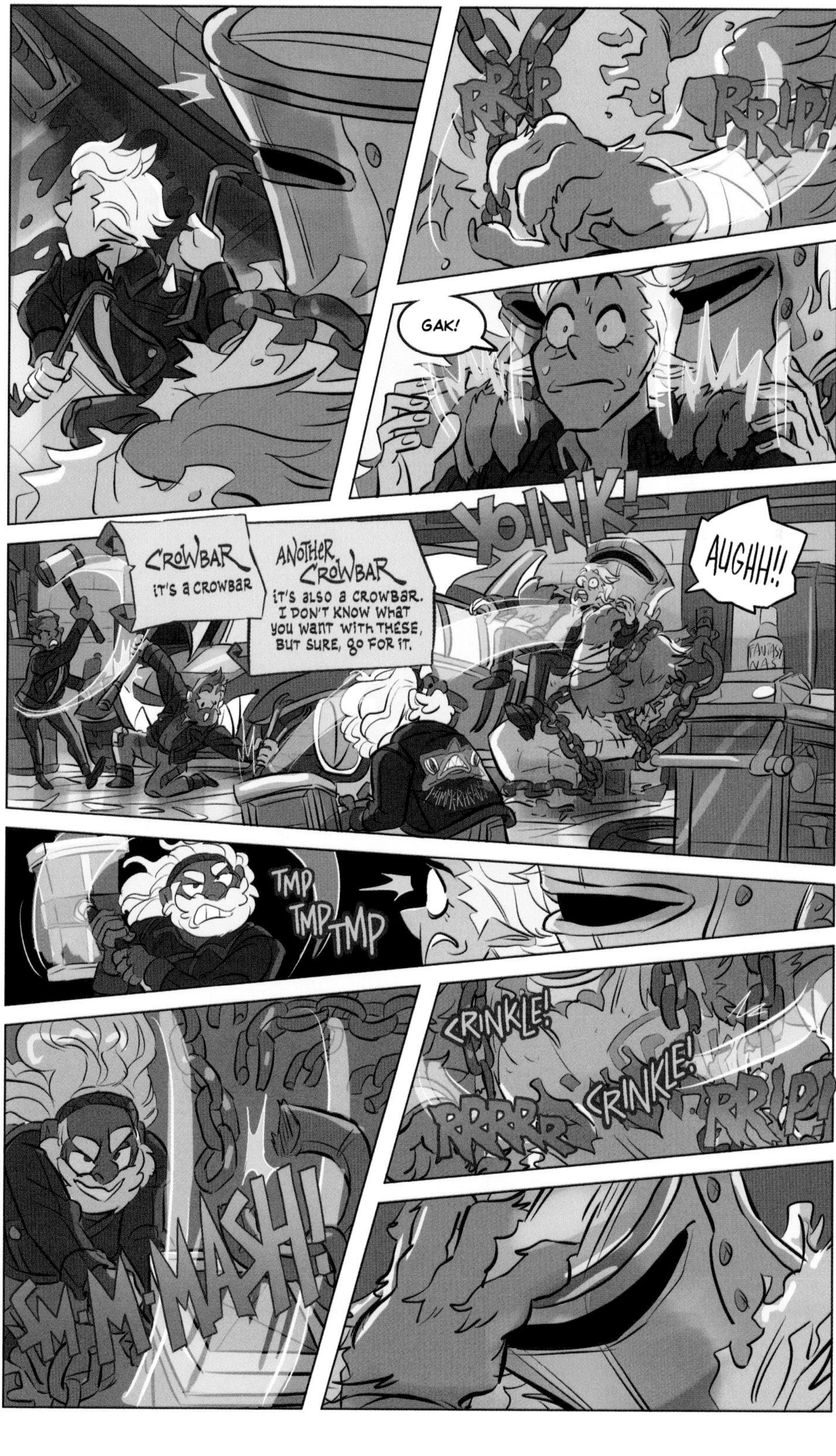
RRIP
RRIP!
GAK!
YOINK!
AUGHH!!
CROWBAR
it's a crowbar
ANOTHER CROWBAR
it's also a crowbar. I don't know what you want with these, but sure, go for it.
TMP
TMP TMP
CRINKLE!
CRINKLE!
RRRRR
RRIP!
SMMMASH!

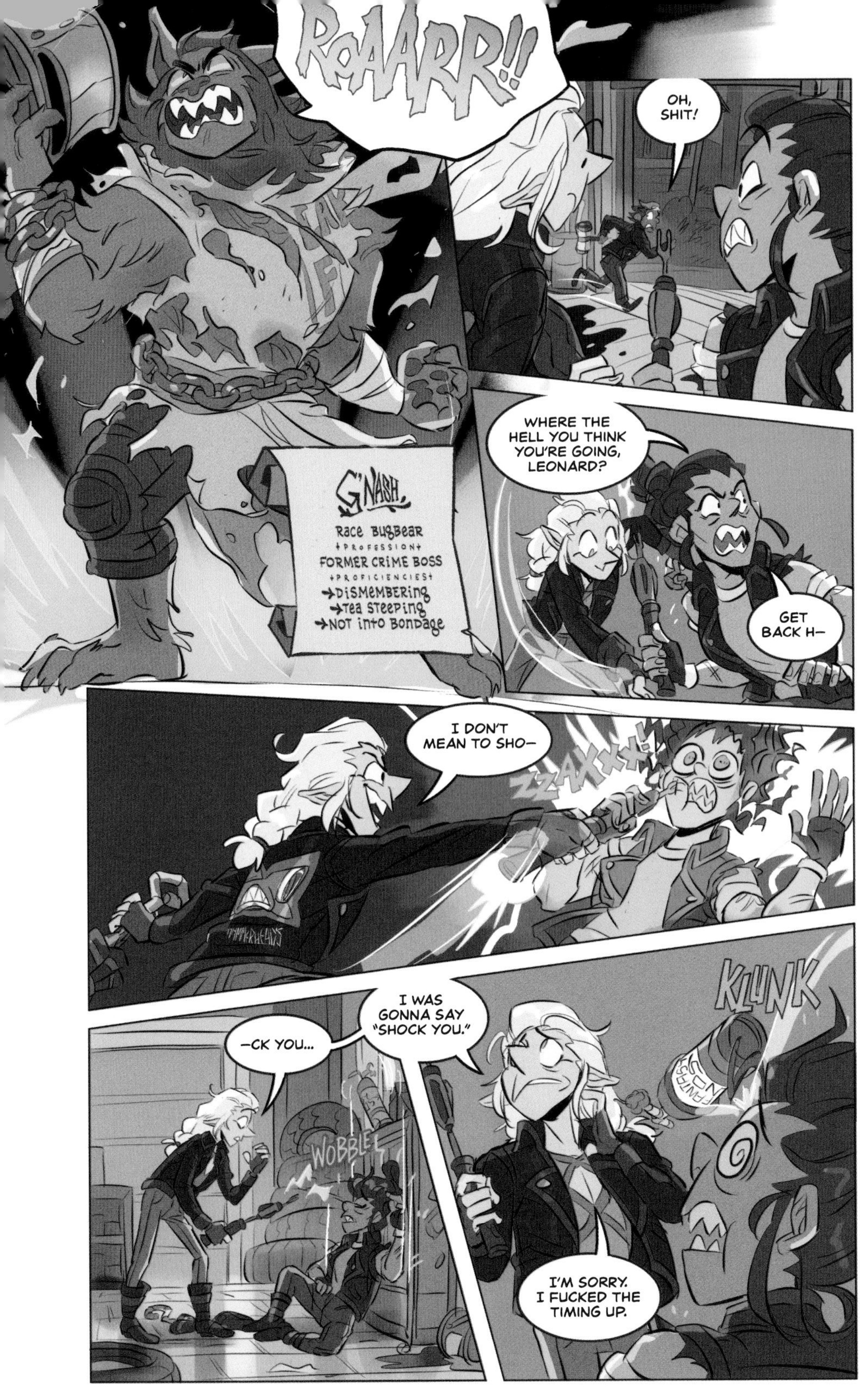
ROAARR!!
OH, SHIT!
G'NASH
Race Bugbear
Profession
FORMER CRIME BOSS
Proficiencies
→DISMEMBERING
→Tea Steeping
→NOT into Bondage
WHERE THE HELL YOU THINK YOU'RE GOING, LEONARD?
GET BACK H—
I DON'T MEAN TO SHO—
ZZAXX
—CK YOU...
I WAS GONNA SAY "SHOCK YOU."
KLUNK
WOBBLE
I'M SORRY. I FUCKED THE TIMING UP.

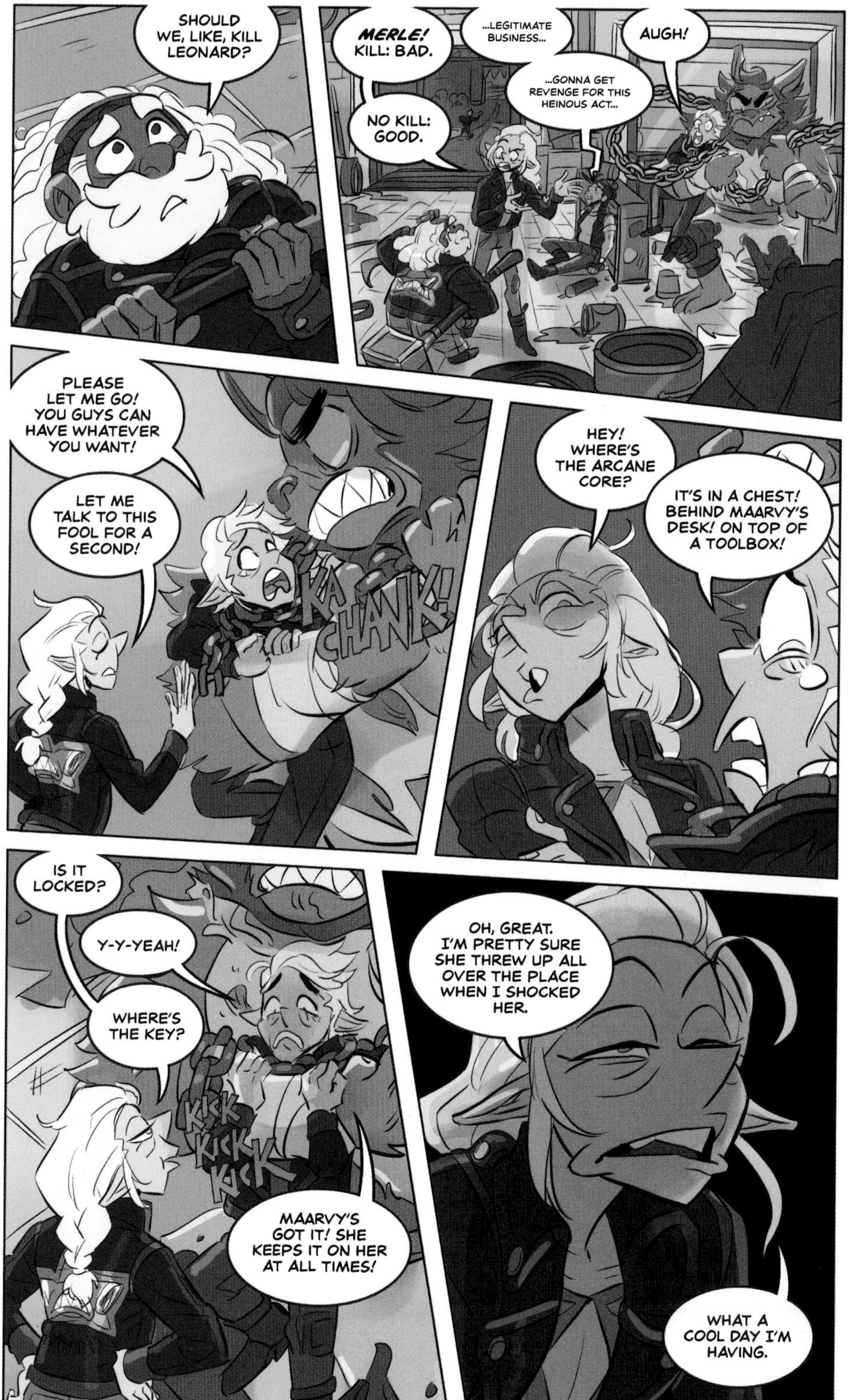
SHOULD WE, LIKE, KILL LEONARD?
MERLE! KILL: BAD.
NO KILL: GOOD.
...LEGITIMATE BUSINESS...
...GONNA GET REVENGE FOR THIS HEINOUS ACT...
AUGH!
PLEASE LET ME GO! YOU GUYS CAN HAVE WHATEVER YOU WANT!
LET ME TALK TO THIS FOOL FOR A SECOND!
KA CHANK!
HEY! WHERE'S THE ARCANE CORE?
IT'S IN A CHEST! BEHIND MAARVY'S DESK! ON TOP OF A TOOLBOX!
IS IT LOCKED?
Y-Y-YEAH!
WHERE'S THE KEY?
KICK KICK KICK
MAARVY'S GOT IT! SHE KEEPS IT ON HER AT ALL TIMES!
OH, GREAT. I'M PRETTY SURE SHE THREW UP ALL OVER THE PLACE WHEN I SHOCKED HER.
WHAT A COOL DAY I'M HAVING.

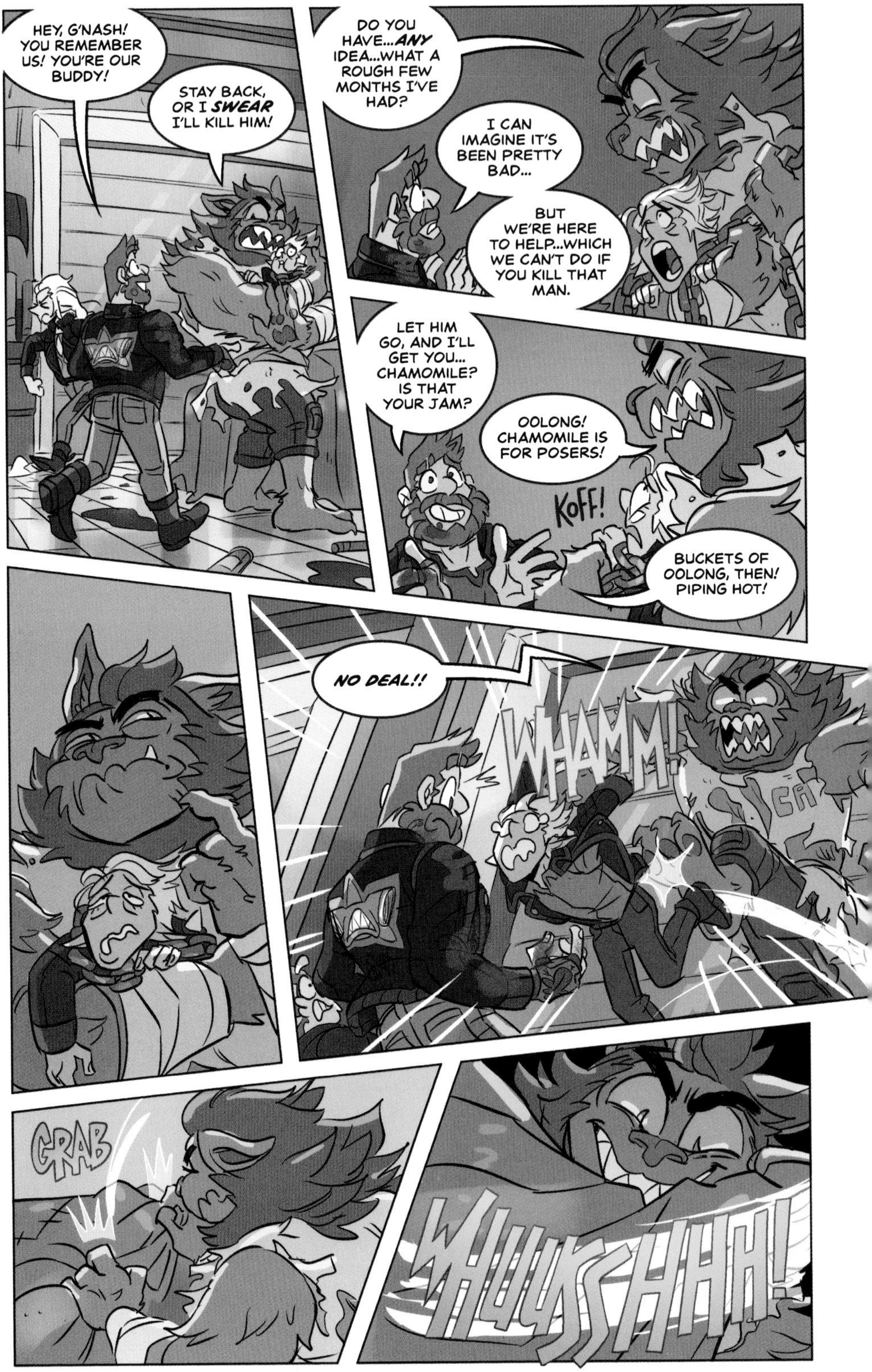
HEY, G'NASH! YOU REMEMBER US! YOU'RE OUR BUDDY!
STAY BACK, OR I SWEAR I'LL KILL HIM!
DO YOU HAVE...ANY IDEA...WHAT A ROUGH FEW MONTHS I'VE HAD?
I CAN IMAGINE IT'S BEEN PRETTY BAD...
BUT WE'RE HERE TO HELP...WHICH WE CAN'T DO IF YOU KILL THAT MAN.
LET HIM GO, AND I'LL GET YOU... CHAMOMILE? IS THAT YOUR JAM?
OOLONG! CHAMOMILE IS FOR POSERS!
KOFF!
BUCKETS OF OOLONG, THEN! PIPING HOT!
NO DEAL!!
WHAMM!
GRAB
WHUUSHHH!

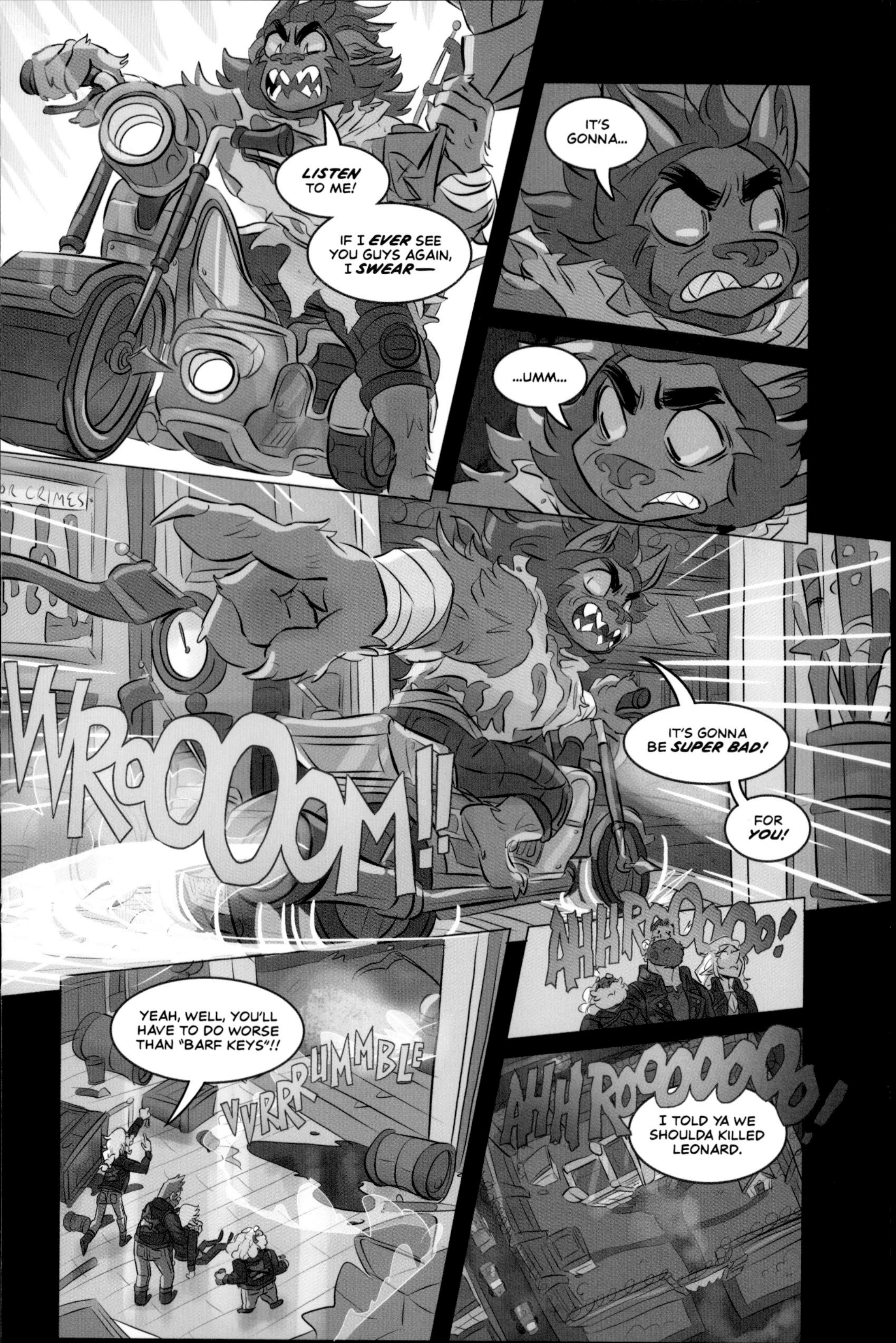
LISTEN TO ME!
IF I EVER SEE YOU GUYS AGAIN, I SWEAR—
IT'S GONNA...
...UMM...
OR CRIMES
VVROOOOM!!
IT'S GONNA BE SUPER BAD!
FOR YOU!
AHHROOOOO!
YEAH, WELL, YOU'LL HAVE TO DO WORSE THAN "BARF KEYS"!!
VVRRRUMMBLE
AHHROOOOOO!
I TOLD YA WE SHOULDA KILLED LEONARD.

Chapter 5

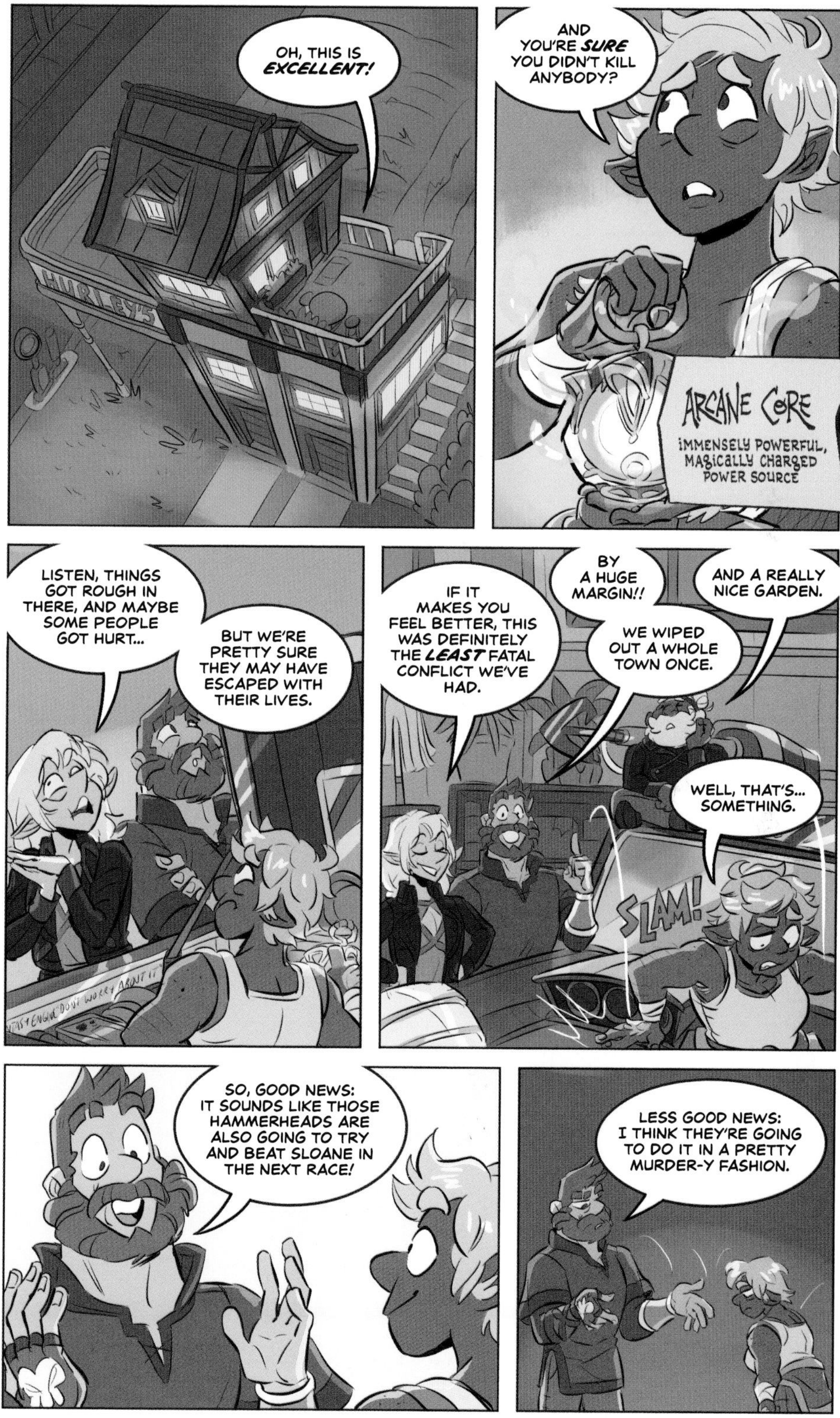
OH, THIS IS EXCELLENT!
AND YOU'RE SURE YOU DIDN'T KILL ANYBODY?
ARCANE CORE
IMMENSELY POWERFUL, MAGICALLY CHARGED POWER SOURCE
LISTEN, THINGS GOT ROUGH IN THERE, AND MAYBE SOME PEOPLE GOT HURT...
BUT WE'RE PRETTY SURE THEY MAY HAVE ESCAPED WITH THEIR LIVES.
IF IT MAKES YOU FEEL BETTER, THIS WAS DEFINITELY THE LEAST FATAL CONFLICT WE'VE HAD.
BY A HUGE MARGIN!!
AND A REALLY NICE GARDEN.
WE WIPED OUT A WHOLE TOWN ONCE.
WELL, THAT'S... SOMETHING.
SLAM!
SO, GOOD NEWS: IT SOUNDS LIKE THOSE HAMMERHEADS ARE ALSO GOING TO TRY AND BEAT SLOANE IN THE NEXT RACE!
LESS GOOD NEWS: I THINK THEY'RE GOING TO DO IT IN A PRETTY MURDER-Y FASHION.

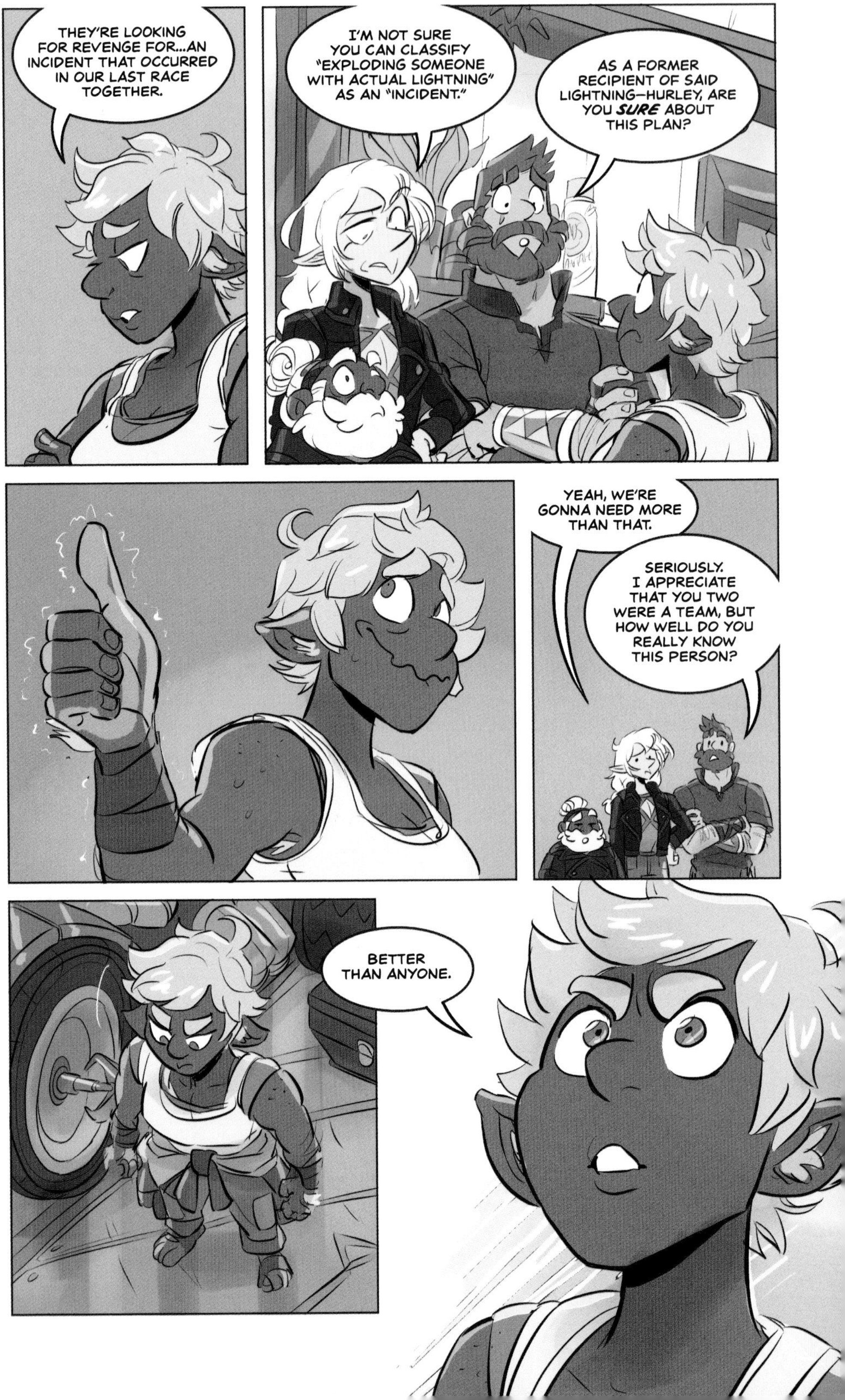
THEY'RE LOOKING FOR REVENGE FOR...AN INCIDENT THAT OCCURRED IN OUR LAST RACE TOGETHER.
I'M NOT SURE YOU CAN CLASSIFY "EXPLODING SOMEONE WITH ACTUAL LIGHTNING" AS AN "INCIDENT."
AS A FORMER RECIPIENT OF SAID LIGHTNING—HURLEY, ARE YOU *SURE* ABOUT THIS PLAN?
YEAH, WE'RE GONNA NEED MORE THAN THAT.
SERIOUSLY. I APPRECIATE THAT YOU TWO WERE A TEAM, BUT HOW WELL DO YOU REALLY KNOW THIS PERSON?
BETTER THAN ANYONE.

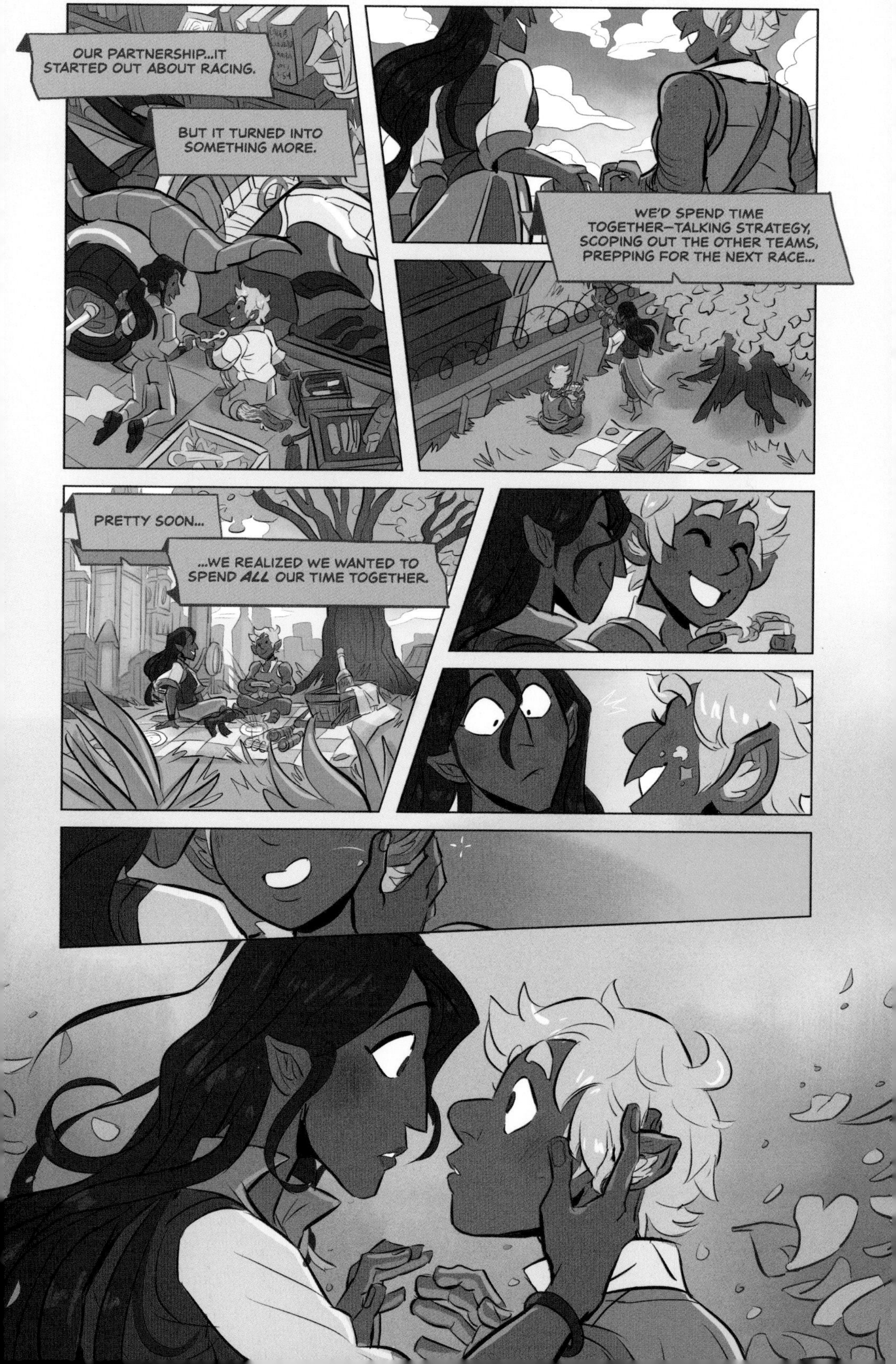
OUR PARTNERSHIP...IT STARTED OUT ABOUT RACING.
BUT IT TURNED INTO SOMETHING MORE.
WE'D SPEND TIME TOGETHER—TALKING STRATEGY, SCOPING OUT THE OTHER TEAMS, PREPPING FOR THE NEXT RACE...
PRETTY SOON...
...WE REALIZED WE WANTED TO SPEND ALL OUR TIME TOGETHER.

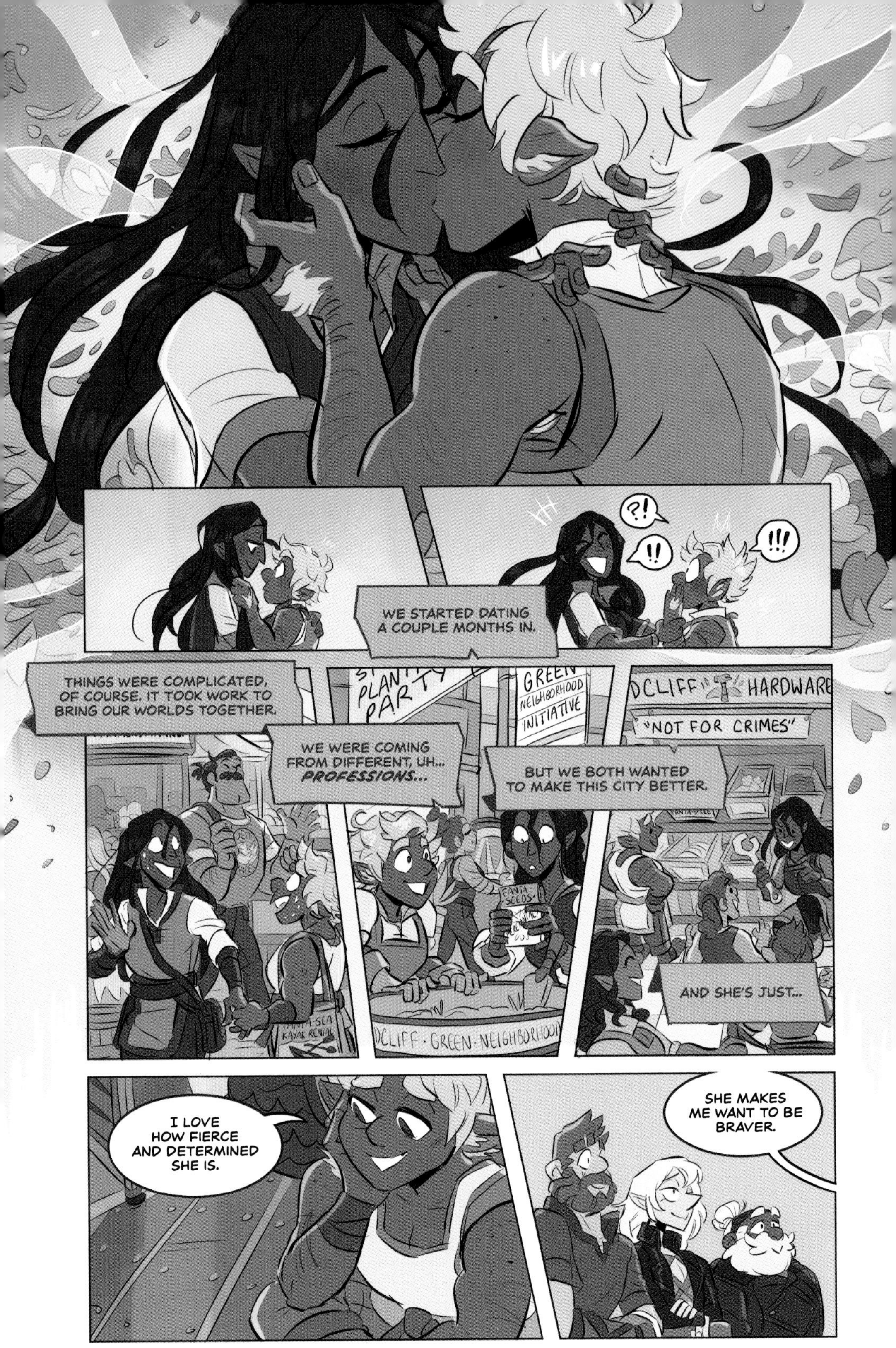
?!
!!
!!!
WE STARTED DATING A COUPLE MONTHS IN.
THINGS WERE COMPLICATED, OF COURSE. IT TOOK WORK TO BRING OUR WORLDS TOGETHER.
PLANT PARTY
GREEN NEIGHBORHOOD INITIATIVE
DCLIFF HARDWARE
"NOT FOR CRIMES"
WE WERE COMING FROM DIFFERENT, UH... ***PROFESSIONS...***
BUT WE BOTH WANTED TO MAKE THIS CITY BETTER.
FANTA SEEDS
FANTA-SEA KAYAK RENTAL
DCLIFF · GREEN · NEIGHBORHOOD
AND SHE'S JUST...
I LOVE HOW FIERCE AND DETERMINED SHE IS.
SHE MAKES ME WANT TO BE BRAVER.

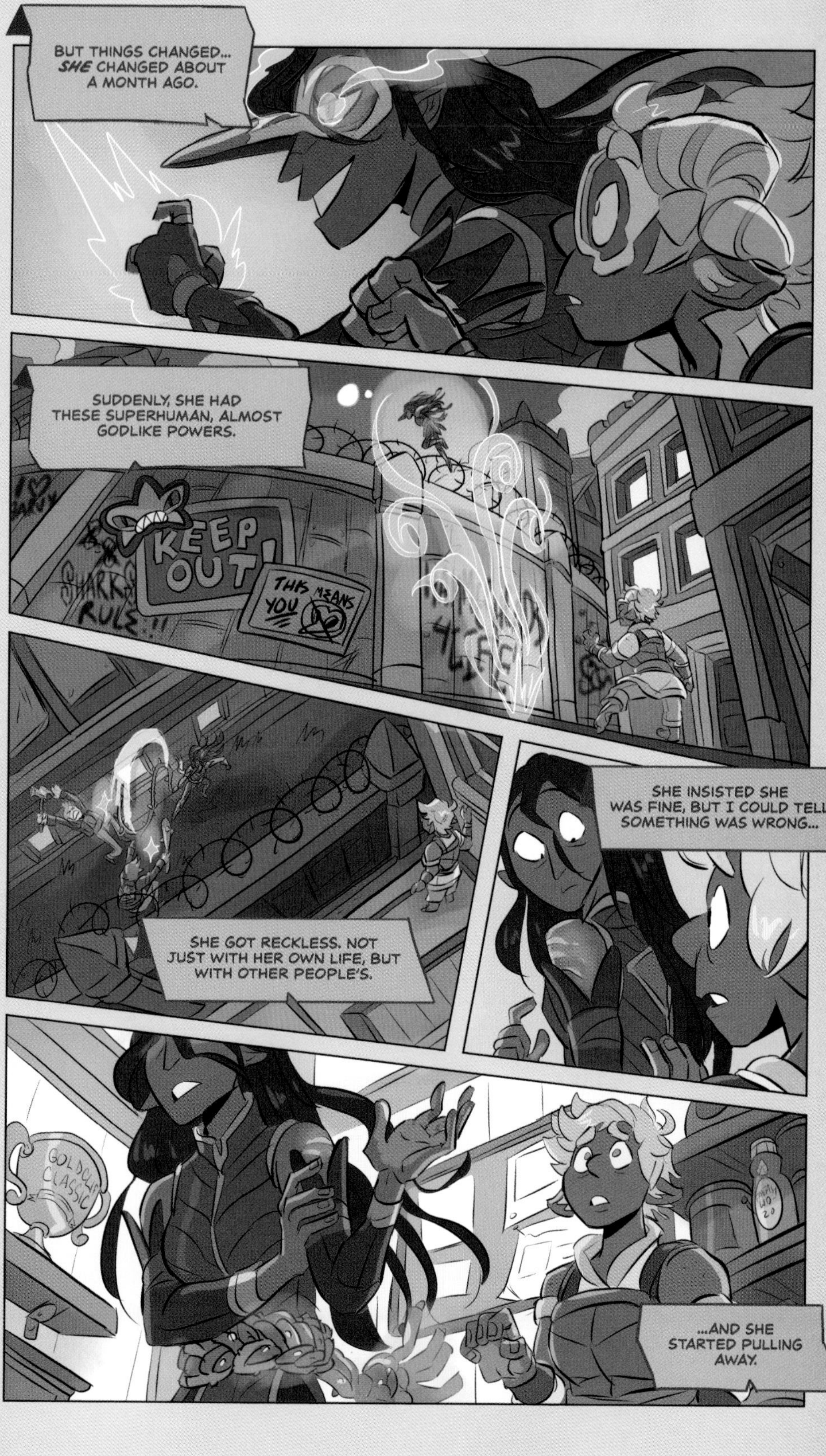
BUT THINGS CHANGED... *SHE* CHANGED ABOUT A MONTH AGO.
SUDDENLY, SHE HAD THESE SUPERHUMAN, ALMOST GODLIKE POWERS.
KEEP OUT!
THIS MEANS YOU
SHARKS RULE!!
SHE GOT RECKLESS. NOT JUST WITH HER OWN LIFE, BUT WITH OTHER PEOPLE'S.
SHE INSISTED SHE WAS FINE, BUT I COULD TELL SOMETHING WAS WRONG...
GOLDCLIFF CLASSIC
...AND SHE STARTED PULLING AWAY.

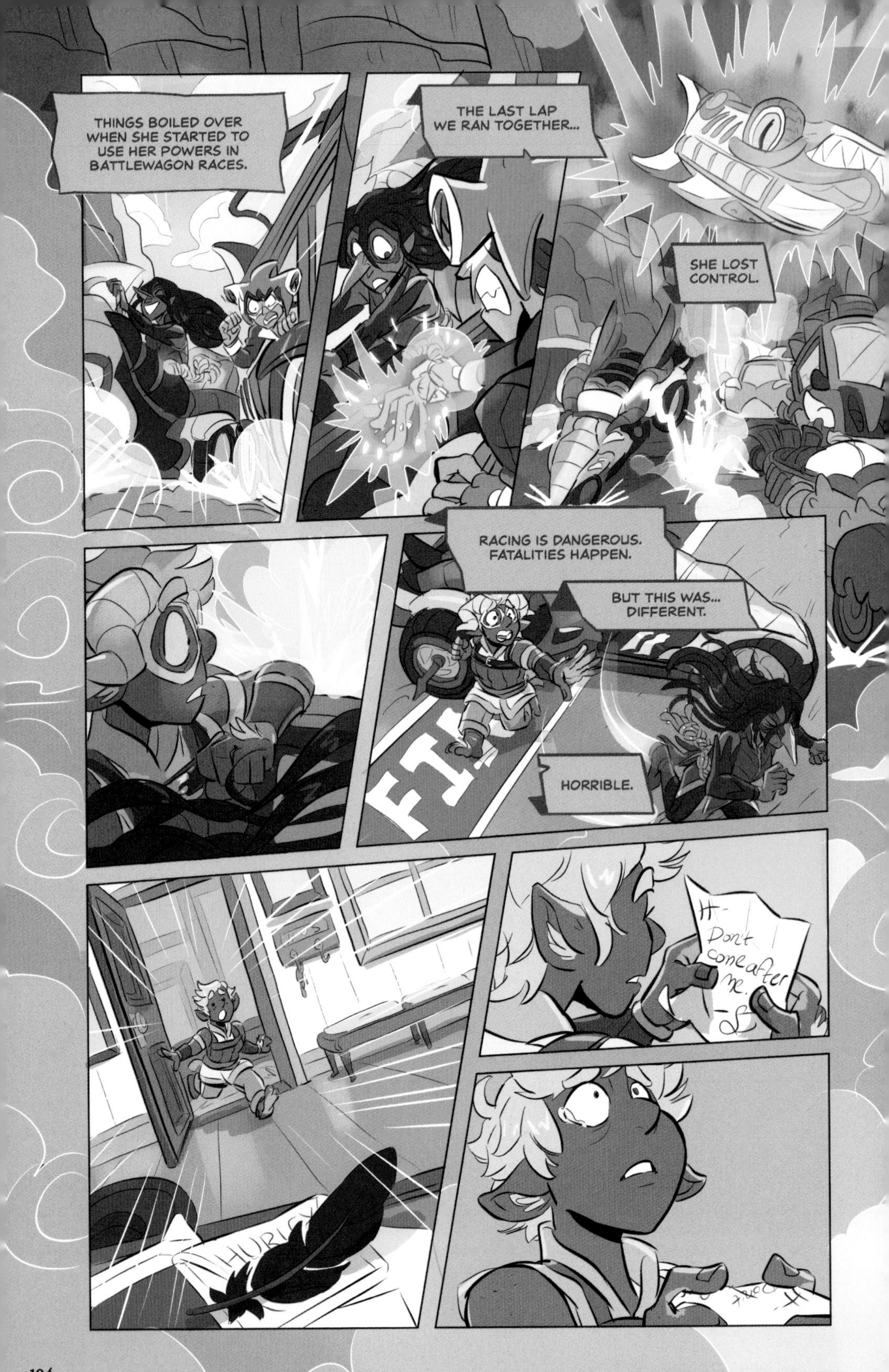
THINGS BOILED OVER WHEN SHE STARTED TO USE HER POWERS IN BATTLEWAGON RACES.
THE LAST LAP WE RAN TOGETHER...
SHE LOST CONTROL.
RACING IS DANGEROUS. FATALITIES HAPPEN.
BUT THIS WAS... DIFFERENT.
HORRIBLE.
H-
Don't come after me.
-B

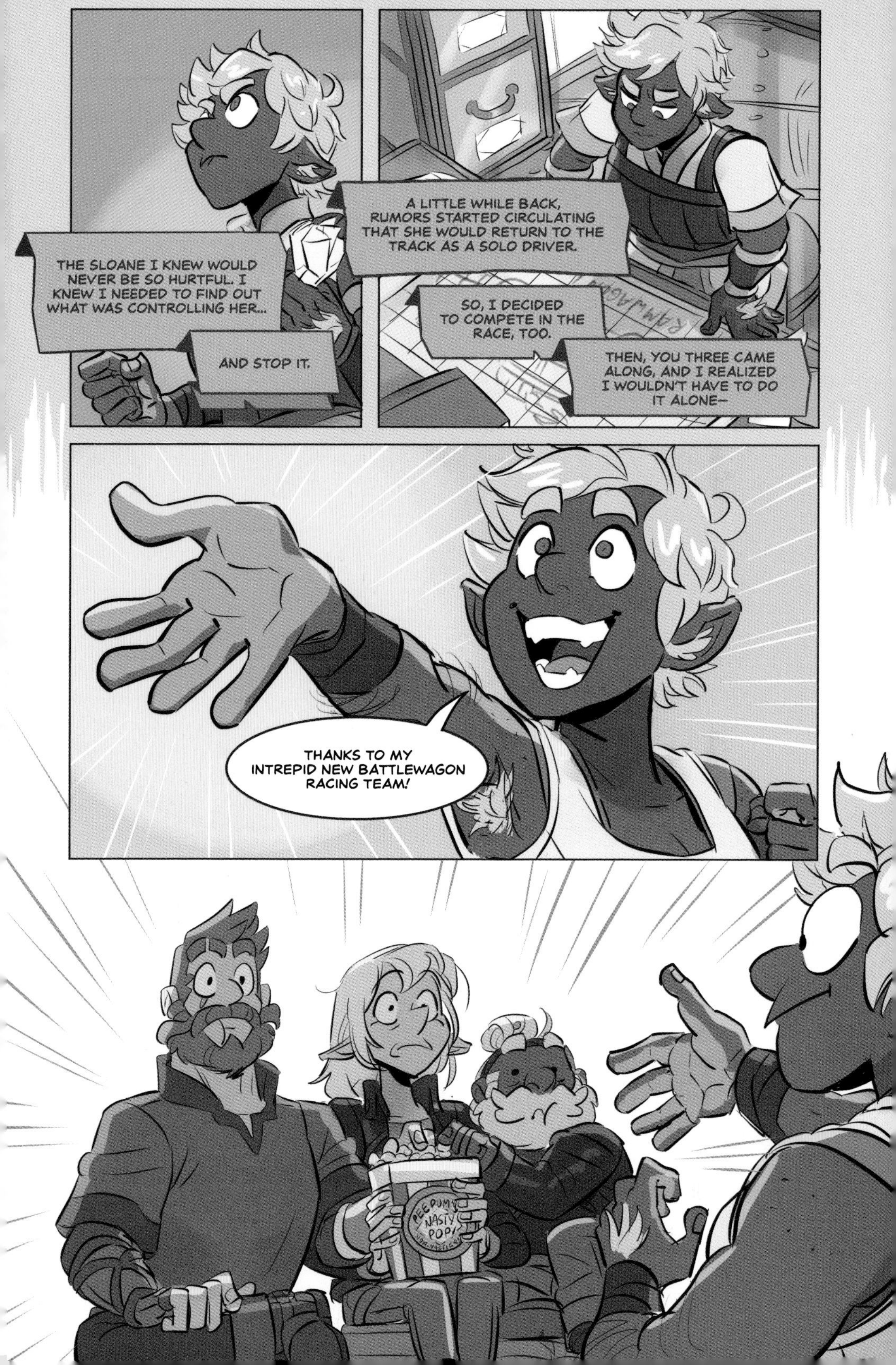

THE SLOANE I KNEW WOULD NEVER BE SO HURTFUL. I KNEW I NEEDED TO FIND OUT WHAT WAS CONTROLLING HER...
AND STOP IT.
A LITTLE WHILE BACK, RUMORS STARTED CIRCULATING THAT SHE WOULD RETURN TO THE TRACK AS A SOLO DRIVER.
SO, I DECIDED TO COMPETE IN THE RACE, TOO.
THEN, YOU THREE CAME ALONG, AND I REALIZED I WOULDN'T HAVE TO DO IT ALONE—
THANKS TO MY INTREPID NEW BATTLEWAGON RACING TEAM!

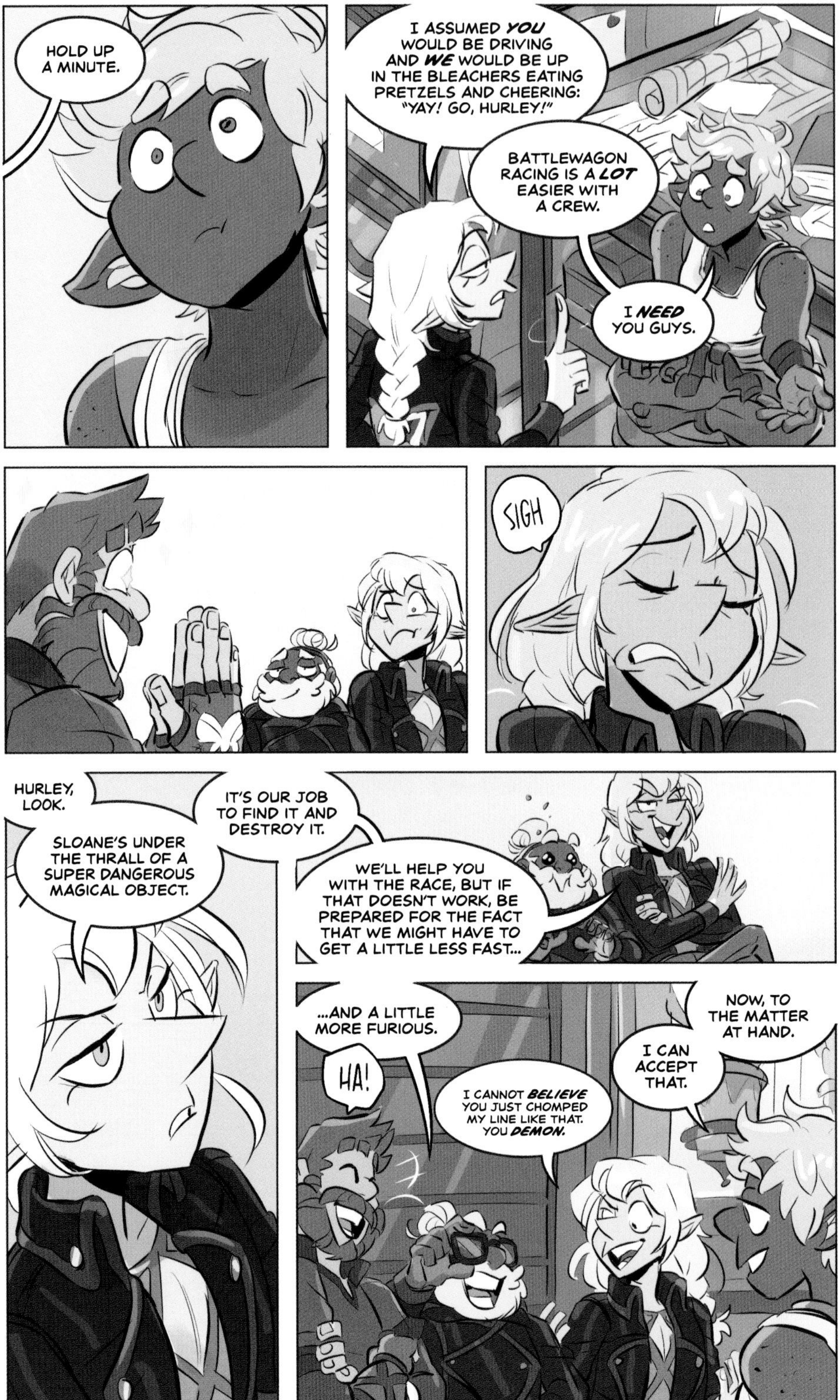
HOLD UP A MINUTE.
I ASSUMED *YOU* WOULD BE DRIVING AND *WE* WOULD BE UP IN THE BLEACHERS EATING PRETZELS AND CHEERING: "YAY! GO, HURLEY!"
BATTLEWAGON RACING IS A *LOT* EASIER WITH A CREW.
I *NEED* YOU GUYS.
SIGH
HURLEY, LOOK.
SLOANE'S UNDER THE THRALL OF A SUPER DANGEROUS MAGICAL OBJECT.
IT'S OUR JOB TO FIND IT AND DESTROY IT.
WE'LL HELP YOU WITH THE RACE, BUT IF THAT DOESN'T WORK, BE PREPARED FOR THE FACT THAT WE MIGHT HAVE TO GET A LITTLE LESS FAST...
...AND A LITTLE MORE FURIOUS.
HA!
I CANNOT *BELIEVE* YOU JUST CHOMPED MY LINE LIKE THAT. YOU *DEMON.*
I CAN ACCEPT THAT.
NOW, TO THE MATTER AT HAND.

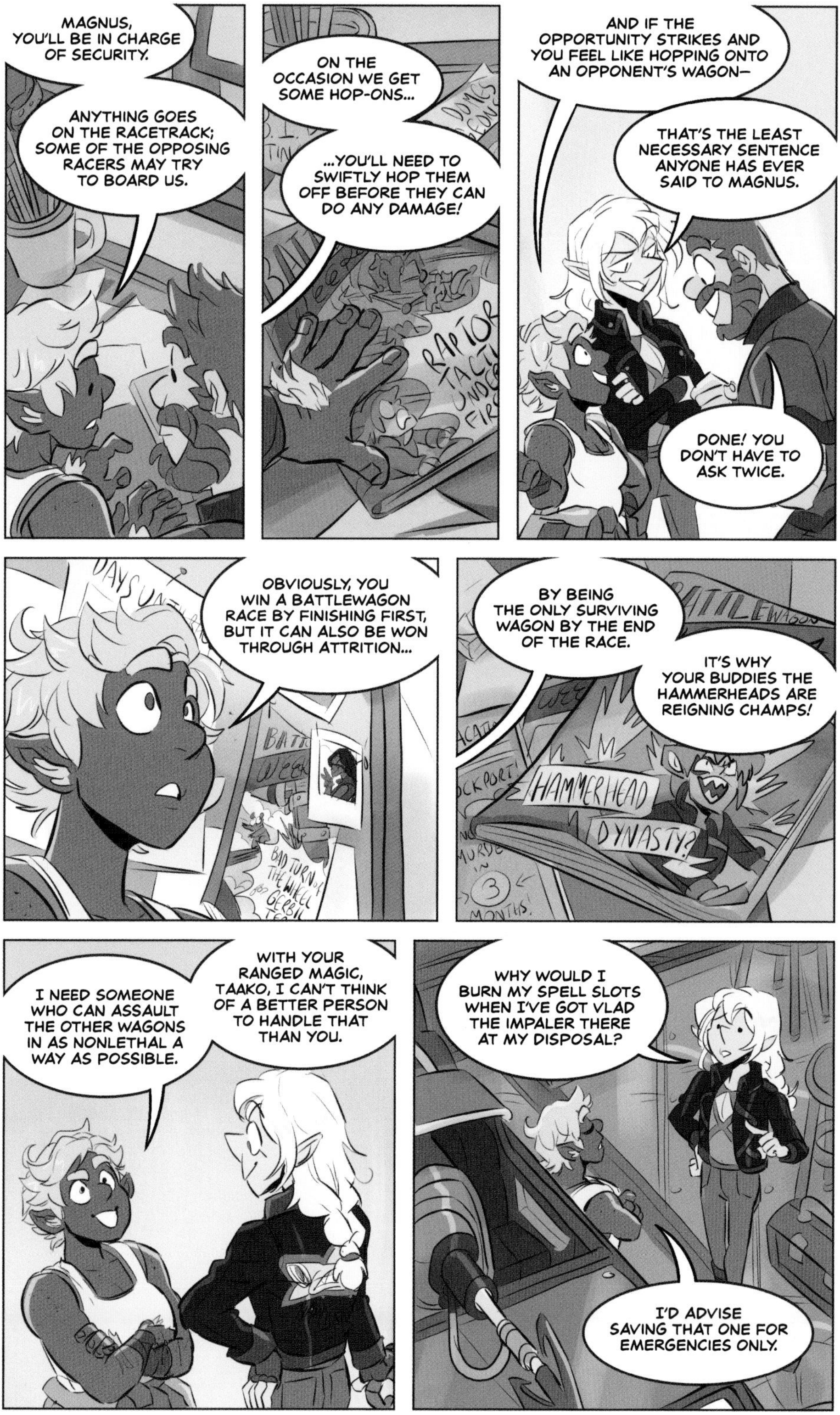
MAGNUS, YOU'LL BE IN CHARGE OF SECURITY.
ANYTHING GOES ON THE RACETRACK; SOME OF THE OPPOSING RACERS MAY TRY TO BOARD US.
ON THE OCCASION WE GET SOME HOP-ONS...
...YOU'LL NEED TO SWIFTLY HOP THEM OFF BEFORE THEY CAN DO ANY DAMAGE!
RAPTOR
AND IF THE OPPORTUNITY STRIKES AND YOU FEEL LIKE HOPPING ONTO AN OPPONENT'S WAGON—
THAT'S THE LEAST NECESSARY SENTENCE ANYONE HAS EVER SAID TO MAGNUS.
DONE! YOU DON'T HAVE TO ASK TWICE.
OBVIOUSLY, YOU WIN A BATTLEWAGON RACE BY FINISHING FIRST, BUT IT CAN ALSO BE WON THROUGH ATTRITION...
BAD TURN of THE WHEEL
BY BEING THE ONLY SURVIVING WAGON BY THE END OF THE RACE.
IT'S WHY YOUR BUDDIES THE HAMMERHEADS ARE REIGNING CHAMPS!
HAMMERHEAD
DYNASTY?
I NEED SOMEONE WHO CAN ASSAULT THE OTHER WAGONS IN AS NONLETHAL A WAY AS POSSIBLE.
WITH YOUR RANGED MAGIC, TAAKO, I CAN'T THINK OF A BETTER PERSON TO HANDLE THAT THAN YOU.
WHY WOULD I BURN MY SPELL SLOTS WHEN I'VE GOT VLAD THE IMPALER THERE AT MY DISPOSAL?
I'D ADVISE SAVING THAT ONE FOR EMERGENCIES ONLY.

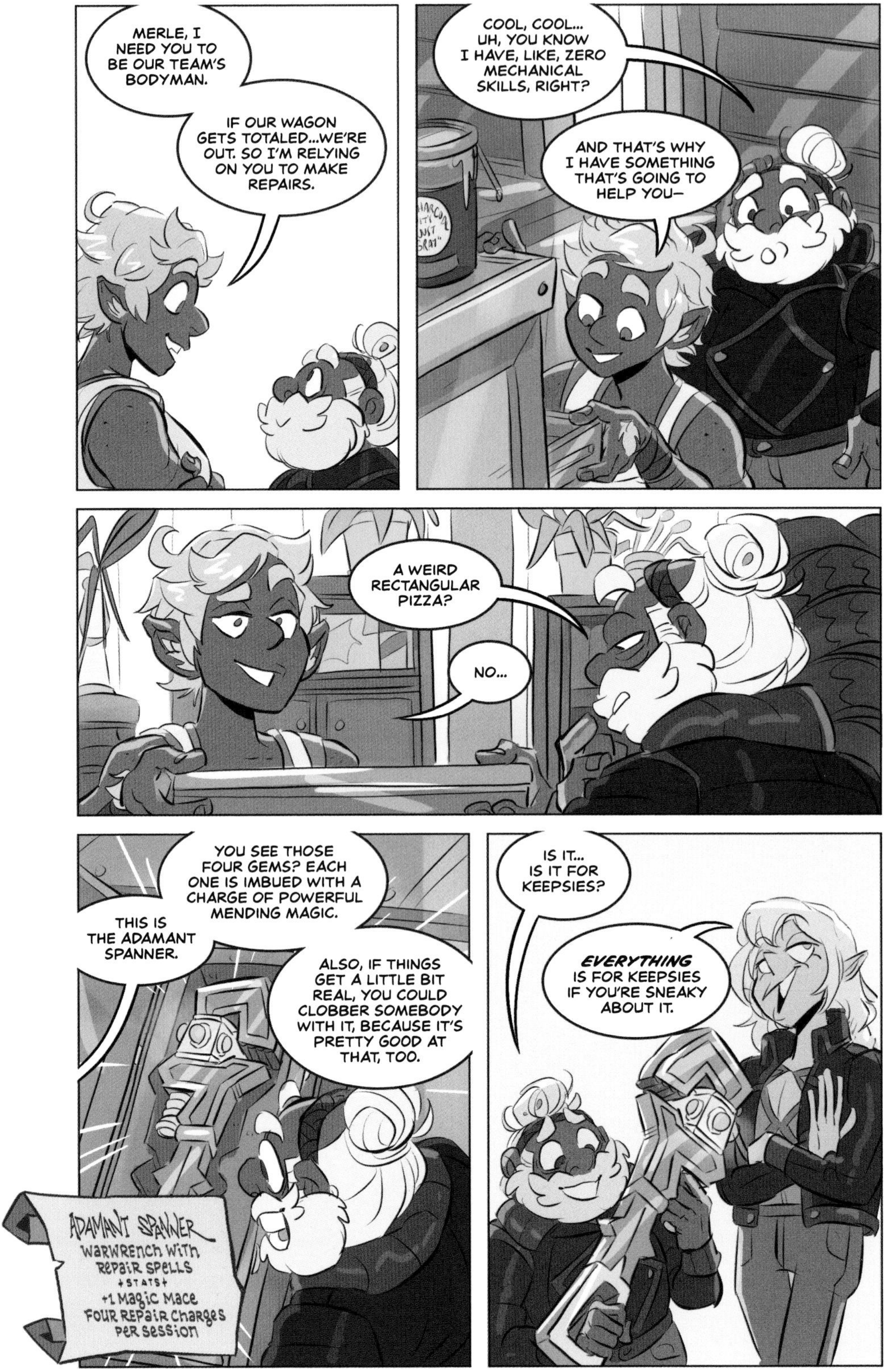
MERLE, I NEED YOU TO BE OUR TEAM'S BODYMAN.
IF OUR WAGON GETS TOTALED...WE'RE OUT. SO I'M RELYING ON YOU TO MAKE REPAIRS.
COOL, COOL... UH, YOU KNOW I HAVE, LIKE, ZERO MECHANICAL SKILLS, RIGHT?
AND THAT'S WHY I HAVE SOMETHING THAT'S GOING TO HELP YOU—
A WEIRD RECTANGULAR PIZZA?
NO...
THIS IS THE ADAMANT SPANNER.
YOU SEE THOSE FOUR GEMS? EACH ONE IS IMBUED WITH A CHARGE OF POWERFUL MENDING MAGIC.
ALSO, IF THINGS GET A LITTLE BIT REAL, YOU COULD CLOBBER SOMEBODY WITH IT, BECAUSE IT'S PRETTY GOOD AT THAT, TOO.
ADAMANT SPANNER
WARWRENCH WITH REPAIR SPELLS
+STATS+
+1 MAGIC MACE
FOUR REPAIR CHARGES PER SESSION
IS IT... IS IT FOR KEEPSIES?
EVERYTHING IS FOR KEEPSIES IF YOU'RE SNEAKY ABOUT IT.

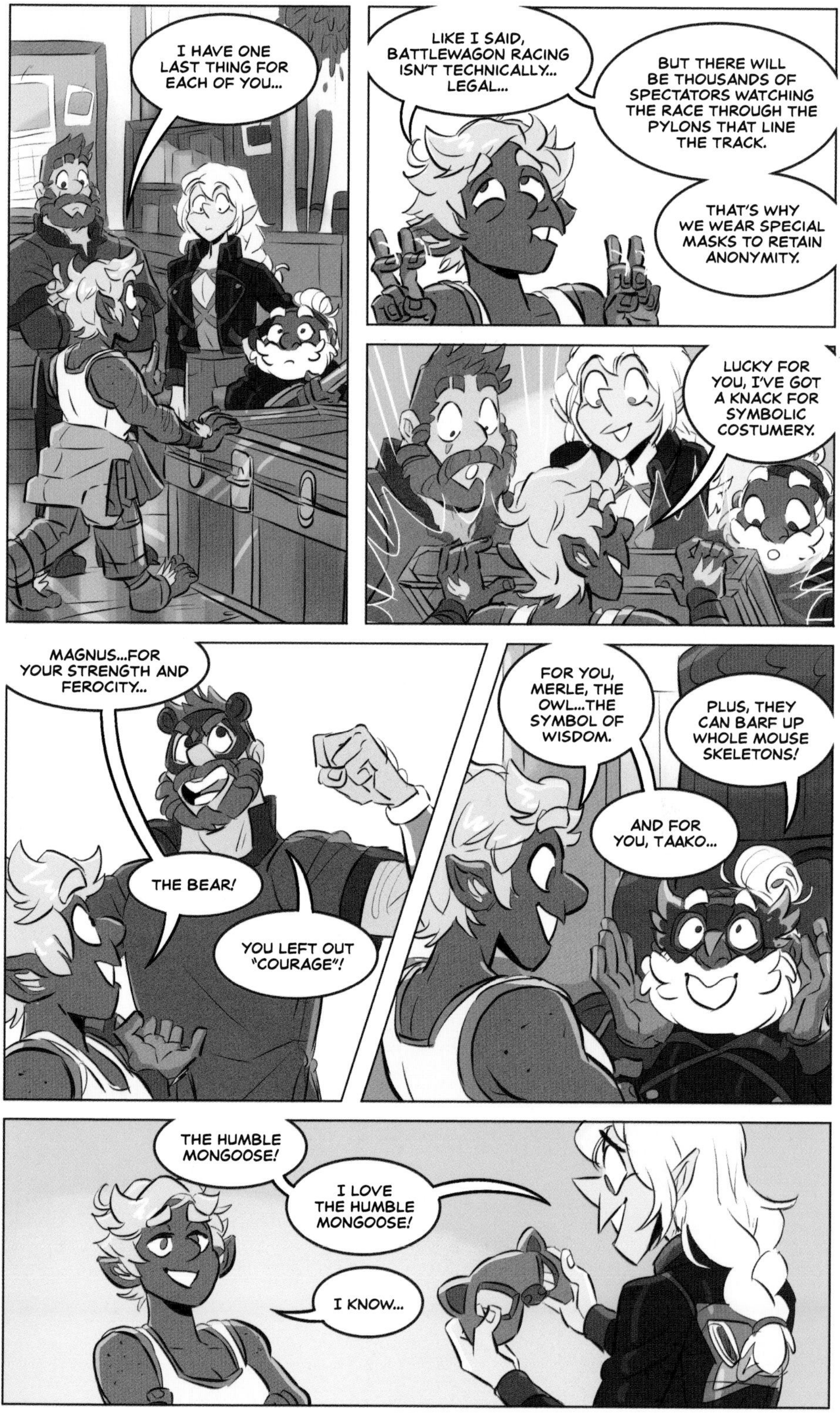
I HAVE ONE LAST THING FOR EACH OF YOU...
LIKE I SAID, BATTLEWAGON RACING ISN'T TECHNICALLY... LEGAL...
BUT THERE WILL BE THOUSANDS OF SPECTATORS WATCHING THE RACE THROUGH THE PYLONS THAT LINE THE TRACK.
THAT'S WHY WE WEAR SPECIAL MASKS TO RETAIN ANONYMITY.
LUCKY FOR YOU, I'VE GOT A KNACK FOR SYMBOLIC COSTUMERY.
MAGNUS...FOR YOUR STRENGTH AND FEROCITY...
THE BEAR!
YOU LEFT OUT "COURAGE"!
FOR YOU, MERLE, THE OWL...THE SYMBOL OF WISDOM.
PLUS, THEY CAN BARF UP WHOLE MOUSE SKELETONS!
AND FOR YOU, TAAKO...
THE HUMBLE MONGOOSE!
I LOVE THE HUMBLE MONGOOSE!
I KNOW...

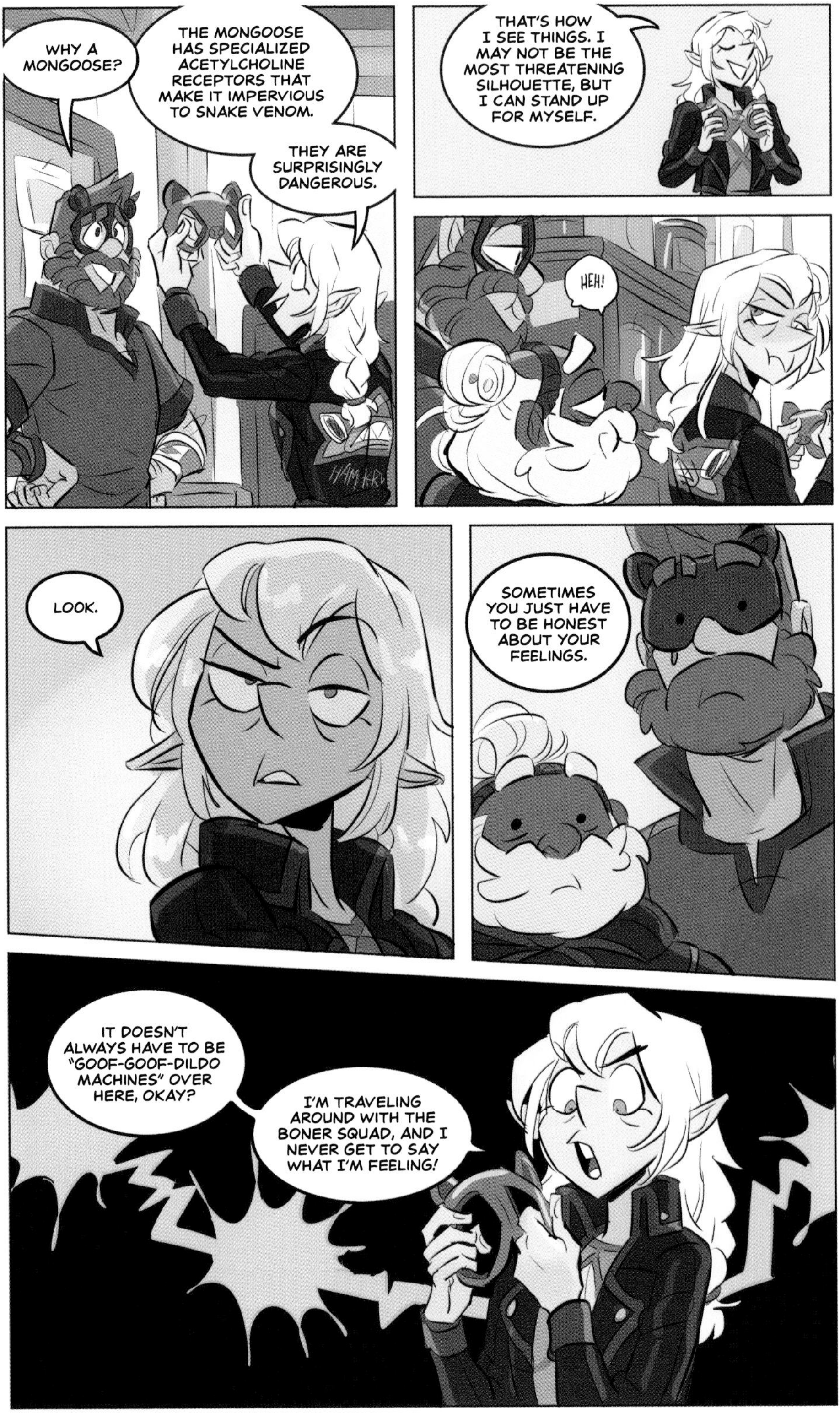
WHY A MONGOOSE?
THE MONGOOSE HAS SPECIALIZED ACETYLCHOLINE RECEPTORS THAT MAKE IT IMPERVIOUS TO SNAKE VENOM.
THEY ARE SURPRISINGLY DANGEROUS.
THAT'S HOW I SEE THINGS. I MAY NOT BE THE MOST THREATENING SILHOUETTE, BUT I CAN STAND UP FOR MYSELF.
HEH!
LOOK.
SOMETIMES YOU JUST HAVE TO BE HONEST ABOUT YOUR FEELINGS.
IT DOESN'T ALWAYS HAVE TO BE "GOOF-GOOF-DILDO MACHINES" OVER HERE, OKAY?
I'M TRAVELING AROUND WITH THE BONER SQUAD, AND I NEVER GET TO SAY WHAT I'M FEELING!

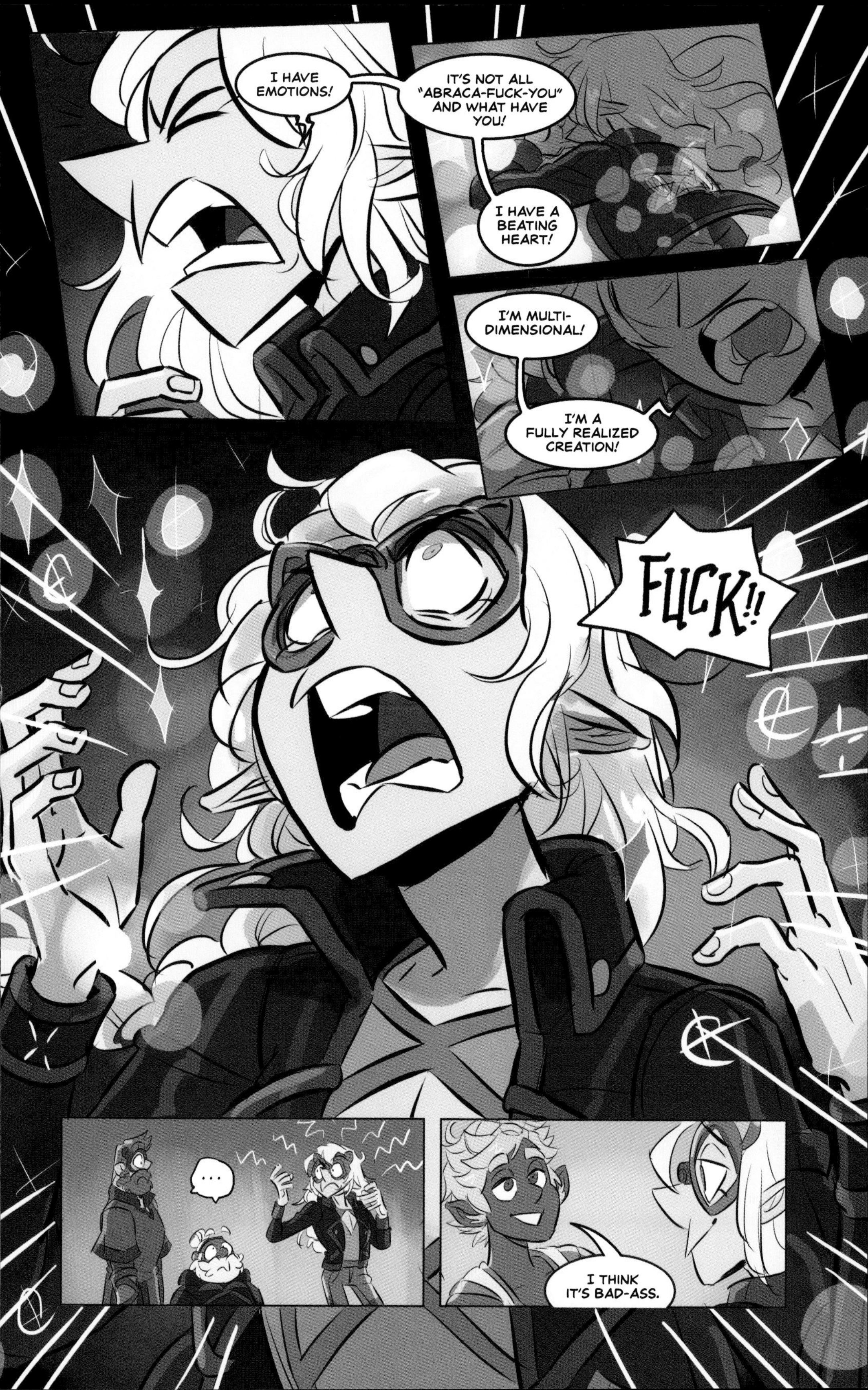
I HAVE EMOTIONS!
IT'S NOT ALL "ABRACA-FUCK-YOU" AND WHAT HAVE YOU!
I HAVE A BEATING HEART!
I'M MULTI-DIMENSIONAL!
I'M A FULLY REALIZED CREATION!
FUCK!!
...
I THINK IT'S BAD-ASS.

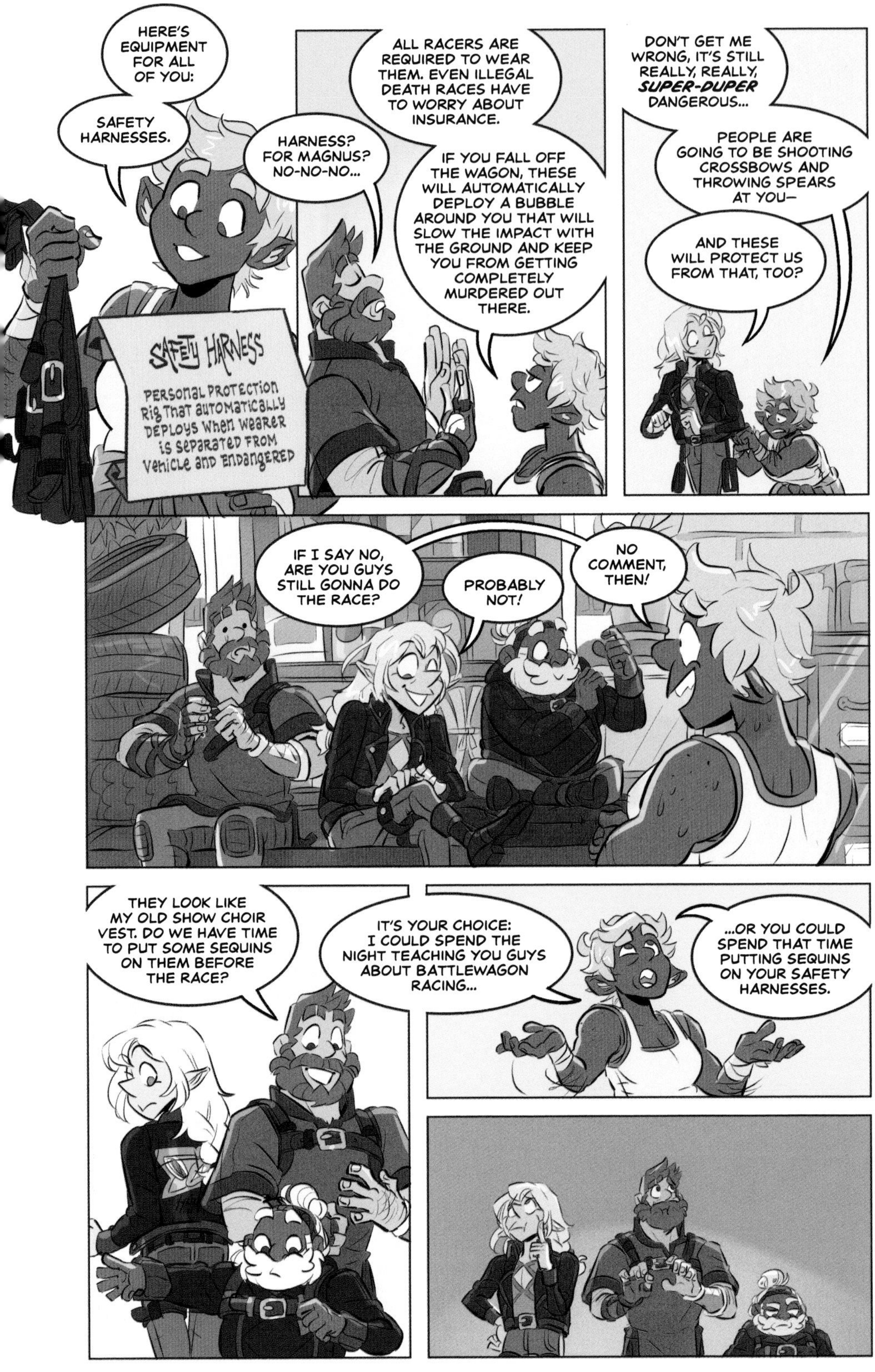
HERE'S EQUIPMENT FOR ALL OF YOU:
SAFETY HARNESSES.
SAFETY HARNESS
PERSONAL PROTECTION RIG THAT AUTOMATICALLY DEPLOYS WHEN WEARER IS SEPARATED FROM VEHICLE AND ENDANGERED
HARNESS? FOR MAGNUS? NO-NO-NO...
ALL RACERS ARE REQUIRED TO WEAR THEM. EVEN ILLEGAL DEATH RACES HAVE TO WORRY ABOUT INSURANCE.
IF YOU FALL OFF THE WAGON, THESE WILL AUTOMATICALLY DEPLOY A BUBBLE AROUND YOU THAT WILL SLOW THE IMPACT WITH THE GROUND AND KEEP YOU FROM GETTING COMPLETELY MURDERED OUT THERE.
DON'T GET ME WRONG, IT'S STILL REALLY, REALLY, ***SUPER-DUPER*** DANGEROUS...
PEOPLE ARE GOING TO BE SHOOTING CROSSBOWS AND THROWING SPEARS AT YOU—
AND THESE WILL PROTECT US FROM THAT, TOO?
IF I SAY NO, ARE YOU GUYS STILL GONNA DO THE RACE?
PROBABLY NOT!
NO COMMENT, THEN!
THEY LOOK LIKE MY OLD SHOW CHOIR VEST. DO WE HAVE TIME TO PUT SOME SEQUINS ON THEM BEFORE THE RACE?
IT'S YOUR CHOICE: I COULD SPEND THE NIGHT TEACHING YOU GUYS ABOUT BATTLEWAGON RACING...
...OR YOU COULD SPEND THAT TIME PUTTING SEQUINS ON YOUR SAFETY HARNESSES.

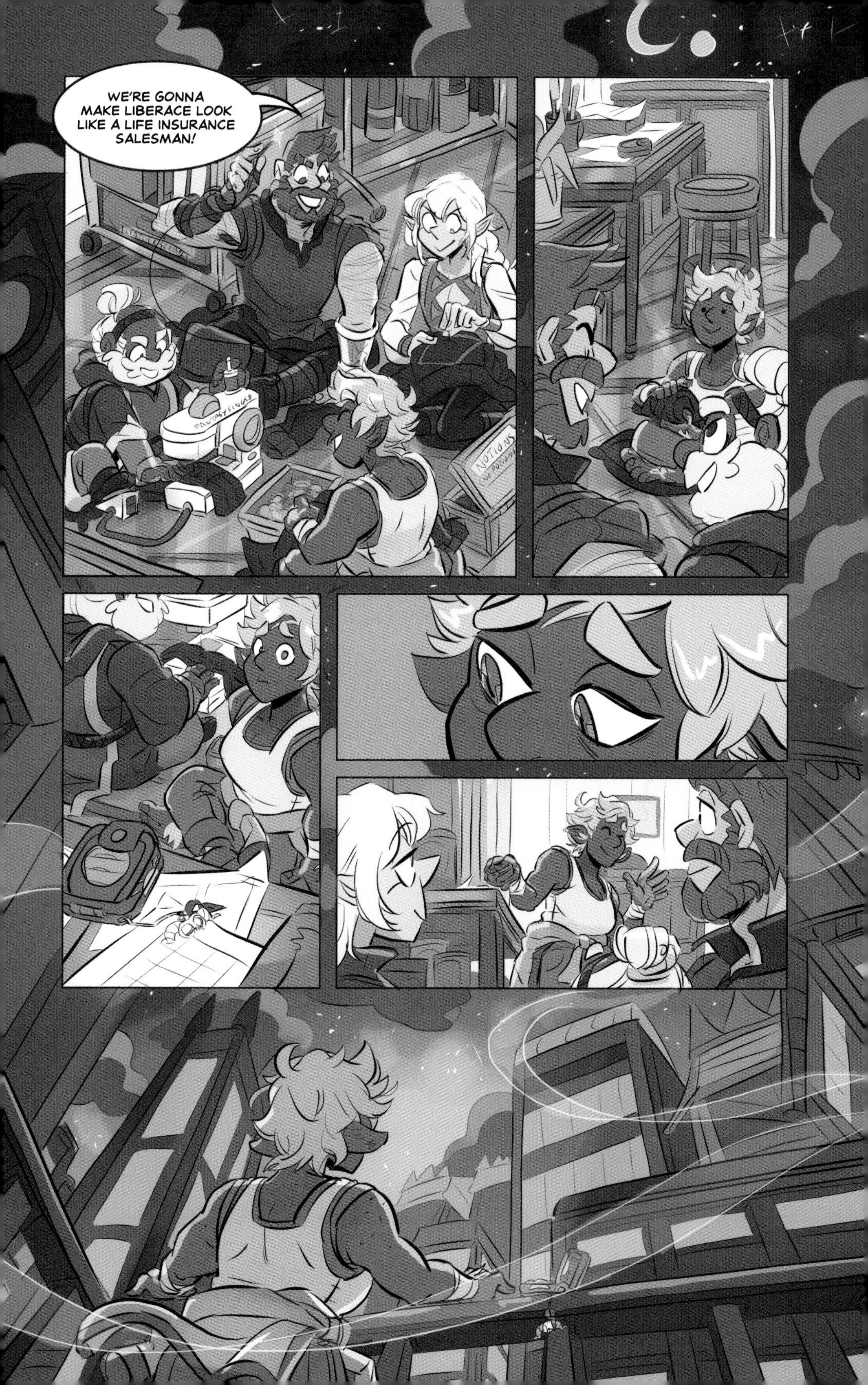
WE'RE GONNA MAKE LIBERACE LOOK LIKE A LIFE INSURANCE SALESMAN!
FANTASY SINGER
NOTIONS

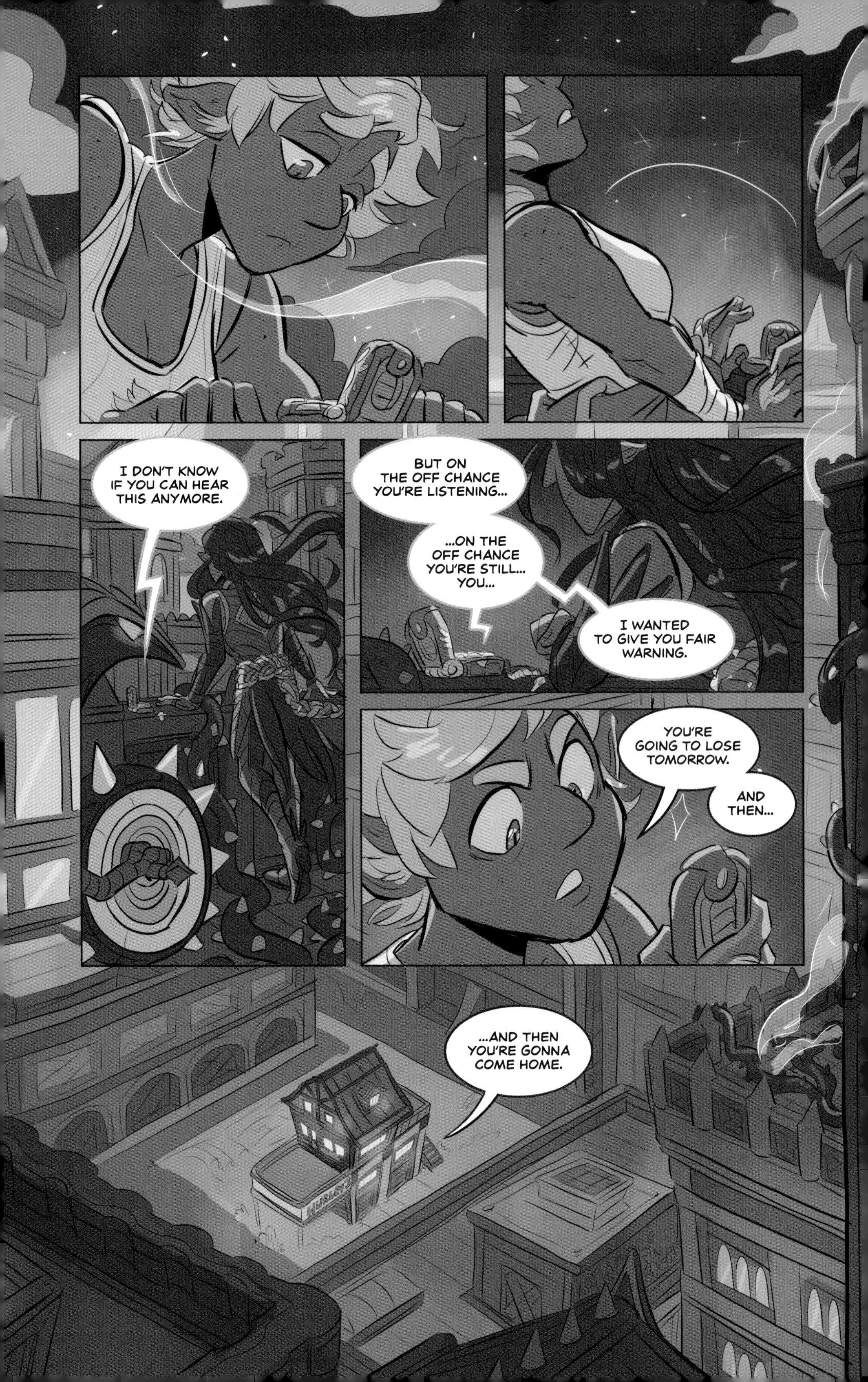
I DON'T KNOW IF YOU CAN HEAR THIS ANYMORE.
BUT ON THE OFF CHANCE YOU'RE LISTENING...
...ON THE OFF CHANCE YOU'RE STILL... YOU...
I WANTED TO GIVE YOU FAIR WARNING.
YOU'RE GOING TO LOSE TOMORROW.
AND THEN...
...AND THEN YOU'RE GONNA COME HOME.

Chapter 6

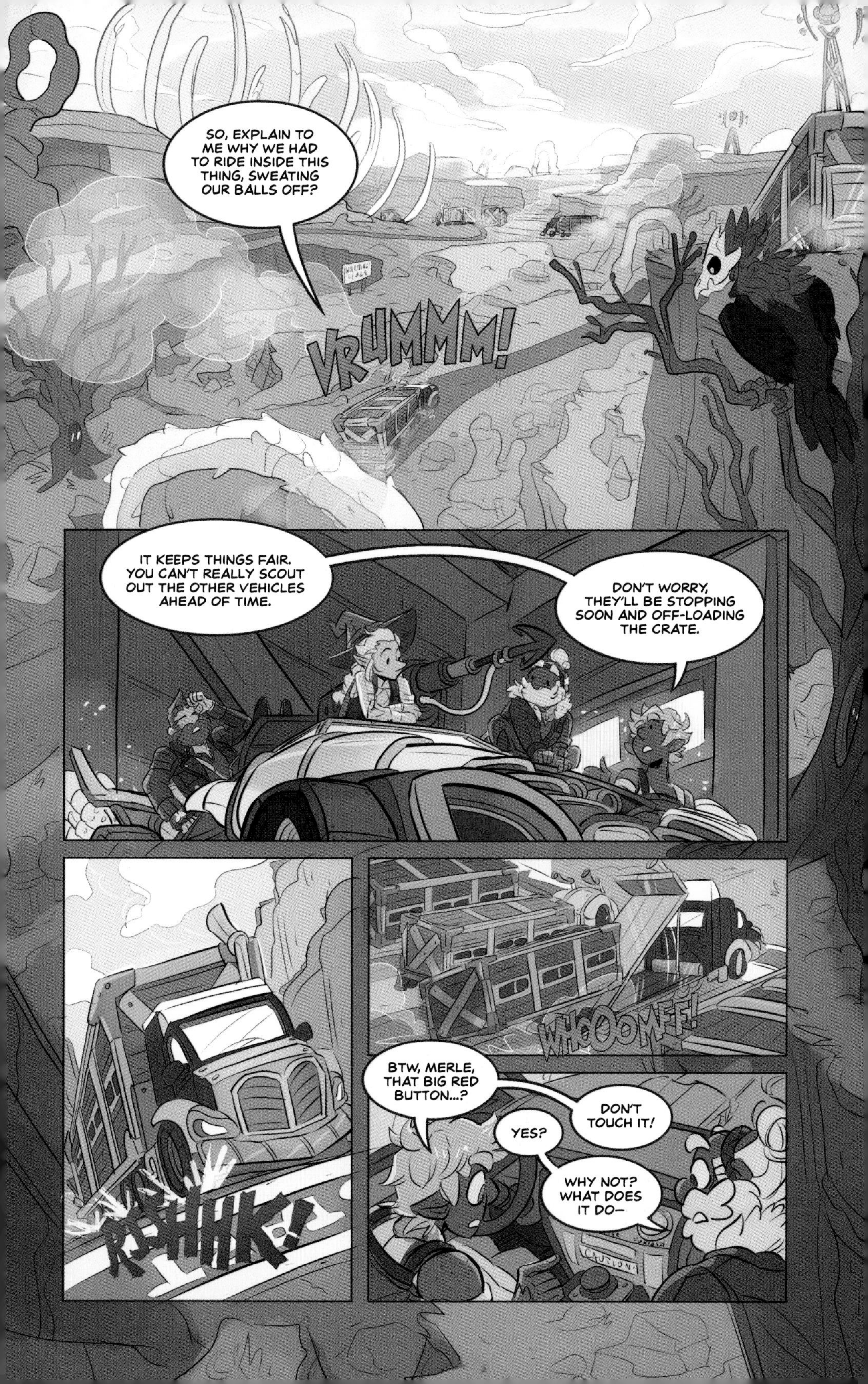
SO, EXPLAIN TO ME WHY WE HAD TO RIDE INSIDE THIS THING, SWEATING OUR BALLS OFF?
VRUMMMM!
IT KEEPS THINGS FAIR. YOU CAN'T REALLY SCOUT OUT THE OTHER VEHICLES AHEAD OF TIME.
DON'T WORRY, THEY'LL BE STOPPING SOON AND OFF-LOADING THE CRATE.
RSHHHK!
WHOOOMFF!
BTW, MERLE, THAT BIG RED BUTTON...?
YES?
DON'T TOUCH IT!
WHY NOT? WHAT DOES IT DO—
CAUTION

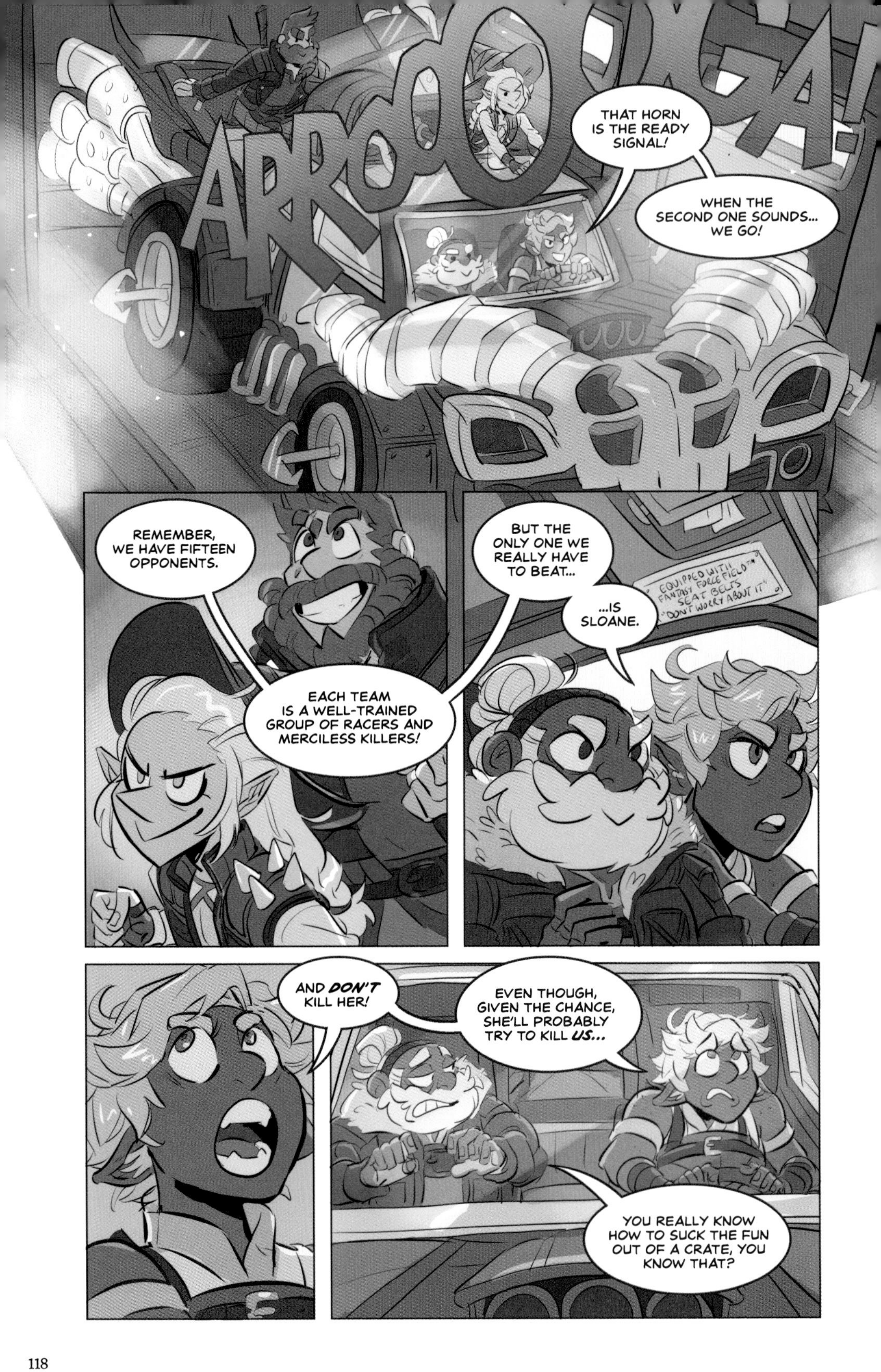
ARROOOOGA!
THAT HORN IS THE READY SIGNAL!
WHEN THE SECOND ONE SOUNDS... WE GO!
REMEMBER, WE HAVE FIFTEEN OPPONENTS.
EACH TEAM IS A WELL-TRAINED GROUP OF RACERS AND MERCILESS KILLERS!
BUT THE ONLY ONE WE REALLY HAVE TO BEAT...
...IS SLOANE.
EQUIPPED WITH FANTASY FORCE FIELD™ SEAT BELTS "DON'T WORRY ABOUT IT"
AND ***DON'T*** KILL HER!
EVEN THOUGH, GIVEN THE CHANCE, SHE'LL PROBABLY TRY TO KILL ***US...***
YOU REALLY KNOW HOW TO SUCK THE FUN OUT OF A CRATE, YOU KNOW THAT?

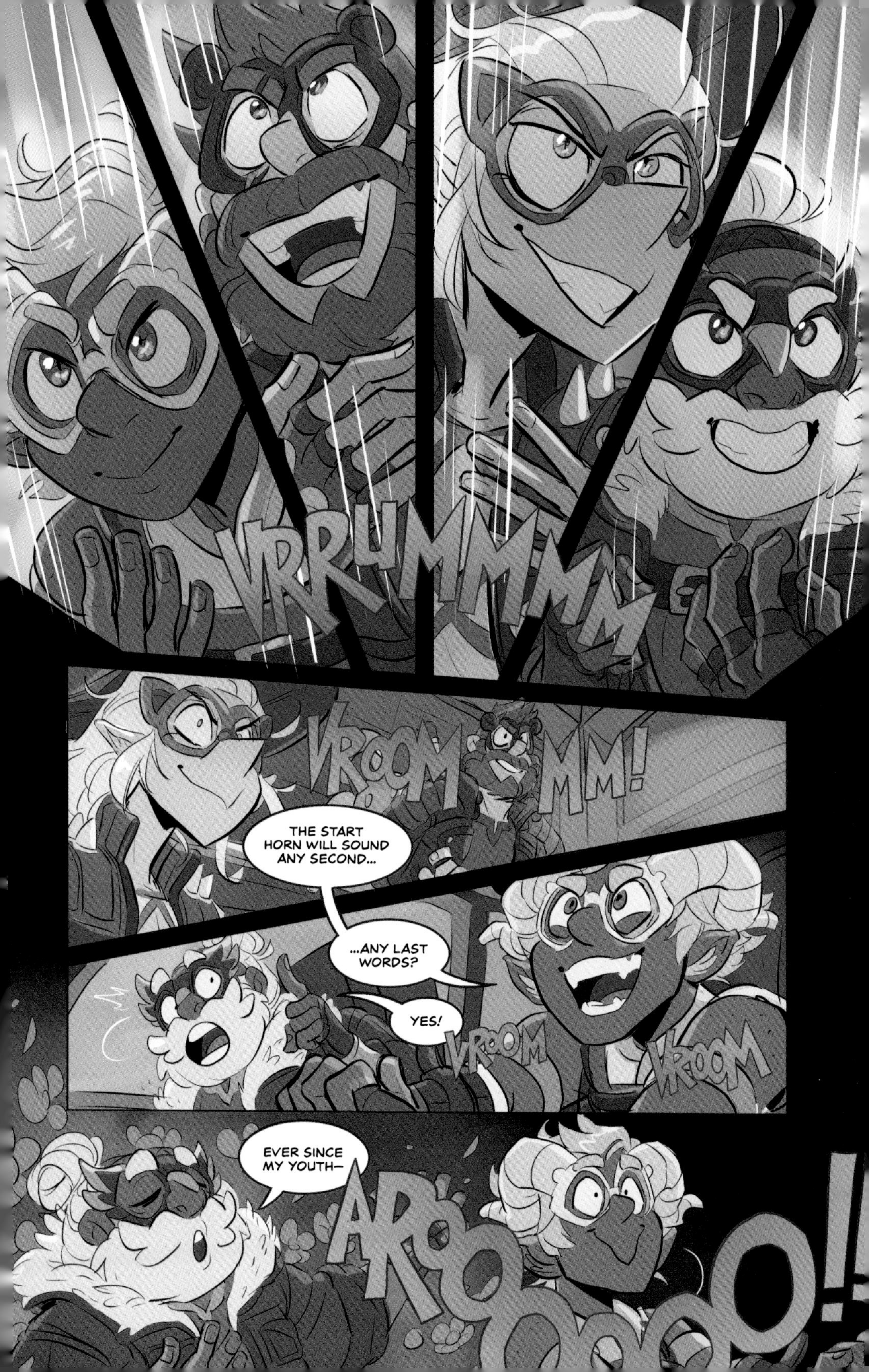
VRRUMMMMM
VROOM MM!
THE START HORN WILL SOUND ANY SECOND...
...ANY LAST WORDS?
YES!
VROOM
VROOM
EVER SINCE MY YOUTH—
AROOOOOO!!

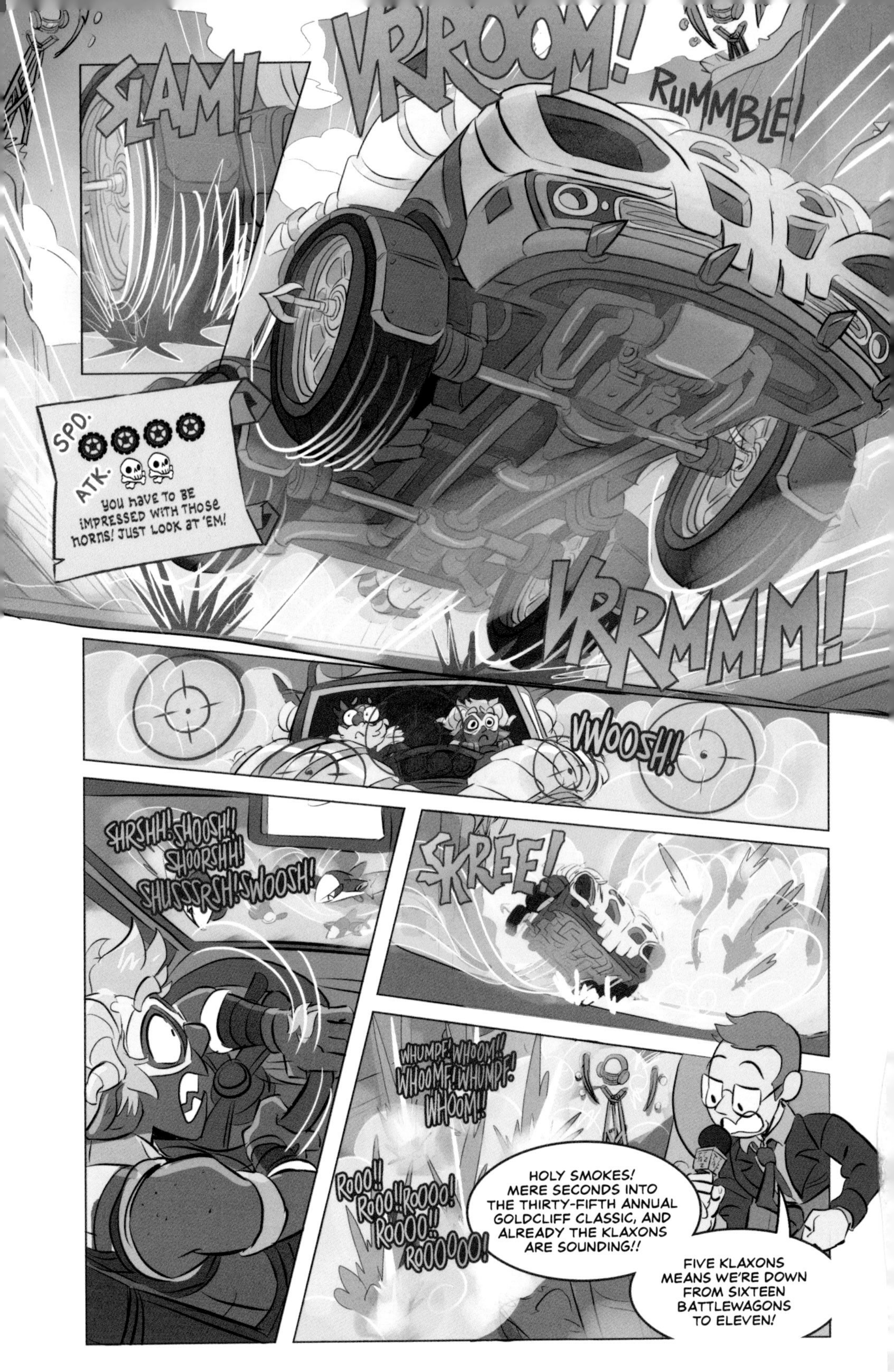
SLAM!
VRROOM!
RUMMBLE!
SPD.
ATK.
YOU HAVE TO BE IMPRESSED WITH THOSE HORNS! JUST LOOK AT 'EM!
VRRMMM!
VWOOSH!
SHRSHH! SHOOSH!! SHOORSHH! SHUSSSRSH! SWOOSH!
SKREE!
WHUMPF! WHOOM!! WHOOMF! WHUMPF! WHOOM!!
ROOO!! ROOO!! ROOOO! ROOOO!! ROOOOOO!
HOLY SMOKES! MERE SECONDS INTO THE THIRTY-FIFTH ANNUAL GOLDCLIFF CLASSIC, AND ALREADY THE KLAXONS ARE SOUNDING!!
FIVE KLAXONS MEANS WE'RE DOWN FROM SIXTEEN BATTLEWAGONS TO ELEVEN!

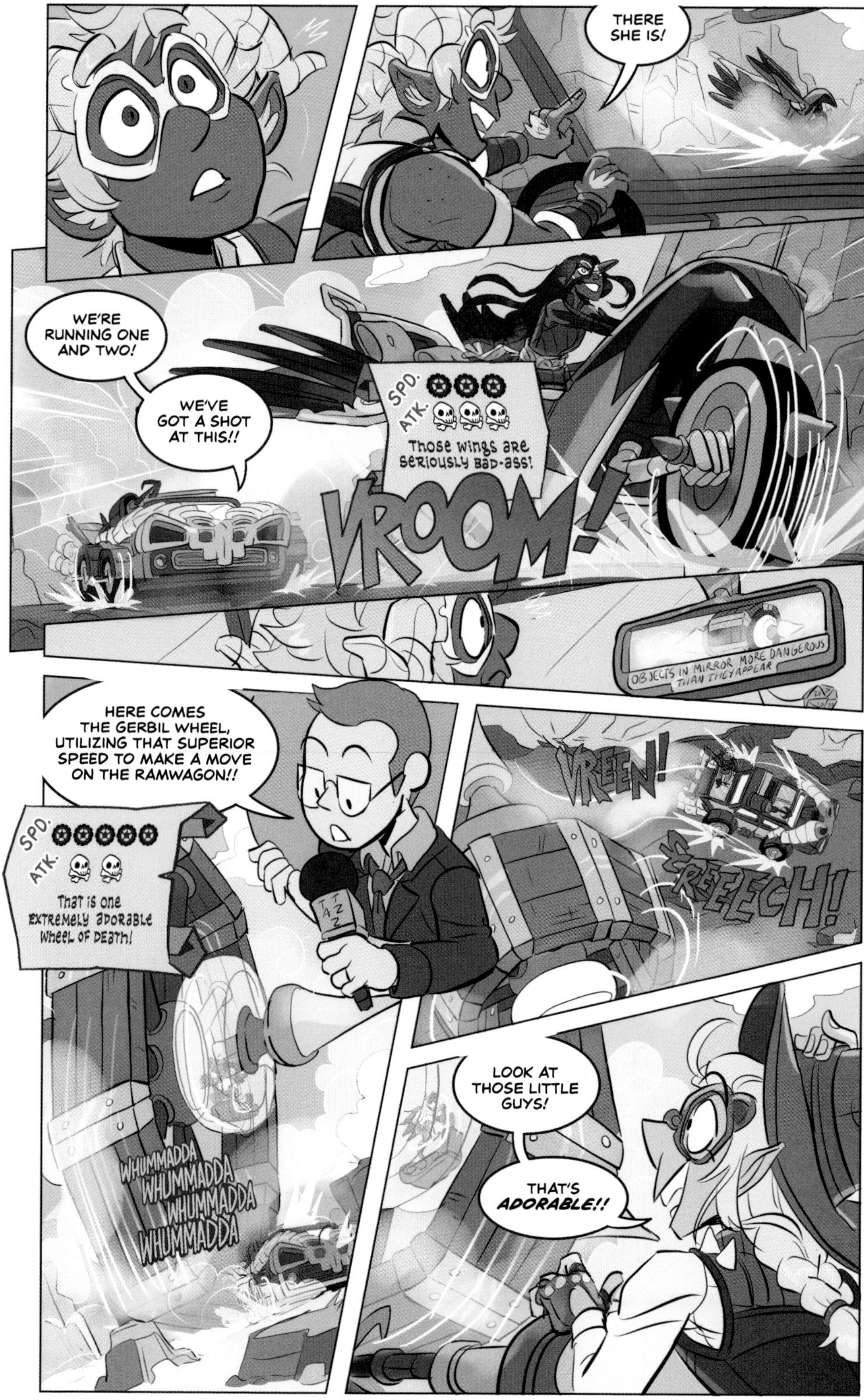
THERE SHE IS!
WE'RE RUNNING ONE AND TWO!
WE'VE GOT A SHOT AT THIS!!
SPD. ATK.
Those wings are seriously bad-ass!
VROOM!
OBJECTS IN MIRROR MORE DANGEROUS THAN THEY APPEAR
HERE COMES THE GERBIL WHEEL, UTILIZING THAT SUPERIOR SPEED TO MAKE A MOVE ON THE RAMWAGON!!
SPD. ATK.
That is one extremely adorable wheel of death!
TAZ
VREEN!
SREEECH!
WHUMMADDA WHUMMADDA WHUMMADDA WHUMMADDA
LOOK AT THOSE LITTLE GUYS!
THAT'S *ADORABLE!!*

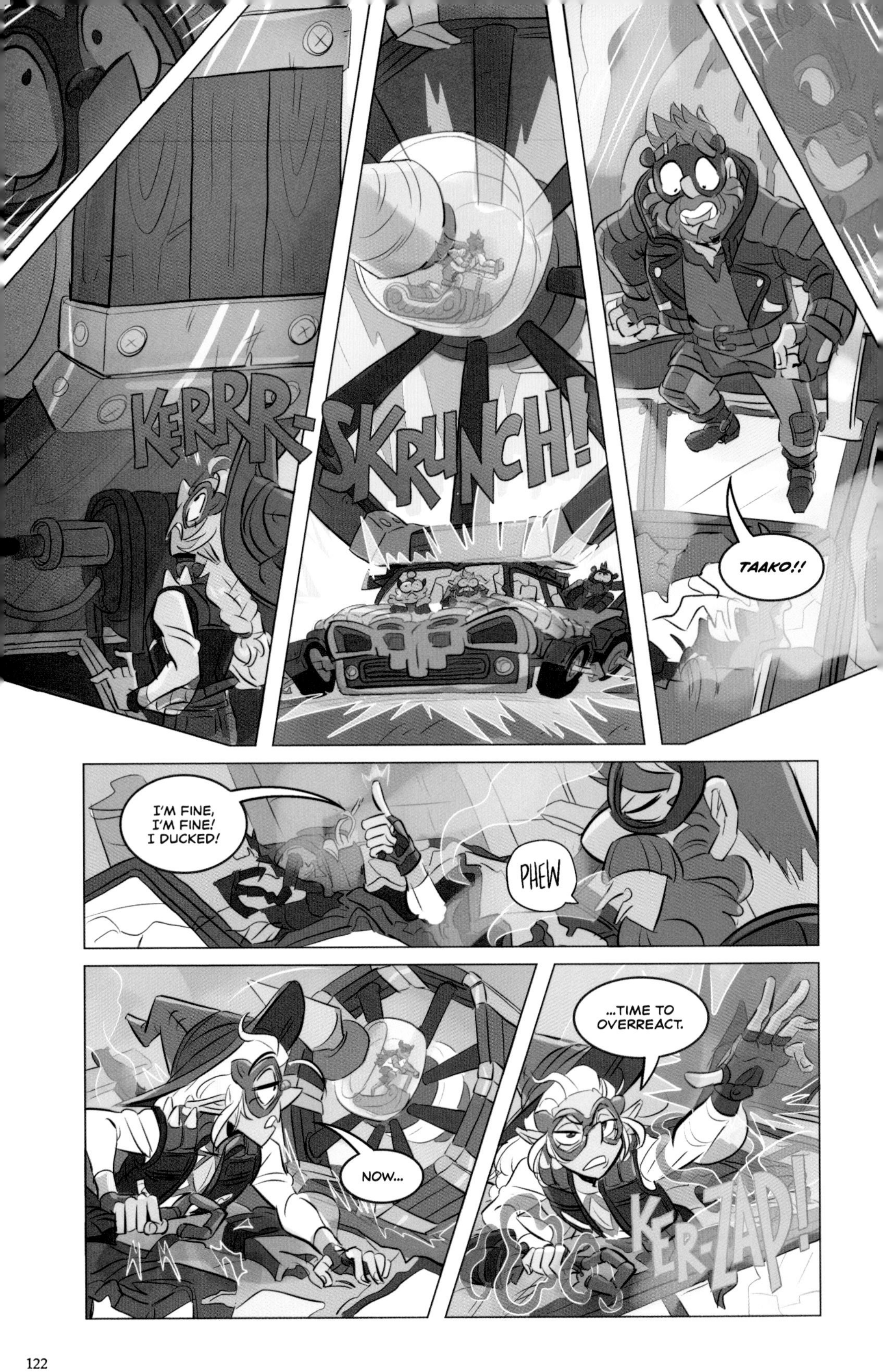
KERRR-SKRUNCH!
TAAKO!!
I'M FINE, I'M FINE! I DUCKED!
PHEW
NOW...
...TIME TO OVERREACT.
KER-ZAP!

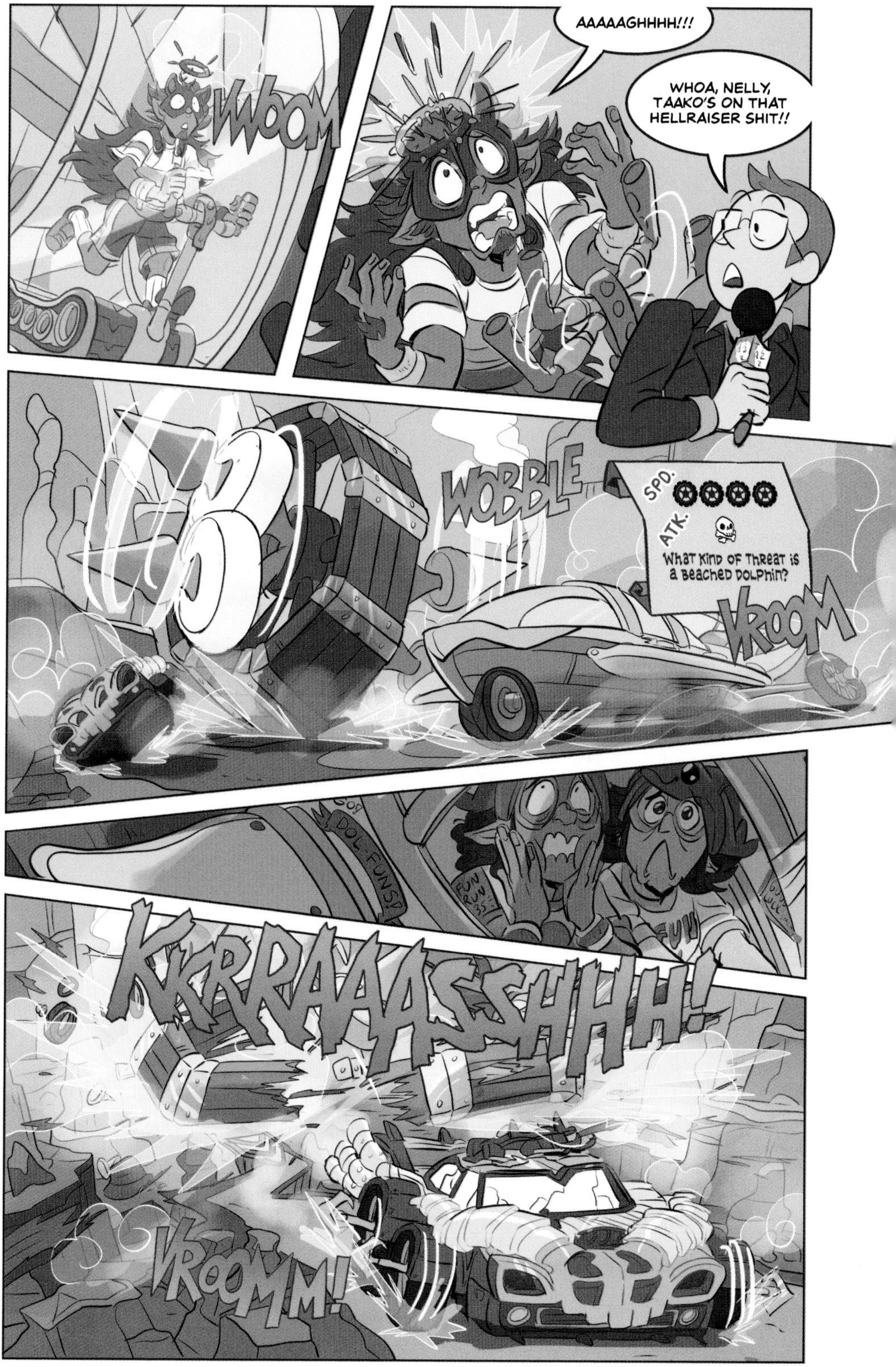
VWOOM
AAAAAGHHHH!!!
WHOA, NELLY, TAAKO'S ON THAT HELLRAISER SHIT!!
WOBBLE
SPD.
ATK.
What kind of threat is a beached dolphin?
VROOM
DOL-FUNS?
FUN RUN
KKRRAAASSHHH!
VROOMM!

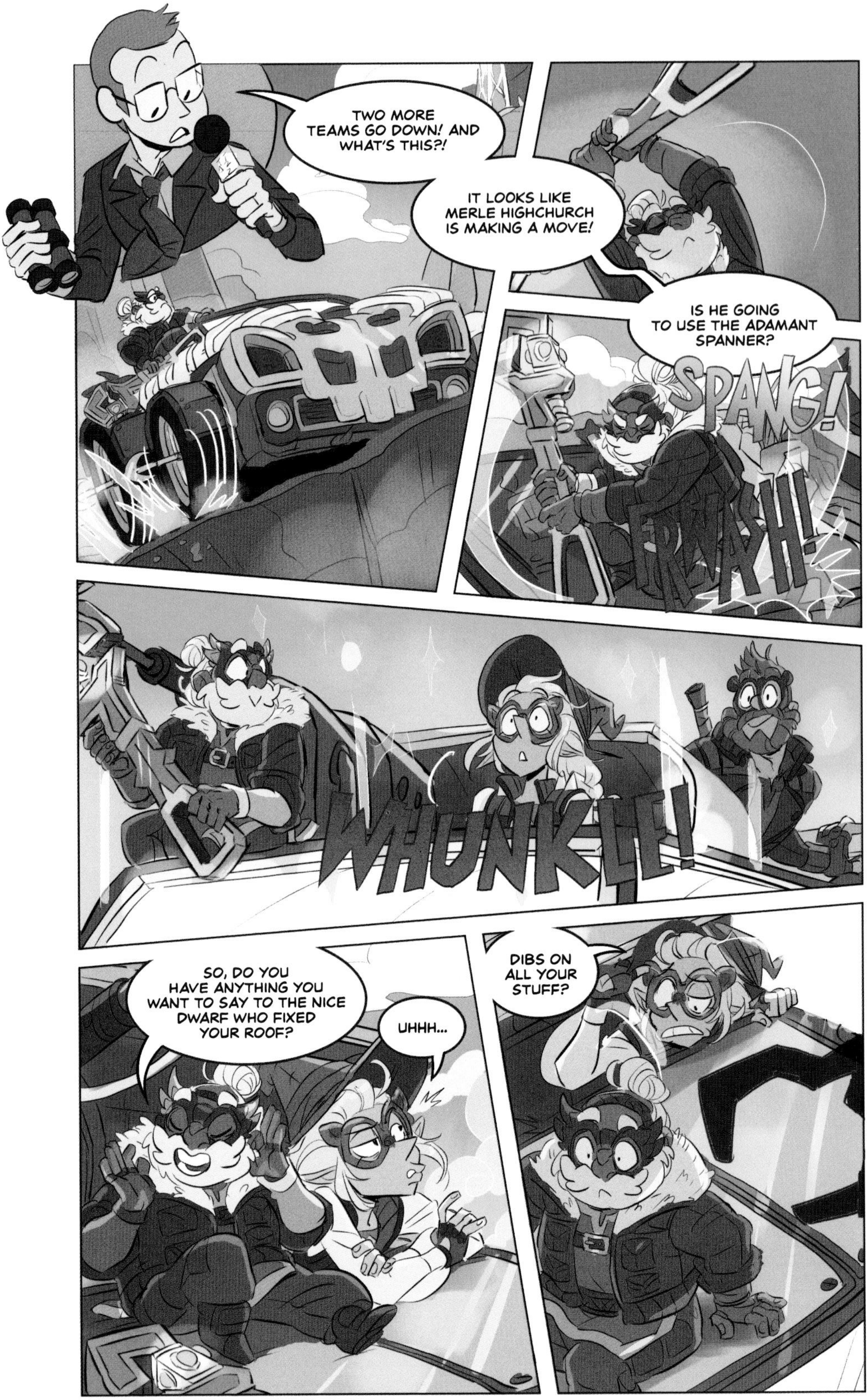
TWO MORE TEAMS GO DOWN! AND WHAT'S THIS?!
IT LOOKS LIKE MERLE HIGHCHURCH IS MAKING A MOVE!
IS HE GOING TO USE THE ADAMANT SPANNER?
SPANG!
WHUNKLE!
SO, DO YOU HAVE ANYTHING YOU WANT TO SAY TO THE NICE DWARF WHO FIXED YOUR ROOF?
UHHH...
DIBS ON ALL YOUR STUFF?

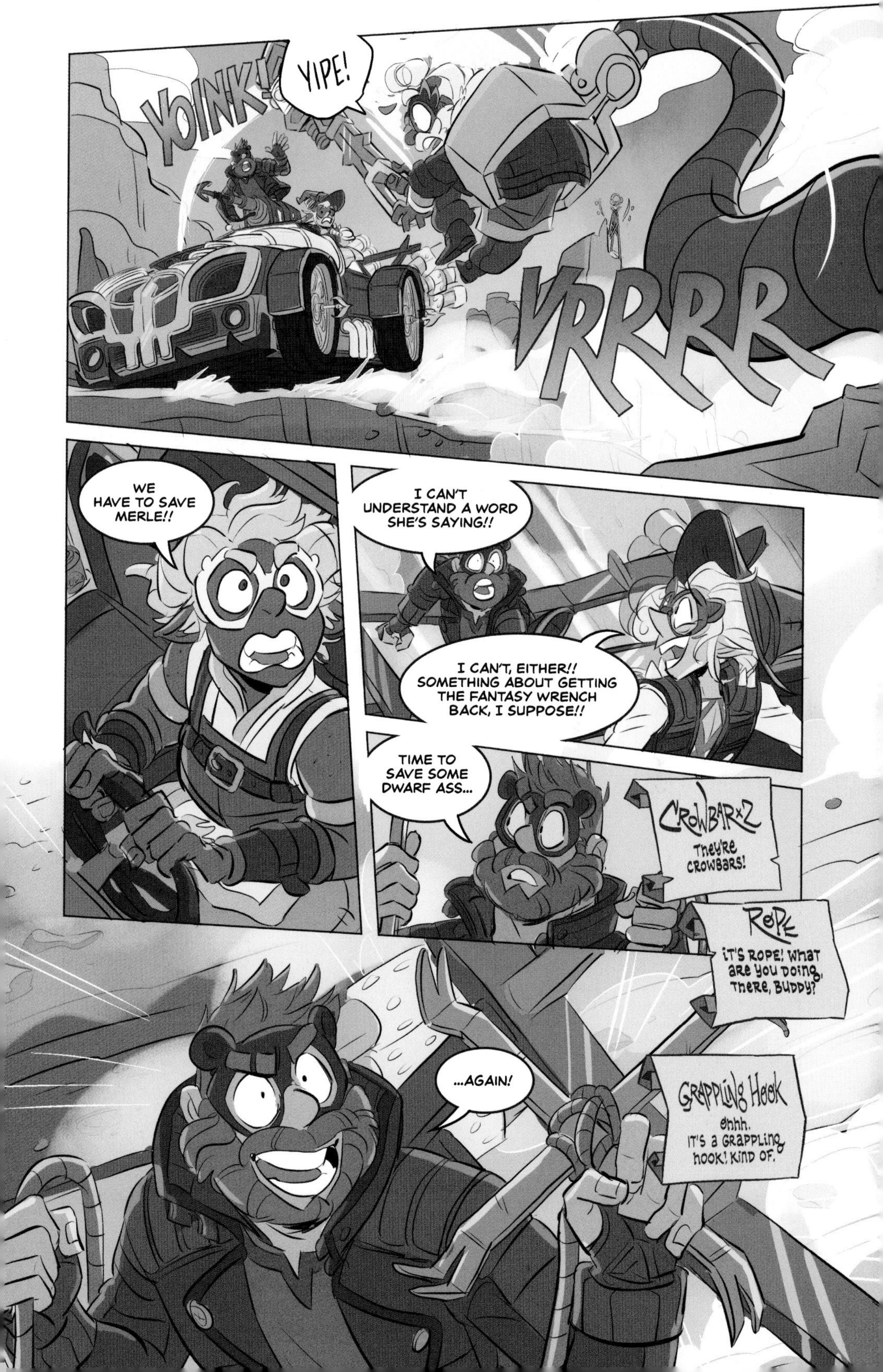
YOINK!!
YIPE!
VRRRR
WE HAVE TO SAVE MERLE!!
I CAN'T UNDERSTAND A WORD SHE'S SAYING!!
I CAN'T, EITHER!! SOMETHING ABOUT GETTING THE FANTASY WRENCH BACK, I SUPPOSE!!
TIME TO SAVE SOME DWARF ASS...
CROWBAR×2
They're CROWBARS!
ROPE
IT'S ROPE! WHAT are you doing, there, BUDDY?
...AGAIN!
GRAPPLING HOOK
Ohhh. IT'S a GRAPPLING hook! Kind of.

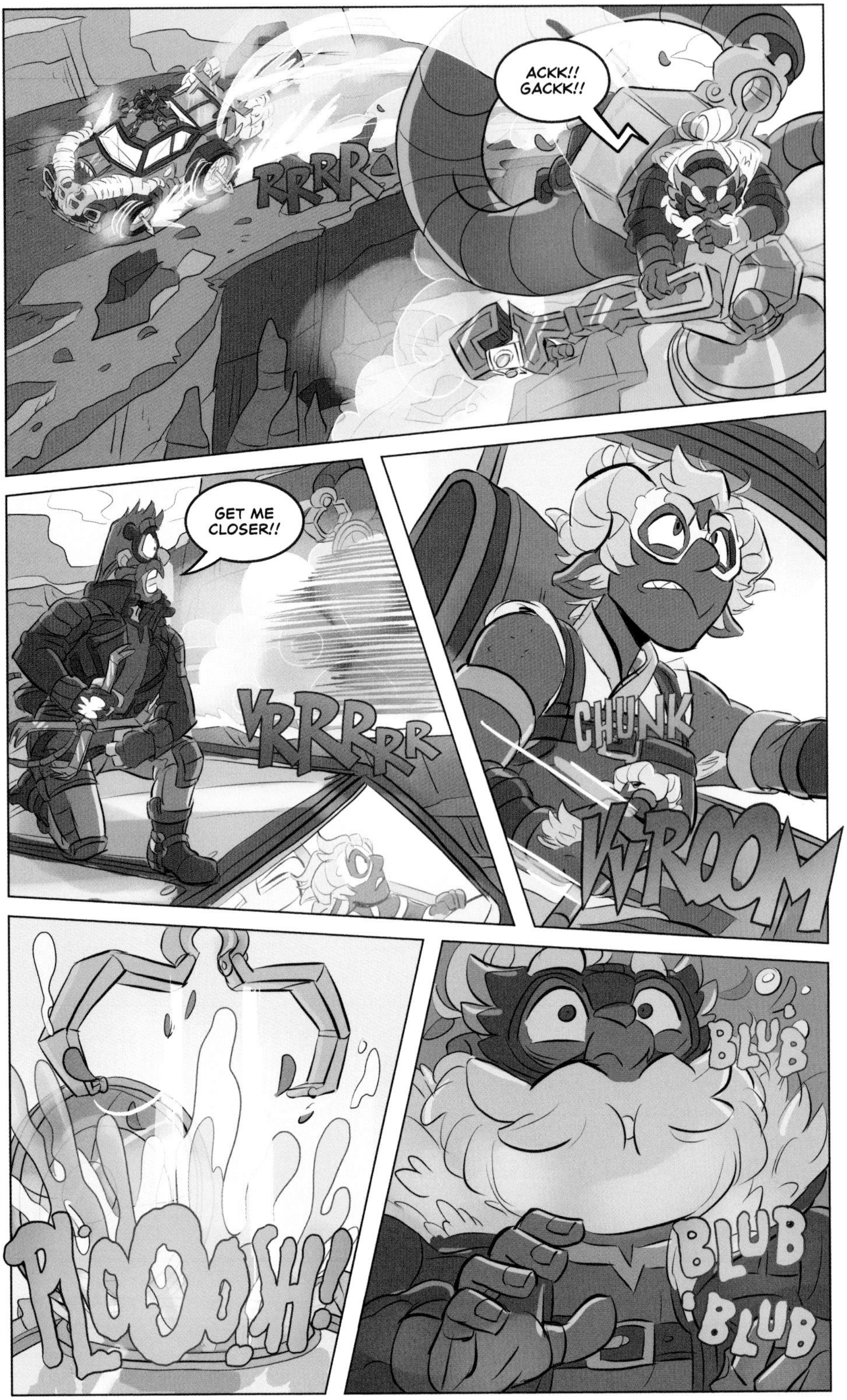
RRRR
ACKK!!
GACKK!!
GET ME
CLOSER!!
VRRRRR
CHUNK
VROOM
PLOOOSH!
BLUB
BLUB
BLUB

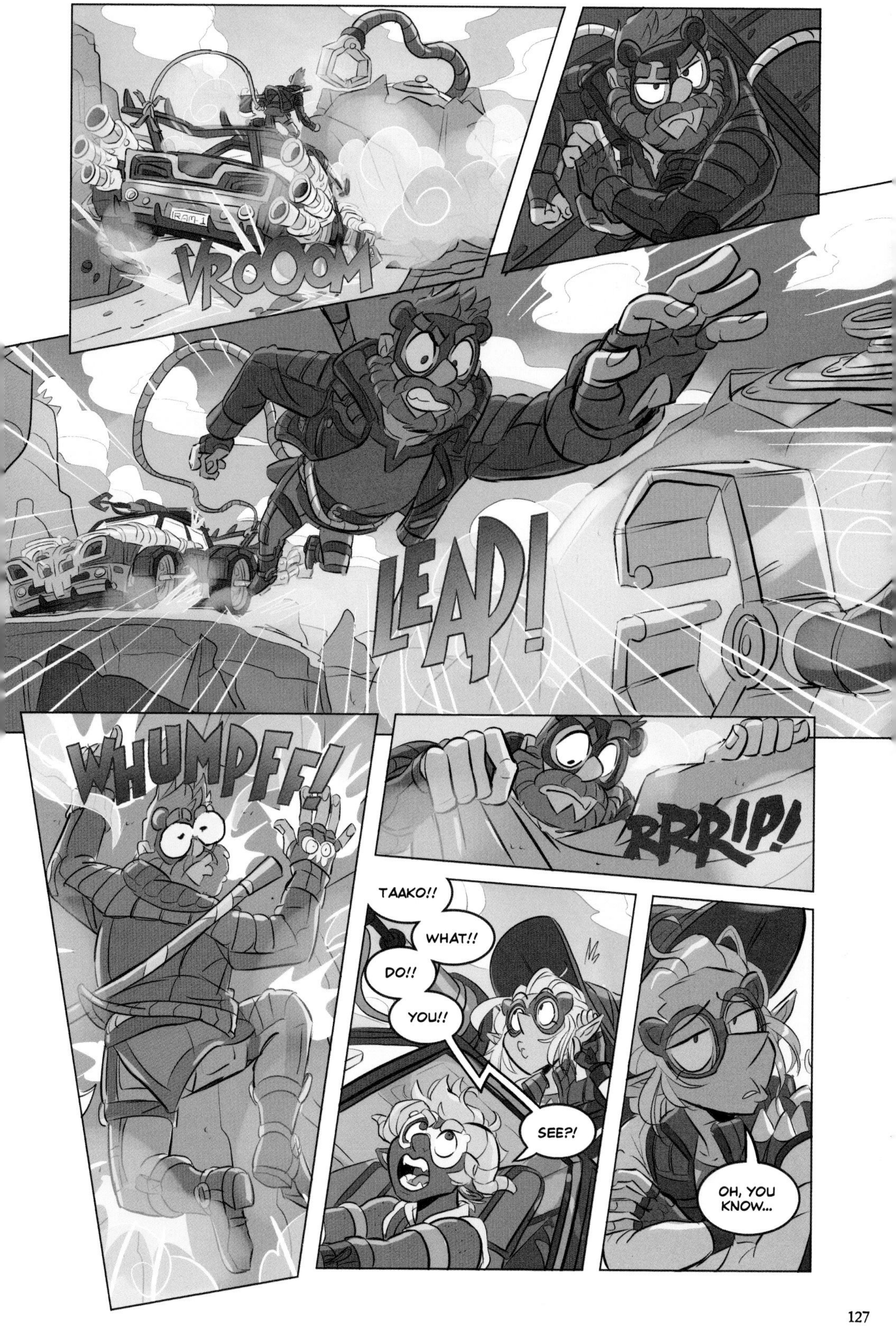
RAM-1
VROOOM
LEAP!
WHUMPFF!
RRRIP!
TAAKO!!
WHAT!!
DO!!
YOU!!
SEE?!
OH, YOU KNOW...

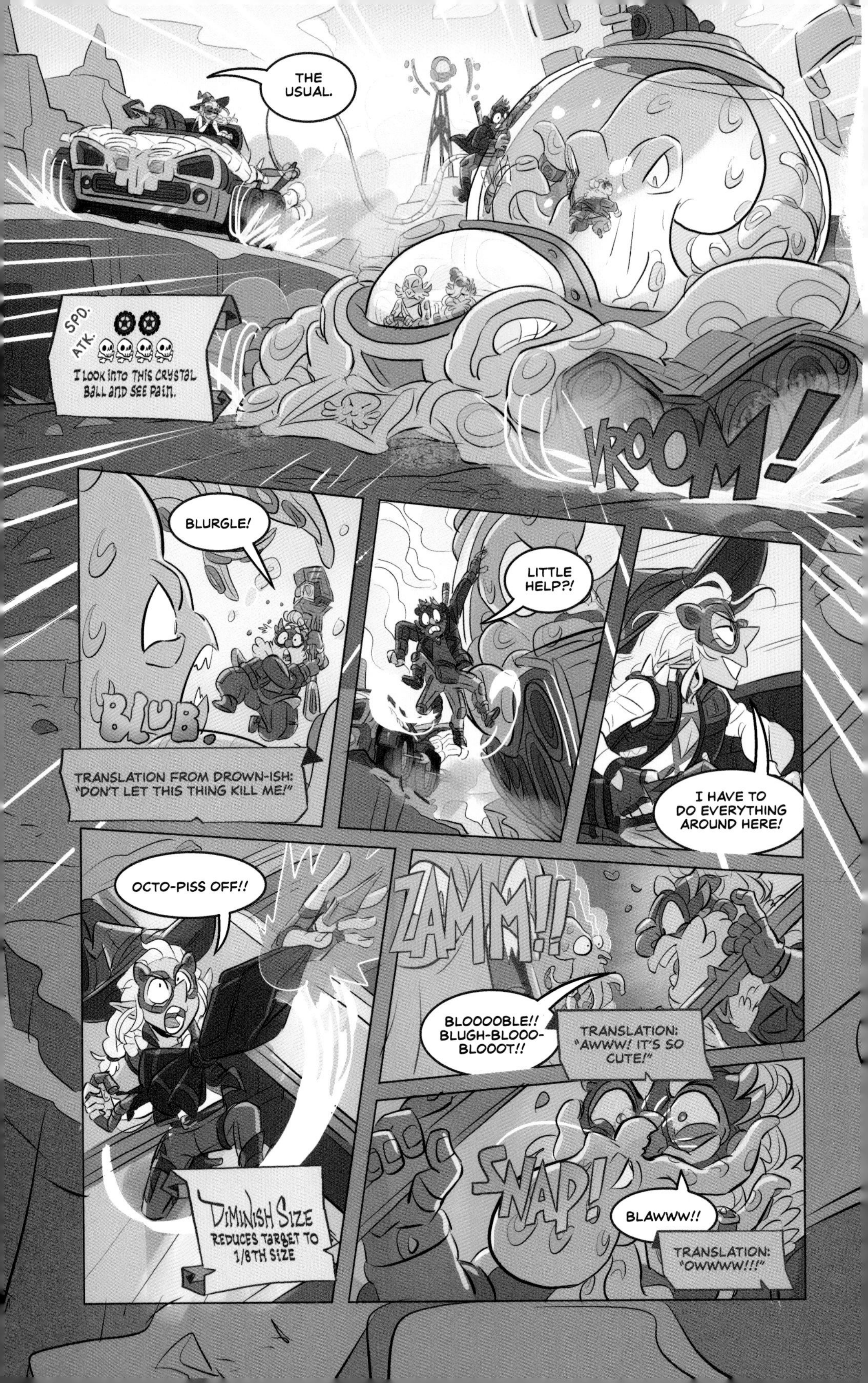
THE USUAL.
SPD.
ATK.
I LOOK INTO THIS CRYSTAL BALL AND SEE PAIN.
VROOM!
BLURGLE!
BLUB
TRANSLATION FROM DROWN-ISH: "DON'T LET THIS THING KILL ME!"
LITTLE HELP?!
I HAVE TO DO EVERYTHING AROUND HERE!
OCTO-PISS OFF!!
DIMINISH SIZE
REDUCES TARGET TO 1/8TH SIZE
ZAMM!!
BLOOOOBLE!! BLUGH-BLOOO-BLOOOT!!
TRANSLATION: "AWWW! IT'S SO CUTE!"
SNAP!
BLAWWW!!
TRANSLATION: "OWWWW!!!"

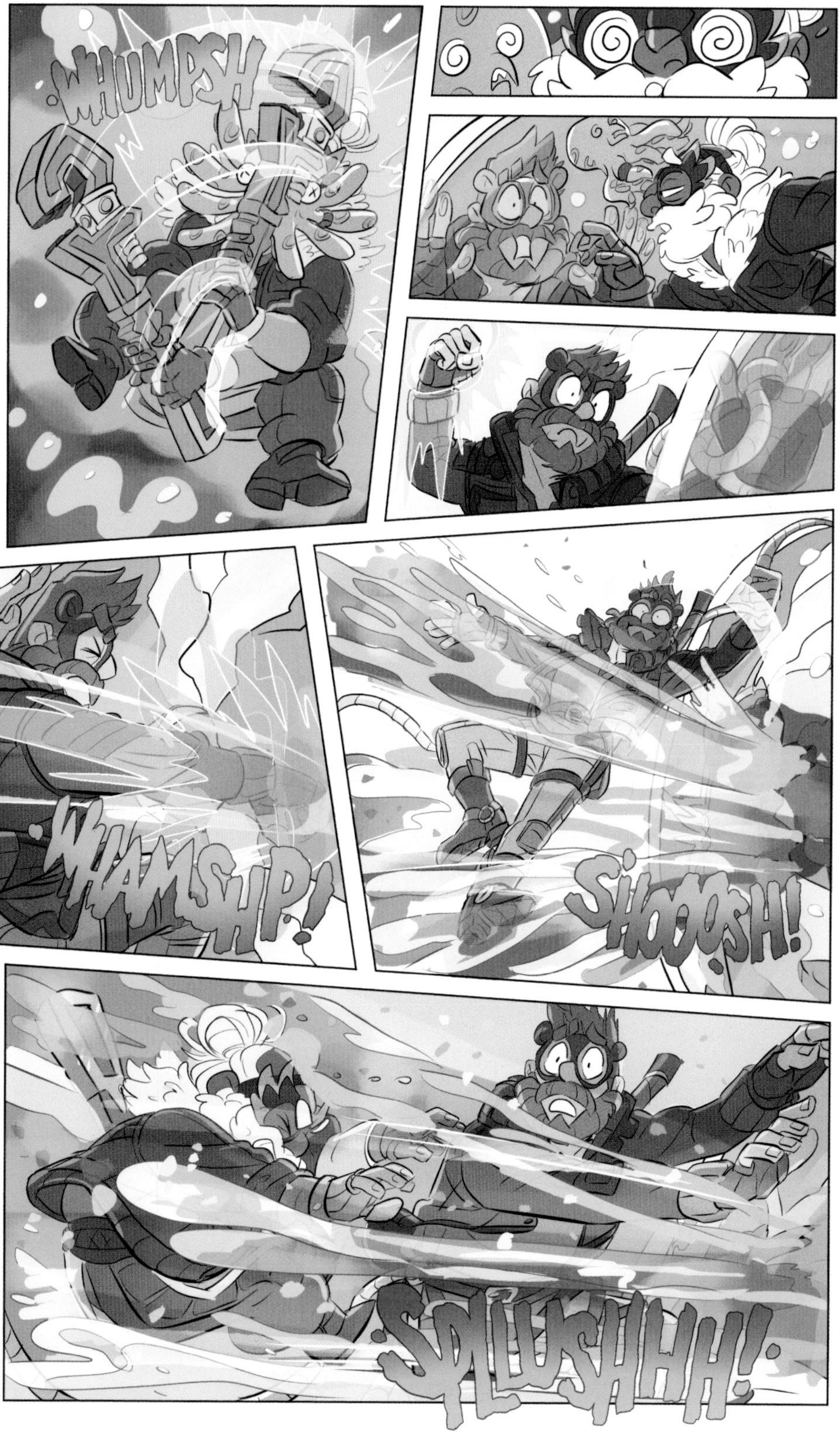
WHUMPSH
WHAMSHP!
SHOOOSH!
SPLUSHHH!

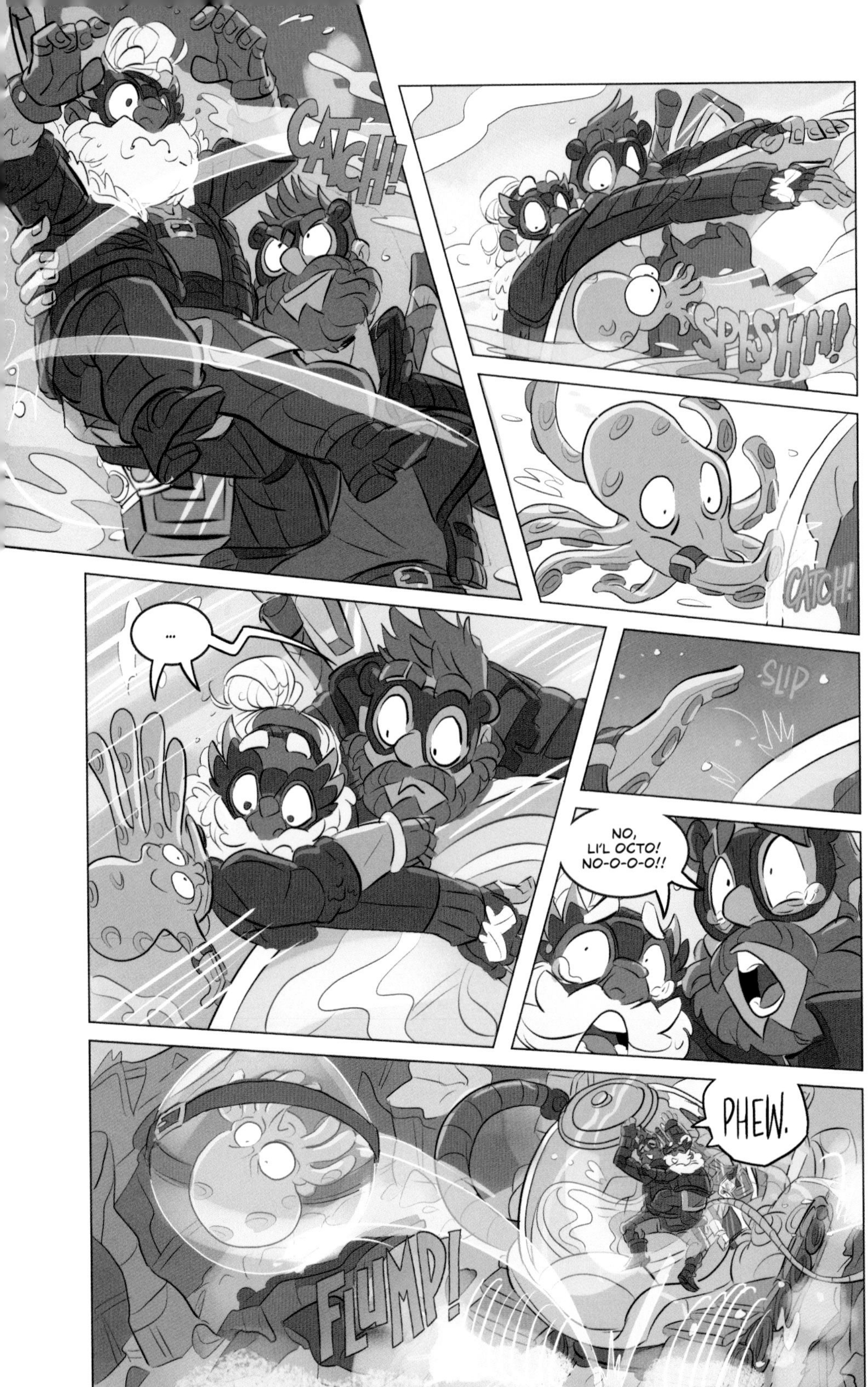
CATCH!
SPLSHH!
CATCH!
...
SLIP
NO, LI'L OCTO! NO-O-O-O!!
PHEW.
FLUMP!

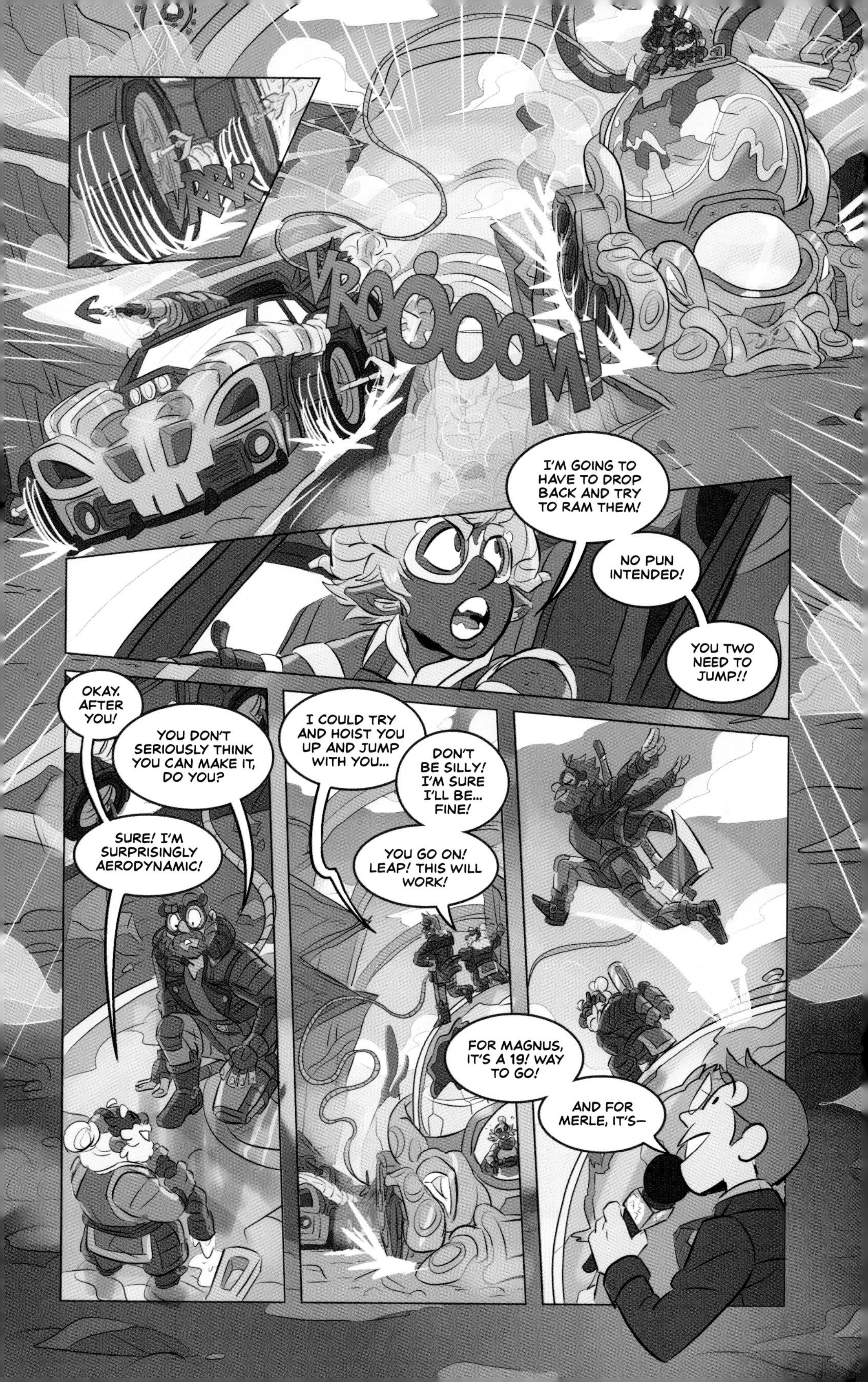
VRRR
VROOOOOM!
I'M GOING TO HAVE TO DROP BACK AND TRY TO RAM THEM!
NO PUN INTENDED!
YOU TWO NEED TO JUMP!!
OKAY. AFTER YOU!
YOU DON'T SERIOUSLY THINK YOU CAN MAKE IT, DO YOU?
SURE! I'M SURPRISINGLY AERODYNAMIC!
I COULD TRY AND HOIST YOU UP AND JUMP WITH YOU...
DON'T BE SILLY! I'M SURE I'LL BE... FINE!
YOU GO ON! LEAP! THIS WILL WORK!
FOR MAGNUS, IT'S A 19! WAY TO GO!
AND FOR MERLE, IT'S—

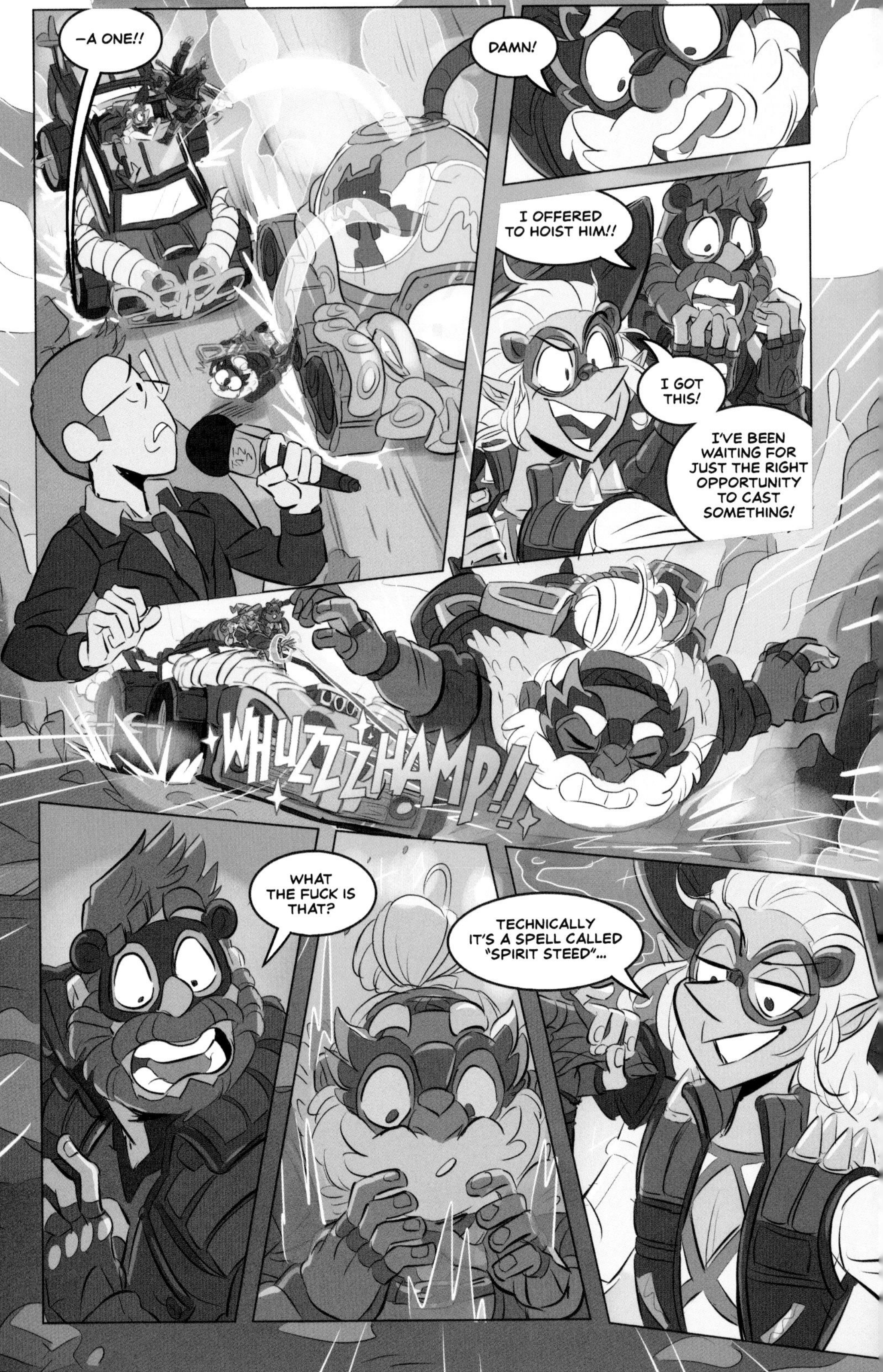
—A ONE!!
DAMN!
I OFFERED TO HOIST HIM!!
I GOT THIS!
I'VE BEEN WAITING FOR JUST THE RIGHT OPPORTUNITY TO CAST SOMETHING!
WHUZZZHAMP!!
WHAT THE FUCK IS THAT?
TECHNICALLY IT'S A SPELL CALLED "SPIRIT STEED"...

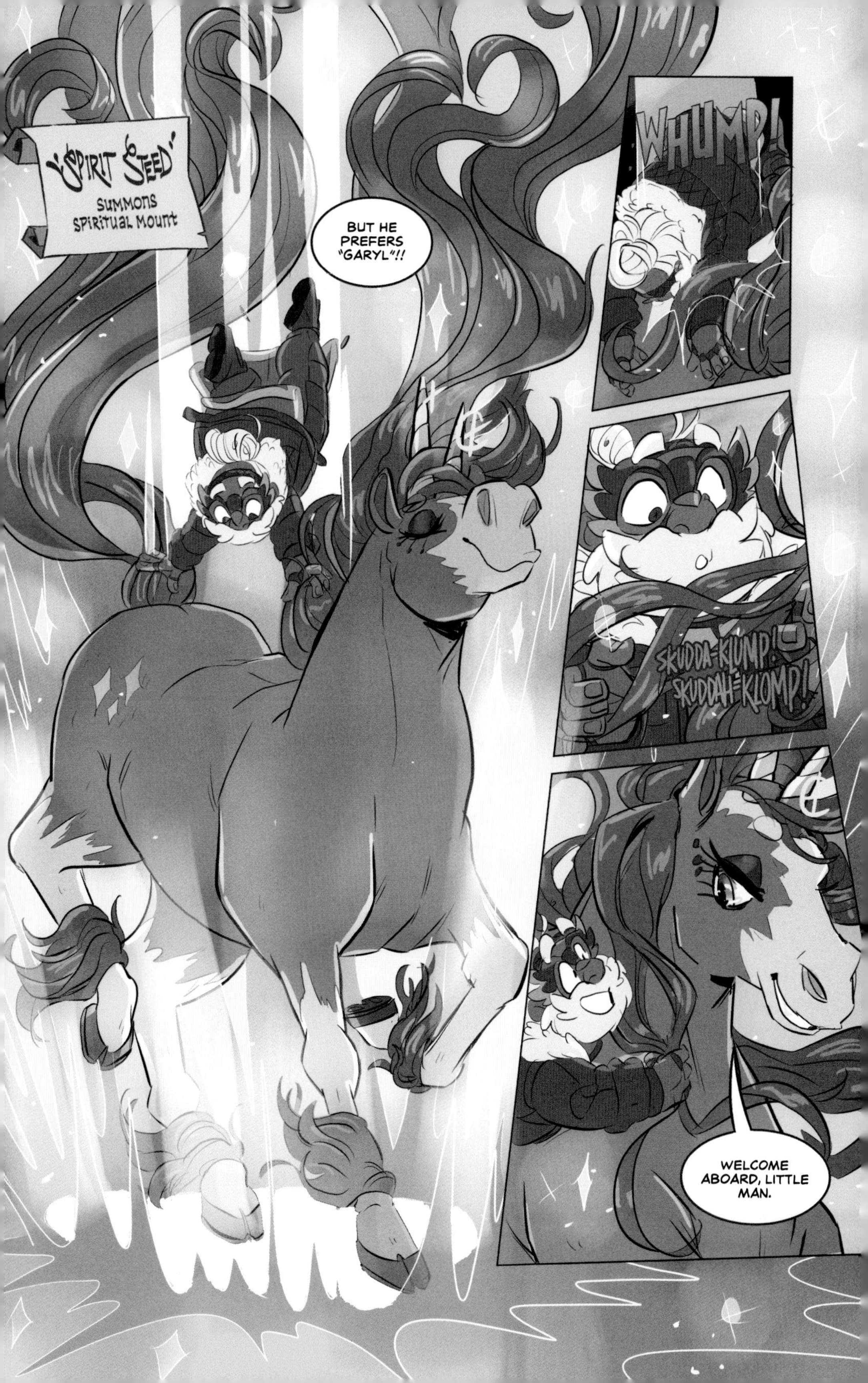
SPIRIT STEED
SUMMONS SPIRITUAL MOUNT
BUT HE PREFERS "GARYL"!!
WHUMP!
SKUDDA-KLUMP! SKUDDAH-KLOMP!
WELCOME ABOARD, LITTLE MAN.

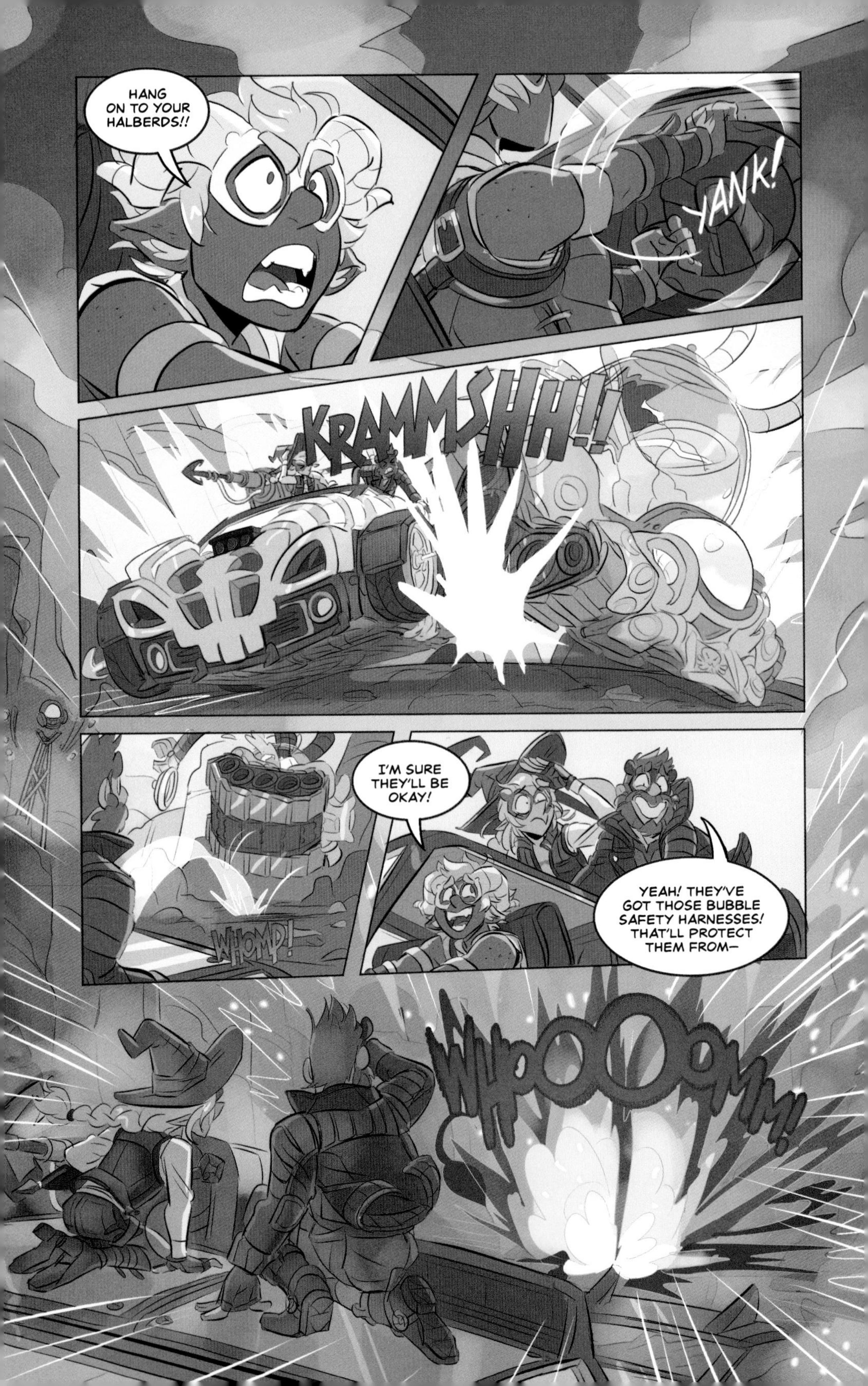
HANG ON TO YOUR HALBERDS!!
YANK!
KRAMMSHH!!
WHOMP!
I'M SURE THEY'LL BE OKAY!
YEAH! THEY'VE GOT THOSE BUBBLE SAFETY HARNESSES! THAT'LL PROTECT THEM FROM—
WHOOOOMM!

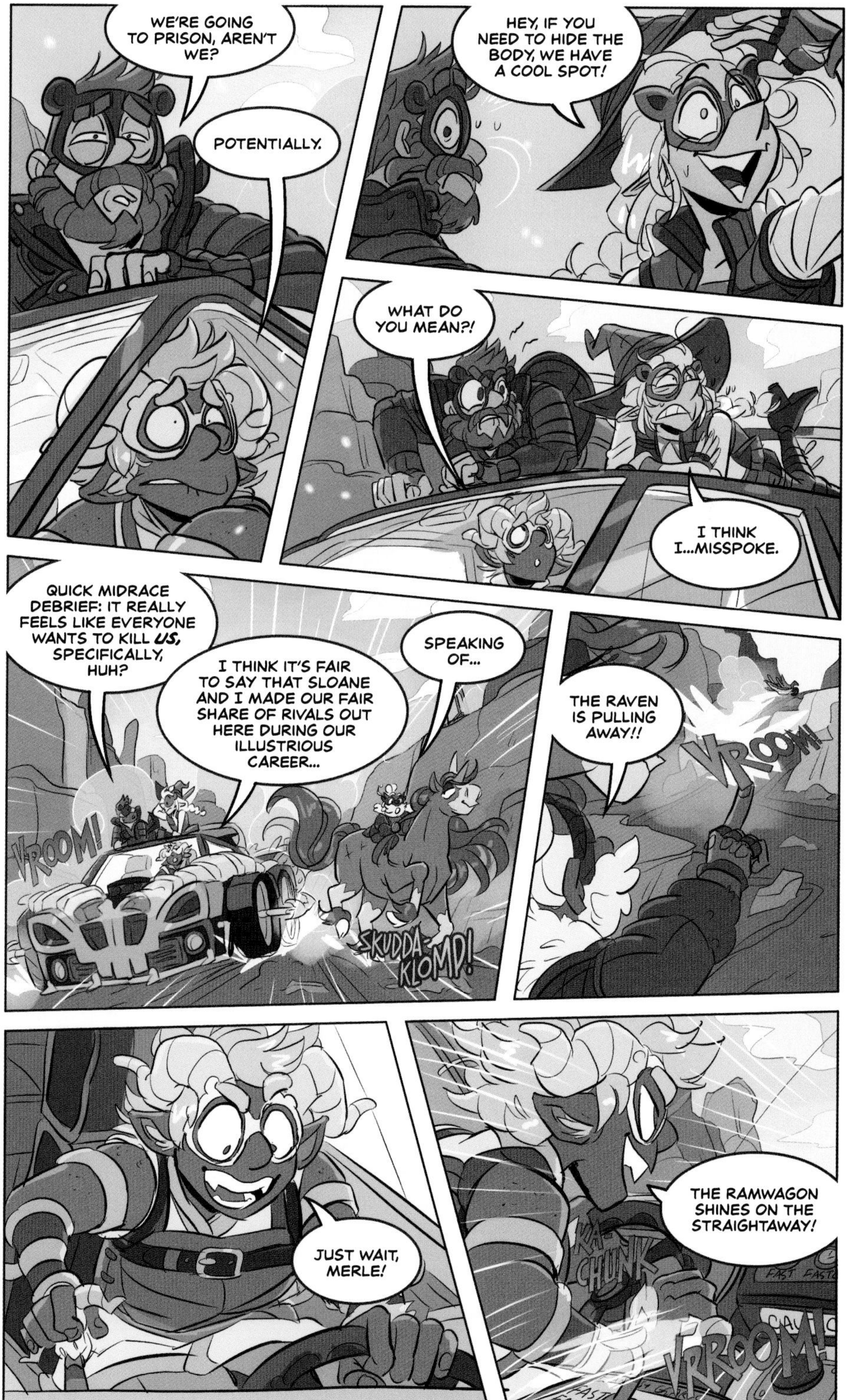
WE'RE GOING TO PRISON, AREN'T WE?
POTENTIALLY.
HEY, IF YOU NEED TO HIDE THE BODY, WE HAVE A COOL SPOT!
WHAT DO YOU MEAN?!
I THINK I...MISSPOKE.
QUICK MIDRACE DEBRIEF: IT REALLY FEELS LIKE EVERYONE WANTS TO KILL US, SPECIFICALLY, HUH?
I THINK IT'S FAIR TO SAY THAT SLOANE AND I MADE OUR FAIR SHARE OF RIVALS OUT HERE DURING OUR ILLUSTRIOUS CAREER...
SPEAKING OF...
VROOM!
SKUDDA-KLOMP!
THE RAVEN IS PULLING AWAY!!
VROOM!
JUST WAIT, MERLE!
THE RAMWAGON SHINES ON THE STRAIGHTAWAY!
KA-CHUNK
VRROOM!

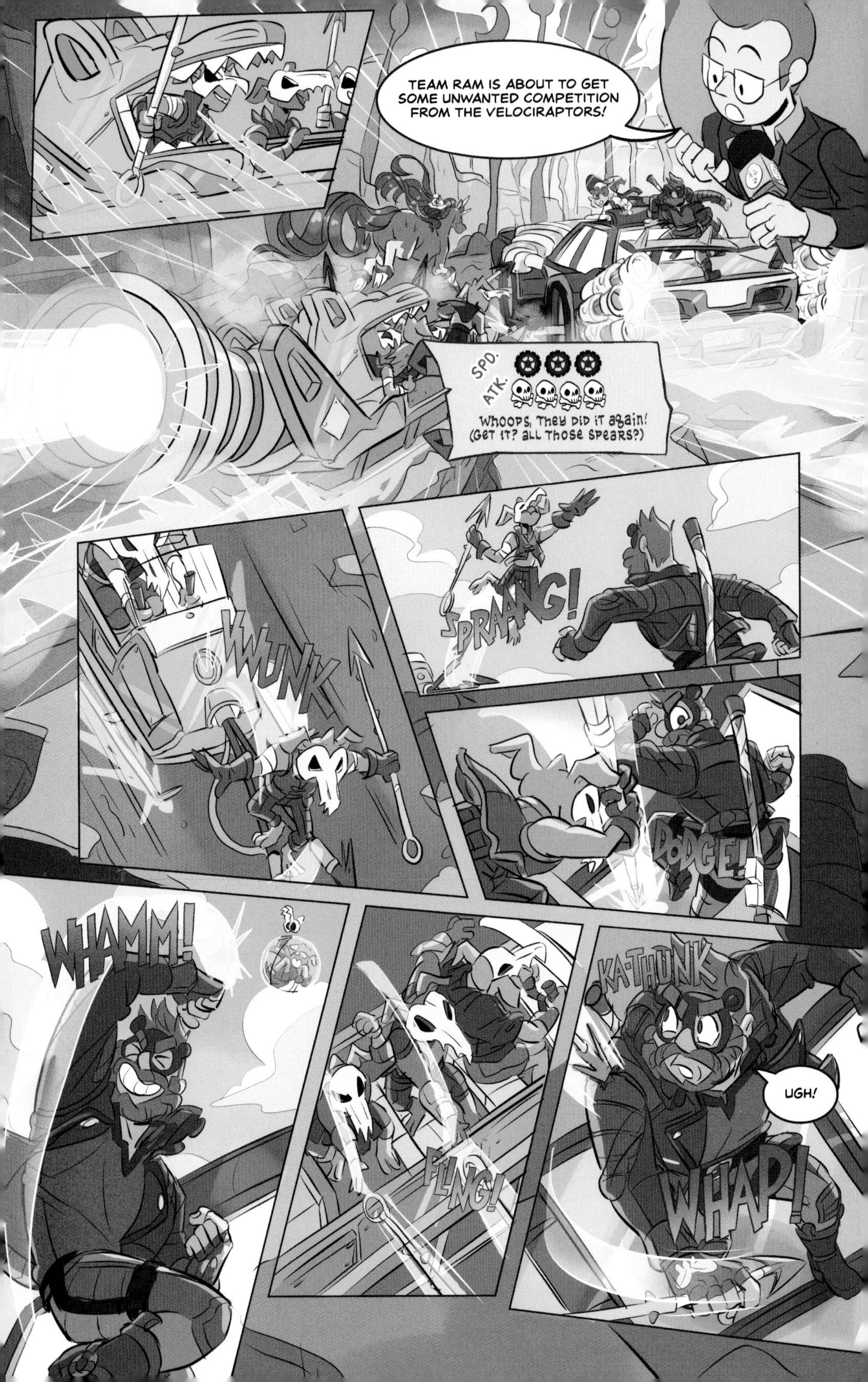
TEAM RAM IS ABOUT TO GET SOME UNWANTED COMPETITION FROM THE VELOCIRAPTORS!
SPD.
ATK.
Whoops, They did it again! (Get it? all those spears?)
WWUNK
SPRAANG!
DODGE!
WHAMM!
FLING!
KA-THUNK
UGH!
WHAP!

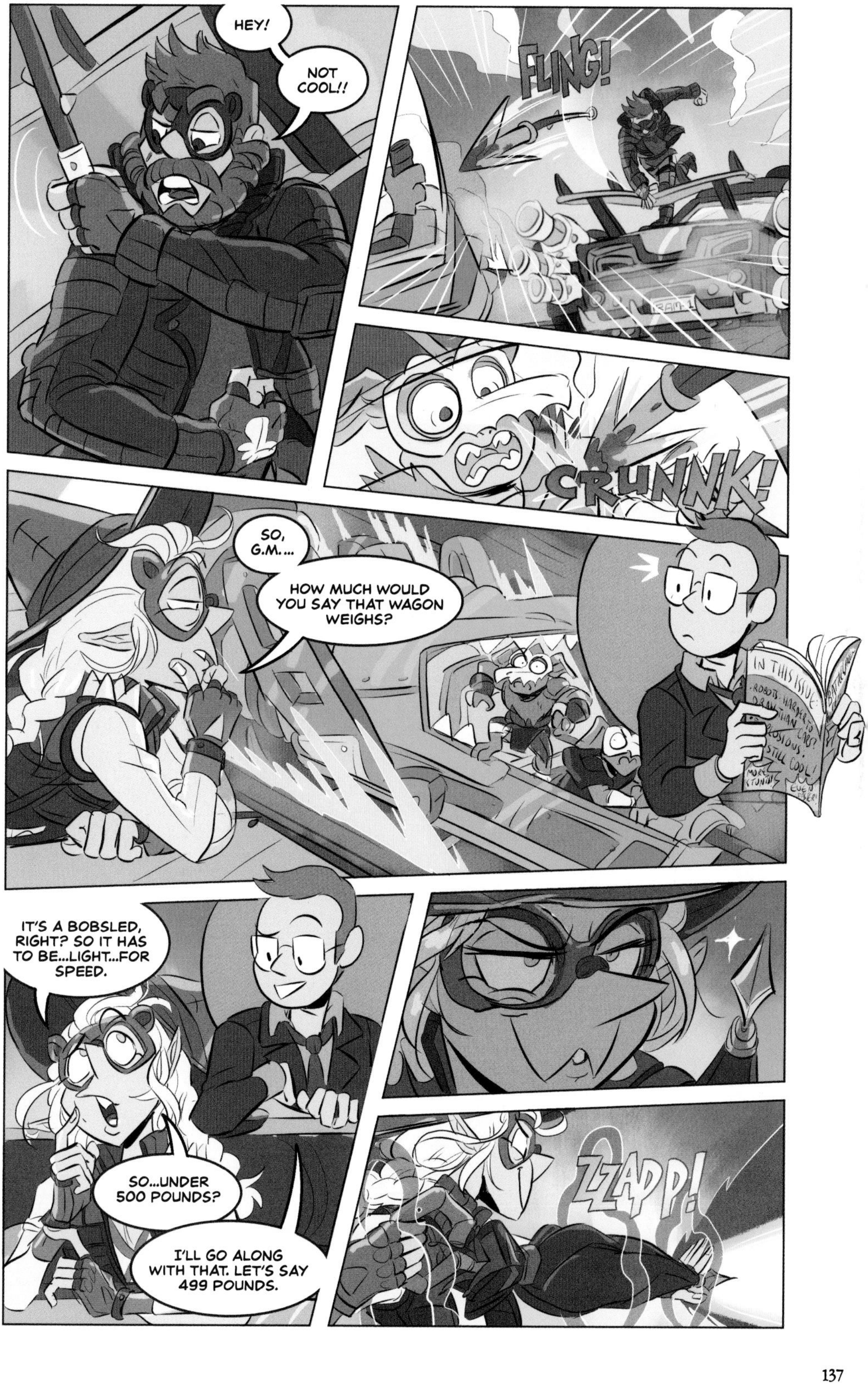
HEY!
NOT COOL!!
FLING!
RAM-1
CRUNNK!
SO, G.M....
HOW MUCH WOULD YOU SAY THAT WAGON WEIGHS?
IN THIS ISSUE
IT'S A BOBSLED, RIGHT? SO IT HAS TO BE...LIGHT...FOR SPEED.
SO...UNDER 500 POUNDS?
I'LL GO ALONG WITH THAT. LET'S SAY 499 POUNDS.
ZZAPP!

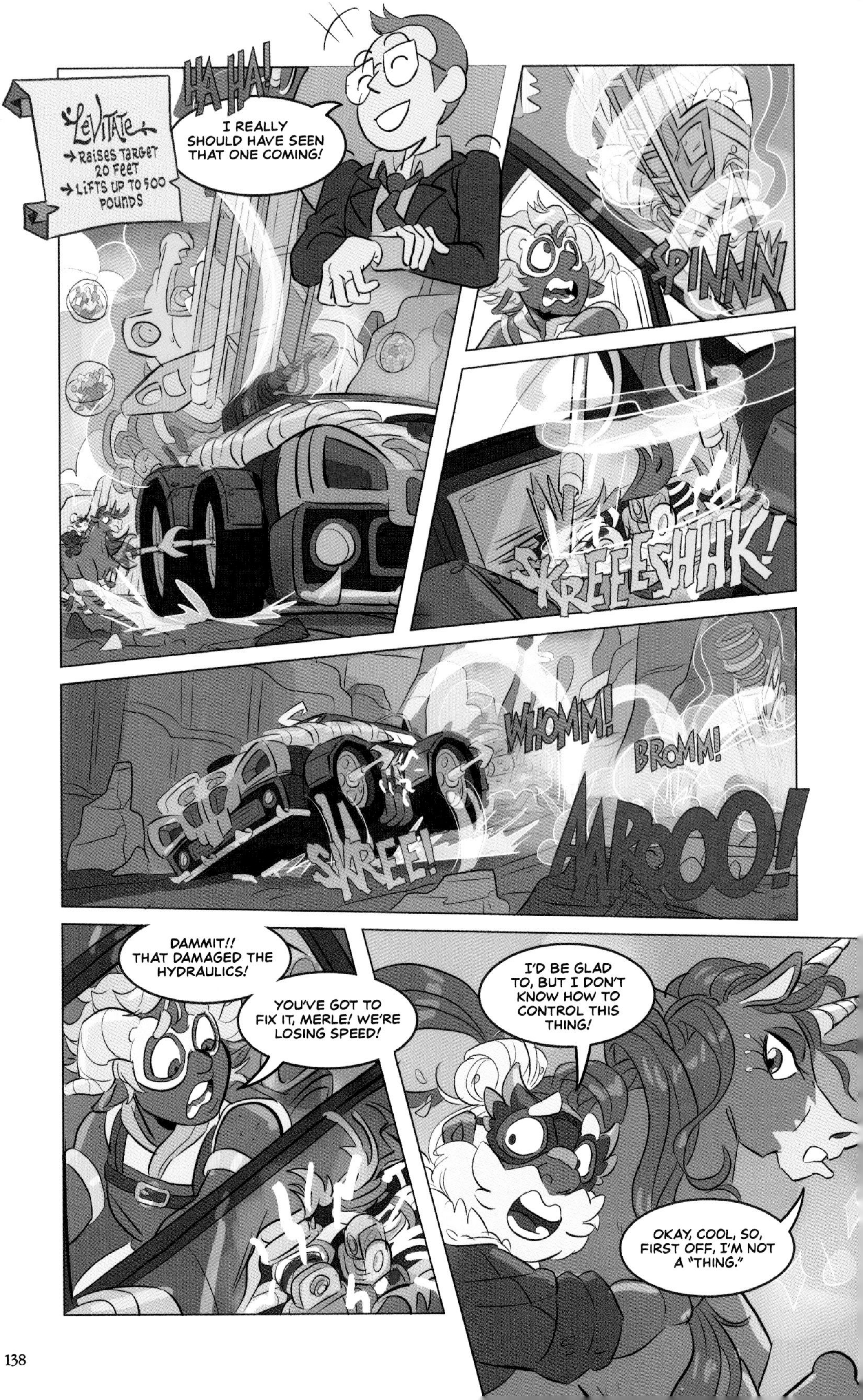
HA HA!
I REALLY SHOULD HAVE SEEN THAT ONE COMING!
Levitate
→ Raises target 20 feet
→ Lifts up to 500 pounds
SPINNN
SKREEESHHK!
WHOMM!
BROMM!
SKREEE!
AAROOO!
DAMMIT!! THAT DAMAGED THE HYDRAULICS!
YOU'VE GOT TO FIX IT, MERLE! WE'RE LOSING SPEED!
I'D BE GLAD TO, BUT I DON'T KNOW HOW TO CONTROL THIS THING!
OKAY, COOL, SO, FIRST OFF, I'M NOT A "THING."

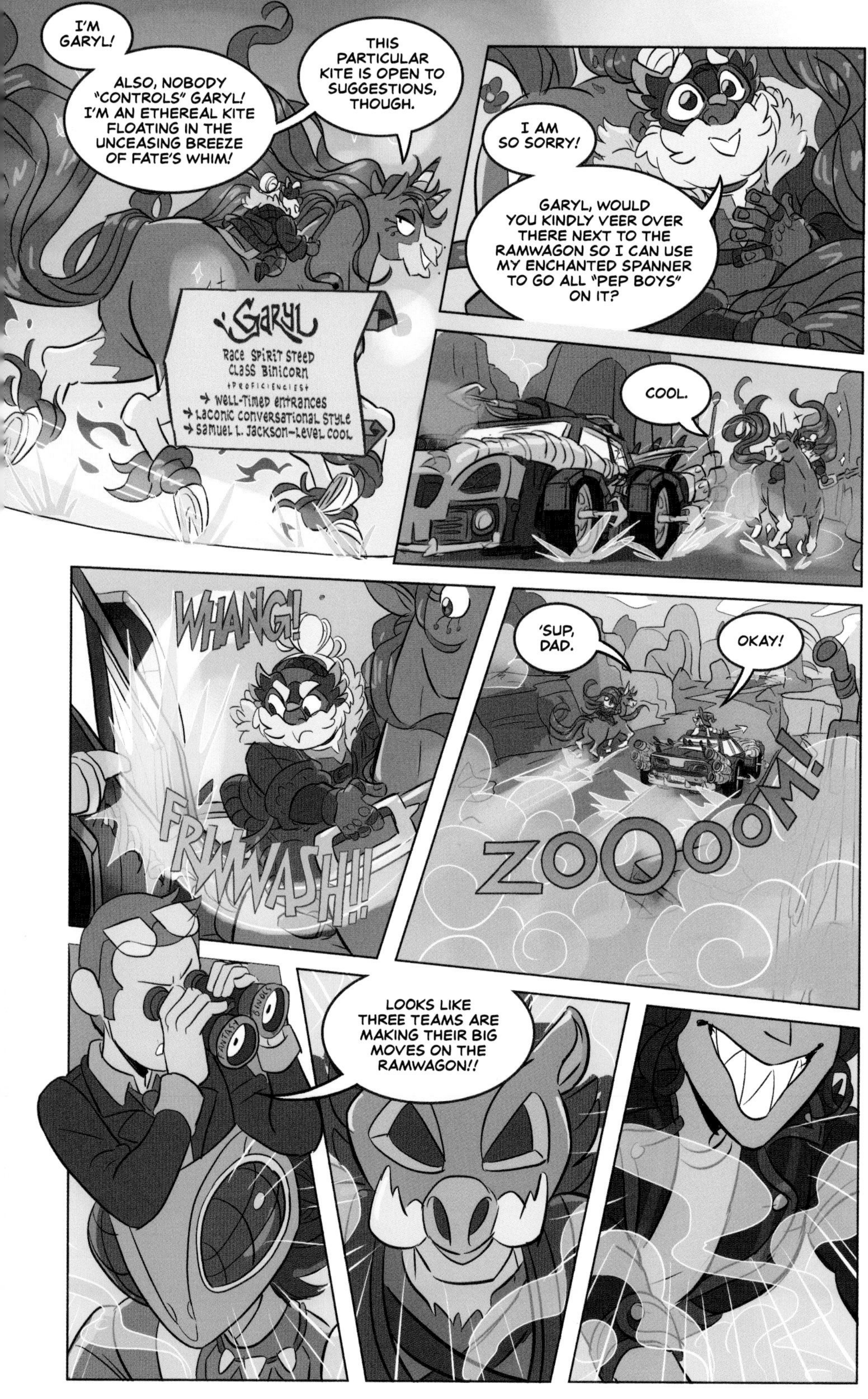
I'M GARYL!
ALSO, NOBODY "CONTROLS" GARYL! I'M AN ETHEREAL KITE FLOATING IN THE UNCEASING BREEZE OF FATE'S WHIM!
THIS PARTICULAR KITE IS OPEN TO SUGGESTIONS, THOUGH.
GARYL
Race Spirit Steed
Class Binicorn
Proficiencies
→ Well-Timed entrances
→ Laconic conversational style
→ Samuel L. Jackson-level cool
I AM SO SORRY!
GARYL, WOULD YOU KINDLY VEER OVER THERE NEXT TO THE RAMWAGON SO I CAN USE MY ENCHANTED SPANNER TO GO ALL "PEP BOYS" ON IT?
COOL.
WHANG!
FRWWASH!!
'SUP, DAD.
OKAY!
ZOOOOOM!
FANTASY BINOCS
LOOKS LIKE THREE TEAMS ARE MAKING THEIR BIG MOVES ON THE RAMWAGON!!

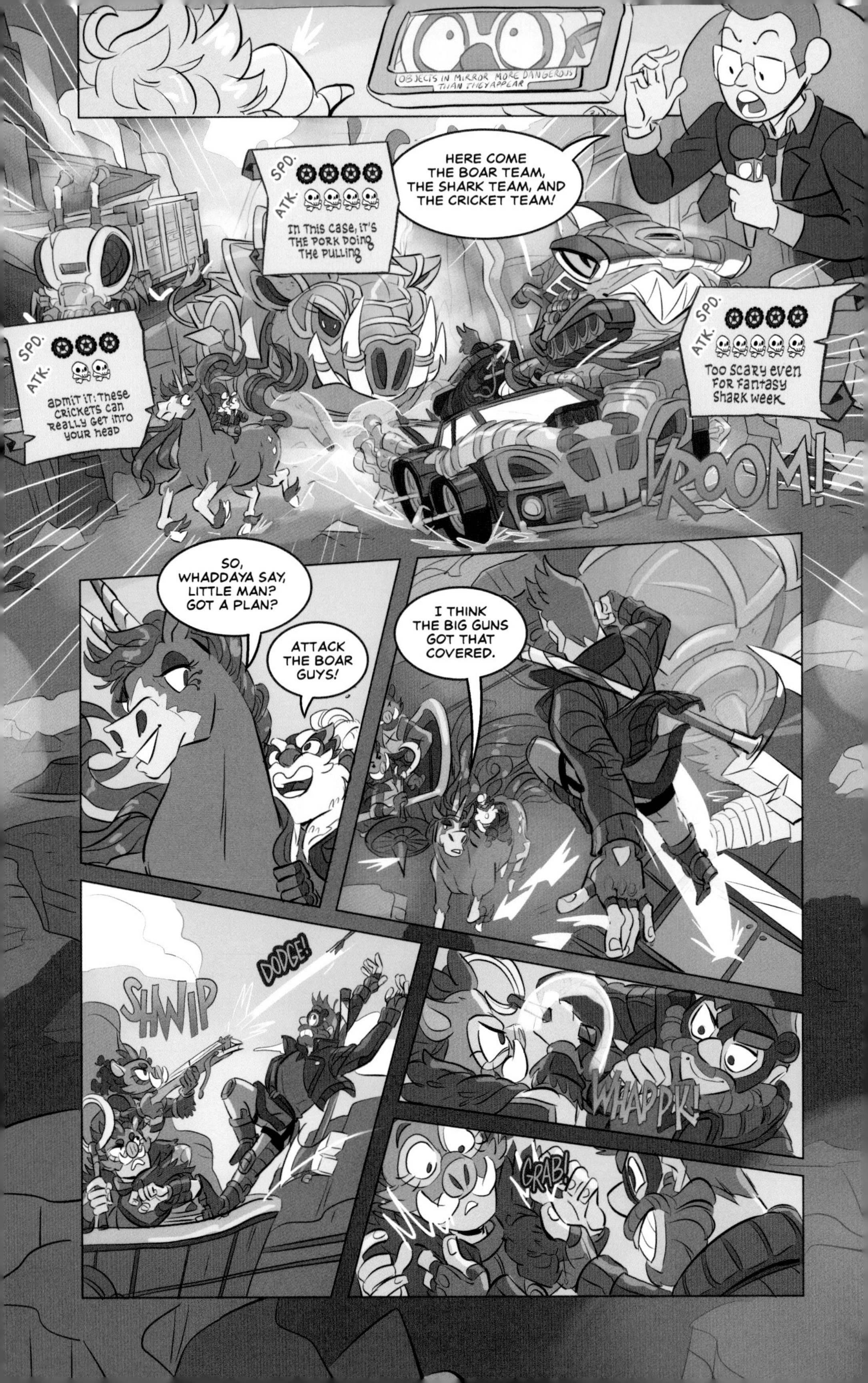
OBJECTS IN MIRROR MORE DANGEROUS THAN THEY APPEAR
SPD. ATK.
In this case, it's the pork doing the pulling
HERE COME THE BOAR TEAM, THE SHARK TEAM, AND THE CRICKET TEAM!
SPD. ATK.
admit it: these crickets can really get into your head
SPD. ATK.
Too scary even for fantasy shark week
VROOM!
SO, WHADDAYA SAY, LITTLE MAN? GOT A PLAN?
ATTACK THE BOAR GUYS!
I THINK THE BIG GUNS GOT THAT COVERED.
SHWIP
DODGE!
WHAPPK!
GRAB!

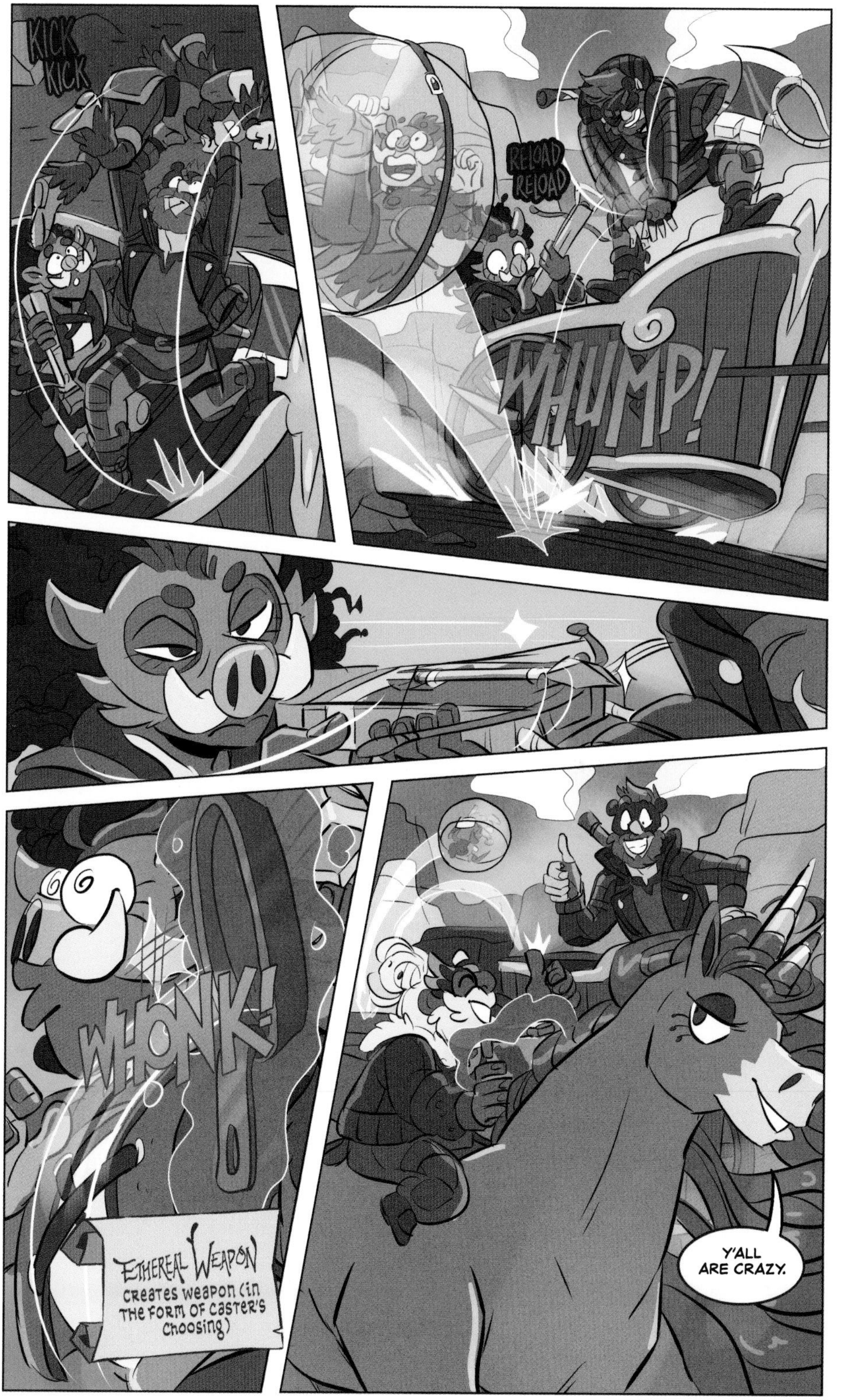
KICK KICK
RELOAD RELOAD
WHUMP!
WHONK!
ETHEREAL WEAPON
Creates weapon (in the form of caster's choosing)
Y'ALL ARE CRAZY.

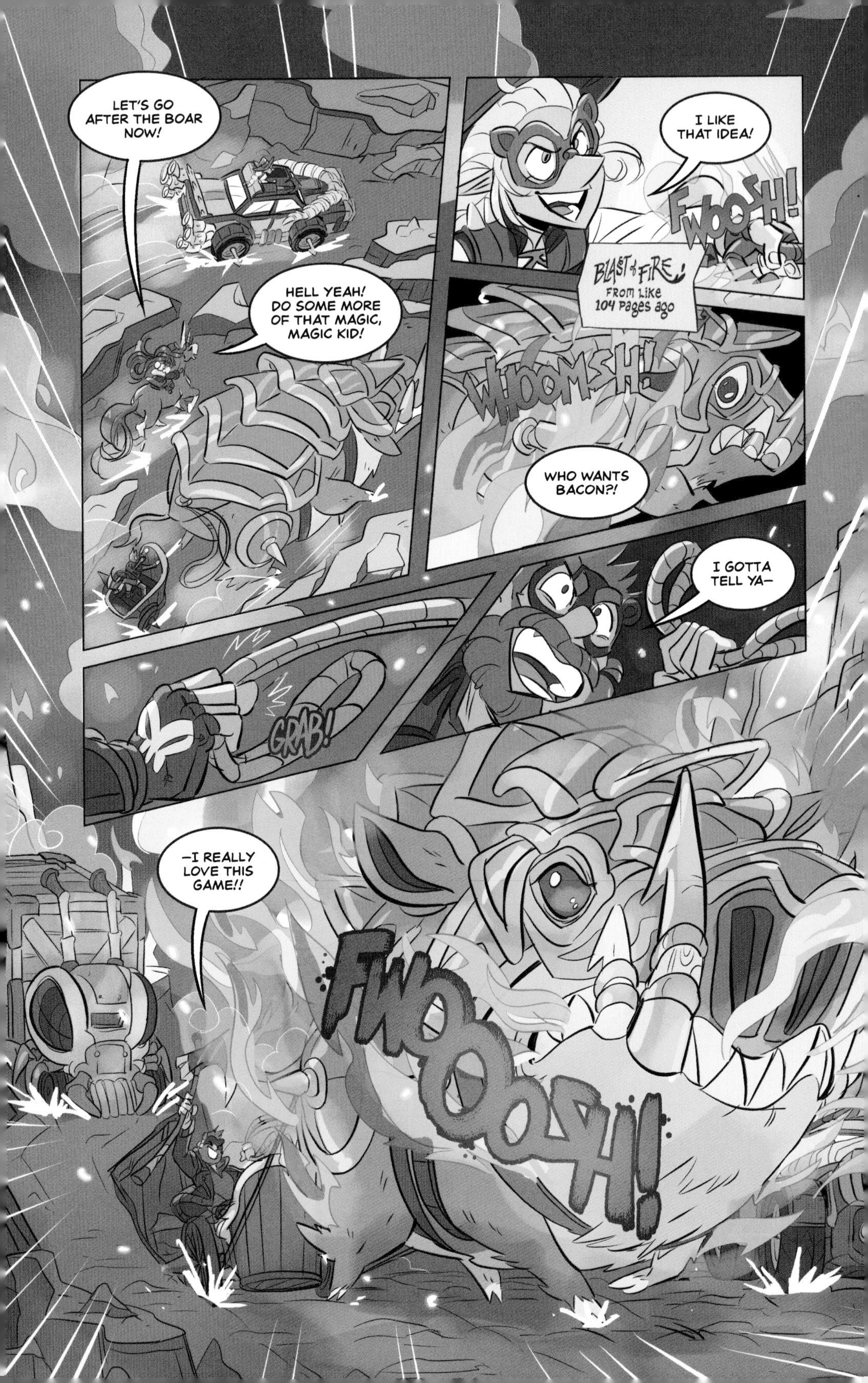
LET'S GO AFTER THE BOAR NOW!
I LIKE THAT IDEA!
FWOOSH!
HELL YEAH! DO SOME MORE OF THAT MAGIC, MAGIC KID!
BLAST of FIRE! FROM LIKE 104 pages ago
WHOOMSH!
WHO WANTS BACON?!
I GOTTA TELL YA—
GRAB!
—I REALLY LOVE THIS GAME!!
FWOOOSH!!

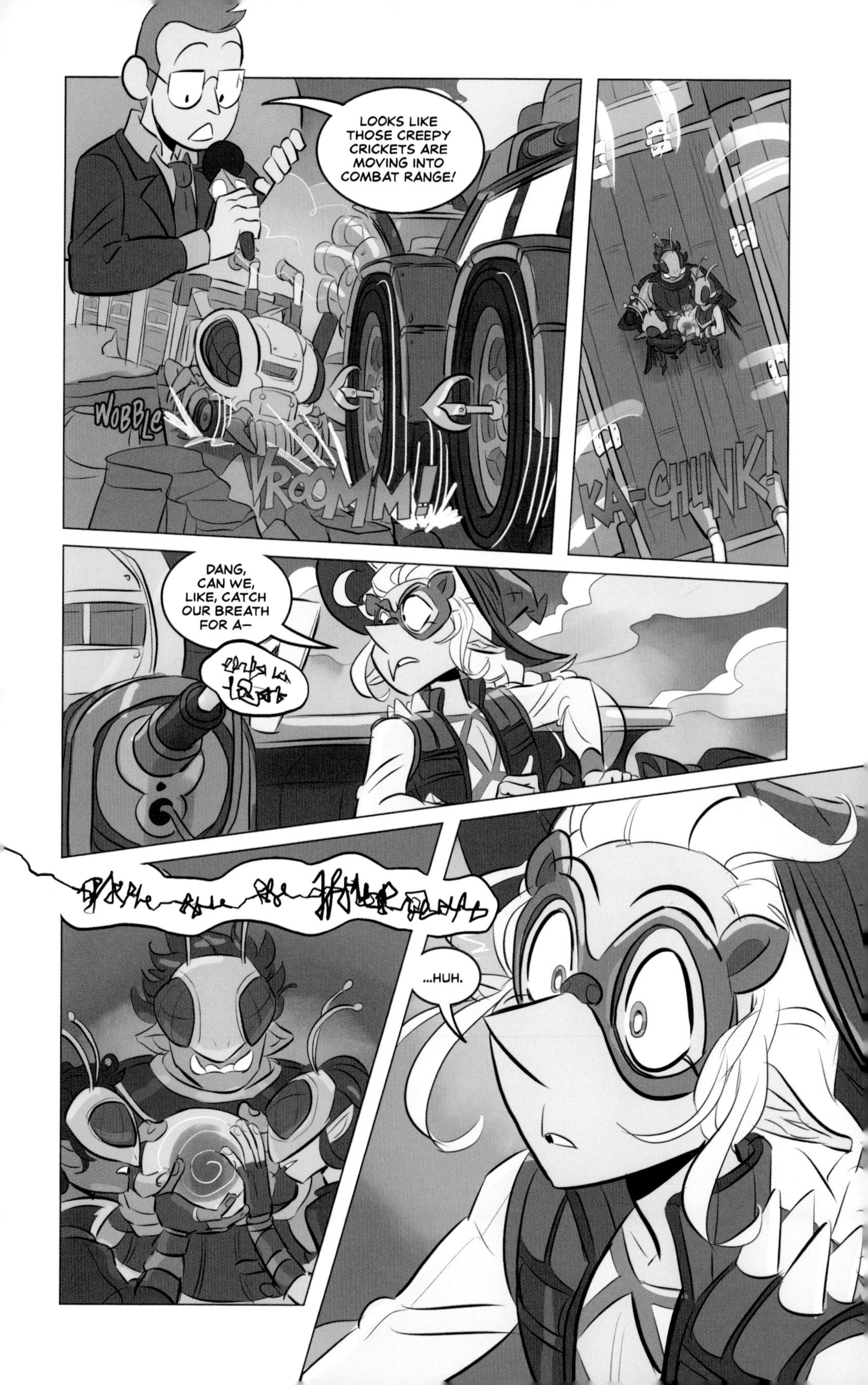
LOOKS LIKE THOSE CREEPY CRICKETS ARE MOVING INTO COMBAT RANGE!
WOBBLE
VROOMM!
KA-CHUNK!
DANG, CAN WE, LIKE, CATCH OUR BREATH FOR A–
...HUH.

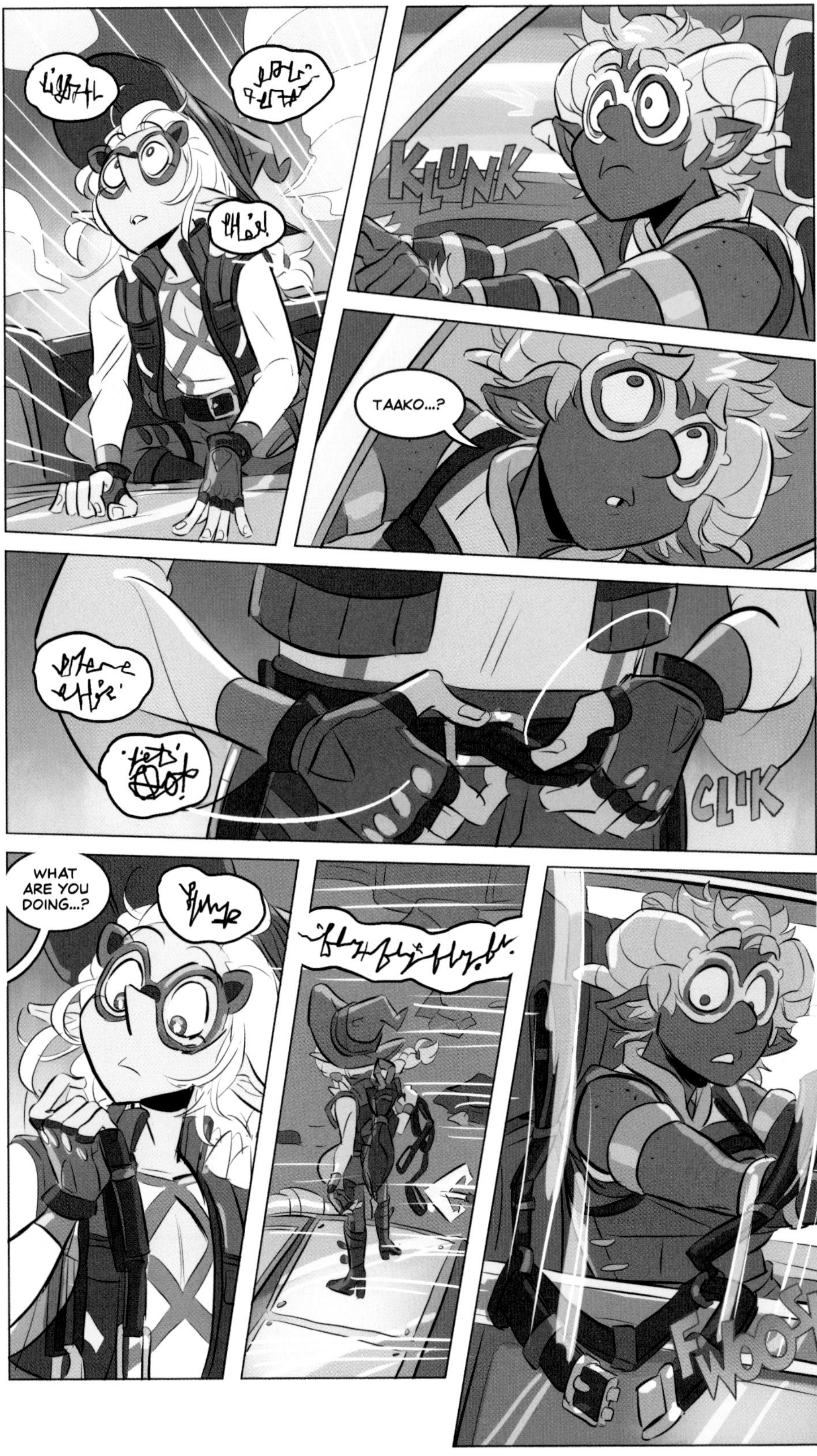
KLUNK
TAAKO...?
CLIK
WHAT ARE YOU DOING...?
FWOOSH!

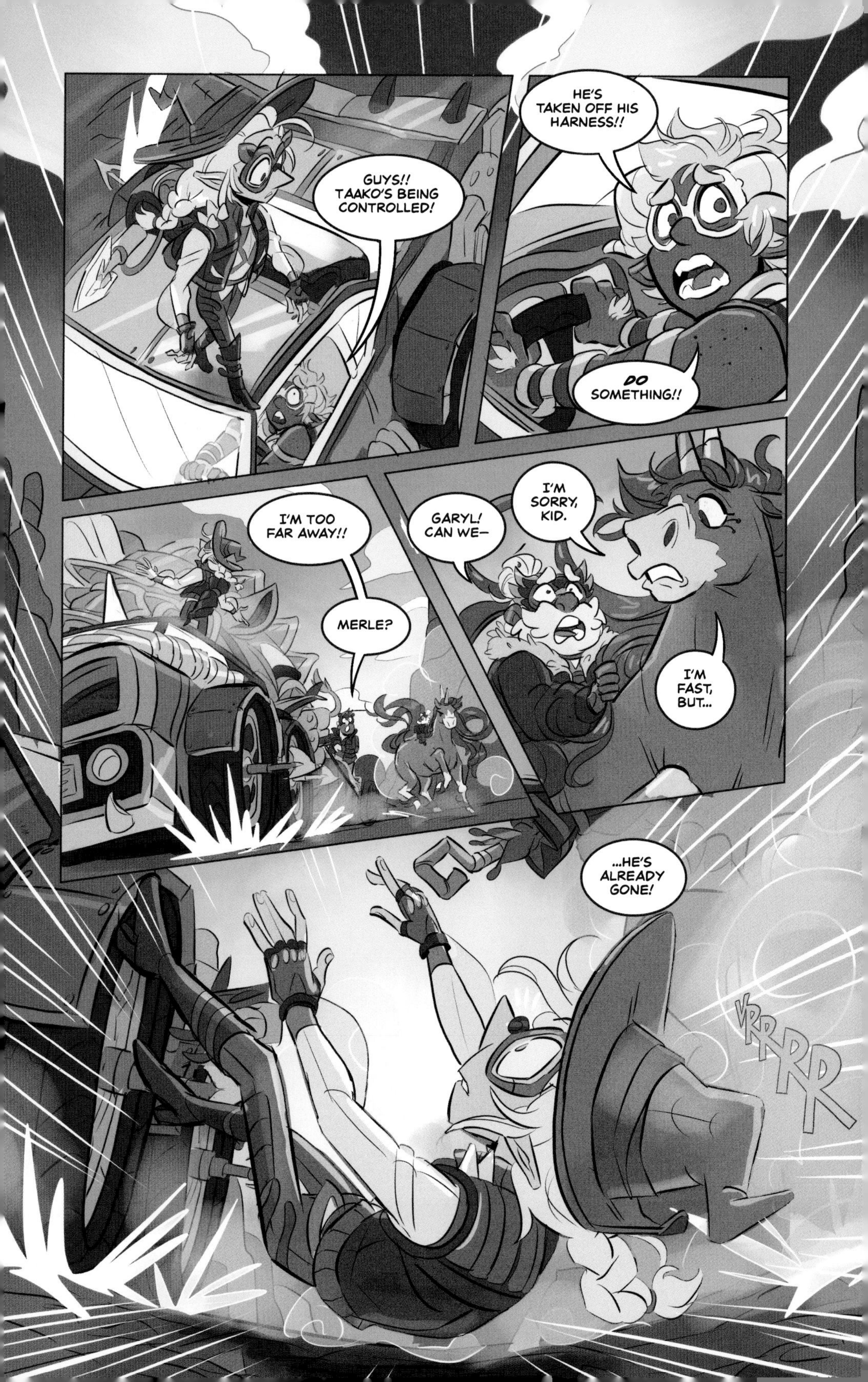
GUYS!! TAAKO'S BEING CONTROLLED!
HE'S TAKEN OFF HIS HARNESS!!
DO SOMETHING!!
I'M TOO FAR AWAY!!
MERLE?
GARYL! CAN WE–
I'M SORRY, KID.
I'M FAST, BUT...
...HE'S ALREADY GONE!
VRRRRR

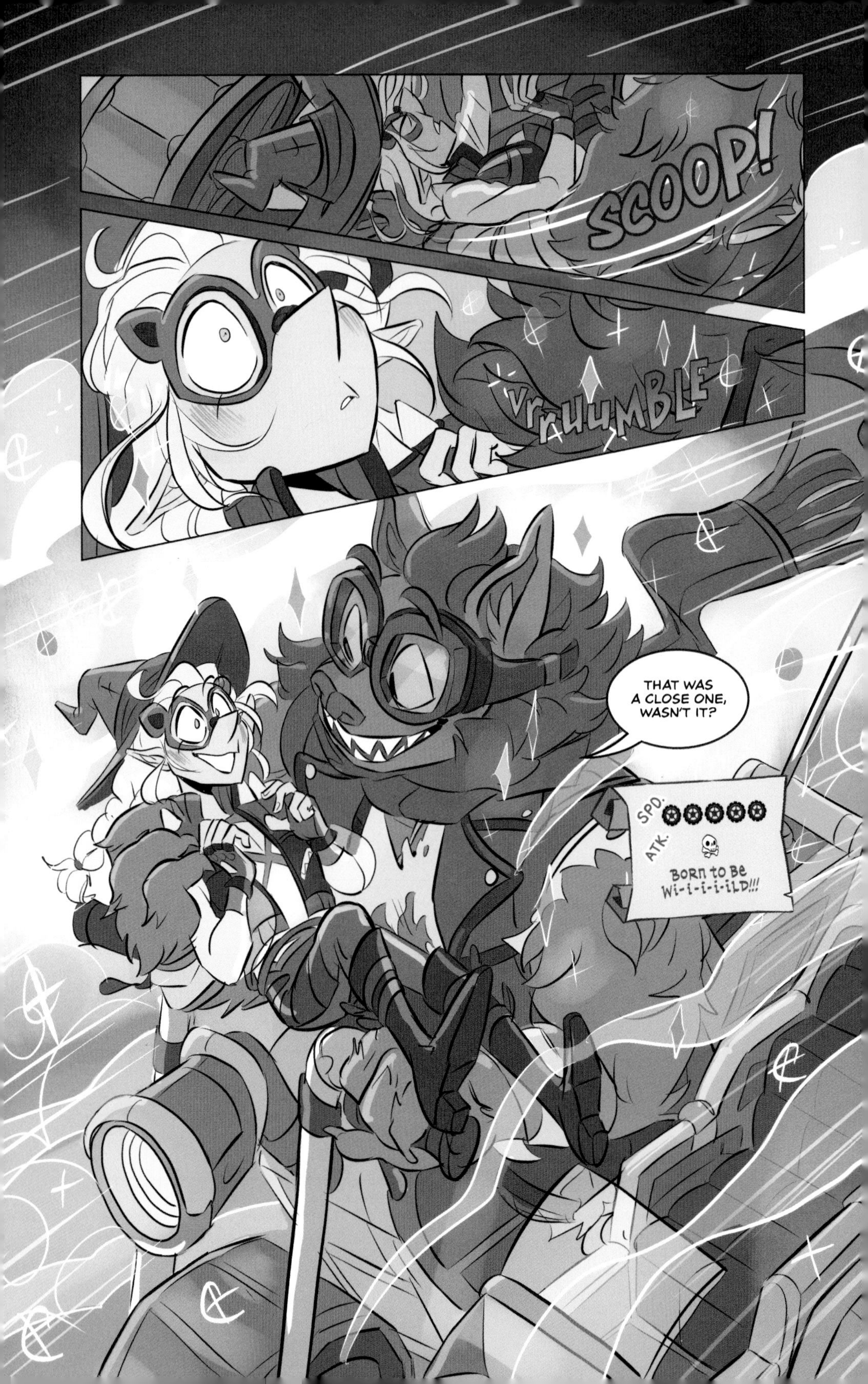
SCOOP!
VRRUUMBLE
THAT WAS A CLOSE ONE, WASN'T IT?
SPD.
ATK.
BORN TO BE WI-I-I-I-ILD!!!

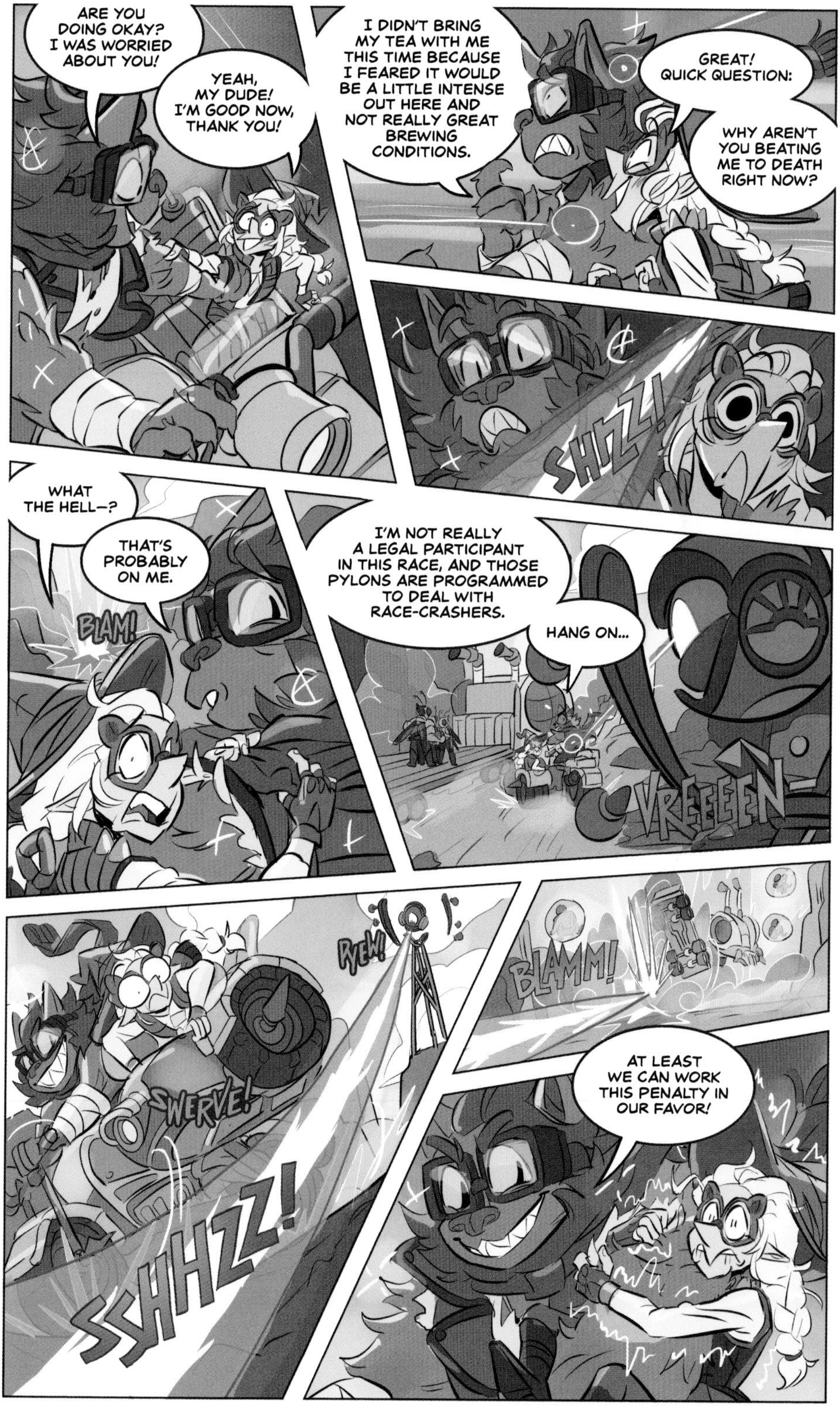

ARE YOU DOING OKAY? I WAS WORRIED ABOUT YOU!
YEAH, MY DUDE! I'M GOOD NOW, THANK YOU!
I DIDN'T BRING MY TEA WITH ME THIS TIME BECAUSE I FEARED IT WOULD BE A LITTLE INTENSE OUT HERE AND NOT REALLY GREAT BREWING CONDITIONS.
GREAT! QUICK QUESTION:
WHY AREN'T YOU BEATING ME TO DEATH RIGHT NOW?
SHIZZ!
WHAT THE HELL—?
THAT'S PROBABLY ON ME.
BLAM!
I'M NOT REALLY A LEGAL PARTICIPANT IN THIS RACE, AND THOSE PYLONS ARE PROGRAMMED TO DEAL WITH RACE-CRASHERS.
HANG ON...
VREEEEN-
PYEW!
SWERVE!
SSHHZZZ!
BLAMM!
AT LEAST WE CAN WORK THIS PENALTY IN OUR FAVOR!

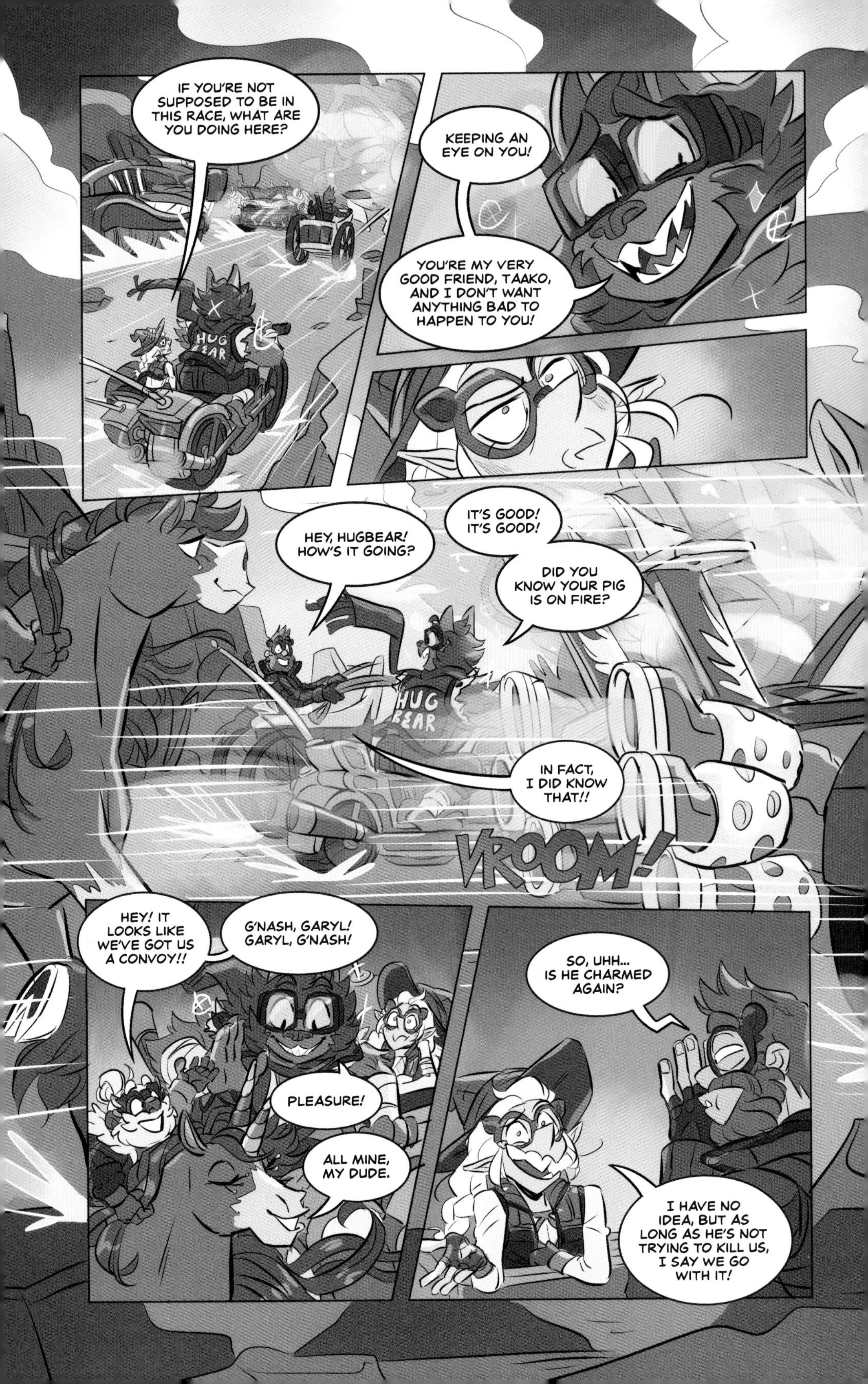
IF YOU'RE NOT SUPPOSED TO BE IN THIS RACE, WHAT ARE YOU DOING HERE?
HUG BEAR
KEEPING AN EYE ON YOU!
YOU'RE MY VERY GOOD FRIEND, TAAKO, AND I DON'T WANT ANYTHING BAD TO HAPPEN TO YOU!
HEY, HUGBEAR! HOW'S IT GOING?
IT'S GOOD! IT'S GOOD!
DID YOU KNOW YOUR PIG IS ON FIRE?
HUG BEAR
IN FACT, I DID KNOW THAT!!
VROOM!
HEY! IT LOOKS LIKE WE'VE GOT US A CONVOY!!
G'NASH, GARYL! GARYL, G'NASH!
PLEASURE!
ALL MINE, MY DUDE.
SO, UHH... IS HE CHARMED AGAIN?
I HAVE NO IDEA, BUT AS LONG AS HE'S NOT TRYING TO KILL US, I SAY WE GO WITH IT!

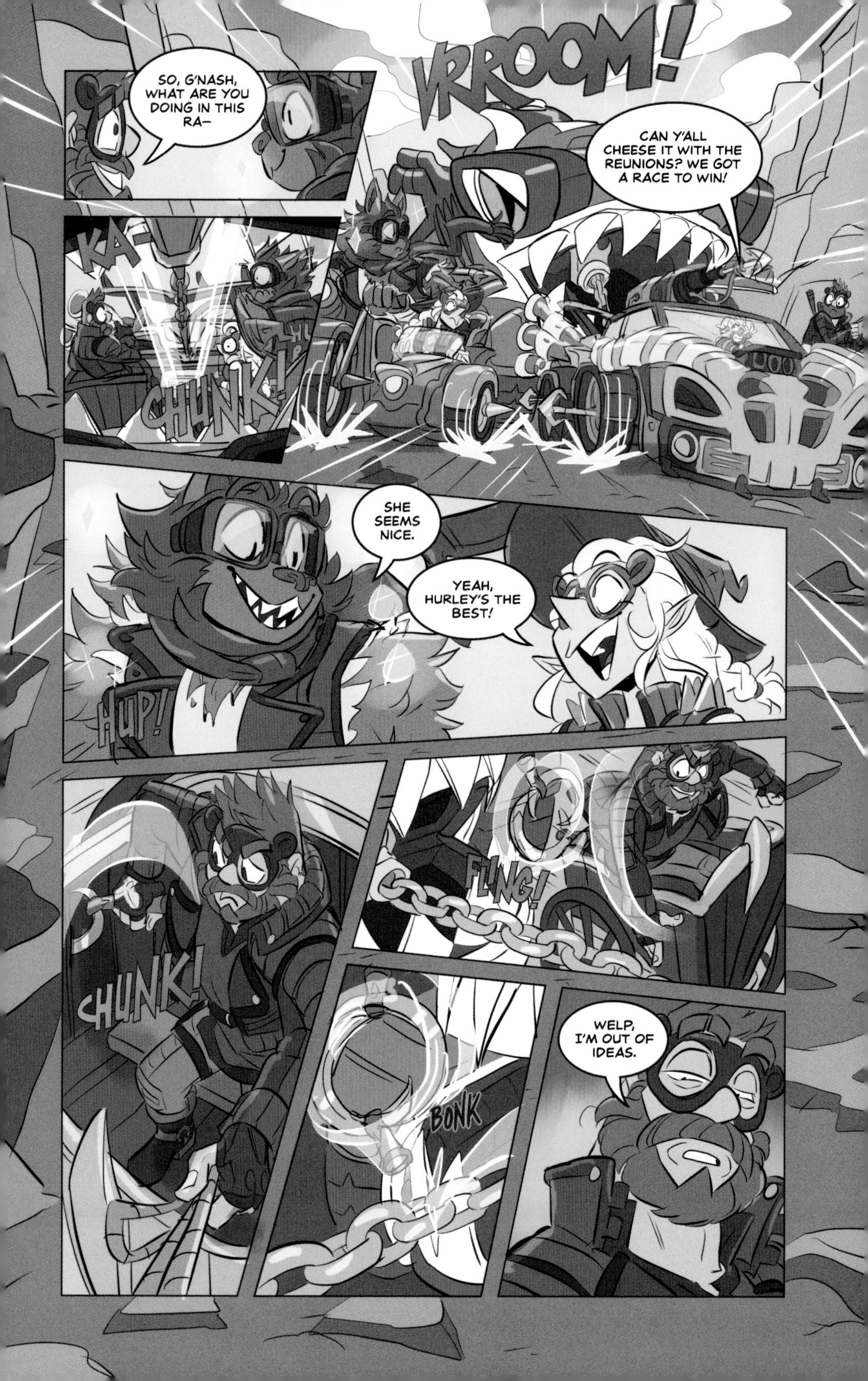
SO, G'NASH, WHAT ARE YOU DOING IN THIS RA—
VRROOM!
CAN Y'ALL CHEESE IT WITH THE REUNIONS? WE GOT A RACE TO WIN!
KA-
CHUNK!
SHE SEEMS NICE.
YEAH, HURLEY'S THE BEST!
HUP!
CHUNK!
FLING!
BONK
WELP, I'M OUT OF IDEAS.

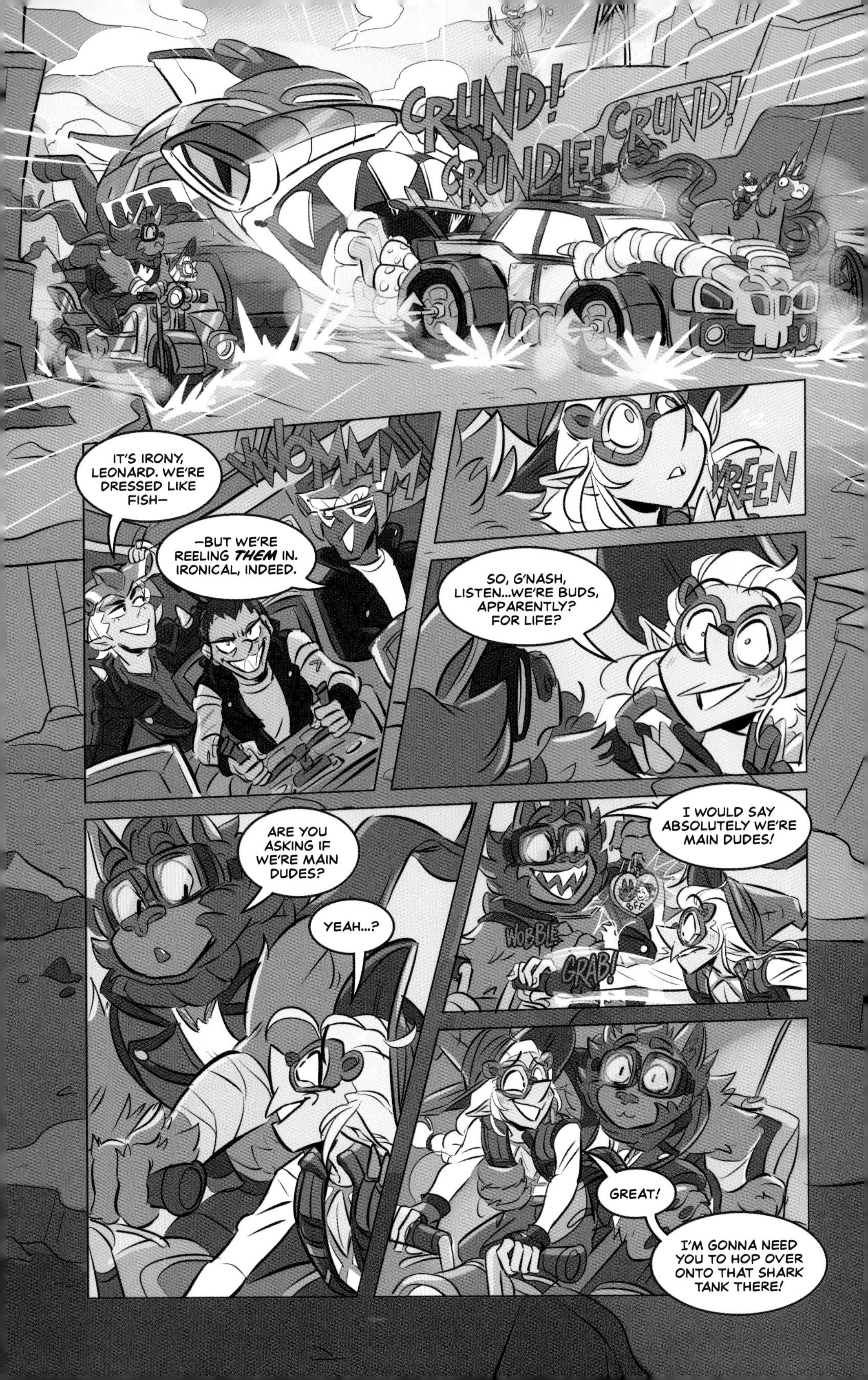

CRUND!
CRUNDLE!
CRUND!
WHOMMM
IT'S IRONY, LEONARD. WE'RE DRESSED LIKE FISH—
—BUT WE'RE REELING *THEM* IN. IRONICAL, INDEED.
VREEN
SO, G'NASH, LISTEN...WE'RE BUDS, APPARENTLY? FOR LIFE?
ARE YOU ASKING IF WE'RE MAIN DUDES?
YEAH...?
I WOULD SAY ABSOLUTELY WE'RE MAIN DUDES!
WOBBLE
GRAB!
GREAT!
I'M GONNA NEED YOU TO HOP OVER ONTO THAT SHARK TANK THERE!

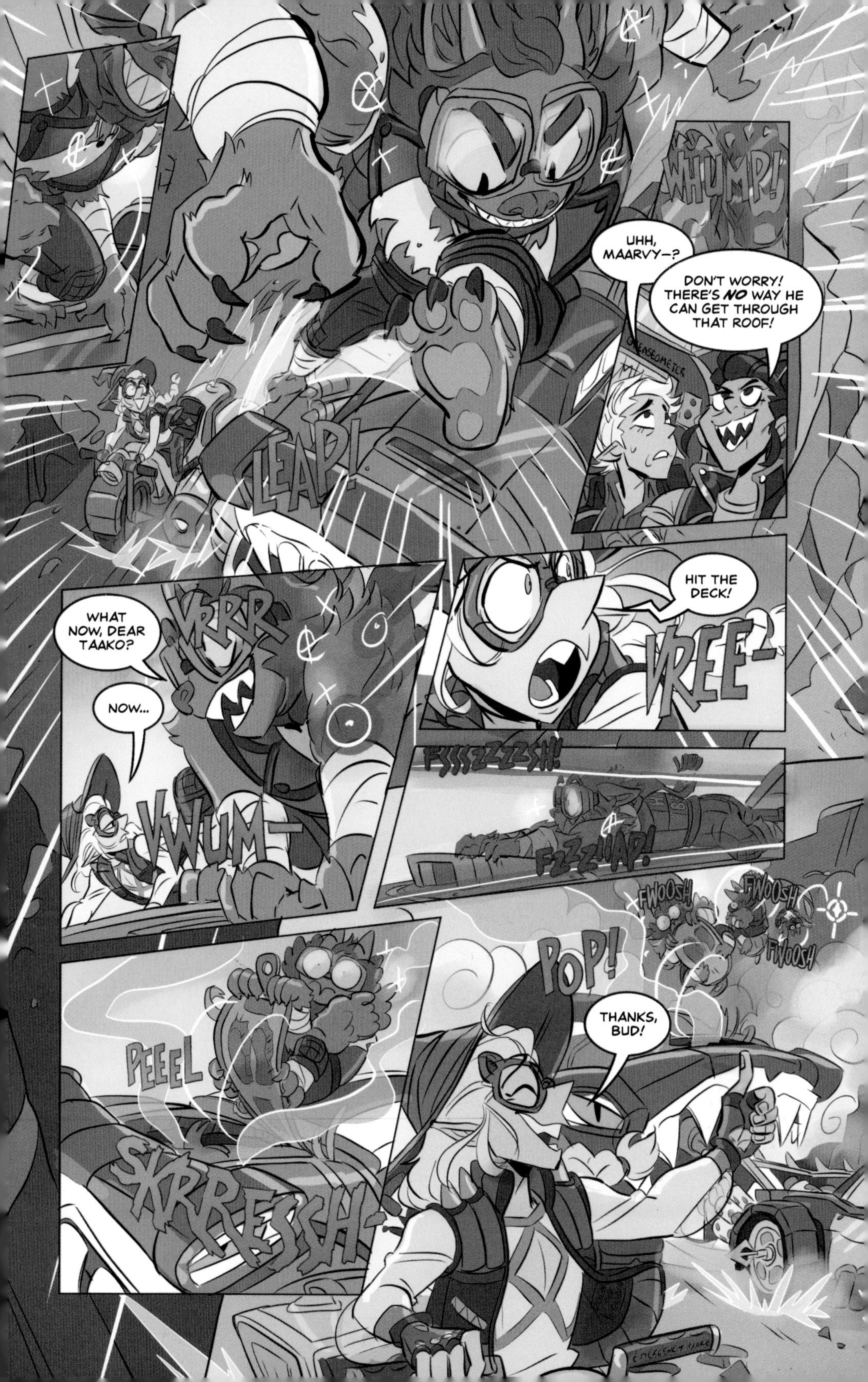
LEAP!
WHUMP!
UHH, MAARVY—?
DON'T WORRY! THERE'S *NO* WAY HE CAN GET THROUGH THAT ROOF!
WHAT NOW, DEAR TAAKO?
VRRR
NOW...
VWUM-
HIT THE DECK!
VREE-
FSSSZZZZSH!
FZZZAP!
FWOOSH
FWOOSH
FWOOSH
POP!
PEEEL
THANKS, BUD!
SKRRESCH-

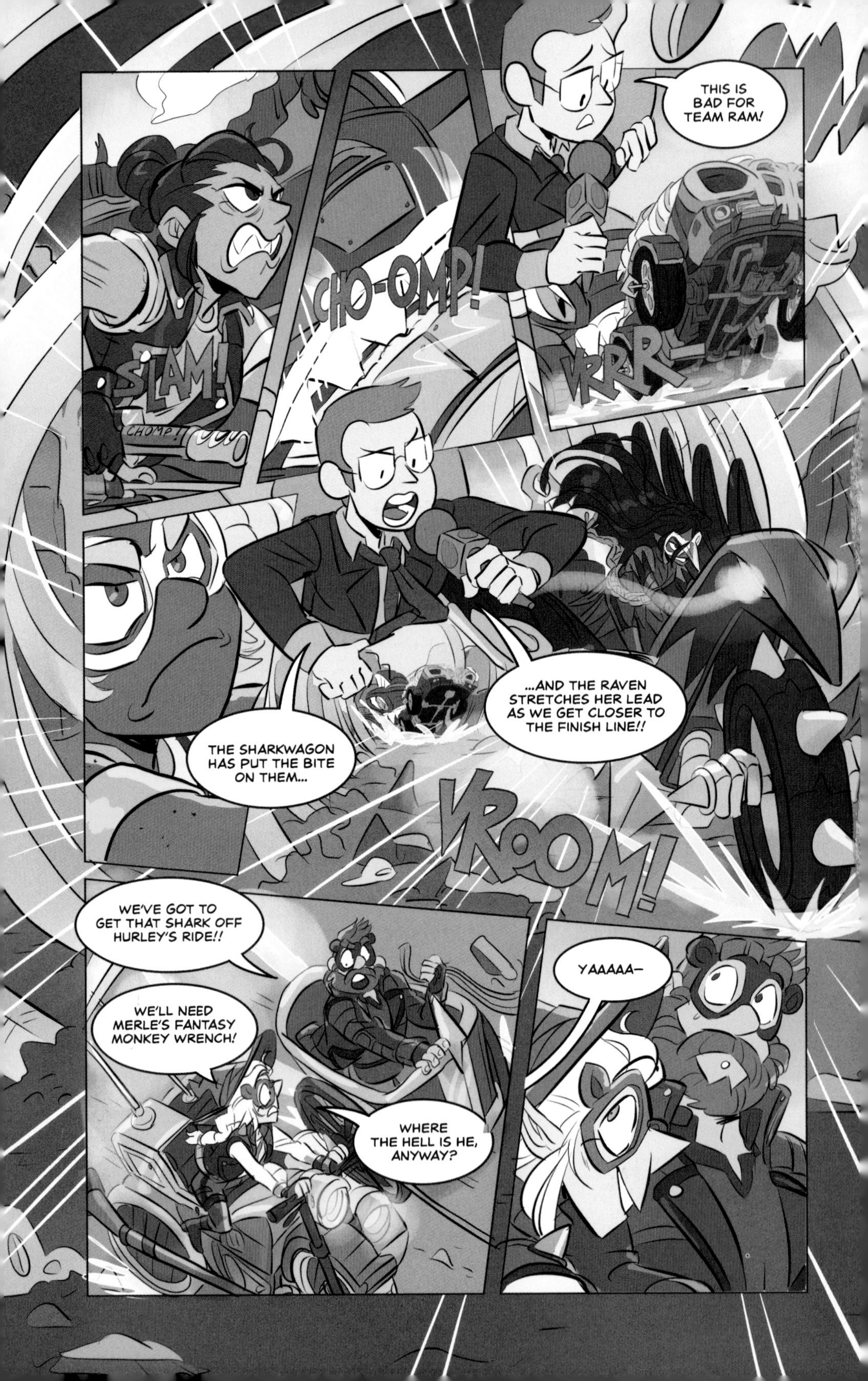
SLAM!
CHOMP!
CHO-OMP!
THIS IS BAD FOR TEAM RAM!
VRRR
THE SHARKWAGON HAS PUT THE BITE ON THEM...
...AND THE RAVEN STRETCHES HER LEAD AS WE GET CLOSER TO THE FINISH LINE!!
VROOOM!
WE'VE GOT TO GET THAT SHARK OFF HURLEY'S RIDE!!
WE'LL NEED MERLE'S FANTASY MONKEY WRENCH!
WHERE THE HELL IS HE, ANYWAY?
YAAAAA–

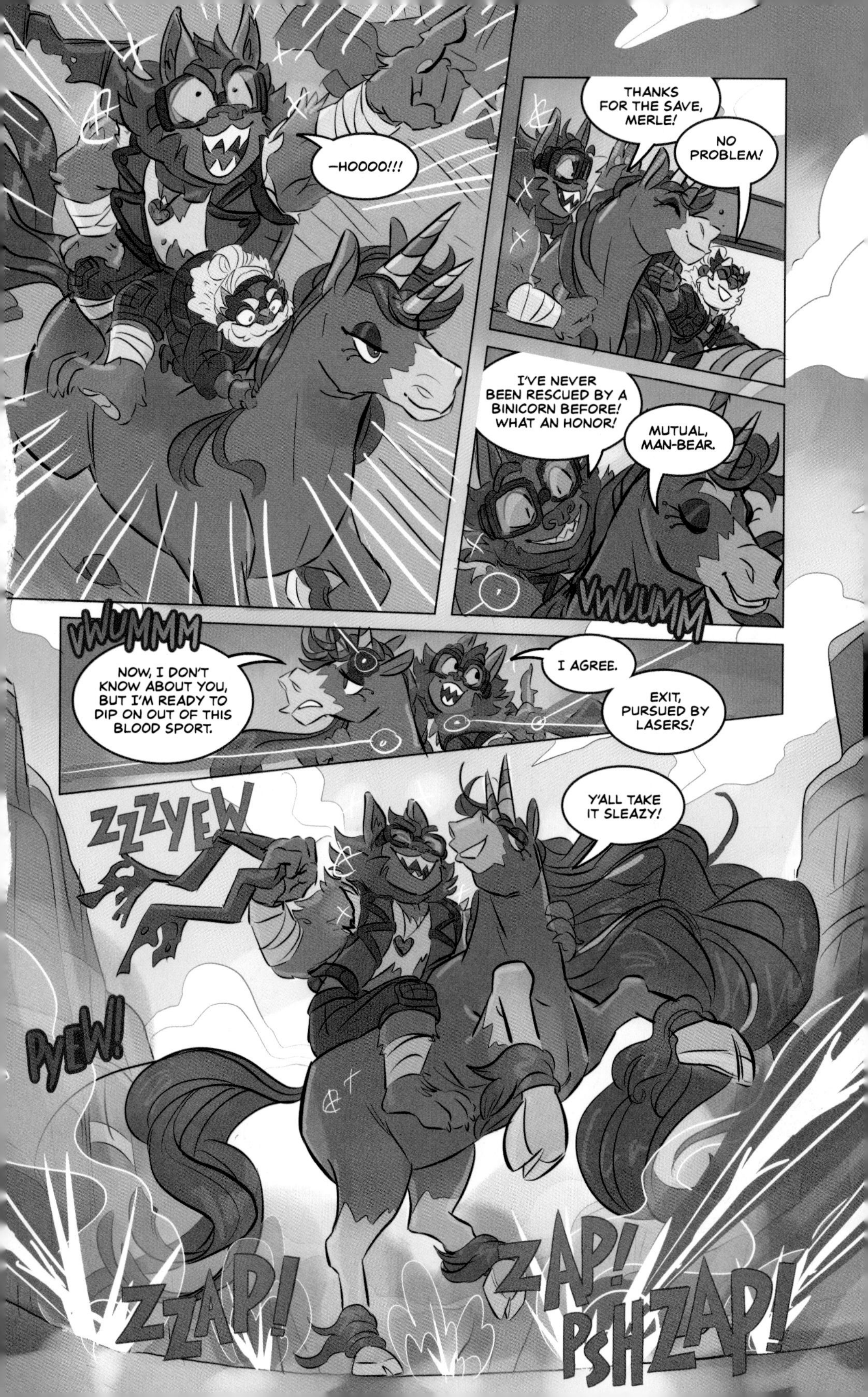
—HOOOO!!!
THANKS FOR THE SAVE, MERLE!
NO PROBLEM!
I'VE NEVER BEEN RESCUED BY A BINICORN BEFORE! WHAT AN HONOR!
MUTUAL, MAN-BEAR.
VWUMM
VWUMMM
NOW, I DON'T KNOW ABOUT YOU, BUT I'M READY TO DIP ON OUT OF THIS BLOOD SPORT.
I AGREE.
EXIT, PURSUED BY LASERS!
ZZZYEW
Y'ALL TAKE IT SLEAZY!
PYEW!
ZZAP!
ZAP!
PSHZAP!

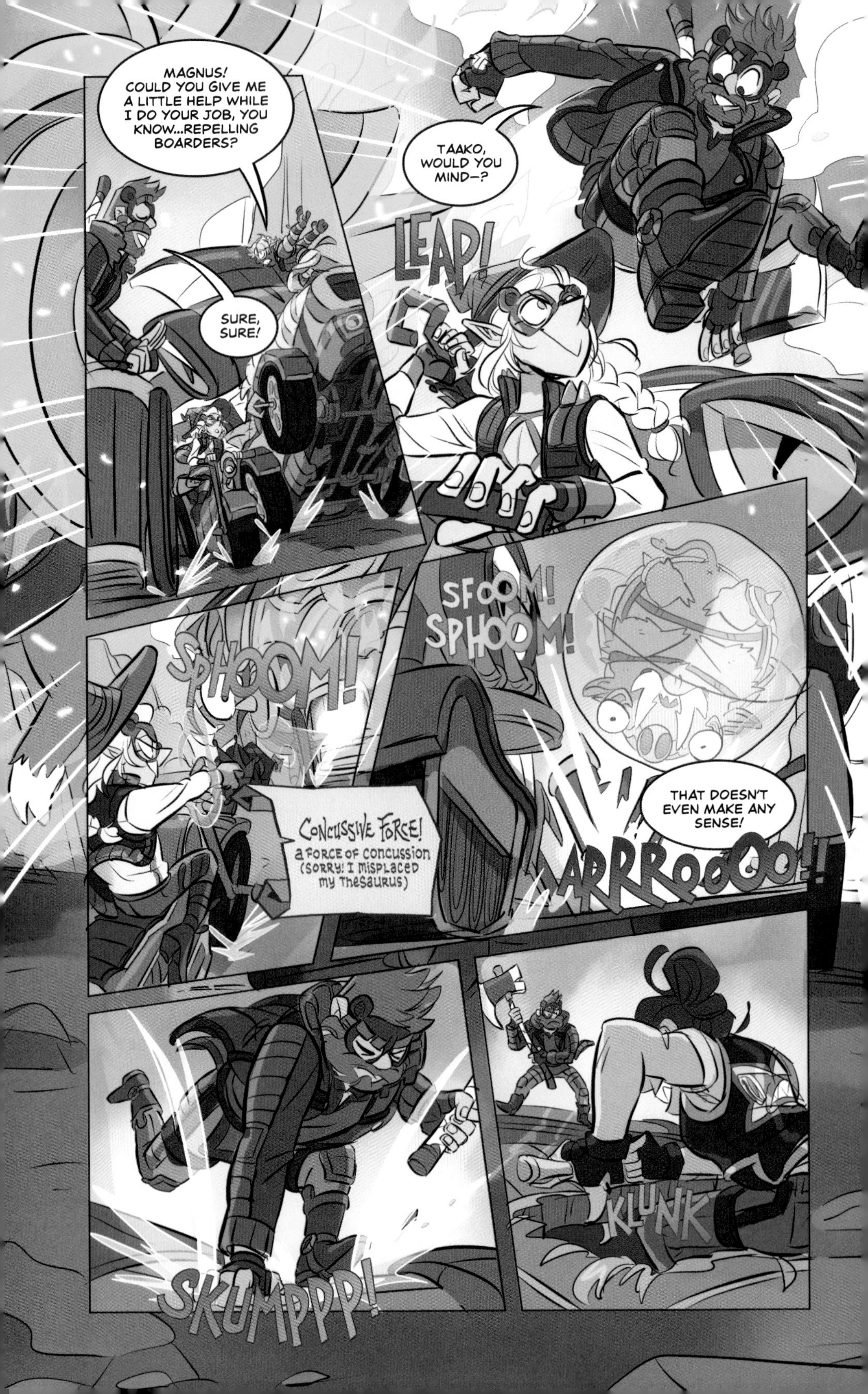
MAGNUS! COULD YOU GIVE ME A LITTLE HELP WHILE I DO YOUR JOB, YOU KNOW...REPELLING BOARDERS?
SURE, SURE!
TAAKO, WOULD YOU MIND—?
LEAP!
SPHOOM!
CONCUSSIVE FORCE! a FORCE OF CONCUSSION (SORRY! I MISPLACED my THESAURUS)
SFOOM! SPHOOM!
THAT DOESN'T EVEN MAKE ANY SENSE!
ARRROOOO!!
SKUMPPP!
KLUNK

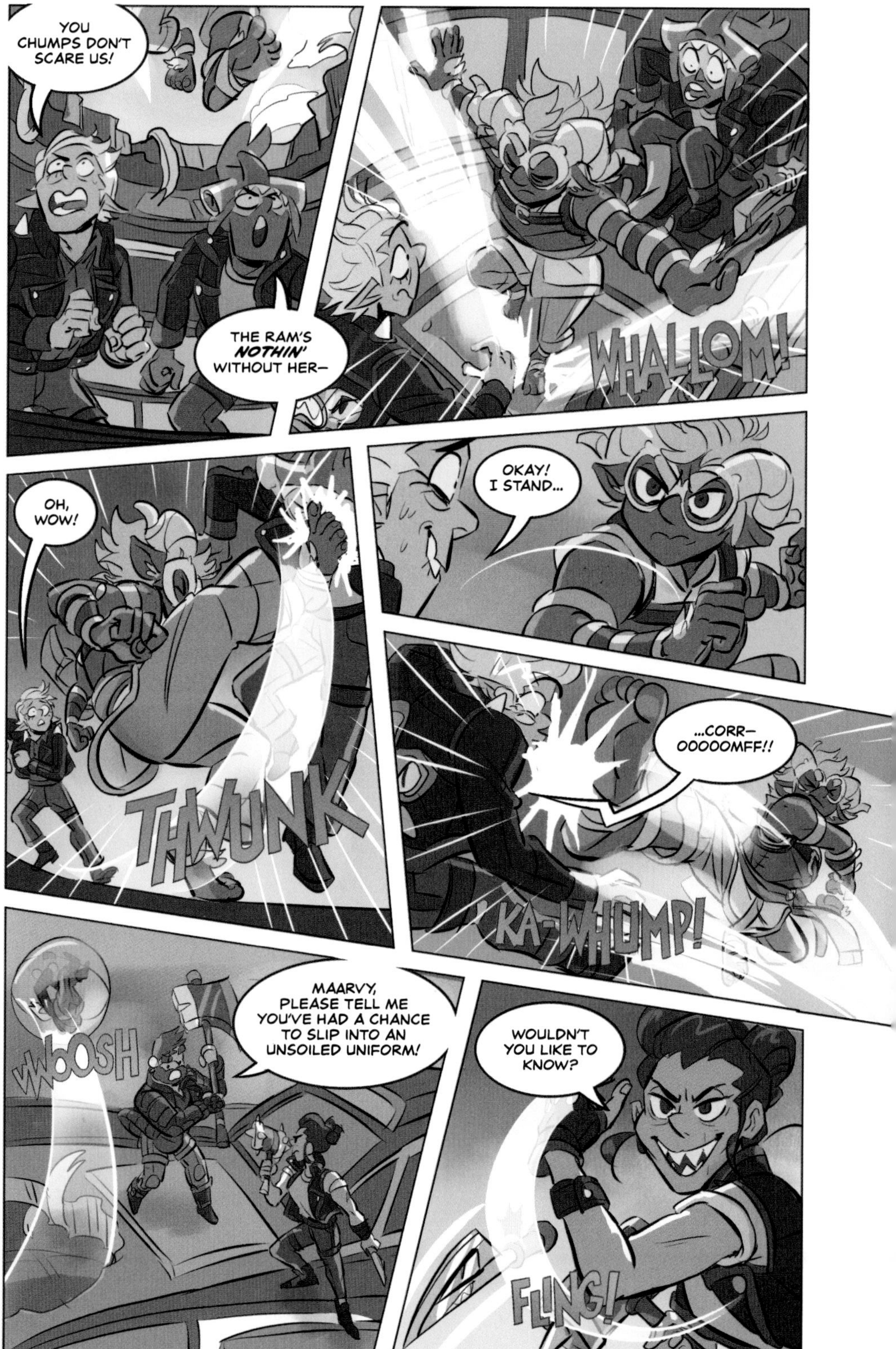
YOU CHUMPS DON'T SCARE US!
THE RAM'S ***NOTHIN'*** WITHOUT HER—
WHALLOM!
OH, WOW!
THWUNK
OKAY! I STAND...
...CORR— OOOOOMFF!!
KA-WHUMP!
WOOSH
MAARVY, PLEASE TELL ME YOU'VE HAD A CHANCE TO SLIP INTO AN UNSOILED UNIFORM!
WOULDN'T YOU LIKE TO KNOW?
FLING!

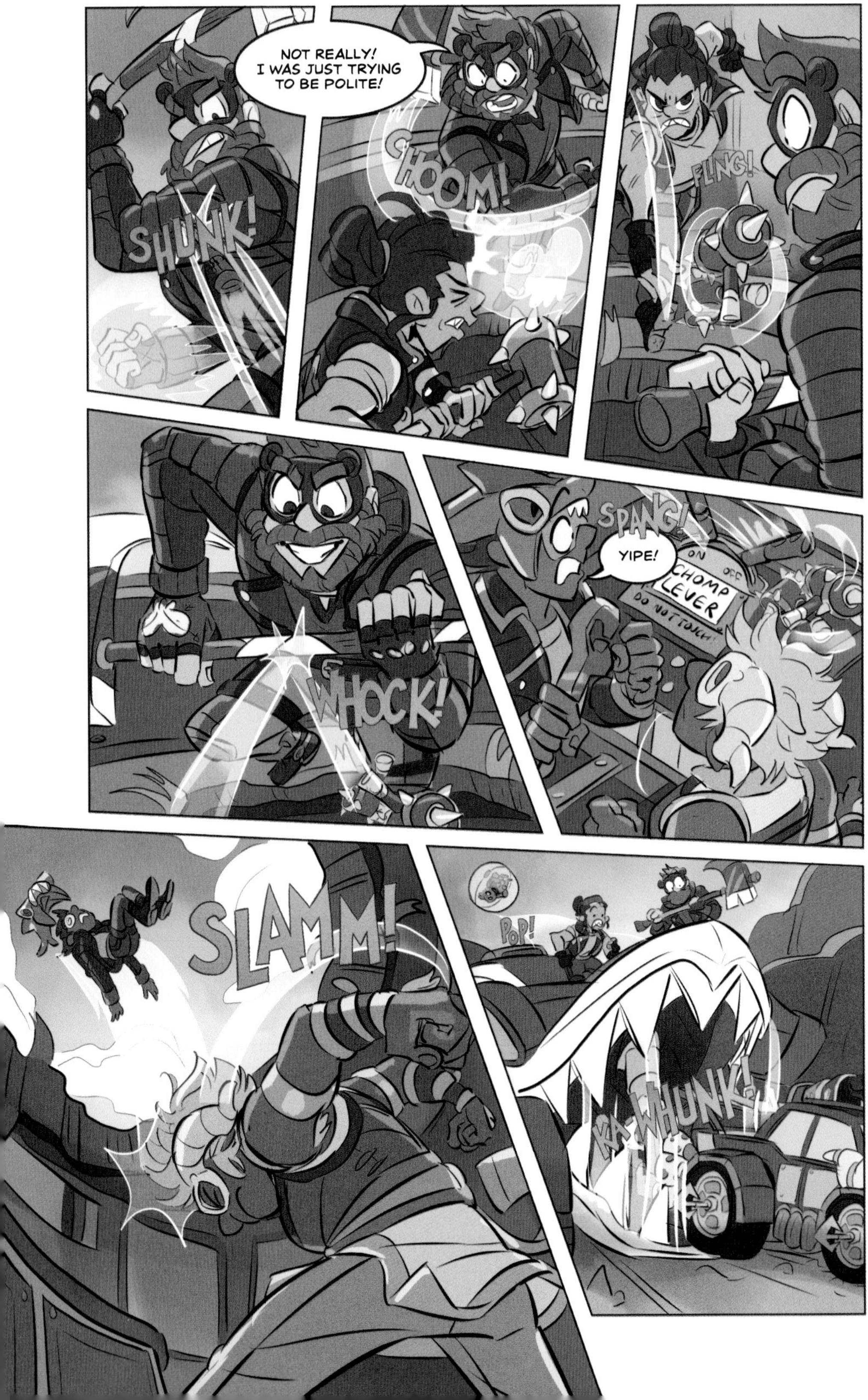
SHUNK!
NOT REALLY! I WAS JUST TRYING TO BE POLITE!
CHOOM!
FLING!
WHOCK!
SPANG!
YIPE!
ON OFF
CHOMP LEVER
DO NOT TOUCH!
SLAMM!
POP!
KA-WHUNK!

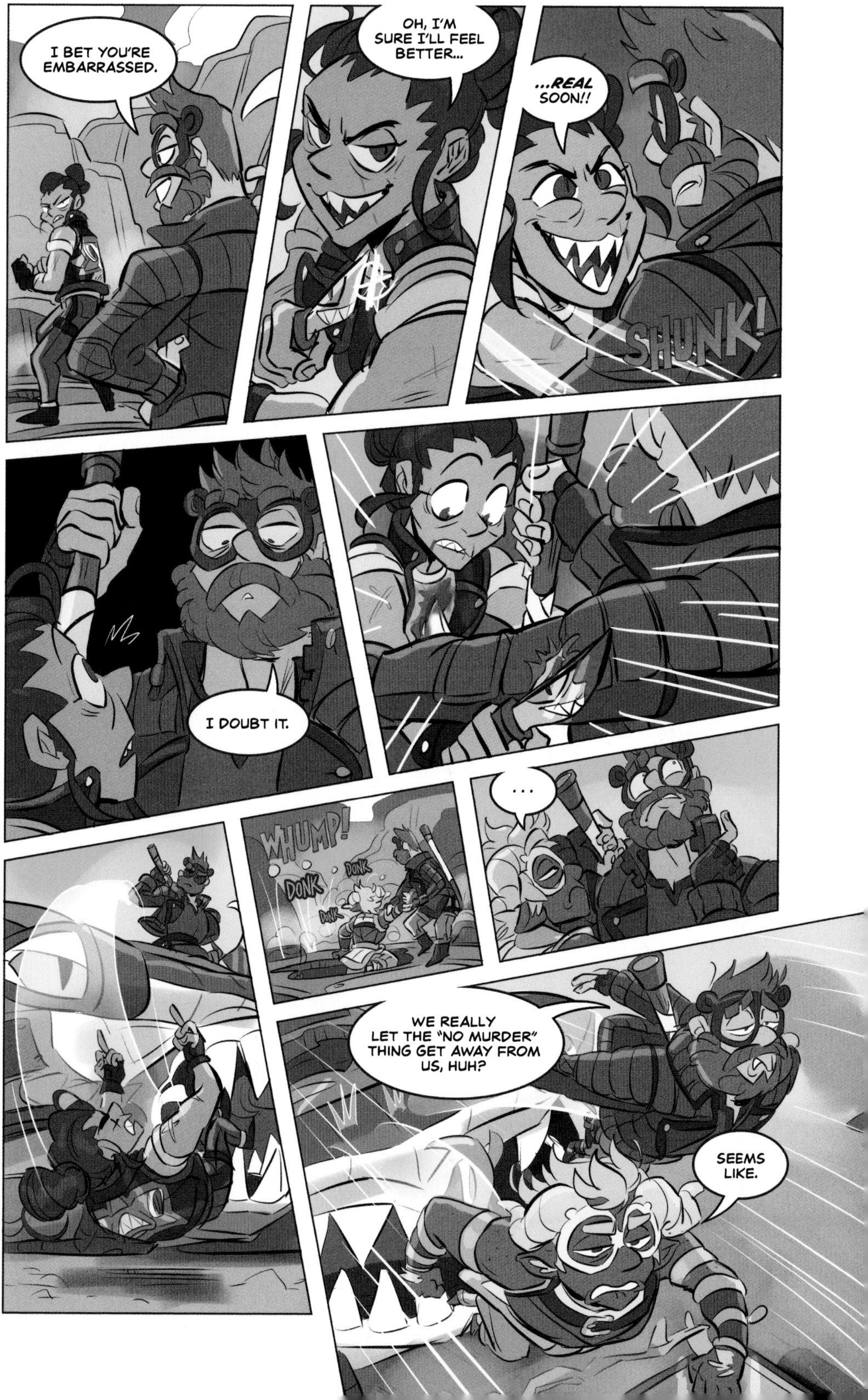
I BET YOU'RE EMBARRASSED.
OH, I'M SURE I'LL FEEL BETTER...
...REAL SOON!!
SHUNK!
I DOUBT IT.
WHUMP!
DONK
DONK
DONK
...
WE REALLY LET THE "NO MURDER" THING GET AWAY FROM US, HUH?
SEEMS LIKE.

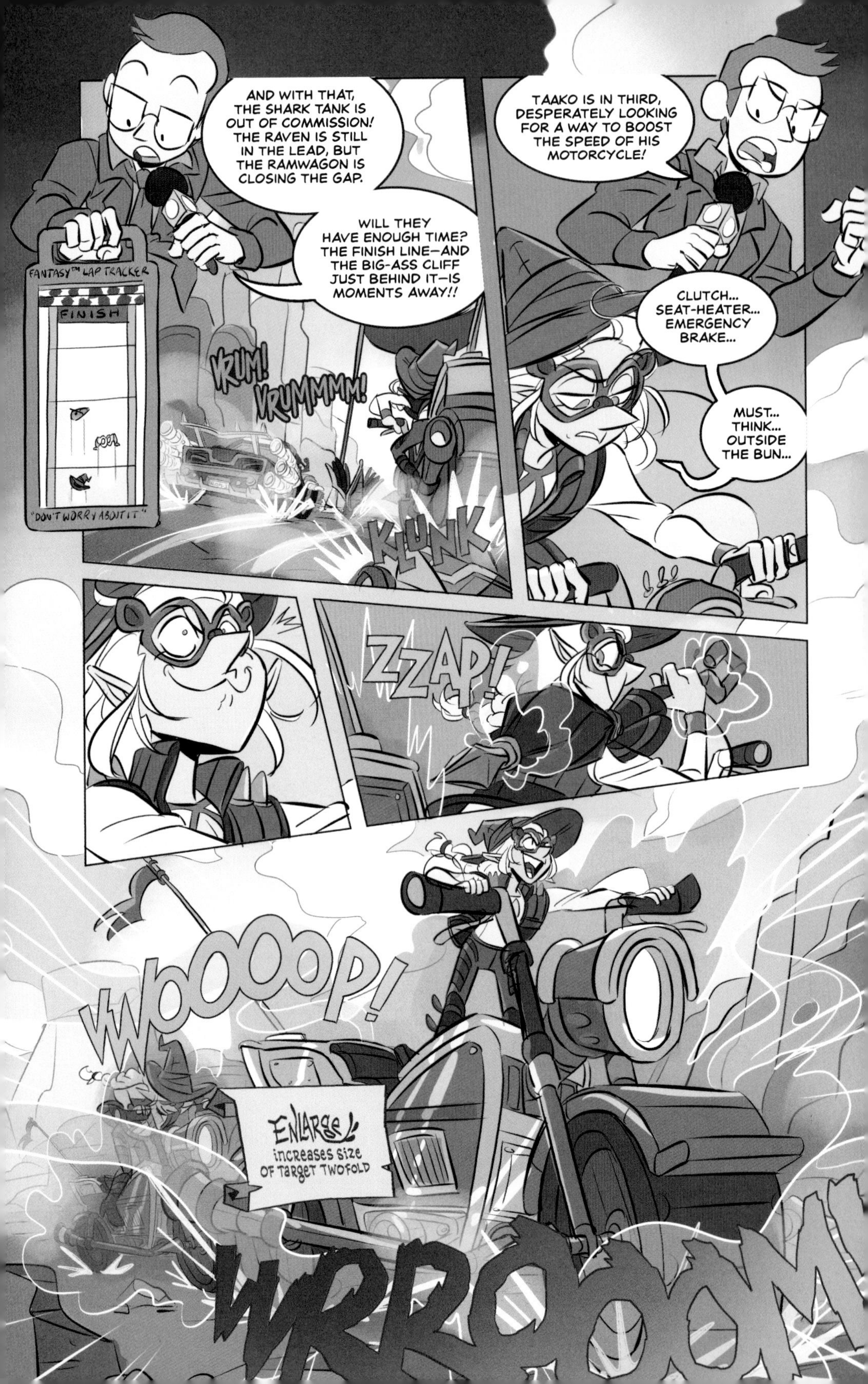
AND WITH THAT, THE SHARK TANK IS OUT OF COMMISSION! THE RAVEN IS STILL IN THE LEAD, BUT THE RAMWAGON IS CLOSING THE GAP.
WILL THEY HAVE ENOUGH TIME? THE FINISH LINE—AND THE BIG-ASS CLIFF JUST BEHIND IT—IS MOMENTS AWAY!!
FANTASY™ LAP TRACKER
FINISH
"DON'T WORRY ABOUT IT"
VRUM!
VRUMMMM!
KLUNK
TAAKO IS IN THIRD, DESPERATELY LOOKING FOR A WAY TO BOOST THE SPEED OF HIS MOTORCYCLE!
CLUTCH... SEAT-HEATER... EMERGENCY BRAKE...
MUST... THINK... OUTSIDE THE BUN...
ZZAP!
WOOOOP!
ENLARGE
increases size of target twofold
WRROOOM

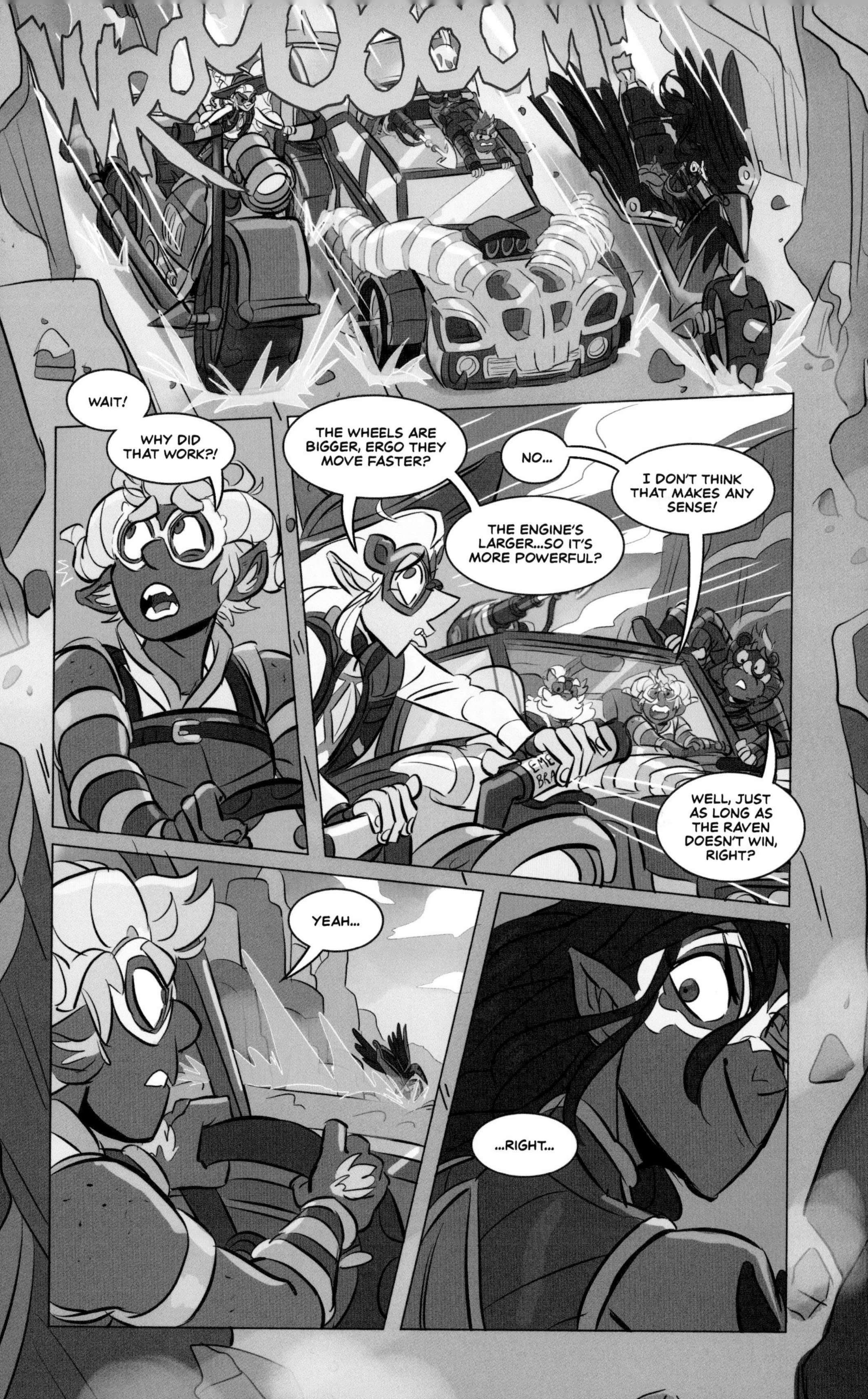
WROOOOOOM!
WAIT!
WHY DID THAT WORK?!
THE WHEELS ARE BIGGER, ERGO THEY MOVE FASTER?
THE ENGINE'S LARGER...SO IT'S MORE POWERFUL?
NO...
I DON'T THINK THAT MAKES ANY SENSE!
WELL, JUST AS LONG AS THE RAVEN DOESN'T WIN, RIGHT?
YEAH...
...RIGHT...

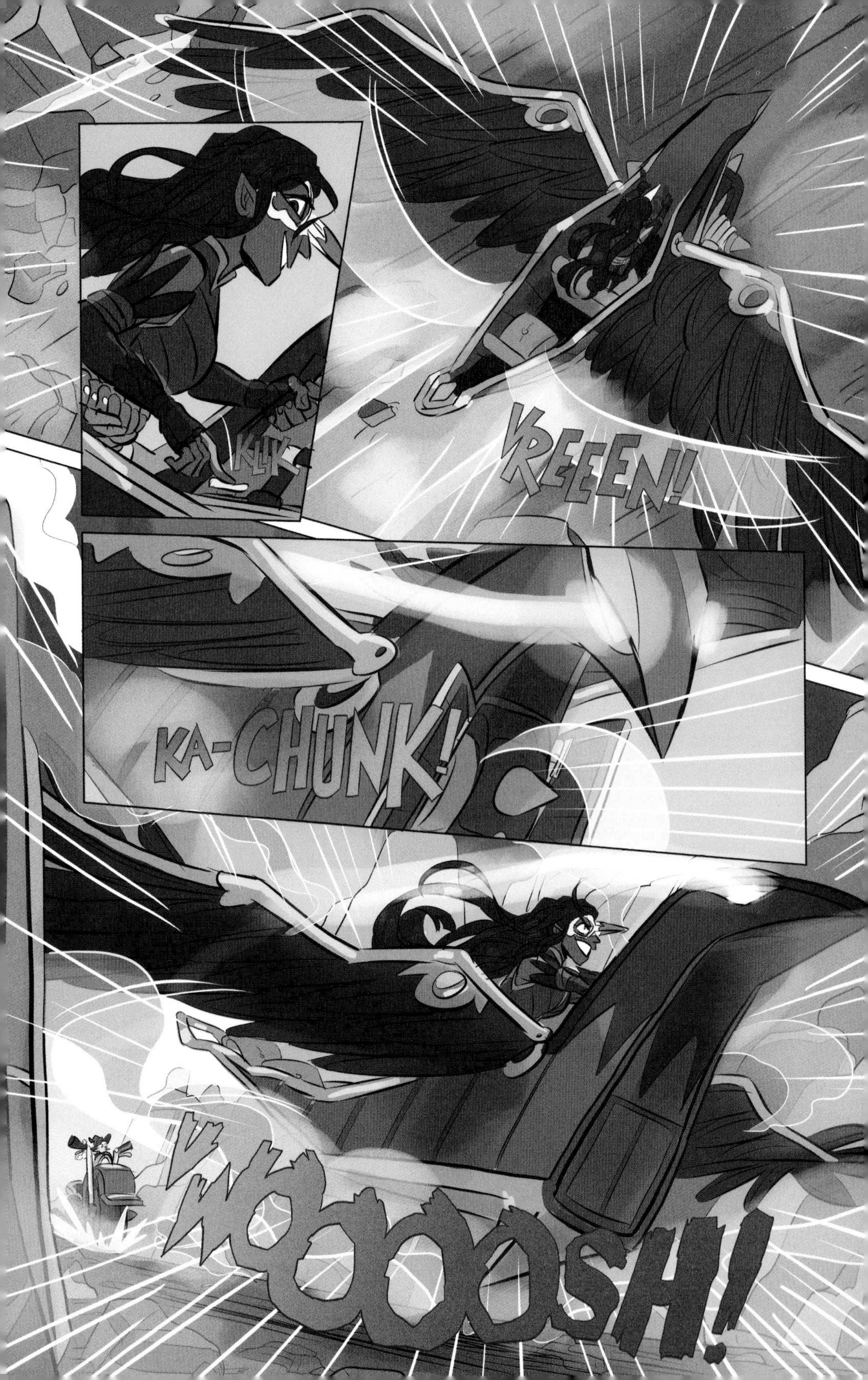
KLIK
VREEEN!
KA-CHUNK!
VWOOOOSH!

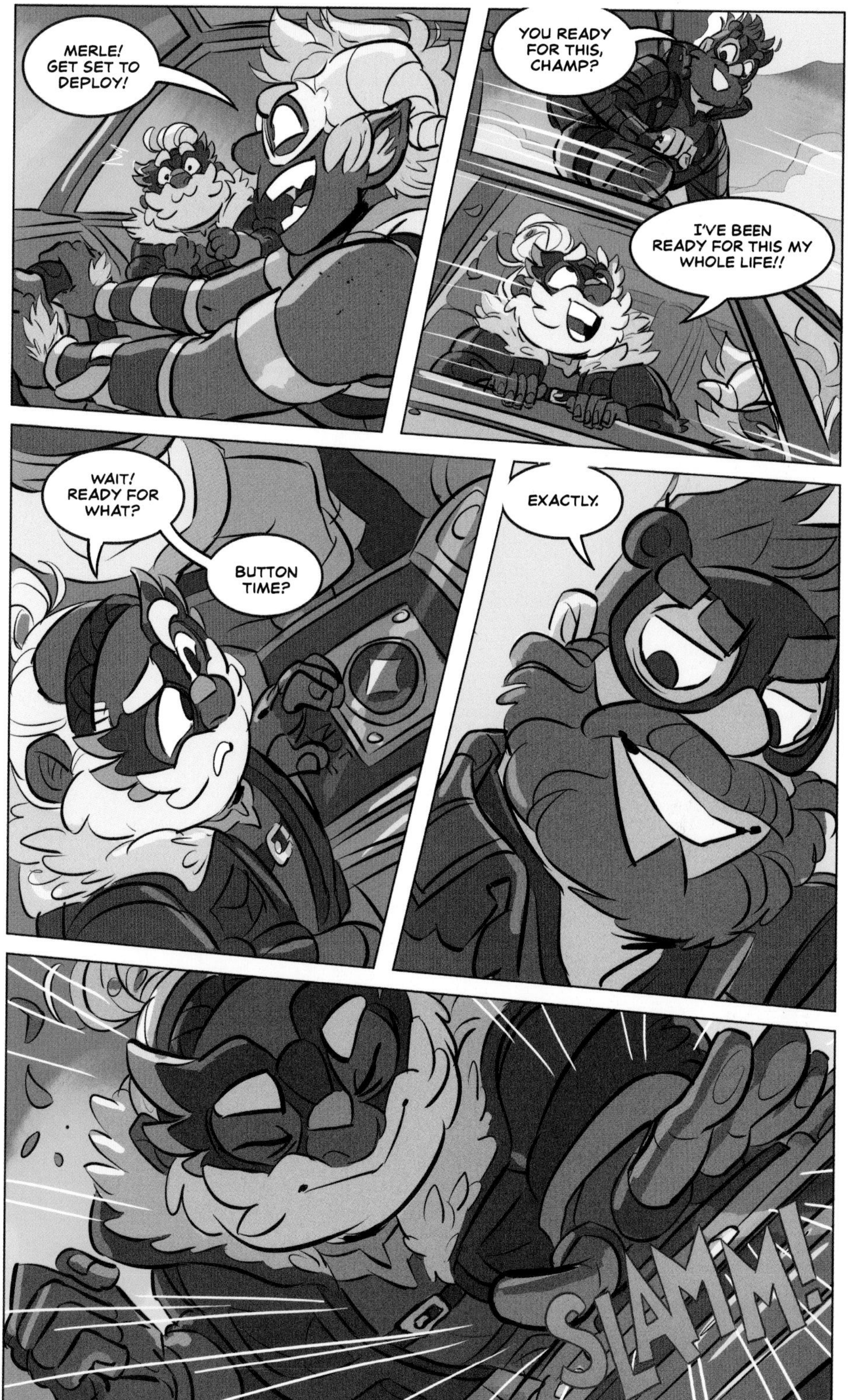
MERLE! GET SET TO DEPLOY!
YOU READY FOR THIS, CHAMP?
I'VE BEEN READY FOR THIS MY WHOLE LIFE!!
WAIT! READY FOR WHAT?
BUTTON TIME?
EXACTLY.
SLAMM!

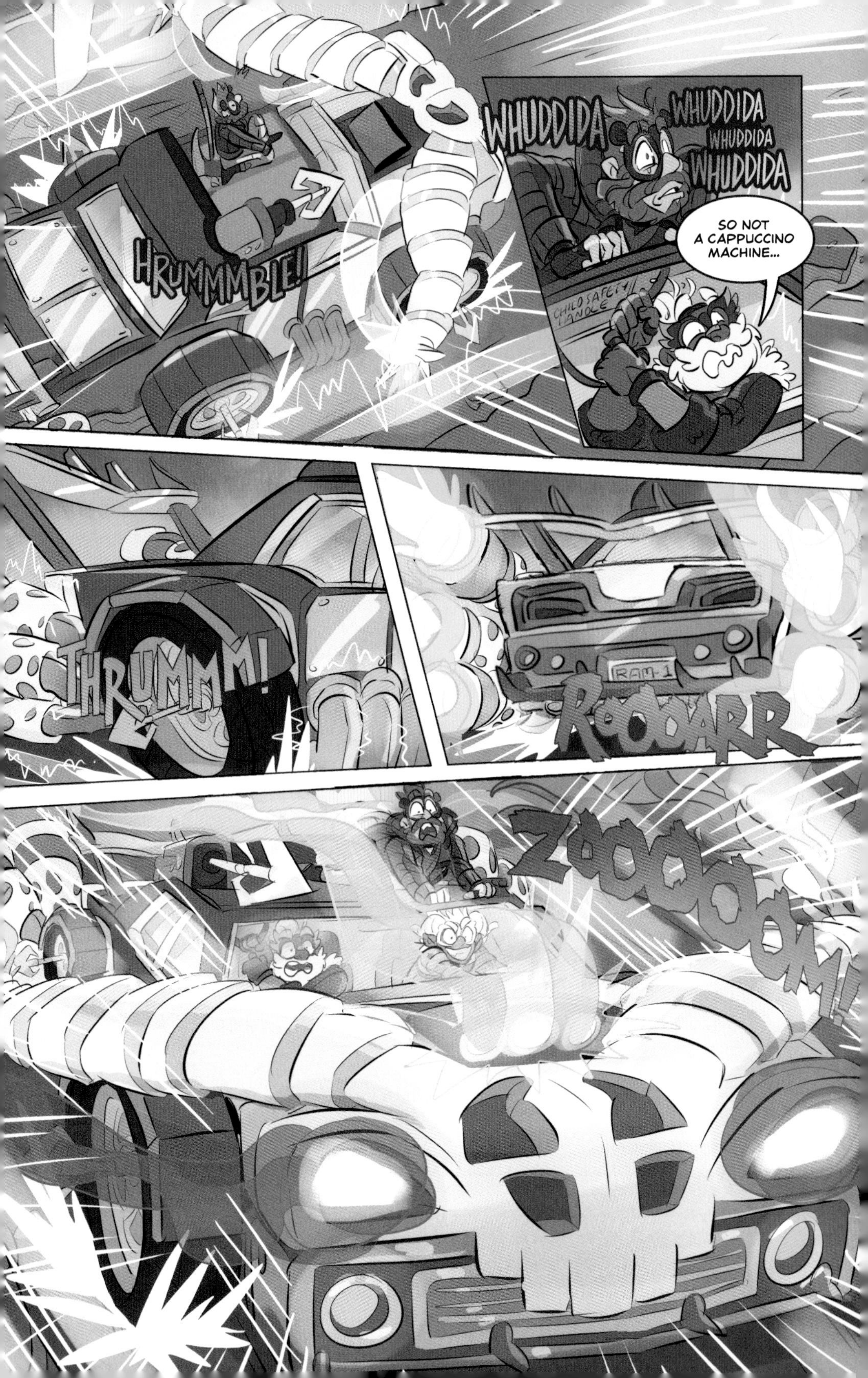
HRUMMMBLE!
WHUDDIDA
WHUDDIDA
WHUDDIDA
WHUDDIDA
SO NOT A CAPPUCCINO MACHINE...
CHILD SAFETY HANDLE
THRUMMM!
RAM-1
ROOOARR
ZOOOOOOM!!

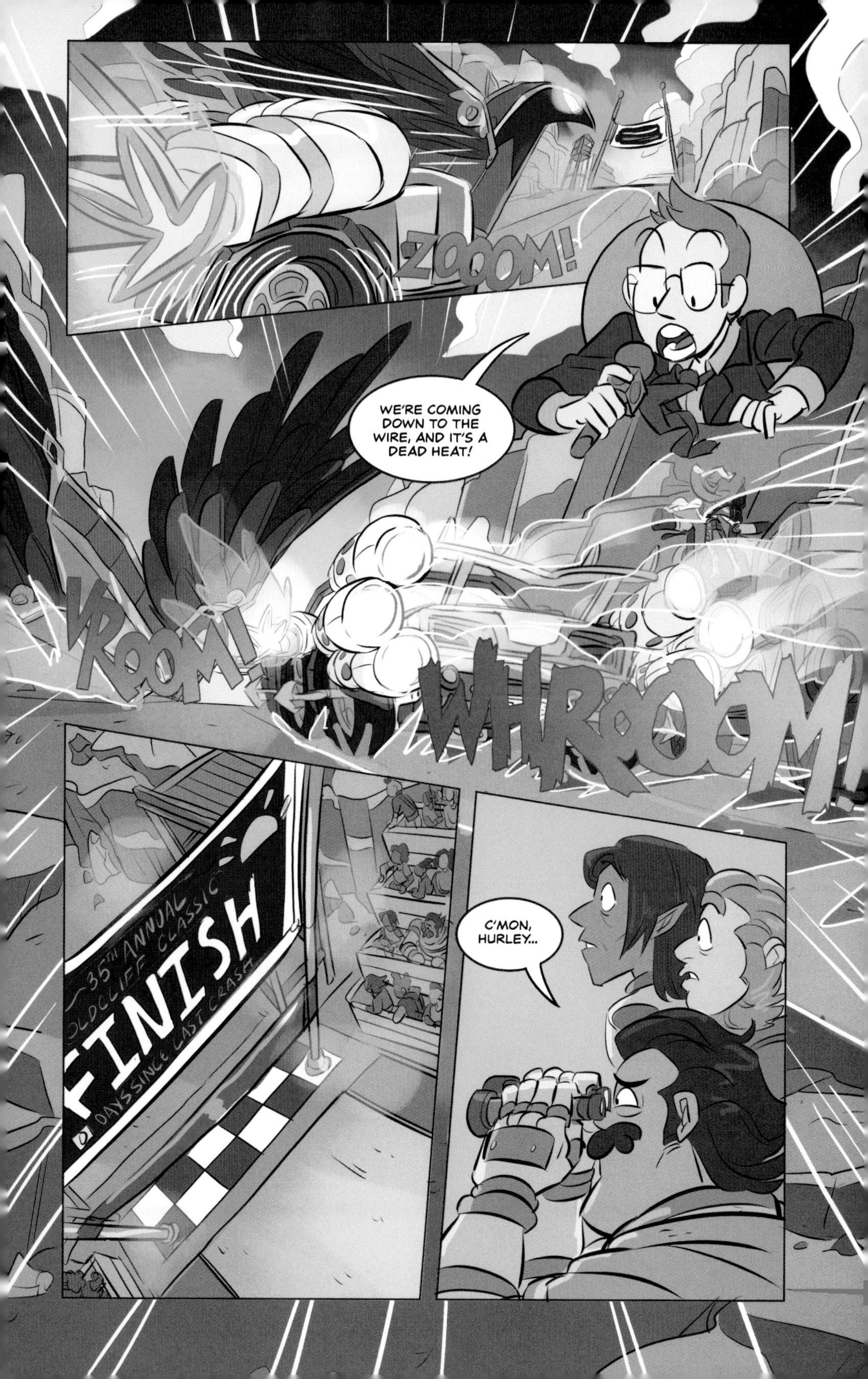
ZOOOM!
WE'RE COMING DOWN TO THE WIRE, AND IT'S A DEAD HEAT!
VROOM!
WHROOOM!
35TH ANNUAL
FINISH
C'MON, HURLEY...

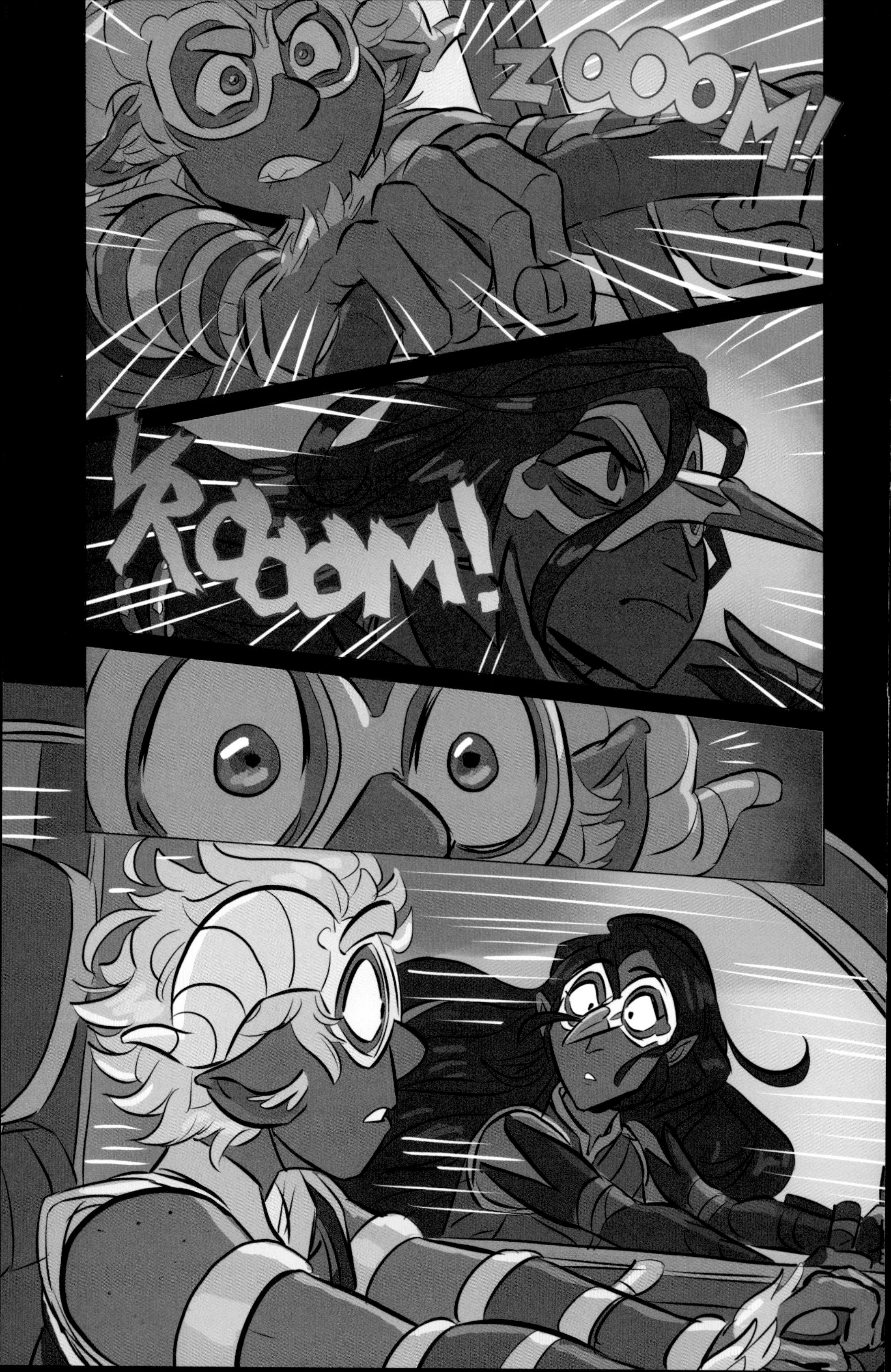
ZOOOOM!
VROOOM!

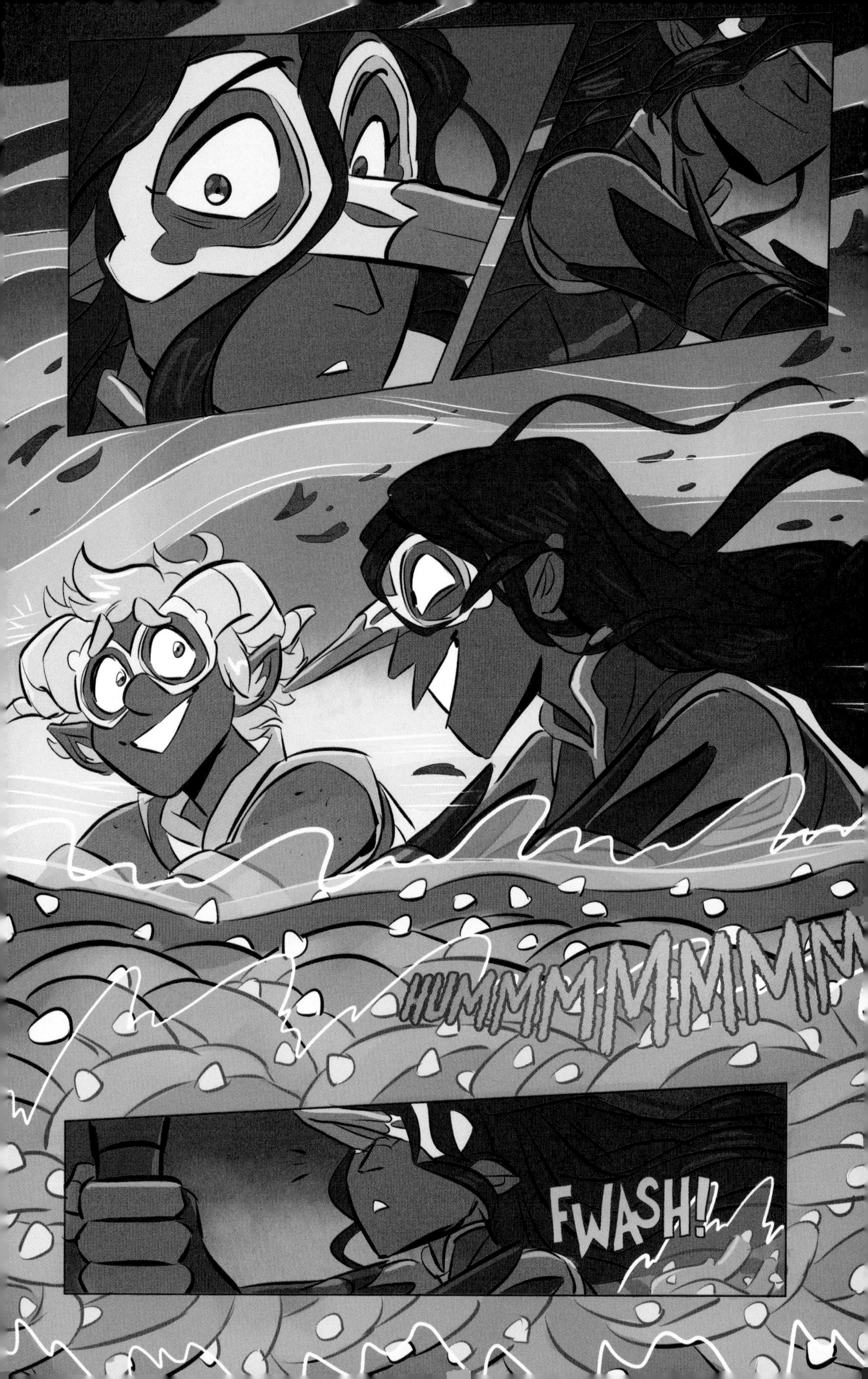
HUMMMMMMMM
FWASH!!

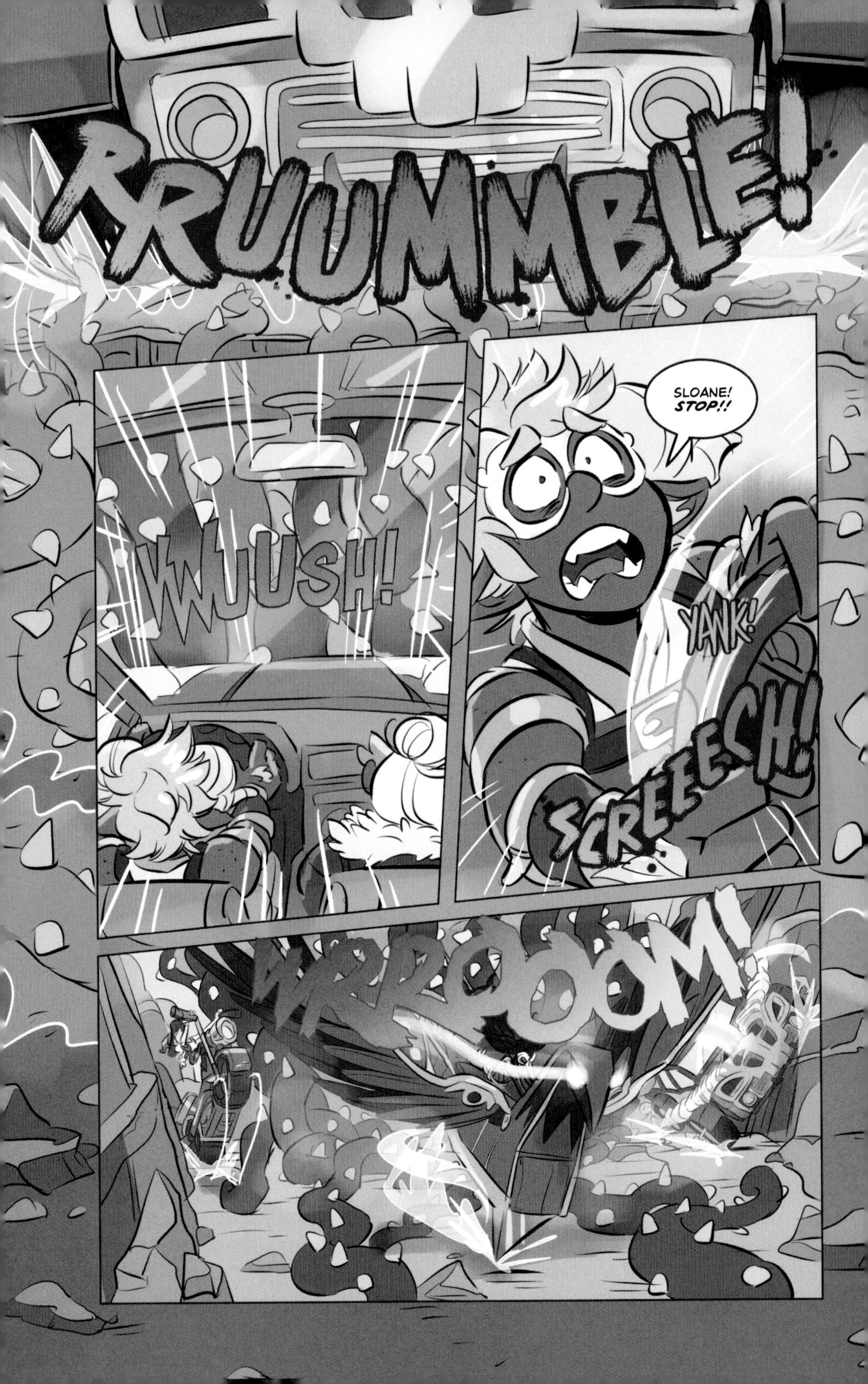
RRUUMMBLE!
VWUUSH!
SLOANE!
STOP!!
YANK!
SCREEECH!
WRROOOM!

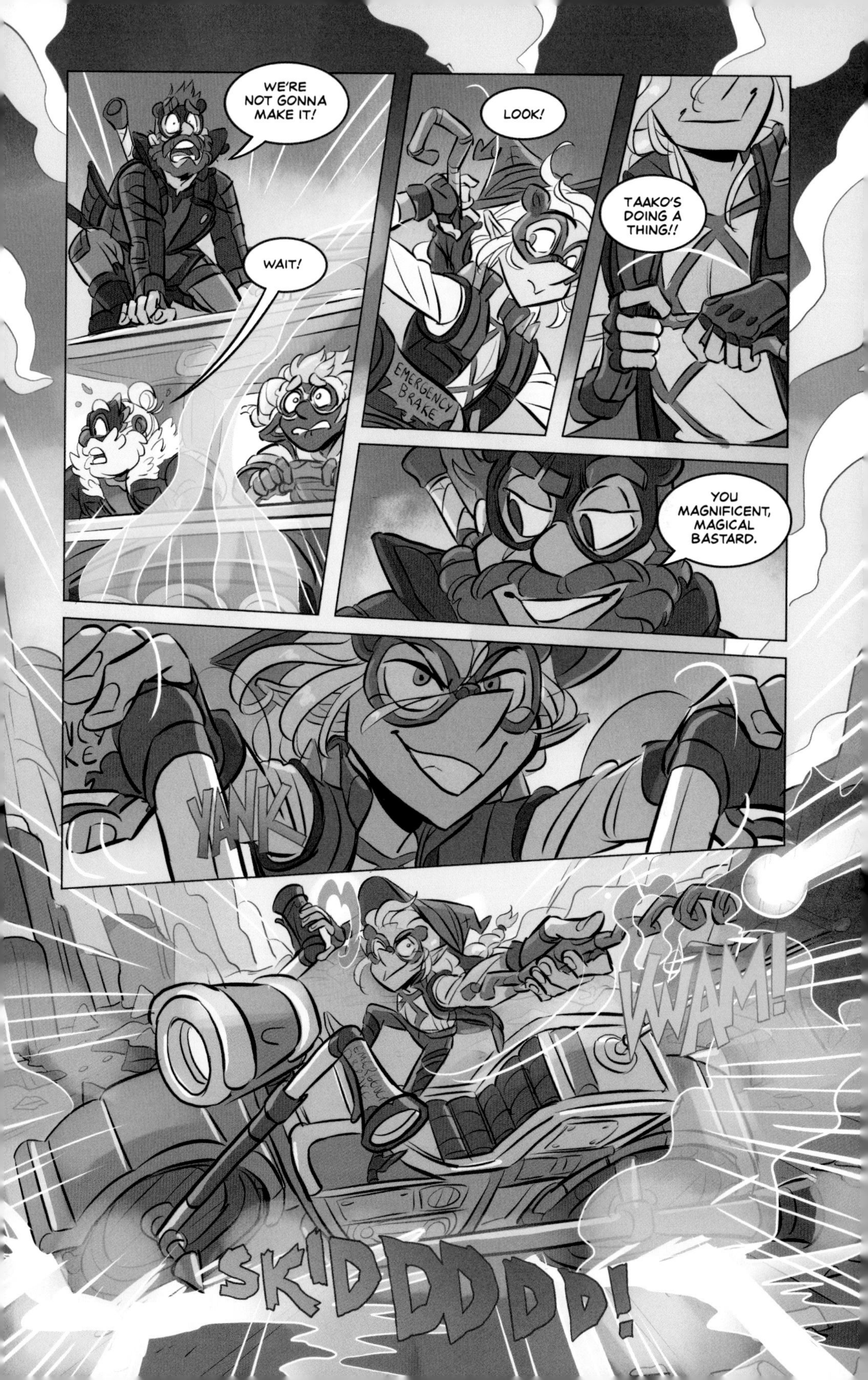

WE'RE NOT GONNA MAKE IT!
WAIT!
LOOK!
EMERGENCY BRAKE
TAAKO'S DOING A THING!!
YOU MAGNIFICENT, MAGICAL BASTARD.
YANK!
WAM!
SKIDDDDD!

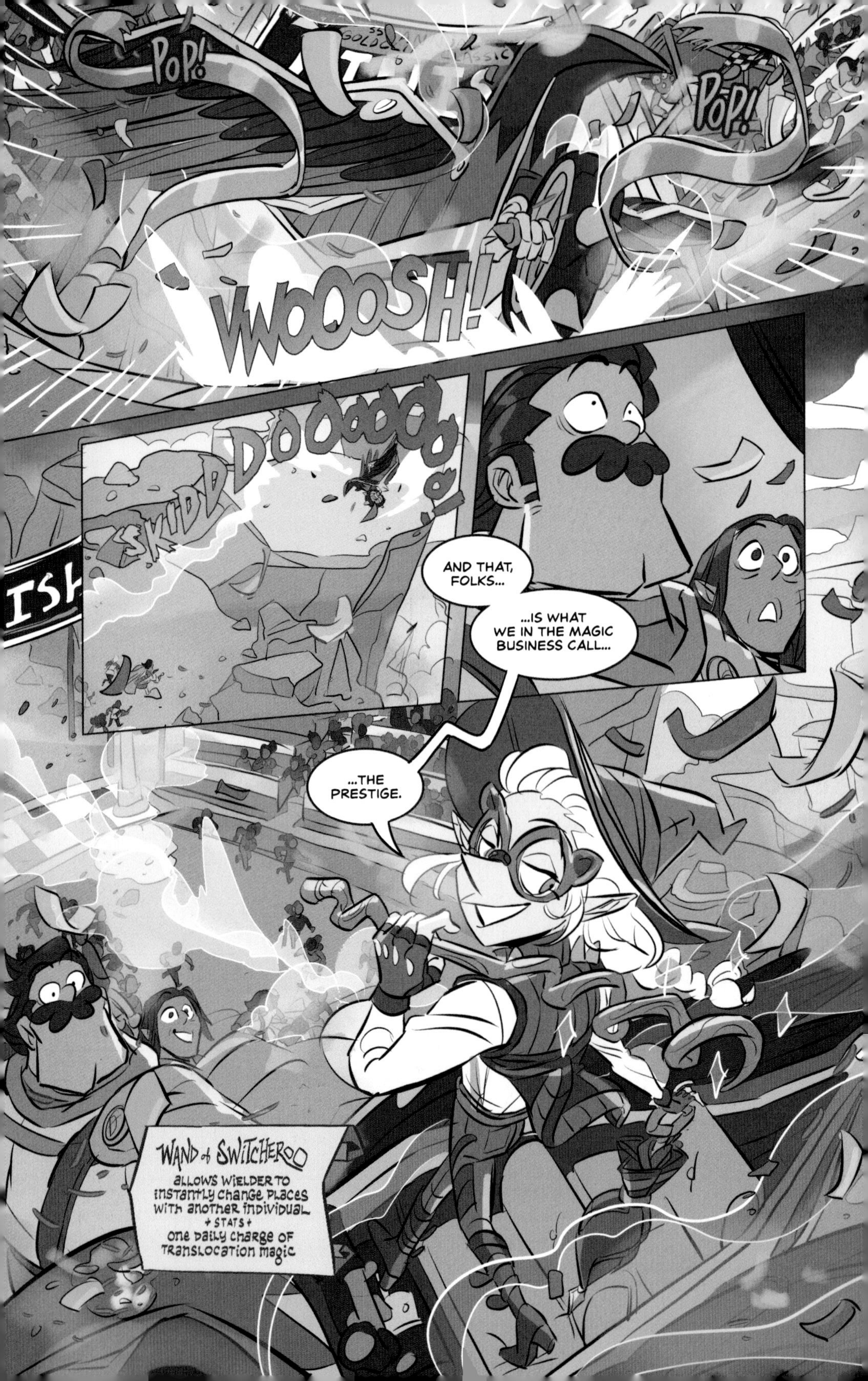
POP!
POP!
WOOOOSH!
SKIDDDOOOOOO
AND THAT, FOLKS...
...IS WHAT WE IN THE MAGIC BUSINESS CALL...
...THE PRESTIGE.
WAND of SWITCHEROO
allows wielder to instantly change places with another individual
+ STATS +
one daily charge of translocation magic

Chapter 7

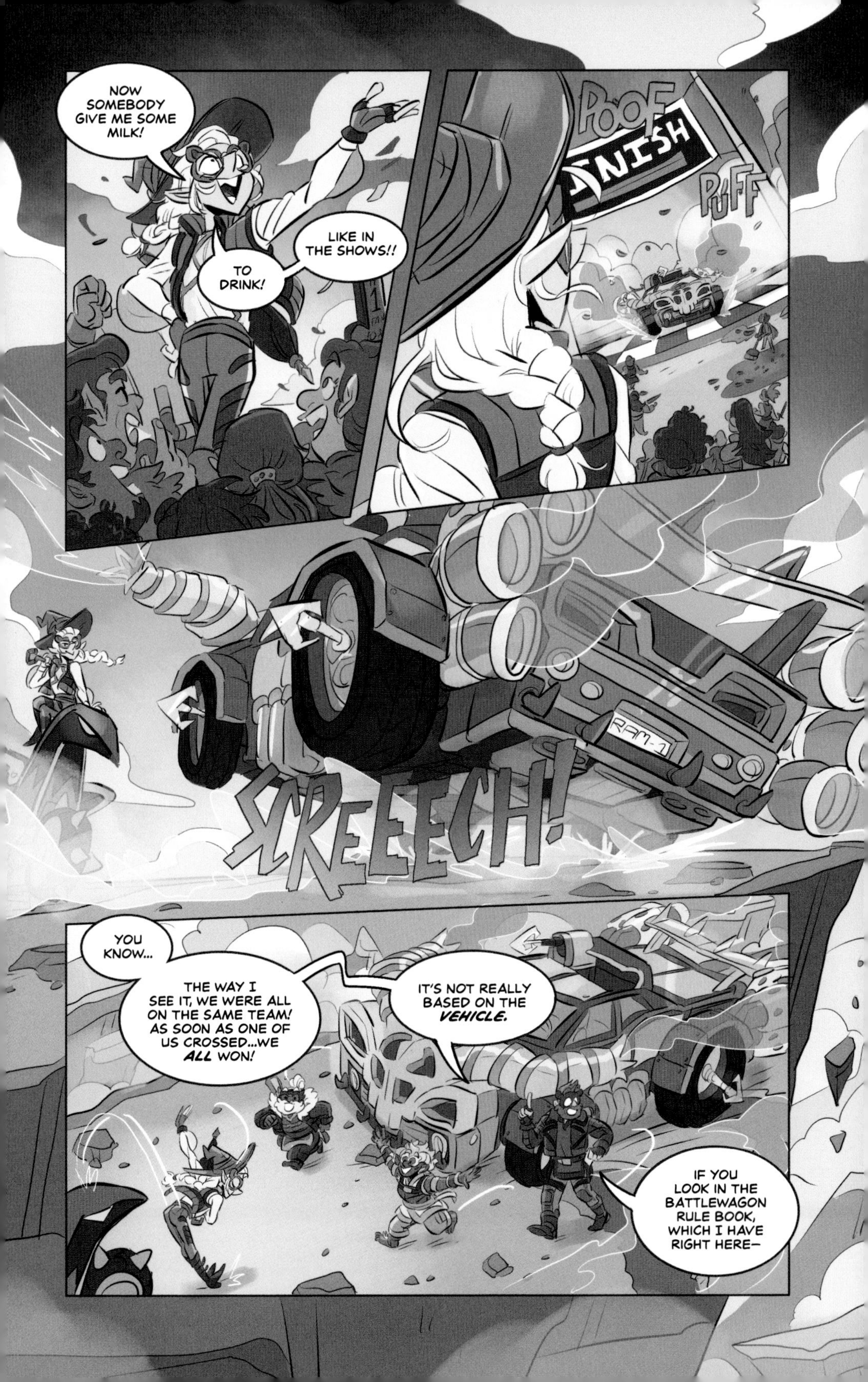
NOW SOMEBODY GIVE ME SOME MILK!
TO DRINK!
LIKE IN THE SHOWS!!
POOF
NISH
PUFF
RAM-1
SCREEECH!
YOU KNOW...
THE WAY I SEE IT, WE WERE ALL ON THE SAME TEAM! AS SOON AS ONE OF US CROSSED...WE ALL WON!
IT'S NOT REALLY BASED ON THE VEHICLE.
IF YOU LOOK IN THE BATTLEWAGON RULE BOOK, WHICH I HAVE RIGHT HERE—

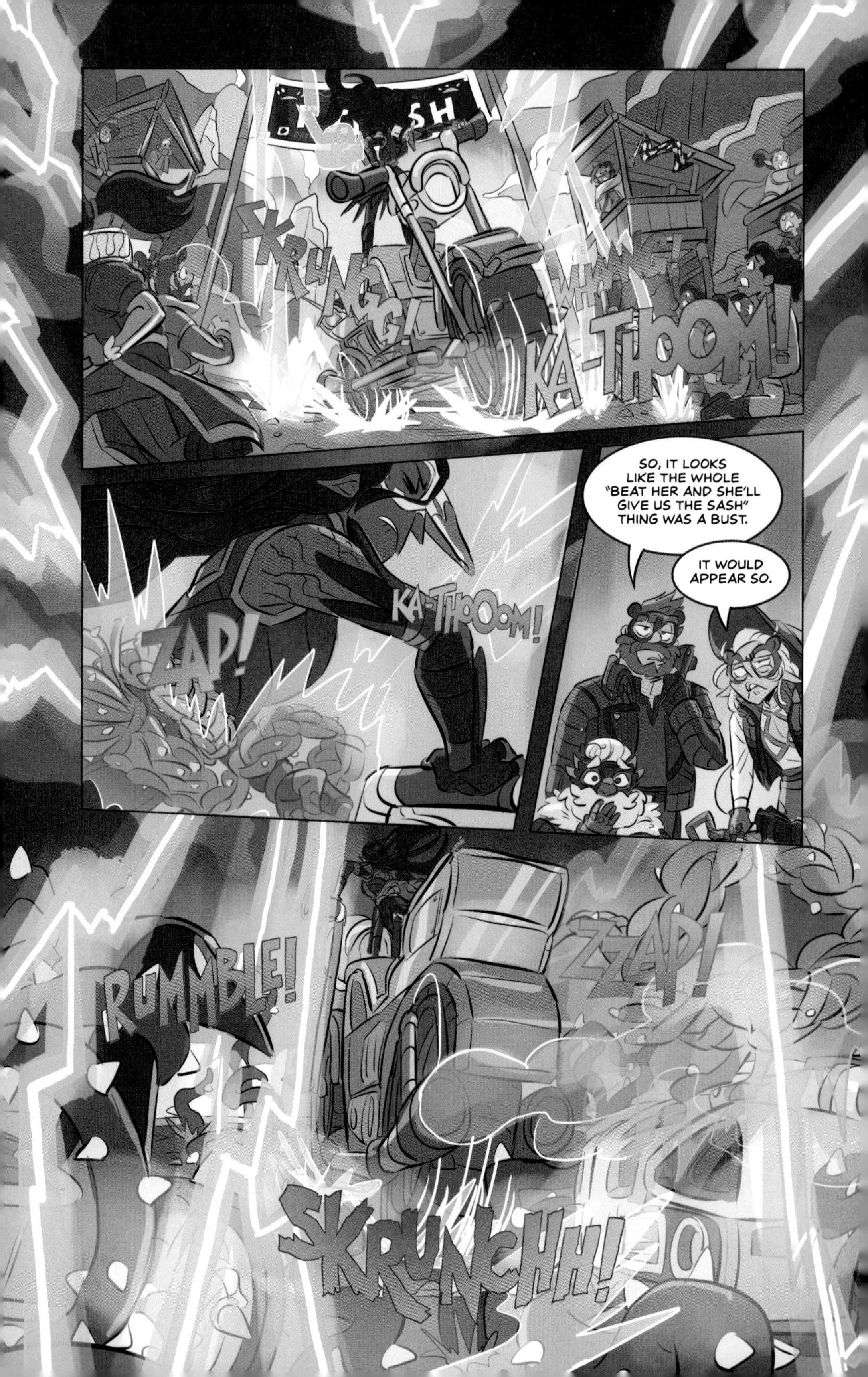
SKRUNGG!
WHANG!
KA-THOOM!
SO, IT LOOKS LIKE THE WHOLE "BEAT HER AND SHE'LL GIVE US THE SASH" THING WAS A BUST.
IT WOULD APPEAR SO.
ZAP!
KA-THOOOM!
RUMMBLE!
ZZAP!
SKRUNCHH!

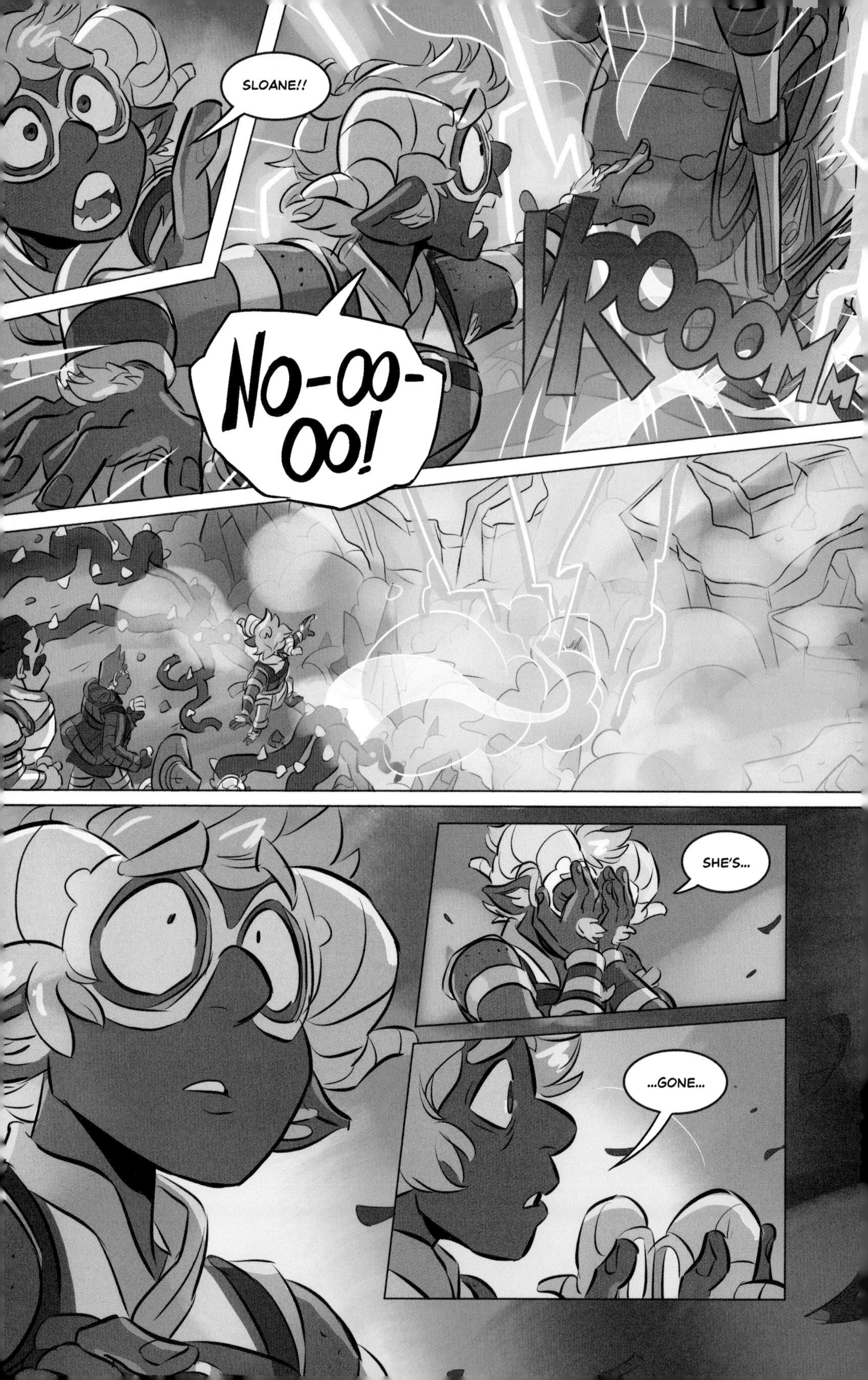
SLOANE!!
NO-OO-OO!
VROOOOM
SHE'S...
...GONE...

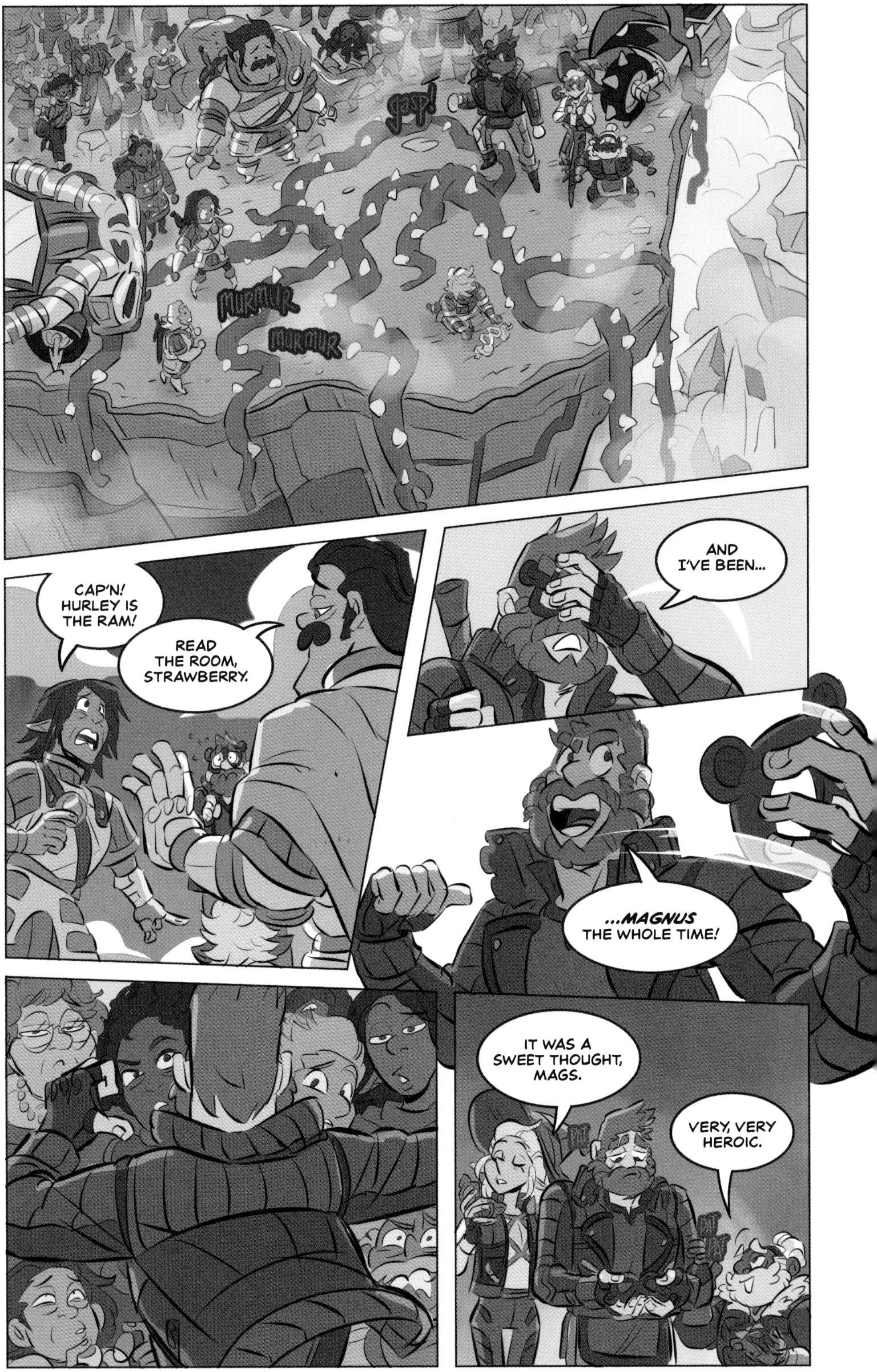
gasp!
MURMUR
MURMUR
CAP'N! HURLEY IS THE RAM!
READ THE ROOM, STRAWBERRY.
AND I'VE BEEN...
...MAGNUS THE WHOLE TIME!
IT WAS A SWEET THOUGHT, MAGS.
VERY, VERY HEROIC.
PAT
PAT PAT

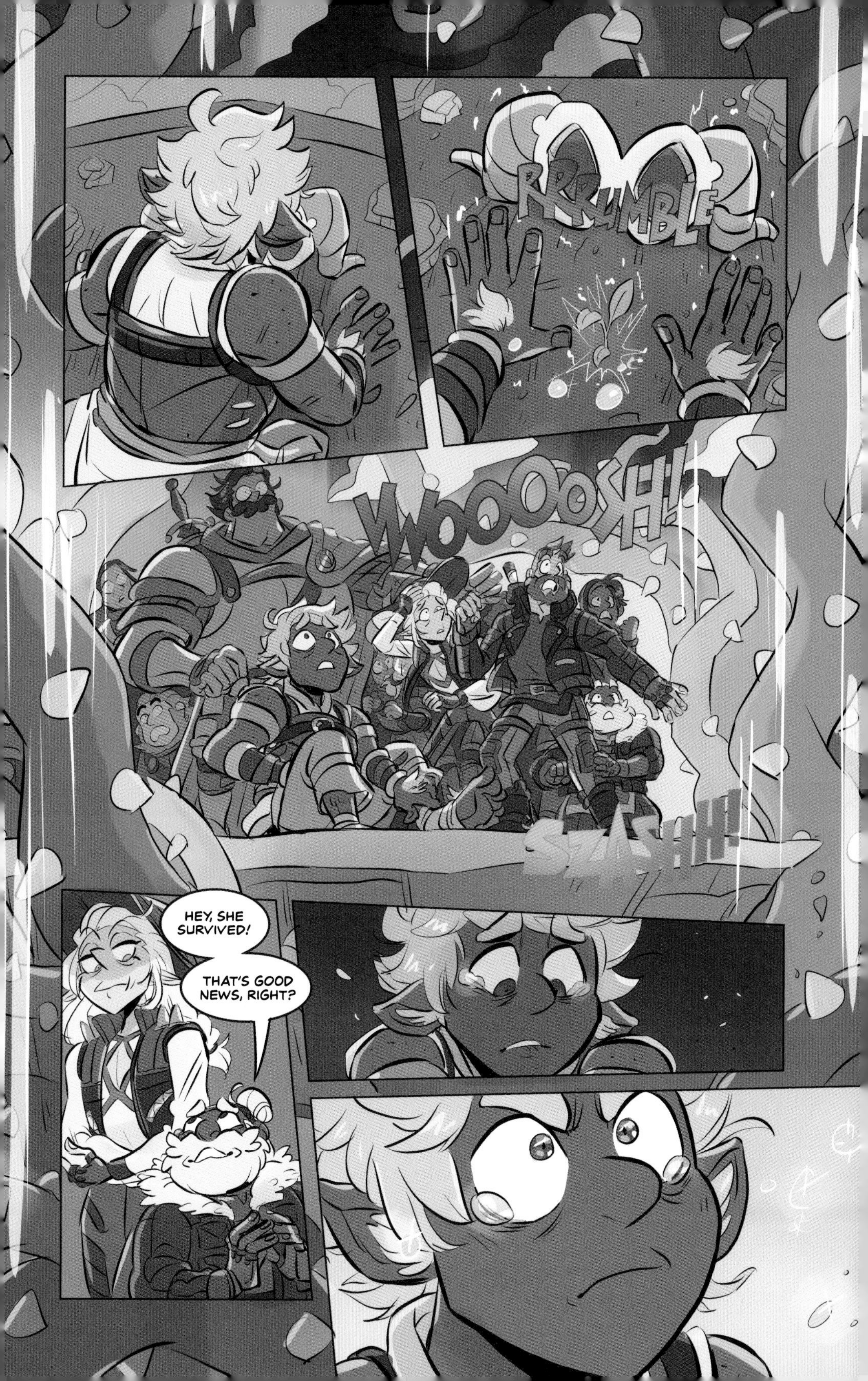
RRRUMBLE
WOOOOOSH!!
SZASHH!!
HEY, SHE SURVIVED!
THAT'S GOOD NEWS, RIGHT?

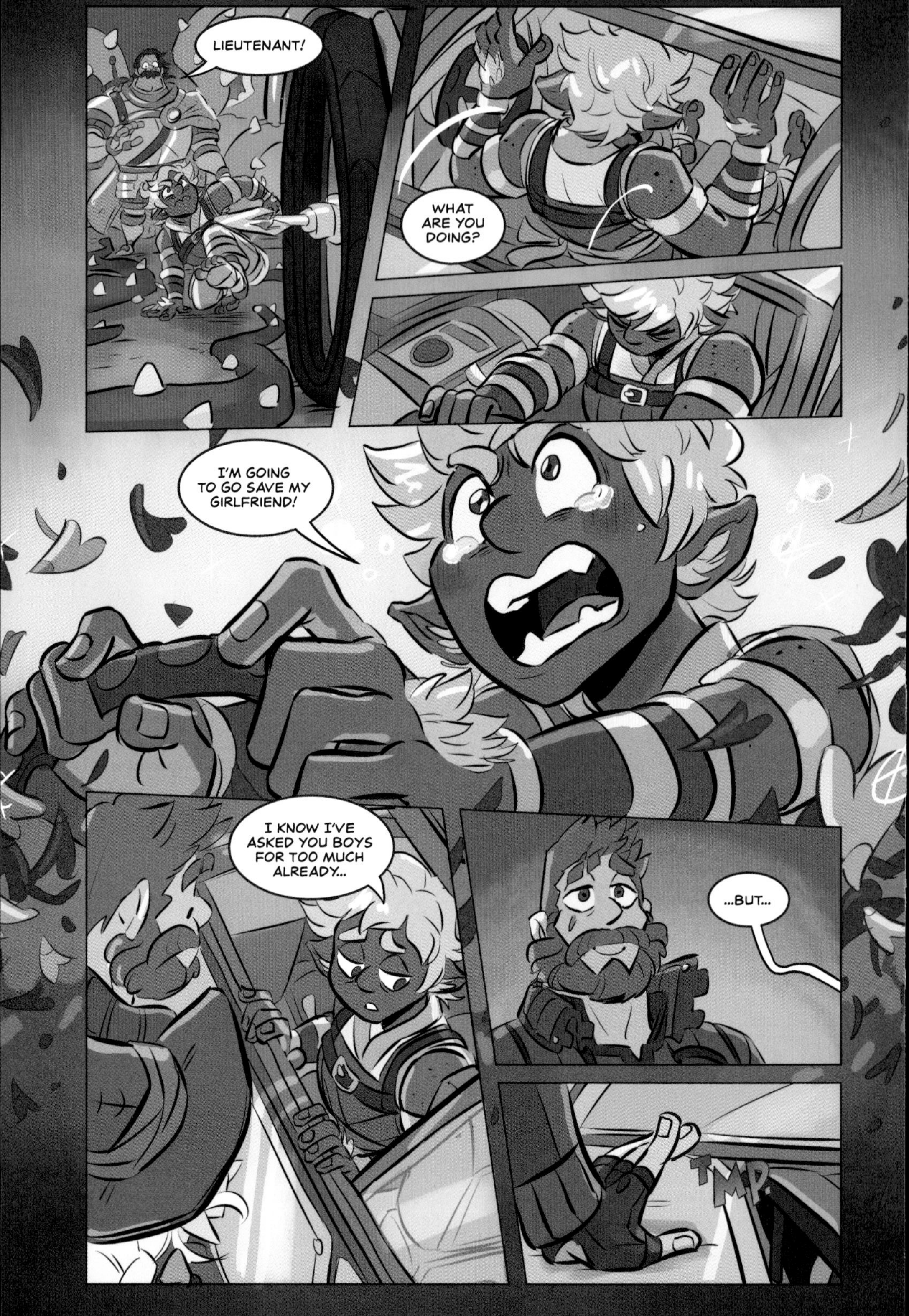
LIEUTENANT!
WHAT ARE YOU DOING?
I'M GOING TO GO SAVE MY GIRLFRIEND!
I KNOW I'VE ASKED YOU BOYS FOR TOO MUCH ALREADY...
...BUT...
TMP

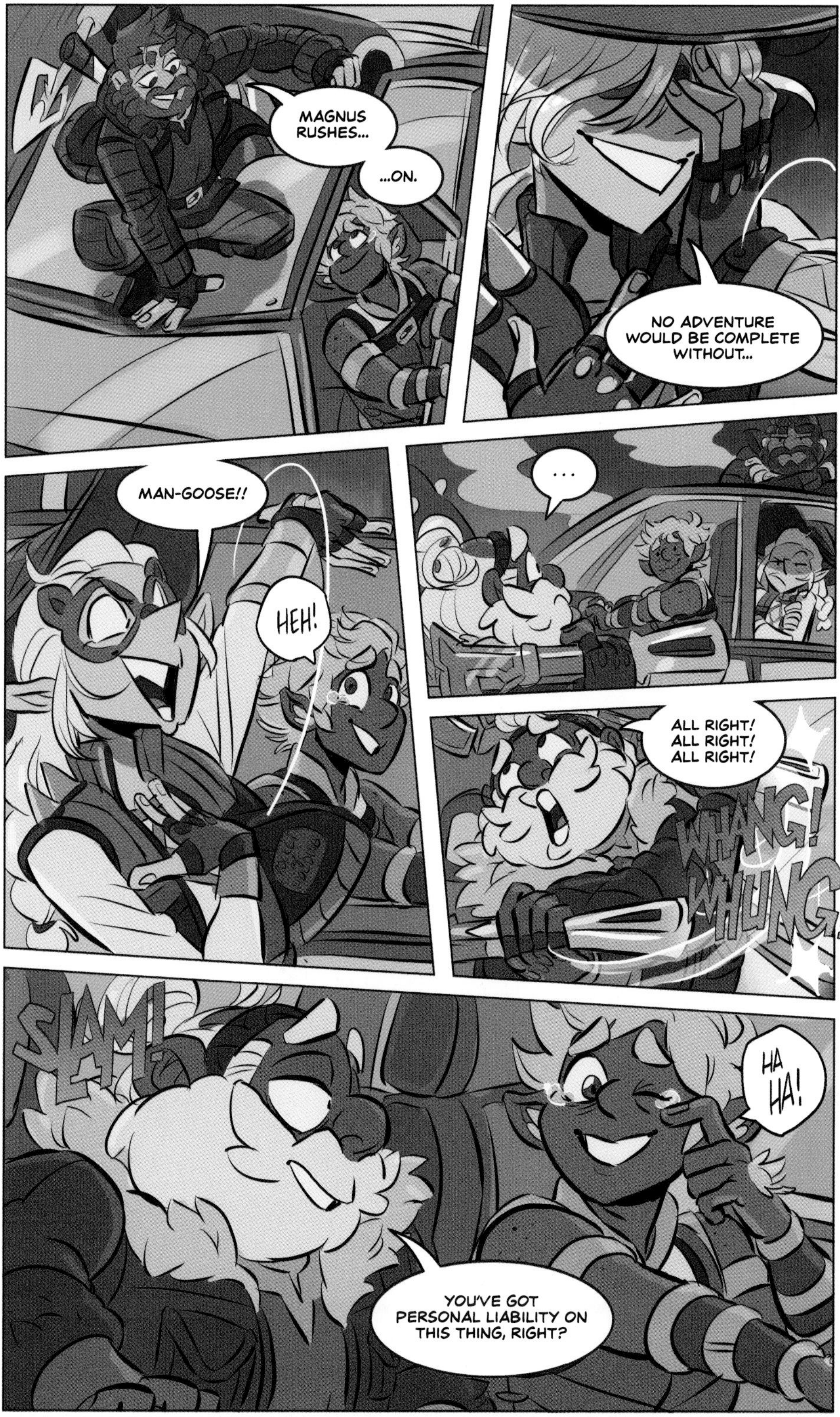
MAGNUS RUSHES...
...ON.
NO ADVENTURE WOULD BE COMPLETE WITHOUT...
MAN-GOOSE!!
HEH!
...
ALL RIGHT! ALL RIGHT! ALL RIGHT!
WHANG!
WHUNG!
SLAM!
HA HA!
YOU'VE GOT PERSONAL LIABILITY ON THIS THING, RIGHT?

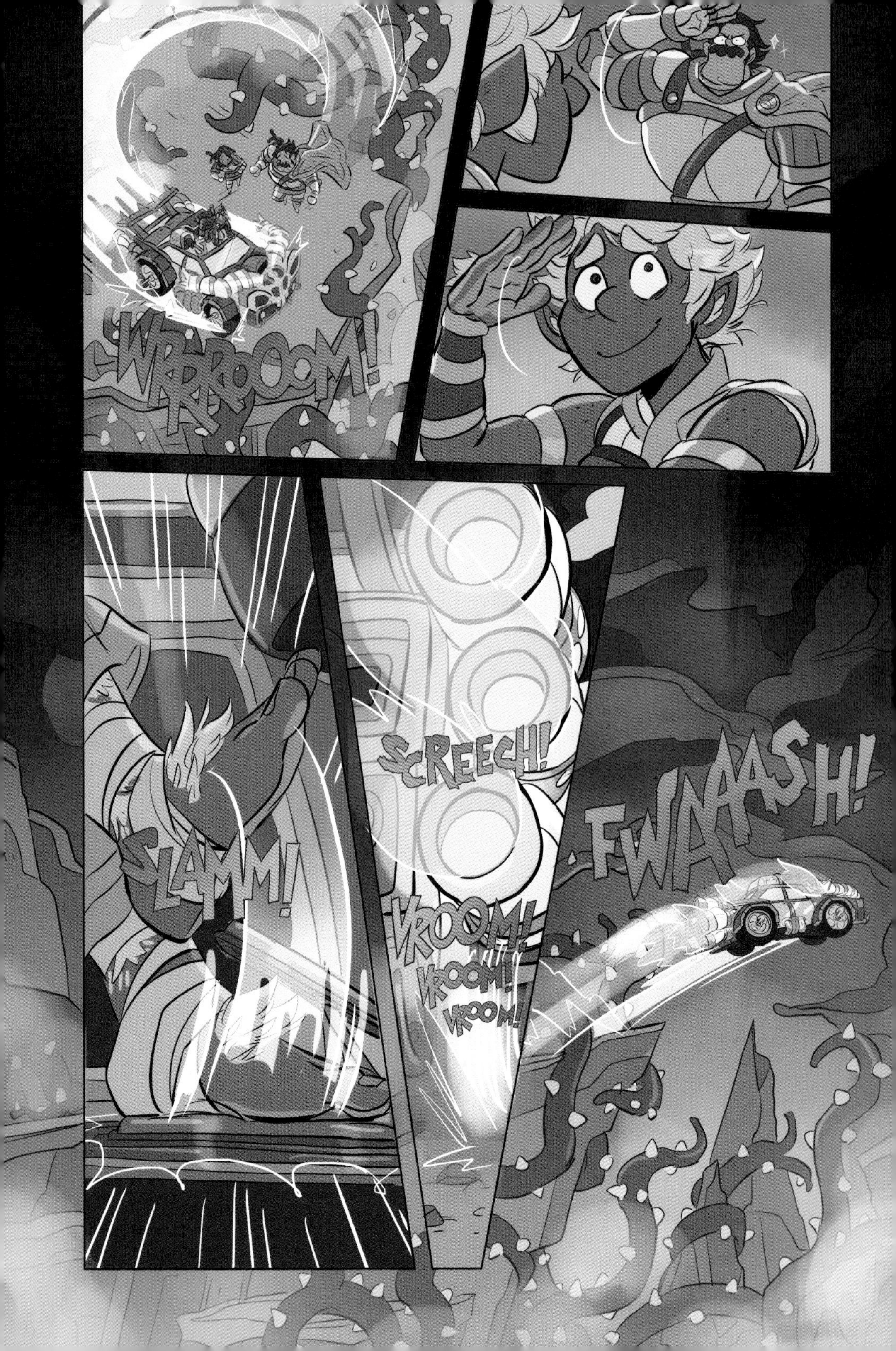
WRRROOOM!
SLAMM!
SCREECH!
VROOM!
VROOM!
VROOM!
FWAAASH!

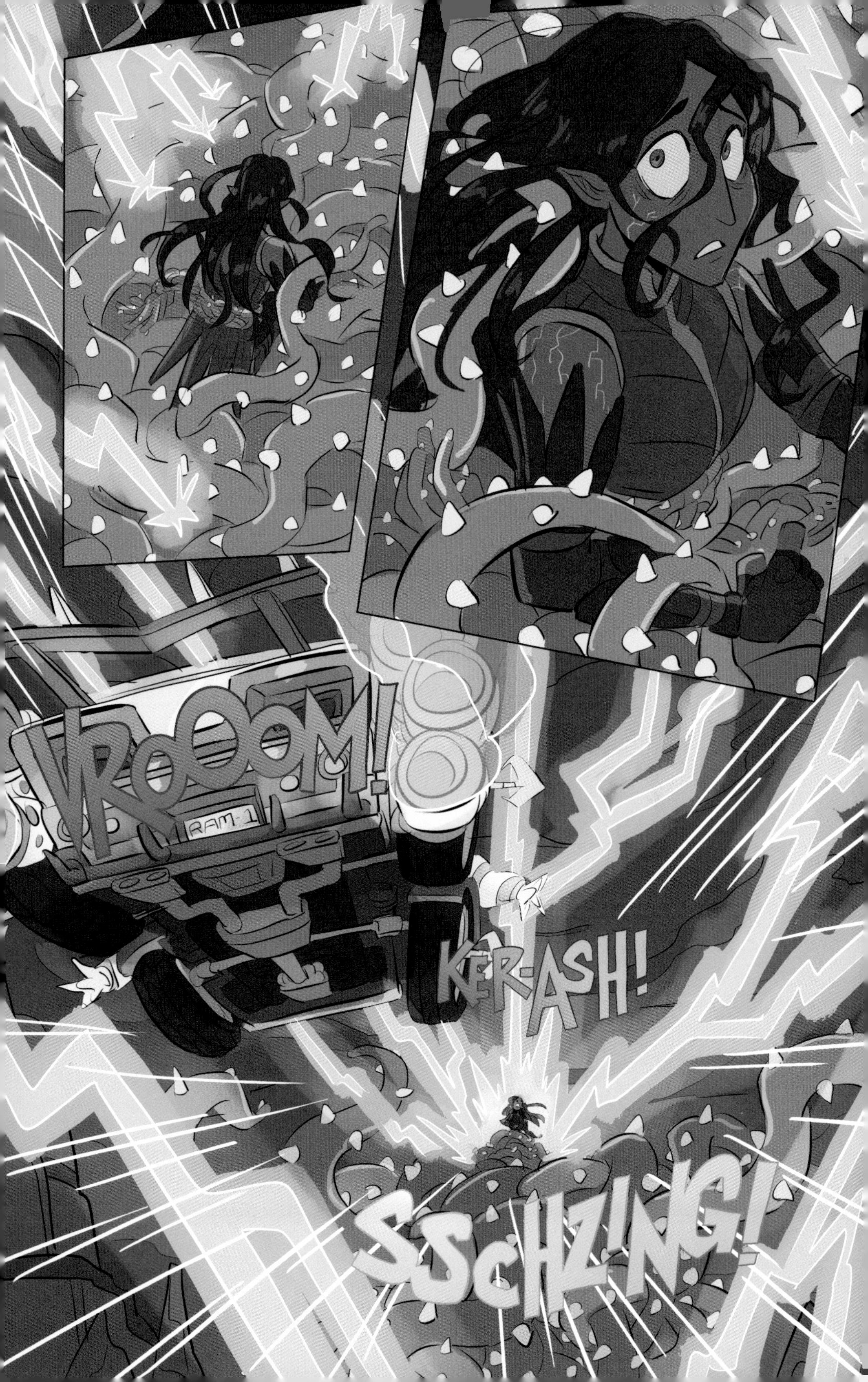
VROOOM!
RAM-1
KER-ASH!
SSCHZING!

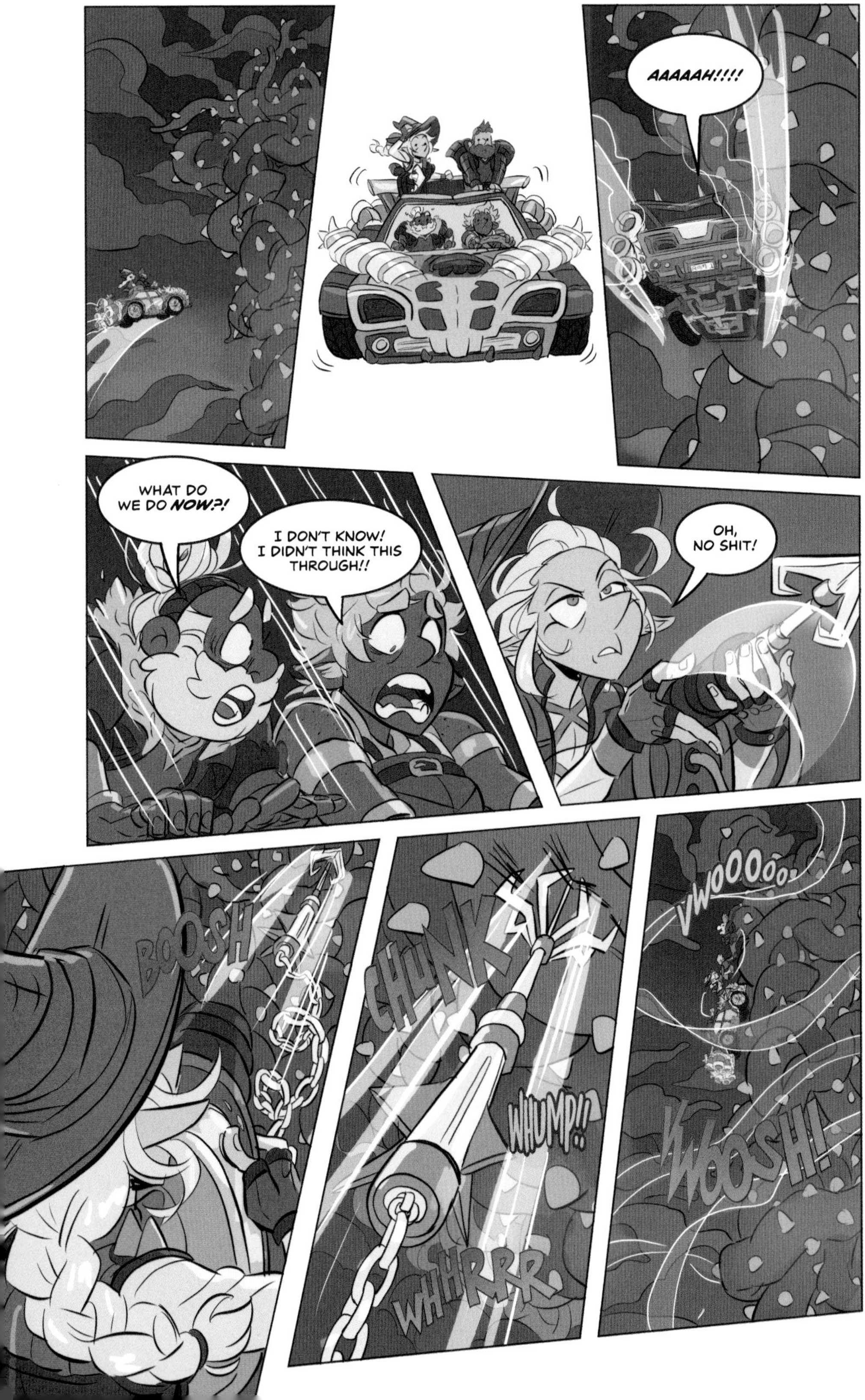

AAAAAH!!!!
WHAT DO WE DO NOW?!
I DON'T KNOW! I DIDN'T THINK THIS THROUGH!!
OH, NO SHIT!
BOOSH
CHUNK
WHUMP!!
WHHRRR
VWOOOOoo
WOOSH!

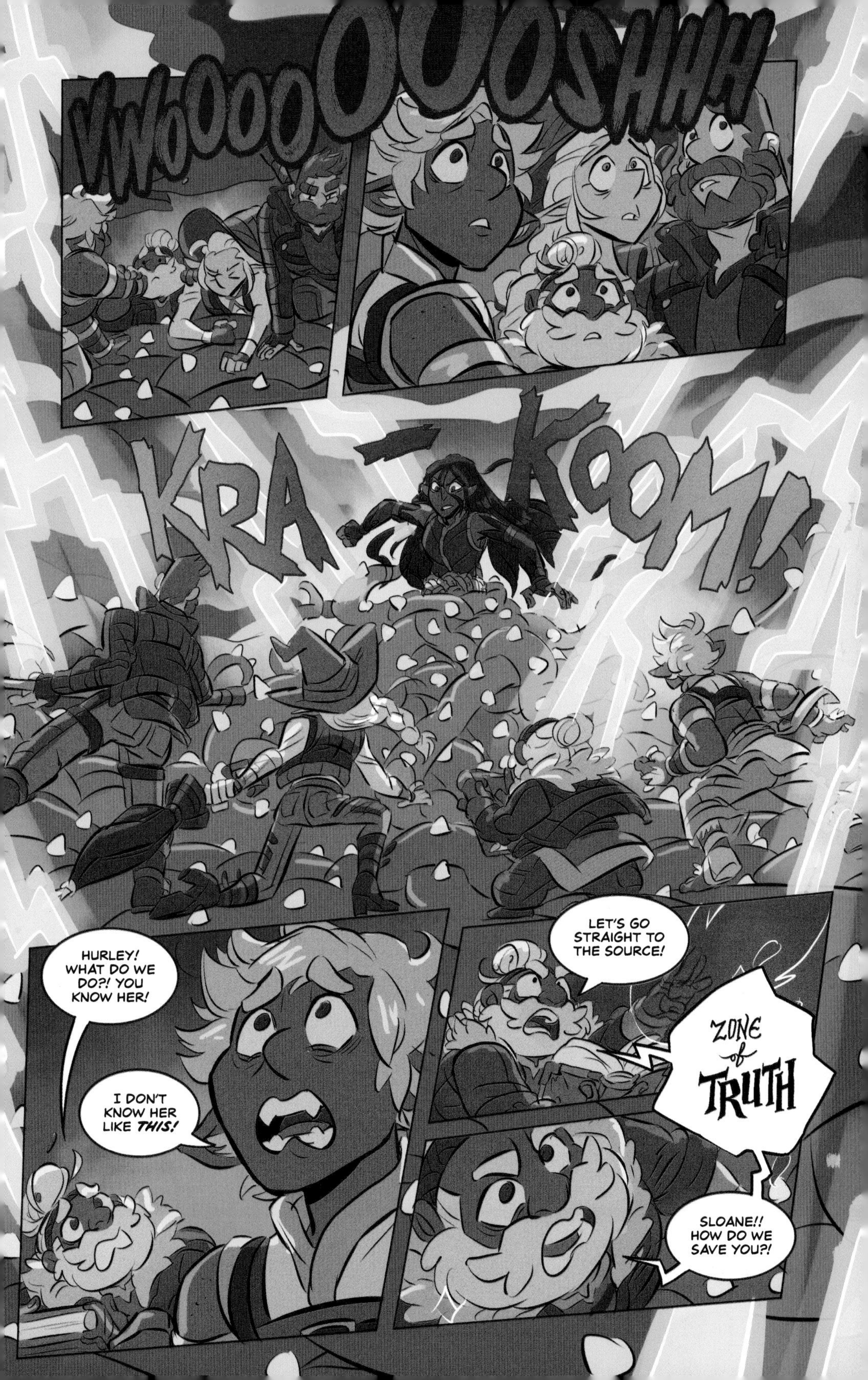
VWOOOOOUUOSHHH
KRA-KOOM!!
HURLEY! WHAT DO WE DO?! YOU KNOW HER!
I DON'T KNOW HER LIKE *THIS!*
LET'S GO STRAIGHT TO THE SOURCE!
ZONE of TRUTH
SLOANE!! HOW DO WE SAVE YOU?!

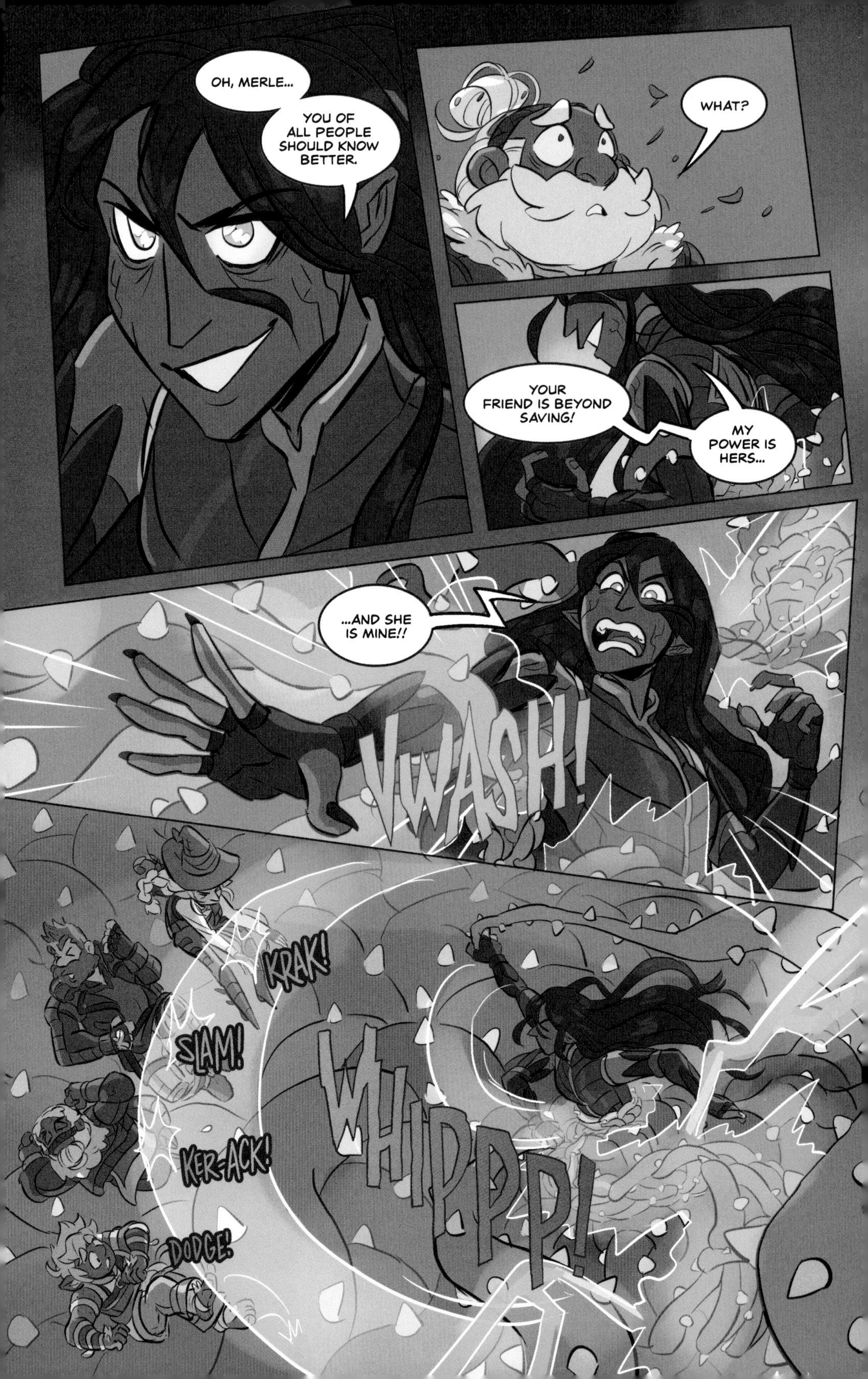
OH, MERLE...
YOU OF ALL PEOPLE SHOULD KNOW BETTER.
WHAT?
YOUR FRIEND IS BEYOND SAVING!
MY POWER IS HERS...
...AND SHE IS MINE!!
VWASH!
KRAK!
SLAM!
KER-ACK!
DODGE!
WHIPPP!

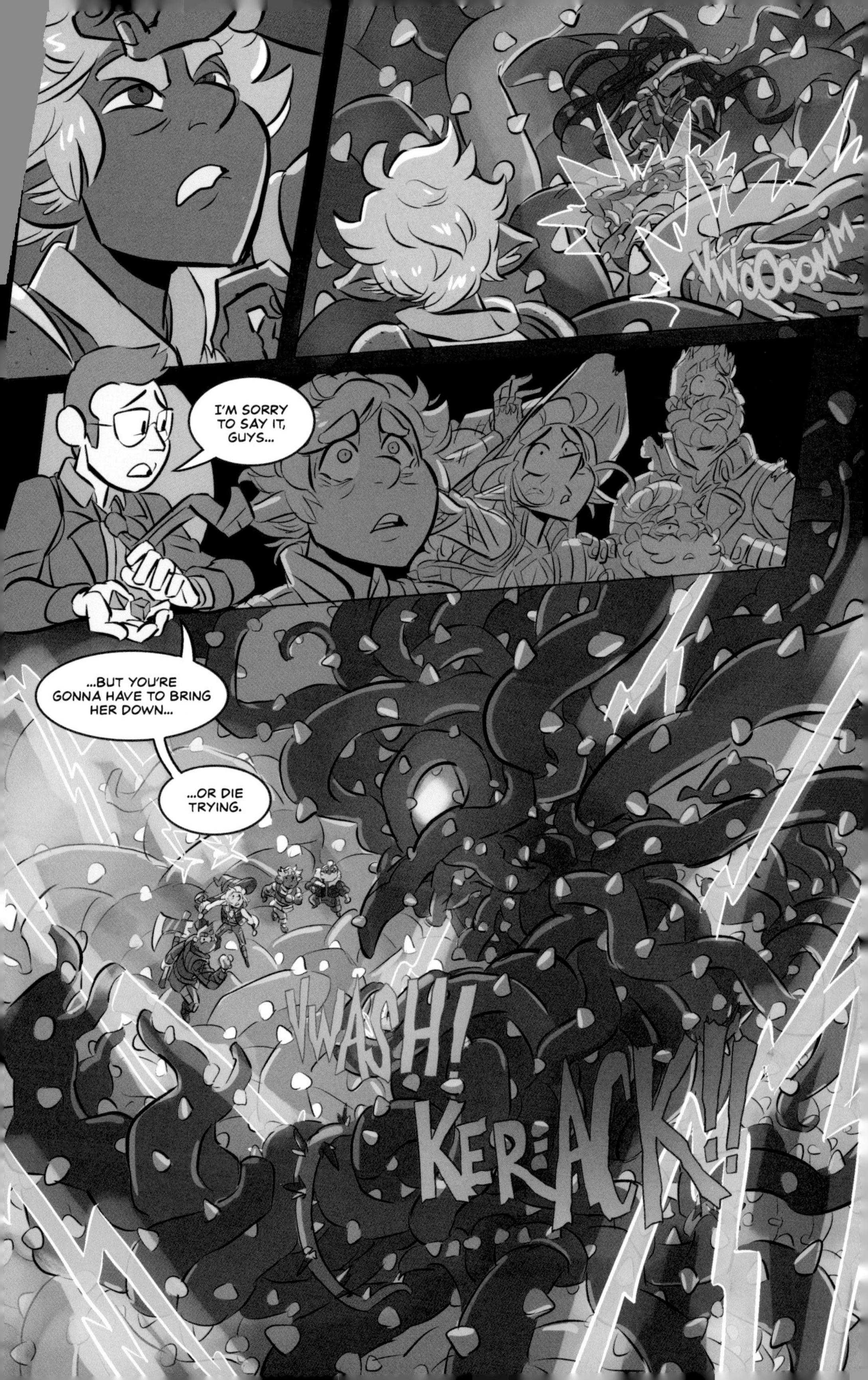
VWOOOOMM
I'M SORRY TO SAY IT, GUYS...
...BUT YOU'RE GONNA HAVE TO BRING HER DOWN...
...OR DIE TRYING.
VWASH!
KER-ACK!

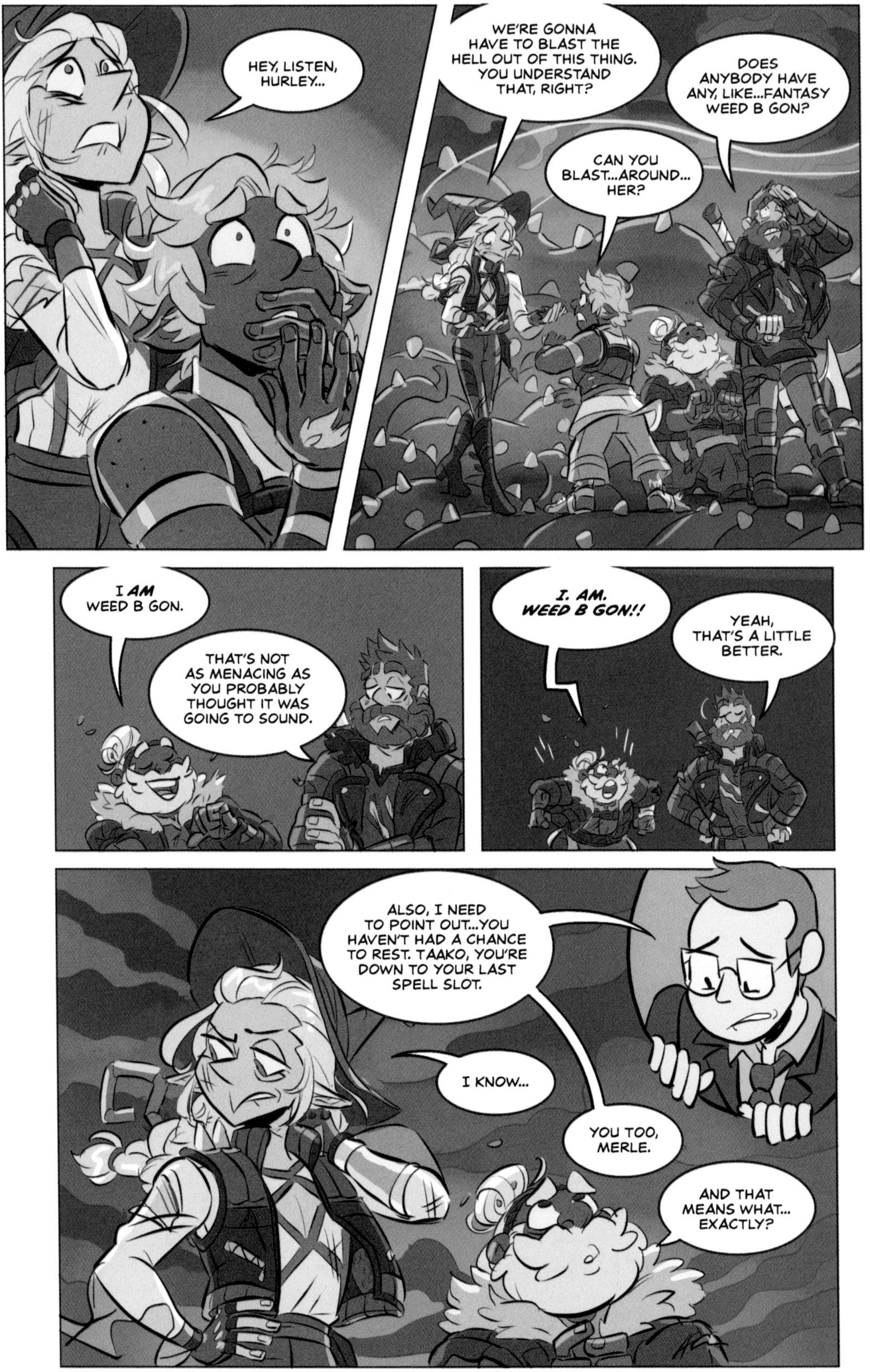
HEY, LISTEN, HURLEY...
WE'RE GONNA HAVE TO BLAST THE HELL OUT OF THIS THING. YOU UNDERSTAND THAT, RIGHT?
DOES ANYBODY HAVE ANY, LIKE...FANTASY WEED B GON?
CAN YOU BLAST...AROUND... HER?
I *AM* WEED B GON.
THAT'S NOT AS MENACING AS YOU PROBABLY THOUGHT IT WAS GOING TO SOUND.
I. AM. WEED B GON!!
YEAH, THAT'S A LITTLE BETTER.
ALSO, I NEED TO POINT OUT...YOU HAVEN'T HAD A CHANCE TO REST. TAAKO, YOU'RE DOWN TO YOUR LAST SPELL SLOT.
I KNOW...
YOU TOO, MERLE.
AND THAT MEANS WHAT... EXACTLY?

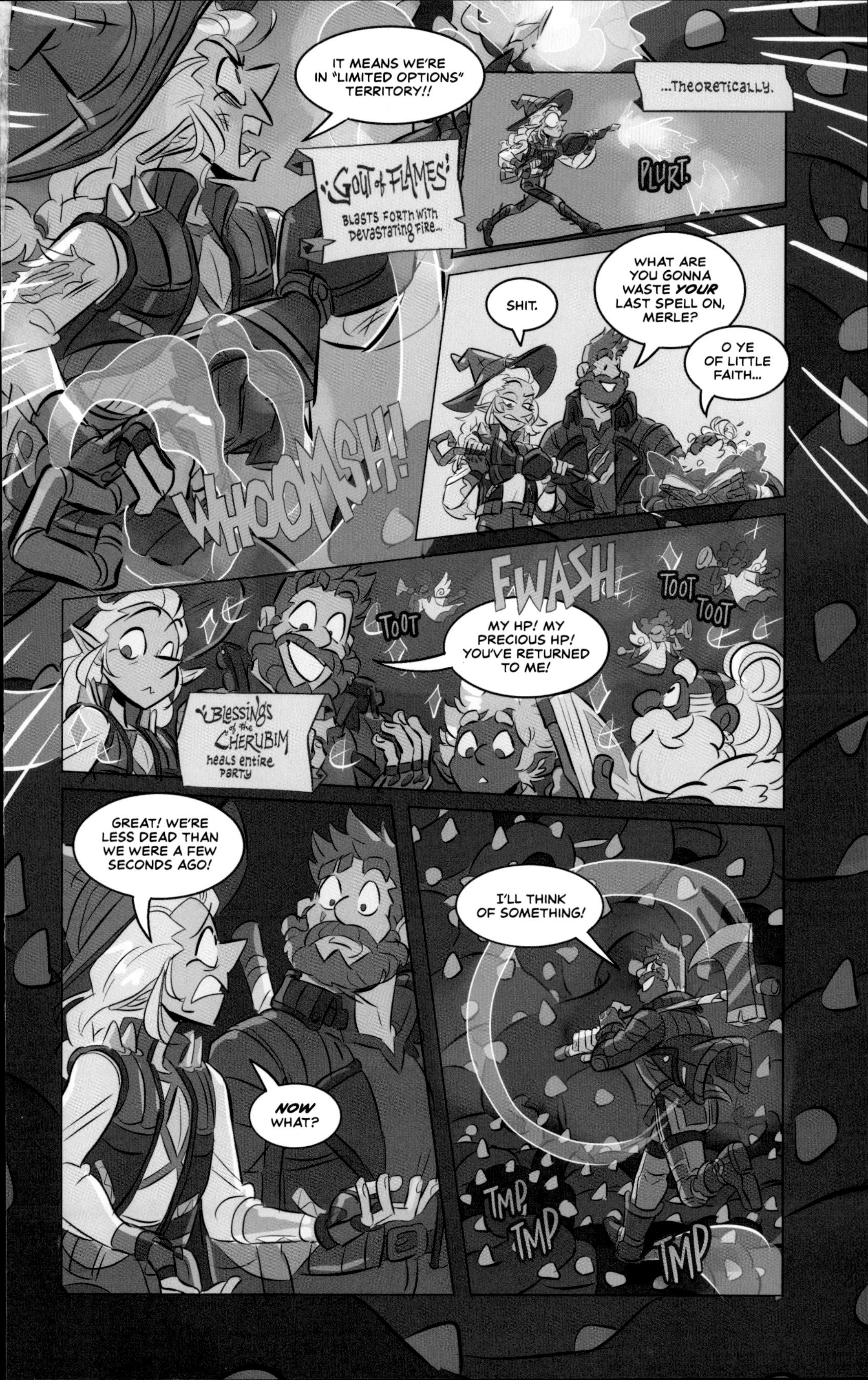
IT MEANS WE'RE IN "LIMITED OPTIONS" TERRITORY!!
Gout of Flames
Blasts forth with devastating fire...
...theoretically.
PLURT.
WHOOMSH!
SHIT.
WHAT ARE YOU GONNA WASTE YOUR LAST SPELL ON, MERLE?
O YE OF LITTLE FAITH...
FWASH
TOOT
TOOT TOOT
MY HP! MY PRECIOUS HP! YOU'VE RETURNED TO ME!
Blessings of the Cherubim
heals entire party
GREAT! WE'RE LESS DEAD THAN WE WERE A FEW SECONDS AGO!
NOW WHAT?
I'LL THINK OF SOMETHING!
TMP
TMP
TMP

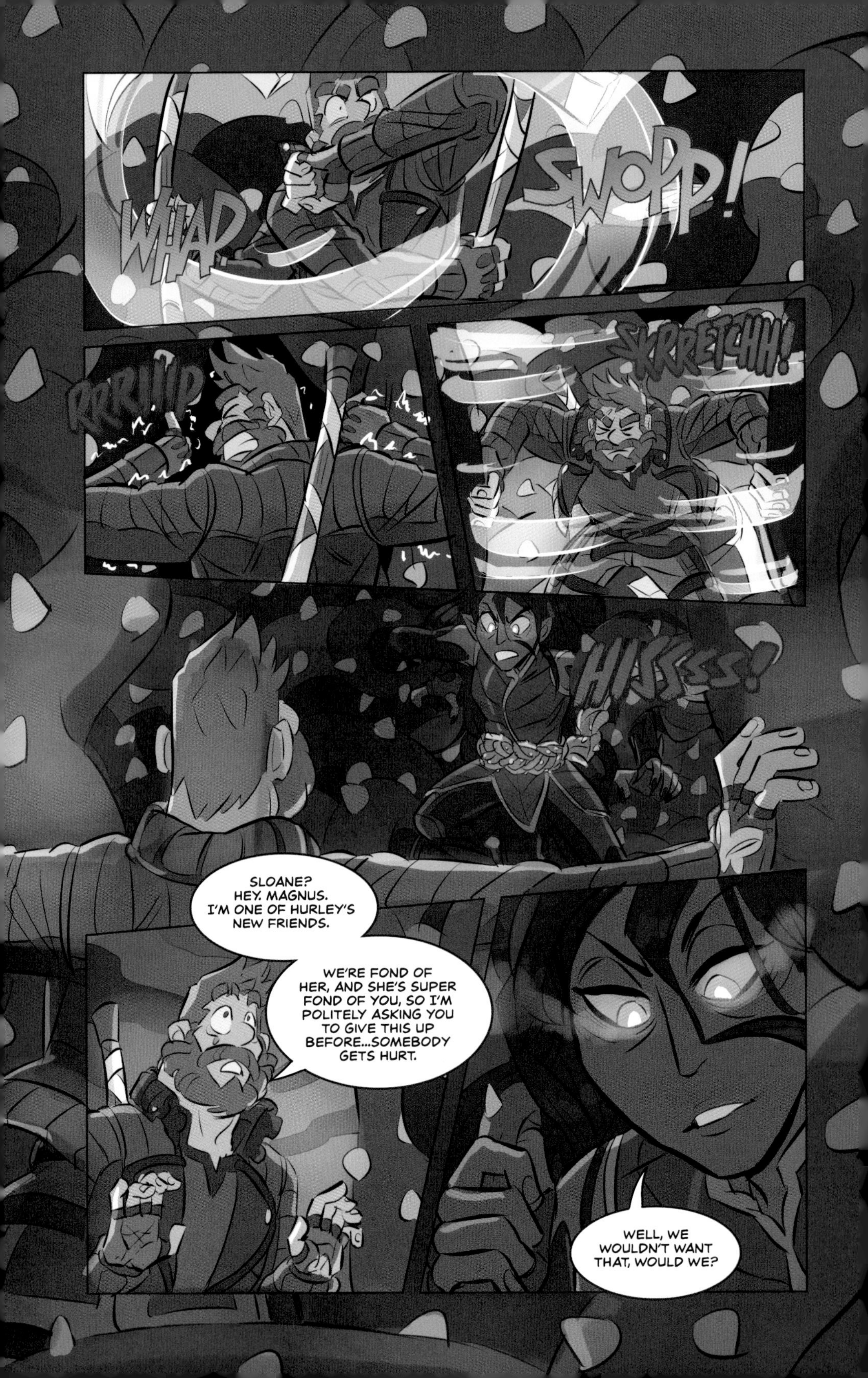
WHAP
SWOPP!
RRRIIIP
SKRRETCHH!
HISSSES!
SLOANE? HEY. MAGNUS. I'M ONE OF HURLEY'S NEW FRIENDS.
WE'RE FOND OF HER, AND SHE'S SUPER FOND OF YOU, SO I'M POLITELY ASKING YOU TO GIVE THIS UP BEFORE...SOMEBODY GETS HURT.
WELL, WE WOULDN'T WANT THAT, WOULD WE?

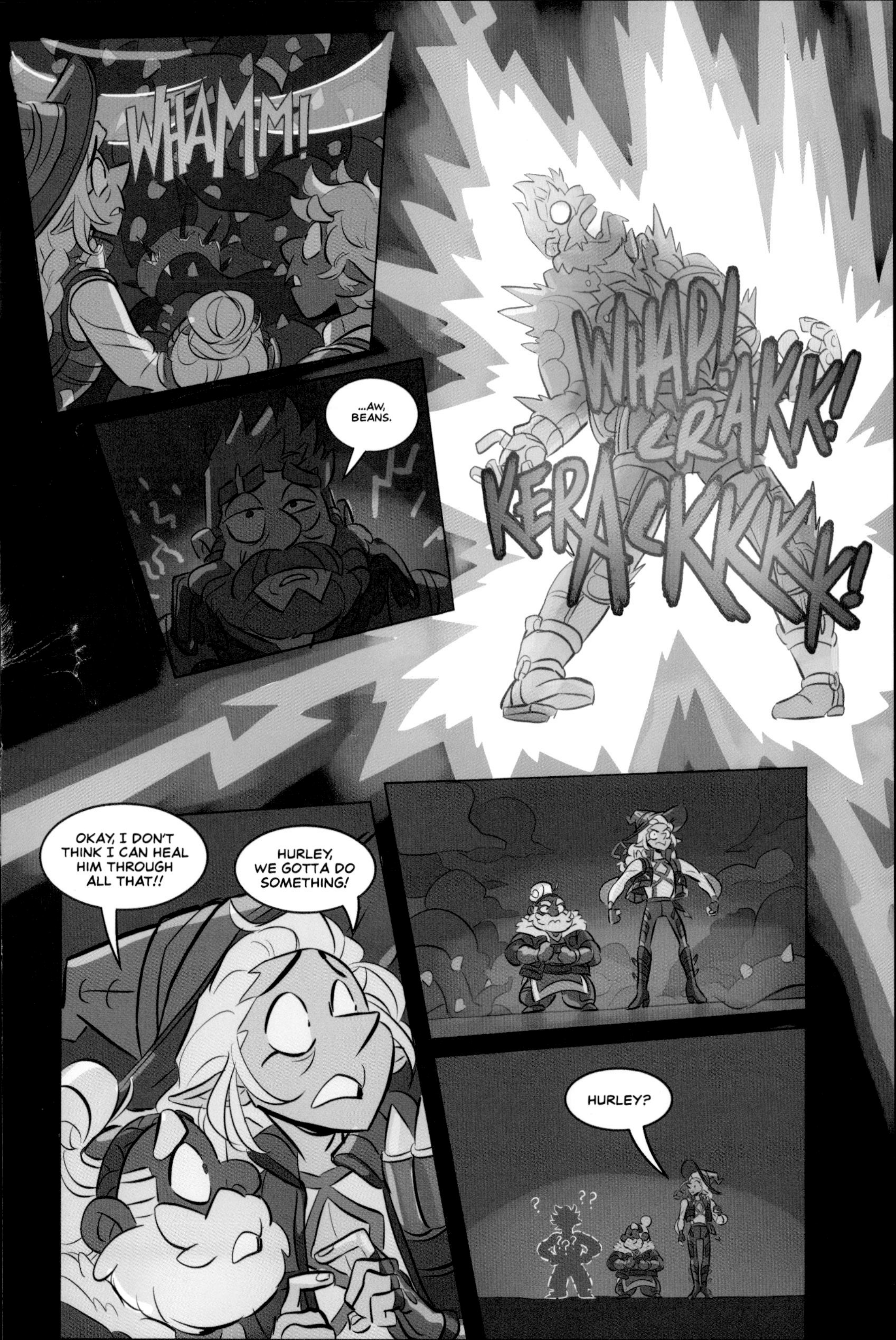
WHAMM!
...AW, BEANS.
WHAP! CRAKK! KERACKKKKK!
OKAY, I DON'T THINK I CAN HEAL HIM THROUGH ALL THAT!!
HURLEY, WE GOTTA DO SOMETHING!
HURLEY?

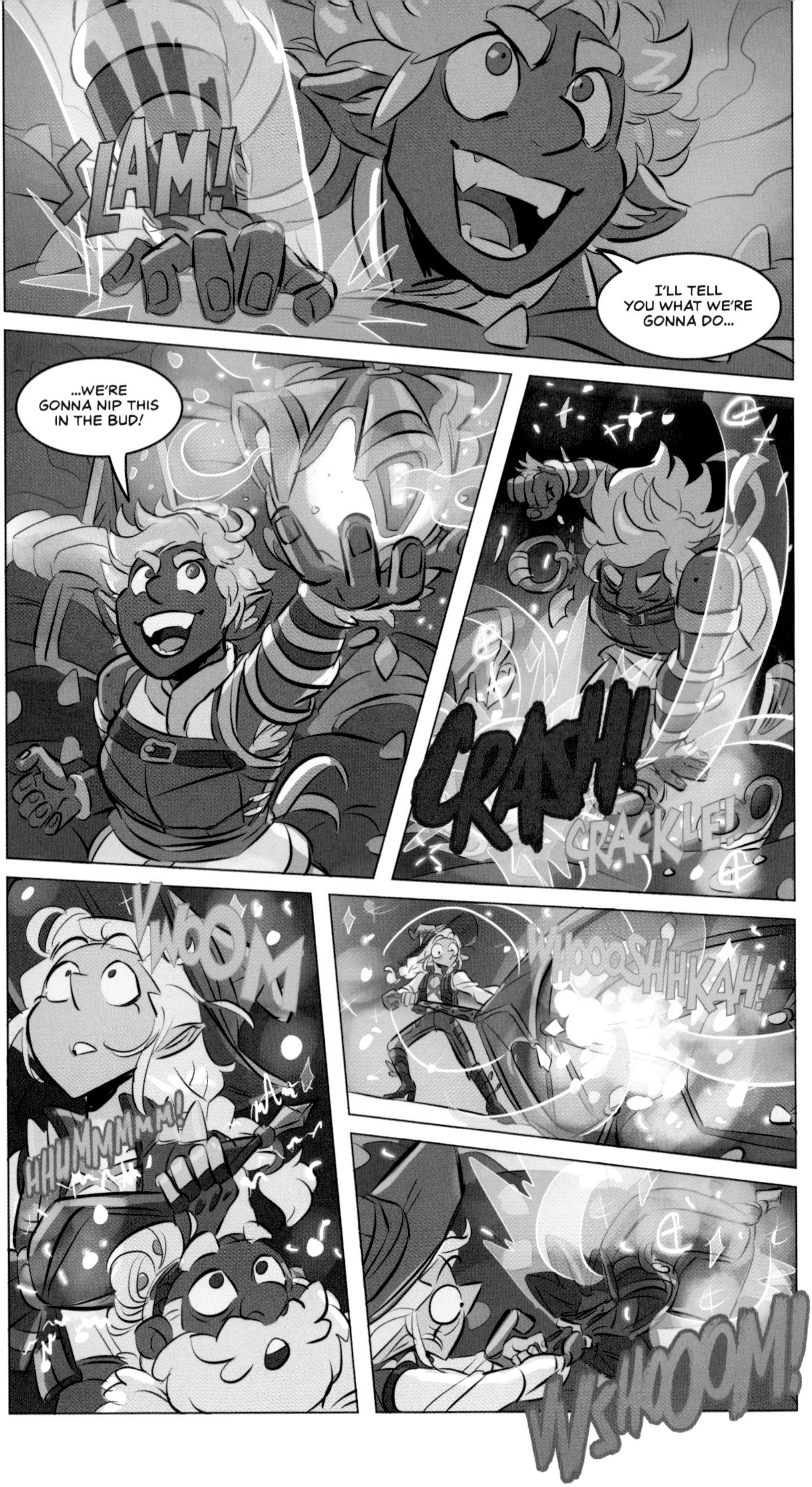
SLAM!
I'LL TELL YOU WHAT WE'RE GONNA DO...
...WE'RE GONNA NIP THIS IN THE BUD!
CRASH!
CRACKLE!
VWOOM
HHUMMMMM!
WHOOOSHHKAH!
WSHOOOM!

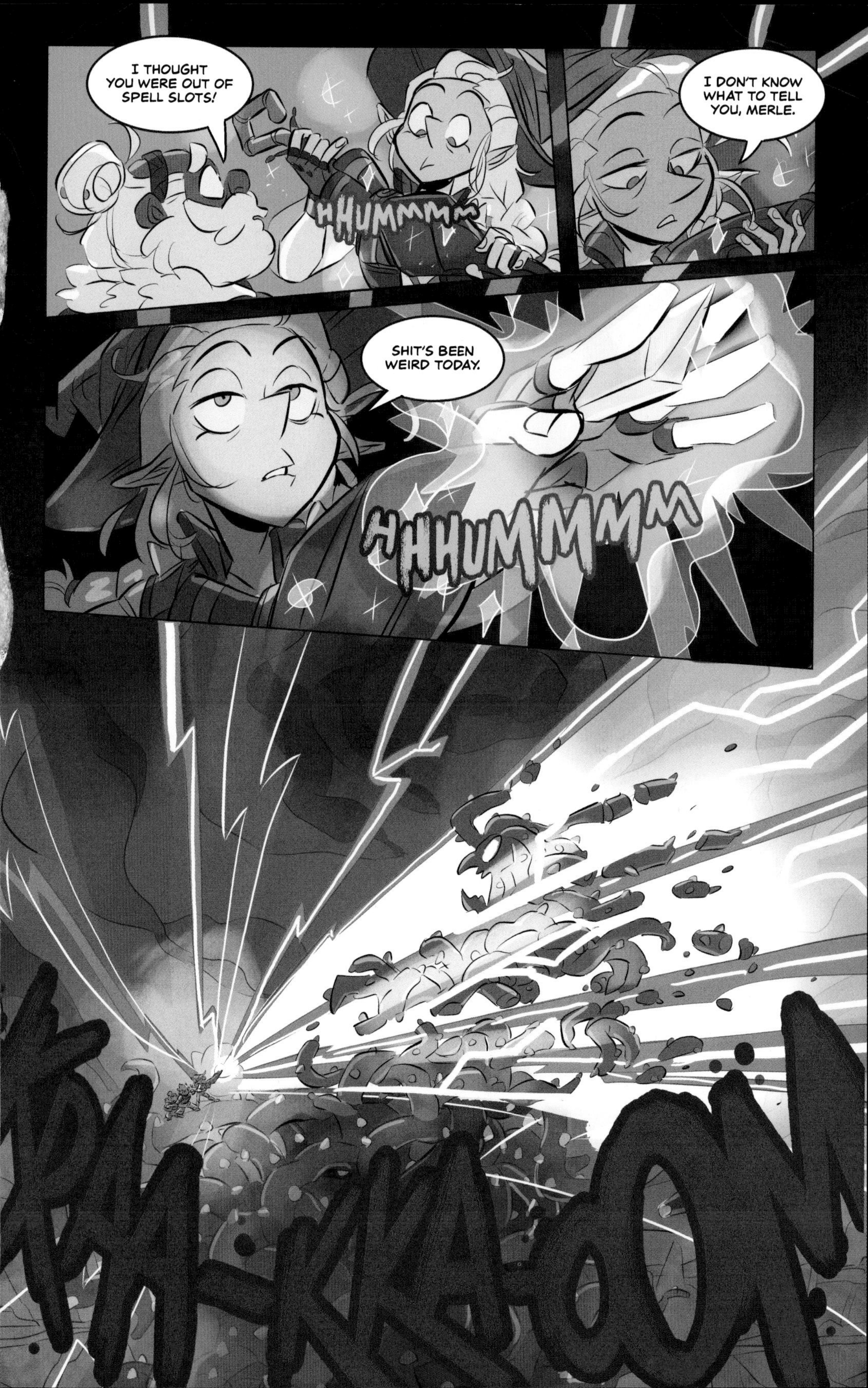
I THOUGHT YOU WERE OUT OF SPELL SLOTS!
HHUMMMM
I DON'T KNOW WHAT TO TELL YOU, MERLE.
SHIT'S BEEN WEIRD TODAY.
HHUMMMMM
KRA-KA-KA-OOOM!

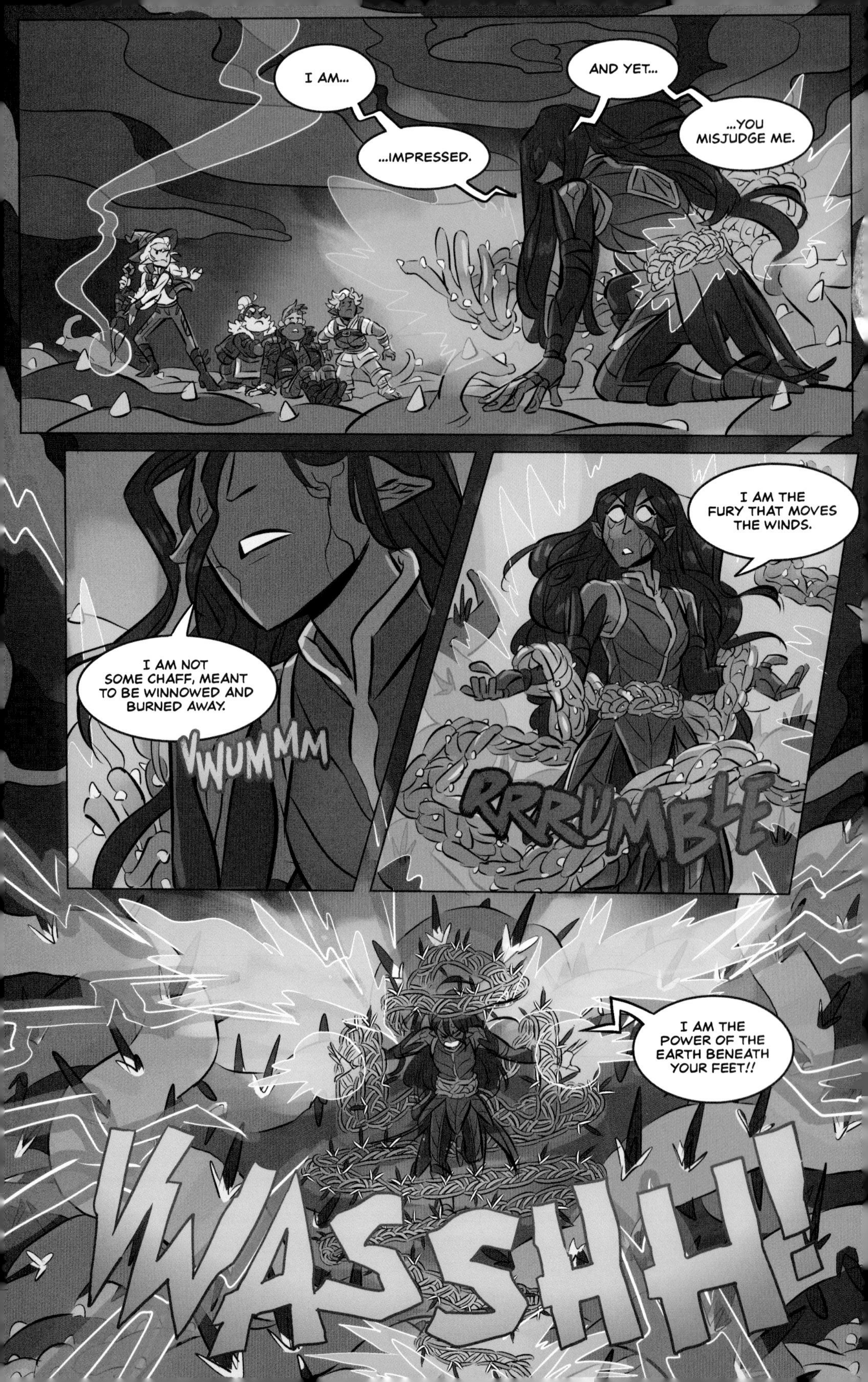
I AM...
...IMPRESSED.
AND YET...
...YOU MISJUDGE ME.
I AM NOT SOME CHAFF, MEANT TO BE WINNOWED AND BURNED AWAY.
VWUMMM
I AM THE FURY THAT MOVES THE WINDS.
RRRUMBLE
I AM THE POWER OF THE EARTH BENEATH YOUR FEET!!
WASHH!

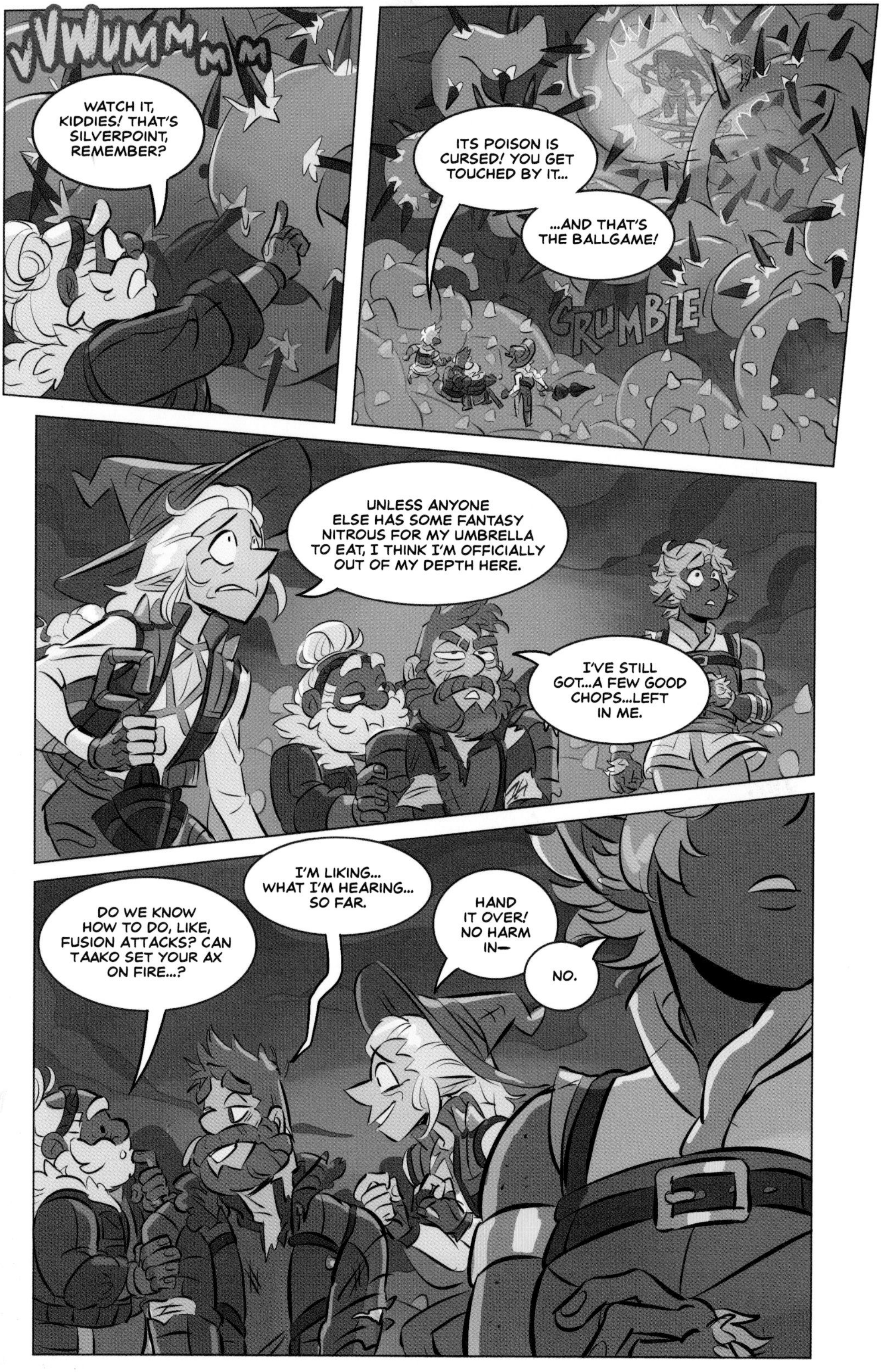
vVWUMMMMM
WATCH IT, KIDDIES! THAT'S SILVERPOINT, REMEMBER?
ITS POISON IS CURSED! YOU GET TOUCHED BY IT...
...AND THAT'S THE BALLGAME!
CRUMBLE
UNLESS ANYONE ELSE HAS SOME FANTASY NITROUS FOR MY UMBRELLA TO EAT, I THINK I'M OFFICIALLY OUT OF MY DEPTH HERE.
I'VE STILL GOT...A FEW GOOD CHOPS...LEFT IN ME.
DO WE KNOW HOW TO DO, LIKE, FUSION ATTACKS? CAN TAAKO SET YOUR AX ON FIRE...?
I'M LIKING... WHAT I'M HEARING... SO FAR.
HAND IT OVER! NO HARM IN—
NO.

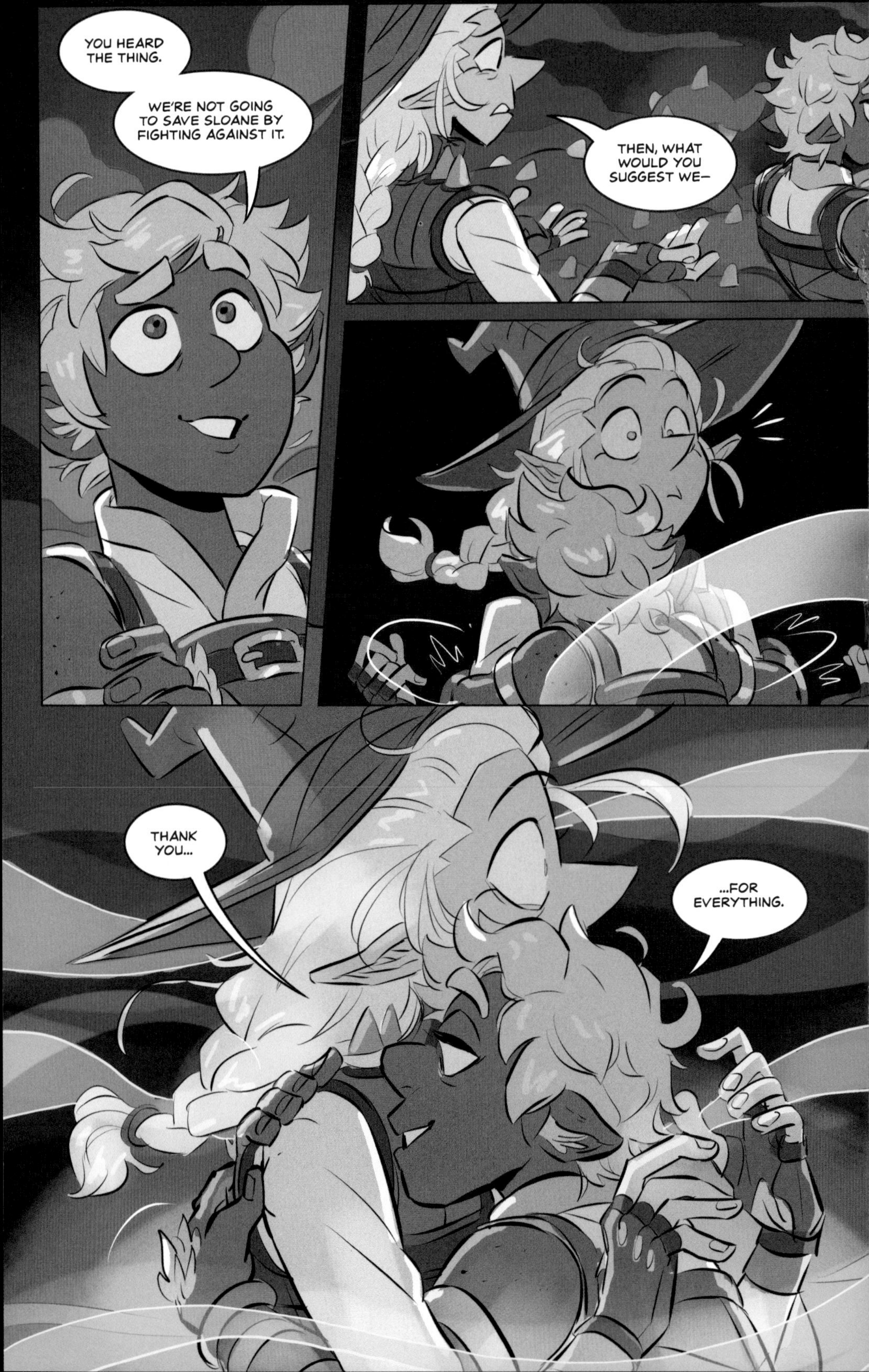
YOU HEARD THE THING.
WE'RE NOT GOING TO SAVE SLOANE BY FIGHTING AGAINST IT.
THEN, WHAT WOULD YOU SUGGEST WE—
THANK YOU...
...FOR EVERYTHING.

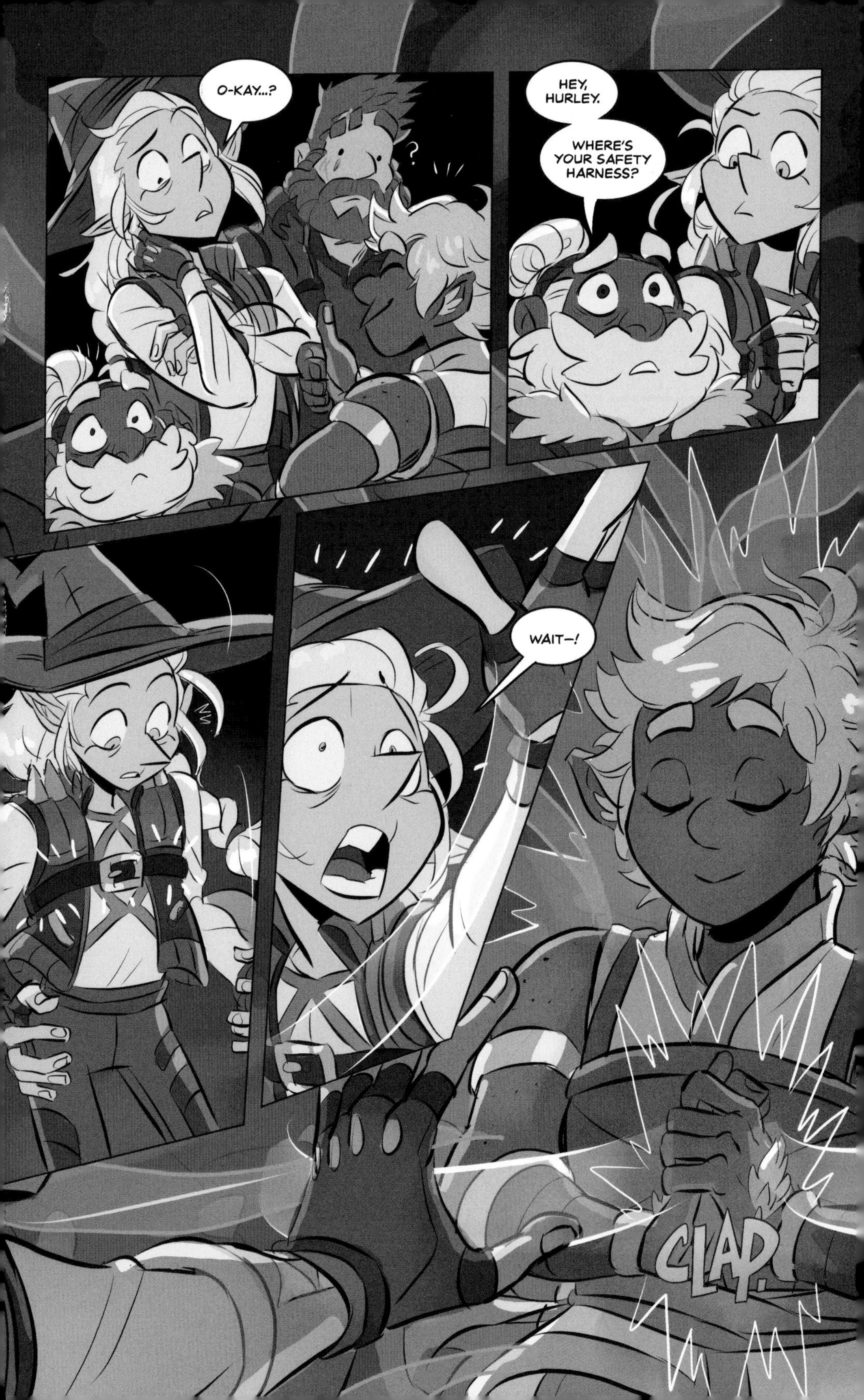
O-KAY...?
?
HEY, HURLEY.
WHERE'S YOUR SAFETY HARNESS?
WAIT—!
CLAP.

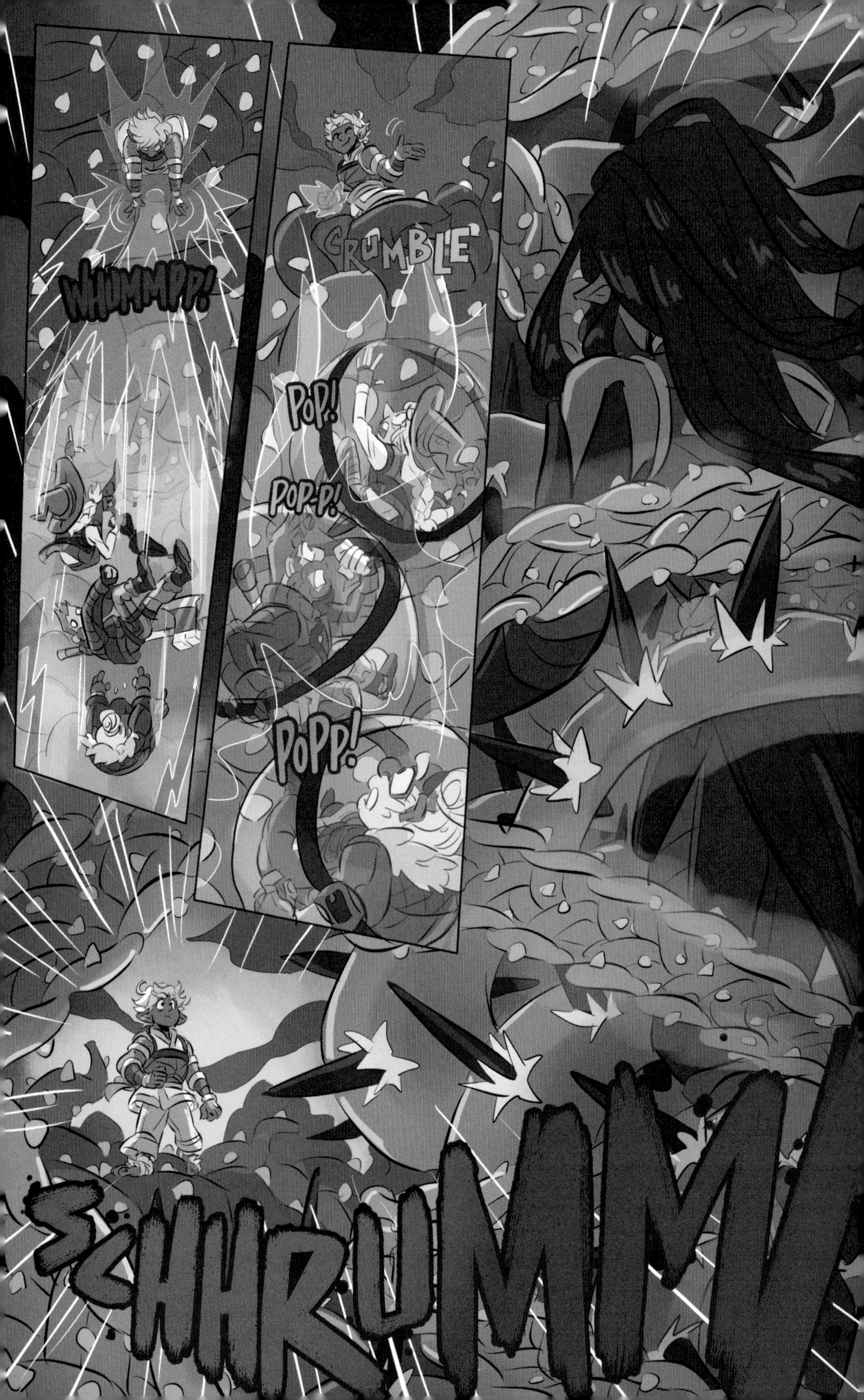
WHUMMPP!
CRUMBLE
POP!
POP-P!
POPP!
SCHHRUMMM

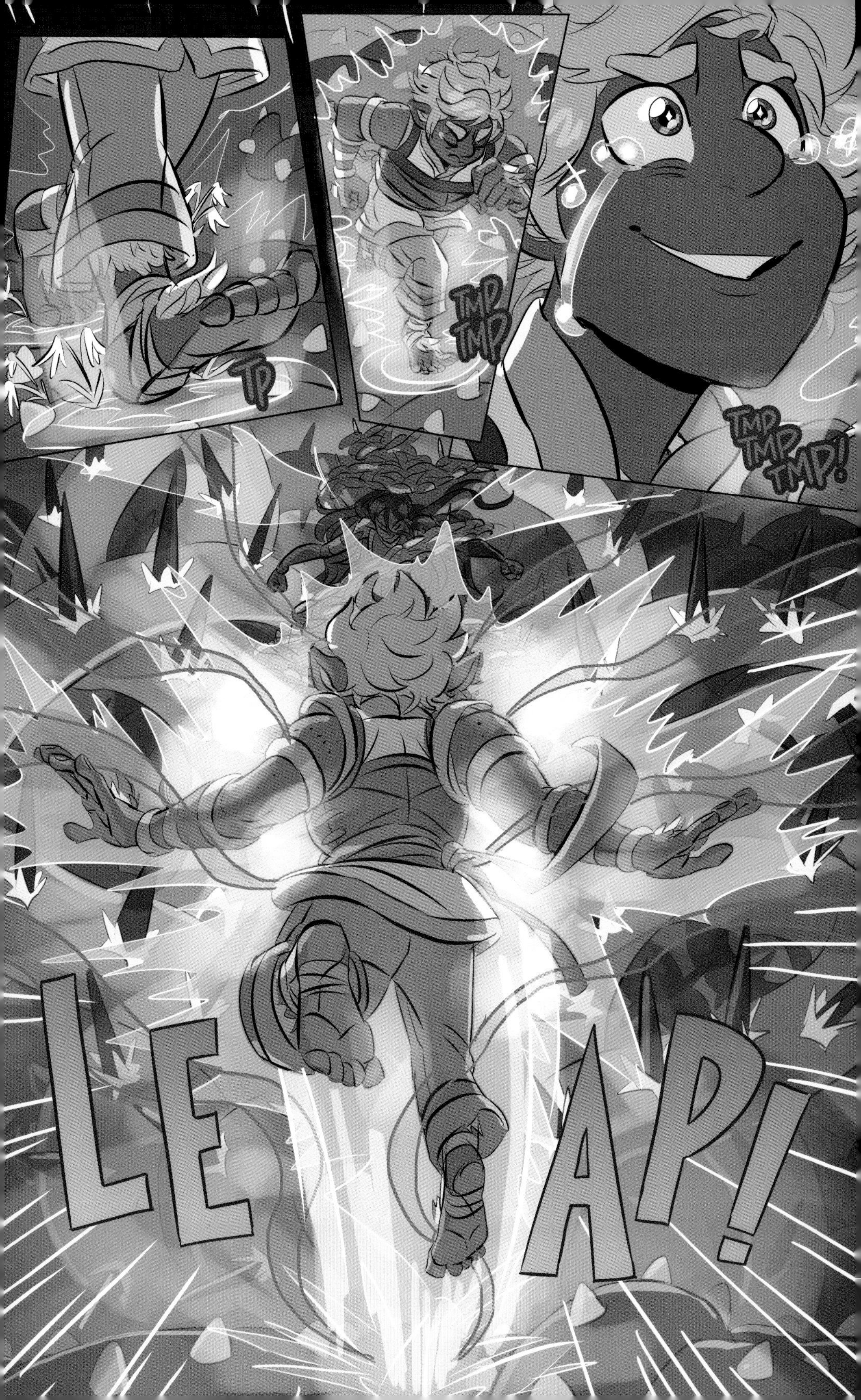
TP
TMP TMP
TMP TMP TMP!
LEAP!

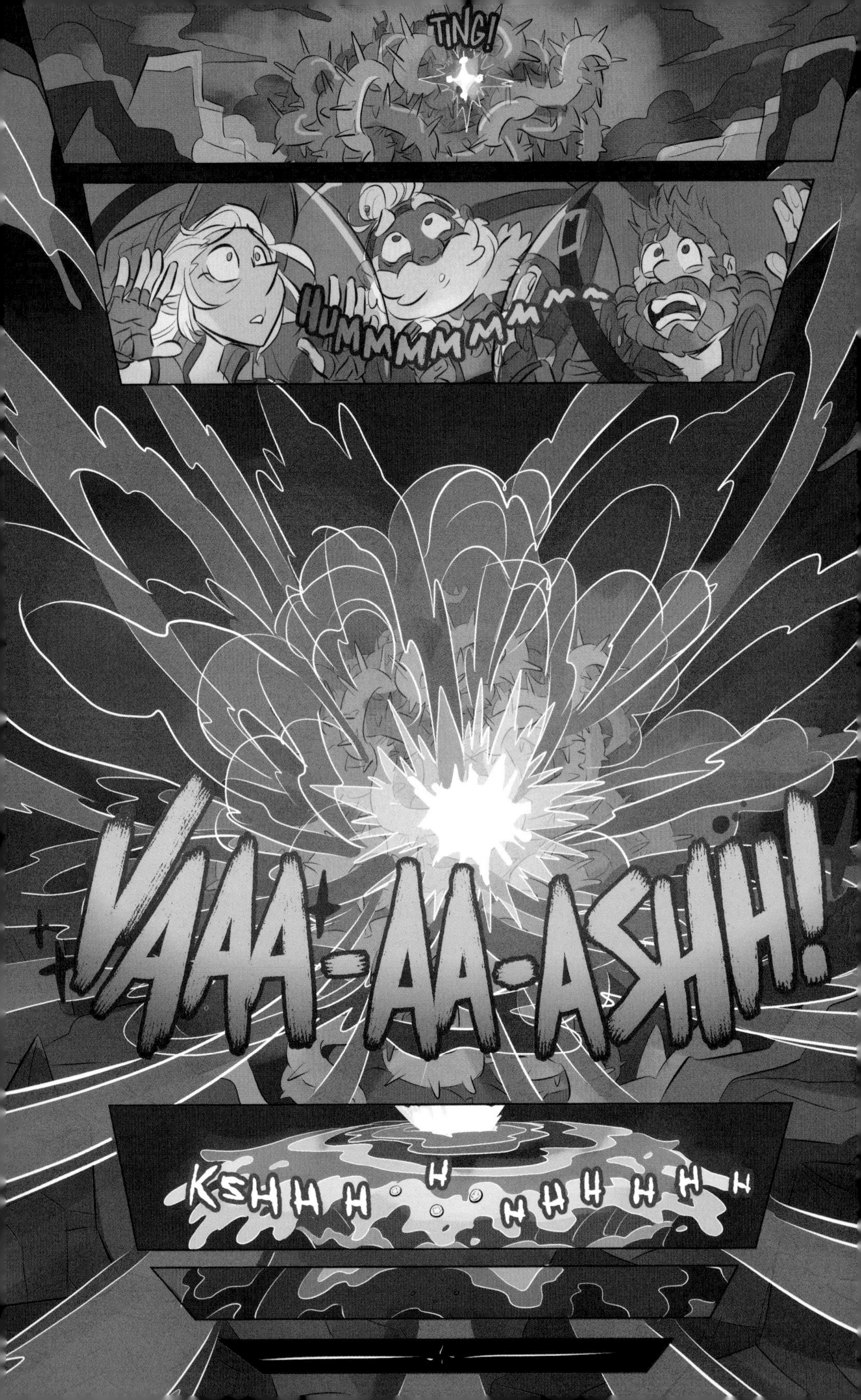
TING!
HUMMMMMMMMM
VAAA-AA-ASHH!
KSHHHHHHHHHHHH

Chapter 8

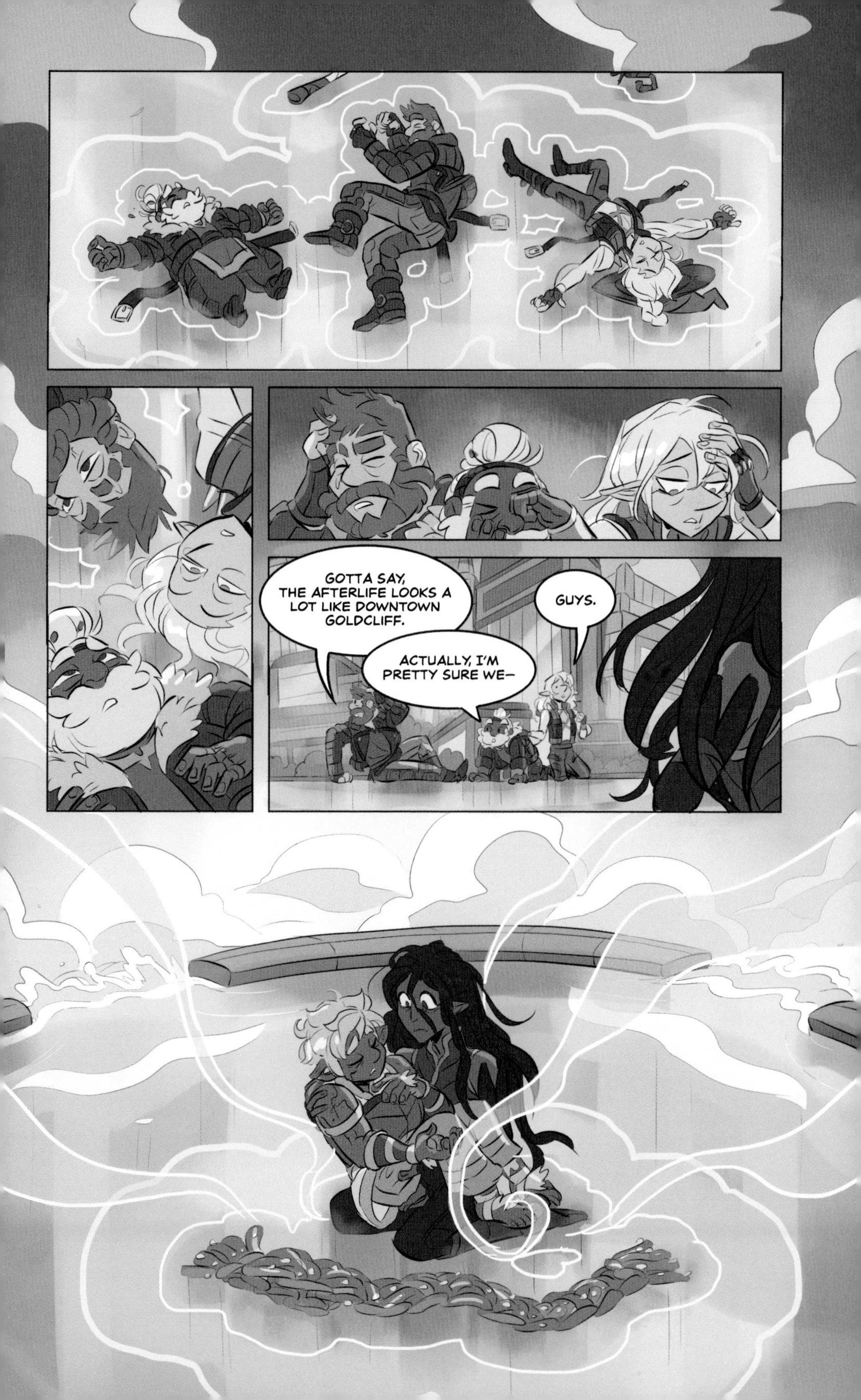
GOTTA SAY, THE AFTERLIFE LOOKS A LOT LIKE DOWNTOWN GOLDCLIFF.
ACTUALLY, I'M PRETTY SURE WE—
GUYS.

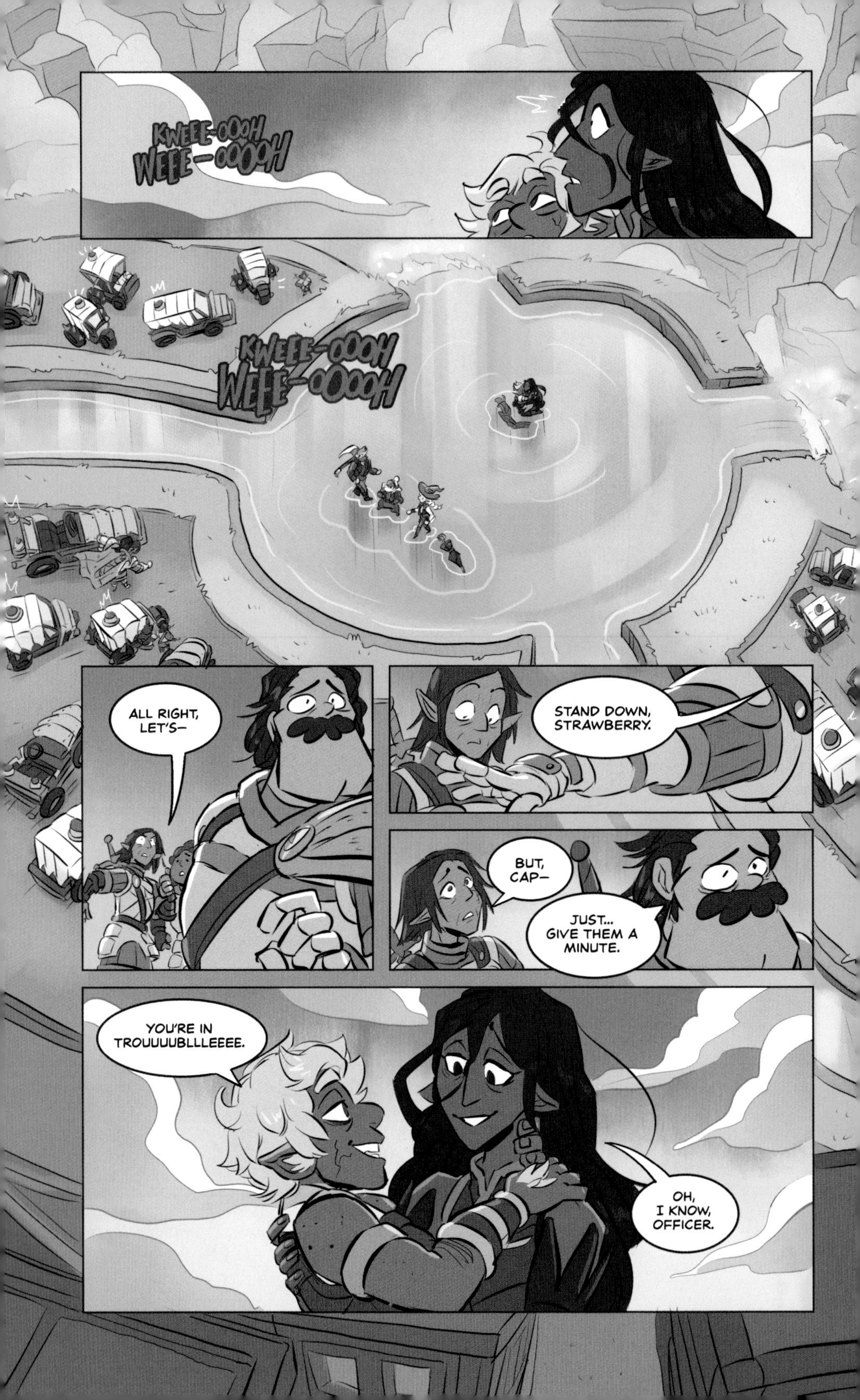
KWEEE-OOOH
WEEE-OOOOH
KWEEE-OOOH
WEEE-OOOOH
ALL RIGHT, LET'S—
STAND DOWN, STRAWBERRY.
BUT, CAP—
JUST... GIVE THEM A MINUTE.
YOU'RE IN TROUUUUBLLLEEEE.
OH, I KNOW, OFFICER.

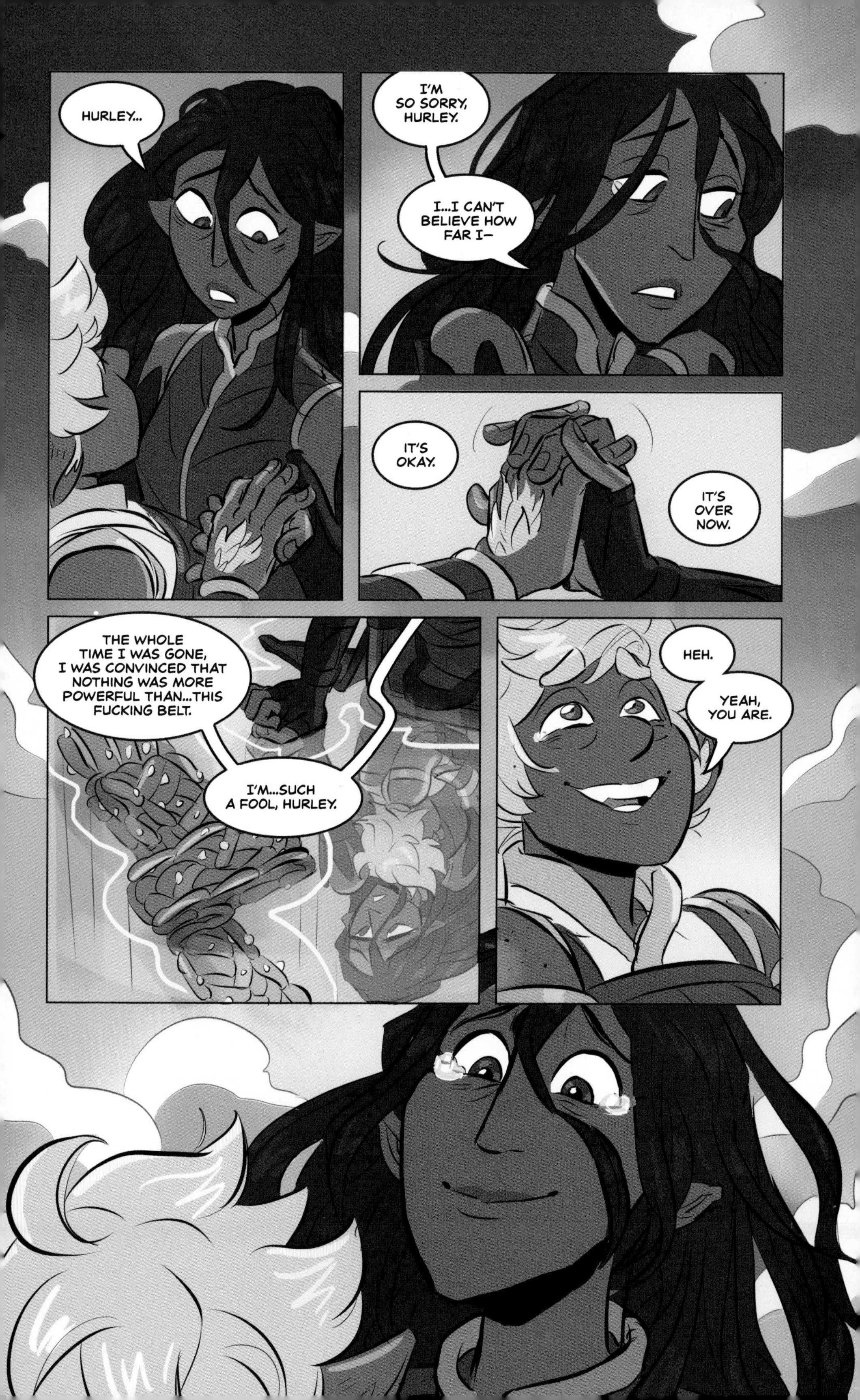
HURLEY...
I'M SO SORRY, HURLEY.
I...I CAN'T BELIEVE HOW FAR I—
IT'S OKAY.
IT'S OVER NOW.
THE WHOLE TIME I WAS GONE, I WAS CONVINCED THAT NOTHING WAS MORE POWERFUL THAN...THIS FUCKING BELT.
I'M...SUCH A FOOL, HURLEY.
HEH.
YEAH, YOU ARE.

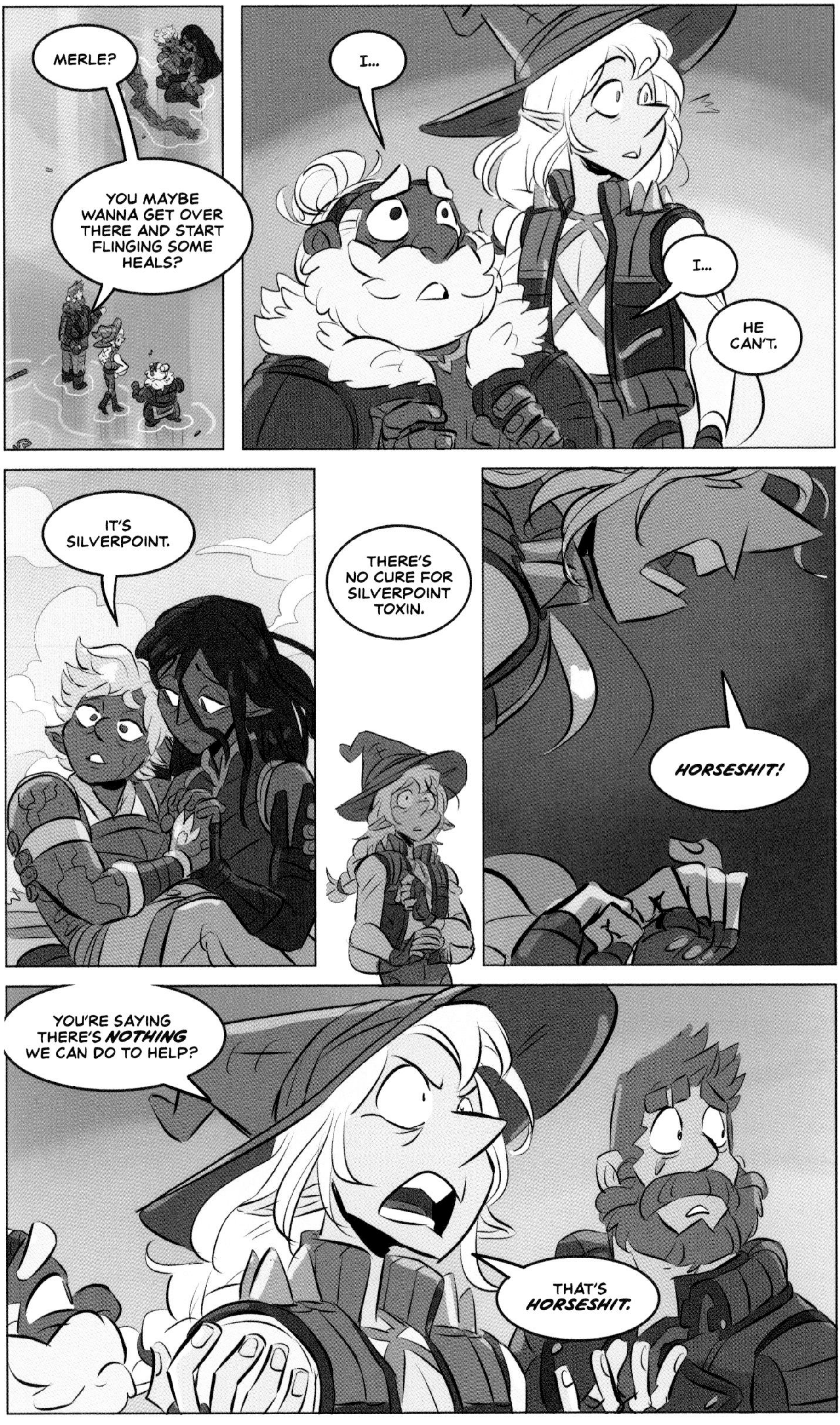
MERLE?
YOU MAYBE WANNA GET OVER THERE AND START FLINGING SOME HEALS?
I...
I...
HE CAN'T.
IT'S SILVERPOINT.
THERE'S NO CURE FOR SILVERPOINT TOXIN.
HORSESHIT!
YOU'RE SAYING THERE'S ***NOTHING*** WE CAN DO TO HELP?
THAT'S ***HORSESHIT.***

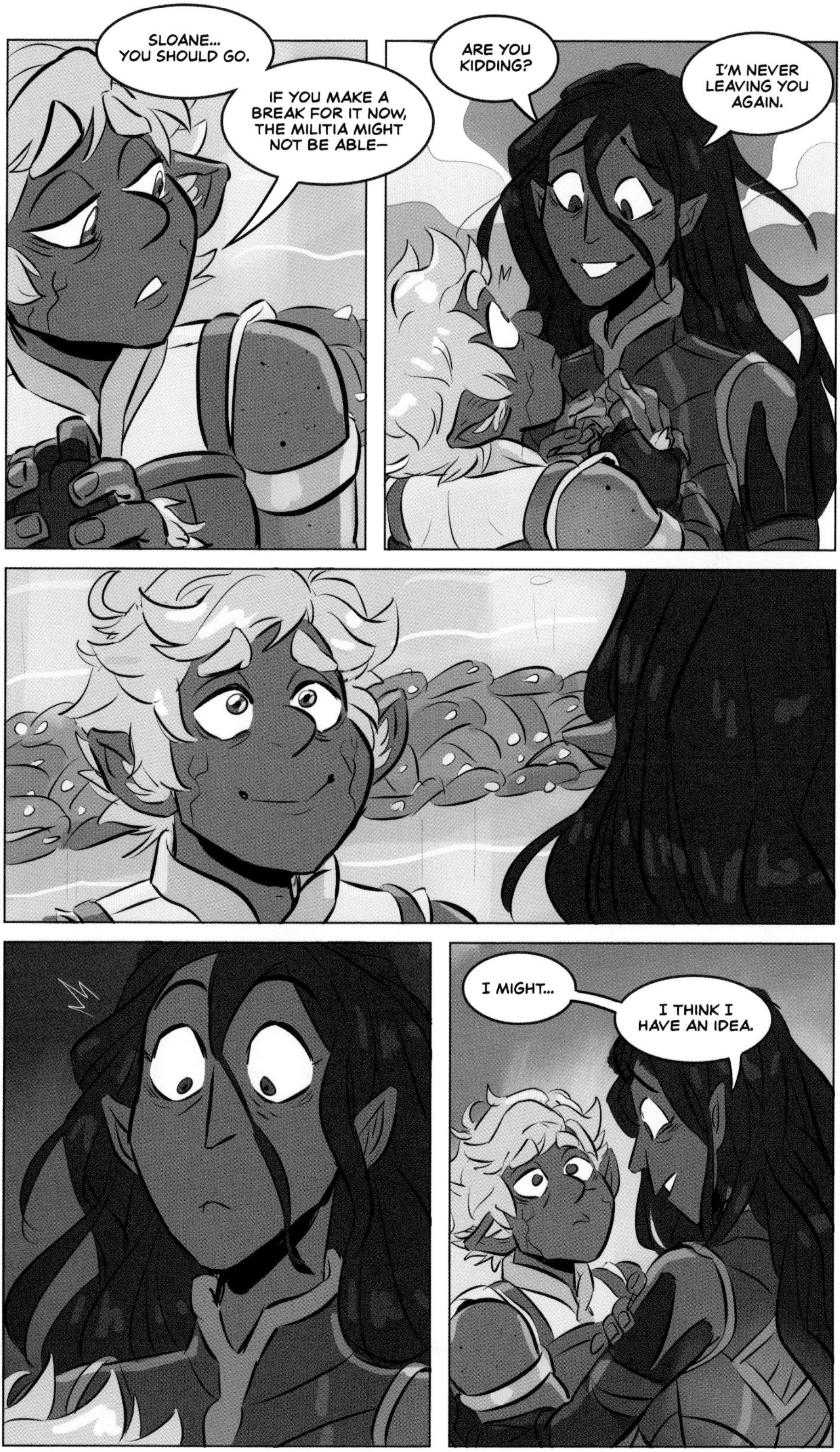
SLOANE... YOU SHOULD GO.
IF YOU MAKE A BREAK FOR IT NOW, THE MILITIA MIGHT NOT BE ABLE—
ARE YOU KIDDING?
I'M NEVER LEAVING YOU AGAIN.
I MIGHT...
I THINK I HAVE AN IDEA.

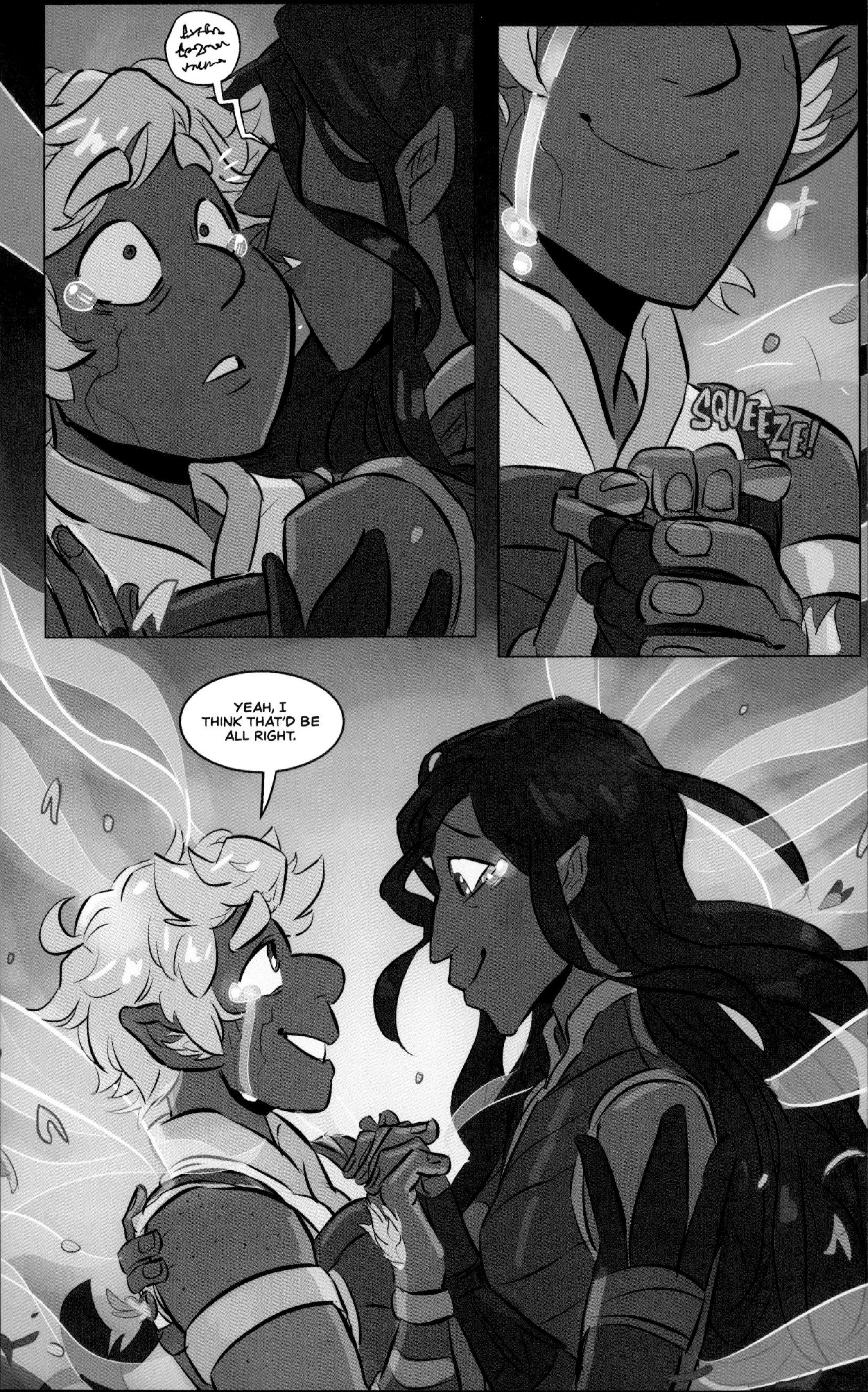
SQUEEZE!
YEAH, I THINK THAT'D BE ALL RIGHT.

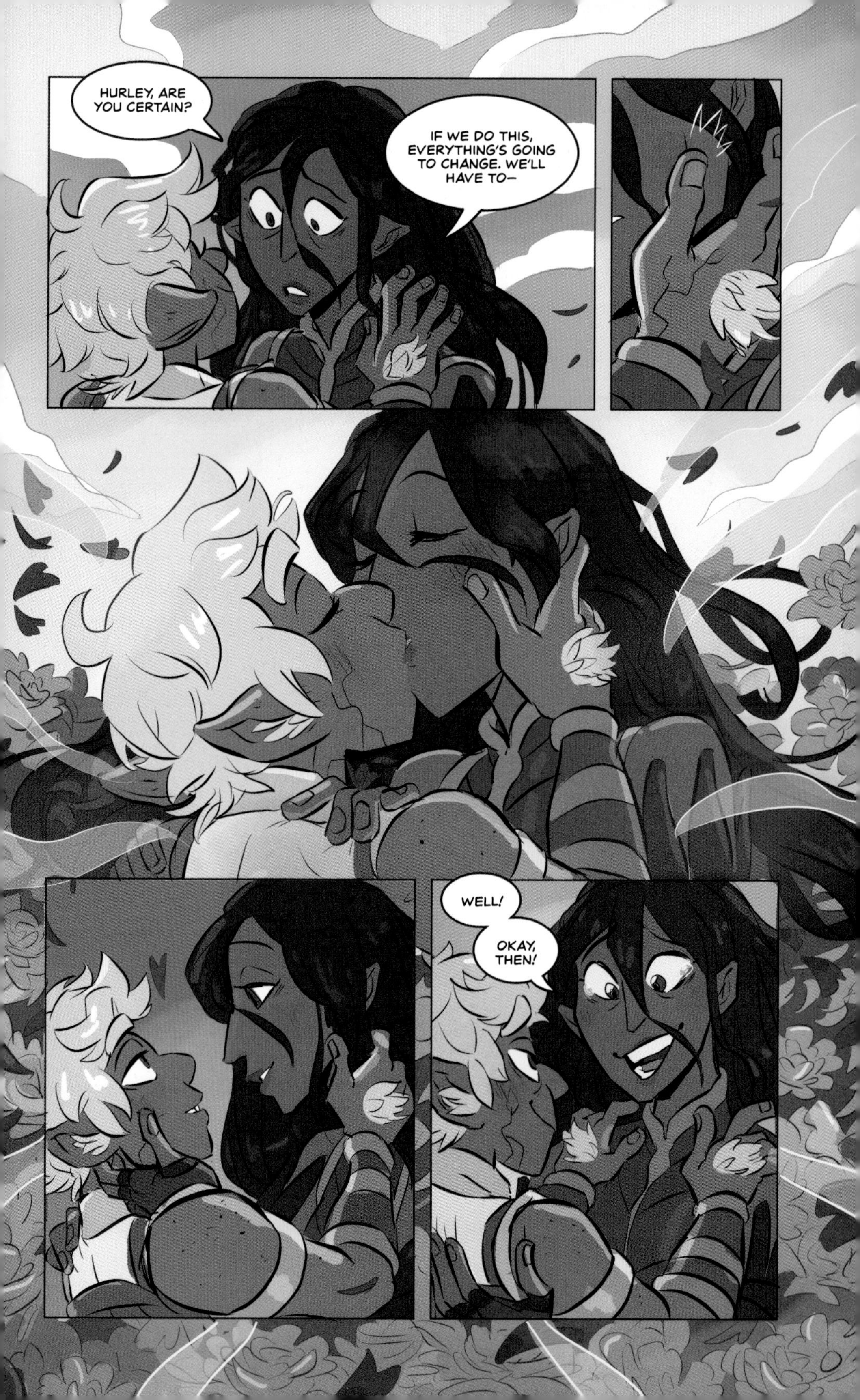
HURLEY, ARE YOU CERTAIN?
IF WE DO THIS, EVERYTHING'S GOING TO CHANGE. WE'LL HAVE TO—
WELL!
OKAY, THEN!

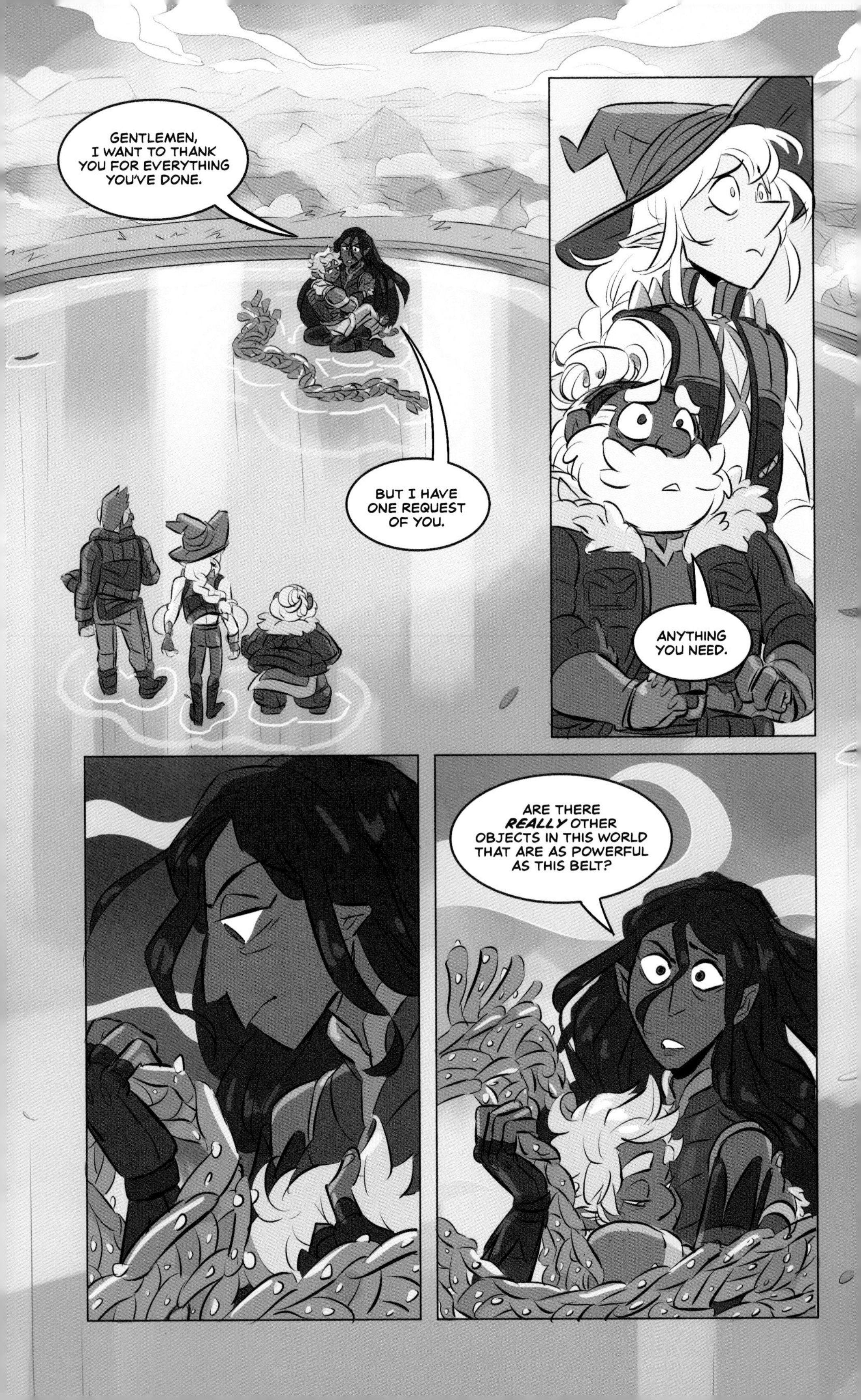
GENTLEMEN, I WANT TO THANK YOU FOR EVERYTHING YOU'VE DONE.
BUT I HAVE ONE REQUEST OF YOU.
ANYTHING YOU NEED.
ARE THERE *REALLY* OTHER OBJECTS IN THIS WORLD THAT ARE AS POWERFUL AS THIS BELT?

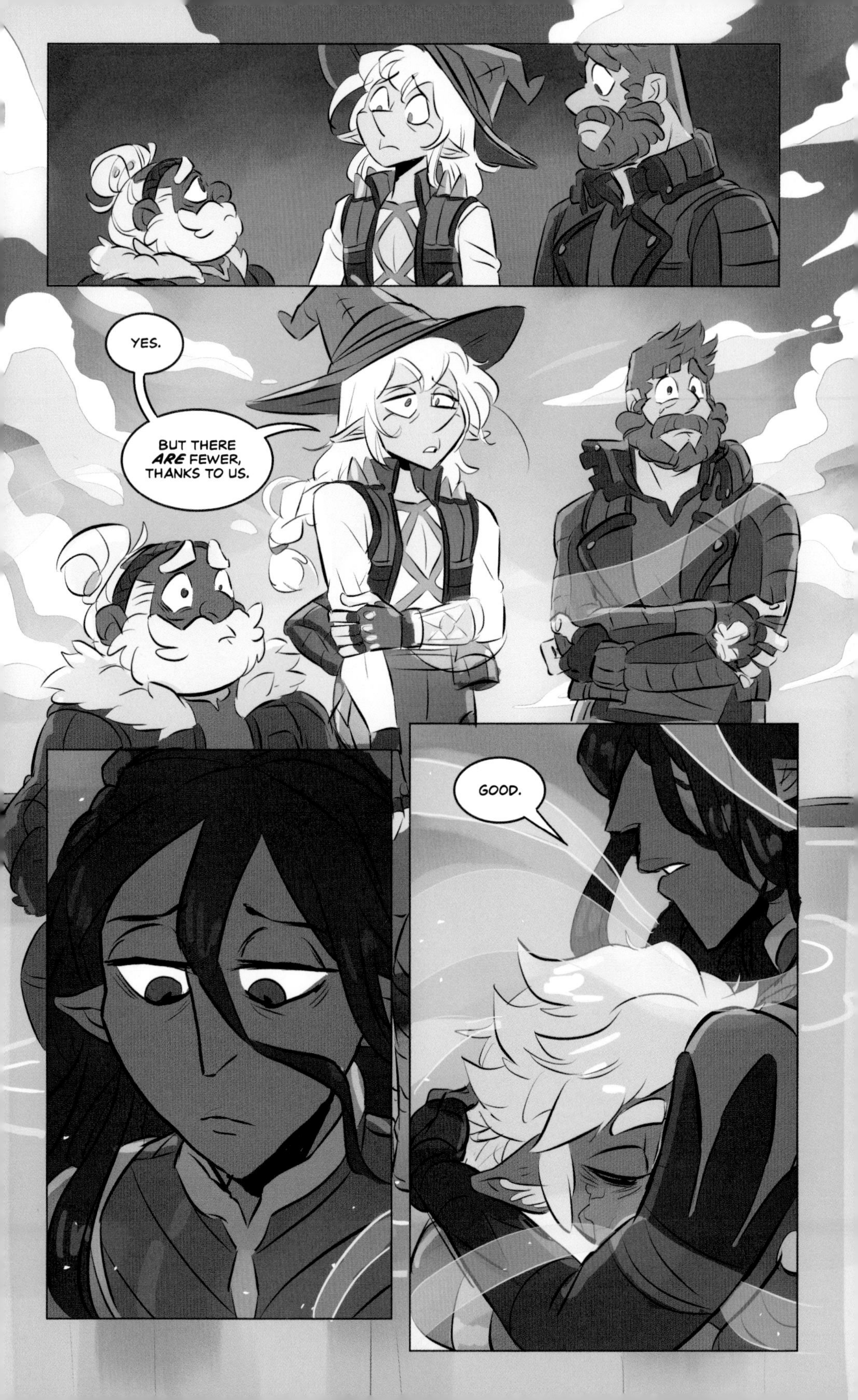
YES.
BUT THERE *ARE* FEWER, THANKS TO US.
GOOD.

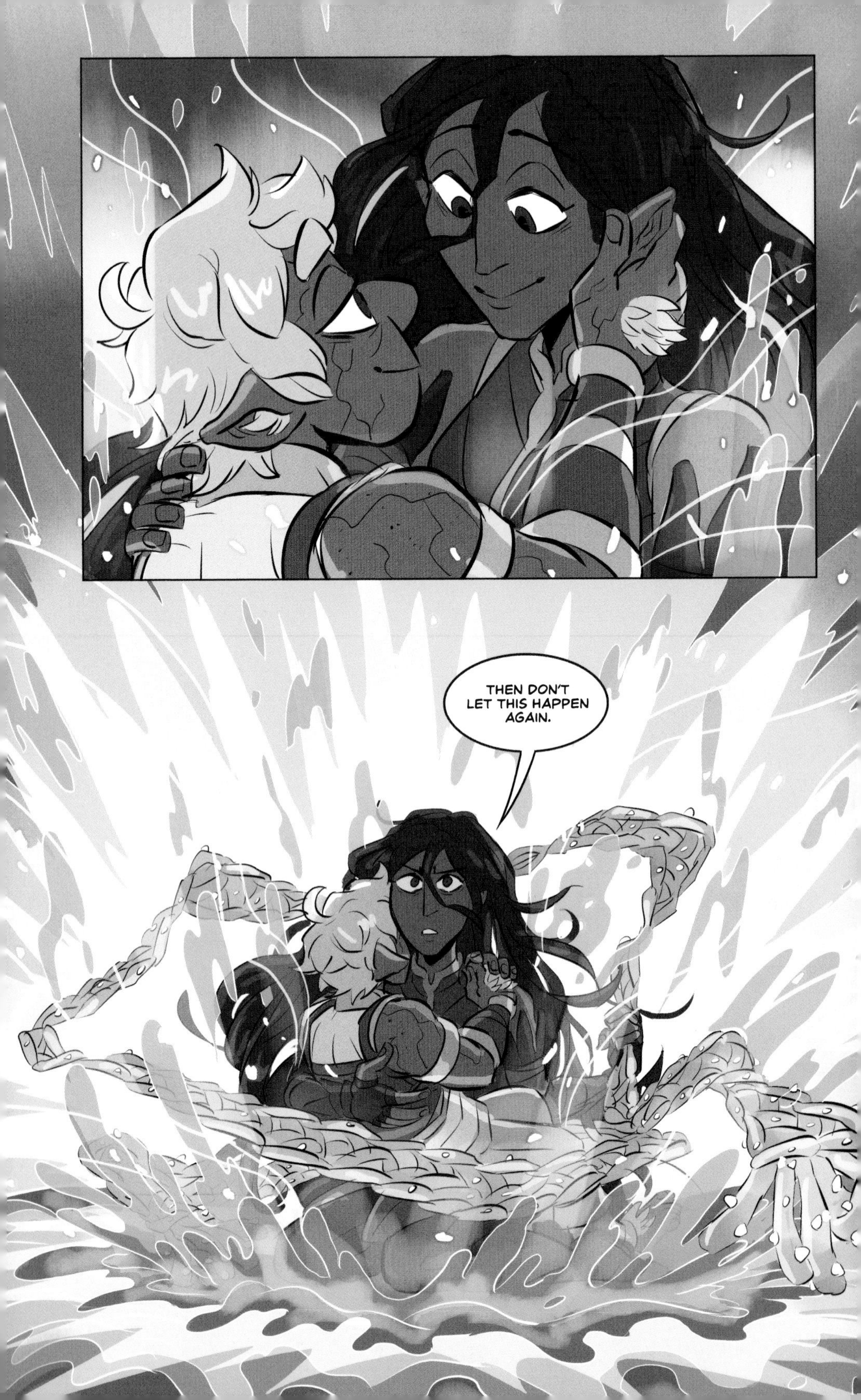
THEN DON'T
LET THIS HAPPEN
AGAIN.

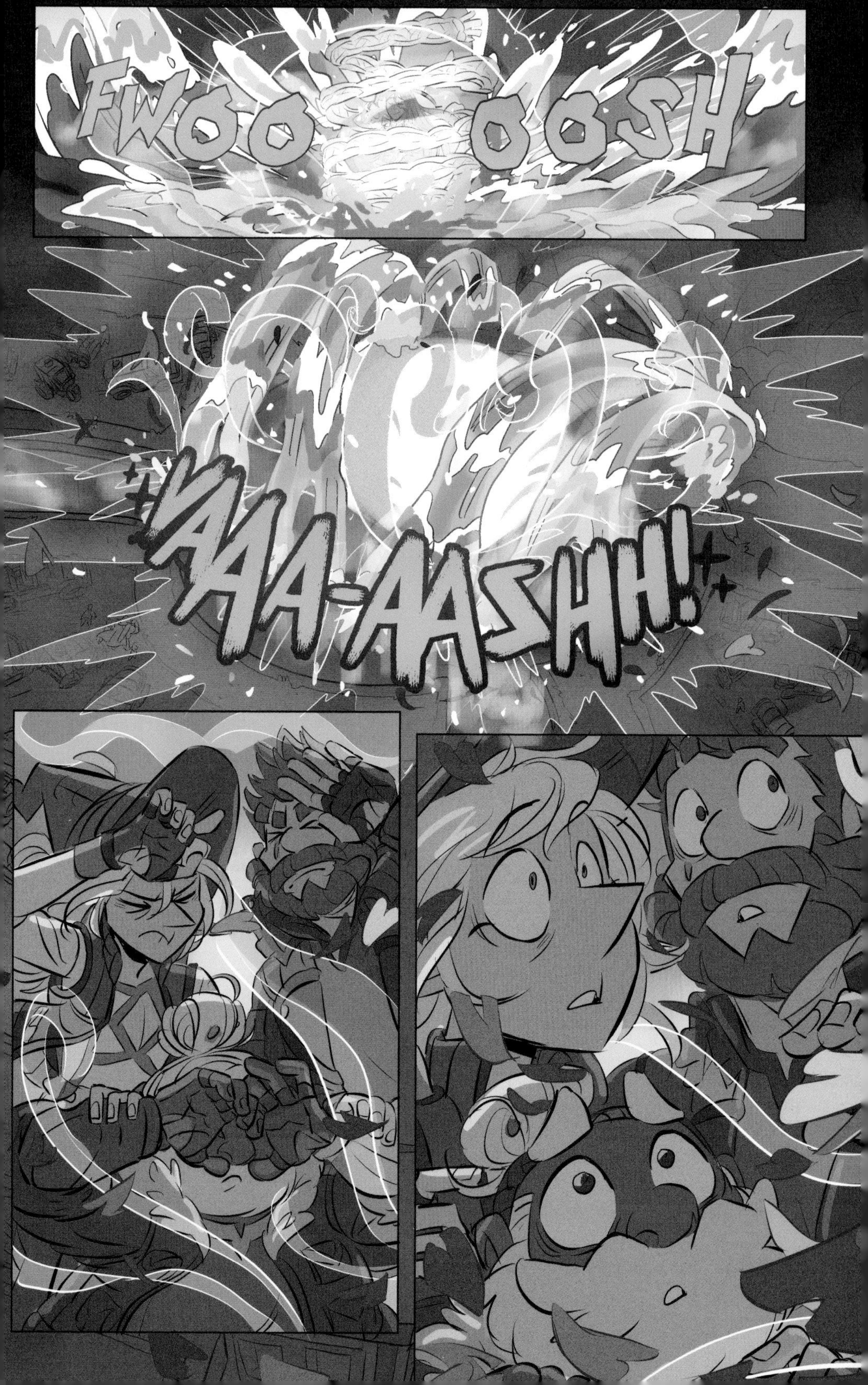
FWOOOOOSH
VAAA-AASHH!

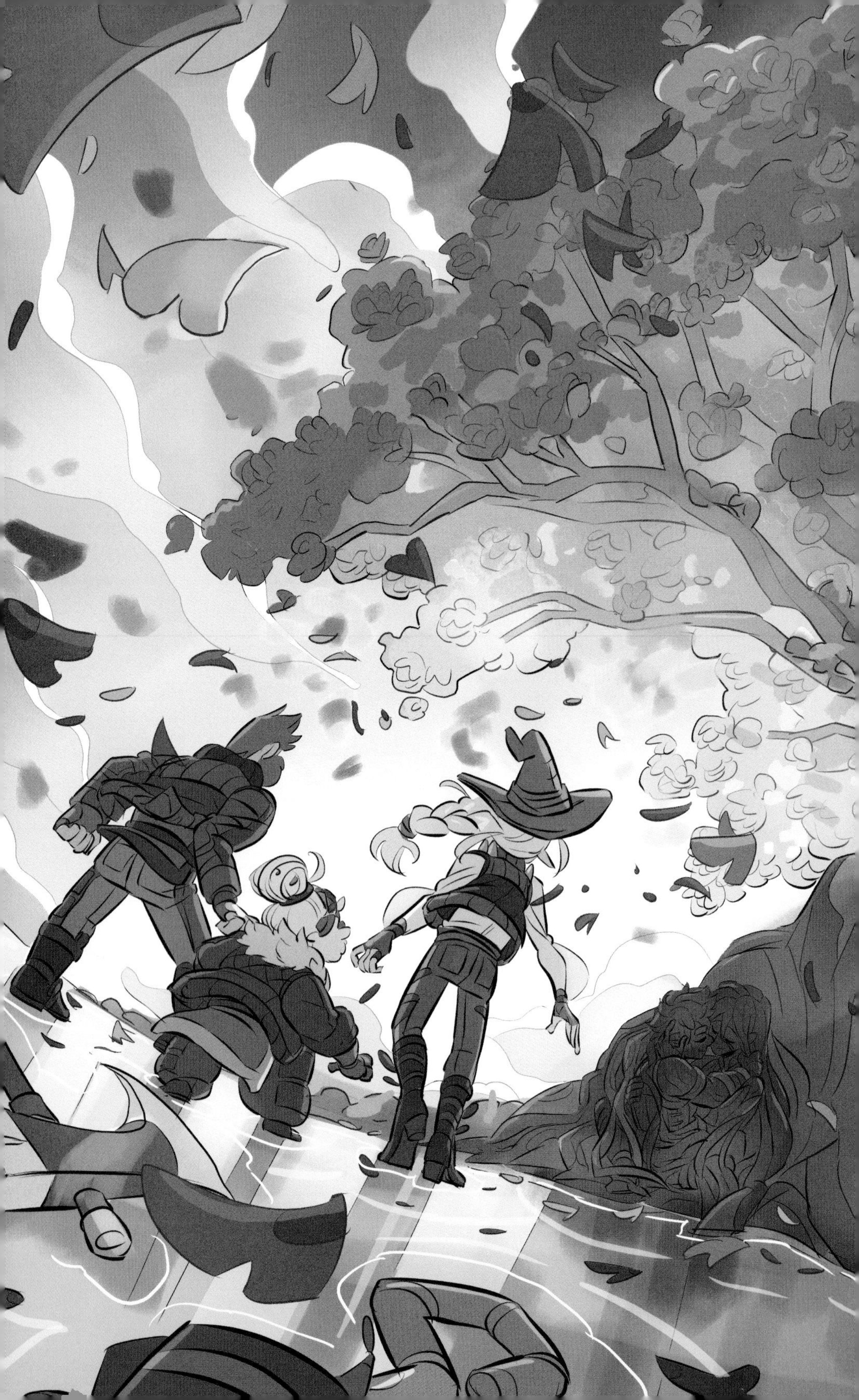

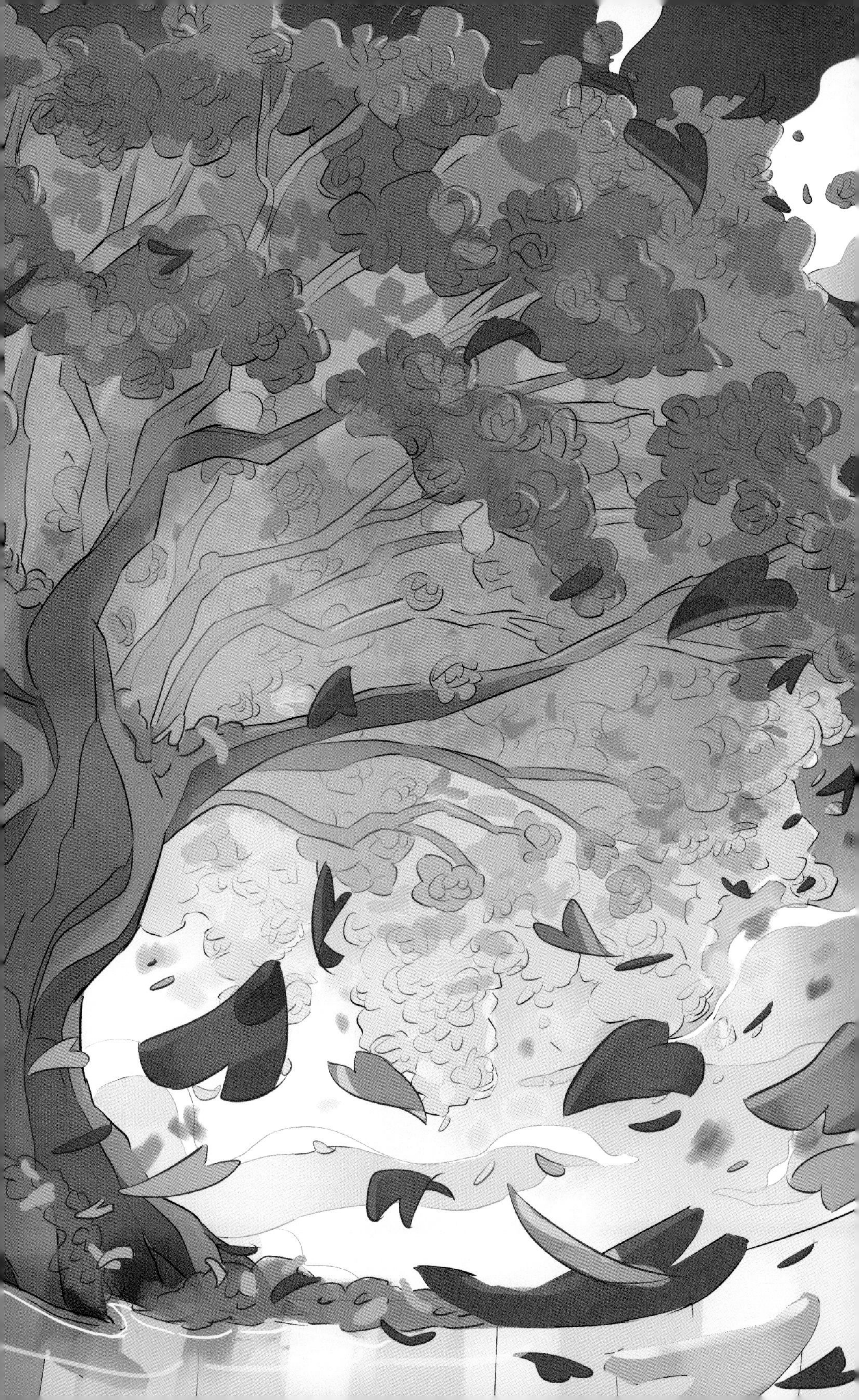

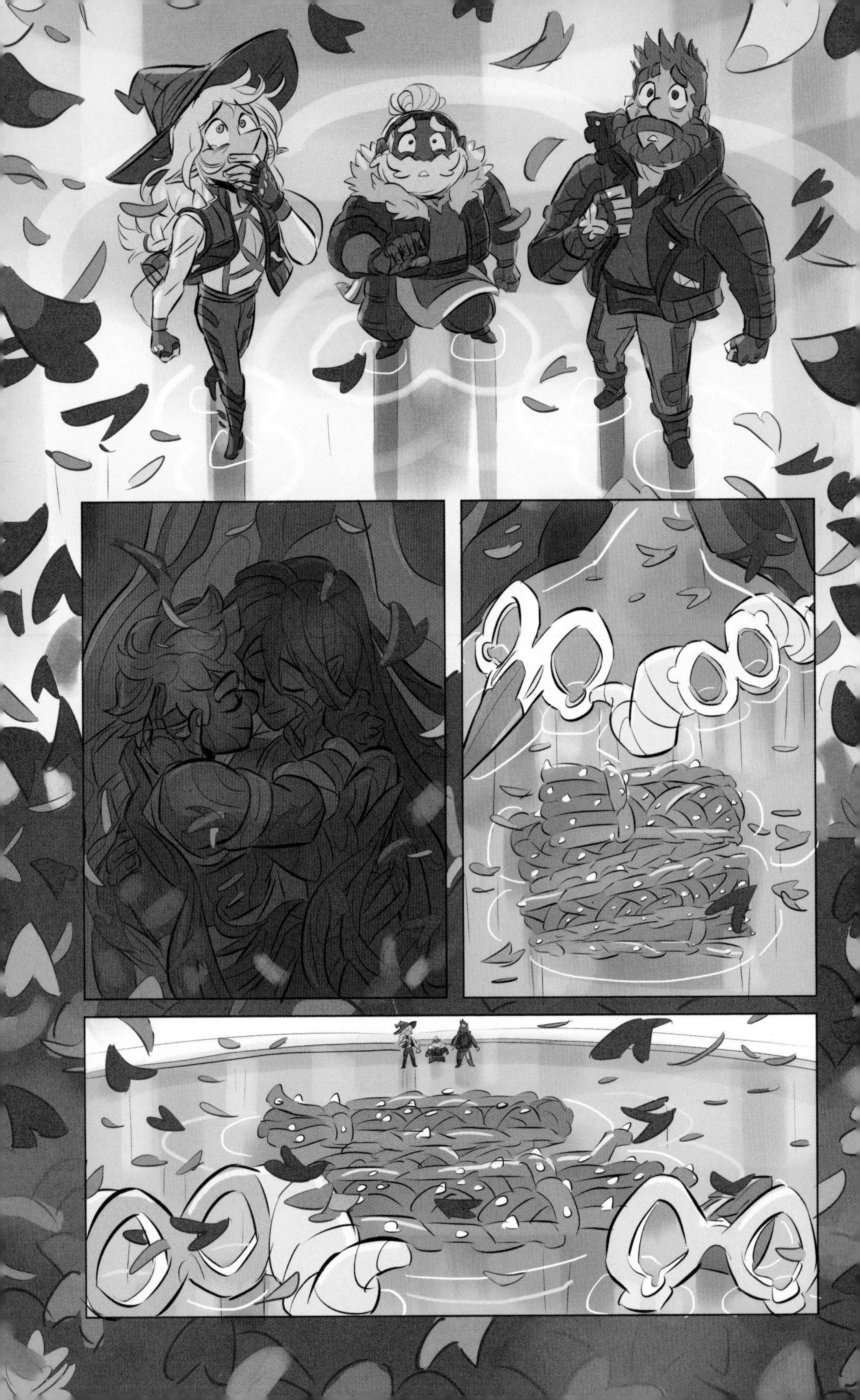

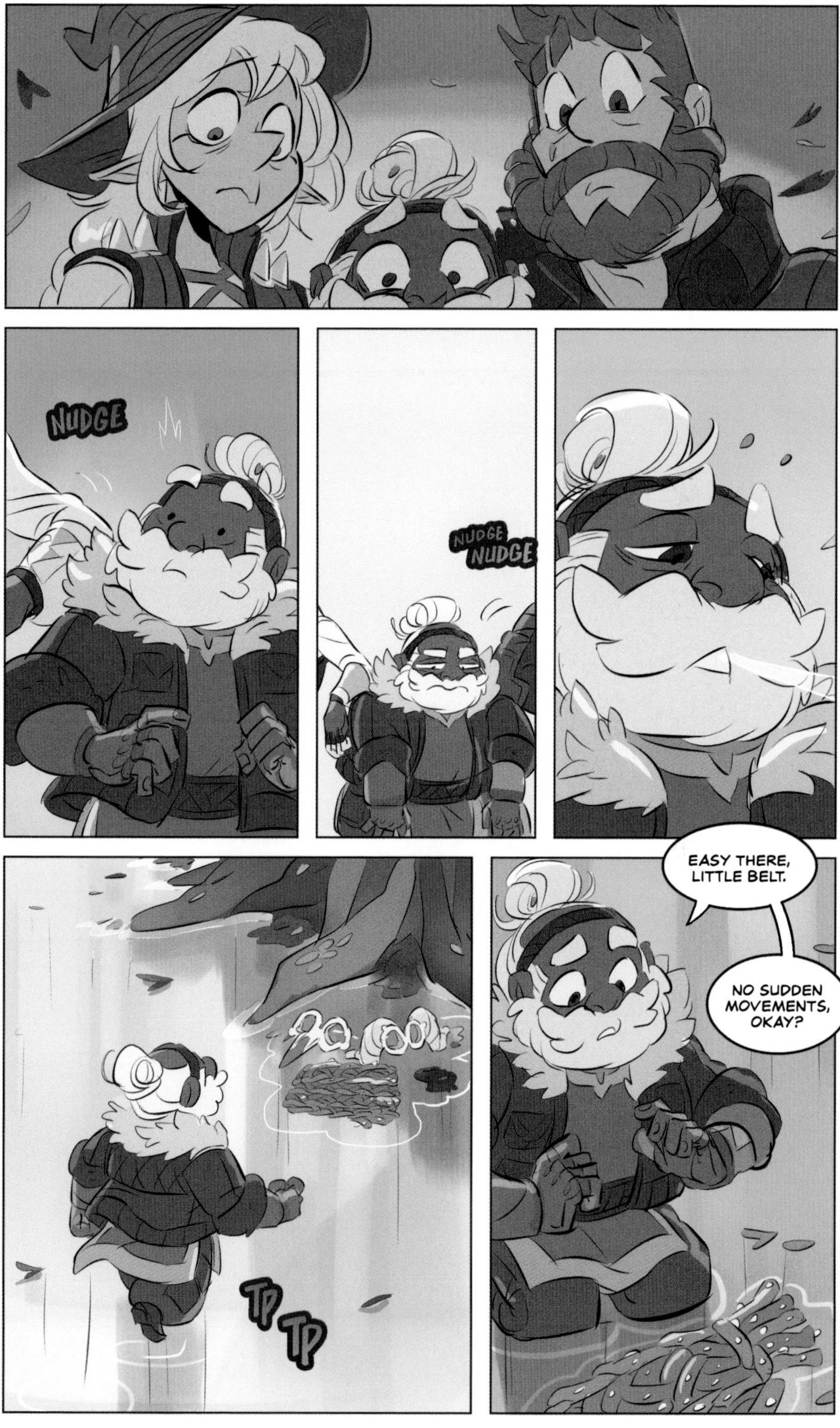
NUDGE
NUDGE
NUDGE
EASY THERE, LITTLE BELT.
NO SUDDEN MOVEMENTS, OKAY?
TP
TP

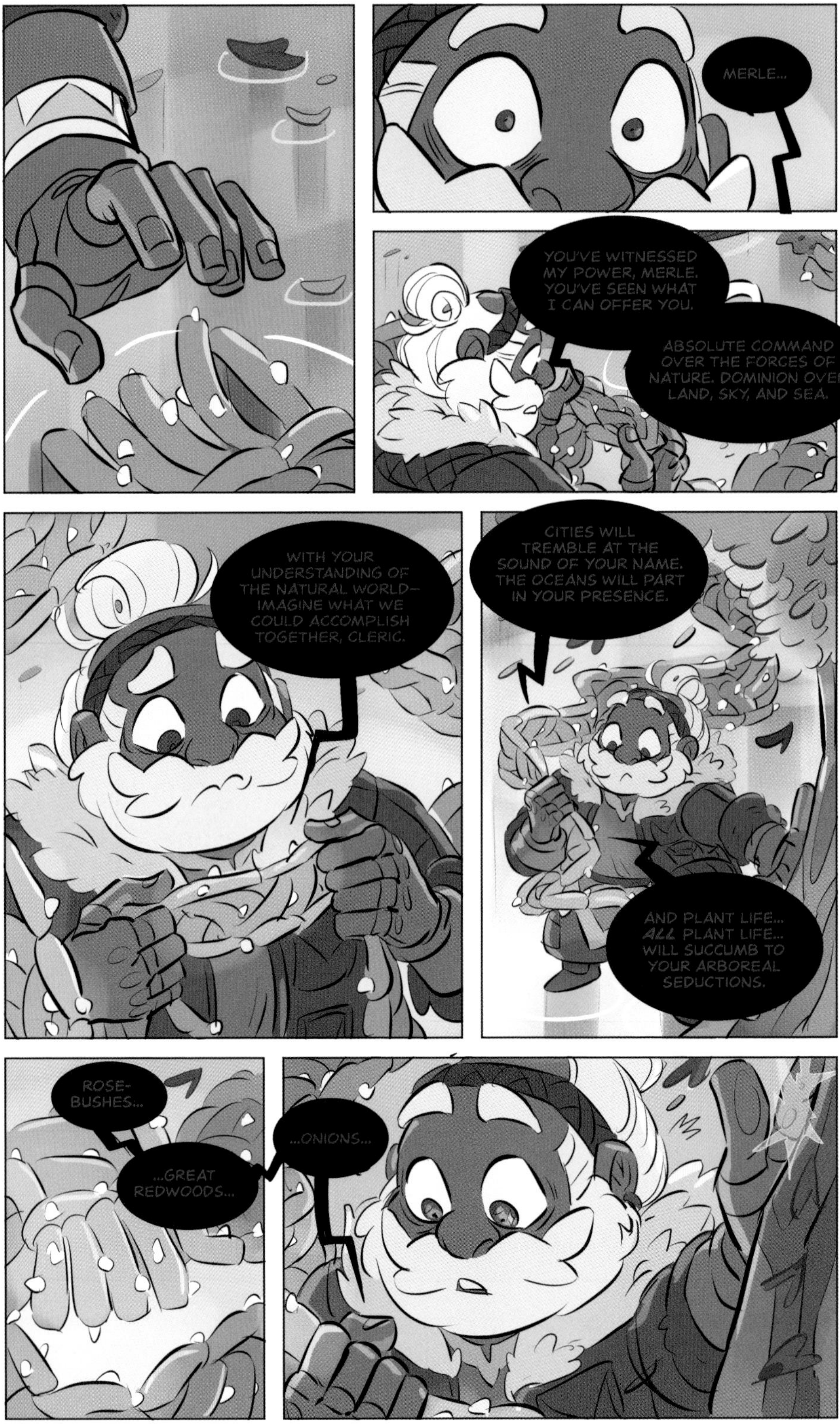
MERLE...
YOU'VE WITNESSED MY POWER, MERLE. YOU'VE SEEN WHAT I CAN OFFER YOU.
ABSOLUTE COMMAND OVER THE FORCES OF NATURE. DOMINION OVER LAND, SKY, AND SEA.
WITH YOUR UNDERSTANDING OF THE NATURAL WORLD— IMAGINE WHAT WE COULD ACCOMPLISH TOGETHER, CLERIC.
CITIES WILL TREMBLE AT THE SOUND OF YOUR NAME. THE OCEANS WILL PART IN YOUR PRESENCE.
AND PLANT LIFE... *ALL* PLANT LIFE... WILL SUCCUMB TO YOUR ARBOREAL SEDUCTIONS.
ROSE-BUSHES...
...GREAT REDWOODS...
...ONIONS...

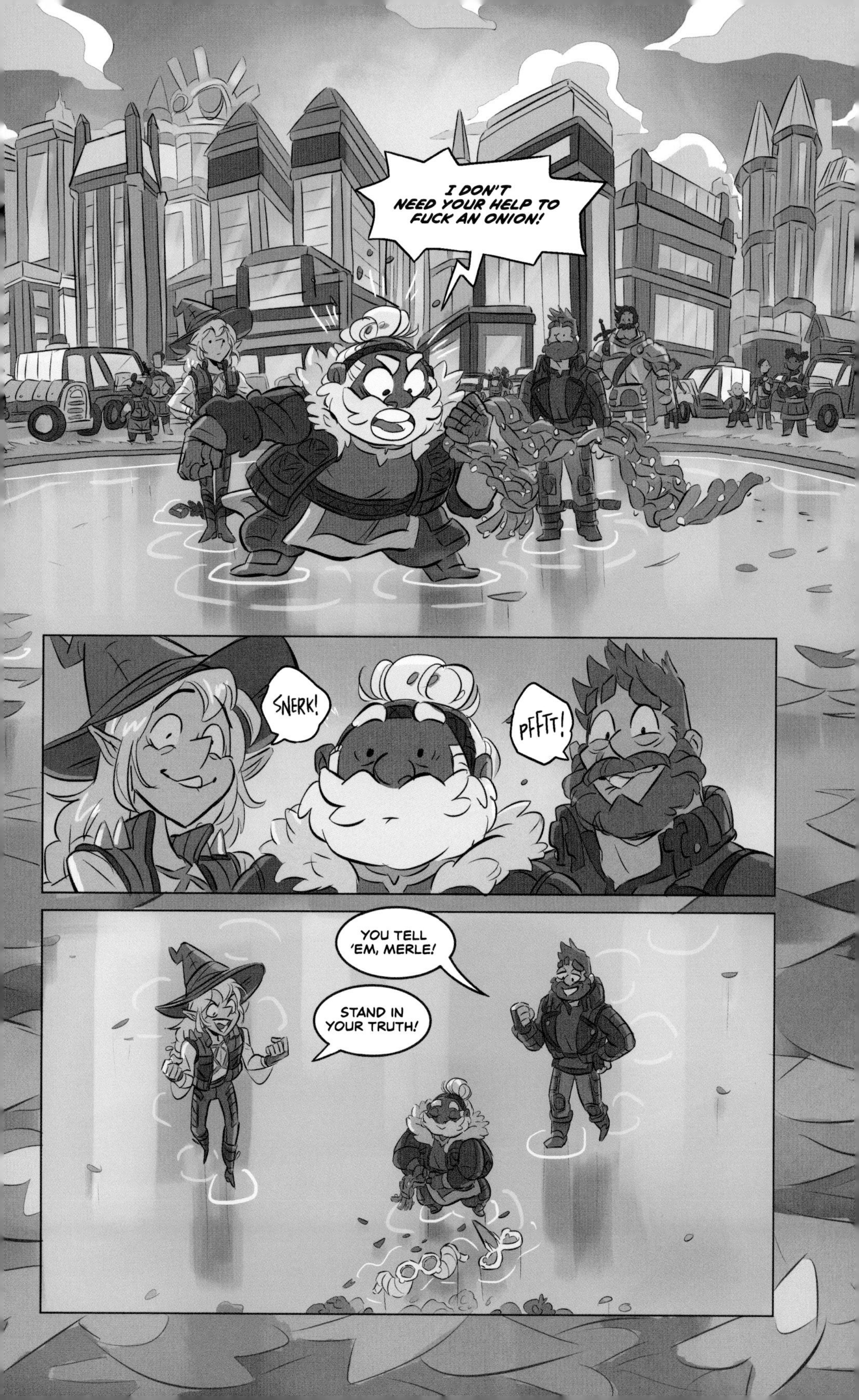
I DON'T NEED YOUR HELP TO FUCK AN ONION!
SNERK!
PFFTT!
YOU TELL 'EM, MERLE!
STAND IN YOUR TRUTH!

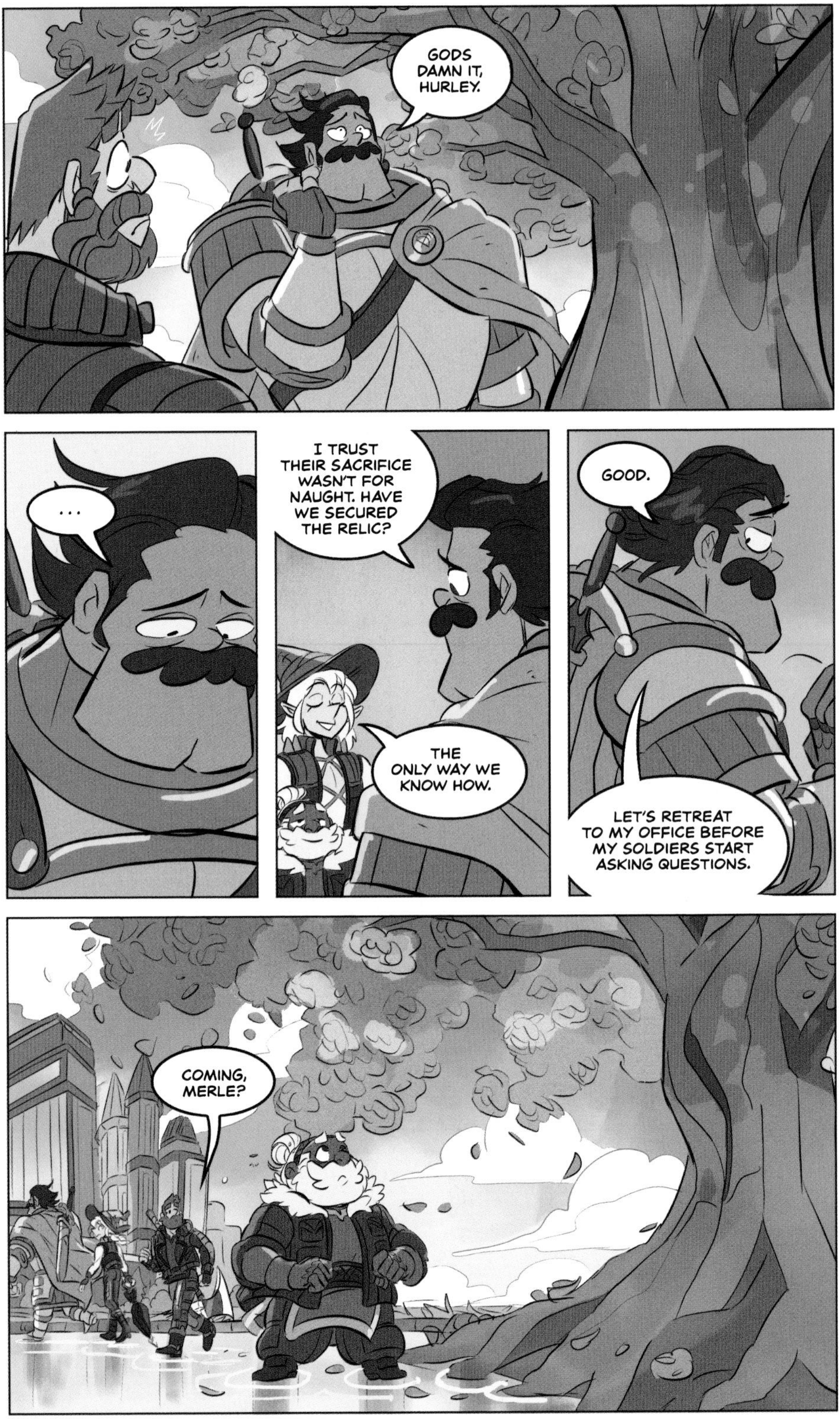
GODS DAMN IT, HURLEY.
...
I TRUST THEIR SACRIFICE WASN'T FOR NAUGHT. HAVE WE SECURED THE RELIC?
THE ONLY WAY WE KNOW HOW.
GOOD.
LET'S RETREAT TO MY OFFICE BEFORE MY SOLDIERS START ASKING QUESTIONS.
COMING, MERLE?

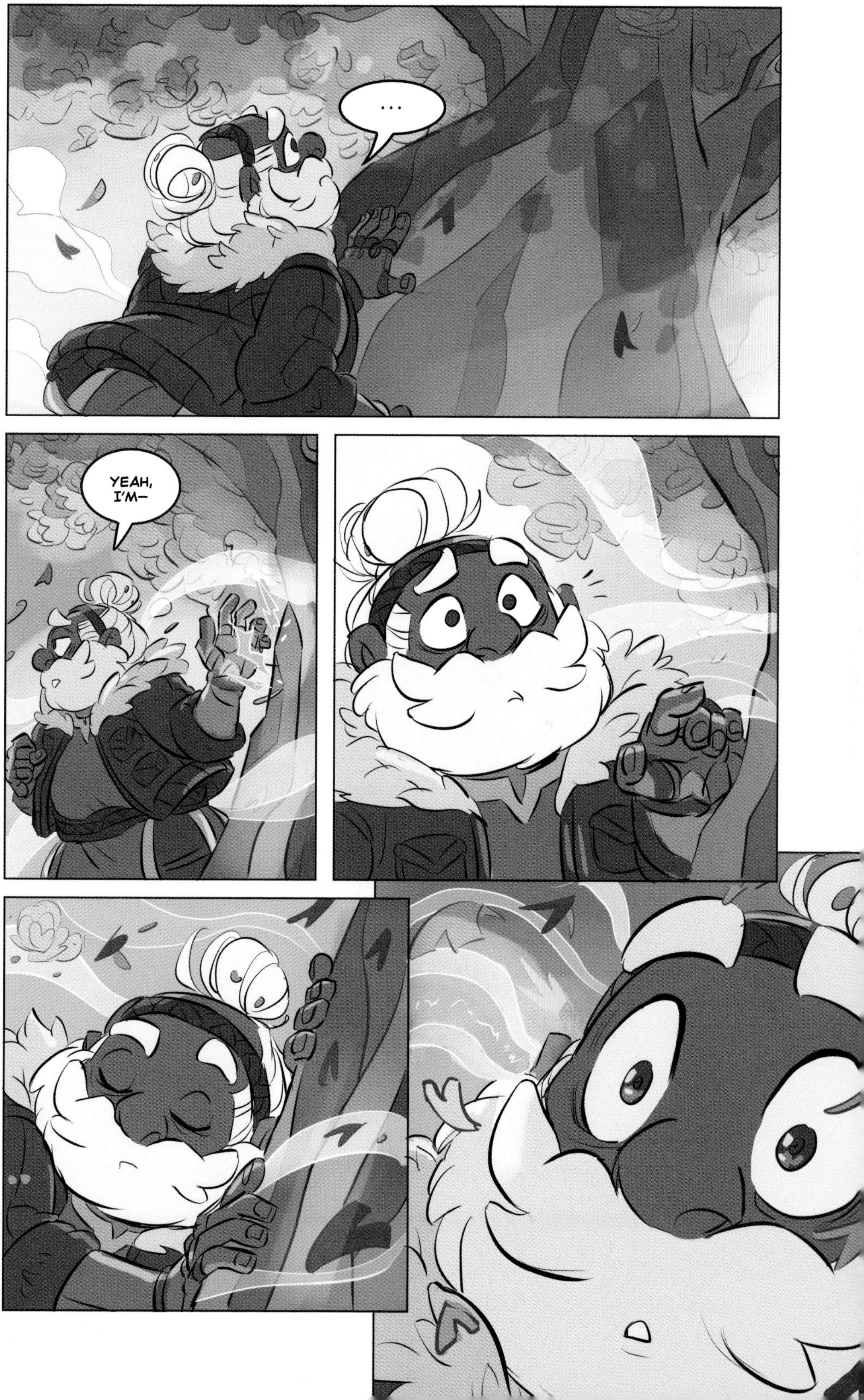
...
YEAH, I'M—

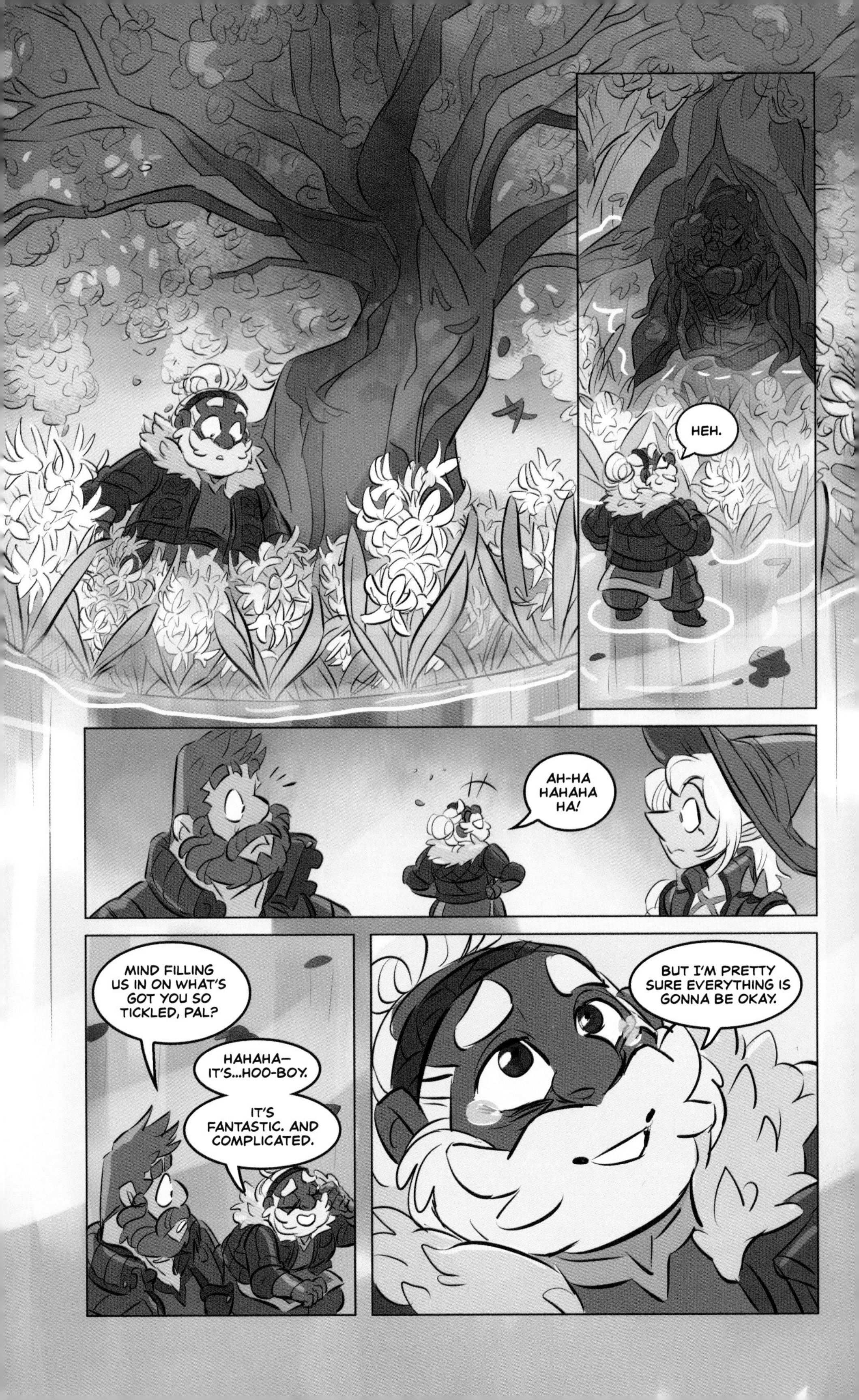
HEH.
AH-HA HAHAHA HA!
MIND FILLING US IN ON WHAT'S GOT YOU SO TICKLED, PAL?
HAHAHA— IT'S...HOO-BOY.
IT'S FANTASTIC. AND COMPLICATED.
BUT I'M PRETTY SURE EVERYTHING IS GONNA BE OKAY.

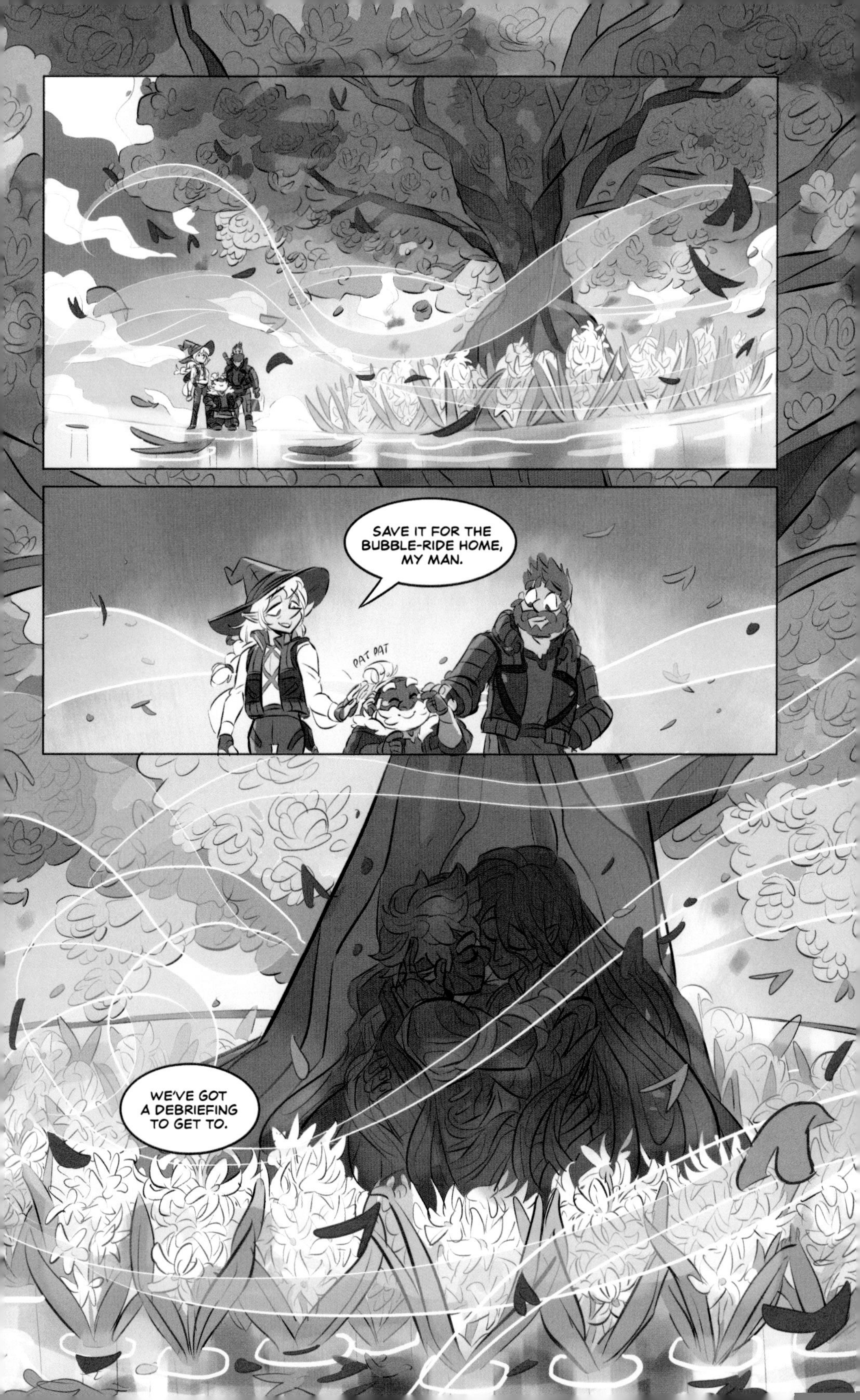
SAVE IT FOR THE BUBBLE-RIDE HOME, MY MAN.
PAT PAT
WE'VE GOT A DEBRIEFING TO GET TO.

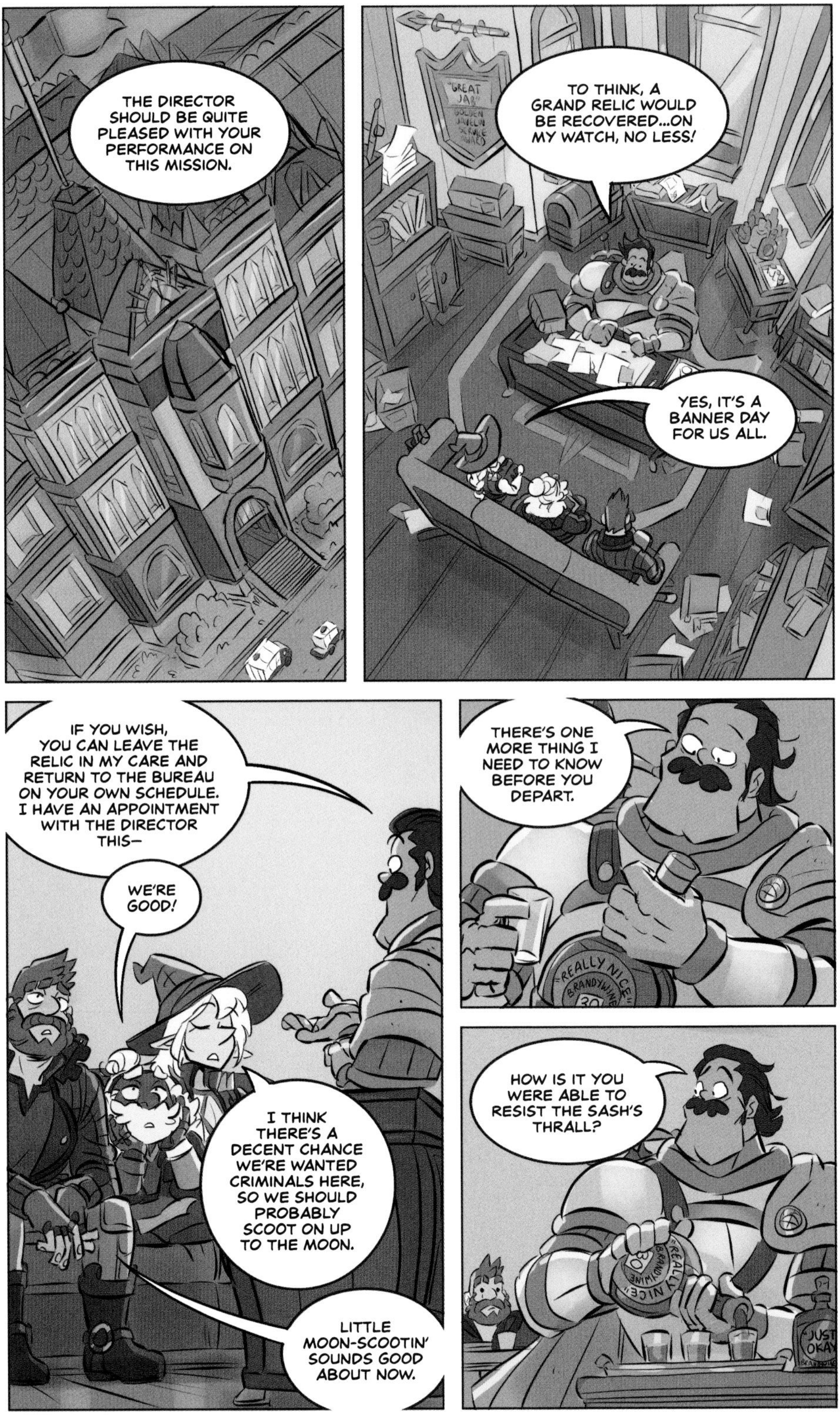
THE DIRECTOR SHOULD BE QUITE PLEASED WITH YOUR PERFORMANCE ON THIS MISSION.
"GREAT JAB" GOLDEN JAVELIN SERVICE AWARD
TO THINK, A GRAND RELIC WOULD BE RECOVERED...ON MY WATCH, NO LESS!
YES, IT'S A BANNER DAY FOR US ALL.
IF YOU WISH, YOU CAN LEAVE THE RELIC IN MY CARE AND RETURN TO THE BUREAU ON YOUR OWN SCHEDULE. I HAVE AN APPOINTMENT WITH THE DIRECTOR THIS—
WE'RE GOOD!
I THINK THERE'S A DECENT CHANCE WE'RE WANTED CRIMINALS HERE, SO WE SHOULD PROBABLY SCOOT ON UP TO THE MOON.
LITTLE MOON-SCOOTIN' SOUNDS GOOD ABOUT NOW.
THERE'S ONE MORE THING I NEED TO KNOW BEFORE YOU DEPART.
REALLY NICE BRANDYWINE 30
HOW IS IT YOU WERE ABLE TO RESIST THE SASH'S THRALL?
REALLY NICE BRANDYWINE 30
JUST OKAY

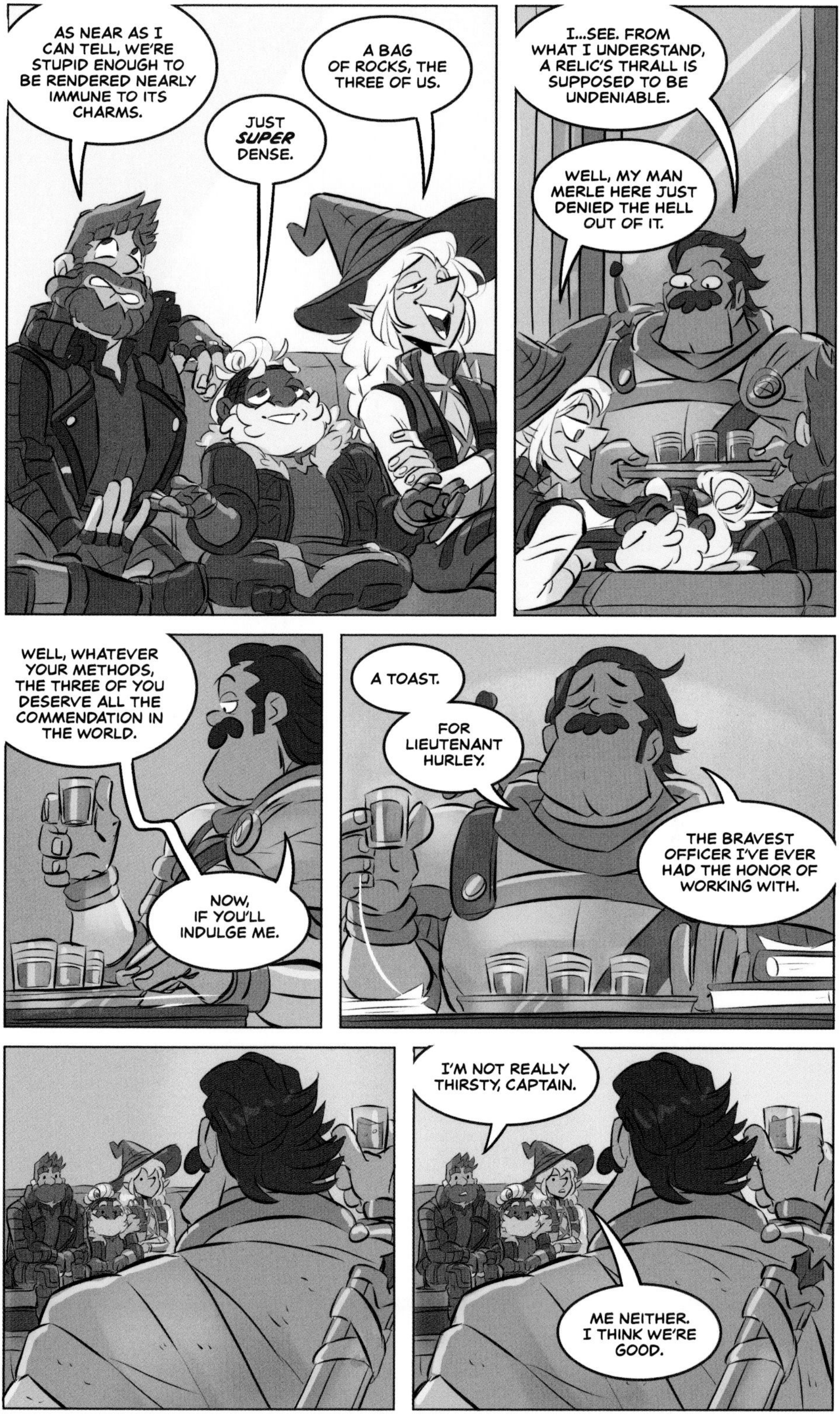
AS NEAR AS I CAN TELL, WE'RE STUPID ENOUGH TO BE RENDERED NEARLY IMMUNE TO ITS CHARMS.
JUST *SUPER* DENSE.
A BAG OF ROCKS, THE THREE OF US.
I...SEE. FROM WHAT I UNDERSTAND, A RELIC'S THRALL IS SUPPOSED TO BE UNDENIABLE.
WELL, MY MAN MERLE HERE JUST DENIED THE HELL OUT OF IT.
WELL, WHATEVER YOUR METHODS, THE THREE OF YOU DESERVE ALL THE COMMENDATION IN THE WORLD.
NOW, IF YOU'LL INDULGE ME.
A TOAST.
FOR LIEUTENANT HURLEY.
THE BRAVEST OFFICER I'VE EVER HAD THE HONOR OF WORKING WITH.
I'M NOT REALLY THIRSTY, CAPTAIN.
ME NEITHER. I THINK WE'RE GOOD.

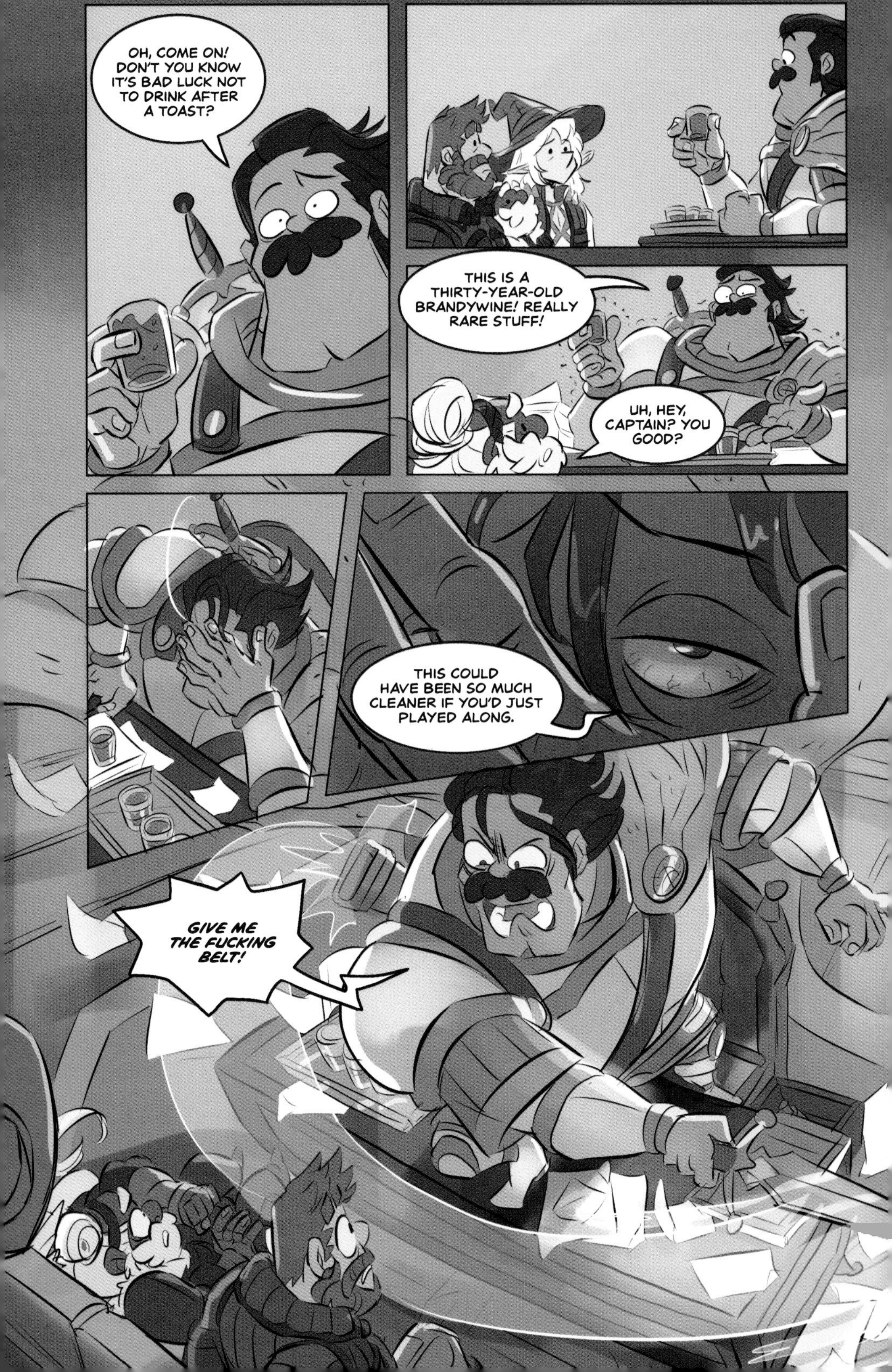
OH, COME ON! DON'T YOU KNOW IT'S BAD LUCK NOT TO DRINK AFTER A TOAST?
THIS IS A THIRTY-YEAR-OLD BRANDYWINE! REALLY RARE STUFF!
UH, HEY, CAPTAIN? YOU GOOD?
THIS COULD HAVE BEEN SO MUCH CLEANER IF YOU'D JUST PLAYED ALONG.
GIVE ME THE FUCKING BELT!

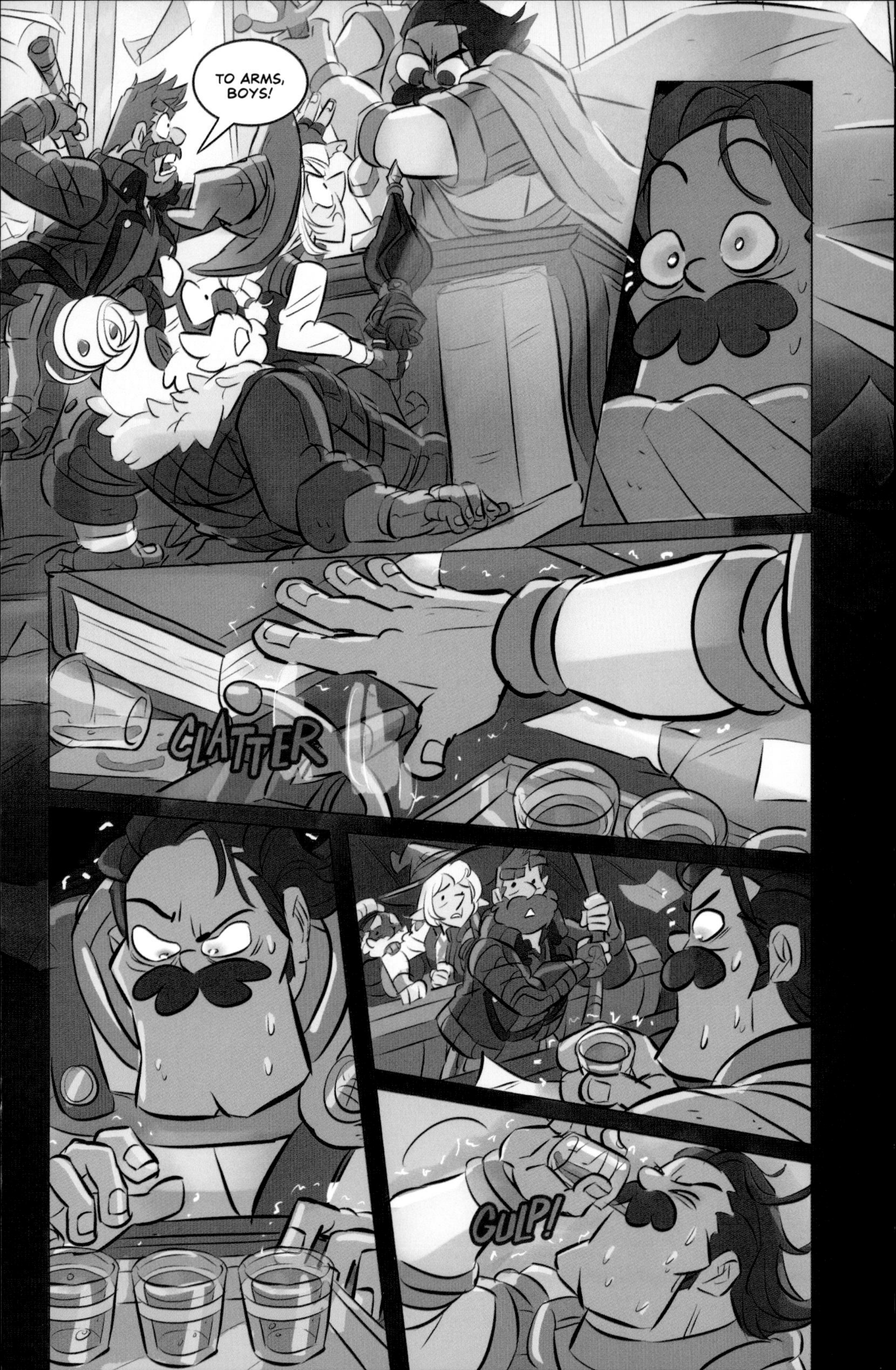
TO ARMS, BOYS!
CLATTER
GULP!

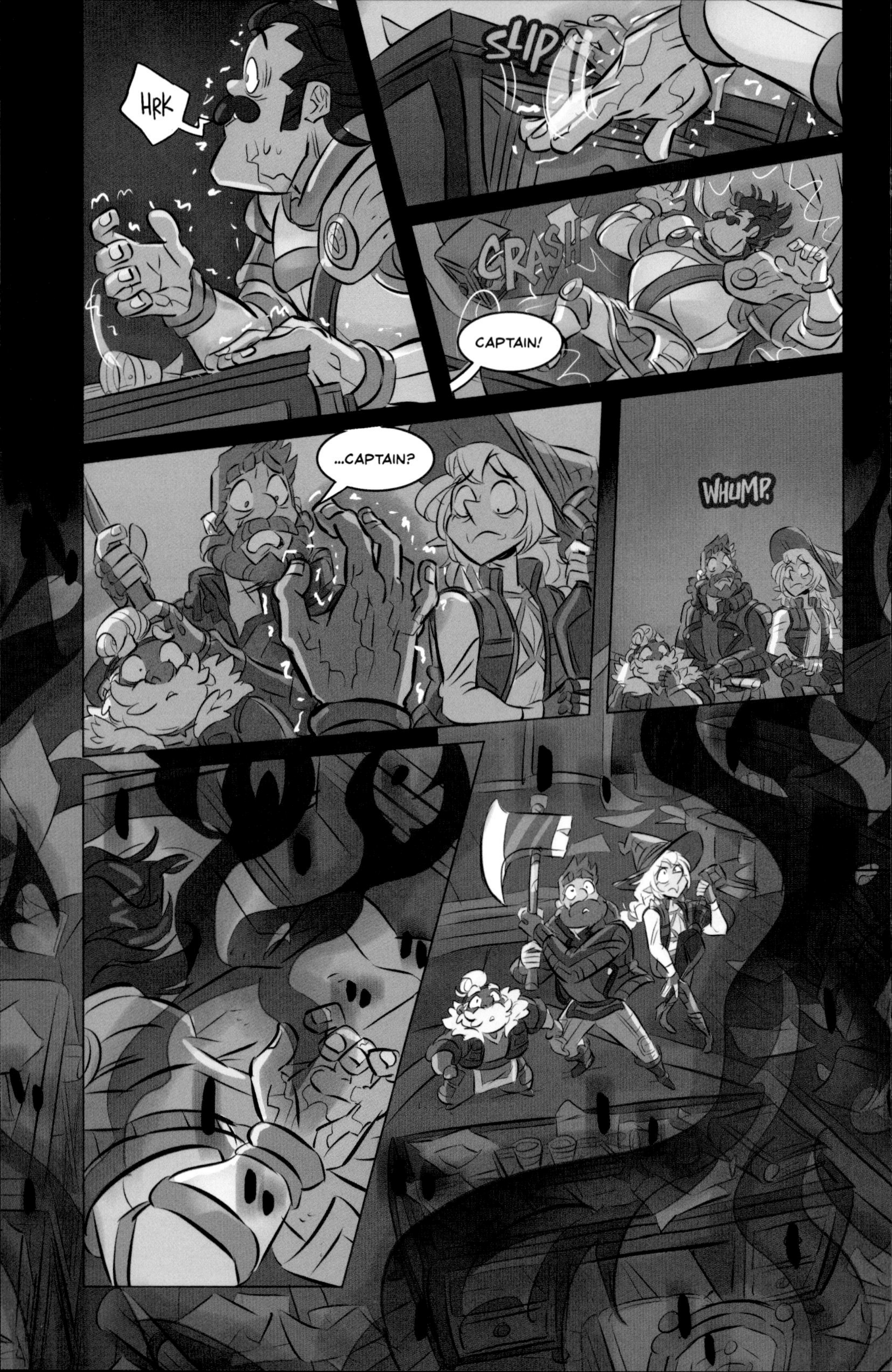
HRK
SLIP
CRASH
CAPTAIN!
...CAPTAIN?
WHUMP.

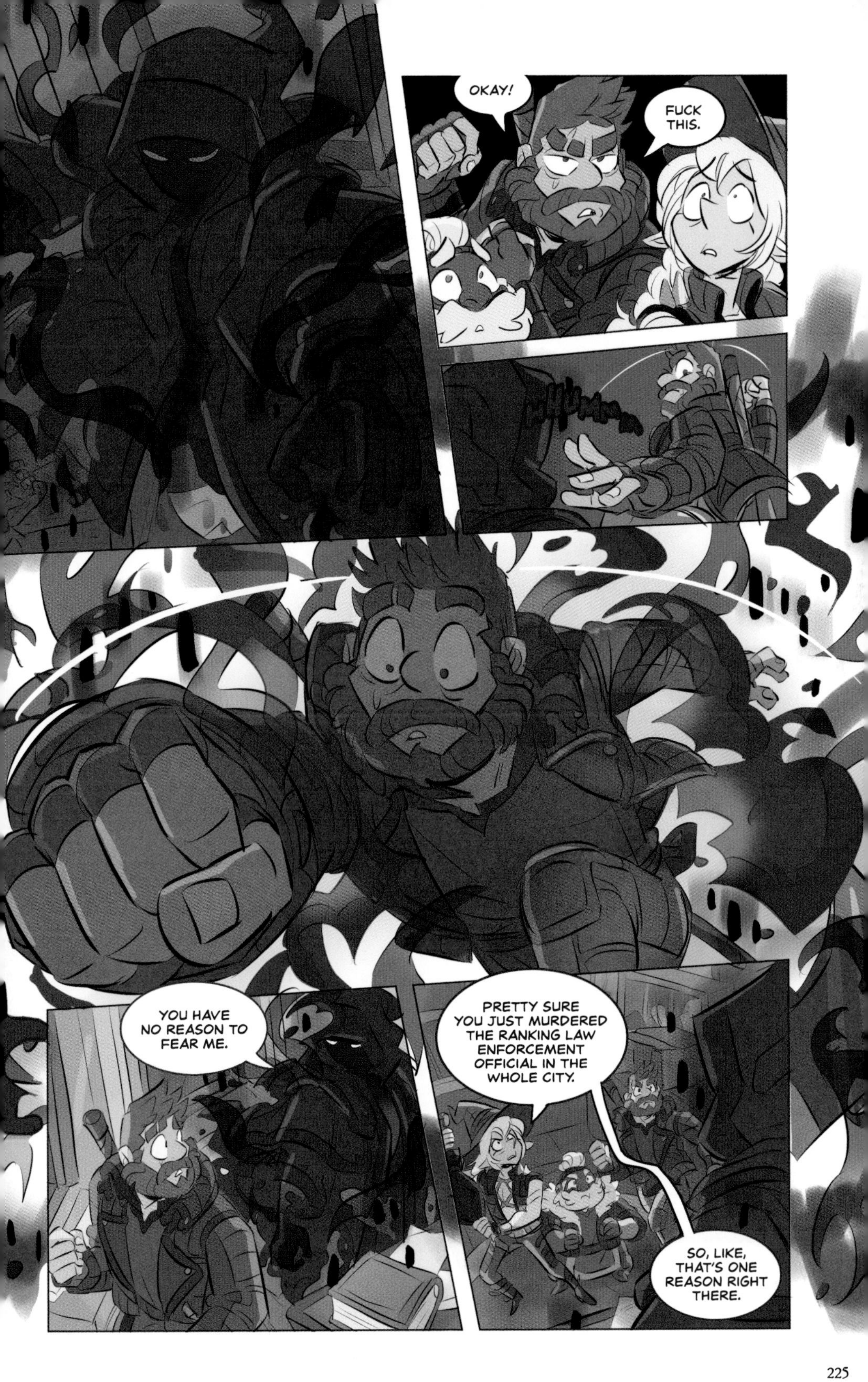
OKAY!
FUCK THIS.
YOU HAVE NO REASON TO FEAR ME.
PRETTY SURE YOU JUST MURDERED THE RANKING LAW ENFORCEMENT OFFICIAL IN THE WHOLE CITY.
SO, LIKE, THAT'S ONE REASON RIGHT THERE.

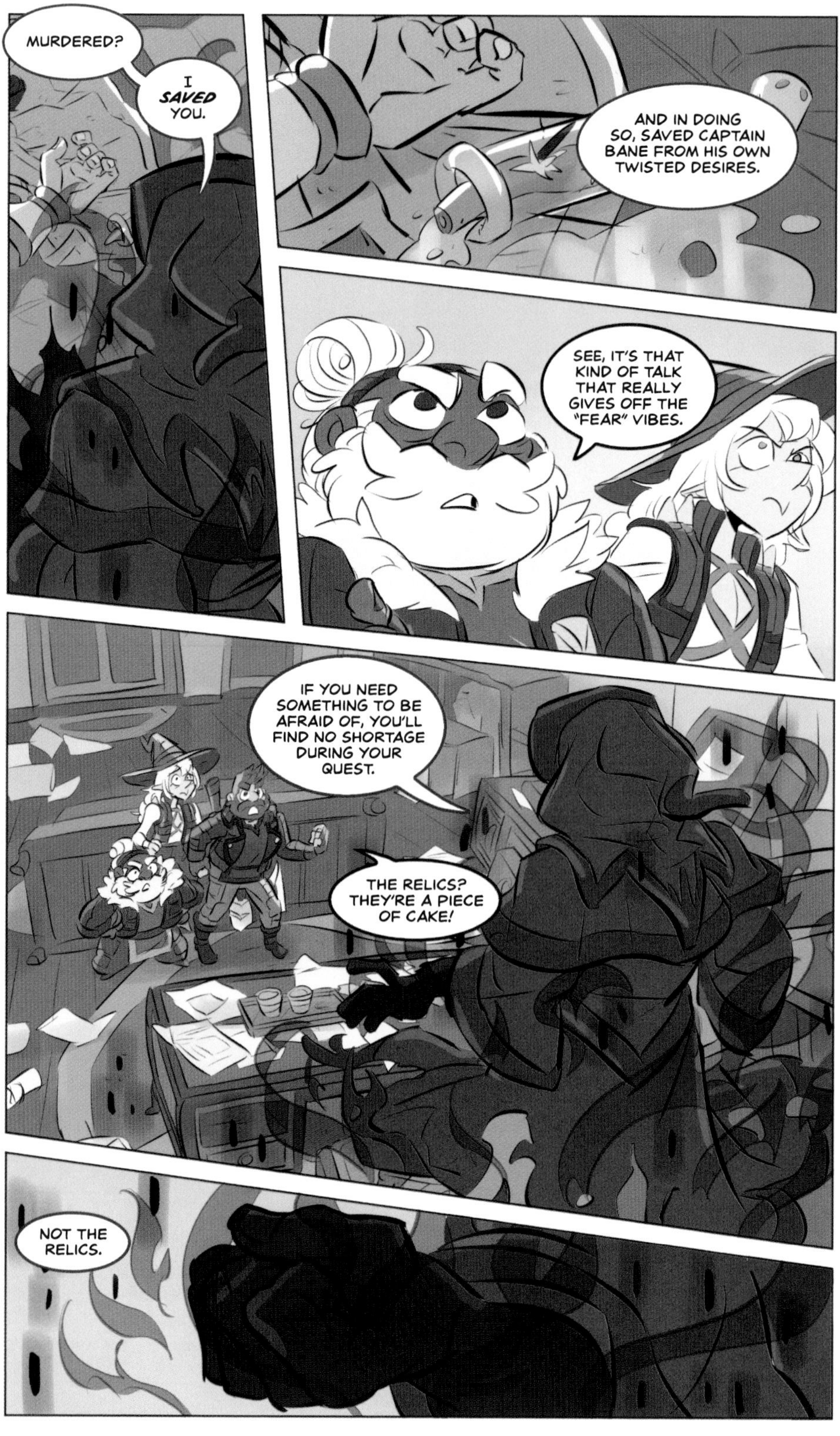
MURDERED?
I SAVED YOU.
AND IN DOING SO, SAVED CAPTAIN BANE FROM HIS OWN TWISTED DESIRES.
SEE, IT'S THAT KIND OF TALK THAT REALLY GIVES OFF THE "FEAR" VIBES.
IF YOU NEED SOMETHING TO BE AFRAID OF, YOU'LL FIND NO SHORTAGE DURING YOUR QUEST.
THE RELICS? THEY'RE A PIECE OF CAKE!
NOT THE RELICS.

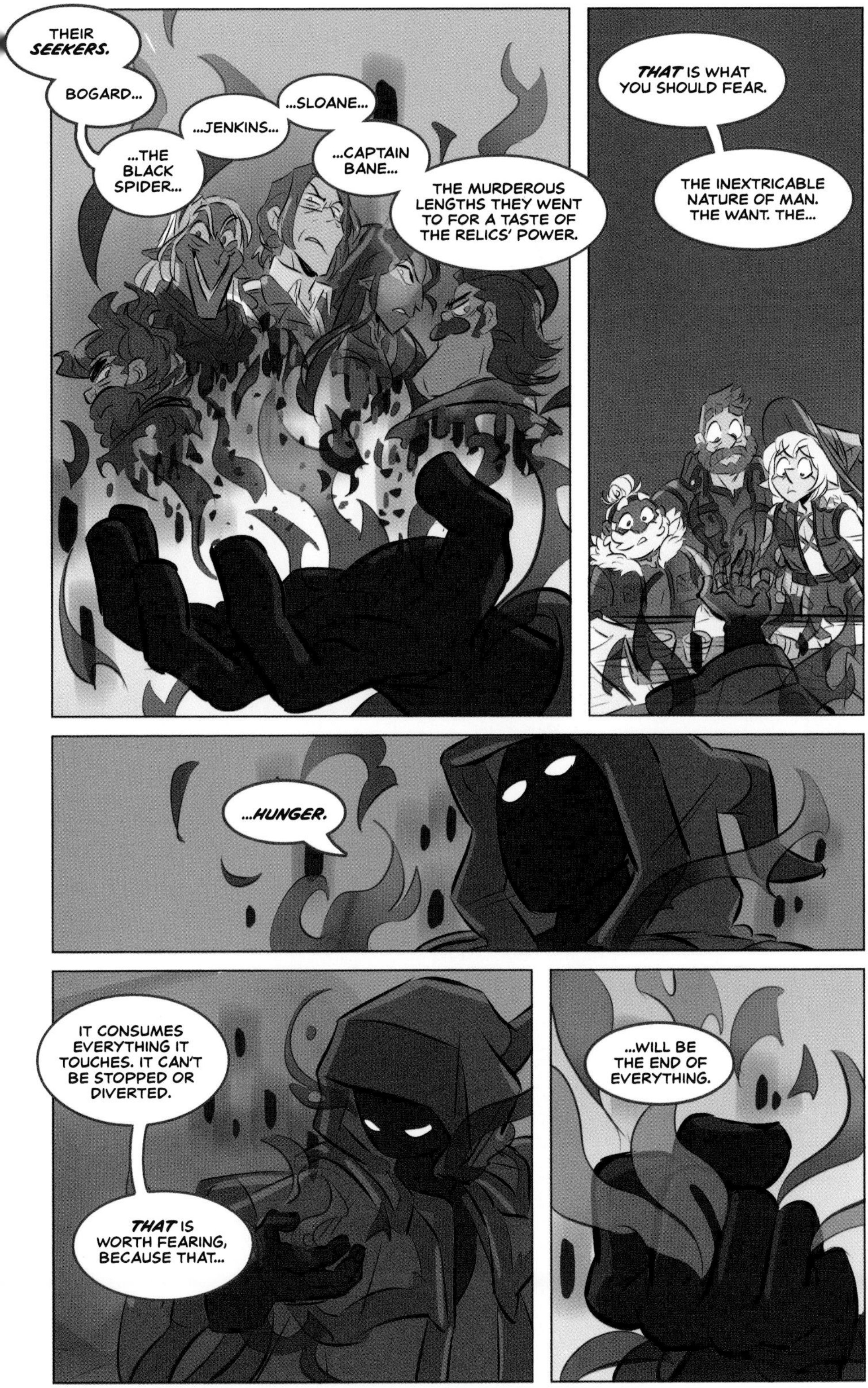
THEIR SEEKERS.
BOGARD...
...JENKINS...
...SLOANE...
...THE BLACK SPIDER...
...CAPTAIN BANE...
THE MURDEROUS LENGTHS THEY WENT TO FOR A TASTE OF THE RELICS' POWER.
THAT IS WHAT YOU SHOULD FEAR.
THE INEXTRICABLE NATURE OF MAN. THE WANT. THE...
...HUNGER.
IT CONSUMES EVERYTHING IT TOUCHES. IT CAN'T BE STOPPED OR DIVERTED.
THAT IS WORTH FEARING, BECAUSE THAT...
...WILL BE THE END OF EVERYTHING.

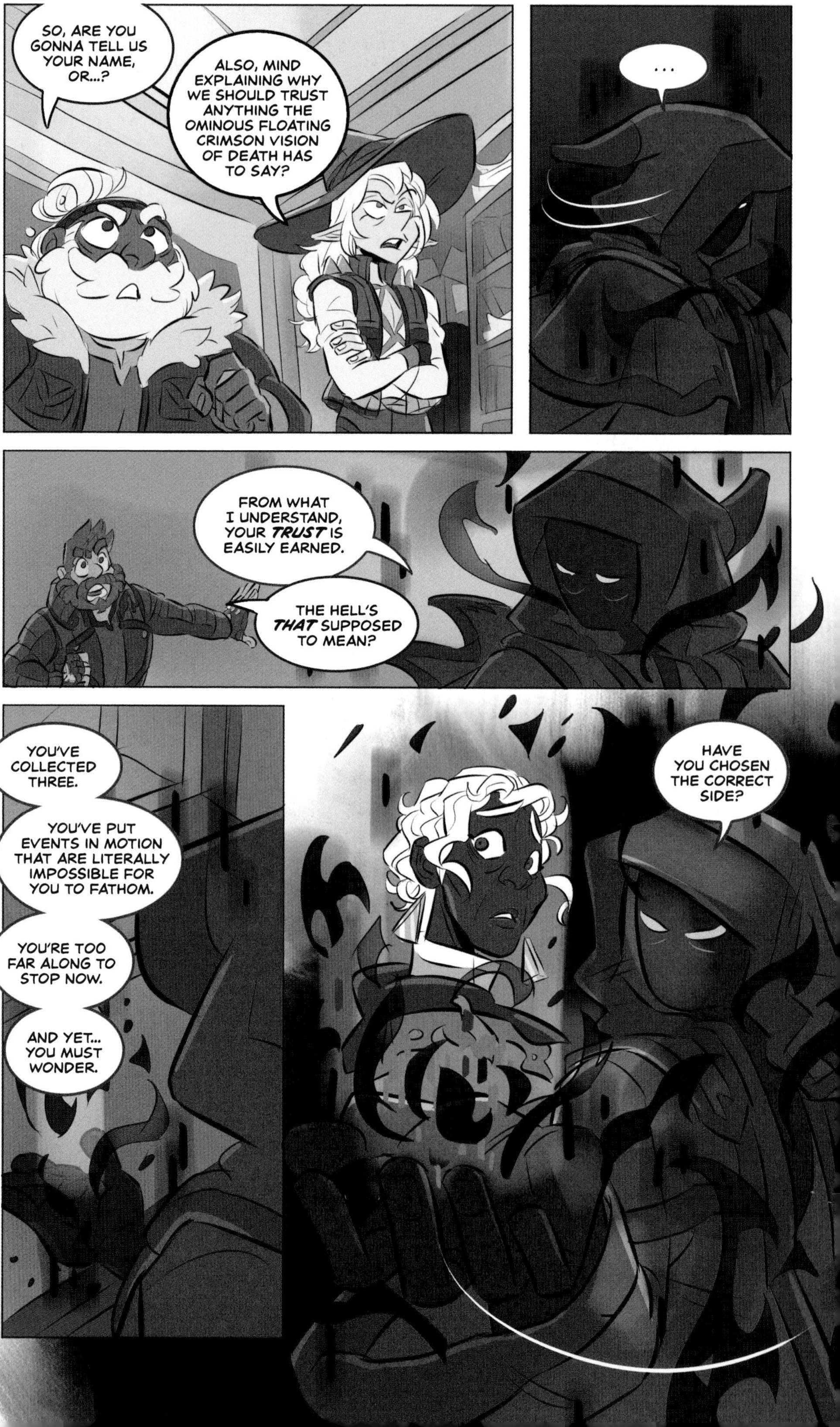
SO, ARE YOU GONNA TELL US YOUR NAME, OR...?
ALSO, MIND EXPLAINING WHY WE SHOULD TRUST ANYTHING THE OMINOUS FLOATING CRIMSON VISION OF DEATH HAS TO SAY?
...
FROM WHAT I UNDERSTAND, YOUR *TRUST* IS EASILY EARNED.
THE HELL'S *THAT* SUPPOSED TO MEAN?
YOU'VE COLLECTED THREE.
YOU'VE PUT EVENTS IN MOTION THAT ARE LITERALLY IMPOSSIBLE FOR YOU TO FATHOM.
YOU'RE TOO FAR ALONG TO STOP NOW.
AND YET... YOU MUST WONDER.
HAVE YOU CHOSEN THE CORRECT SIDE?

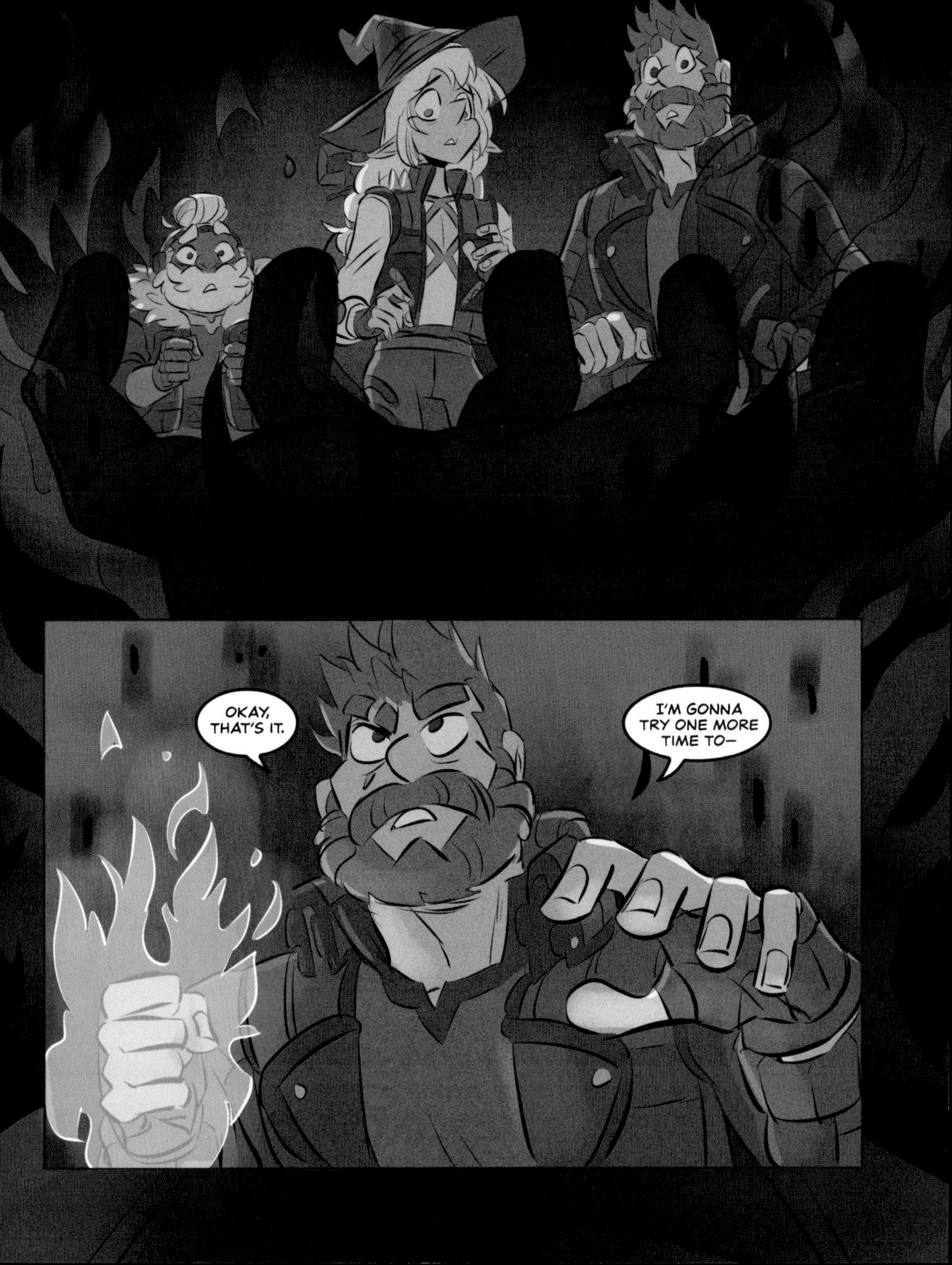
OKAY, THAT'S IT.
I'M GONNA TRY ONE MORE TIME TO—

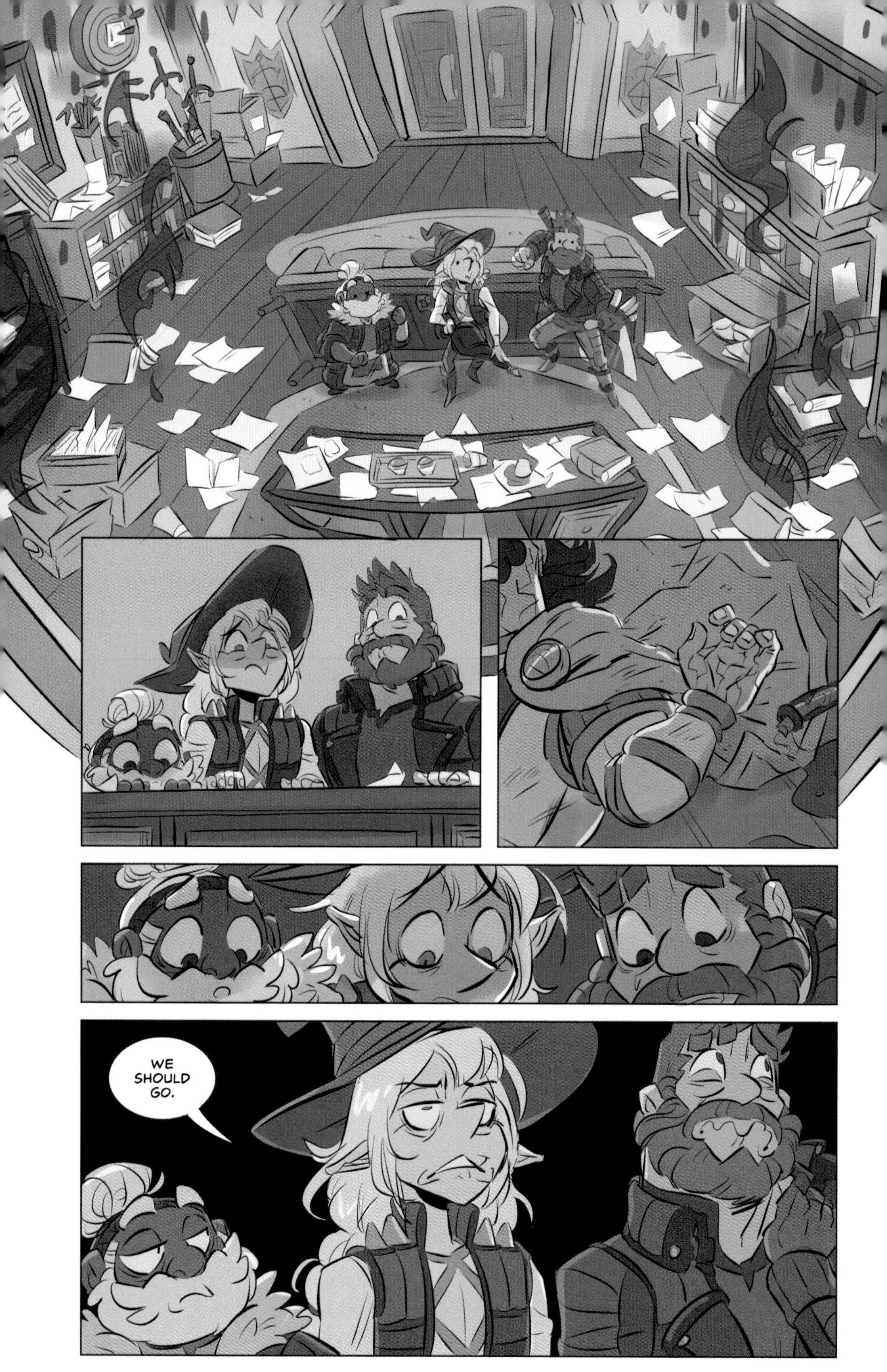
WE SHOULD GO.

Chapter 9

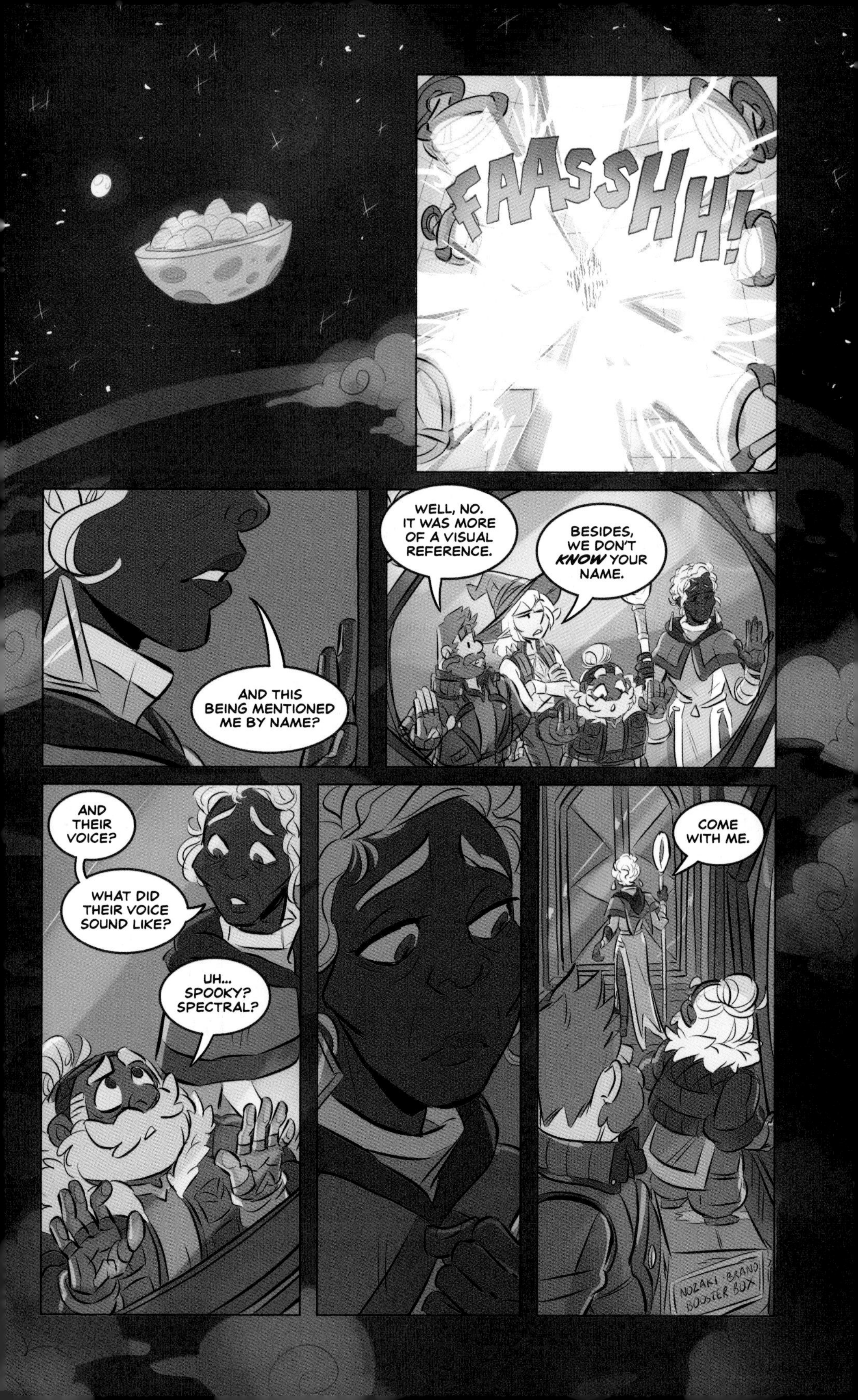
FAASSHH!
AND THIS BEING MENTIONED ME BY NAME?
WELL, NO. IT WAS MORE OF A VISUAL REFERENCE.
BESIDES, WE DON'T ***KNOW*** YOUR NAME.
AND THEIR VOICE?
WHAT DID THEIR VOICE SOUND LIKE?
UH... SPOOKY? SPECTRAL?
COME WITH ME.
NOZAKI-BRAND BOOSTER BOX

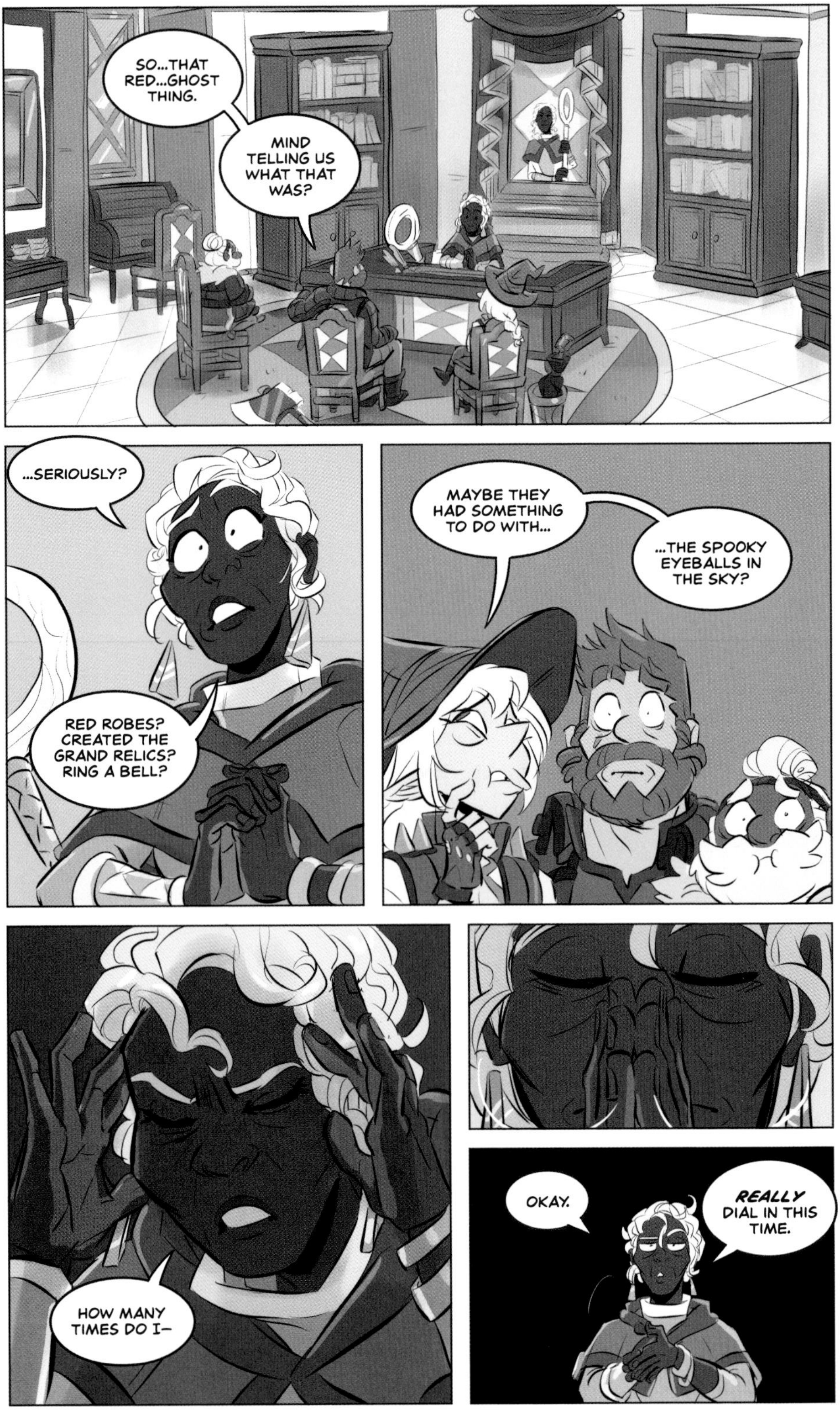
SO...THAT RED...GHOST THING.
MIND TELLING US WHAT THAT WAS?
...SERIOUSLY?
RED ROBES? CREATED THE GRAND RELICS? RING A BELL?
MAYBE THEY HAD SOMETHING TO DO WITH...
...THE SPOOKY EYEBALLS IN THE SKY?
HOW MANY TIMES DO I—
OKAY.
REALLY DIAL IN THIS TIME.

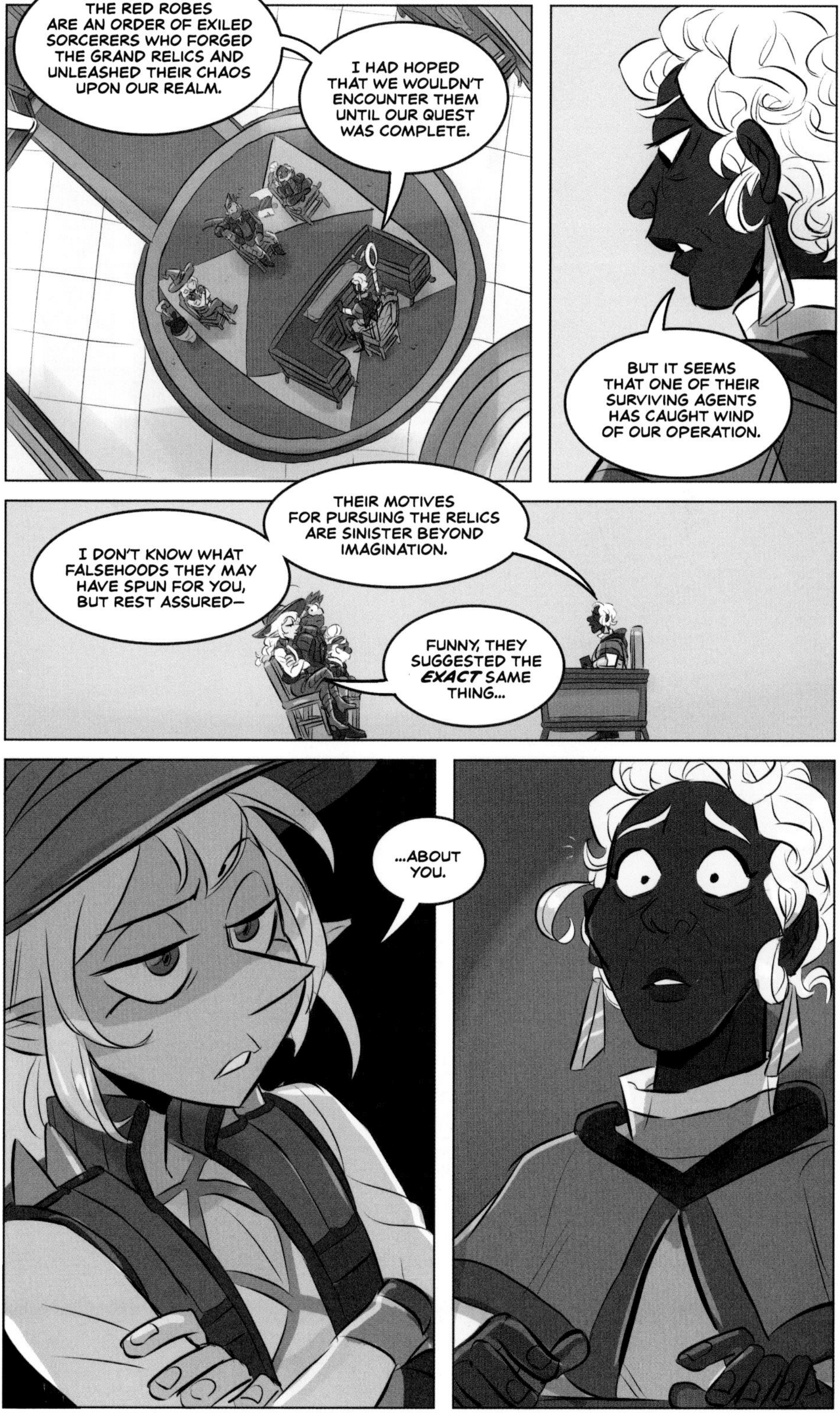
THE RED ROBES ARE AN ORDER OF EXILED SORCERERS WHO FORGED THE GRAND RELICS AND UNLEASHED THEIR CHAOS UPON OUR REALM.
I HAD HOPED THAT WE WOULDN'T ENCOUNTER THEM UNTIL OUR QUEST WAS COMPLETE.
BUT IT SEEMS THAT ONE OF THEIR SURVIVING AGENTS HAS CAUGHT WIND OF OUR OPERATION.
I DON'T KNOW WHAT FALSEHOODS THEY MAY HAVE SPUN FOR YOU, BUT REST ASSURED—
THEIR MOTIVES FOR PURSUING THE RELICS ARE SINISTER BEYOND IMAGINATION.
FUNNY, THEY SUGGESTED THE *EXACT* SAME THING...
...ABOUT YOU.

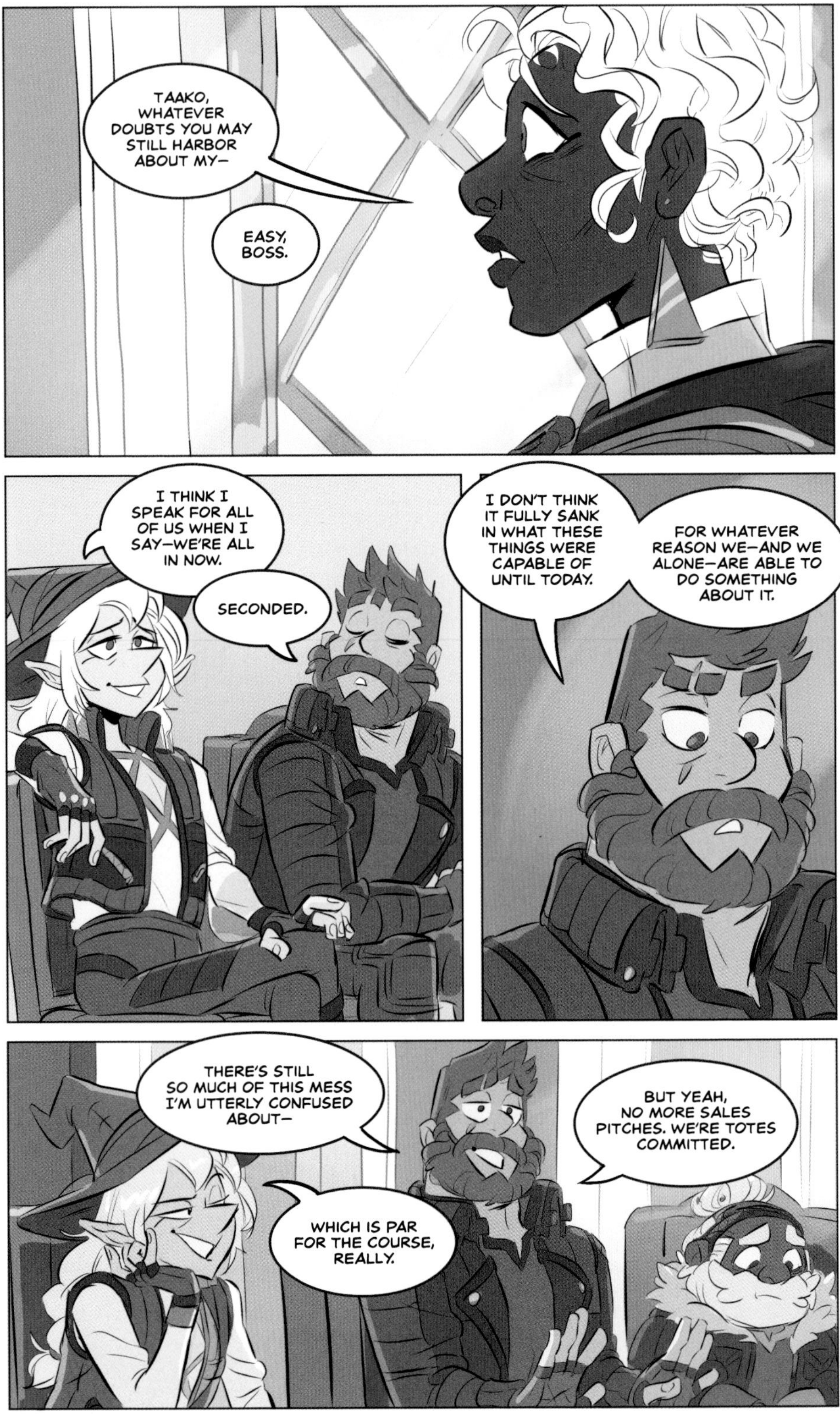
TAAKO, WHATEVER DOUBTS YOU MAY STILL HARBOR ABOUT MY—
EASY, BOSS.
I THINK I SPEAK FOR ALL OF US WHEN I SAY—WE'RE ALL IN NOW.
SECONDED.
I DON'T THINK IT FULLY SANK IN WHAT THESE THINGS WERE CAPABLE OF UNTIL TODAY.
FOR WHATEVER REASON WE—AND WE ALONE—ARE ABLE TO DO SOMETHING ABOUT IT.
THERE'S STILL SO MUCH OF THIS MESS I'M UTTERLY CONFUSED ABOUT—
WHICH IS PAR FOR THE COURSE, REALLY.
BUT YEAH, NO MORE SALES PITCHES. WE'RE TOTES COMMITTED.

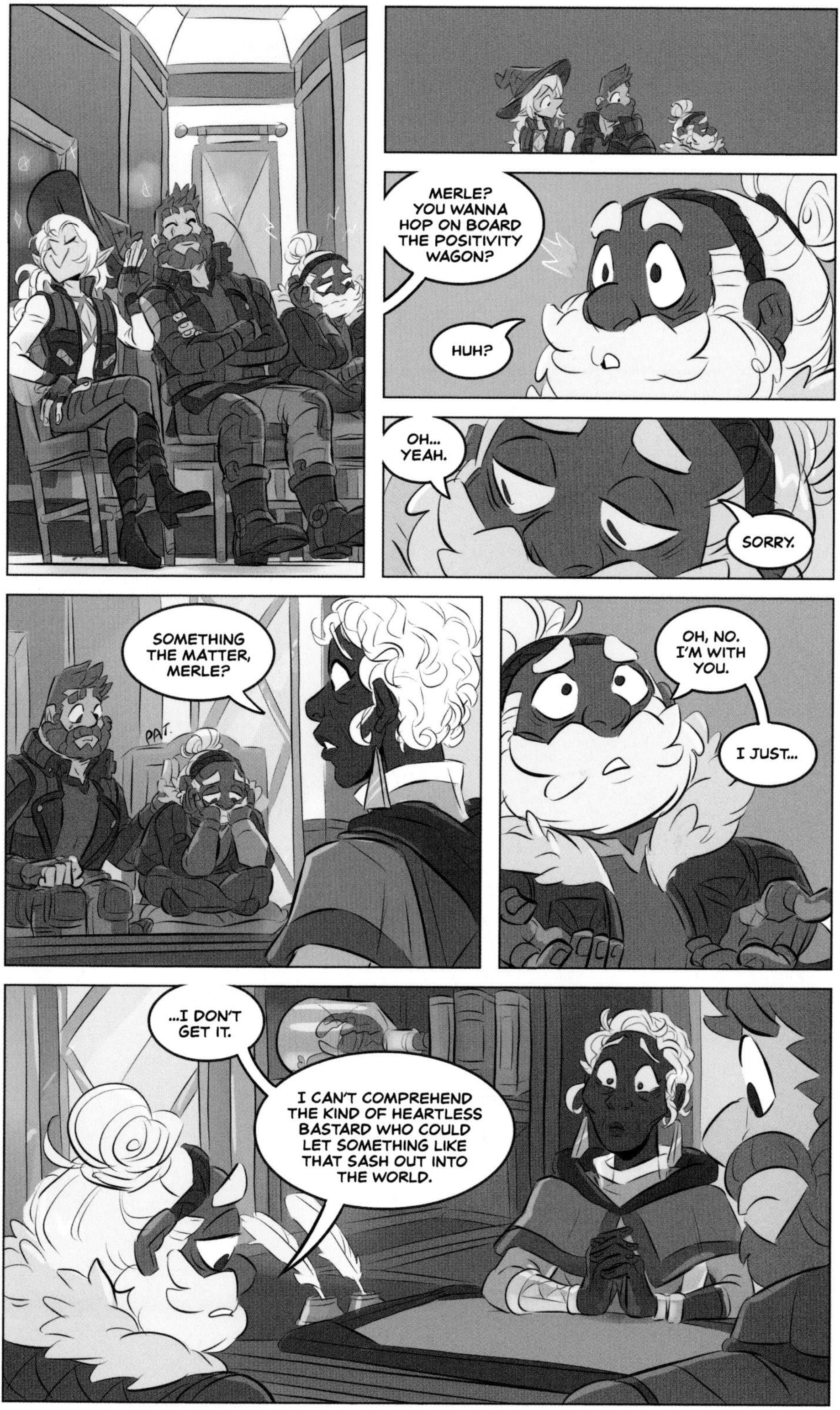
MERLE? YOU WANNA HOP ON BOARD THE POSITIVITY WAGON?
HUH?
OH... YEAH.
SORRY.
SOMETHING THE MATTER, MERLE?
PAT.
OH, NO. I'M WITH YOU.
I JUST...
...I DON'T GET IT.
I CAN'T COMPREHEND THE KIND OF HEARTLESS BASTARD WHO COULD LET SOMETHING LIKE THAT SASH OUT INTO THE WORLD.

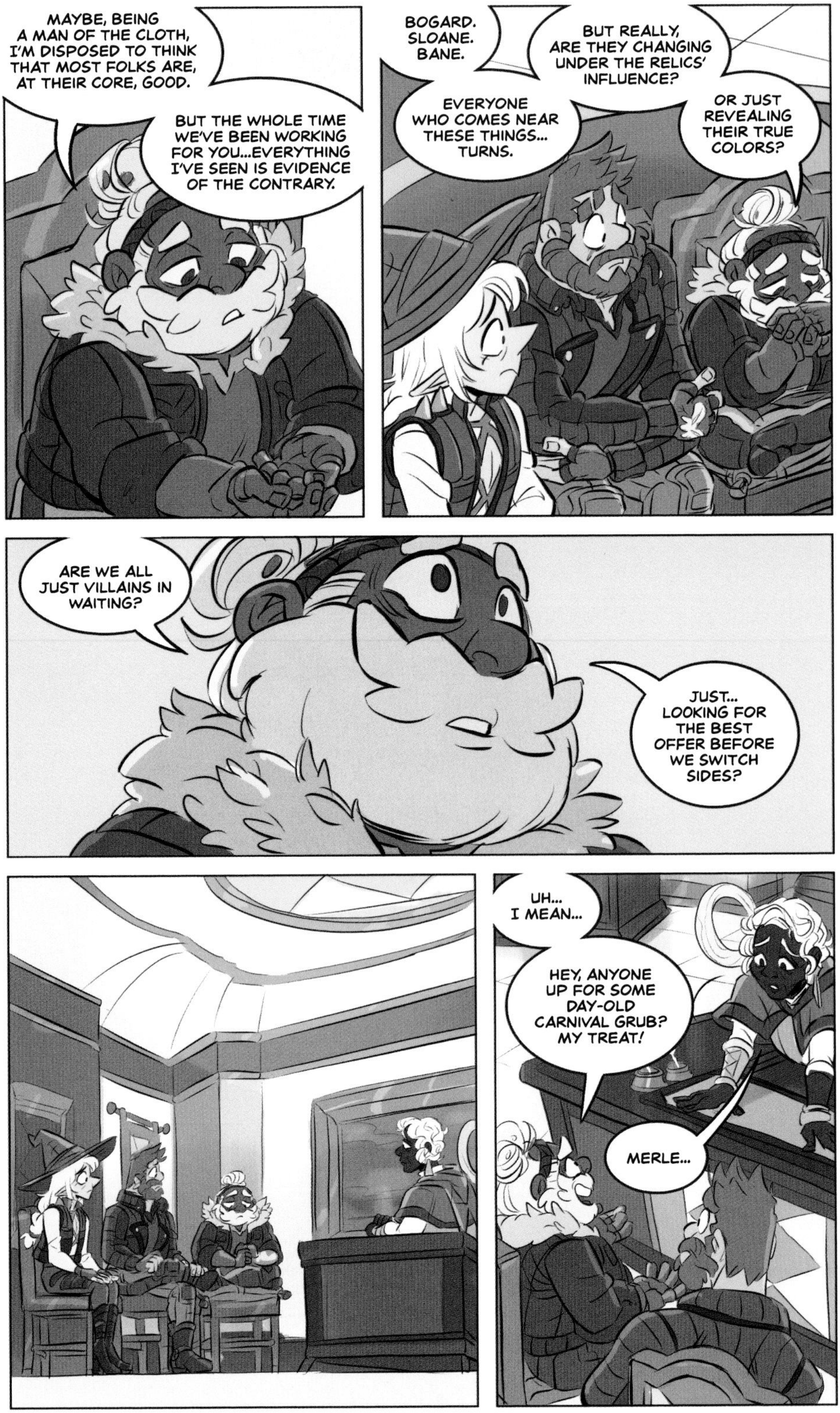
MAYBE, BEING A MAN OF THE CLOTH, I'M DISPOSED TO THINK THAT MOST FOLKS ARE, AT THEIR CORE, GOOD.
BUT THE WHOLE TIME WE'VE BEEN WORKING FOR YOU...EVERYTHING I'VE SEEN IS EVIDENCE OF THE CONTRARY.
BOGARD. SLOANE. BANE.
EVERYONE WHO COMES NEAR THESE THINGS... TURNS.
BUT REALLY, ARE THEY CHANGING UNDER THE RELICS' INFLUENCE?
OR JUST REVEALING THEIR TRUE COLORS?
ARE WE ALL JUST VILLAINS IN WAITING?
JUST... LOOKING FOR THE BEST OFFER BEFORE WE SWITCH SIDES?
UH... I MEAN...
HEY, ANYONE UP FOR SOME DAY-OLD CARNIVAL GRUB? MY TREAT!
MERLE...

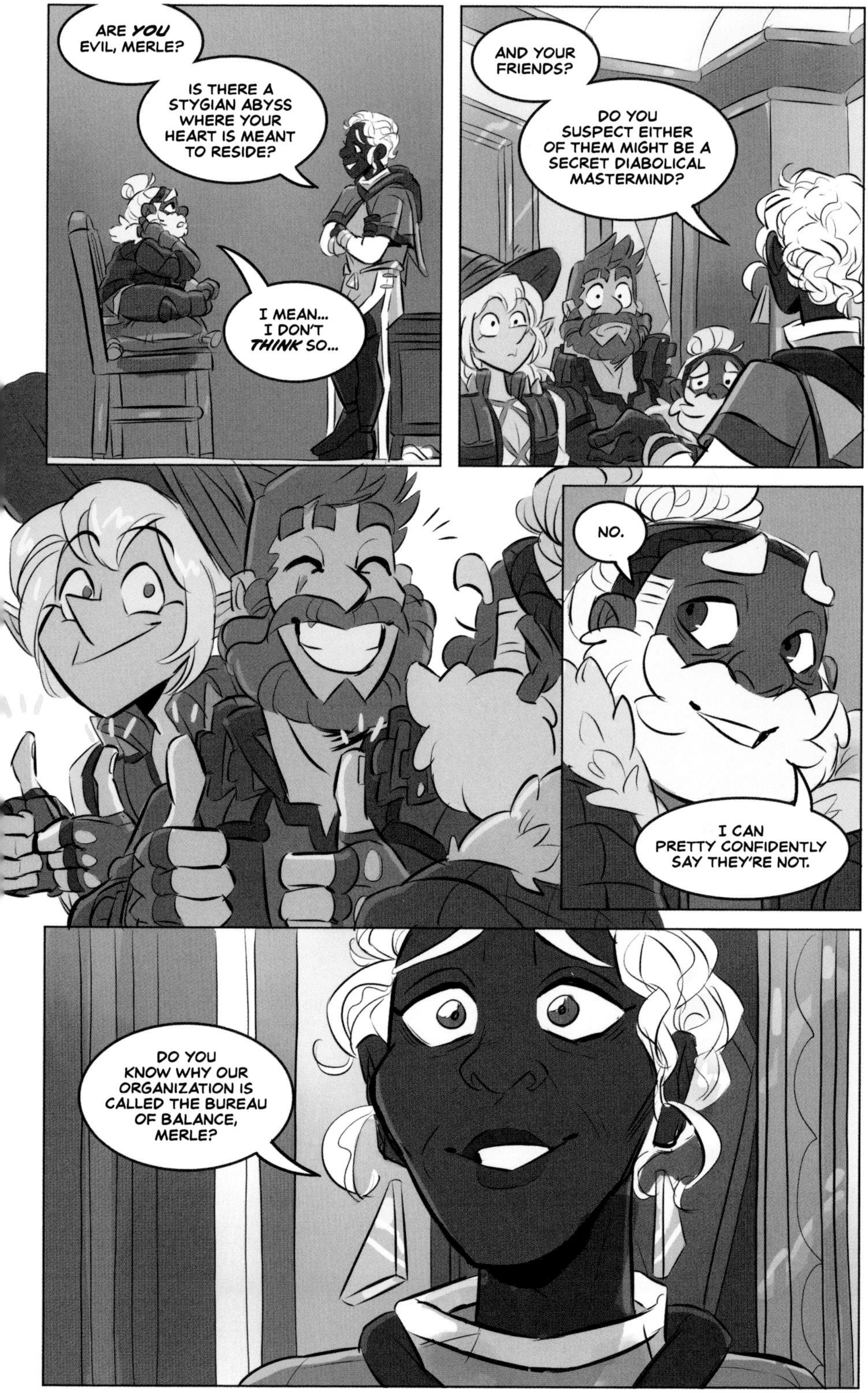
ARE *YOU* EVIL, MERLE?
IS THERE A STYGIAN ABYSS WHERE YOUR HEART IS MEANT TO RESIDE?
I MEAN... I DON'T *THINK* SO...
AND YOUR FRIENDS?
DO YOU SUSPECT EITHER OF THEM MIGHT BE A SECRET DIABOLICAL MASTERMIND?
NO.
I CAN PRETTY CONFIDENTLY SAY THEY'RE NOT.
DO YOU KNOW WHY OUR ORGANIZATION IS CALLED THE BUREAU OF BALANCE, MERLE?

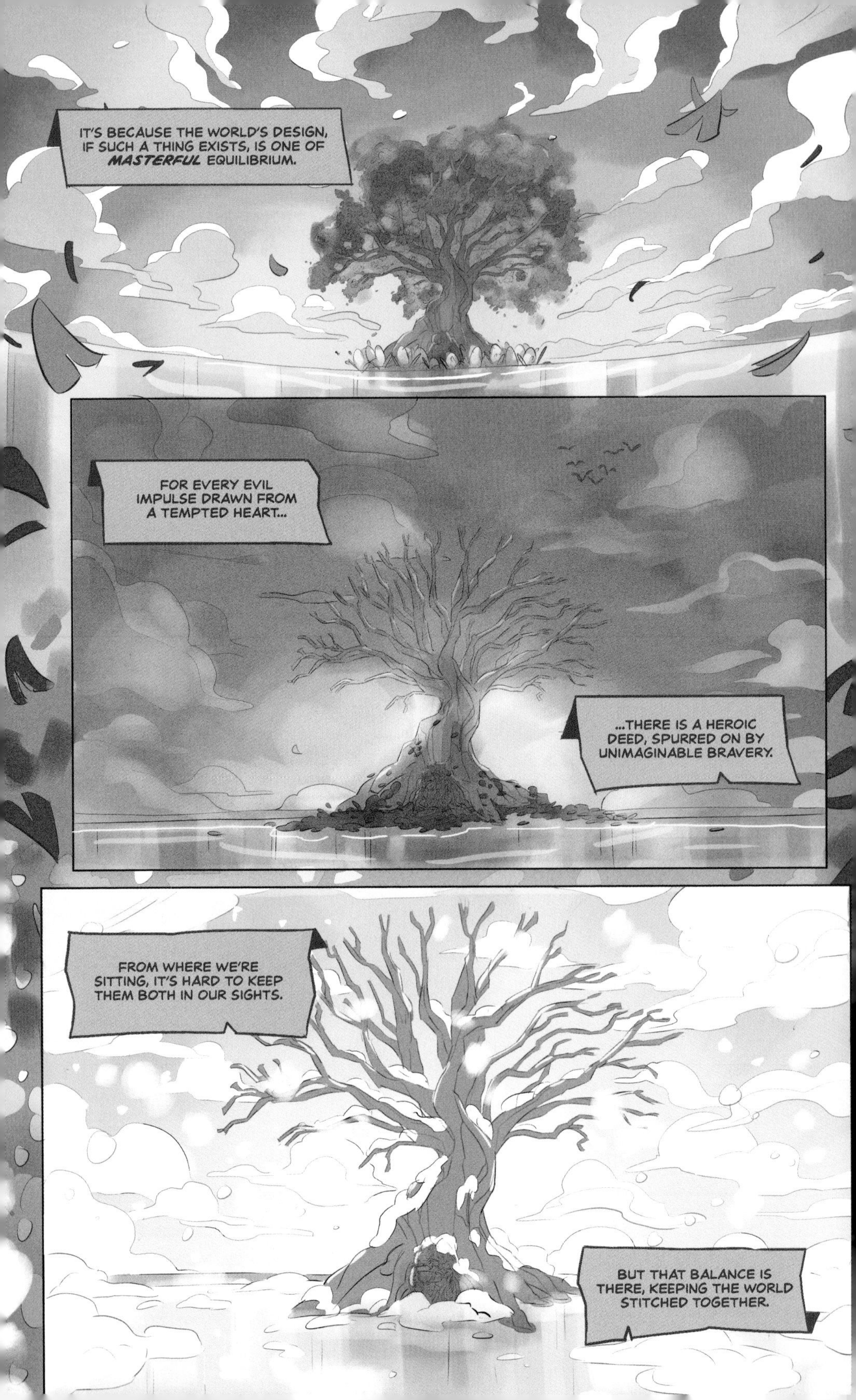
IT'S BECAUSE THE WORLD'S DESIGN, IF SUCH A THING EXISTS, IS ONE OF *MASTERFUL* EQUILIBRIUM.
FOR EVERY EVIL IMPULSE DRAWN FROM A TEMPTED HEART...
...THERE IS A HEROIC DEED, SPURRED ON BY UNIMAGINABLE BRAVERY.
FROM WHERE WE'RE SITTING, IT'S HARD TO KEEP THEM BOTH IN OUR SIGHTS.
BUT THAT BALANCE IS THERE, KEEPING THE WORLD STITCHED TOGETHER.

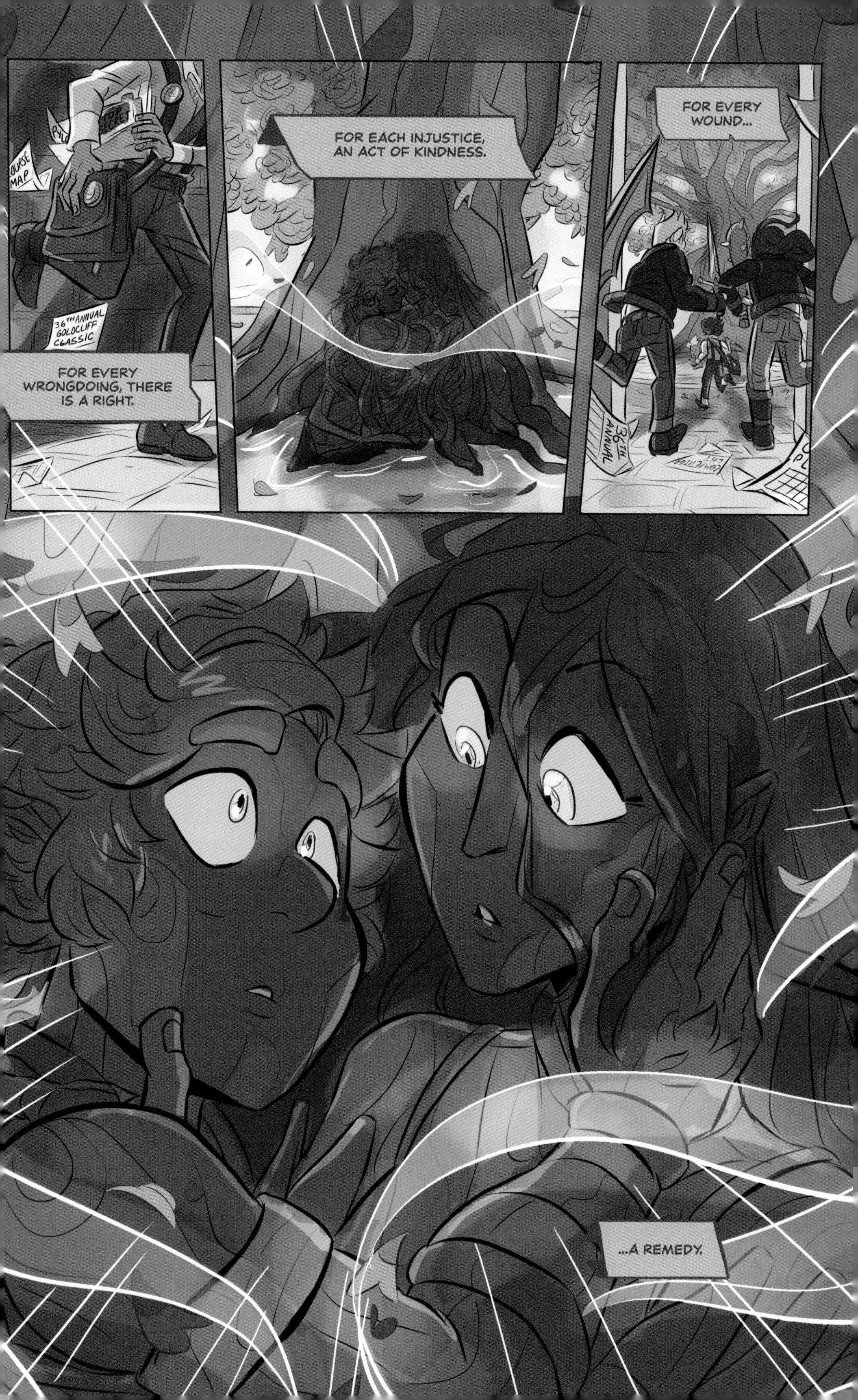

FOR EVERY WRONGDOING, THERE IS A RIGHT.
FOR EACH INJUSTICE, AN ACT OF KINDNESS.
FOR EVERY WOUND...
...A REMEDY.

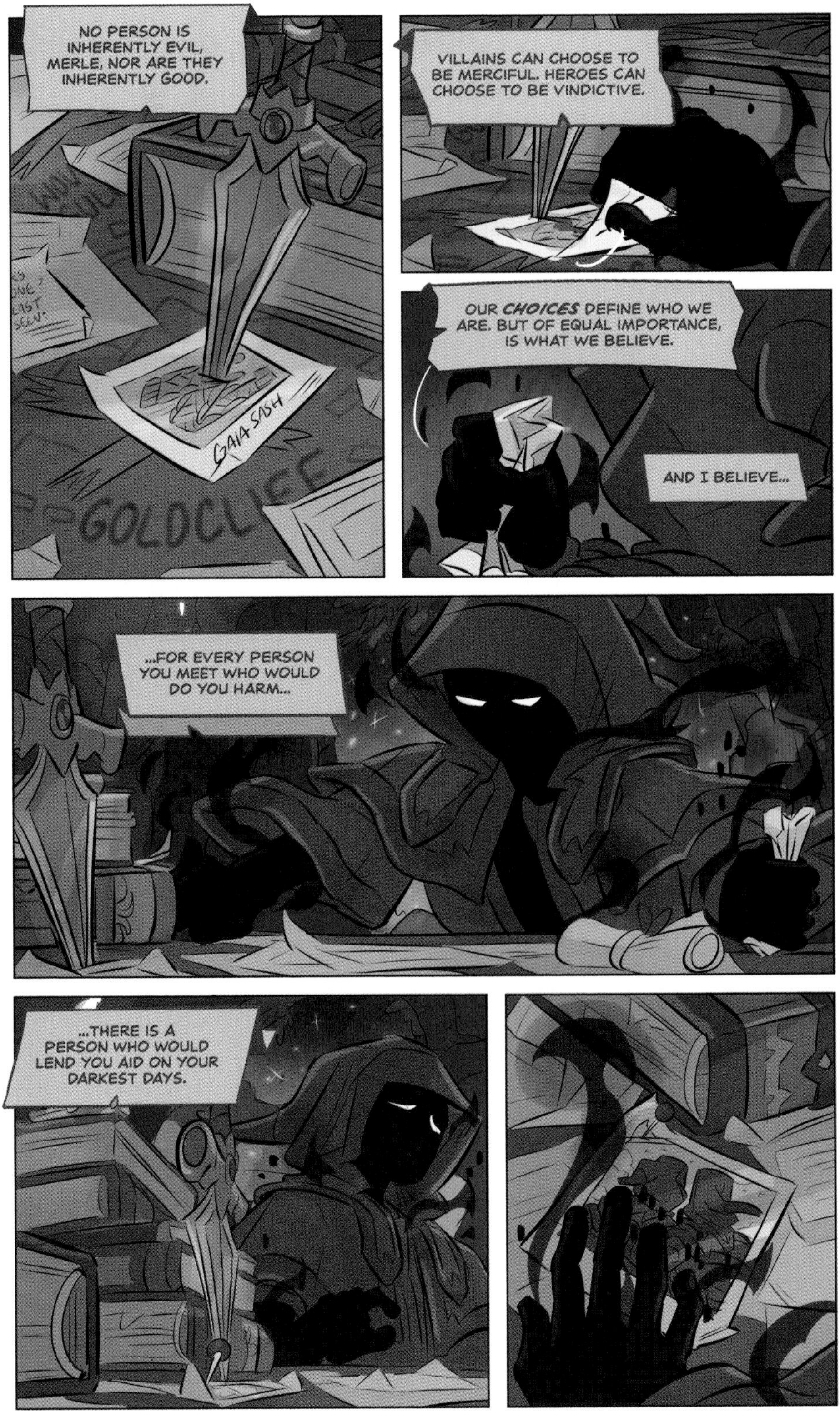
NO PERSON IS INHERENTLY EVIL, MERLE, NOR ARE THEY INHERENTLY GOOD.
GAIA SASH
GOLDCLIFF
VILLAINS CAN CHOOSE TO BE MERCIFUL. HEROES CAN CHOOSE TO BE VINDICTIVE.
OUR CHOICES DEFINE WHO WE ARE. BUT OF EQUAL IMPORTANCE, IS WHAT WE BELIEVE.
AND I BELIEVE...
...FOR EVERY PERSON YOU MEET WHO WOULD DO YOU HARM...
...THERE IS A PERSON WHO WOULD LEND YOU AID ON YOUR DARKEST DAYS.

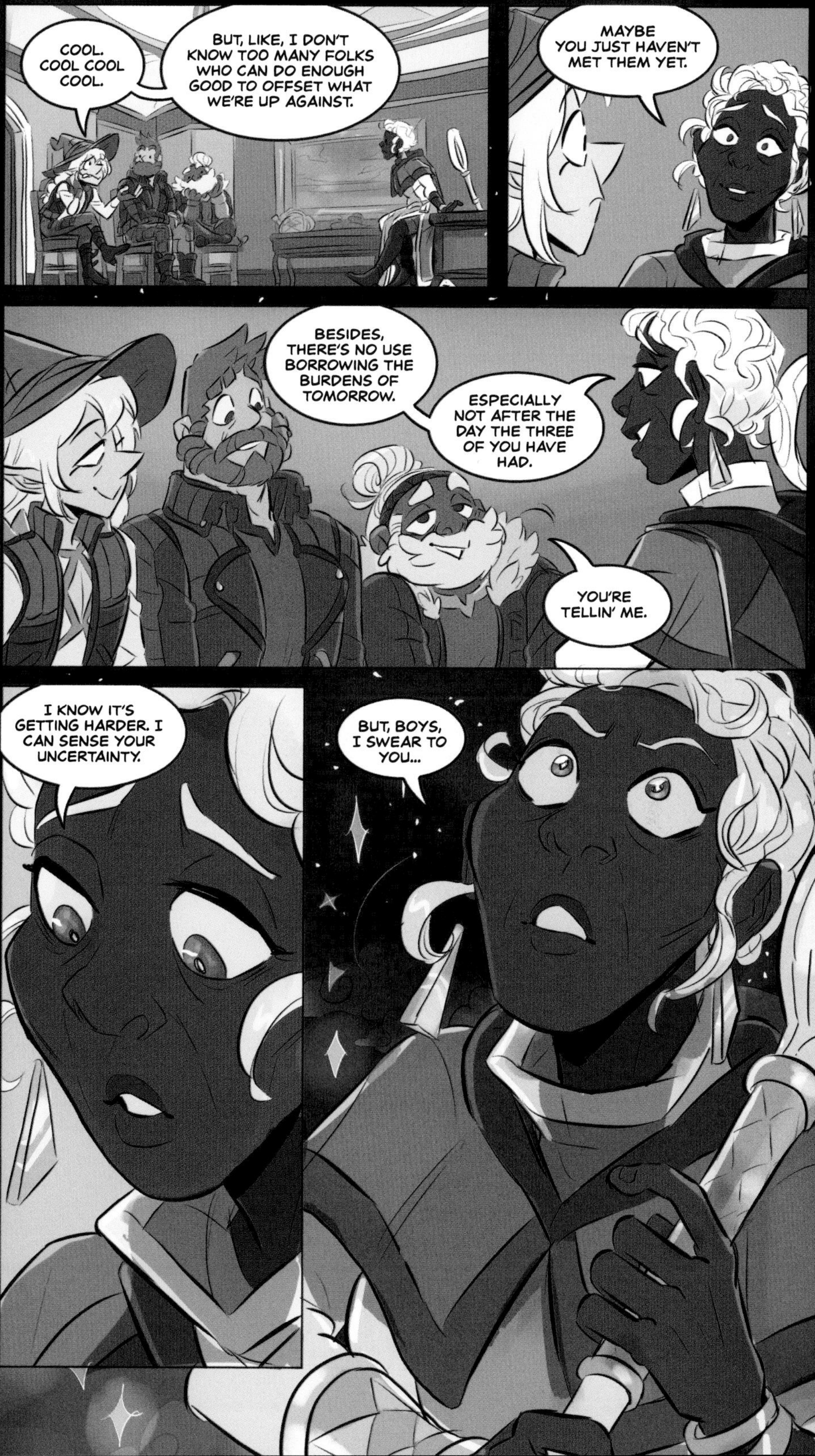
COOL. COOL COOL COOL.
BUT, LIKE, I DON'T KNOW TOO MANY FOLKS WHO CAN DO ENOUGH GOOD TO OFFSET WHAT WE'RE UP AGAINST.
MAYBE YOU JUST HAVEN'T MET THEM YET.
BESIDES, THERE'S NO USE BORROWING THE BURDENS OF TOMORROW.
ESPECIALLY NOT AFTER THE DAY THE THREE OF YOU HAVE HAD.
YOU'RE TELLIN' ME.
I KNOW IT'S GETTING HARDER. I CAN SENSE YOUR UNCERTAINTY.
BUT, BOYS, I SWEAR TO YOU...

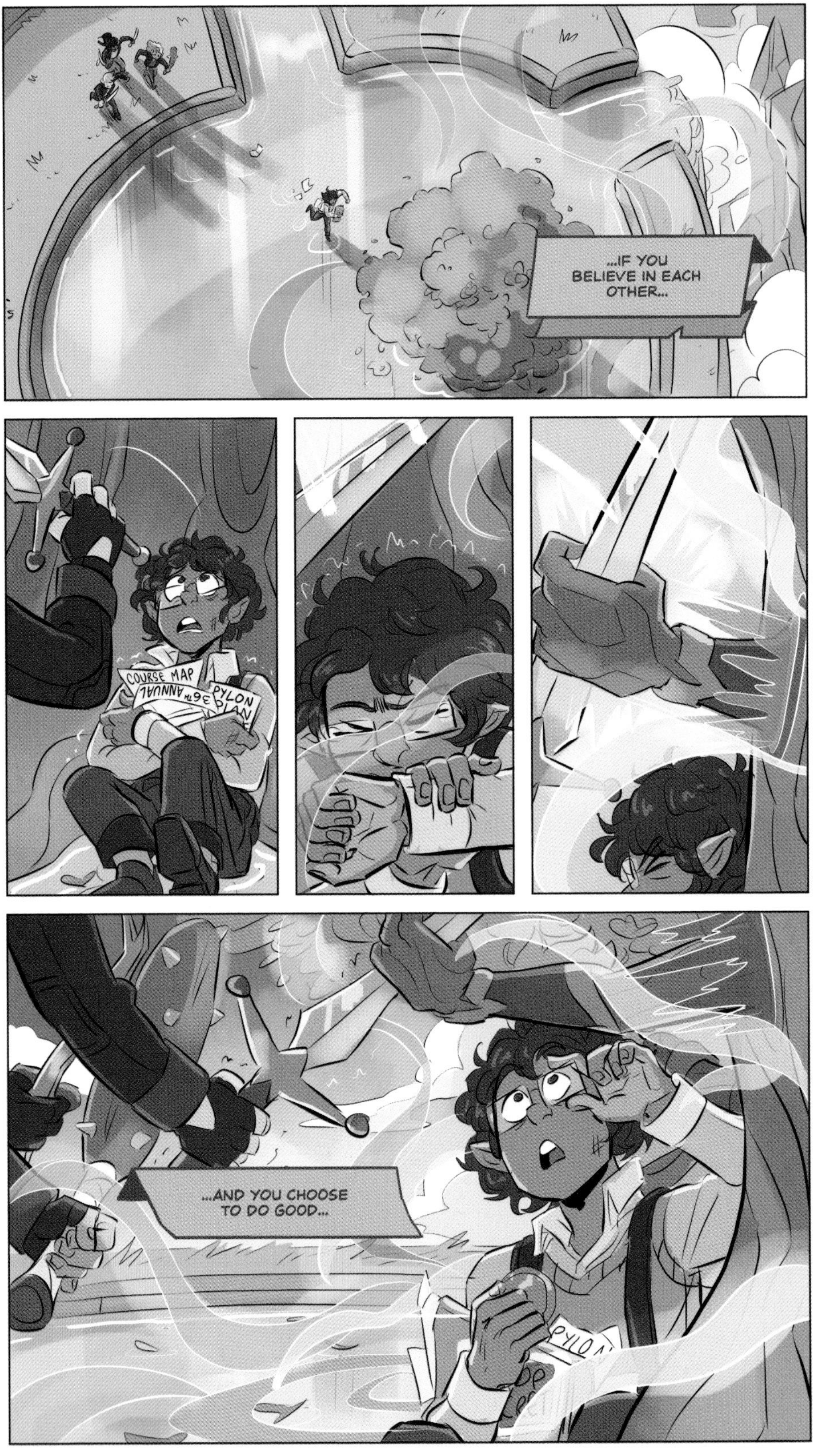
...IF YOU BELIEVE IN EACH OTHER...
COURSE MAP
PYLON PLAN
...AND YOU CHOOSE TO DO GOOD...

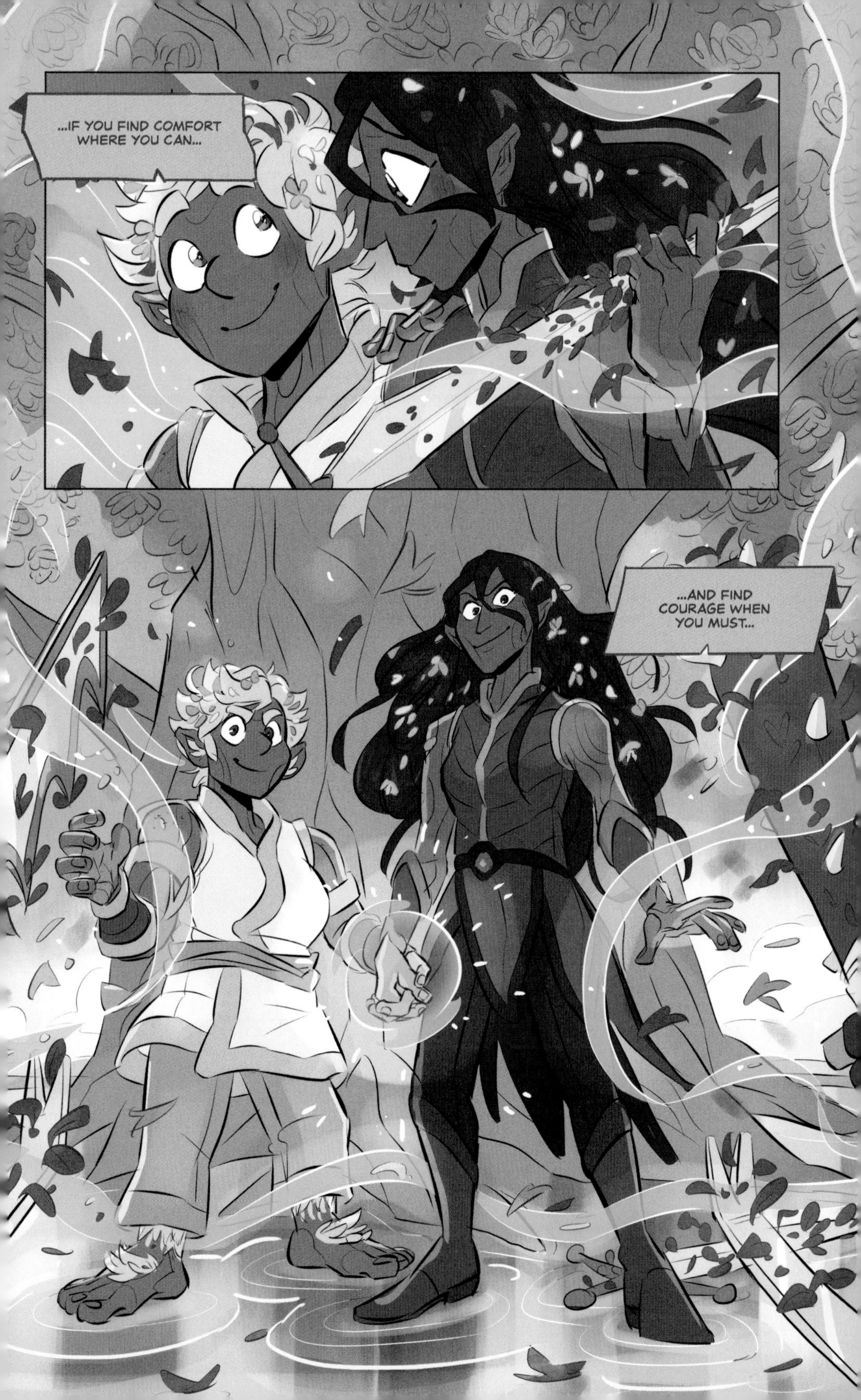
...IF YOU FIND COMFORT WHERE YOU CAN...
...AND FIND COURAGE WHEN YOU MUST...

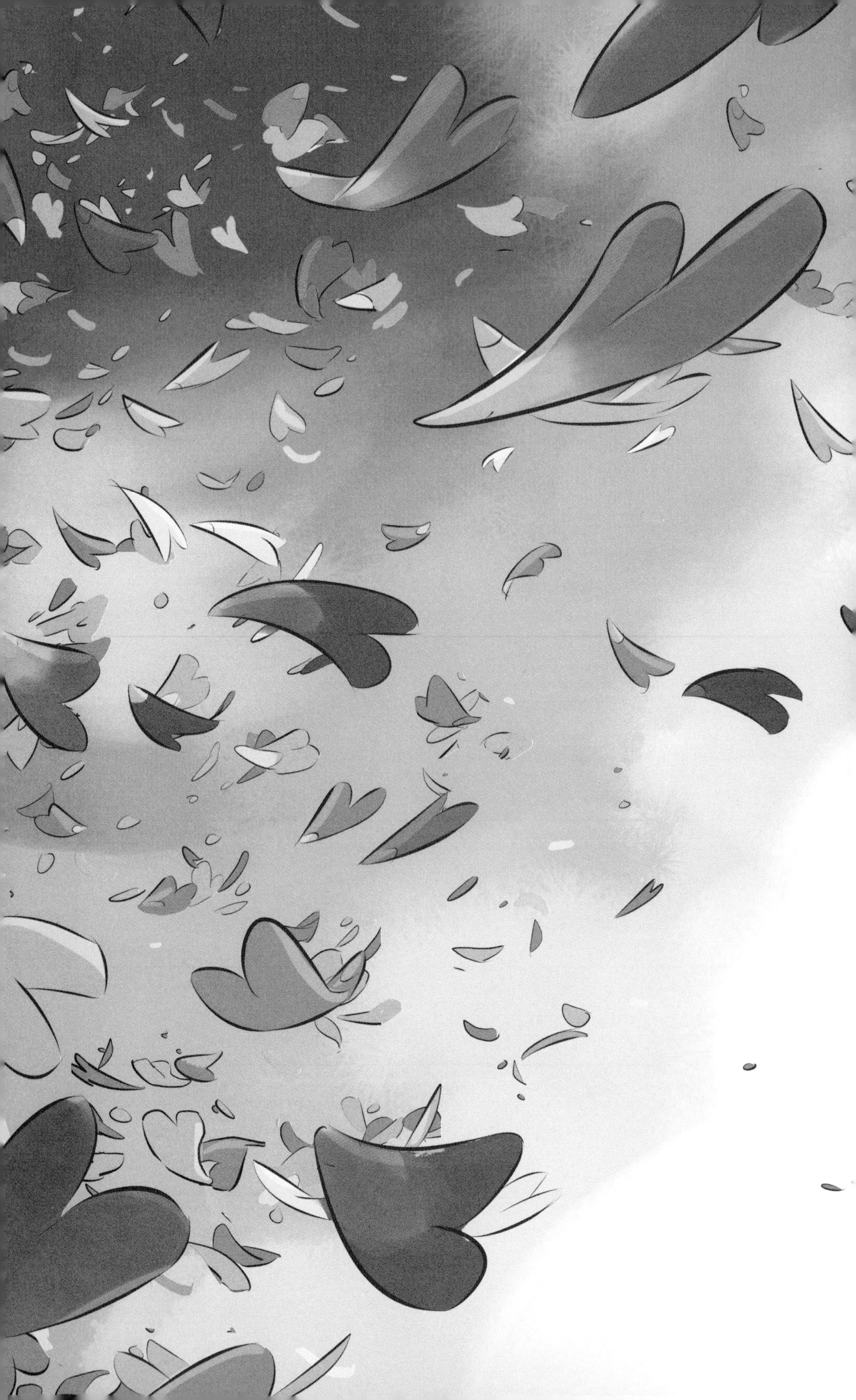

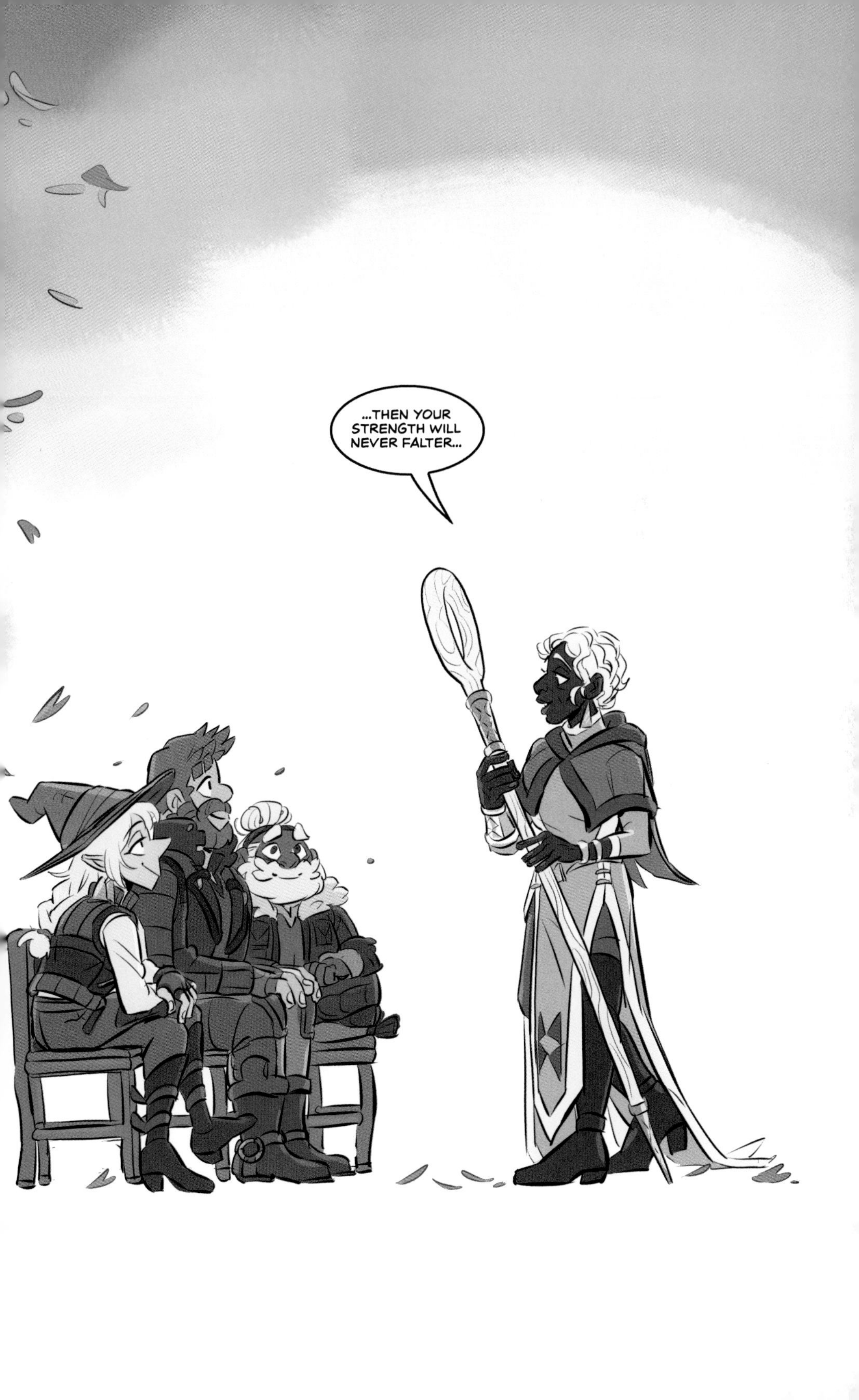
...THEN YOUR STRENGTH WILL NEVER FALTER...

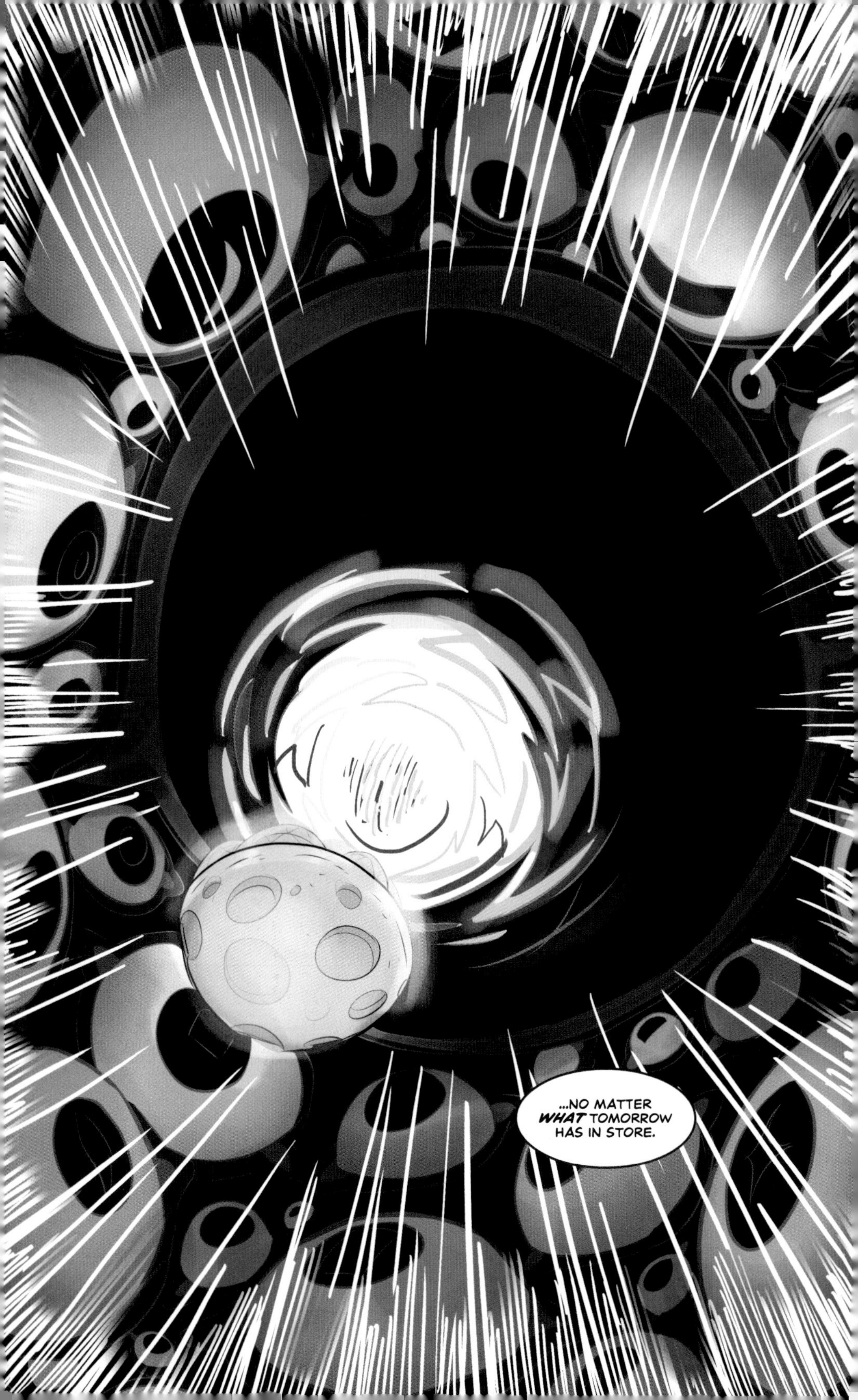
...NO MATTER *WHAT* TOMORROW HAS IN STORE.

The ADVENTURE CONTINUES in

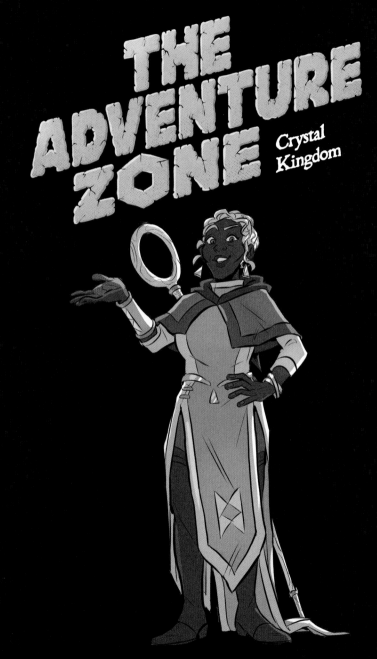

THE ADVENTURE ZONE

Crystal Kingdom

Coming Soon!

Fan Art Gallery

The *Adventure Zone* has been lucky enough to garner a passionate and deeply creative fandom. Many thanks to the fan artists who contributed pieces to this gallery—and to all the writers, artists, creators, and fans of all stripes who have made *The Adventure Zone* what it is. ♥

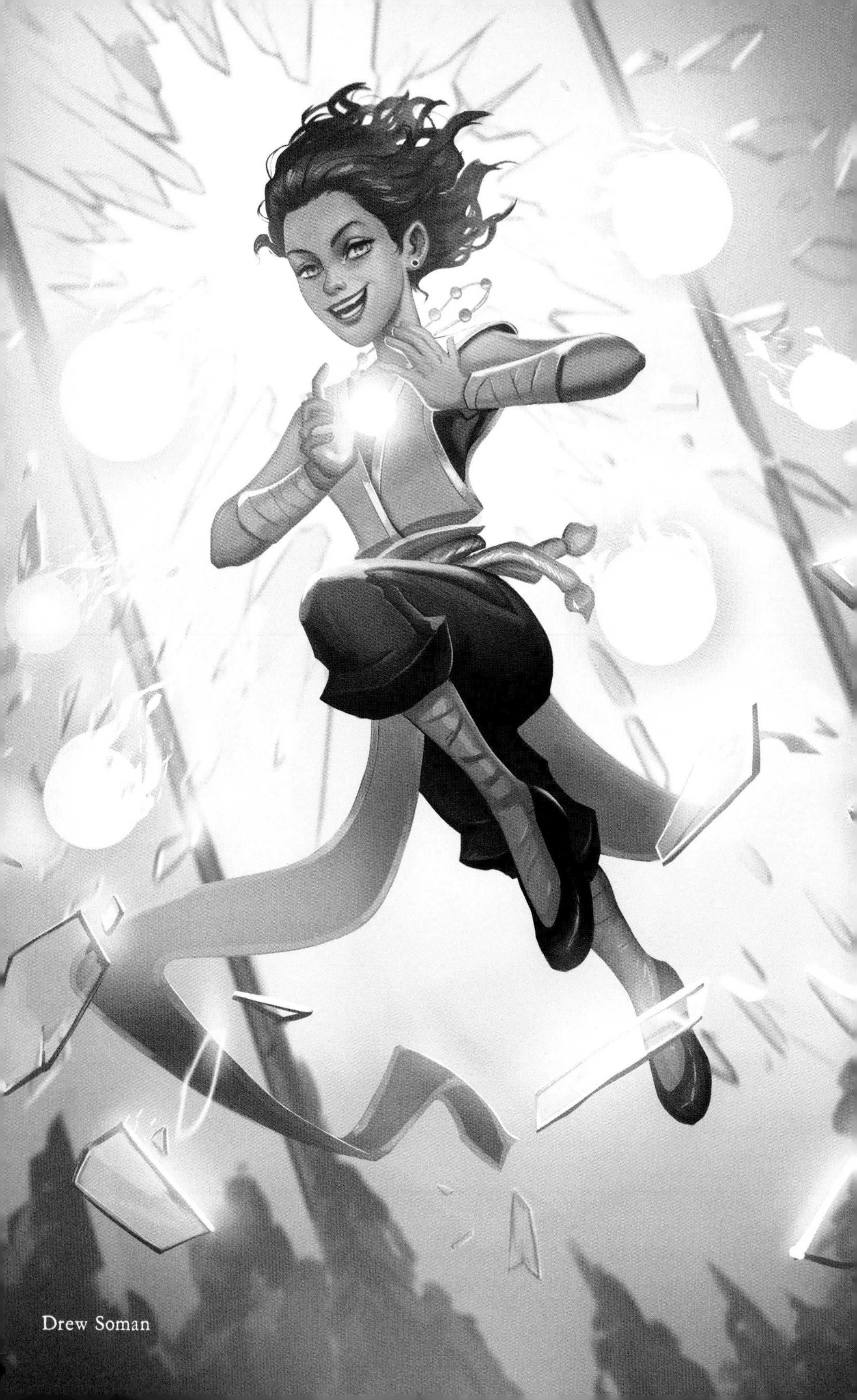

Drew Soman

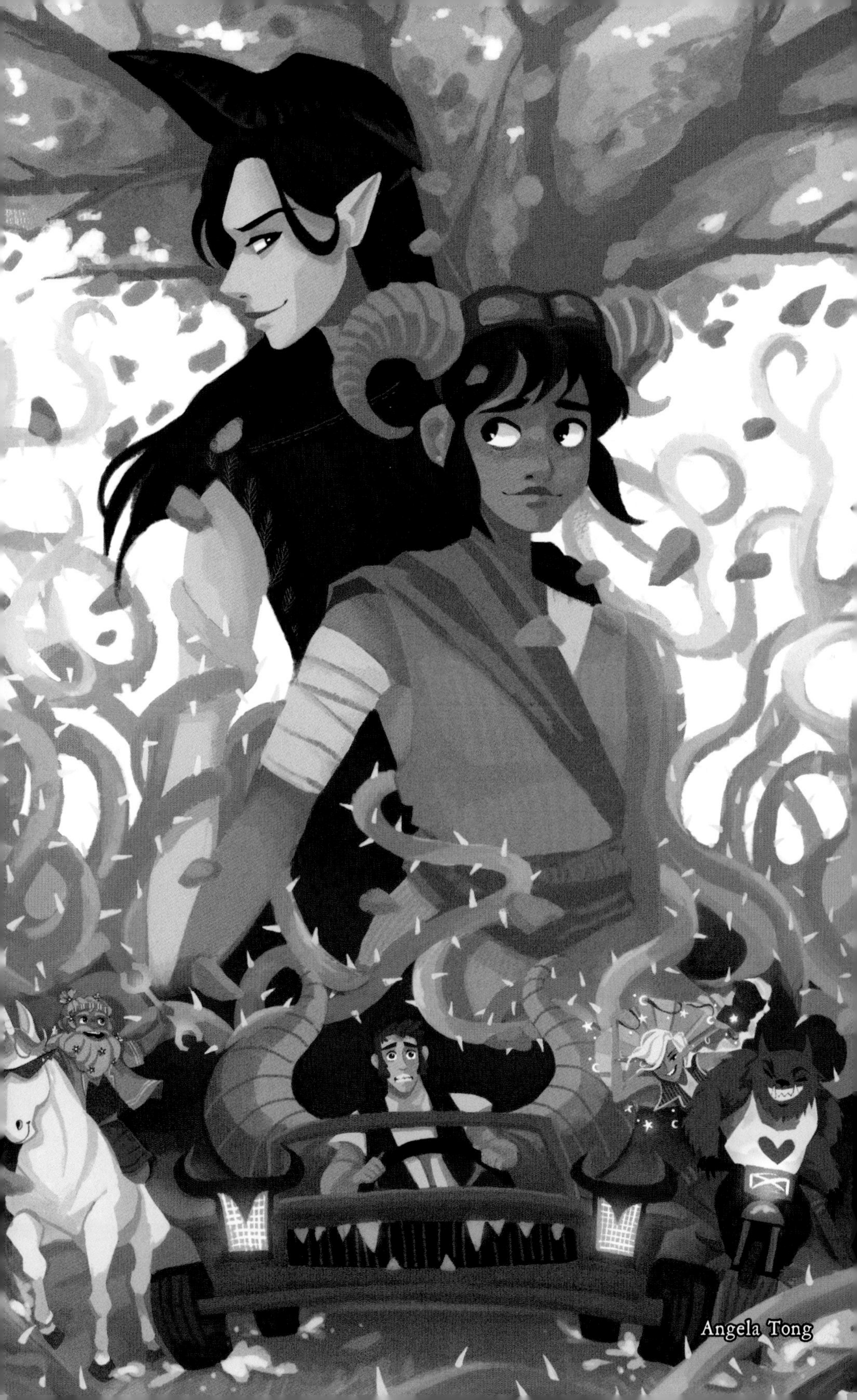
Angela Tong

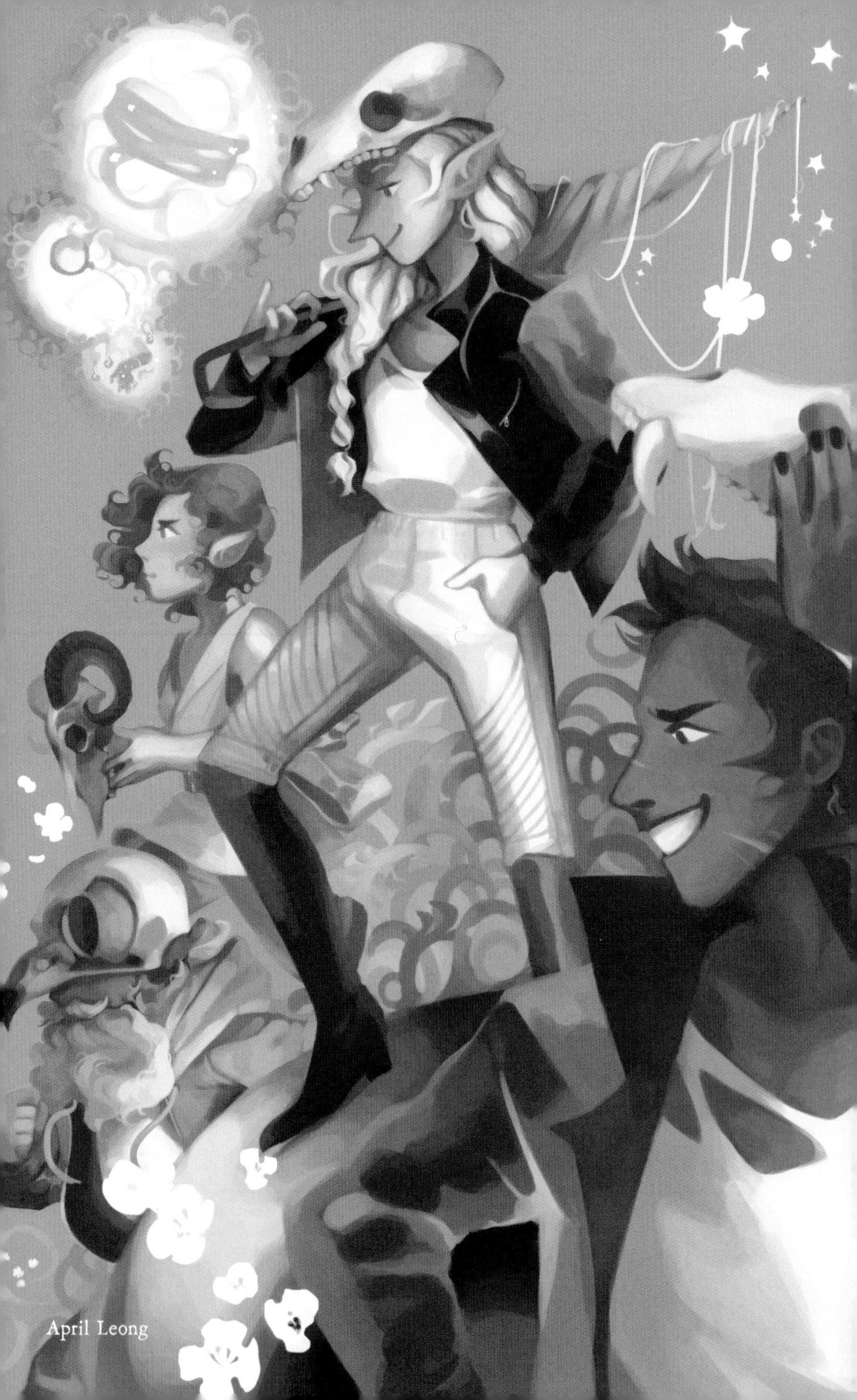

April Leong

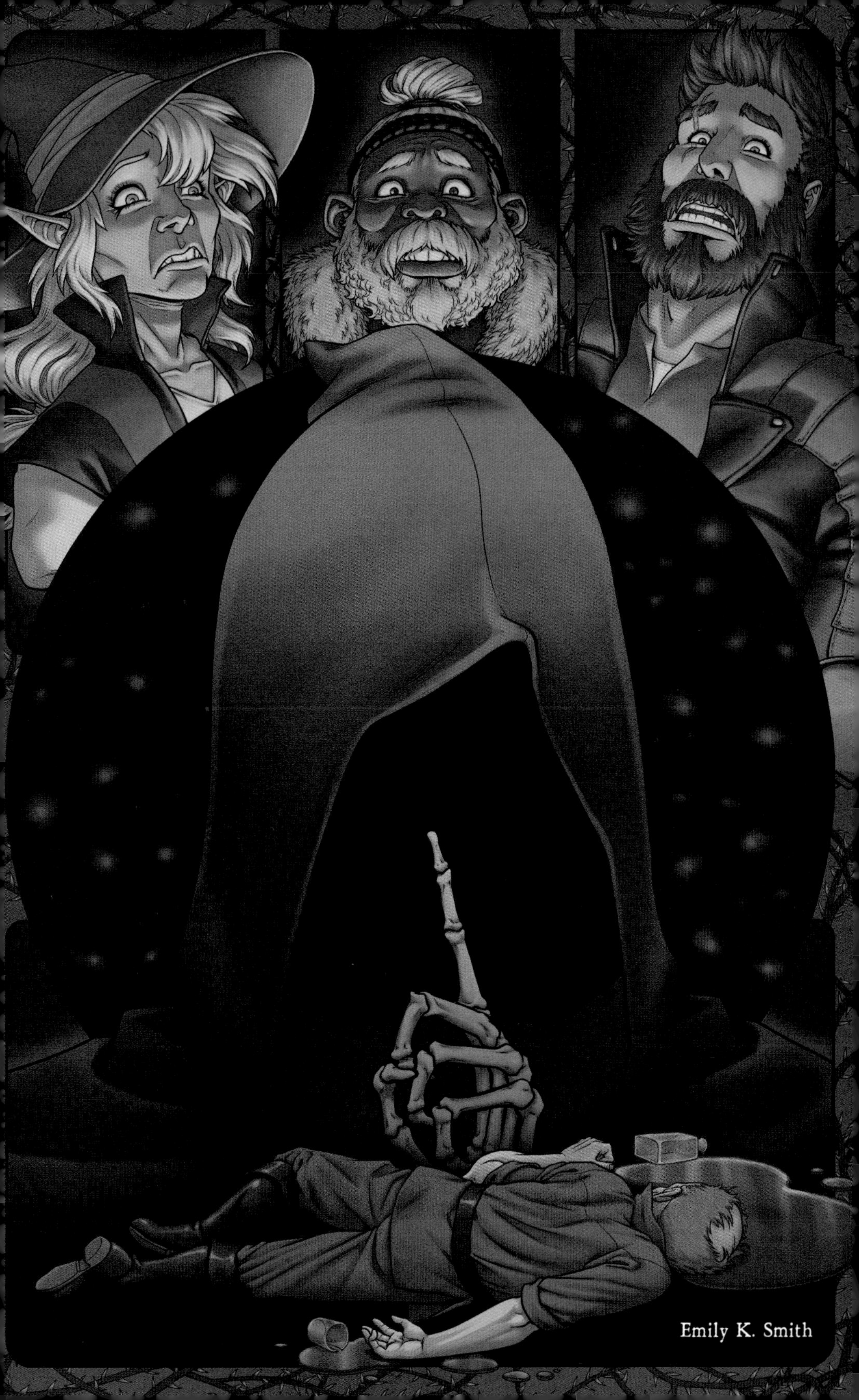
Emily K. Smith

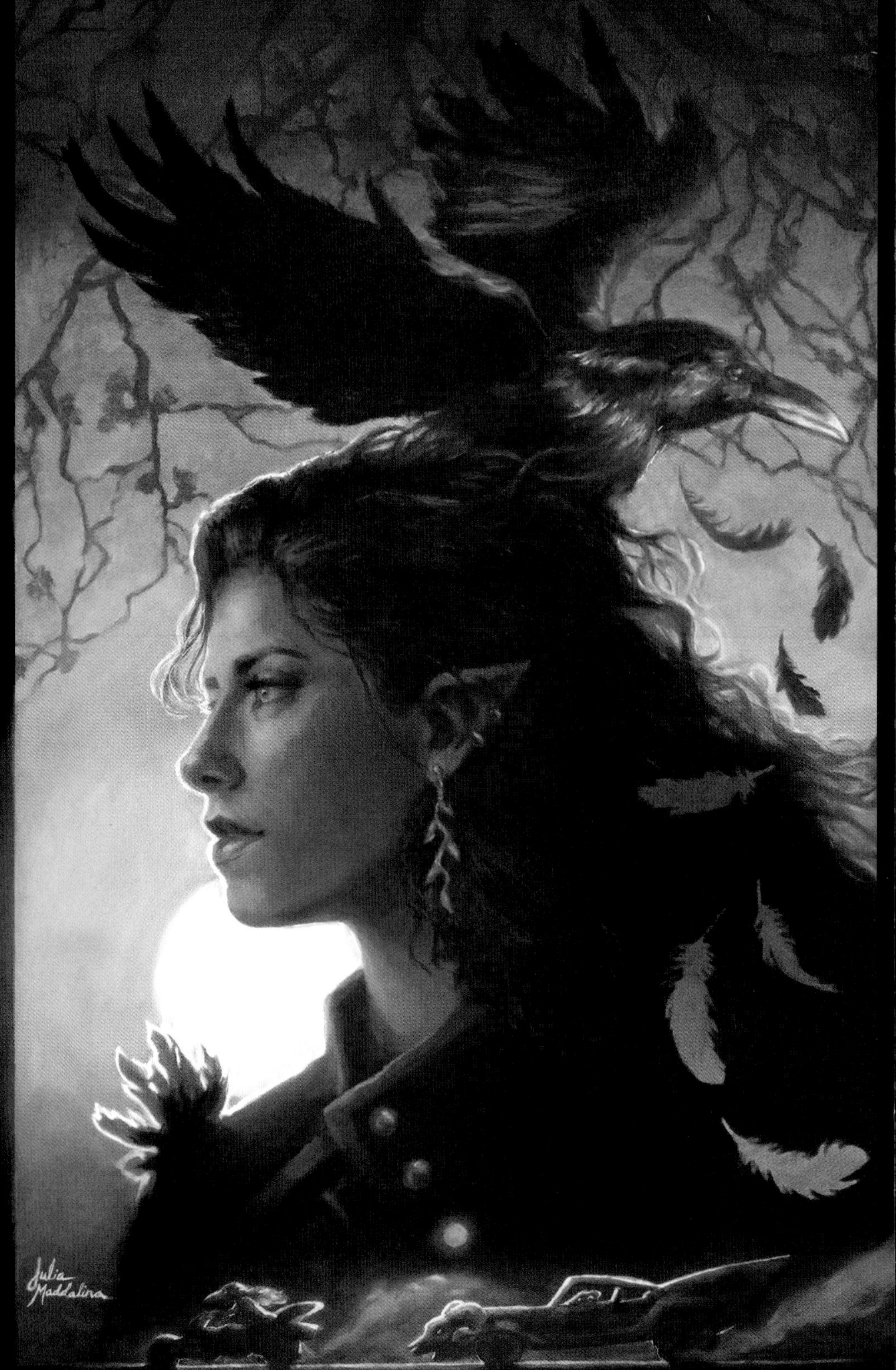
Julia Maddalina

Julia Maddalina

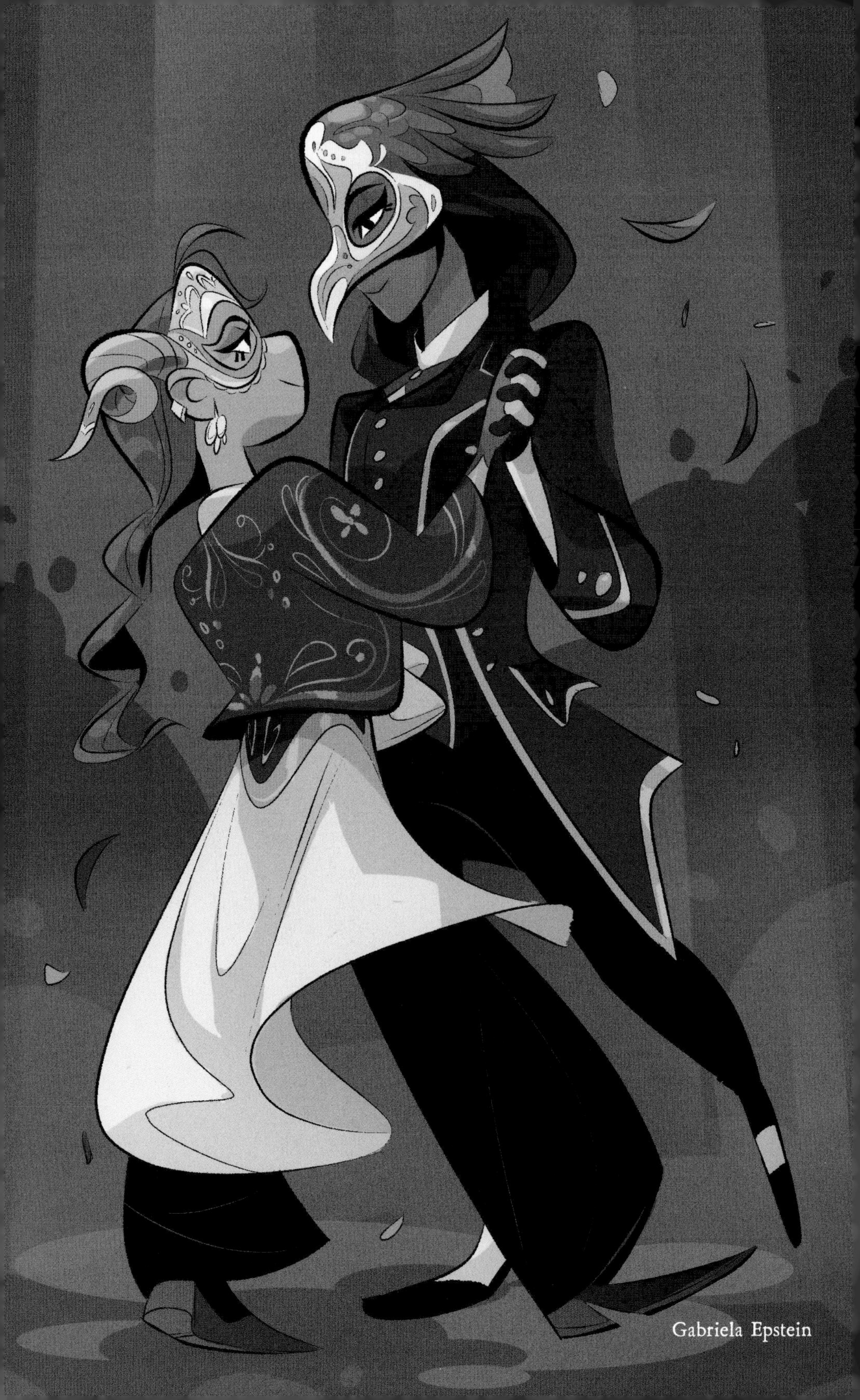

Gabriela Epstein

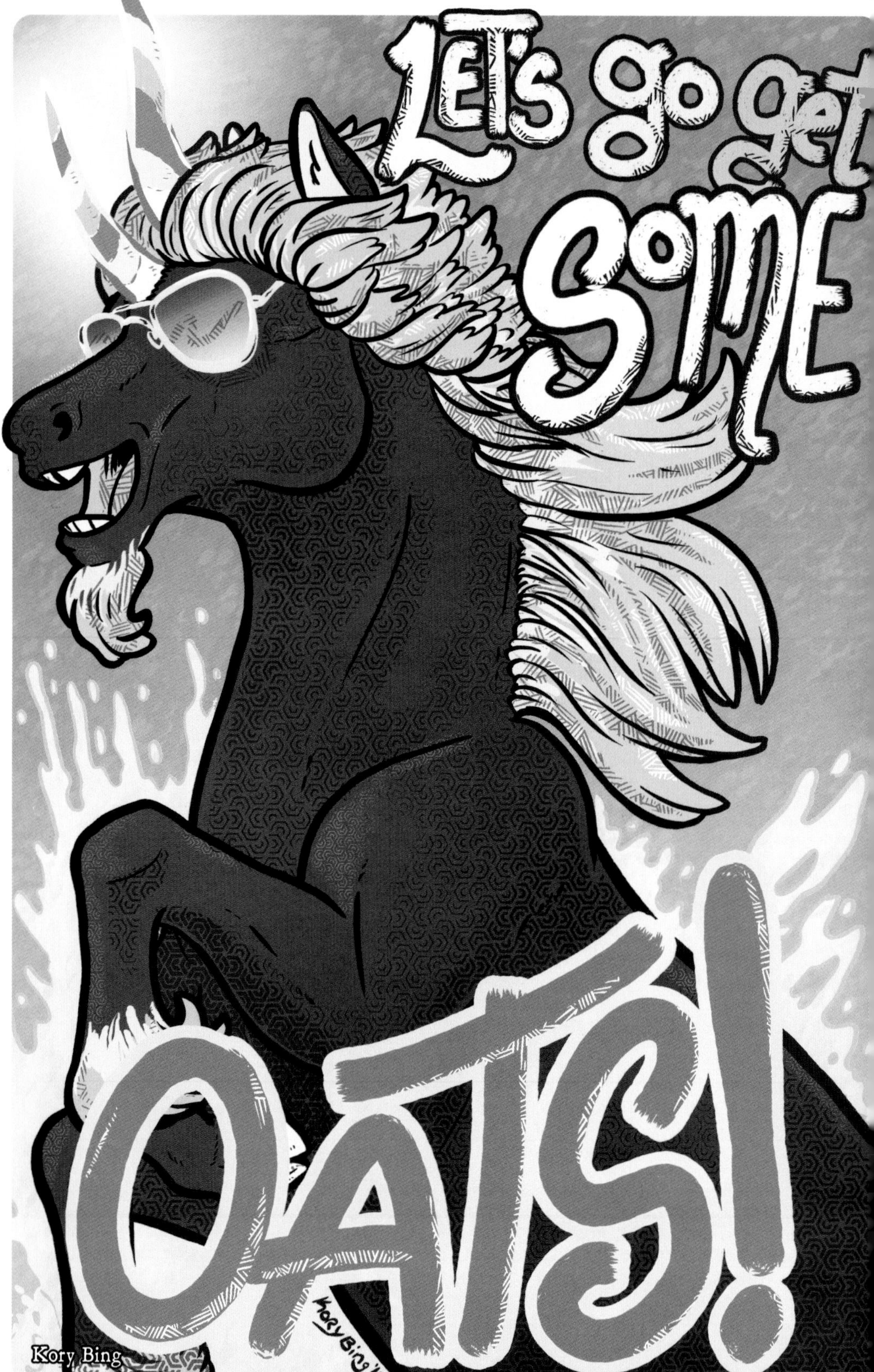
LET'S go get
SOME
OATS!
Kory Bing '19
Kory Bing

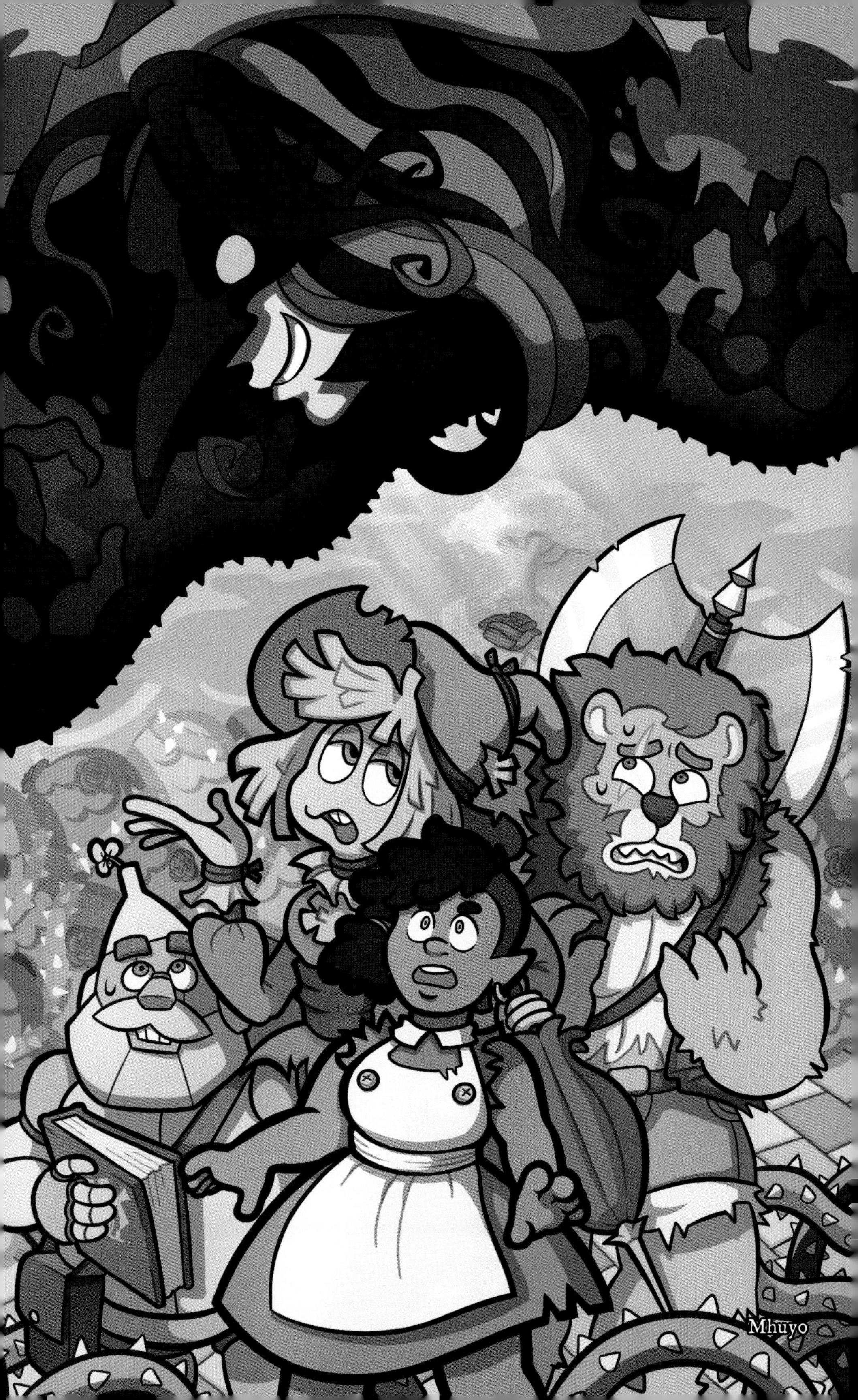
Mhuyo

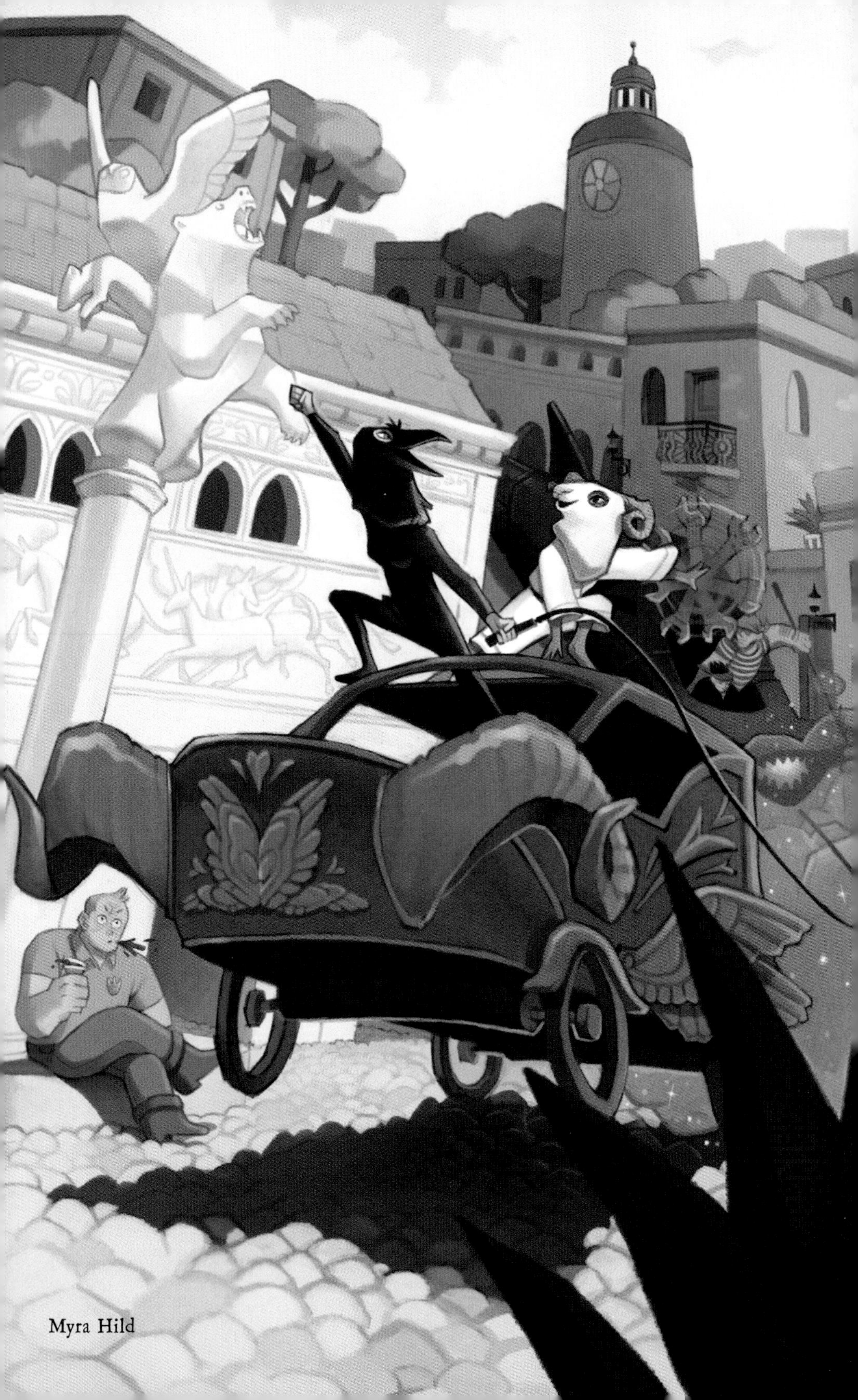

Myra Hild

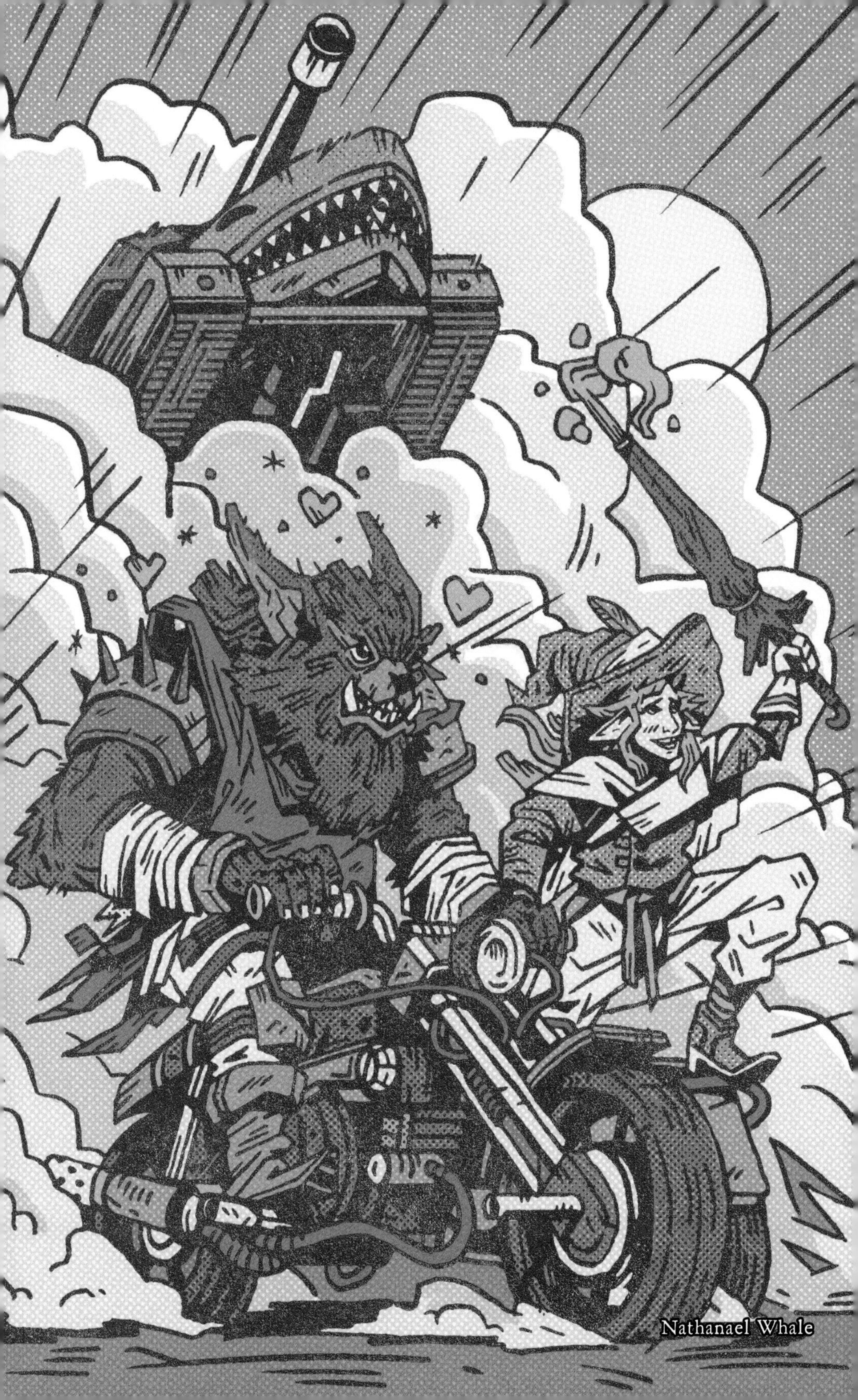
Nathanael Whale

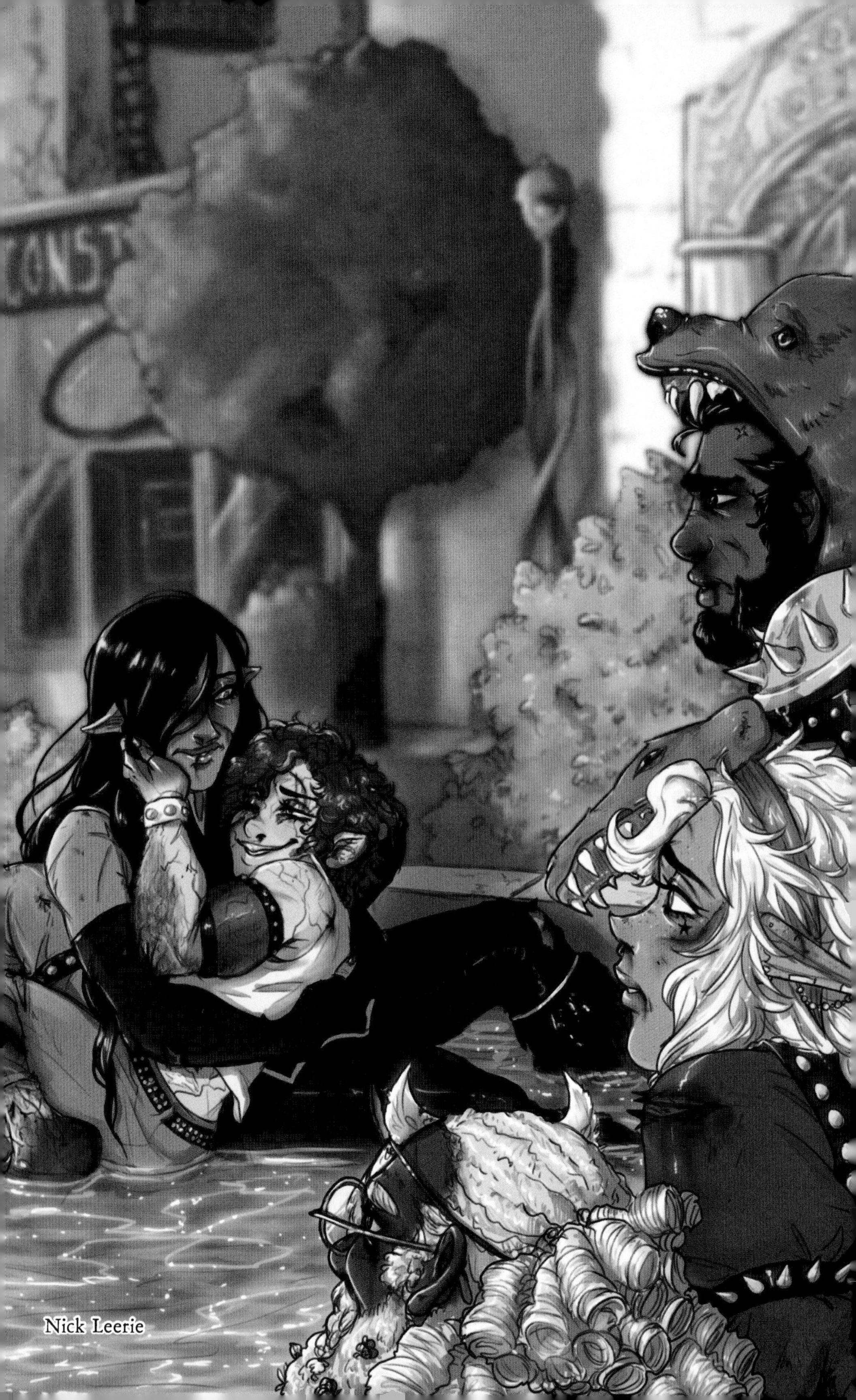
Nick Leerie

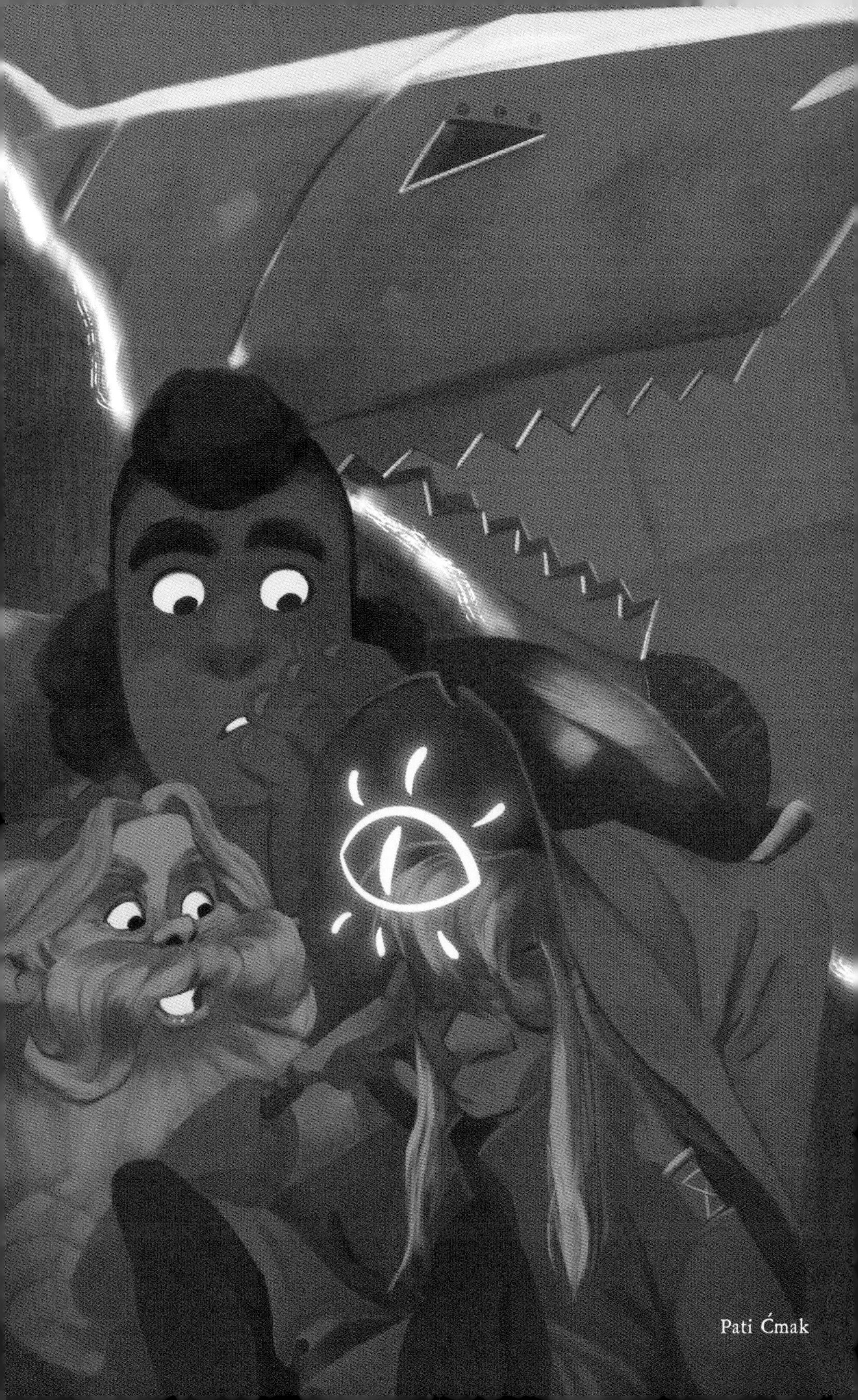

Pati Ćmak

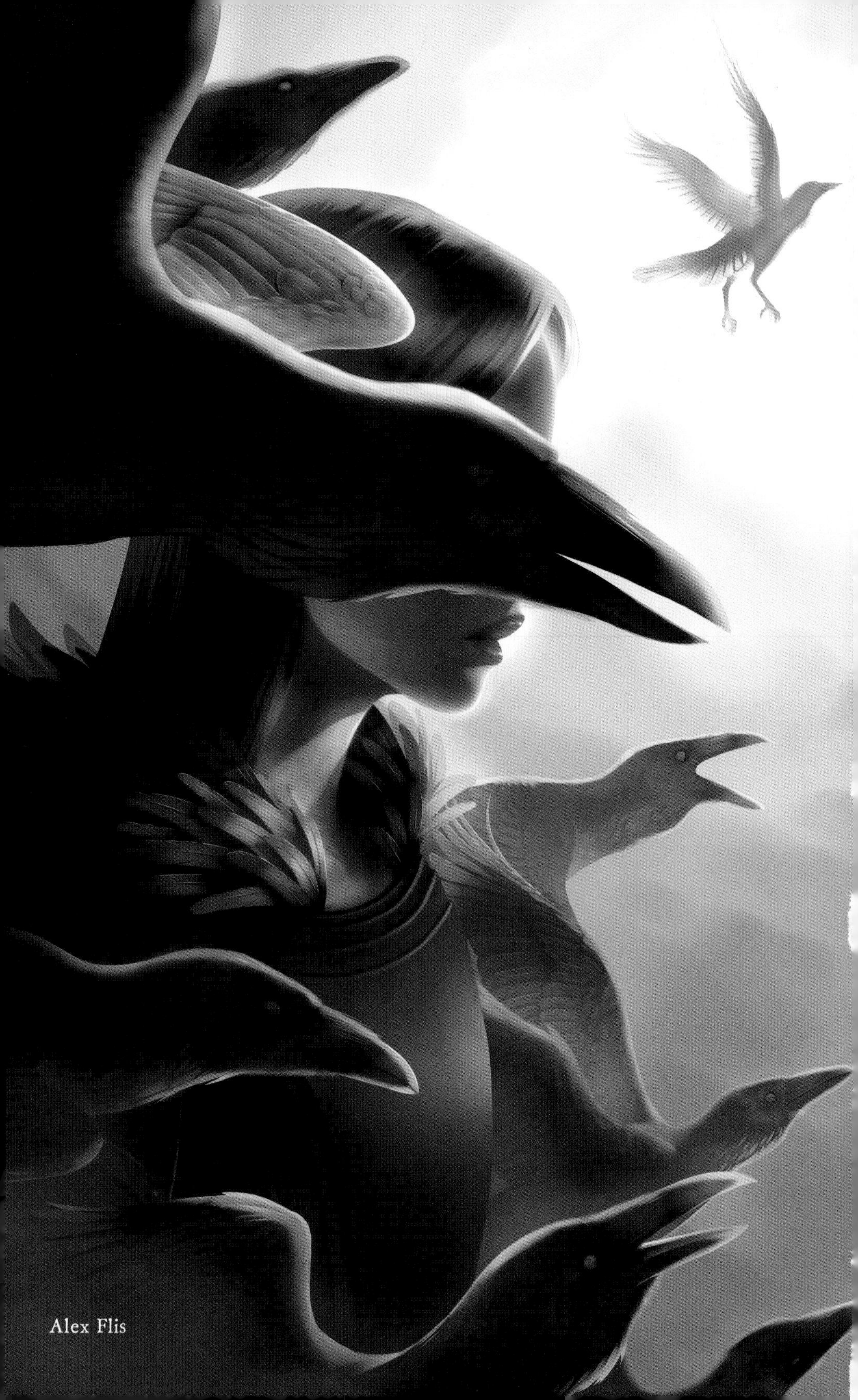
Alex Flis